MW01622184

IF FOUND, please notify and arrange return to o[covered by sticker] **or** the owner's career and/or exam preparation.

Name: ______________________

Address: ______________________

City, State, ZIP: ______________________

Telephone: (____) ______________ Email: ______________

Gleim Publications, Inc., offers five university-level study systems:

Auditing & Systems Exam Questions and Explanations with Test Prep CD-Rom
Business Law/Legal Studies Exam Questions and Explanations with Test Prep CD-Rom
Federal Tax Exam Questions and Explanations with Test Prep CD-Rom
Financial Accounting Exam Questions and Explanations with Test Prep CD-Rom
Cost/Managerial Accounting Exam Questions and Explanations with Test Prep CD-Rom

The following is a list of Gleim certification examination review systems:

CIA Review: Part I, Internal Audit Role in Governance, Risk, and Control
CIA Review: Part II, Conducting the Internal Audit Engagement
CIA Review: Part III, Business Analysis and Information Technology
CIA Review: Part IV, Business Management Skills

CMA Review: Part 1, Business Analysis
CMA Review: Part 2, Management Accounting and Reporting
CMA Review: Part 3, Strategic Management
CMA Review: Part 4, Business Applications

CPA Review: Financial
CPA Review: Auditing
CPA Review: Business
CPA Review: Regulation

EA Review: Part 1, Individuals
EA Review: Part 2, Businesses
EA Review: Part 3, Representation, Practice, and Procedures

An order form is provided at the back of this book, or contact us at www.gleim.com or (800) 87-GLEIM (800-874-5346).

All orders must be prepaid. Shipping and handling charges will be added to all orders. Library and company orders may be purchased on account. Add applicable sales tax to shipments within Florida. All payments must be in U.S. funds and payable on a U.S. bank. Please write or call for prices and availability of all foreign country shipments. Orders will usually be shipped the day your request is received. Allow 10 days for delivery in the United States. Please contact us if you do not receive your shipment within 2 weeks.

Gleim Publications, Inc. guarantees the immediate refund of all resalable texts and unopened software and audios purchased directly from Gleim Publications, Inc. if they are returned within 30 days. Shipping and handling charges are nonrefundable. Returns of books purchased from bookstores and other resellers should be made to the respective bookstore or reseller.

Groundwood Paper and Highlighters — All Gleim books are printed on high-quality groundwood paper. We recommend you use a non-bleed-through (dry) highlighter (e.g., the Avery *Glidestick*™ – ask for it at your local office supply store) when highlighting page items within these books.

REVIEWERS AND CONTRIBUTORS

Garrett W. Gleim, B.S., CPA (not in public practice), is a graduate of The Wharton School at the University of Pennsylvania. Mr. Gleim coordinated the production staff, reviewed the manuscript, and provided production assistance throughout the project.

Grady M. Irwin, J.D., is a graduate of the University of Florida College of Law and has taught in the University of Florida College of Business. Mr. Irwin provided substantial editorial assistance throughout the project.

Scott Lawton, B.S., is a graduate of Brigham Young University-Idaho and Utah Valley University. He has passed the EA exam and has been employed by the Utah State Tax Commission.

John F. Rebstock, B.S.A., is a graduate of the Fisher School of Accounting at the University of Florida. He has passed the CIA and CPA exams. Mr. Rebstock reviewed portions of the manuscript.

A PERSONAL THANKS

This manual would not have been possible without the extraordinary effort and dedication of Jacob Brunny, Kyle Cadwallader, Julie Cutlip, Mumbi Ngugi, Eileen Nickl, Teresa Soard, and Joanne Strong, who typed the entire manuscript and all revisions, and drafted and laid out the diagrams and illustrations in this book.

The authors also appreciate the production and editorial assistance of Christine Bertrand, Ellen Buhl, Katherine Goodrich, James Harvin, Jean Marzullo, Shane Rapp, Victoria Rodriguez, Laura Ter Keurst, and Martha Willis.

The authors also appreciate the critical reading assistance of Corinne Contento, Margaret Curtis, Ellie Gonzalez, and Holly Johnson.

Finally, we appreciate the encouragement, support, and tolerance of our families throughout this project.

THIRTEENTH EDITION

CIA REVIEW

PART I

INTERNAL AUDIT ROLE IN GOVERNANCE, RISK, AND CONTROL

by

Irvin N. Gleim, Ph.D., CPA, CIA, CMA, CFM

with the assistance of
Grady M. Irwin, J.D.

ABOUT THE AUTHOR

Irvin N. Gleim is Professor Emeritus in the Fisher School of Accounting at the University of Florida and is a member of the American Accounting Association, Academy of Legal Studies in Business, American Institute of Certified Public Accountants, Association of Government Accountants, Florida Institute of Certified Public Accountants, The Institute of Internal Auditors, and the Institute of Management Accountants. He has had articles published in the *Journal of Accountancy*, *The Accounting Review*, and *The American Business Law Journal* and is author/coauthor of numerous accounting and aviation books and CPE courses.

Gleim Publications, Inc.
P.O. Box 12848
University Station
Gainesville, Florida 32604
(800) 87-GLEIM or (800) 874-5346
(352) 375-0772
FAX: (352) 375-6940
Internet: www.gleim.com
Email: admin@gleim.com

This is the first printing of the thirteenth edition of ***CIA Review: Part I, Internal Audit Role in Governance, Risk, and Control***. Please email update@gleim.com with **CIA I 13-1** included in the subject or text. You will receive our current update as a reply. Updates are available until the next edition is published.

EXAMPLE:

To: update@gleim.com
From: *your email address*
Subject: **CIA I 13-1**

ISSN: 1547-8041

ISBN: 978-1-58194-631-4

First Printing: February 2008

ACKNOWLEDGMENTS FOR PART I

The author is grateful for permission to reproduce the following materials copyrighted by The Institute of Internal Auditors: Certified Internal Auditor Examination Questions and Suggested Solutions (copyright © 1980 - 2007), excerpts from *The Practice of Modern Internal Auditing* and from *Sawyer's Internal Auditing* (5th ed.), The IIA Code of Ethics, *International Standards for the Professional Practice of Internal Auditing*, and Practice Advisories.

The authors also appreciate and thank the Institute of Certified Management Accountants for permission to use questions from past CMA examinations, copyright © 1982 - 2007 by the Institute of Management Accountants.

TABLE OF CONTENTS

PREFACE

The purpose of this book is to help **you** prepare **yourself** to pass Part I of the CIA examination. The overriding consideration is to provide an inexpensive, effective, and easy-to-use study program. This manual

1. Defines topics tested on Part I of the CIA examination.
2. Includes all recent changes in Part I of the CIA program.
3. Explains how to optimize your grade by analyzing how the CIA exam is constructed and graded.
4. Suggests exam-taking techniques to help you maximize your exam score.
5. Outlines all of the subject matter tested on Part I of the CIA exam in 10 easy-to-use study units, including all relevant authoritative pronouncements.
6. Reorganizes past exam questions according to the subunits within each of the 10 study units and presents an intuitively appealing explanation of each objective question answer.
7. Provides an opportunity for professional accountants to obtain CPE credit while preparing to pass the CIA exam. See the following page for more information.

The outline format and spacing and the question and answer formats are designed to facilitate learning, understanding, and readability. Please read the Introduction of this book carefully.

Even though Gleim's four-volume *CIA Review* constitutes a complete self-study program for the CIA exam, candidates may consider enrolling in a formal review program. Local IIA chapters throughout the world have, in the past, coordinated their CIA review programs with our materials. All candidates should invest in our *CIA Complete System with Gleim Online*, which is designed to maximize your limited studying time. Our *System* includes our *CIA Test Prep* CD-Rom, which is a powerful supplemental study aid. Also, our *System* includes our audio series, books, and online review course. If you have not already purchased our *CIA Complete System with Gleim Online*, you may call us at (800) 874-5346 to purchase the remaining components at a reduced price.

Thank you for your interest in our materials. We deeply appreciate the thousands of letters and suggestions we have received from CIA, CMA, CPA, and EA candidates and accounting students and professors during the last four decades.

Please send us your suggestions, comments, and corrections concerning *CIA Review: Part I*. The last page in this book has been designed to help you note corrections and suggestions throughout your study process. It is imperative that we receive your feedback after you take the CIA exam. We pledge to continue to improve the product (with your suggestions, we hope) in subsequent editions.

To continue providing our customers with first-rate service, we request that questions about our materials be sent to us via mail, email, or fax. The appropriate staff member will give each question thorough consideration and a prompt response. Questions concerning orders, prices, shipments, or payments will be handled via telephone by our competent and courteous customer service staff.

Good Luck on the Exam,

Irvin N. Gleim

February 2008

EARN CPE CREDITS WHILE STUDYING FOR THE CIA EXAM

The Gleim approach to CPE is both interactive and intense. You should be continually challenged to answer each question correctly. When you answer a question incorrectly or have difficulty, you should pursue a complete understanding by reading the answer explanation and consulting reference sources as necessary.

We offer CPE credit online that correlates with this Thirteenth Edition text. Please call us at 800-87-GLEIM (800-874-5346) for more information.

Most of the questions in the study guide were taken from various professional examinations. Each question is revised, adapted, etc., to provide broader, up-to-date coverage of the internal auditing body of technical knowledge. In addition, publisher questions cover material added since examinations became "closed."

To continue providing our customers with first-rate service, we request that questions about our materials be sent to us via mail, email, or fax. The appropriate staff member will give each question thorough consideration and a prompt response. Questions concerning orders, prices, shipments, or payments will be handled via telephone by our competent and courteous customer service staff.

Thank you for your interest, and we look forward to hearing from you.

Best Wishes in Your CPE Endeavors,

Irvin N. Gleim

February 2008

PREPARING FOR AND TAKING THE CIA EXAM

ABOUT THE CIA EXAM

Introduction

CIA is the acronym for Certified Internal Auditor. The CIA designation is international, with the examination administered in numerous countries. The CIA exam has been administered by The Institute of Internal Auditors (The IIA) since 1974. The exam consists of four 3-hour parts that are given on demand throughout the year. Each part consists of 100 four-answer multiple-choice questions.

Computer-Based Testing

The CIA exam is computerized to facilitate easier testing. The computerized environment allows you more freedom in choosing when and where to take the test and ensures that your score is available to you immediately at the conclusion of your test. Additionally, the risk of committing mistakes when transferring answers to a booklet is eliminated with computer-based testing.

Part I	The Internal Audit Activity's Role in Governance, Risk, and Control	3 hours
Part II	Conducting the Internal Audit Engagement	3 hours
Part III	Business Analysis and Information Technology	3 hours
Part IV	Business Management Skills	3 hours
		12 hours

Each part consists of 100 questions, and testing lasts 2 hours and 45 minutes with 15 minutes given for tutorials and a survey. Pearson VUE, the testing company that The IIA contracts to proctor the exams, has over 400 testing centers worldwide, and candidates can choose test dates throughout the year. The Gleim Test Prep CD-Rom and Gleim Online provide tutorials and exact exam emulations of the Pearson VUE computer screens and procedures to prepare you to PASS. The exam application fee is $60. The price to register per part is $130 for members and $160 for non-members.

Please note as you read through this introduction that CIA program rules and prices are subject to change. Please visit Gleim's CIA Candidate Forum at www.gleim.com/account/forum/CIA for the most up-to-date information.

Development of Internal Auditing

Internal auditing is a management-oriented discipline that has evolved rapidly since World War II. Once a function primarily concerned with financial and accounting matters, internal auditing now addresses the entire range of operating activities. Thus, it performs a correspondingly wide variety of **assurance** and **consulting** services. The development of internal auditing was fostered by the increased size and decentralization of organizations and the greater complexity and sophistication of their operations. The result is a need for an independent, objective means of evaluating and improving risk management, control, and governance processes. Accordingly, The IIA's **definition of internal auditing** is as follows:

> *Internal auditing is an independent, objective assurance and consulting activity designed to add value and improve an organization's operations. It helps an organization accomplish its objectives by bringing a systematic, disciplined approach to evaluate and improve the effectiveness of risk management, control, and governance processes.*

Public policy considerations have contributed to the improved status and broadened scope of internal auditing. For example, U.S. organizations are expected to maintain reasonably detailed and accurate accounting records and a reasonably effective system of internal accounting control. Moreover, U.S. public companies must have an internal audit activity and an audit committee composed of nonmanagement directors.

The Institute of Internal Auditors (IIA)

The IIA was organized in 1941 to develop the professional status of internal auditing. The organization's headquarters was in New York City until 1972, when it moved to Altamonte Springs, about 5 miles north of Orlando, Florida.

The IIA has an annual budget of approximately $17 million and employs a full-time staff of 100+. Presently, over 60,000 individuals have attained The Institute of Internal Auditors' CIA designation.

The IIA has chapters in more than 200 metropolitan areas and has affiliated national institutes in many countries around the world. The chapters and institutes hold regular meetings, seminars, and conferences that encourage members to network with peers, develop professional contacts, and stay informed about current issues and practices in internal auditing.

The Institute of Internal Auditors' mission is to be the primary international professional association, organized on a worldwide basis, dedicated to the promotion and development of the practice of internal auditing.

The IIA is committed to:

- Providing, on an international scale, comprehensive professional development activities, standards for the practice of internal auditing, and certification.
- Researching, disseminating, and promoting to its members and to the public throughout the world, knowledge and information concerning internal auditing, including internal control and related subjects.
- Establishing meetings worldwide in order to educate members and others as to the practice of internal auditing as it exists in various countries throughout the world.
- Bringing together internal auditors from all countries to share information and experiences in internal auditing and promoting education in the field of internal auditing.

The IIA's annual dues in the United States, Canada, and Caribbean nations:

1.	Regular Member	$130	4.	Life Member	$2,100
2.	Government Audit Program	$65	5.	Retired Member	$30
3.	Educational Member	$65	6.	Student Member	$30

For non-Chapter members outside the United States, Canada, and the Caribbean nations, dues are $115. These members are also required to pay a $30 bank collection charge for drafts drawn on banks outside the U.S., Canada, and the Caribbean. All applicants except students also must pay a membership application fee of $25.

CIA Board of Regents

The Board of Regents is a special committee of The Institute of Internal Auditors established to direct the certification program for internal auditors as established or modified by The IIA's Board of Directors.

The Board of Regents consists of at least nine regents. The regents are appointed by the Chairman of the Board of Directors to serve 3-year terms. Membership on the Board of Regents rotates, with two or three regents being appointed each year. The responsibilities of the Board of Regents include:

a. Defining the common body of knowledge for the Certified Internal Auditor examination and other Institute certification examinations
b. Defining the education, experience, character, examination, and other program requirements relating to The Institute certifications
c. Defining continuing professional education (CPE) requirements for Institute certifications
d. Maintaining the quality and security of examinations
e. Promoting The Institute's certifications globally

CIA Program

The following is the official statement of The IIA Board of Directors regarding the CIA program:

Professional Qualifications

To assist in achieving the goals and objectives of The Institute, the Certified Internal Auditor (CIA) Program was established. The Board of Directors will develop, approve and modify as necessary, such policies and procedures as may be required to stimulate and encourage this program.

While "Certified Internal Auditor" is intended to be the worldwide designation of qualified internal audit professionals, it is recognized for various reasons other professional organizations of internal auditors may develop similar designations. The Board of Directors will develop, approve and modify as necessary, such procedures as may be deemed desirable to recognize those designations.

The Board may also approve additional certifications as appropriate.

The IIA Certification Department

The Vice Presidents of the Learning Center and the Certification Department staff, who are located in The IIA's Florida offices, administer the program. They undertake all of the day-to-day work with respect to the Board of Regents' responsibilities.

The chair of the Board of Regents divides the members into subcommittees. Each subcommittee is responsible for one part of the exam; i.e., each subcommittee makes the initial recommendations concerning the content and grading of its part of the examination to the Board of Regents as a whole.

Well-Planned Evolution Rather than Abrupt Change

One of the responsibilities of The IIA Board of Regents is to continually update and enhance the sources of exam questions, which in their entirety constitute the **common body of knowledge**.

At the same time, the scope and content of the CIA exam appear to evolve so as to be predictable to CIA candidates. Addition of new topics and deletion of currently tested topics are announced at least one year in advance so that candidates may plan and prepare accordingly. The **common body of knowledge**, referred to in The IIA's materials, is reflected in this edition of *CIA Review*.

Pass rates on the exam are low enough to give the examination credibility relative to the CMA and CPA exams but are high enough to encourage accounting and auditing professionals to participate in the CIA certification program. Everyone, including The IIA Board of Directors, the Board of Regents, the certification staff, CIAs, noncertified internal auditors, and the accounting/auditing profession in general, is interested in the continual upgrading and improvement of the CIA exam.

Objectives and Content of the CIA Examination

The CIA exam tests a candidate's knowledge and ability regarding the current practice of internal auditing. It enables candidates and prospective managers to adapt to professional changes and challenges by

- Addressing nearly all management skills
- Focusing on the principles of management control
- Measuring a candidate's understanding of risk management and internal controls

THE IIA'S CIA CONTENT SPECIFICATION OUTLINES

Part I:	**The Internal Audit Activity's Role in Governance, Risk, and Control**	
A.	Comply with The IIA's Attribute Standards	20%
B.	Establish a risk-based plan to determine the priorities of the internal audit activity	20%
C.	Understand the internal audit activity's role in organizational governance	15%
D.	Perform other internal audit roles and responsibilities	5%
E.	Governance, risk, and control knowledge elements	20%
F.	Plan Engagements	20%
Part II:	**Conducting the Internal Audit Engagement**	
A.	Conduct Engagements	30%
B.	Conduct Specific Engagements	30%
C.	Monitor Engagement Outcomes	10%
D.	Fraud Knowledge Elements	10%
E.	Engagement Tools	20%
Part III:	**Business Analysis and Information Technology**	
A.	Business Processes	20%
B.	Financial Accounting and Finance	20%
C.	Managerial Accounting	15%
D.	Regulatory, Legal, and Economics	10%
E.	Information Technology (IT)	35%
Part IV:	**Business Management Skills**	
A.	Strategic Management	25%
B.	Global Business Environments	20%
C.	Organizational Behavior	20%
D.	Management Skills	25%
E.	Negotiating	10%

See Appendix A for complete details and cross references to this book.

The IIA publishes a Content Specification Outline (CSO), also known as a Content Syllabus, to outline topics covered on each part of the CIA exam. The percentage coverage of each exam part is indicated to the right of each topic. (Note that The IIA "percentage coverage" is given in ranges, e.g., 15-25%, as presented in Appendix A. Above, we present the midpoint of each range to simplify and provide more relevant information to CIA candidates, e.g., 20% instead of 15-25%.) In other words, the percentages listed are plus or minus 5% of the percentage coverages you can expect to encounter during the actual exam. We continually adjust the content of our materials to changes in The IIA's CSOs and changes to CIA exam questions.

Appendix A contains the CSOs in their entirety as well as cross references to the subunits in our text where topics are covered. Remember that we have studied and restudied the CSOs in developing our *CIA Review* materials. Accordingly, you do not need to spend time with Appendix A. Rather, it should give you confidence that Gleim's *CIA Review* is the best review source available to help you PASS the CIA exam. The CSOs refer to proficiency and awareness levels. The IIA definitions of these levels are presented below.

> **Proficiency** -- *Candidate is able to exhibit the competency in understanding and applying the subject matter in the workplace on a regular basis with skill and expertise.*
>
> **Awareness** -- *Candidate exhibits awareness and knowledge. Candidate is able to define terms, recognize issues, and recall facts about the issues.*

Gleim Study Unit Listing

We believe our 10 study unit titles better describe the content of each part of the CIA exam. Our study unit titles and content also reflect feedback from CIA candidates. Please use the last page in this book to give us feedback after each exam. Thank you.

LISTING OF GLEIM STUDY UNITS

Part I: Internal Audit Role in Governance, Risk, and Control

1. Standards and Proficiency
2. Charter, Independence, and Objectivity
3. Internal Audit Roles I
4. Internal Audit Roles II
5. Control I
6. Control II
7. Planning and Supervising the Engagement
8. Managing the Internal Audit Activity I
9. Managing the Internal Audit Activity II
10. Engagement Procedures, Ethics, and Fraud

Part II: Conducting the Internal Audit Engagement

1. Engagement Information
2. Communicating Results and Monitoring Progress
3. Specific Engagements I
4. Specific Engagements II
5. Information Technology I
6. Information Technology II
7. Specific IT Engagements
8. Statistics and Sampling
9. Other Engagement Tools
10. Ethics and Fraud

Part III: Business Analysis and Information Technology

1. Business Performance
2. Managing Resources and Pricing
3. Financial Accounting I
4. Financial Accounting II
5. Finance
6. Managerial Accounting
7. Regulatory, Legal, and Economic Issues
8. Information Technology I
9. Information Technology II
10. Information Technology III

Part IV: Business Management Skills

1. Structural Analysis and Strategies
2. Industry and Market Analysis
3. Industry Environments
4. Strategic Decisions
5. Global Business Issues
6. Motivation and Communications
7. Organizational Structure and Effectiveness
8. Managing Groups
9. Influence and Leadership
10. Time Management, Conflict, and Negotiation

Admission to the CIA Program

Anyone who satisfies these character, educational, and professional requirements may sit for the examination.

1. **Bachelor's degree or equivalent.** Candidates must have an undergraduate (4-year) degree or its equivalent from an accredited college-level institution.
   a. Educational programs outside the United States and the qualifications of candidates who have completed most but not all of a degree program are evaluated by The IIA's Board of Regents to determine equivalency.
   b. The IIA's affiliates have been given the authority to recommend educational and experience criteria for their countries to ensure adequate consideration of cultural and societal differences around the world. In addition, certain international professional designations (such as Chartered Accountant) may be accepted as equivalent to a bachelor's degree.
   c. A major in accounting is not required.
2. **Character reference.** CIA candidates must exhibit high moral and professional character and must submit a character reference from a responsible person such as a CIA, supervisor, manager, or educator. The character reference must accompany the candidate's exam application.
3. **Work experience.** Candidates are required to have 24 months of internal auditing experience (or the equivalent) prior to receiving the CIA certificate. A candidate may sit for the exam before completing the work experience requirements, but (s)he will not be certified until the experience requirement is met.
   a. An advanced academic degree beyond the bachelor's or work experience in related business professions (such as accounting, law, or finance) can be substituted for one year of work experience (1-year maximum).
   b. Equivalent work experience means experience in audit/assessment disciplines, including external auditing, quality assurance, compliance, and internal control.
   c. Full-time college or university-level teaching in the subject matter of the examination is considered equivalent to work experience. Two years of teaching equals one year of internal auditing work experience.
   d. Work experience must be verified by a CIA or the candidate's supervisor. An Experience Verification Form is available on The IIA's website or in the CIA brochure for use in verifying professional experience. This may accompany the candidate's application or be submitted later when criteria have been met.

If you have questions about the acceptability of your work experience, contact The IIA Certification Department at certification@theiia.org or by fax at (407) 937-1101. If you do not possess a bachelor's degree and are unsure whether your educational achievements or professional designation qualify as equivalents to a bachelor's degree, you should submit related educational/professional information with your exam application and include a cover letter requesting review by the Board of Regents. Include a complete description of your situation. Please submit these materials to:

IIA Certification
The Institute of Internal Auditors
247 Maitland Avenue
Altamonte Springs, FL 32701-4201

You will receive a response from The IIA as soon as the certification staff or the Board of Regents evaluates your request. Applicants for equivalency may be registered for the exam pending review but should expect a separate letter regarding the outcome of the review. Applicants who do not receive an equivalency status letter within four weeks of submission of the application and equivalency request should contact The IIA.

Application/Registration for the CBT Exam

Our initial information on applying/registering for the CBT CIA exam includes the following:

1. The application/registration process for the CBT CIA exam will be available online in most countries. Go to www.theiia.org for information on how to apply in countries where an online application is not available.
2. Once you have registered for a part of the exam, you will have 6 months to sit for that part.
3. You may register to take as many parts as you wish in the same time period.
4. If you have previously passed any part(s) of the the CIA exam in the paper and pencil format, you will be able to retain the credit you received for those parts. You will take any remaining parts in the CBT format.
5. A candidate has an initial eligibility period of two years (five examinations) after his/her first registration is approved. The eligibility period is subsequently extended for two years each time a candidate sits for a part. A candidate's eligibility will expire only if the candidate does not take a single exam part within any two-year period. If eligibility expires, the candidate loses credit for any part or parts previously passed and must reregister for consideration as a candidate for future examinations.
6. If you fail an exam part, you must wait 90 days to retake that part.

For more information on the registration process for the CBT exam as it is released by The IIA, check Gleim's CIA Candidate Forum at www.gleim.com/account/forum/CIA.

Professional Recognition Credit for Part IV

The IIA offers a Part IV Professional Recognition Credit for qualified professional certifications. Registered candidates and new CIA candidates who have successfully completed the examination requirements for many designations are eligible to receive credit for Part IV of the CIA exam. In the U.S., these designations include

CBA	CCSA	CFIRS	CISA	CPEA
CBM	CDFM	CGAP	CISSP	CPA
NCCO	CFSA	CGFM	CIDA	CRCM
CCBIA	CFE	CHFP	CMA	CRP

Please visit The IIA's website (www.theiia.org) for a complete list of certifications approved for credit in other countries. Hence, candidates who attain the credit for Part IV and pass Parts I, II, and III satisfy the examination requirement for the CIA designation.

Nondisclosed Exam

The CIA exam is a **nondisclosed** exam. **Nondisclosed** means that exam questions and solutions are NOT released after each examination. You will be asked to read and sign the Non-Disclosure Agreement prior to taking the CIA exam.

In order to keep our materials up to date and relevant to CIA candidates, we request feedback after each CIA exam. We need to know what topics need to be added or enhanced in our *CIA Review* materials. Note that we are not asking for information about CIA questions. Rather, we are asking for feedback on our outlines, questions, and answer explanations. This approach has been approved by The IIA.

CIA Exam Fees

Fees	IIA Members	Nonmembers	Professors/ Full-Time Students
Exam Application (initial nonrefundable fee)	US $60	US $75	US $30
Exam Parts Registration (per part/per sitting)	US $130	US $160	US $85
Part IV Professional Recognition Credit (PRC-IV) (non-refundable fee; waived for CCSAs, CGAPs and CFSAs)	US $130	US $160	US $85
Canadian Exam Site Tax (*percent of total exam part fees paid, including PRC-IV credit)	GST 6%* HST 14%*	GST 6%* HST 14%*	GST 6%* HST 14%*
Deferrals/Cancelations/Changes			
...by the application deadline (without exam fee refund)	US $0	US $0	US $0
...by the application deadline (with exam fee refund)	US $25	US $25	US $25
....after the application deadline	US $35	US $35	US $35
...beginning Wednesday of week before exam or no-shows	US $85	US $110	US $35

Special Professor and Student Examination Fee

The exam application fee is the charge for enrolling candidates in the CIA program. The CIA examination is available to professors and full-time students at reduced fees. For them, the exam application fee is $30 (instead of $60), plus an exam registration fee of $85 (instead of $130) per part. Professors and students may sit for each part at this special rate one time only.

1. To be eligible for the reduced rate, a student must
   a. Be enrolled as a senior in an undergraduate program or as a graduate student
   b. Be a full-time student as defined by the institution in which the student is enrolled (a minimum of 12 semester hours or its equivalent for senior-level undergraduate students and 9 semester hours for graduate students)
   c. Register for and take the CIA exam while enrolled in school
2. In addition to the requirements above, the following items should be submitted to the Certification Department of The Institute of Internal Auditors while the student is still enrolled in school:
   a. A Certified Internal Auditor Examination Registration/Application Form *(with school address substituted for business address)*
   b. A completed and signed Full-Time Student Status Form in lieu of a transcript
   c. A completed and signed Character Reference Form
   d. Payment for the $30 exam application fee and the $85 exam registration fee for each part

Maintaining Your CIA Designation

After certification, CIAs are required to maintain and update their knowledge and skills. Practicing CIAs must complete and report 80 hours of Continuing Professional Education (CPE) every two years. Every February, CIAs who are required to report in the current year will receive reporting forms and instructions from The IIA. Completed forms should be filed with The IIA by May 31 of the required reporting year. Each July, participants in the current year's CPE program will receive a status report acknowledging acceptance of the number of hours reported. Even-numbered certificates report in even years and odd-numbered certificates in odd years.

Examination Sites

The CBT CIA examinations are administered at Pearson VUE testing centers, which are located in the United States, the United Kingdom, India, Japan, and China. A complete list of these test centers, addresses, and driving directions can be found at www.pearsonvue.com. Click on the "Locate a Test Center" link at the top of the screen, and then choose the country and region in which you would like to take your exam.

If you require testing accommodations because of a special need, call a Pearson VUE agent at the time of registration for assistance.

PREPARING TO PASS THE CIA EXAM

Control: How To Be In

You have to be in control to be successful during exam preparation and execution. Control can also contribute greatly to your personal and other professional goals. The objective is to be confident that the best possible performance is being generated. Control is a process whereby you

1. Develop expectations, standards, budgets, and plans
2. Undertake activity, production, study, and learning
3. Measure the activity, production, output, and knowledge
4. Compare actual activity with expected and budgeted activity
5. Modify the activity, behavior, or study to better achieve the desired outcome
6. Revise expectations and standards in light of actual experience
7. Continue the process or restart the process in the future

Every day you rely on control systems implicitly. For example, when you groom your hair, you use a control system. You have expectations about the desired appearance of your hair and the time required to style it. You monitor your progress and make adjustments as appropriate. The control process, however, is applicable to all of your endeavors, both professional and personal. You should refine your personal control processes specifically toward passing the CIA exam.

In this book, we suggest explicit control systems for

1. Preparing to take the CIA exam
2. Studying an individual Gleim study unit
3. Answering individual multiple-choice questions

Most endeavors will improve with explicit control. This is particularly true of the CIA examination.

1. Develop an explicit control system over your study process.
2. Practice your question-answering techniques (and develop control) as you prepare solutions to recent CIA questions during your study program.
3. Prepare a detailed plan of steps you will take at the CIA exam.

How Many Parts to Take

The CIA examination consists of four parts: Parts I and II cover internal auditing subject matter, whereas Part III, Business Analysis and Information Technology, and Part IV, Business Management Skills, cover a wide variety of material.

According to The IIA, you may choose to take only one part at each sitting, which is what Gleim recommends for the CBT exam. Unless you have a strong preference to do otherwise, it is best to take the parts in numerical order, from Part I to Part IV.

Candidates have an initial eligibility period of 2 years from the first exam after their registration is approved. In addition, each time a candidate sits for an exam part, the candidate's eligibility period is extended 2 years from the date of the last exam part taken. A candidate's eligibility expires only if the candidate does not take a single exam part within any 2-year period. If a candidate's eligibility expires, the candidate loses credit for any part or parts passed and must submit a new CIA Exam Application Form and appropriate fees in order to take future examinations.

Study Plan, Time Budget, and Calendar

Complete one ***CIA Review*** study unit at a time. Initially, budget 3 to 4 hours per study unit (1 to 2 hours studying the outline and 1 to 2 minutes each on all the multiple-choice questions). Depending on your background, your time to prepare will vary.

This Introduction	2	Hours
10 study units at 3.5 hours each	35	
Review	10	
Total	47	Hours

Each week, you should evaluate your progress and review your preparation plans for the time remaining prior to the exam. Marking a calendar will facilitate your planning. Note the exam dates and the weeks to go before the exam. Review your commitments, e.g., out-of-town assignments, personal responsibilities, etc., and note them on your calendar to assist you in keeping to your schedule.

Core Concepts

Core concepts are included at the beginning of each study unit. The core concepts provide an overview of the key points that serve as the foundation for learning. In many cases, the core concepts are concise statements of attribute, performance, and implementation standards. As part of your review, you should make sure that you understand each of them.

Study Unit Summaries

Study unit summaries also are included in each study unit. These summaries are similar to the core concepts, but they provide more in-depth synopses of the material. They should help reinforce the main points within each of the study units.

Practice Advisory Summaries

Gleim *CIA Review* also provides the summarization of practice advisories (PA). Each PA is followed by a synopsis of its crucial aspects. The PA summaries provide the reinforcement of key issues that The IIA expects CIA candidates to know.

How to Study a Study Unit Using Gleim's Complete System

To ensure that you are using your time effectively, we recommend that you follow the steps listed below when using all of the materials together (books, CD-Rom, audios, and Gleim Online):

1. (25-30 minutes) In the *CIA Gleim Online* course, complete Multiple-Choice Quiz #1 in 20-25 minutes (excluding the review session). It is expected that your scores will be low on the first quiz.
   a. Immediately following the quiz, you will be prompted to review the questions you marked and/or answered incorrectly. For each question, analyze and understand why you marked it or answered it incorrectly. This step is an essential learning activity.
2. (15-30 minutes) Use the audiovisual presentation for an overview of the study unit. The Gleim *CIA Review Audios* can be substituted for audiovisual presentations and can be used while driving to work, exercising, etc.
3. (30-45 minutes) Complete the 30-question True/False quiz. It is interactive and most effective if used prior to studying the Knowledge Transfer Outline.
4. (60 minutes) Study the Knowledge Transfer Outline, specifically the troublesome areas identified from the multiple-choice questions in the Gleim Online course. The Knowledge Transfer Outlines can be studied either online or from the books.
5. (25-30 minutes) Complete Multiple-Choice Quiz #2 in the Gleim Online course.
   a. Immediately following the quiz, you will be prompted to review the questions you marked and/or answered incorrectly. For each question, analyze and understand why you marked it or answered it incorrectly. This step is an essential learning activity.
6. (40-50 minutes) Complete two 20-question quizzes while in Test Mode from the *CIA Test Prep* CD-Rom.

When following these steps, you will complete all 10 units in about 30-40 hours. Then spend about 5-10 hours using the *CIA Test Prep* CD-Rom to create customized tests for the problem areas that you identified. To review the entire part before the exam, use the *CIA Test Prep* CD-Rom to create 20-question quizzes that draw questions from all ten study units. Continue taking 20-question quizzes until you approach your desired proficiency level, e.g., 75%+.

CIA Gleim Online

Gleim's *CIA Gleim Online* is a versatile, interactive, self-study review program delivered via the Internet. With *CIA Gleim Online*, Gleim guarantees that you will pass the CIA exam on your first sitting. It is divided into four courses (one for each part of the CIA exam).

Each course is broken down into 10 individual, manageable study units. Completion time per study unit will vary from 3-5 hours. Each study unit in the course contains an audiovisual presentation, 30 true/false study questions, 10-20 pages of Knowledge Transfer Outlines, and two 20-question multiple-choice quizzes.

CIA Gleim Online provides you with a Personal Counselor, who will provide support to ensure your competitive edge. Gleim Online is a great way to get confidence as you prepare with Gleim. This confidence will continue during and after the exam.

Gleim Books and Test Prep CD-Rom

Twenty-question tests in the ***CIA Test Prep*** CD-Rom will help you focus on your weaker areas. Make it a game: How much can you improve?

Our *CIA Test Prep* CD-Rom forces you to commit to your answer choice before looking at answer explanations; thus, you are preparing under true exam conditions. It also keeps track of your time and performance history for each study unit, which is available in either a table or graphical format.

Simplify the exam preparation process by following our suggested steps listed below. DO NOT omit the step in which you diagnose the reasons for answering questions incorrectly; i.e., learn from your mistakes while studying so you avoid making similar mistakes on the CIA exam.

1. In test mode, answer a 20-question diagnostic test from each study unit before studying any other information.
2. Study the Knowledge Transfer Outline for the corresponding study unit in your Gleim book. Place special emphasis on the weaker areas that you identified with the initial diagnostic quiz in Step 1.
3. Take two or three 20-question tests in test mode after you have studied the Knowledge Transfer Outline.
4. Immediately following the quiz, you will be prompted to review the questions you marked and/or answered incorrectly. For each question, analyze and understand why you answered it incorrectly. This step is an essential learning activity.
5. Continue this process until you approach a predetermined proficiency level, e.g., 75%+.
6. Modify this process to suit your individual learning process.
   a. Learning from questions you answer incorrectly is very important. Each question you answer incorrectly is an **opportunity** to avoid missing actual test questions on your CIA exam. Thus, you should carefully study the answer explanations provided to understand why you chose the incorrect answer so you can avoid similar errors on your exam. This study technique is clearly the difference between passing and failing for many CIA candidates.

b. You **must** determine why you answered questions incorrectly and learn how to avoid the same error in the future. Reasons for missing questions include:
   1) Misreading the requirement (stem)
   2) Not understanding what is required
   3) Making a math error
   4) Applying the wrong rule or concept
   5) Being distracted by one or more of the answers
   6) Incorrectly eliminating answers from consideration
   7) Not having any knowledge of the topic tested
   8) Employing bad intuition (WHY?) when guessing
c. It is also important to verify that you answered correctly for the right reasons. Otherwise, if the material is tested on the CIA exam in a different manner, you may not answer it correctly.
d. It is imperative that you complete your predetermined number of study units per week so you can review your progress and realize how attainable a comprehensive CIA review program is when using Gleim's Complete System. Remember to meet or beat your schedule to give yourself confidence.

> Avoid studying Gleim questions to learn the correct answers. Use Gleim questions to help you learn how to answer CIA questions under exam conditions. Expect the unexpected and be prepared to deal with it. Become an educated guesser when you encounter questions in doubt; you will outperform the inexperienced exam taker.

Gleim Audio Reviews

Gleim *CIA Review* audios provide a 15- to 40-minute introductory review for each study unit. Each review provides a comprehensive overview of the outline in the *CIA Review* book. The purpose is to get candidates "started" so they can relate to the questions they will answer before reading the study outlines in each study unit.

The audios are short and to the point, as is the entire Gleim System for Success. We are working to get you through the CIA exam with minimum time, cost, and frustration.

If You Failed One or More Parts

The pass rate on each part of the CIA exam averages about 45%. Thus, you may not pass all parts attempted. If you failed a part, you must wait at least 90 days to retake it.

1. Once you have put the reaction to the bad news behind you, you should regroup and begin implementing the suggestions in this introduction. The Gleim system really works! Avoid thinking "I knew that" or "I don't have to study that again." What you knew and how you took the exam last time did NOT work. Develop new and improved perspectives.
2. Avoid failure on the next exam by **identifying**, **correcting**, and **understanding** your mistakes as you practice answering multiple-choice questions during your study sessions. Use the Gleim system as described on the previous pages. This methodology applies to all CIA candidates. Understand your mistakes while you study so you can avoid them on the exam.

As you practice answering multiple-choice questions under exam conditions, it is imperative that you re-study each question you answer incorrectly.

Multiple-Choice Question-Answering Technique

The following suggestions are to assist you in maximizing your score on each part of the CIA exam. Remember, knowing how to take the exam and how to answer individual questions is as important as studying/reviewing the subject matter tested on the exam.

1. **Budget your time.**
   a. We make this point with emphasis. Just as you would fill up your gas tank prior to reaching empty, so too should you finish your exam before time expires.
   b. You have 165 minutes to answer 100 questions, i.e., 1.65 minutes per question. We suggest you attempt to answer eight questions every 10 minutes, which is 1.25 minutes per question. This would result in completing 100 questions in 125 minutes to give you almost 40 minutes to review questions that you have flagged.
   c. Use the wipeboard provided by Pearson VUE for your Gleim Time Management System at the exam. List the question numbers for every 20 questions (i.e., 1, 21, 41, etc.) in a column on the left side of the wipeboard. The right side of the wipeboard will have your start time at the top and will be used for you to fill in the time you have remaining at each question checkpoint. Stay consistent with 1.25 minutes per question.
2. **Answer the items in numerical order.**
   a. Do **not** agonize over any one item. Stay within your time budget.
   b. Note any items you are unsure of by clicking the "Flag for Review" button in the upper-right corner of your screen, and return to them later if time allows. Plan on going back to all the questions you flagged.
3. **For each item,**
   a. **Read the question** stem carefully (the part of the question that precedes the answer choices) to determine the precise requirement.
      1) Focusing on what is required enables you to ignore extraneous information and to proceed directly to determining the correct answer.
         a) Be especially careful to note when the requirement is an **exception**; e.g., "Which of the following is **not** an indication of fraud?"
   b. **Determine the correct answer** before reading the answer choices. The objective is to avoid allowing the answer choices to affect your reading of the question.
      1) **Cover up the answer choices** by scrolling to view only the question or, if necessary, with your hand. Do not allow the answer choices to affect your reading of the item stem.
      2) When four answer choices are presented, three of them are incorrect. They are called distractors for a very good reason.
      3) Read each answer choice with close attention.
         a) Even if answer (A) appears to be the correct choice, do not skip the remaining answer choices. Answer (B), (C), or (D) may be better.
         b) Treat each answer choice as a true/false question.
   c. **Select the best answer.** Select the most likely or best answer choice. If you are uncertain, make an educated guess.
      1) The CIA exam does not penalize guessing, because your score is determined by the number of correct responses. Thus, you should answer every question.

If You Don't Know the Answer

Guess, but make it an educated guess, which means select the best possible answer. First, rule out answers that you feel are obviously incorrect. Second, speculate on The IIA's purpose and/or the rationale behind the question. These steps may lead you to the correct answer. Third, select the best answer, or guess between equally appealing answers. Flag the question in case you have time to return to it for further analysis. However, unless you made an obvious mistake or computational error, try to avoid changing answers at the last minute. Your first guess is usually the most intuitive.

If you cannot make an educated guess, read the item and each answer and pick the best or most intuitive answer. Never leave a question unanswered.

Do **not** look at the previous answer to try to detect an answer. The answers are random, but it is possible to have four or more consecutive questions with the same answer letter, e.g., answer B.

NOTE: Do not waste time beyond the amount budgeted. Move ahead and stay on or ahead of schedule.

CBT Exam Components

Time and Progress

The upper-right corner of the screen will continually display the time you have remaining in your exam. Below the time remaining, the question number you are currently working on is displayed in contrast to how many total questions there are on the exam (e.g., 14 of 100).

You can choose to allow these reminders to show during the exam, or you can minimize them by clicking on their icons. If you minimize the time remaining, it will automatically reappear when you have 5 minutes left.

Navigation

The following Navigation buttons will be available at the bottom of every screen during your exam:

Previous – Moves you back to the preceding screen
Next – Moves you forward to the following screen

Using the Scroll Bar

If you encounter a question that does not fit on the screen in its entirety, use the scroll bar that will appear along the side of the screen. To scroll down, you can either click on the scroll bar and drag it down or click on the arrow at the bottom of the scroll bar. To show the top part of the question again, either click and drag the scroll bar back up or click on the arrow at the top of the scroll bar.

Make certain that you have seen the entire question by always checking to see if the scroll bar appears. If you attempt to complete a question without scrolling to the bottom of the screen, a prompt may appear to remind you to scroll down.

English Display Screen

If you are taking the CIA exam in a language other than English, you may choose to view an English translation of any question on the exam.

To view the translation, click on the English button below the question. A separate screen will open and display the English translation of the current question. Close the translation when you are finished with it by clicking on the X in the lower-right corner of the translation screen.

Calculator

There will be an online calculator available for every question on the CIA exam. To use the calculator, click on the Calculator button in the upper-left corner of the screen. To enter numbers, you can either use your mouse to click the numbers on the calculator display or use the number keypad on your keyboard. Close the calculator when you are finished with it by clicking on the X in the upper-right corner of the calculator display screen.

Flag for Review

To flag a question so you can go back and review it later, click the Flag for Review button in the upper-right corner of the question screen. A flag image will appear in the flag icon on the question screen and to the left of that question number on the review screen. You can flag both answered and unanswered questions for review, but you must complete your review of flagged questions (and answer any unanswered questions) in the allotted exam time.

To unflag a flagged question, click on the Flag for Review button again.

The CIA's Review Screen

Once you get to the end of the exam, the Review Screen will be displayed. Each question is displayed with the status of that question: answered, flagged for review, or incomplete (unanswered).

You will be able to review your questions by choosing to either

Review All questions and answers
Review Incomplete questions and answers only
Review Flagged questions and answers only

The computer will then generate your review based on which questions you chose to be included. During this review, you will be able to go back to your main Review Screen by selecting the Review Screen button. Once you are done with your review, you will click on the End Review/Exam button and then confirm that you are, in fact, done with the review/exam. Once you have clicked Yes on this screen, you will no longer be able to return to your review/exam.

TAKING THE CIA EXAM

CIA Examination Preparation Checklist

1. **Apply online** to the exam program (see page 8).
2. **Register online** for the desired part on the same application form (for the initial application and registration), or file the reapplication form.
   a. As soon as your examination location is confirmed, make travel and lodging reservations if necessary.
3. Acquire your study materials. Rely on our *CIA Complete System with Gleim Online* as your primary study source.
4. Plan your study program.
5. Locate a suitable place to study.
6. Implement your study program.
7. Periodically review, reassess, and revise your study program as needed.
8. Recognize that an orderly, controlled study program builds confidence, reduces anxiety, and produces success!
9. **Pass the examination!**

Exam Psychology

Plan ahead for the exam and systematically prepare for it. Go to the exam and give it your best. Neither you nor anyone else can expect more. If you have undertaken a systematic preparation program, you will do well.

Maintain a positive attitude and do not become anxious or depressed if you encounter difficulties before or during the exam. An optimist will usually do better than an equally well-prepared pessimist. Remember, you are not in a position to be objective about your results during the exam. Many well-prepared examination candidates have been pleasantly surprised by their scores. Indeed, you should be confident because you are competing with many less-qualified persons who have not prepared as well as you. Optimism and a fighting spirit are worth points on every exam; fear, anxiety, and depression tend to impair performance.

Proper exercise, diet, and rest during the weeks before the exam are very important. High energy levels, reduced tension, and a positive attitude are among the benefits. A good aerobic fitness program, a nutritious and well-balanced diet, and a regular sleep pattern will promote your long-term emotional and physical well-being as well as contribute significantly to a favorable exam result. Of course, the use of health-undermining substances should be avoided.

CBT Preparation

Your examination will be taken on a computer at the Pearson VUE testing center. You do not need any computer experience or typing skills to take your examination. Before you start the examination, you will be able to take a tutorial on the testing system if you wish. If you have used the Gleim *CIA Test Prep* CD-Rom and Gleim Online, you will be completely familiar and comfortable with the CBT format.

Examination Tactics

1. Arrive 15-30 minutes before your scheduled appointment. This early check-in allows time for you to sign in and for staff to verify your identification.
2. Before you are allowed to enter the testing room, you will be required to show 2 forms of identification, including one government-issued photo identification. Both must have signatures.
3. Dressing for exam success means emphasizing comfort, not appearance. Be prepared to adjust for changes in temperature, e.g., remove a sweater or put on a coat. Do not bring notes, this text, other books, etc., to the exam. You will only make yourself nervous and confused by trying to cram during the last 5 minutes before the exam. Books are not allowed in the exam room anyway.
4. Read the exam instructions carefully.
5. Answer the 100 questions in chronological order. Flag any questions that you are leaving for later or you wish to review.
6. You have 165 minutes (2 hours 45 minutes) to answer 100 questions. If you allocate 1.25 minutes per question, you will use only 125 minutes, leaving 40 minutes to complete Steps 7 and 8. If you use the Gleim Time Management System to pace yourself during the exam, you will have adequate time to complete each part.
7. After you worked through all 100 questions, you should return to the questions you flagged and make a final selection, i.e., your best answer.
    a. Review each question carefully. If you made an obvious mistake, e.g., misread the question, make the correction. DO NOT, however, begin changing answers and second guessing yourself. Your first answer to each question should be based on the systematic question-answering technique that you have practiced throughout your preparation program.
8. As soon as you return home from your exam, please email, fax, or write to us with your comments on our materials. We are particularly interested in which topics need to be added or expanded. We are NOT asking about specific CIA questions. Rather, we are asking for feedback on our materials. Use the last two pages in each Gleim book to send us your comments. This approach is approved by The IIA.
9. Re-review this tactics list and be confident in maximizing your score.

STUDY UNIT ONE
STANDARDS AND PROFICIENCY

(26 pages of outline)

The mandatory auditing pronouncements of The Institute of Internal Auditors (The IIA) -- the **International Standards for the Professional Practice of Internal Auditing (Standards)** -- are reproduced here, along with a listing (Glossary) of useful terms. The Standards are included in full in this study unit as a convenient reference for the examination candidate. However, they will be repeated in other study units and subunits as appropriate. Thus, they are integrated with nonmandatory pronouncements of The IIA and other outline material.

The **environments and organizations** in which internal audit activities are performed throughout the world or even within one country are highly diverse. Moreover, these activities may be **insourced** or **outsourced**. This diversity of laws, customs, and cultures affects the practice of internal auditing in each environment and organization. Nevertheless, **individuals** and **entities** providing internal auditing services must still comply with the Standards. Thus, the Standards and other pronouncements of The IIA have no geographic limits. Accordingly, the Standards are presented as broad principles because they may be applied in very different circumstances.

According to The IIA, the Standards are part of the **International Professional Practices Framework (PPF)**. They are intended to

a. State basic principles for the practice of internal auditing
b. Provide a framework for performing and promoting value-added internal audit activities
c. Establish the basis for evaluating internal auditing performance
d. Improve organizational processes and operations

The Standards consist of Attribute Standards (currently 1000-1340), Performance Standards (currently 2000-2600), and Implementation Standards (integrated with the other Standards). **Attribute Standards** concern the traits of entities and parties providing internal auditing services. **Performance Standards** describe internal audit activities and criteria for evaluation of their performance. Attribute and Performance Standards apply regardless of the service performed. Thus, they furnish guidance for assurance, consulting, and other internal auditing services.

Each group of **implementation standards** applies only to a major category of engagements. They apply the other standards in a more specific context. To date, final Implementation Standards have been issued for assurance services (e.g., 1110.A1) and consulting services (e.g., 1000.C1).

a. An internal auditor who provides an **assurance service** determines the nature and scope of the engagement and objectively assesses (evaluates) the evidence gathered. The evidence and its evaluation form the basis for expressing an opinion or stating a conclusion about the subject matter of the engagement, such as a process or system. The **three parties** to an assurance service are the process owner (the party directly involved with the process or system), the internal auditor (the assessor), and the user of the assessment.

b. An internal auditor who provides a **consulting service** ordinarily does so at the client's request. The nature and scope of this advisory service are agreed upon with the client. The **two parties** to a consulting service are the internal auditor (the advisor) and the client (the advisee).

The final subunits address the **proficiency** of internal auditors individually and collectively.

Core Concepts

- Attribute Standards describe the characteristics of entities and individuals that provide internal auditing services.
- Performance Standards provide criteria for guiding and evaluating all internal audit activities.
- Implementation Standards apply the other standards in the context of specific categories of engagements, e.g., assurance and consulting.
- *Internal auditing is an independent, objective assurance and consulting activity designed to add value and improve an organization's operations. It helps an organization accomplish its objectives by bringing a systematic, disciplined approach to evaluate and improve the effectiveness of risk management, control, and governance processes.*
- Engagements should be performed with proficiency and due professional care.
- Internal auditors should continue their professional education.

1.1 INTERNATIONAL PROFESSIONAL PRACTICES FRAMEWORK (PPF)

1. The **Internal Auditing Standards Board (IASB)** is charged by The IIA with developing professional standards for internal auditing. Its primary responsibility is to provide guidance to practitioners.

2. The **Ethics Committee** considers needed changes in the The IIA Code of Ethics and investigates complaints against members of The IIA and CIAs.

   a. A change in The IIA's content specification outline for Part I added a topic about compliance (and promoting compliance) with The IIA Code of Ethics. Thus, candidates should review Study Unit 10, which covers The IIA Code of Ethics.

3. **Guidance-setting processes and due diligence.** The IPPF is the **conceptual framework** that organizes authoritative guidance promulgated by The IIA. The scope of the IPPF extends only to **authoritative guidance** developed by an IIA international technical committee following appropriate **due process**. Technical committees are those committees and boards reporting to the Professional Practices Council (Internal Auditing Standards Board, Professional Issues Committee, Advanced Technology Committee, Board of Regents, Committee on Quality, and the Ethics Committee). Authoritative guidance consists of two categories:
   a. **Mandatory.** Compliance is required, and the guidance is developed following **due process**, which includes public exposure. Compliance with the principles set forth in mandatory guidance is essential for the professional practice of internal auditing.
   b. **Strongly recommended.** Compliance is strongly recommended, and the guidance is endorsed by The IIA through a formal review and approval process. It describes practices to implement effectively the Code of Ethics and Standards.
4. **Categories of Guidance.** The IPPF consists of
   a. Mandatory guidance (Definition of Internal Auditing, Standards, Interpretations, and the Code of Ethics)
   b. Strongly recommended but not mandatory guidance (Position Papers, Practice Advisories, and Practice Guides)
5. The foundation of the IPPF is the **definition of internal auditing**. It should be memorized.

   Internal auditing is an independent, objective assurance and consulting activity designed to add value and improve an organization's operations. It helps an organization accomplish its objectives by bringing a systematic, disciplined approach to evaluate and improve the effectiveness of risk management, control, and governance processes.

   a. **Key elements of the definition.** Internal auditing
      1) Is independent and objective
      2) Engages in assurance and consulting activities
      3) Adds value and improves operations
      4) Has a systematic, disciplined approach
      5) Evaluates risk management, control, and governance

6. The following is an overview of the IPPF:

<table>
<tr><th>Description</th><th>Final Approval</th></tr>
<tr><td colspan="2">Definition of Internal Auditing</td></tr>
<tr><td>The Definition is a statement of the fundamental purpose, nature, and scope of internal auditing.</td><td>Board of Directors</td></tr>
<tr><td colspan="2">Code of Ethics</td></tr>
<tr><td>The Code is a statement of the principles and expectations governing the behavior of individuals and organizations in the conduct of internal auditing.

The Code is a description of the minimum requirements for conduct. The Code describes behavioral expectations rather than specific activities.</td><td>Board of Directors</td></tr>
<tr><td colspan="2">Standards</td></tr>
<tr><td>The Standards consist of Statements and Interpretations. Both must be considered to understand and apply the Standards correctly.

1. Statements are basic requirements for the professional practice of internal auditing and for evaluating the effectiveness of its performance. They are internationally applicable at the organizational and individual level, are principle-focused, and provide a framework for performing and promoting internal auditing as defined. The Statements include the following:
a. Attribute Standards relate to the attributes of the internal auditing organization or attributes personal to the internal auditor, including objectivity and independence, professional proficiency, and compliance with standards.
b. Performance Standards are applicable to the performance of work and address managing the internal audit processes; assessing risk, control, and governance processes; planning the engagement; testing and analyzing information; evaluating evidential matter; and communicating results.
c. Implementation Standards address appropriate means of applying Attribute and Performance Standards. Currently, they have been issued only for assurance and consulting activities. Such assurance and consulting services cover a broad range of topics. They include reporting on internal control, information technology, fraud investigations, directed topics, and standards issued by other standards setting bodies and adopted by The IIA.

2. Interpretations clarify terms or concepts within the Statements.</td><td>• Internal Auditing Standards Board
• Internal Audit Standards Oversight Board</td></tr>
<tr><td colspan="2">Position Papers</td></tr>
<tr><td>A Position Paper is an IIA statement to assist a wide range of interested parties, including those not in the internal auditing profession in (1) understanding significant governance, risk, or control issues and (2) delineating the related roles and responsibilities of the internal audit profession.</td><td>Executive Committee</td></tr>
<tr><td colspan="2">Practice Advisories</td></tr>
<tr><td>Practice Advisories address approach, methodology, and considerations, but not detailed processes and procedures, addressed in Practice Guides.

Practice Advisories provide concise and timely guidance to assist internal auditors in applying the Code of Ethics and the Standards and promoting good practices.

These practices relate to:
• International, country, or industry-specific issues;
• Specific types of engagements; and
• Legal or regulatory issues.</td><td>Professional Practices Council</td></tr>
<tr><td colspan="2">Practice Guides</td></tr>
<tr><td>Practice Guides provide detailed guidance for conducting internal audit activities. They describe detailed processes and procedures, such as tools and techniques, programs, step-by-step approaches, and examples of deliverables.</td><td>Professional Practices Council</td></tr>
</table>

a. **The IIA Code of Ethics** is in Study Unit 10.
b. The full text of the **Standards** is in Study Unit 1, Subunits 1.2 and 1.3. Individual sections also appear in the appropriate study units in *CIA Review* Parts I and II.
c. **Practice Advisories** are presented with the related sections of the Standards.

7. Stop and review! You have completed the outline for this subunit. Study multiple-choice questions 1 through 5 beginning on page 46.

1.2 ATTRIBUTE STANDARDS

1. These Standards apply to all who provide internal auditing services, regardless of the nature of the services.
2. **Implementation Standards** are integrated with the Attribute Standards. They pertain to specific types of services and are designated by **A (assurance)** or **C (consulting)**.
3. The following are the Attribute Standards and the related Implementation Standards:

1000 ***Purpose, Authority, and Responsibility*** – *The purpose, authority, and responsibility of the internal audit activity should be formally defined in a charter, consistent with the Standards, and approved by the board.*

1000.A1 – *The nature of assurance services provided to the organization should be defined in the audit charter. If assurance services are to be provided to parties outside the organization, the nature of these assurances should also be defined in the charter.*

1000.C1 – *The nature of consulting services should be defined in the audit charter.*

1100 ***Independence and Objectivity*** – *The internal audit activity should be independent, and internal auditors should be objective in performing their work.*

1110 ***Organizational Independence*** – *The chief audit executive should report to a level within the organization that allows the internal audit activity to fulfill its responsibilities.*

1110.A1 – *The internal audit activity should be free from interference in determining the scope of internal auditing, performing work, and communicating results.*

1120 ***Individual Objectivity*** – *Internal auditors should have an impartial, unbiased attitude and avoid conflicts of interest.*

1130 ***Impairments to Independence or Objectivity*** – *If independence or objectivity is impaired in fact or appearance, the details of the impairment should be disclosed to appropriate parties. The nature of the disclosure will depend upon the impairment.*

1130.A1 – *Internal auditors should refrain from assessing specific operations for which they were previously responsible. Objectivity is presumed to be impaired if an internal auditor provides assurance services for an activity for which the internal auditor had responsibility within the previous year.*

1130.A2 – *Assurance engagements for functions over which the chief audit executive has responsibility should be overseen by a party outside the internal audit activity.*

1130.C1 – *Internal auditors may provide consulting services relating to operations for which they had previous responsibilities.*

1130.C2 – *If internal auditors have potential impairments to independence or objectivity relating to proposed consulting services, disclosure should be made to the engagement client prior to accepting the engagement.*

1200 ***Proficiency and Due Professional Care*** – *Engagements should be performed with proficiency and due professional care.*

1210 ***Proficiency*** – *Internal auditors should possess the knowledge, skills, and other competencies needed to perform their individual responsibilities. The internal audit activity collectively should possess or obtain the knowledge, skills, and other competencies needed to perform its responsibilities.*

1210.A1 – *The chief audit executive should obtain competent advice and assistance if the internal audit staff lacks the knowledge, skills, or other competencies needed to perform all or part of the engagement.*

1210.A2 – *The internal auditor should have sufficient knowledge to identify the indicators of fraud but is not expected to have the expertise of a person whose primary responsibility is detecting and investigating fraud.*

1210.A3 – *Internal auditors should have knowledge of key information technology risks and controls and available technology-based audit techniques to perform their assigned work. However, not all internal auditors are expected to have the expertise of an internal auditor whose primary responsibility is information technology auditing.*

1210.C1 – *The chief audit executive should decline the consulting engagement or obtain competent advice and assistance if the internal audit staff lacks the knowledge, skills, or other competencies needed to perform all or part of the engagement.*

1220 ***Due Professional Care*** – *Internal auditors should apply the care and skill expected of a reasonably prudent and competent internal auditor. Due professional care does not imply infallibility.*

1220.A1 – *The internal auditor should exercise due professional care by considering the:*

- *Extent of work needed to achieve the engagement's objectives.*
- *Relative complexity, materiality, or significance of matters to which assurance procedures are applied.*
- *Adequacy and effectiveness of risk management, control, and governance processes.*
- *Probability of significant errors, irregularities, or noncompliance.*
- *Cost of assurance in relation to potential benefits.*

1220.A2 – *In exercising due professional care, the internal auditor should consider the use of computer-assisted audit tools and other data analysis techniques.*

1220.A3 – *The internal auditor should be alert to the significant risks that might affect objectives, operations, or resources. However, assurance procedures alone, even when performed with due professional care, do not guarantee that all significant risks will be identified.*

1220.C1 – *The internal auditor should exercise due professional care during a consulting engagement by considering the:*

- *Needs and expectations of engagement clients, including the nature, timing, and communication of engagement results.*
- *Relative complexity and extent of work needed to achieve the engagement's objectives.*
- *Cost of the consulting engagement in relation to potential benefits.*

1230 ***Continuing Professional Development*** – *Internal auditors should enhance their knowledge, skills, and other competencies through continuing professional development.*

***1300 <u>Quality Assurance and Improvement Program</u>** – The chief audit executive should develop and maintain a quality assurance and improvement program that covers all aspects of the internal audit activity and continuously monitors its effectiveness. This program includes periodic internal and external quality assessments and ongoing internal monitoring. Each part of the program should be designed to help the internal auditing activity add value and improve the organization's operations and to provide assurance that the internal audit activity is in conformity with the Standards and the Code of Ethics.*

***1310 <u>Quality Program Assessments</u>** – The internal audit activity should adopt a process to monitor and assess the overall effectiveness of the quality program. The process should include both internal and external assessments.*

***1311 <u>Internal Assessments</u>** – Internal assessments should include:*

- *Ongoing reviews of the performance of the internal audit activity; and*
- *Periodic reviews performed through self-assessment or by other persons within the organization with knowledge of internal auditing practices and the Standards.*

***1312 <u>External Assessments</u>** – External assessments should be conducted at least once every five years by a qualified, independent reviewer or review team from outside the organization. The potential need for more frequent external assessments as well as the qualifications and independence of the external reviewer or review team, including any potential conflict of interest, should be discussed by the CAE with the Board. Such discussions should also consider the size, complexity, and industry of the organization in relation to the experience of the reviewer or review team.*

***1320 <u>Reporting on the Quality Program</u>** – The chief audit executive should communicate the results of external assessments to the board.*

***1330 <u>Use of "Conducted in Accordance with the Standards"</u>** – Internal auditors are encouraged to report that their activities are "conducted in accordance with the International Standards for the Professional Practice of Internal Auditing." However, internal auditors may use the statement only if assessments of the quality improvement program demonstrate that the internal audit activity is in compliance with the Standards.*

***1340 <u>Disclosure of Noncompliance</u>** – Although the internal audit activity should achieve full compliance with the Standards and internal auditors with the Code of Ethics, there may be instances in which full compliance is not achieved. When noncompliance impacts the overall scope or operation of the internal audit activity, disclosure should be made to senior management and the board.*

4. **Attribute Standards Review**

   1000 Purpose, Authority, and Responsibility
   1100 Independence and Objectivity
   1200 Proficiency and Due Professional Care
   1300 Quality Assurance and Improvement Program

5. Stop and review! You have completed the outline for this subunit. Study multiple-choice question 6 on page 48.

1.3 PERFORMANCE STANDARDS

1. These Standards describe the activities of internal auditors. They also state criteria for measuring the quality of services rendered.
2. **Implementation Standards** are integrated with the Performance Standards. They pertain to specific types of services and are designated by **A (assurance)** or **C (consulting)**.
3. The following are the Performance Standards and the related Implementation Standards:

2000 *__Managing the Internal Audit Activity__ – The chief audit executive should effectively manage the internal audit activity to ensure it adds value to the organization.*

2010 *__Planning__ – The chief audit executive should establish risk-based plans to determine the priorities of the internal audit activity, consistent with the organization's goals.*

2010.A1 *– The internal audit activity's plan of engagements should be based on a risk assessment, undertaken at least annually. The input of senior management and the board should be considered in this process.*

2010.C1 *– The chief audit executive should consider accepting proposed consulting engagements based on the engagement's potential to improve management of risks, add value, and improve the organization's operations. Those engagements that have been accepted should be included in the plan.*

2020 *__Communication and Approval__ – The chief audit executive should communicate the internal audit activity's plans and resource requirements, including significant interim changes, to senior management and to the board for review and approval. The chief audit executive should also communicate the impact of resource limitations.*

2030 *__Resource Management__ – The chief audit executive should ensure that internal audit resources are appropriate, sufficient, and effectively deployed to achieve the approved plan.*

2040 *__Policies and Procedures__ – The chief audit executive should establish policies and procedures to guide the internal audit activity.*

2050 *__Coordination__ – The chief audit executive should share information and coordinate activities with other internal and external providers of relevant assurance and consulting services to ensure proper coverage and minimize duplication of efforts.*

2060 *__Reporting to the Board and Senior Management__ – The chief audit executive should report periodically to the board and senior management on the internal audit activity's purpose, authority, responsibility, and performance relative to its plan. Reporting should also include significant risk exposures and control issues, corporate governance issues, and other matters needed or requested by the board and senior management.*

2100 **Nature of Work** – *The internal audit activity evaluates and contributes to the improvement of risk management, control, and governance processes using a systematic and disciplined approach.*

2110 **Risk Management** – *The internal audit activity should assist the organization by identifying and evaluating significant exposures to risk and contributing to the improvement of risk management and control systems.*

2110.A1 – *The internal audit activity should monitor and evaluate the effectiveness of the organization's risk management system.*

2110.A2 – *The internal audit activity should evaluate risk exposures relating to the organization's governance, operations, and information systems regarding the*

- *Reliability and integrity of financial and operational information.*
- *Effectiveness and efficiency of operations.*
- *Safeguarding of assets.*
- *Compliance with laws, regulations, and contracts.*

2110.C1 – *During consulting engagements, internal auditors should address risk consistent with the engagement's objectives and should be alert to the existence of other significant risks.*

2110.C2 – *Internal auditors should incorporate knowledge of risks gained from consulting engagements into the process of identifying and evaluating significant risk exposures of the organization.*

2120 **Control** – *The internal audit activity should assist the organization in maintaining effective controls by evaluating their effectiveness and efficiency and by promoting continuous improvement.*

2120.A1 – *Based on the results of the risk assessment, the internal audit activity should evaluate the adequacy and effectiveness of controls encompassing the organization's governance, operations, and information systems. This should include:*

- *Reliability and integrity of financial and operational information.*
- *Effectiveness and efficiency of operations.*
- *Safeguarding of assets.*
- *Compliance with laws, regulations, and contracts.*

2120.A2 – *Internal auditors should ascertain the extent to which operating and program goals and objectives have been established and conform to those of the organization.*

2120.A3 – *Internal auditors should review operations and programs to ascertain the extent to which results are consistent with established goals and objectives to determine whether operations and programs are being implemented or performed as intended.*

2120.A4 – *Adequate criteria are needed to evaluate controls. Internal auditors should ascertain the extent to which management has established adequate criteria to determine whether objectives and goals have been accomplished. If adequate, internal auditors should use such criteria in their evaluation. If inadequate, internal auditors should work with management to develop appropriate evaluation criteria.*

2120.C1 – *During consulting engagements, internal auditors should address controls consistent with the engagement's objectives and should be alert to the existence of any significant control weaknesses.*

2120.C2 – *Internal auditors should incorporate knowledge of controls gained from consulting engagements into the process of identifying and evaluating significant risk exposures of the organization.*

2130 ***Governance*** *– The internal audit activity should assess and make appropriate recommendations for improving the governance process in its accomplishment of the following objectives:*

- *Promoting appropriate ethics and values within the organization.*
- *Ensuring effective organizational performance management and accountability.*
- *Effectively communicating risk and control information to appropriate areas of the organization.*
- *Effectively coordinating the activities of and communicating information among the board, external and internal auditors and management.*

2130.A1 *– The internal audit activity should evaluate the design, implementation, and effectiveness of the organization's ethics-related objectives, programs, and activities.*

2130.C1 *– Consulting engagement objectives should be consistent with the overall values and goals of the organization.*

2200 ***Engagement Planning*** *– Internal auditors should develop and record a plan for each engagement, including the scope, objectives, timing, and resource allocations.*

2201 ***Planning Considerations*** *– In planning the engagement, internal auditors should consider:*

- *The objectives of the activity being reviewed and the means by which the activity controls its performance.*
- *The significant risks to the activity, its objectives, resources, and operations and the means by which the potential impact of risk is kept to an acceptable level.*
- *The adequacy and effectiveness of the activity's risk management and control systems compared to a relevant control framework or model.*
- *The opportunities for making significant improvements to the activity's risk management and control systems.*

2201.A1 *– When planning an engagement for parties outside the organization, internal auditors should establish a written understanding with them about objectives, scope, respective responsibilities, and other expectations, including restrictions on distribution of the results of the engagement and access to engagement records.*

2201.C1 *– Internal auditors should establish an understanding with consulting engagement clients about objectives, scope, respective responsibilities, and other client expectations. For significant engagements, this understanding should be documented.*

2210 ***Engagement Objectives*** *– Objectives should be established for each engagement.*

2210.A1 *– Internal auditors should conduct a preliminary assessment of the risks relevant to the activity under review. Engagement objectives should reflect the results of this assessment.*

2210.A2 *– The internal auditor should consider the probability of significant errors, irregularities, noncompliance, and other exposures when developing the engagement objectives.*

2210.C1 *– Consulting engagement objectives should address risks, controls, and governance processes to the extent agreed upon with the client.*

***2220 Engagement Scope** – The established scope should be sufficient to satisfy the objectives of the engagement.*

__2220.A1__ – The scope of the engagement should include consideration of relevant systems, records, personnel, and physical properties, including those under the control of third parties.

__2220.A2__ – If significant consulting opportunities arise during an assurance engagement, a specific written understanding as to the objectives, scope, respective responsibilities, and other expectations should be reached and the results of the consulting engagement communicated in accordance with consulting standards.

__2220.C1__ – In performing consulting engagements, internal auditors should ensure that the scope of the engagement is sufficient to address the agreed-upon objectives. If internal auditors develop reservations about the scope during the engagement, these reservations should be discussed with the client to determine whether to continue with the engagement.

***2230 Engagement Resource Allocation** – Internal auditors should determine appropriate resources to achieve engagement objectives. Staffing should be based on an evaluation of the nature and complexity of each engagement, time constraints, and available resources.*

***2240 Engagement Work Program** – Internal auditors should develop work programs that achieve the engagement objectives. These work programs should be recorded.*

__2240.A1__ – Work programs should establish the procedures for identifying, analyzing, evaluating, and recording information during the engagement. The work program should be approved prior to its implementation, and any adjustments approved promptly.

__2240.C1__ – Work programs for consulting engagements may vary in form and content depending upon the nature of the engagement.

***2300 Performing the Engagement** – Internal auditors should identify, analyze, evaluate, and record sufficient information to achieve the engagement's objectives.*

***2310 Identifying Information** – Internal auditors should identify sufficient, reliable, relevant, and useful information to achieve the engagement's objectives.*

***2320 Analysis and Evaluation** – Internal auditors should base conclusions and engagement results on appropriate analyses and evaluations.*

***2330 Recording Information** – Internal auditors should record relevant information to support the conclusions and engagement results.*

__2330.A1__ – The chief audit executive should control access to engagement records. The chief audit executive should obtain the approval of senior management and/or legal counsel prior to releasing such records to external parties, as appropriate.

__2330.A2__ – The chief audit executive should develop retention requirements for engagement records. These retention requirements should be consistent with the organization's guidelines and any pertinent regulatory or other requirements.

__2330.C1__ – The chief audit executive should develop policies governing the custody and retention of engagement records, as well as their release to internal and external parties. These policies should be consistent with the organization's guidelines and any pertinent regulatory or other requirements.

***2340 Engagement Supervision** – Engagements should be properly supervised to ensure objectives are achieved, quality is assured, and staff is developed.*

2400 ***<u>Communicating Results</u>*** *– Internal auditors should communicate the engagement results.*

2410 ***<u>Criteria for Communicating</u>*** *– Communications should include the engagement's objectives and scope as well as applicable conclusions, recommendations, and action plans.*

2410.A1 *– Final communication of engagement results should, where appropriate, contain the internal auditor's overall opinion and/or conclusions.*

2410.A2 *– Internal auditors are encouraged to acknowledge satisfactory performance in engagement communications.*

2410.A3 *– When releasing engagement results to parties outside the organization, the communication should include limitations on distribution and use of the results.*

2410.C1 *– Communication of the progress and results of consulting engagements will vary in form and content depending upon the nature of the engagement and the needs of the client.*

2420 ***<u>Quality of Communications</u>*** *– Communications should be accurate, objective, clear, concise, constructive, complete, and timely.*

2421 ***<u>Errors and Omissions</u>*** *– If a final communication contains a significant error or omission, the chief audit executive should communicate corrected information to all parties who received the original communication.*

2430 ***<u>Engagement Disclosure of Noncompliance with the Standards</u>*** *– When noncompliance with the Standards impacts a specific engagement, communication of the results should disclose the:*

- *Standard(s) with which full compliance was not achieved,*
- *Reason(s) for noncompliance, and*
- *Impact of noncompliance on the engagement.*

2440 ***<u>Disseminating Results</u>*** *– The chief audit executive should disseminate results to the appropriate parties.*

2440.A1 *– The chief audit executive is responsible for communicating the final results to parties who can ensure that the results are given due consideration.*

2440.A2 *– If not otherwise mandated by legal, statutory or regulatory requirements, prior to releasing results to parties outside the organization, the chief audit executive should:*

- *Assess the potential risk to the organization.*
- *Consult with senior management and/or legal counsel as appropriate.*
- *Control dissemination by restricting the use of the results.*

2440.C1 *– The chief audit executive is responsible for communicating the final results of consulting engagements to clients.*

2440.C2 *– During consulting engagements, risk management, control, and governance issues may be identified. Whenever these issues are significant to the organization, they should be communicated to senior management and the board.*

***2500 Monitoring Progress** – The chief audit executive should establish and maintain a system to monitor the disposition of results communicated to management.*

__2500.A1__ – The chief audit executive should establish a follow-up process to monitor and ensure that management actions have been effectively implemented or that senior management has accepted the risk of not taking action.

__2500.C1__ – The internal audit activity should monitor the disposition of results of consulting engagements to the extent agreed upon with the client.

***2600 Resolution of Management's Acceptance of Risks** – When the chief audit executive believes that senior management has accepted a level of residual risk that may be unacceptable to the organization, the chief audit executive should discuss the matter with senior management. If the decision regarding residual risk is not resolved, the chief audit executive and senior management should report the matter to the board for resolution.*

4. **Performance Standards Review**

   2000 Managing the Internal Audit Activity
   2100 Nature of Work
   2200 Engagement Planning
   2300 Performing the Engagement
   2400 Communicating Results
   2500 Monitoring Progress
   2600 Resolution of Management's Acceptance of Risks

5. Stop and review! You have completed the outline for this subunit. Study multiple-choice questions 7 and 8 on page 48.

1.4 GLOSSARY

1. The **Glossary** that accompanies the Standards contains important terminology.
   a. For example, "internal audit activity" and "chief audit executive" replaced "internal auditing department" and "internal auditing director," respectively. These changes follow from the reality that the internal auditing function is often outsourced.
   b. Furthermore, the term "internal audit activity" is stated in terms of the definition of internal auditing.
   c. Other key definitions include those related to the nature of the work of the internal audit activity ("risk," "risk management," "control," and "governance") and the kinds of engagements performed ("assurance services" and "consulting services").

Glossary

***Add Value** - Value is provided by improving opportunities to achieve organizational objectives, identifying operational improvement, and/or reducing risk exposure through both assurance and consulting services.*

***Adequate Control** - Present if management has planned and organized (designed) in a manner that provides reasonable assurance that the organization's risks have been managed effectively and that the organization's goals and objectives will be achieved efficiently and economically.*

***Assurance Services** - An objective examination of evidence for the purpose of providing an independent assessment on risk management, control, or governance processes for the organization. Examples may include financial, performance, compliance, system security, and due diligence engagements.*

Board *- A board is an organization's governing body, such as a board of directors, supervisory board, head of an agency or legislative body, board of governors or trustees of a nonprofit organization, or any other designated body of the organization, including the audit committee, to whom the chief audit executive may functionally report.*

Charter *- The charter of the internal audit activity is a formal written document that defines the activity's purpose, authority, and responsibility. The charter should (a) establish the internal audit activity's position within the organization; (b) authorize access to records, personnel, and physical properties relevant to the performance of engagements; and (c) define the scope of internal audit activities.*

Chief Audit Executive (CAE) *- Top position within the organization responsible for internal audit activities. Normally, this would be the internal audit director. In the case where internal audit activities are obtained from outside service providers, the chief audit executive is the person responsible for overseeing the service contract and the overall quality assurance of these activities, reporting to senior management and the board regarding internal audit activities, and follow-up of engagement results. The term also includes such titles as general auditor, chief internal auditor, and inspector general.*

Code of Ethics *- The Code of Ethics of The Institute of Internal Auditors (IIA) consists of Principles relevant to the profession and practice of internal auditing and Rules of Conduct that describe behavior expected of internal auditors. The Code of Ethics applies to both parties and entities that provide internal audit services. The purpose of the Code of Ethics is to promote an ethical culture in the global profession of internal auditing.*

Compliance *- Conformity and adherence to policies, plans, procedures, laws, regulations, contracts, or other requirements.*

Conflict of Interest *- Any relationship that is or appears to be not in the best interest of the organization. A conflict of interest would prejudice an individual's ability to perform his or her duties and responsibilities objectively.*

Consulting Services *- Advisory and related client service activities, the nature and scope of which are agreed with the client and which are intended to add value and improve an organization's governance, risk management, and control processes without the internal auditor assuming management responsibility. Examples include counsel, advice, facilitation, and training.*

Control *- Any action taken by management, the board, and other parties to manage risk and increase the likelihood that established objectives and goals will be achieved. Management plans, organizes, and directs the performance of sufficient actions to provide reasonable assurance that objectives and goals will be achieved.*

Control Environment *- The attitude and actions of the board and management regarding the significance of control within the organization. The control environment provides the discipline and structure for the achievement of the primary objectives of the system of internal control. The control environment includes the following elements:*

- *Integrity and ethical values*
- *Management's philosophy and operating style*
- *Organizational structure*
- *Assignment of authority and responsibility*
- *Human resource policies and practices*
- *Competence of personnel*

Control Processes *- The policies, procedures, and activities that are part of a control framework designed to ensure that risks are contained within the risk tolerances established by the risk management process.*

Engagement *- A specific internal audit assignment, task, or review activity, such as an internal audit, Control Self-Assessment review, fraud examination, or consultancy. An engagement may include multiple tasks or activities designed to accomplish a specific set of related objectives.*

Engagement Objectives *- Broad statements developed by internal auditors that define intended engagement accomplishments.*

Engagement Work Program *- A document that lists the procedures to be followed during an engagement designed to achieve the engagement plan.*

External Service Provider *- A person or firm outside of the organization who has special knowledge, skill, and experience in a particular discipline.*

Fraud *- Any illegal acts characterized by deceit, concealment, or violation of trust. These acts are not dependent upon the application of threat of violence or of physical force. Frauds are perpetrated by parties and organizations to obtain money, property, or services; to avoid payment or loss of services; or to secure personal or business advantage.*

Governance *- The combination of processes and structures implemented by the board in order to inform, direct, manage, and monitor the activities of the organization toward the achievement of its objectives.*

Impairments *- Impairments to individual objectivity and organizational independence may include personal conflicts of interest; scope limitations; restrictions on access to records, personnel, and properties; and resource limitations (funding).*

Independence *- The freedom from conditions that threaten objectivity or the appearance of objectivity. Such threats to objectivity must be managed at the individual auditor, engagement, functional, and organizational levels.*

Internal Audit Activity (IAA) *- A department, division, team of consultants, or other practitioner(s) that provides independent, objective assurance and consulting services designed to add value and improve an organization's operations. The internal audit activity helps an organization accomplish its objectives by bringing a systematic, disciplined approach to evaluate and improve the effectiveness of risk management, control, and governance processes.*

Objectivity *- An unbiased mental attitude that allows internal auditors to perform engagements in such a manner that they have an honest belief in their work product and that no significant quality compromises are made. Objectivity requires internal auditors not to subordinate their judgment on audit matters to that of others.*

Residual Risks *- The risk remaining after management takes action to reduce the impact and likelihood of an adverse event, including control activities, in responding to a risk.*

Risk *- The possibility of an event occurring that could have an impact on the achievement of objectives. Risk is measured in terms of impact and likelihood.*

Risk Management *- A process to identify, assess, manage, and control potential events or situations to provide reasonable assurance regarding the achievement of the organization's objectives.*

Should *- The use of the word "should" in the Standards represents a mandatory obligation.*

Standard *- A professional pronouncement promulgated by the Internal Auditing Standards Board that delineates the requirements for performing a broad range of internal audit activities and evaluating internal audit performance.*

2. **Glossary Review**
   a. Among the key definitions given, the following are the most basic:
      1) Assurance services
      2) Consulting services
      3) Control
      4) Governance
      5) Internal audit activity (compare the definition of internal auditing in Subunit 1.1)
      6) Risk management
3. Stop and review! You have completed the outline for this subunit. Study multiple-choice questions 9 through 15 beginning on page 49.

1.5 PROFICIENCY

1. Maintenance of a high degree of **competence** in the performance of work is a characteristic of a profession. Accordingly, The IIA issues pronouncements to
   a. Impart an understanding of the roles and responsibilities of internal auditing to its constituencies,
   b. Establish the basis for the guidance and measurement of internal auditing performance, and
   c. Improve the practice of internal auditing.
2. Proficiency is also an **ethical obligation** of entities and individuals that provide internal auditing services. The Principles and Rules of Conduct from The IIA Code of Ethics are pertinent to this aspect of proficiency. Thus, internal auditors

   1.1 Shall perform their work with honesty, diligence, and responsibility

   4.1 Shall engage only in those services for which they have the necessary knowledge, skills, and experience

   4.2 Shall perform internal auditing services in accordance with the International Standards for the Professional Practice of Internal Auditing

   4.3 Shall continually improve their proficiency and the effectiveness and quality of their services
3. This subunit describes the attributes of individual internal auditors and of the internal audit activity (IAA) that allow services to be performed with proficiency. These matters are covered in one General Attribute Standard, one Specific Attribute Standard, three Assurance Implementation Standards, one Consulting Implementation Standard, and four Practice Advisories.
4. ***1200*** ***Proficiency and Due Professional Care*** *– Engagements should be performed with proficiency and due professional care.*
   a. ***PRACTICE ADVISORY 1200-1: PROFICIENCY AND DUE PROFESSIONAL CARE***
      1. *Professional proficiency is the responsibility of the* ***chief audit executive*** *and* ***each internal auditor****. The chief audit executive should ensure that persons assigned to each engagement collectively possess the necessary knowledge, skills, and other competencies to conduct the engagement properly.*
      2. *Internal auditors should* ***comply with professional standards of conduct****. The Institute of Internal Auditors' Code of Ethics extends beyond the definition of internal auditing to include two essential components:*
         - ***Principles*** *that are relevant to the profession and practice of internal auditing -- specifically, integrity, objectivity, confidentiality, and competency; and*

- ***Rules of Conduct** that describe behavior norms expected of internal auditors. These rules are an aid to interpreting the Principles into practical applications and are intended to guide the ethical conduct of internal auditors.*

PA Summary

- The CAE and each auditor are responsible for the **collective proficiency** of the IAA and his/her own proficiency, respectively.
- The CAE should ensure that persons assigned to each engagement collectively possess the necessary **knowledge, skills, and other competencies**.
- Internal auditors should comply with **The IIA Code of Ethics**.

5. ***1210*** ***Proficiency*** *– Internal auditors should possess the knowledge, skills, and other competencies needed to perform their individual responsibilities. The internal audit activity collectively should possess or obtain the knowledge, skills, and other competencies needed to perform its responsibilities.*

a. ***PRACTICE ADVISORY 1210-1: PROFICIENCY***

1. *Each internal auditor should possess certain knowledge, skills, and other competencies:*
   - ***Proficiency in applying internal auditing standards, procedures, and techniques** is required in performing engagements. Proficiency means the ability to apply knowledge to situations likely to be encountered and to deal with them without extensive recourse to technical research and assistance.*
   - ***Proficiency in accounting principles and techniques** is required of auditors who work extensively with financial records and reports.*
   - *An **understanding of management principles** is required to recognize and evaluate the materiality and significance of deviations from good business practices. An understanding means the ability to apply broad knowledge to situations likely to be encountered, to recognize significant deviations, and to be able to carry out the research necessary to arrive at reasonable solutions.*
   - *An **appreciation** is required of the fundamentals of subjects such as accounting, economics, commercial law, taxation, finance, quantitative methods, and information technology. An appreciation means the ability to recognize the existence of problems or potential problems and to determine the further research to be undertaken or the assistance to be obtained.*
2. *Internal auditors should be skilled in **dealing with people and in communicating** effectively. Internal auditors should understand human relations and maintain satisfactory relationships with engagement clients.*
3. *Internal auditors should be skilled in **oral and written communications** so that they can clearly and effectively convey such matters as engagement objectives, evaluations, conclusions, and recommendations.*
4. *The chief audit executive should establish suitable **criteria of education and experience** for filling internal auditing positions, giving due consideration to scope of work and level of responsibility. Reasonable assurance should be obtained as to each prospective auditor's qualifications and proficiency.*
5. *The internal auditing staff should **collectively possess** the knowledge and skills essential to the practice of the profession within the organization.*

PA Summary

- Each auditor should be proficient in applying **auditing standards** and methods. **Proficiency** means the ability to apply knowledge to situations likely to be encountered and to deal with them without extensive recourse to technical research and assistance.
- Each auditor should be proficient in **accounting principles** if (s)he works extensively with financial data.
- Each auditor should have an understanding of **management principles** so as to be able to evaluate deviations from good practices. An **understanding** means the ability to apply broad knowledge to situations likely to be encountered, to recognize significant deviations, and to be able to do the research necessary for reasonable solutions.
- Each auditor should have an appreciation of other subjects such as accounting, economics, commercial law, taxation, finance, quantitative methods, and IT. An **appreciation** means the ability to recognize problems and to determine the research to be undertaken or the assistance to be obtained.
- Internal auditors should be skilled in **dealing with people and in communicating** effectively, both orally and in writing.
- The CAE should establish suitable **criteria or education and experience** for auditors, given their scope of work and level of responsibility.

6. ***1210.A1*** – *The chief audit executive should obtain competent advice and assistance if the internal audit staff lacks the knowledge, skills, or other competencies needed to perform all or part of the engagement.*

   a. ***PRACTICE ADVISORY 1210.A1-1: OBTAINING SERVICES TO SUPPORT OR COMPLEMENT THE INTERNAL AUDIT ACTIVITY***

      1. *The internal audit activity should have employees or use* ***outside service providers*** *who are qualified in disciplines such as accounting, auditing, economics, finance, statistics, information technology, engineering, taxation, law, environmental affairs, and such other areas as needed to meet the internal audit activity's responsibilities. Each member of the internal audit activity, however, need not be qualified in all disciplines.*
      2. *An outside service provider is a person or firm, independent of the organization, who has* ***special knowledge, skill, and experience*** *in a particular discipline. Outside service providers include, among others, actuaries, accountants, appraisers, environmental specialists, fraud investigators, lawyers, engineers, geologists, security specialists, statisticians, information technology specialists, the organization's external auditors, and other auditing organizations. An outside service provider may be engaged by the board, senior management, or the chief audit executive.*

3. ***Functions.*** *Outside service providers may be used by the internal audit activity in connection with, among other things:*
   - *Auditing activities for which a specialized skill and knowledge are required, such as information technology, statistics, taxes, language translations, or to achieve the objectives in the engagement work schedule*
   - *Valuations of assets such as land and buildings, works of art, precious gems, investments, and complex financial instruments*
   - *Determination of quantities or physical condition of certain assets, such as mineral and petroleum reserves*
   - *Measuring the work completed and to be completed on contracts in progress*
   - *Fraud and security investigations*
   - *Determination of amounts by using specialized methods, such as actuarial determinations of employee benefit obligations*
   - *Interpretation of legal, technical, and regulatory requirements*
   - *Evaluating the internal audit activity's quality improvement program in accordance with Section 1300 of the Standards*
   - *Mergers and acquisitions*
4. *When the chief audit executive intends to use and rely on the work of an outside service provider, the chief audit executive should* ***assess the competency, independence, and objectivity of the outside service provider*** *as it relates to the particular assignment to be performed. This assessment should also be made when the outside service provider is selected by senior management or the board, and the chief audit executive intends to use and rely on the outside service provider's work. When the selection is made by others and the chief audit executive's assessment determines that he or she should not use and rely on the work of an outside service provider, the results of the assessment should be communicated to senior management or the board, as appropriate.*
5. *The chief audit executive should determine that the outside service provider possesses the* ***necessary knowledge, skills, and other competencies*** *to perform the engagement. When assessing competency, the chief audit executive should consider the following:*
   - *Professional certification, license, or other recognition of the outside service provider's competency in the relevant discipline.*
   - *Membership of the outside service provider in an appropriate professional organization and adherence to that organization's code of ethics.*
   - *The reputation of the outside service provider. This may include contacting others familiar with the outside service provider's work.*
   - *The outside service provider's experience in the type of work being considered.*
   - *The extent of education and training received by the outside service provider in disciplines that pertain to the particular engagement.*
   - *The outside service provider's knowledge and experience in the industry in which the organization operates.*

6. *The chief audit executive should assess the **relationship of the outside service provider to the organization and to the internal audit activity** to ensure that independence and objectivity are maintained throughout the engagement. In performing the assessment, the chief audit executive should determine that there are no financial, organizational, or personal relationships that will prevent the outside service provider from rendering impartial and unbiased judgments and opinions when performing or reporting on the engagement.*

7. *In assessing the **independence and objectivity** of the outside service provider, the chief audit executive should consider:*
   - *The financial interest the provider may have in the organization*
   - *The personal or professional affiliation the provider may have with the board, senior management, or others within the organization*
   - *The relationship the provider may have had with the organization or the activities being reviewed*
   - *The extent of other ongoing services the provider may be performing for the organization*
   - *Compensation or other incentives that the provider may have*

8. *If the outside service provider is also the organization's **external auditor** and the nature of the engagement is **extended audit services**, the chief audit executive should ascertain that work performed does not **impair** the external auditor's **independence**. Extended audit services refers to those services beyond the requirements of auditing standards generally accepted by external auditors. If the organization's external auditors act or appear to act as members of senior management, management, or as employees of the organization, then their independence is impaired. Additionally, external auditors may provide the organization with other services such as tax and consulting. Independence, however, should be assessed in relation to the full range of services provided to the organization.*

9. *The chief audit executive should obtain sufficient information regarding the **scope of the outside service provider's work**. This is necessary in order to ascertain that the scope of work is adequate for the purposes of the internal auditing activity. It may be prudent to have these and other matters **documented** in an engagement letter or contract. The chief audit executive should review with the outside service provider:*
   - *Objectives and scope of work*
   - *Specific matters expected to be covered in the engagement communications*
   - *Access to relevant records, personnel, and physical properties*
   - *Information regarding assumptions and procedures to be employed*
   - *Ownership and custody of engagement working papers, if applicable*
   - *Confidentiality and restrictions on information obtained during the engagement*

10. *When the outside service provider performs **internal auditing activities**, the chief audit executive should specify and ensure that the work complies with the International Standards for the Professional Practice of Internal Auditing. In reviewing the work of an outside service provider, the chief audit executive should evaluate the **adequacy of work performed**. This evaluation should include **sufficiency of information** obtained to afford a reasonable basis for the conclusions reached and the resolution of significant exceptions or other unusual matters.*

11. *When the chief audit executive issues* ***engagement communications*** *and an outside service provider was used, the chief audit executive may, as appropriate, refer to such services provided. The outside service provider should be informed and, if appropriate, concurrence should be obtained prior to such reference being made in engagement communications.*

PA Summary

- The IAA should have employees or use **outside service providers** who are qualified in disciplines needed to meet its responsibilities. But each member of the IAA need not be qualified in all disciplines.
- An outside service provider (OSP) is an independent person or firm with **special knowledge, skill, and experience**. An OSP may be engaged by the board, senior management, or the CAE. Examples of functions of OSPs are (1) specialized auditing activities (e.g., taxes, IT, or language translations); (2) valuations of assets; (3) determination of quantities or condition of assets (e.g., mineral and petroleum reserves); (4) measuring work on contracts in progress; (5) fraud investigations; (6) actuarial determinations of employee benefit obligations; (7) interpretation of legal, technical, and regulatory requirements; (8) evaluating the IAA's quality improvement program; and (9) mergers and acquisitions.
- The CAE should assess the **competency, independence, and objectivity** of an OSP if the CAE will rely on the OSP's work, regardless of who selected the OSP.
- The CAE should determine that the OSP possesses the **necessary knowledge, skills, and other competencies**. The CAE considers such factors as (1) licensure, (2) experience, (3) reputation, (4) education, (5) training, and (6) membership in a professional organization and adherence to its ethics code.
- The CAE should assess the **relationship of the OSP to the organization and to the IAA** to ensure that **independence and objectivity** are maintained. No financial, organizational, or personal relationships should prevent the OSP from being impartial.
- The OSP may be the **external auditor** and perform **extended audit services** or other services. The CAE should determine that the work does not **impair the external auditor's independence**. Extended audit services are beyond the requirements of auditing standards. If the external auditors appear to act as members of management or employees, their independence is impaired. Moreover, independence is assessed relative to all services provided.
- The CAE should determine that the OSP's **scope of work** is adequate. This matter and others usually should be **documented** in an engagement letter or contract. The CAE should review with the OSP (1) objectives and scope of work, (2) matters to be covered in communications, (3) access, (4) assumptions and procedures, (5) ownership and custody of working papers, and (6) confidentiality and restrictions on information.
- An OSP may perform **internal auditing activities**. The CAE should specify that the work complies with the Standards and is adequate. Information should be **sufficient** to afford a reasonable basis for conclusions and resolution of unusual matters.
- The CAE may in appropriate cases refer in **engagement communications** to the OSP's services. Appropriate prior concurrence by the OSP should be obtained.

7. ***1210.A2*** – *The internal auditor should have sufficient knowledge to identify the indicators of fraud but is not expected to have the expertise of a person whose primary responsibility is detecting and investigating fraud.*

8. ***1210.A3*** – *Internal auditors should have knowledge of key information technology risks and controls and available technology-based audit techniques to perform their assigned work. However, not all internal auditors are expected to have the expertise of an internal auditor whose primary responsibility is information technology auditing.*

9. ***1210.C1*** – *The chief audit executive should decline the consulting engagement or obtain competent advice and assistance if the internal audit staff lacks the knowledge, skills, or other competencies needed to perform all or part of the engagement.*

   a. ***PRACTICE ADVISORY 1000.C1-2: ADDITIONAL CONSIDERATIONS FOR FORMAL CONSULTING ENGAGEMENTS***

   The following is the portion of this comprehensive Practice Advisory relevant to Standards 1210.C1 (above) and 1220.C1 (see Subunit 1.6).

   9. *The internal auditor should exercise **due professional care** in conducting a **formal consulting engagement** by understanding the following:*

   - ***Needs of management** officials, including the nature, timing, and **communication** of engagement results*
   - *Possible **motivations and reasons** of those requesting the service*
   - ***Extent of work** needed to achieve the engagement's objectives*
   - ***Skills and resources** needed to conduct the engagement*
   - *Effect on the **scope of the audit plan** previously approved by the audit committee*
   - ***Potential impact** on future audit assignments and engagements*
   - *Potential organizational **benefits** to be derived from the engagement*

   10. *In addition to the independence and objectivity evaluation and due professional care considerations, the internal auditor should:*

   - *Conduct appropriate meetings and gather necessary information to **assess** the **nature and extent of the service** to be provided.*
   - *Confirm that **those receiving the service** understand and **agree with the relevant guidance** contained in the **internal audit charter**, internal audit activity's **policies and procedures**, and other related guidance governing the conduct of consulting engagements. The internal auditor should **decline to perform consulting engagements** that are prohibited by the terms of the internal audit charter, conflict with the policies and procedures of the internal audit activity, or do not add value and promote the best interests of the organization.*
   - ***Evaluate** the consulting engagement for **compatibility** with the internal audit activity's **overall plan of engagements**. The internal audit activity's risk-based plan of engagements may incorporate and rely on consulting engagements, to the extent deemed appropriate, to provide necessary audit coverage to the organization.*
   - ***Document** general terms, understandings, deliverables, and other **key factors** of the **formal consulting engagement** in a **written agreement** or plan. It is essential that both the internal auditor and those receiving the consulting engagement understand and agree with the reporting and communication requirements.*

PA Summary

- **Due professional care** for a **formal consulting engagement** requires an understanding of the (1) needs of management, (2) reasons for the service, (3) extent of work, (4) resources required, (5) effect on the audit plan, (6) effect on future engagements, and (7) engagement benefits.
- The auditor should assess the **nature and extent of the service**.
- The auditor should confirm that service recipients **agree with related guidance** (e.g., the IAA's charter, policies, and procedures). Engagements should not be performed when they (1) are prohibited by the charter, (2) conflict with policy, or (3) do not add value.
- An engagement should be compatible with the IAA's **overall plan of engagements**. In appropriate circumstances, consulting engagements may provide necessary audit coverage.
- **Key engagement factors** should be **documented** in a **written agreement**.

10. Stop and review! You have completed the outline for this subunit. Study multiple-choice questions 16 through 29 beginning on page 51.

1.6 DUE PROFESSIONAL CARE

1. This subunit defines due professional care. The relevant pronouncements are one General Attribute Standard, one Specific Attribute Standard, three Assurance Implementation Standards, one Consulting Implementation Standard, and two Practice Advisories (PA 1200-1 is in Subunit 1.5).
2. ***1200*** ***<u>Proficiency and Due Professional Care</u>*** *– Engagements should be performed with proficiency and due professional care.*
   a. ***<u>PRACTICE ADVISORY 1200-1: PROFICIENCY AND DUE PROFESSIONAL CARE</u>***
      1. *Professional proficiency is the responsibility of the* ***chief audit executive*** *and* ***each internal auditor****. The chief audit executive should ensure that persons assigned to each engagement collectively possess the necessary knowledge, skills, and other competencies to conduct the engagement properly.*
      2. *Internal auditors should* ***comply with professional standards of conduct****. The Institute of Internal Auditors' Code of Ethics extends beyond the definition of internal auditing to include two essential components:*
         - ***Principles*** *that are relevant to the profession and practice of internal auditing -- specifically, integrity, objectivity, confidentiality, and competency; and*
         - ***Rules of Conduct*** *that describe behavior norms expected of internal auditors. These rules are an aid to interpreting the Principles into practical applications and are intended to guide the ethical conduct of internal auditors.*

PA Summary

- The CAE and each auditor are responsible for the **collective proficiency** of the IAA and his/her own proficiency, respectively.
- The CAE should ensure that persons assigned to each engagement collectively possess the necessary **knowledge, skills, and other competencies**.
- Internal auditors should comply with **The IIA Code of Ethics**.

3. ***1220*** ***Due Professional Care*** *– Internal auditors should apply the care and skill expected of a reasonably prudent and competent internal auditor. Due professional care does not imply infallibility.*

   a. ***PRACTICE ADVISORY 1220-1: DUE PROFESSIONAL CARE***

      1. *Due professional care calls for the application of the care and skill expected of a* ***reasonably prudent and competent internal auditor in the same or similar circumstances****. Professional care should, therefore, be appropriate to the complexities of the engagement being performed. In exercising due professional care, internal auditors should be alert to the possibility of intentional wrongdoing, errors and omissions, inefficiency, waste, ineffectiveness, and conflicts of interest. They should also be alert to those conditions and activities where irregularities are most likely to occur. In addition, they should* ***identify inadequate controls*** *and recommend improvements to promote compliance with acceptable procedures and practices.*

      2. *Due care implies* ***reasonable care and competence****, not infallibility or extraordinary performance. Due care requires the auditor to conduct examinations and verifications to a reasonable extent but does not require detailed reviews of all transactions. Accordingly, internal auditors cannot give absolute assurance that noncompliance or irregularities do not exist. Nevertheless, the possibility of material irregularities or noncompliance should be considered whenever an internal auditor undertakes an internal auditing assignment.*

PA Summary

- **Due professional care** is the care exercised by a **reasonably prudent and competent auditor in similar circumstances**. The auditor should be alert to intentional wrongdoing, inefficiency, and ineffectiveness. The auditor also must identify controls.
- The auditor provides reasonable, not absolute, assurance.

4. ***1220.A1*** *– The internal auditor should exercise due professional care by considering the:*
   - *Extent of work needed to achieve the engagement's objectives*
   - *Relative complexity, materiality, or significance of matters to which assurance procedures are applied*
   - *Adequacy and effectiveness of risk management, control, and governance processes*
   - *Probability of significant errors, irregularities, or noncompliance*
   - *Cost of assurance in relation to potential benefits*

5. ***1220.A2*** *– In exercising due professional care, the internal auditor should consider the use of computer-assisted audit tools and other data analysis techniques.*

6. ***1220.A3*** *– The internal auditor should be alert to the significant risks that might affect objectives, operations, or resources. However, assurance procedures alone, even when performed with due professional care, do not guarantee that all significant risks will be identified.*
7. ***1220.C1*** *– The internal auditor should exercise due professional care during a consulting engagement by considering the:*
   - *Needs and expectations of clients, including the nature, timing, and communication of engagement results*
   - *Relative complexity and extent of work needed to achieve the engagement's objectives*
   - *Cost of the consulting engagement in relation to potential benefits*

   a. Also see the portion of Practice Advisory 1000.C1-2 reproduced after Standard 1210.C1 in Subunit 1.5.
8. Stop and review! You have completed the outline for this subunit. Study multiple-choice questions 30 through 39 beginning on page 55.

1.7 CONTINUING PROFESSIONAL DEVELOPMENT (CPD)

1. This subunit presents The IIA's CPD requirements. The relevant pronouncements are one Specific Attribute Standard and one Practice Advisory.
2. ***1230*** ***Continuing Professional Development*** *– Internal auditors should enhance their knowledge, skills, and other competencies through continuing professional education.*

   a. ***PRACTICE ADVISORY 1230-1: CONTINUING PROFESSIONAL DEVELOPMENT***

      1. Internal auditors are responsible for ***continuing their education*** *in order to maintain their proficiency. They should keep informed about improvements and current developments in internal auditing standards, procedures, and techniques. Continuing education may be obtained through membership and participation in professional societies; attendance at conferences, seminars, college courses, and in-house training programs; and participation in research projects.*

      2. Internal auditors are encouraged to demonstrate their proficiency by obtaining appropriate ***professional certification****, such as the Certified Internal Auditor designation and other designations offered by The Institute of Internal Auditors.*

      3. Internal auditors with professional certifications should obtain ***sufficient continuing professional education*** *to satisfy requirements related to the professional certification held.*

      4. Internal auditors not presently holding appropriate certifications are encouraged to pursue an educational program that supports efforts to obtain professional certification.

PA Summary

- Internal auditors must continue their education to maintain proficiency and to meet certification requirements. They should keep informed about improvements and current developments in internal auditing through participation in professional societies; attendance at conferences, seminars, and college courses; in-house training; and research.
- Internal auditors are encouraged to obtain **professional certification**.

3. Stop and review! You have completed the outline for this subunit. Study multiple-choice question 40 on page 59.

1.8 STUDY UNIT 1 SUMMARY

1. The following is the definition of internal auditing:

   Internal auditing is an independent, objective assurance and consulting activity designed to add value and improve an organization's operations. It helps an organization accomplish its objectives by bringing a systematic, disciplined approach to evaluate and improve the effectiveness of risk management, control, and governance processes.

2. The IIA's mandatory guidance consists of Attribute, Performance, and Implementation Standards.
3. Practice Advisories provide nonmandatory guidance. But they represent best practices endorsed by The IIA.
4. The CAE and each internal auditor are responsible for the collective proficiency of the IAA and his/her own proficiency, respectively.
5. Internal auditors should apply reasonable care and skill and continue their education to enhance their competencies.

QUESTIONS

1.1 International Professional Practices Framework (PPF)

1. The purposes of the Standards include all of the following except

A. Establishing the basis for the measurement of internal audit performance.

B. Guiding the ethical conduct of internal auditors.

C. Stating basic principles that represent the practice of internal auditing as it should be.

D. Fostering improved organizational processes and operations.

Answer (B) is correct. *(CIA, adapted)*

REQUIRED: The item not a purpose of the Standards.

DISCUSSION: The IIA Code of Ethics describes Rules of Conduct that constitute "behavior norms expected of internal auditors. These rules are intended as an aid to interpreting the Principles into practical applications and are intended to guide the ethical conduct of internal auditors." The purposes of the Standards are to

1. State basic principles that represent the practice of internal auditing as it should be.
2. Provide a framework for performing and promoting a broad range of value-added internal audit activities.
3. Establish the basis for the measurement of internal audit performance.
4. Foster improved organizational processes and operations.

(Introduction to the Standards)

2. The proper organizational role of internal auditing is to

A. Assist the external auditor in order to reduce external audit fees.

B. Perform studies to assist in the attainment of more efficient operations.

C. Serve as the investigative arm of the board.

D. Serve as an independent, objective assurance and consulting activity that adds value to operations.

Answer (D) is correct. *(CIA, adapted)*

REQUIRED: The role of internal auditing.

DISCUSSION: According to the definition of internal auditing, "Internal auditing is an independent, objective assurance and consulting activity designed to add value and improve an organization's operations. It helps an organization accomplish its objectives by bringing a systematic, disciplined approach to evaluate and improve the effectiveness of risk management, control, and governance processes."

Answer (A) is incorrect because reducing external audit fees may be a direct result of internal audit work, but it is not a reason for staffing an internal audit activity. Answer (B) is incorrect because the primary role of internal auditing includes, but is not limited to, assessing the efficiency of operations. Answer (C) is incorrect because internal auditors serve management as well as the board.

3. One of the purposes of the International Standards for the Professional Practice of Internal Auditing as stated in the Introduction to the current version of the Standards is to

A. Encourage the professionalization of internal auditing.

B. Establish the independence of the internal audit activity and emphasize the objectivity of internal auditing.

C. Encourage external auditors to make more extensive use of the work of internal auditors.

D. Establish the basis for evaluating internal auditing performance.

Answer (D) is correct. *(CIA, adapted)*

REQUIRED: The purpose of the Standards.

DISCUSSION: The Introduction states the following purposes of the current version of the Standards:

1. State basic principles that represent the practice of internal auditing as it should be.
2. Provide a framework for performing and promoting a broad range of value-added internal audit activities.
3. Establish the basis for evaluating internal auditing performance.
4. Foster improved organizational processes and operations.

Answer (A) is incorrect because the professionalization of internal auditing is important but is not a purpose of the Standards. Answer (B) is incorrect because independence and objectivity are but two aspects of the practice of internal auditing as it should be. Answer (C) is incorrect because the Standards do not formally encourage external auditors to make more extensive use of the work of internal auditors.

4. Internal audit activities may involve which of the following?

A. Assurance services.

B. Consulting services.

C. Both assurance and consulting services.

D. Neither assurance nor consulting services.

Answer (C) is correct. *(Publisher, adapted)*

REQUIRED: The services that may be included in internal audit activities.

DISCUSSION: Internal audit activities may involve both assurance and consulting services. Assurance services are objective examinations of evidence for the purpose of providing an independent assessment on risk management, control, or governance processes for the organization. Consulting services are advisory and related client service activities. Their nature and scope are agreed upon with the client and are intended to add value and improve an organization's governance, risk management, and control processes without assumption of responsibility by the internal auditor.

5. Which Standards apply to organizations and individuals performing specific types of internal auditing services?

A. Performance Standards.

B. Attribute Standards.

C. Implementation Standards.

D. All of the Standards listed in the other answer choices.

Answer (C) is correct. *(Publisher, adapted)*

REQUIRED: The Standards that apply to organizations and individuals performing the specific types of internal auditing services.

DISCUSSION: According to the Professional Practices Framework, Implementation Standards apply to organizations and individuals performing specific types of internal auditing services. Implementation Standards have been issued for assurance services and consulting services.

Answer (A) is incorrect because Performance Standards apply to all internal auditing services. Answer (B) is incorrect because Attribute Standards apply to all internal auditing services. Answer (D) is incorrect because only Implementation Standards apply to specific types of internal auditing services.

1.2 Attribute Standards

6. The Standards consist of three types of standards. Which standards apply to the characteristics of organizations and parties providing internal auditing services?

A. Implementation Standards.

B. Performance Standards.

C. Attribute Standards.

D. Independence Standards.

Answer (C) is correct. *(Publisher, adapted)*

REQUIRED: The standards describing the traits of entities and individuals providing internal auditing services.

DISCUSSION: The Standards consist of Attribute Standards, Performance Standards, and Implementation Standards. Attribute Standards concern the characteristics of organizations and parties providing internal auditing services. Performance Standards describe the nature of internal audit activities and quality criteria for evaluation of their performance. Attribute and Performance Standards furnish guidance for all internal auditing services (assurance, consulting, and other).

Answer (A) is incorrect because Implementation Standards apply to specific types of engagements. Answer (B) is incorrect because Performance Standards describe the nature of internal audit activities and quality criteria for evaluation of their performance. Answer (D) is incorrect because Independence Standards are not one of the three types of Standards. The Attribute Standards address organizational independence.

1.3 Performance Standards

7. According to the Professional Practices Framework of The IIA, which pronouncements represent mandatory guidance for implementing the Standards?

A. Development Aids.

B. Practice Aids.

C. Performance Standards.

D. Practice Advisories.

Answer (C) is correct. *(Publisher, adapted)*

REQUIRED: The pronouncements that represent mandatory guidance for implementing the Standards.

DISCUSSION: Compliance with Development Aids and Practice Aids is not required. They are provided to assist organizations and individuals to which such guidance is relevant. Practice Advisories are nonmandatory interpretations of the Standards or their application in specific situations. They represent best practices endorsed by The IIA as a means of implementing the Standards. The Code of Ethics, Attribute Standards, Implementation Standards, and Performance Standards constitute mandatory guidance.

8. Which of the following are closely related to engagement objectives?

I. The engagement work program
II. Engagement communications
III. The engagement plan

A. I and III only.

B. I and II only.

C. II and III only.

D. I, II, and III.

Answer (D) is correct. *(Publisher, adapted)*

REQUIRED: The items closely related to engagement objectives.

DISCUSSION: Engagement objectives are broad statements developed by internal auditors that define intended engagement accomplishments (Glossary). The engagement work program is a document that lists the procedures to be followed during an engagement that are designed to achieve the engagement objectives (Glossary). An engagement communication includes the engagement's objectives and scope as well as applicable conclusions, recommendations, and action plans (Standard 2410). The engagement plan should include the engagement scope and objectives as well as the timing of procedures and resource allocations.

Answer (A) is incorrect because engagement communications include the engagement's objectives and scopes as well as conclusions, recommendations, and action plans. Answer (B) is incorrect because the engagement plan includes the scope, objectives, timing, and resource allocations. Answer (C) is incorrect because internal auditors develop work programs to achieve engagement objectives.

1.4 Glossary

9. Internal auditing is an assurance and consulting activity. An example of an assurance service is a(n)

A. Advisory engagement. – Consulting

B. Facilitation engagement.

C. Training engagement.

D. Compliance engagement.

Answer (D) is correct. *(Publisher, adapted)*

REQUIRED: The example of an assurance service.

DISCUSSION: An assurance service is "an objective examination of evidence for the purpose of providing an independent assessment on risk management, control, or governance processes for the organization. Examples may include financial, performance, compliance, system security, and due diligence engagements." Consulting services are "advisory and related client service activities, the nature and scope of which are agreed with the client and which are intended to add value and improve an organization's governance, risk management, and control processes without the internal auditor assuming management responsibility. Examples include counsel, advice, facilitation, and training" (Glossary).

10. The work of the internal audit activity includes evaluating and contributing to the improvement of risk management systems. Risk is

I. The negative effect of events certain to occur
II. Measured in terms of impact
III. Measured in terms of likelihood

A. I only.

B. I and II only.

C. II and III only.

D. I, II, and III.

Answer (C) is correct. *(Publisher, adapted)*

REQUIRED: The nature of risk.

DISCUSSION: The IAA should assist the organization by identifying and evaluating significant exposures to risk and contributing to the improvement of risk management and control systems (Standard 2110). Risk is the possibility that an event will occur having an effect on the achievement of objectives. It is measured in terms of impact and likelihood (Glossary).

11. The chief audit executive is best defined as the

A. Inspector general.

B. Person responsible for the internal audit function.

C. Outside provider of internal audit services.

D. Person responsible for overseeing the contract with the outside provider of internal audit services.

Answer (B) is correct. *(Publisher, adapted)*

REQUIRED: The best definition of the chief audit executive.

DISCUSSION: The chief audit executive is the "top position within the organization responsible for internal audit activities." Normally, this person is the internal audit director. When internal auditing services are obtained from outside service providers, the CAE is the person responsible for overseeing the service contract and overall quality assurance, reporting to senior management and the board regarding internal audit activities, and follow-up of engagement results. The term also includes such titles as general auditor, chief internal auditor, and inspector general (Glossary).

12. A major reason for establishing an internal audit activity is to

A. Relieve overburdened management of the responsibility for establishing effective controls.

B. Safeguard resources entrusted to the organization.

C. Ensure the reliability and integrity of financial and operational information.

D. Evaluate and improve the effectiveness of control processes.

Answer (D) is correct. *(CIA, adapted)*

REQUIRED: The major reason for establishing an internal audit activity.

DISCUSSION: Control processes are "The policies, procedures, and activities that are part of a control framework, designed to ensure that risks are contained within the risk tolerances established by the risk management process." Hence, they have a prominent role in internal auditing, which "helps an organization accomplish its objectives by bringing a systematic, disciplined approach to evaluate and improve the effectiveness of risk management, control, and governance processes" (Glossary).

Answer (A) is incorrect because management is responsible for the establishment of internal control. Answer (B) is incorrect because risk management, control, and governance processes ultimately serve to safeguard the organization's resources. Answer (C) is incorrect because the IAA cannot ensure the reliability and integrity of financial and operational information. Its responsibility is to evaluate risk exposures relating to governance, operations, and information systems regarding the reliability and integrity of financial and operational information (Standard 2110.A2). Based on the risk assessment, it then evaluates the adequacy and effectiveness of controls (Standard 2110.A1).

13. What is the most accurate term for the procedures used by the board to oversee activities performed to achieve organizational objectives?

A. Governance.

B. Control.

C. Risk management.

D. Monitoring.

Answer (A) is correct. *(Publisher, adapted)*

REQUIRED: The most accurate term for the means of providing oversight of processes administered by management.

DISCUSSION: Governance is the combination of processes and structures implemented by the board to inform, direct, manage, and monitor the activities of the organization performed to achieve its objectives (Glossary).

Answer (B) is incorrect because control is any action taken by management, the board, and other parties to manage risk and increase the likelihood that established objectives and goals will be achieved. Management plans, organizes, and directs the performance of sufficient actions to provide reasonable assurance that objectives and goals will be achieved. Answer (C) is incorrect because risk management is a process to identify, assess, manage, and control potential events or situations. The purpose is to provide reasonable assurance regarding the achievement of the organization's objectives. It is currently defined in the Glossary. Answer (D) is incorrect because monitoring consists of actions taken by management and others to assess the quality of internal control system performance over time. It is not currently defined in the Standards and Glossary.

14. The actions taken to manage risk and increase the likelihood that established objectives and goals will be achieved are best described as

A. Supervision.

B. Quality assurance.

C. Control.

D. Compliance.

Answer (C) is correct. *(Publisher, adapted)*

REQUIRED: The term for actions taken to manage risk and increase the likelihood that established objectives and goals will be achieved.

DISCUSSION: Control is any action taken by management, the board, and other parties to manage risk and increase the likelihood that established objectives and goals will be achieved. Management plans, organizes, and directs the performance of sufficient actions to provide reasonable assurance that objectives and goals will be achieved.

Answer (A) is incorrect because supervision is just one means of achieving control. Answer (B) is incorrect because quality assurance relates to just one set of objectives and goals. It does not pertain to achievement of all established organizational objectives and goals. Answer (D) is incorrect because compliance is conformity and adherence to policies, plans, procedures, laws, regulations, contracts, or other requirements (Glossary).

15. Which of the following is the most accurate term for the attitudes and actions of the board and management regarding the significance of control within the organization?

A. Control processes.

B. Control environment.

C. Governance process.

D. Management's philosophy and operating style.

Answer (B) is correct. *(Publisher, adapted)*

REQUIRED: The term for the attitudes and actions of the board and management regarding control.

DISCUSSION: The control environment encompasses the attitude and actions of the board and management regarding the significance of control within the organization (Glossary). The control environment provides the discipline and structure for the achievement of the primary objectives of the system of internal control. The control environment includes the following elements:

- Integrity and ethical values
- Management's philosophy and operating style
- Organizational structure
- Assignment of authority and responsibility
- Human resource policies and practices
- Competence of personnel

Answer (A) is incorrect because control processes are the policies, procedures, and activities that are part of a control framework designed to ensure that risks are contained within the risk tolerances established by the risk management process. Answer (C) is incorrect because the governance process is the combination of processes and structures implemented by the board to inform, direct, manage, and monitor the activities of the organization performed to achieve its objectives. Answer (D) is incorrect because management's philosophy and operating style is just one element of the control environment.

1.5 Proficiency

16. Use of outside service providers with expertise in health care benefits is appropriate when the internal audit activity is

A. Evaluating the organization's estimate of its liability for postretirement benefits, which include health care benefits.

B. Comparing the cost of the organization's health care program with other programs offered in the industry.

C. Training its staff to conduct an audit of health care costs in a major division of the organization.

D. All of the answers are correct.

Answer (D) is correct. *(CIA, adapted)*

REQUIRED: The reason(s) for using specialists in health care benefits.

DISCUSSION: The IAA should collectively possess or obtain the knowledge, skills, and other competencies needed to perform its responsibilities (Standard 1210). In regard to an assurance engagement, the CAE should obtain competent advice and assistance if the internal audit staff lacks the knowledge, skills, and other competencies needed to perform all or part of the engagement (Standard 1210.A1). In regard to a consulting engagement, the CAE should decline the engagement or obtain competence advice and assistance if the internal audit staff lacks the knowledge, skills, and other competencies needed to perform all or part of the engagement (Standard 1210.C1). Accordingly, if the internal audit staff lacks expertise with regard to health care costs, outside service providers should be employed who can provide the requisite knowledge, skills, and other competencies. These outside service providers can provide assistance in estimating the company's liability for postretirement benefits, in developing a comparative analysis of health care costs, and in training the staff to audit health care costs.

17. A chief audit executive has reviewed credentials, checked references, and interviewed a candidate for a staff position. The CAE concludes that the candidate has a thorough understanding of internal auditing techniques, accounting, and finance. However, the candidate has limited knowledge of economics and information technology. Which action is most appropriate?

A. Reject the candidate because of the lack of knowledge required by the Standards.

B. Offer the candidate a position despite lack of knowledge in certain essential areas.

C. Encourage the candidate to obtain additional training in economics and information technology and then reapply.

D. Offer the candidate a position if other staff members possess sufficient knowledge in economics and information technology.

Answer (D) is correct. *(CIA, adapted)*

REQUIRED: The proper hiring decision for an internal audit activity.

DISCUSSION: The internal audit activity should collectively possess or obtain the knowledge, skills, and other competencies needed to perform its responsibilities (Standard 1210). These attributes include proficiency in applying internal auditing standards, procedures, and techniques. The IAA should have employees or use outside service providers who are qualified in such disciplines as accounting, auditing, economics, finance, statistics, information technology, engineering, taxation, law, environmental affairs, and such other areas as needed to meet the IAA's responsibilities. Each member of the IAA, however, need not be qualified in all of these disciplines (PA 1210.A1-1).

Answer (A) is incorrect because the Standards do not require each internal auditor to possess a knowledge of all relevant subjects. Answer (B) is incorrect because the IAA's needs may be for additional expertise in economics or information technology. Answer (C) is incorrect because encouraging the candidate to obtain additional training does not adequately address the IAA's current needs.

18. An internal audit activity has scheduled an engagement relating to a construction contract. One portion of this engagement will include comparing materials purchased with those specified in the engineering drawings. The IAA does not have anyone on staff with sufficient expertise to complete this procedure. The chief audit executive should

A. Delete the engagement from the schedule.

B. Perform the entire engagement using current staff.

C. Engage an engineering consultant to perform the comparison.

D. Accept the contractor's written representations.

Answer (C) is correct. *(CIA, adapted)*

REQUIRED: The appropriate action when internal auditors lack the expertise to make a crucial determination.

DISCUSSION: The IAA should have employees or use outside service providers who are qualified in such disciplines as accounting, auditing, economics, finance, statistics, information technology, engineering, taxation, law, environmental affairs, and such other areas as needed to meet the IAA's responsibilities. Each member of the IAA, however, need not be qualified in all of these disciplines (PA 1210.A1-1). Thus, hiring an outside service provider is also necessary as an exercise of due professional care.

Answer (A) is incorrect because the engagement is within the scope of the IAA. Answer (B) is incorrect because performing the engagement using the current (unqualified) staff is inappropriate. Answer (D) is incorrect because accepting the contractor's representations without adequate testing is inappropriate.

19. A chief audit executive for a large manufacturer is considering revising the internal audit activity's charter with respect to the minimum educational and experience qualifications required. The CAE wants to require all staff auditors to possess specialized training in accounting and a professional auditing certification such as the Certified Internal Auditor or the Chartered Accountant (CA). One of the disadvantages of imposing this requirement would be

A. The policy might negatively affect the internal audit activity's ability to perform quality engagements relating to the organization's financial and accounting systems.

B. The policy would not promote the professionalism of the internal audit activity.

C. The policy would prevent the internal audit activity from using outside service providers when it did not have the knowledge, skills, and other competencies required in certain engagements.

D. The policy could limit the range of services that could be performed due to the internal audit activity's narrow expertise and backgrounds.

Answer (D) is correct. *(CIA, adapted)*

REQUIRED: The disadvantage of requiring all staff auditors to possess specialized training in accounting and a professional auditing certification.

DISCUSSION: The IAA should have employees or use outside service providers who are qualified in such disciplines as accounting, auditing, economics, finance, statistics, information technology, engineering, taxation, law, environmental affairs, and such other areas as needed to meet the IAA's responsibilities. Each member of the IAA, however, need not be qualified in all of these disciplines (PA 1210.A1-1). Thus, the IAA should have an appropriate balance of experience, training, and skills to permit the performance of a wide range of services.

Answer (A) is incorrect because the policy might result in better engagements relating to financial and accounting systems. Answer (B) is incorrect because setting minimum professional standards promotes professionalism. Answer (C) is incorrect because this requirement would not affect whether outside service providers were used.

20. If the internal audit activity of a non-public company does not have the skills to perform a particular task, an outside service provider could be brought in from

I. The organization's external audit firm
II. An outside consulting firm
III. The engagement client
IV. A college or university

A. I and II only.

B. II and IV only.

C. I, II, and III only.

D. I, II, and IV only.

Answer (D) is correct. *(CIA, adapted)*

REQUIRED: The appropriate sources of outside service providers.

DISCUSSION: The IAA should have employees or use outside service providers who are qualified in such disciplines as accounting, auditing, economics, finance, statistics, information technology, engineering, taxation, law, environmental affairs, and such other areas as needed to meet the IAA's responsibilities. Each member of the IAA, however, need not be qualified in all of these disciplines (PA 1210.A1-1). Qualified outside service providers may be recruited from a variety of sources. However, an outside service provider from the engagement client is unacceptable because the person would not be independent or objective.

Answer (A) is incorrect because an outside service provider from a college or university is acceptable. Answer (B) is incorrect because an outside service provider from a non-public organization's external audit firm is acceptable. Note that Sarbanes-Oxley prohibits the external audit firm from providing internal audit services to the public company's client(s). Answer (C) is incorrect because an outside service provider from the engagement client is unacceptable.

21. A professional engineer applied for a position in the internal audit activity of a high technology firm. The engineer became interested in the position after observing several internal auditors while they were performing an engagement in the engineering department. The chief audit executive

A. Should not hire the engineer because of the lack of knowledge of internal auditing standards.

B. May hire the engineer despite the lack of knowledge of internal auditing standards.

C. Should not hire the engineer because of the lack of knowledge of accounting and taxes.

D. May hire the engineer because of the knowledge of internal auditing gained in the previous position.

Answer (B) is correct. *(CIA, adapted)*

REQUIRED: The appropriate decision whether to hire a specialist.

DISCUSSION: The IAA should have employees or use outside service providers who are qualified in such disciplines as accounting, auditing, economics, finance, statistics, information technology, engineering, taxation, law, environmental affairs, and such other areas as needed to meet the IAA's responsibilities. Each member of the IAA, however, need not be qualified in all of these disciplines (PA 1210.A1-1).

Answer (A) is incorrect because each new employee of an IAA is not required to have knowledge of internal auditing standards. However, the IAA collectively must have this knowledge. Answer (C) is incorrect because each individual internal auditor is not required to have knowledge of accounting or taxes. Answer (D) is incorrect because the knowledge acquired by observation is irrelevant to the skills necessary for internal auditing.

22. Your organization has selected you to develop an internal audit activity (IAA). Your approach will most likely be to hire

A. Internal auditors each of whom possesses all the skills required to handle all engagements.

B. Inexperienced personnel and train them the way the organization wants them trained.

C. Degreed accountants because most internal audit work is accounting related.

D. Internal auditors who collectively have the knowledge and skills needed to perform the responsibilities of the internal audit activity.

Answer (D) is correct. *(CIA, adapted)*

REQUIRED: The personnel required by an IAA.

DISCUSSION: The internal audit activity should collectively possess or obtain the knowledge, skills, and other competencies needed to perform its responsibilities (Standard 1210). The IAA should have employees or use outside service providers who are qualified in such disciplines as accounting, auditing, economics, finance, statistics, information technology, engineering, taxation, law, environmental affairs, and such other areas as needed to meet the IAA's responsibilities. Each member of the IAA, however, need not be qualified in all of these disciplines (PA 1210.A1-1).

Answer (A) is incorrect because the scope of internal auditing is so broad that one individual cannot have the requisite expertise in all areas. Answer (B) is incorrect because the IAA should have personnel with various skill levels to permit appropriate matching of internal auditors with varying engagement complexities. Furthermore, experienced internal auditors should be available to train and supervise less experienced staff members. Answer (C) is incorrect because many skills are needed in internal auditing. For example, computer skills are needed in engagements involving information technology.

23. Reasonable assurance should be obtained as to each prospective internal auditor's qualifications and proficiency. Which of the following is the least useful application of this principle?

A. Determining that all applicants have an accounting degree.

B. Obtaining college transcripts.

C. Checking an applicant's references.

D. Determining previous job experience.

Answer (A) is correct. *(CIA, adapted)*

REQUIRED: The least useful application of the principle concerning internal auditor qualifications and proficiency.

DISCUSSION: "Internal auditors should possess the knowledge, skills, and other competencies needed to perform their individual responsibilities. The internal audit activity collectively should possess or obtain the knowledge, skills, and other competencies needed to perform its responsibilities" (Standard 1210). Each member of the IAA, however, need not be qualified in all disciplines (PA 1210.A1-1).

Answer (B) is incorrect because obtaining college transcripts is an appropriate procedure to determine a prospective auditor's qualifications. Answer (C) is incorrect because checking an applicant's references is an appropriate procedure to determine a prospective auditor's qualifications. Answer (D) is incorrect because determining previous job experience is appropriate during the hiring process.

24. Internal auditing is unique in that its scope often encompasses all areas of an organization. Thus, it is not possible for each internal auditor to possess detailed competence in all areas that might be the subject of engagements. Which of the following competencies should every internal auditor have?

A. Understanding of taxation and law as it applies to operation of the organization.

B. Proficiency in accounting principles.

C. Understanding of management principles.

D. Proficiency in information technology.

Answer (C) is correct. *(CIA, adapted)*

REQUIRED: The competencies an internal auditor should have.

DISCUSSION: All internal auditors should have an understanding of management principles. An understanding is "the ability to apply broad knowledge to situations likely to be encountered, to recognize significant deviations, and to be able to carry out the research necessary to arrive at reasonable solutions" (PA 1210-1).

Answer (A) is incorrect because an internal auditor should have only an appreciation of taxation and law. Answer (B) is incorrect because only those auditors who work extensively with financial records and reports should have proficiency in accounting principles. Answer (D) is incorrect because an auditor need only have an appreciation of IT. An internal auditor whose primary responsibility is not IT auditing should at least have knowledge of key IT risks and controls and available IT-based audit tools (Standard 1210.A3).

25. Internal auditors should be proficient with respect to which discipline?

A. Internal auditing procedures and techniques.
B. Accounting principles and techniques.
C. Management principles.
D. Marketing techniques.

Answer (A) is correct. *(CIA, adapted)*

REQUIRED: The organizational discipline that matches the skill level described.

DISCUSSION: Internal auditors should be proficient in applying internal auditing standards, procedures, and techniques in performing engagements. Proficiency means the ability to apply knowledge to situations likely to be encountered and to deal with them without extensive recourse to technical research and assistance (PA 1210-1).

Answer (B) is incorrect because only auditors who work extensively with financial records and reports should have proficiency in accounting principles and techniques. Answer (C) is incorrect because an internal auditor should have an understanding of, not a proficiency in, management principles. Answer (D) is incorrect because internal auditors ordinarily need not be proficient in marketing techniques.

26. Internal auditors should have an understanding with respect to which discipline?

A. Internal auditing procedures and techniques.
B. Accounting principles and techniques.
C. Management principles.
D. Marketing techniques.

Answer (C) is correct. *(CIA, adapted)*

REQUIRED: The organizational discipline that matches the skill level described.

DISCUSSION: An internal auditor should have an understanding of management principles to recognize and evaluate the materiality and significance of deviations from good business practice. An understanding means the ability to apply broad knowledge to situations likely to be encountered, to recognize significant deviations, and to be able to carry out the research necessary to arrive at reasonable solutions (PA 1210-1).

Answer (A) is incorrect because internal auditors should have proficiency in, not an understanding of, internal auditing standards, procedures, and techniques. Answer (B) is incorrect because only auditors who work extensively with financial records and reports should have proficiency in accounting principles and techniques. Answer (D) is incorrect because internal auditors ordinarily need not be proficient in, or have an understanding or appreciation of, marketing techniques.

27. Internal auditors should have an appreciation of which discipline?

A. Internal auditing procedures and techniques.
B. Accounting principles and techniques.
C. Management principles.
D. Marketing techniques.

Answer (B) is correct. *(CIA, adapted)*

REQUIRED: The organizational discipline that matches the skill level described.

DISCUSSION: An internal auditor should have an appreciation of the fundamentals of such subjects as accounting, economics, commercial law, taxation, finance, quantitative methods, and information technology. An appreciation means the ability to recognize the existence of problems or potential problems and to determine the further research to be undertaken or the assistance to be obtained. Auditors who work extensively with financial records and reports should have proficiency in accounting principles and techniques (PA 1210-1).

Answer (A) is incorrect because internal auditors should be proficient in applying internal auditing standards, procedures, and techniques. Answer (C) is incorrect because an internal auditor should have an understanding, not an appreciation, of management principles. Answer (D) is incorrect because internal auditors ordinarily need not be proficient in, or have an understanding or appreciation of, marketing techniques.

28. Internal auditors should possess all of the following except

A. Proficiency in applying internal auditing standards.

B. An understanding of management principles.

C. The ability to maintain good interpersonal relations.

D. The ability to conduct training sessions in quantitative methods.

Answer (D) is correct. *(CIA, adapted)*

REQUIRED: The item that is not one of the qualifications of internal auditors.

DISCUSSION: Internal auditors should have an appreciation of the fundamentals of such subjects as accounting, economics, commercial law, taxation, finance, quantitative methods, and information technology. An appreciation means the ability to recognize the existence of problems or potential problems and to determine the further research to be undertaken or the assistance to be obtained (PA 1210-1).

Answer (A) is incorrect because an internal auditor should be proficient in applying internal auditing standards, procedures, and techniques. Answer (B) is incorrect because an internal auditor should have an understanding of management principles sufficient to recognize and evaluate the materiality and significance of deviations from good business practice. Answer (C) is incorrect because internal auditors should understand human relations and maintain satisfactory relationships with engagement clients.

29. Communication skills are important to internal auditors. They should be able to convey effectively all of the following to engagement clients except

A. The objectives designed for a specific engagement.

B. The engagement evaluations based on a preliminary survey.

C. The risk assessment used in selecting the area for investigation.

D. Recommendations that are generated in relationship to a specific engagement client.

Answer (C) is correct. *(CIA, adapted)*

REQUIRED: The matter that internal auditors need not communicate to engagement clients.

DISCUSSION: Internal auditors should be skilled in oral and written communications so that they can clearly and effectively convey such matters as engagement objectives, evaluations, conclusions, and recommendations (PA 1210-1). However, the risk assessment is not necessarily a matter that must be communicated.

1.6 Due Professional Care

30. In exercising due professional care, an internal auditor should consider which of the following?

I. The relative complexity, materiality, or significance of matters to which assurance procedures are applied

II. The extent of assurance procedures necessary to ensure that all significant risks will be identified

III. The probability of significant errors, irregularities, or noncompliance

A. I and II only.

B. II and III only.

C. I and III only.

D. I, II, and III.

Answer (C) is correct. *(Publisher, adapted)*

REQUIRED: The items that should be considered by an internal auditor when exercising due professional care.

DISCUSSION: According to Standard 1220.A1, the internal auditor should exercise due professional care by considering the:

- Extent of work needed to achieve the engagement's objectives
- Relative complexity, materiality, or significance of matters to which assurance procedures are applied
- Adequacy and effectiveness of risk management, control, and governance processes
- Probability of significant errors, irregularities, or noncompliance
- Cost of assurance in relation to potential benefits

Assurance procedures alone, even when performed with due professional care, do not guarantee that all significant risks will be identified (Standard 1220.A3).

31. The internal auditor should exercise due professional care in conducting a formal consulting engagement by understanding all of the following except

A. Possible motivations and reasons of those requesting the service.

B. Potential benefits in the form of compensation to be derived from the engagement.

C. Skills and resources needed to conduct the engagement.

D. Potential impact on future audit assignments and engagements.

Answer (B) is correct. *(Publisher, adapted)*

REQUIRED: The item that the internal auditor of a formal consulting engagement should not consider when exercising due professional care.

DISCUSSION: The internal auditor should exercise due professional care in conducting a formal consulting engagement by understanding the following (PA 1000.C1-2):

- Needs of management officials, including the nature, timing, and communication of engagement results
- Possible motivations and reasons of those requesting the service
- Extent of work needed to achieve the engagement's objectives
- Skills and resources needed to conduct the engagement
- Effect on the scope of the audit plan previously approved by the audit committee
- Potential impact on future audit assignments and engagements
- Potential organizational benefits to be derived from the engagement

Any benefit related to compensation for the engagement is not one of the considerations for an internal auditor who is exercising due professional care.

32. The chief audit executive (CAE) is conducting a formal consulting engagement for XYZ Corp. In addition to the independence and objectivity evaluation and due professional care considerations, the CAE should do which of the following?

I. Document general terms, understandings, deliverables, and other key factors of the formal consulting engagement in a written agreement or plan.

II. Evaluate the consulting engagement for comparability with the internal audit activity's overall plan of engagements.

III. Conduct appropriate meetings and gather necessary information to assess the nature and extent of the services to be provided.

A. I and II only.

B. II and III only.

C. I and III only.

D. I, II, and III.

Answer (D) is correct. *(Publisher, adapted)*

REQUIRED: The procedures the CAE should perform when conducting a formal consulting engagement.

DISCUSSION: In addition to the independence and objectivity evaluation and due professional care considerations, the CAE should:

- Conduct appropriate meetings and gather necessary information to assess the nature and extent of the service to be provided.
- Confirm that those receiving the service understand and agree with the relevant guidance contained in the internal audit charter, internal audit activity's policies and procedures, and other related guidance governing the conduct of consulting engagements. The CAE should decline to perform consulting engagements that are prohibited by the terms of the internal audit charter, conflict with the policies and procedures of the internal audit activity, or do not add value and promote the best interests of the organization.
- Evaluate the consulting engagement for compatibility with the internal audit activity's overall plan of engagements. The internal audit activity's risk-based plan of engagements may incorporate and rely on consulting engagements, to the extent deemed appropriate, to provide necessary audit coverage to the organization.
- Document general terms, understandings, deliverables, and other key factors of the formal consulting engagement in a written agreement or plan. It is essential that both the CAE and those receiving the consulting engagement understand and agree with the reporting and communication requirements (PA 1000.C1-2).

33. Which of the following statements is true with respect to due professional care?

A. An internal auditor should perform detailed tests of all transactions before communicating results.

B. An item should not be mentioned in an engagement communication unless the internal auditor is absolutely certain of the item.

C. An engagement communication should never be viewed as providing an infallible truth about a subject.

D. An internal auditor has no responsibility to recommend improvements.

Answer (C) is correct. *(CIA, adapted)*

REQUIRED: The true statement about due professional care.

DISCUSSION: Due professional care implies reasonable care and competence, not infallibility or extraordinary performance. Due professional care requires the internal auditor to conduct examinations and verifications to a reasonable extent, but it does not require detailed reviews of all transactions. Accordingly, internal auditors cannot give absolute assurance that noncompliance or irregularities do not exist. Nevertheless, the possibility of material irregularities or noncompliance should be considered whenever an internal auditor undertakes an internal auditing assignment (PA 1220-1).

Answer (A) is incorrect because an internal auditor should conduct reasonable examinations and verifications, but detailed tests of all transactions are not required. Answer (B) is incorrect because absolute assurance need not, and cannot, be given. Answer (D) is incorrect because an internal auditor should recommend improvements to promote compliance with acceptable procedures and practices.

34. An internal auditor observes that a receivables clerk has physical access to and control of cash receipts. The auditor worked with the clerk several years before and has a high level of trust in the individual. Accordingly, the auditor notes in the engagement working papers that controls over receipts are adequate. Has the auditor exercised due professional care?

A. Yes, reasonable care has been taken.

B. No, irregularities were not noted.

C. No, alertness to conditions most likely indicative of irregularities was not shown.

D. Yes, the engagement working papers were annotated.

Answer (C) is correct. *(CIA, adapted)*

REQUIRED: The true statement as to whether the internal auditor has exercised due professional care.

DISCUSSION: These facts indicate that the internal auditor has failed to exercise due professional care. Internal auditors must be alert to those conditions and activities where irregularities are most likely to occur (PA 1220-1). Cash has a high degree of inherent risk and should therefore be subject to stringent controls. Access to cash and the record-keeping functions should be separated regardless of the personal qualities of the individuals involved. That the clerk is a friend of the internal auditor is irrelevant. Management still needs to be aware that internal control over receivables is inadequate.

Answer (A) is incorrect because the auditor's engagement observation is inappropriate given the lack of segregation of functions. Answer (B) is incorrect because no indication is given that irregularities have occurred. Answer (D) is incorrect because following instructions by rote is unacceptable. Professional judgment and alertness are necessary.

35. Due professional care implies reasonable care and competence, not infallibility or extraordinary performance. Thus, which of the following is unnecessary?

A. The conduct of examinations and verifications to a reasonable extent.

B. The conduct of extensive examinations.

C. The reasonable assurance that compliance does exist.

D. The consideration of the possibility of material irregularities.

Answer (B) is correct. *(CIA, adapted)*

REQUIRED: The obligation not imposed by the due professional care standard.

DISCUSSION: Due professional care implies reasonable care and competence, not infallibility or extraordinary performance. It requires the internal auditor to conduct examinations and verifications to a reasonable extent, but it does not require detailed reviews of all transactions. Accordingly, the internal auditor cannot give absolute assurance that noncompliance or irregularities do not exist. Nevertheless, the possibility of material irregularities or noncompliance should be considered whenever an internal auditor undertakes an internal auditing assignment (PA 1220-1).

Answer (A) is incorrect because examination and verification need only be undertaken to a reasonable extent. Answer (C) is incorrect because an internal auditor cannot give absolute assurance. Answer (D) is incorrect because the possibility of material irregularities should be considered.

36. An internal auditor judged an item to be immaterial when planning an assurance engagement. However, the assurance engagement may still include the item if it is subsequently determined that

A. Sufficient staff is available.

B. Adverse effects related to the item are likely to occur.

C. Related information is reliable.

D. Miscellaneous income is affected.

Answer (B) is correct. *(CIA, adapted)*
REQUIRED: The basis for including an item in the engagement although it is immaterial.
DISCUSSION: Internal auditors should exercise due professional care by considering the relative complexity, materiality, or significance of matters to which assurance procedures are applied (Standard 1220.A1). Materiality judgments are made in the light of all the circumstances and involve qualitative as well as quantitative considerations. Moreover, internal auditors must also consider the interplay of risk with materiality. Consequently, engagement effort may be required for a quantitatively immaterial item if adverse effects are likely to occur, for example, a material contingent liability arising from an illegal payment that is otherwise immaterial.
Answer (A) is incorrect because, in the absence of other considerations, devoting additional engagement effort to an immaterial item is inefficient. Answer (C) is incorrect because additional engagement procedures might not be needed if related information is reliable. Answer (D) is incorrect because the item is more likely to be included if it affects recurring income items rather than miscellaneous income.

37. The internal audit activity can perform an important role in preventing and detecting significant fraud by being assigned all but which one of the following tasks?

A. Review large, abnormal, or unexplained expenditures.

B. Review sensitive expenses such as legal fees, consultant fees, and foreign sales commissions.

C. Review every control feature pertaining to petty cash receipts.

D. Review contributions by the organization that appear to be unusual.

Answer (C) is correct. *(CIA, adapted)*
REQUIRED: The task not appropriate to the prevention and detection of significant fraud.
DISCUSSION: The internal auditor should exercise due professional care by considering the relative complexity, materiality, or significance of matters to which assurance procedures are applied. The cost of assurance in relation to potential benefits also should be considered (Standard 1220.A1). Hence, an exhaustive review of petty cash is not an efficient and effective use of limited IAA resources because it will not prevent or detect significant fraud. The amount of any theft of petty cash will not be substantial.

38. Assurance engagements should be performed with proficiency and due professional care. Accordingly, the Standards require internal auditors to

I. Consider the probability of significant noncompliance

II. Perform assurance procedures with due professional care so that all significant risks are identified

III. Weigh the cost of assurance against the benefits

A. I and II only.

B. I and III only.

C. II and III only.

D. I, II, and III.

Answer (B) is correct. *(Publisher, adapted)*
REQUIRED: The responsibility(ies) of internal auditors regarding proficiency and due professional care.
DISCUSSION: Standard 1220.A1 states that the exercise of due professional care involves considering the extent of work needed to achieve management's objectives; the relative complexity, materiality, or significance of matters to which assurance procedures are applied; the adequacy and effectiveness of risk management, control, and governance processes; the probability of significant errors, irregularities, or noncompliance; and the cost of assurance in relation to the benefits. Moreover, the internal auditor should be alert to the significant risks that might affect objectives, operations, or resources (Standard 1220.A3). However, assurance procedures alone, even when performed with due professional care, do not guarantee that all significant risks will be identified.

Question 39 is based on the following information. An organization has two manufacturing facilities. Each facility has two manufacturing processes and a separate packaging process. The processes are similar at both facilities. Raw materials used include aluminum, materials to make plastic, various chemicals, and solvents. Pollution occurs at several operational stages, including raw materials handling and storage, process chemical use, finished goods handling, and disposal. Waste products produced during the manufacturing processes include several that are considered hazardous. The nonhazardous waste is transported to the local landfill. An outside waste vendor is used for the treatment, storage, and disposal of all hazardous waste.

Management is aware of the need for compliance with environmental laws. The organization recently developed an environmental policy including a statement that each employee is responsible for compliance with environmental laws.

39. If the internal audit activity is assigned the responsibility of conducting an environmental audit, which of the following actions should be performed first?

A. Conduct risk assessments for each site.

B. Review organizational policies and procedures and verify compliance.

C. Provide the assigned staff with technical training.

D. Review the environmental management system.

Answer (C) is correct. *(CIA, adapted)*

REQUIRED: The first step in an environmental audit.

DISCUSSION: All internal auditing engagements should be performed with proficiency and due professional care. The internal audit activity collectively should possess or obtain the necessary knowledge, skills, and other competencies needed to conduct the audit properly. Thus, providing the assigned staff with adequate training or employing qualified outside service providers is a first step in an environmental audit.

Answer (A) is incorrect because the internal auditors should conduct risk assessments for each site only after qualified people have been assigned to the project. Answer (B) is incorrect because audit procedures to verify compliance with company policies and procedures are performed only after an audit staff with the needed knowledge, skills, and other competencies is assigned to the audit. Answer (D) is incorrect because internal auditors should review the environmental management system only after qualified people have been assigned to the project.

1.7 Continuing Professional Development (CPD)

40. Internal auditors are responsible for continuing their education in order to maintain their proficiency. Which of the following is true regarding the continuing education requirements of the practicing internal auditor?

A. Internal auditors are required to obtain 40 hours of continuing professional education each year and a minimum of 120 hours over a 3-year period.

B. CIAs have formal requirements that must be met in order to continue as CIAs.

C. Attendance, as an officer or committee member, at formal Institute of Internal Auditors meetings does not meet the criteria of continuing professional development.

D. In-house programs meet continuing professional education requirements only if they have been preapproved by The Institute of Internal Auditors.

Answer (B) is correct. *(CIA, adapted)*

REQUIRED: The true statement about continuing education requirements.

DISCUSSION: Internal auditors should enhance their knowledge, skills, and other competencies through continuing professional development (Standard 1230). To maintain the CIA designation, the CIA must commit to a formal program of continuing professional development and report to the Certification Department of The IIA.

Answer (A) is incorrect because the Standards do not state formal hour requirements for internal auditors. The intent of the Standards is to provide flexibility in meeting the requirements. Answer (C) is incorrect because continuing education may be obtained by participation in professional societies. Answer (D) is incorrect because prior approval by The IIA is not necessary for CPE courses.

STUDY UNIT TWO
CHARTER, INDEPENDENCE, AND OBJECTIVITY

(28 pages of outline)

The **purpose, authority, and responsibility** of internal auditing should be adequate to enable the internal audit activity to accomplish its objectives. For that reason, the purpose, authority, and responsibility should be stated in a **written charter** and periodically reassessed.

Internal auditing is an independent, objective assurance and consulting activity designed to add value and improve an organization's operations. Accordingly, the Standards require the internal audit activity to be **independent** and the internal auditors to be **objective** in performing their work. Thus, independence is an attribute of an organizational unit, and objectivity is an attribute of individuals. In this context, independence means that internal auditors can carry out their duties freely and objectively. Objectivity means independence in mental attitude.

Core Concepts

- The purpose, authority, and responsibility of the internal audit activity should be defined in a formal charter.
- The nature of assurance and consulting services should be defined in the charter.
- The internal audit activity should be independent, and the internal auditor should be objective.
- The chief audit executive should report functionally to the audit committee.
- Impairment of independence or objectivity should be disclosed.
- Internal auditors should not assess operations for which they were previously responsible.

2.1 CHARTER

1. This subunit concerns the content of the charter of the internal audit activity. One General Attribute Standard, an Assurance Implementation Standard, a Consulting Implementation Standard, and four Practice Advisories currently address this topic.

2. ***1000*** ***Purpose, Authority, and Responsibility*** – *The purpose, authority, and responsibility of the internal audit activity should be formally defined in a charter, consistent with the Standards, and approved by the board.**

   *The term "board" here and elsewhere in pronouncements of The IIA includes "an organization's governing body, such as a board of directors, supervisory board, head of an agency or legislative body, board of governors or trustees of a non-profit organization, or any other designated body of the organization, including the audit committee, to whom the chief audit executive may functionally report" (Glossary).

a. ***PRACTICE ADVISORY 1000-1: INTERNAL AUDIT CHARTER***

1. *The purpose, authority, and responsibility of the internal audit activity should be defined in a charter. The chief audit executive should seek **approval** of the charter by **senior management** as well as **acceptance by the board**, audit committee, or appropriate governing authority. The charter should (a) establish the internal audit activity's **position** within the organization; (b) **authorize access** to records, personnel, and physical properties relevant to the performance of engagements; and (c) **define the scope** of internal audit activities.*

2. *The internal audit activity's charter should be **in writing**. A written statement provides formal communication for review and approval by management and for acceptance by the board. It also facilitates a **periodic assessment** of the adequacy of the internal audit activity's purpose, authority, and responsibility. Providing a formal, written document containing the charter of the internal audit activity is critical in **managing the auditing function** within the organization. The purpose, authority, and responsibility should be defined and communicated to establish the role of the internal audit activity and to provide a basis for management and the board to use in evaluating the operations of the function. If a question should arise, the charter also provides a formal, written agreement with management and the board about the role and responsibilities of the internal audit activity within the organization.*

3. *The chief audit executive should **periodically assess** whether the purpose, authority, and responsibility, as defined in the charter, continue to be adequate to enable the internal audit activity to accomplish its objectives. The result of this periodic assessment should be communicated to senior management and the board.*

PA Summary

- The **purpose, authority, and responsibility** of the IAA (internal audit activity) should be defined in a formal written charter approved by senior management and accepted by the board.
- The **charter** establishes the position of the IAA, authorizes access relevant to engagement performance, and defines the scope of its activities.
- A charter is critical in managing the auditing function. It establishes the **IAA's role** and provides a basis for its evaluation.
- The CAE should periodically **reassess the adequacy** of the charter. The result should be communicated to senior management and the board.

3. ***1000.A1** – The nature of assurance services provided to the organization should be defined in the audit charter. If assurances are to be provided to parties outside the organization, the nature of these assurances should also be defined in the charter.*

4. ***1000.C1** – The nature of consulting services should be defined in the audit charter.*

a. ***PRACTICE ADVISORY 1000.C1-1: PRINCIPLES GUIDING THE PERFORMANCE OF CONSULTING ACTIVITIES OF INTERNAL AUDITORS***

1. ***Value Proposition** – The value proposition of the internal audit activity is realized within every organization that employs internal auditors in a manner that suits the culture and resources of that organization. That value proposition is captured in the **definition of internal auditing** and includes assurance and consulting activities designed to add value to the organization by bringing a systematic, disciplined approach to the areas of governance, risk, and control.*

2. ***Consistency with Internal Audit Definition*** – *A disciplined, systematic evaluation methodology is incorporated in each internal audit activity. The list of services can generally be incorporated into the broad categories of assurance and consulting. However, the services may also include* ***evolving forms of value-adding services*** *that are consistent with the broad definition of internal auditing.*
3. ***Audit Activities Beyond Assurance and Consulting*** – *There are multiple internal auditing services. Assurance and consulting are not mutually exclusive and do not preclude other auditing services, such as investigations and nonauditing roles. Many audit services will have both an assurance and consultative (advising) role.*
4. ***Interrelationship between Assurance and Consulting*** – *Internal audit consulting enriches value-adding internal auditing. While consulting is often the direct result of assurance services, it should also be recognized that assurance could also be generated from consulting engagements.*
5. ***Empower Consulting Through the Internal Audit Charter*** – *Internal auditors have traditionally performed many types of consulting services, including the analysis of controls built into developing systems, analysis of security products, serving on task forces to analyze operations and make recommendations, and so forth. The board (or audit committee) should empower the internal audit activity to perform additional services if they do* ***not represent a conflict of interest*** *or detract from its obligations to the committee. That empowerment should be reflected in the internal audit charter.*
6. ***Objectivity*** – *Consulting services may enhance the auditor's* ***understanding of business processes or issues*** *related to an assurance engagement and do not necessarily impair the auditor's or the internal audit activity's objectivity. Internal auditing is not a management decision-making function. Decisions to adopt or implement recommendations made as a result of an internal auditing advisory service should be made by management. Therefore, internal auditing objectivity should not be impaired by the decisions made by management.*
7. ***Internal Audit Foundation for Consulting Services*** – *Much of consulting is a natural* ***extension of assurance*** *and investigative services and may represent informal or formal advice, analysis, or assessments. The internal audit activity is* ***uniquely positioned*** *to perform this type of consulting work based on (a) its adherence to the highest standards of objectivity and (b) its breadth of knowledge about organizational processes, risk, and strategies.*
8. ***Communication of Fundamental Information*** – *A primary internal auditing value is to provide* ***assurance*** *to senior management and audit committee directors. Consulting engagements cannot be performed in a manner that masks information that in the judgment of the chief audit executive (CAE) should be presented to senior executives and board members. All consulting is to be understood in that context.*
9. ***Principles of Consulting Understood by the Organization*** – *Organizations must have ground rules for the performance of consulting services that are understood by all members of an organization, and these rules should be codified in the audit charter approved by the audit committee and promulgated in the organization.*

10. ***Formal Consulting Engagements*** – *Management often engages* ***outside consultants*** *for formal consulting engagements that last a significant period of time. However, an organization may find that the internal audit activity is uniquely qualified for some formal consulting tasks. If an internal audit activity undertakes to perform a formal consulting engagement, the internal audit group should bring a* ***systematic, disciplined approach*** *to the conduct of the engagement.*
11. ***CAE Responsibilities*** – *Consulting services permit the CAE to enter into dialogue with management to address specific managerial issues. In this dialogue, the breadth of the engagement and time frames are made responsive to management needs. However, the CAE retains the prerogative of* ***setting the audit techniques*** *and the* ***right of reporting*** *to senior executives and audit committee members when the nature and materiality of results pose significant risks to the organization.*
12. ***Criteria for Resolving Conflicts or Evolving Issues*** – *An internal auditor is first and foremost an internal auditor. Thus, in the performance of all services, the internal auditor is guided by The IIA Code of Ethics and the Attribute and Performance Standards of the International Standards for the Professional Practice of Internal Auditing. The resolution of any unforeseen conflicts or activities should be consistent with the Code of Ethics and Standards.*

PA Summary

- The **value proposition** of the IAA is realized in a way suiting the organization's culture and resources. It is reflected in the **definition of internal auditing**. It extends to assurance, consulting, and other evolving forms of value-adding services, including nonaudit roles, investigations, and activities that combine assurance and consulting. Moreover, consulting may result from assurance or vice versa.
- The IAA performs consulting, e.g., analysis of controls in systems development. The board and charter should therefore empower consulting that is not a conflict of interest. Consulting may enhance understanding of business processes and does not necessarily impair objectivity because management makes decisions about adoption of IAA recommendations.
- Consulting is often an **extension of assurance**. It may consist of formal (informal) advice, analysis, or assessments. The IAA is uniquely positioned to do such work because of its objectivity and breadth of knowledge.
- A primary IAA value is to **provide assurance** to senior management and the audit committee. Consulting must not conceal information that should be reported as part of that function.
- The **organization's rules for consulting** should be understood by all its members. They should be codified in the charter.
- Instead of hiring outsiders for **formal consulting** tasks, the organization may find that the IAA is uniquely qualified for some of these engagements. In formal consulting, the IAA should adopt a systematic, disciplined approach.
- The breadth and time frame of an engagement are based on **managerial needs**. But the **CAE** should set audit techniques and be able to report to senior managers and the board when results indicate significant risk.
- Internal auditors should follow the **Code of Ethics** and the **Standards** when performing all services, even those involving unforeseen conflicts and activities.

b. ***PRACTICE ADVISORY 1000.C1-2: ADDITIONAL CONSIDERATIONS FOR FORMAL CONSULTING ENGAGEMENTS***

The following is the portion of this comprehensive Practice Advisory relevant to Standard 1000.C1:

Definition of Consulting Services

1. *The **Glossary** in the **Standards** defines "consulting services" as follows: "Advisory and related client service activities, the nature and scope of which are agreed with the client and which are intended to add value and improve an organization's governance, risk management, and control processes without the internal auditor assuming management responsibility. Examples include counsel, advice, facilitation, and training."*

2. *The chief audit executive should determine the methodology to use for **classifying engagements** within the organization. In some circumstances, it may be appropriate to conduct a "blended" engagement that incorporates elements of both consulting and assurance activities into one consolidated approach. In other cases, it may be appropriate to distinguish between the assurance and consulting components of the engagement.*

3. *Internal auditors may conduct consulting services as part of their **normal or routine activities** as well as in response to **requests by management**. Each organization should consider the type of consulting activities to be offered and determine if specific policies or procedures should be developed for each type of activity. Possible categories could include:*

- ***Formal consulting** engagements – planned and subject to written agreement.*
- ***Informal consulting** engagements – routine activities, such as participation on standing committees, limited-life projects, ad-hoc meetings, and routine information exchange.*
- ***Special consulting** engagements – participation on a merger and acquisition team or system conversion team.*
- ***Emergency consulting** engagements – participation on a team established for recovery or maintenance of operations after a disaster or other extraordinary business event or a team assembled to supply temporary help to meet a special request or unusual deadline.*

4. *Auditors generally should not agree to conduct a consulting engagement simply to circumvent, or to allow others to circumvent, requirements that would normally apply to an **assurance engagement** if the service in question is more appropriately conducted as an assurance engagement. This does not preclude adjusting methodologies if services once conducted as assurance engagements are deemed more suitable to being performed as a consulting engagement.*

PA Summary

- The **Glossary** in the Standards defines "consulting services." The CAE determines the methods for classifying engagements. Blended rather than separate assurance and consulting engagements may be appropriate.
- Consulting may be done as a routine IAA function or in response to requests by management.
- Consulting engagements may be formal, informal, special, and emergency. **Formal engagements** are planned and subject to written agreement. **Informal engagements** are routine, such as ad-hoc meetings and routine information exchange. An example of a **special engagement** is participation on a system conversion team. **Emergency engagements** involve participation on a team established (1) for recovery operations after an extraordinary business event or (2) to supply temporary help to meet a special request or unusual deadline.
- Consulting should **not** be done to **avoid the requirements** of an assurance engagement. But adjusting methods is appropriate if services once conducted as assurance engagements are more suitably performed as consulting engagements.

c. ***PRACTICE ADVISORY 1000.C1-3: ADDITIONAL CONSIDERATIONS FOR CONSULTING ENGAGEMENTS IN GOVERNMENT ORGANIZATIONAL SETTINGS***

1. *This Practice Advisory provides guidance for government audit organizations conducting work in compliance with IIA Standards, but whose local governance rules, audit standards, policies, or legislation more strictly limit* ***non-assurance (consulting) services****. The* ***parameters*** *within which an organization plans to provide non-assurance (consulting) services should be included in the internal audit* ***charter****. They should be supported by the policies and procedures of the internal audit activity. The guidance in this PA may assist organizations in developing relevant language and policies to manage the provision of non-assurance (consulting) services.*

2. ***Core Elements of the Role of Auditors.*** *Through their assurance (audit) engagements, auditors help to ensure that management is accountable for meeting organizational objectives and complying with internal and external requirements for how operations and activities are carried out. Although these engagements can include an "assistance" dimension through the inclusion of* ***recommendations for improvement****, the auditor does not bear ultimate responsibility for making or authorizing the improvement. Should an auditor* ***take responsibility for implementing or authorizing*** *operational improvements, whether recommended in the course of an audit (assurance) engagement, or as a separate non-audit (consulting) engagement, the auditor is very likely* ***jeopardizing*** *the* ***independence and objectivity*** *that are essential to the role of audit.*

*Even when assisting an organization through non-audit (consulting) activities, auditors should keep their activities within boundaries that define the **core elements of the audit function**. These core elements include:*

- *Auditors should be **independent**. They should avoid relationships and situations that compromise their **objectivity**.*
- *Auditors should **not audit their own work**.*
- *Auditors should not perform **management functions** or make management decisions.*[1]

*The elements are "core" because they support the fundamental value proposition of audit, namely, the principle that an objective third party is **attesting to** (or providing assurance to) the credibility of **management's assertions**. Accordingly, to protect their ability to provide assurance, auditors must minimize potential threats to auditor independence that can arise when the same audit function is also providing non-audit (consulting) services.*

In addition to the core elements above, other threats to auditor independence have been identified, including the conduct of non-audit (consulting) work that

- *Creates a mutuality of interest; or*
- *Places auditors in the role of advocate for the company.*[2]

3. ***Governing Rules.** Specific jurisdictional rules that set restrictions on the work of auditors outside the audit (assurance) role may apply only to auditors conducting the external (financial statement or statutory) audit, or they may apply to auditors performing all types of audits. Moreover, the rules may have been established in the audit function's enabling legislation, imposed by oversight or regulatory bodies, or included in codes of ethics or auditing standards required for audits of specific organizations or jurisdictions.*[3] *It is the Chief Audit Executive's responsibility to ensure that the audit function's **charter** and its **policies and procedures** comply with relevant governing rules.*

   *Moreover, even where the audit function is not subject to governing rules that restrict non-audit (consulting) services, CAEs will nevertheless need to ensure that the **quality assurance system** is designed to manage or minimize threats to auditor independence or objectivity. Otherwise, non-audit (consulting) assignments could have the long-term effect of compromising the audit function's ability to carry out its audit (assurance) role. In addition, an audit function's engagement in non-audit (consulting) work that compromises its independence could prevent other auditors from relying on the audit function's work.*

---

[1] *This principle has been articulated by numerous standard-setting bodies, including guidance published by IAASB/IFAC in its Code of Professional Ethics and the U.S. Government Accountability Office in its Generally Accepted Government Auditing Standards.*

[2] *This risk is raised in the January 2003 Smith Report on Audit Committees and Combined Code Guidance, appointed by the Financial Reporting Council, and is addressed in guidance published by ICAEW (Institute of Chartered Accountants in England and Wales), among others.*

[3] *Examples of specific restrictions include U.K.'s Government Internal Audit Standard 2.4.2, which states: "Objectivity is presumed to be impaired when individual auditors review any activity in which they have previously had executive responsibility, or in which they have provided consultancy advice." This standard is supplemented by Good Practice Guidance on Consultancy, which states: "In this role it is important that the internal auditor offers advice to management and does not undertake the task on behalf of, or as a substitute for, management. Acceptance by management of the advice offered by the internal auditor does not transfer or reduce management's accountability for their own areas of responsibility." (3.5.3)*

4. ***Activities that Compromise Objectivity or Independence.*** *Auditors' ability to engage in non-audit (consulting) work without compromising their independence depends to some extent on where they "draw the line" between assisting or consulting in the sense of advising, versus assisting by doing work that is the responsibility of management. For example, providing advice on appropriate controls during system design with the clear understanding that management has responsibility for accepting or rejecting the advice would have a limited impact on the auditor's objectivity toward that system in the future. By contrast, if the auditor led the system design team, decided which controls to select, or oversaw the implementation of the recommended controls, the auditor's future ability to objectively evaluate that system would be significantly impaired. However, other non-audit assignments may not be as clear-cut. Accordingly, audit functions need to develop procedures for* ***reviewing potential non-audit (consulting) assignments*** *and determining whether they present a* ***threat to independence or objectivity****. The review used to determine the effect on future independence and objectivity should be documented. This* ***documentation*** *should be provided to external quality control reviewers during the QAR engagement.*

5. ***Processes for Minimizing Threats to Objectivity or Independence.*** *The audit function should implement controls that assist in reducing the potential for non-audit (consulting) projects to compromise objectivity of individual auditors, or the independence of the audit function as a whole. Techniques may include:*

   a. *Charter language defining non-audit (consulting) service parameters.*
   b. *Policies and procedures limiting type, nature, or level of participation in non-audit (consulting) projects.*
   c. *Use of a screening process for non-audit (consulting) projects, with limits on accepting engagements that might threaten objectivity.*
   d. *Segregation of non-audit (consulting) units from units conducting audits (assurance engagements) within the same audit function.*
   e. *Rotation of auditors on engagements.*
   f. *Employing outside providers for carrying out non-audit (consulting) engagements, or for conducting assurance engagements in activities where the audit function's prior involvement in non-audit (consulting) work has been determined to impair objectivity/independence.*
   g. *Disclosure in audit reports where objectivity was impaired by participation in a prior non-audit (consulting) project.*

   Attachment A provides examples of relevant language for some of these types of control techniques.

Attachment A
Example Language for Control Techniques Minimizing Threats to Auditor Independence

Charter language defining non-audit (consulting) service parameters. *Charter language will establish the boundaries within which the audit function will operate but is not expected to detail the specific services that would or would not be provided. Accordingly, if a baseline for independence has been described elsewhere in the Charter document, or is included in specifically applicable auditing standards that are referenced; the Charter may need only to include a reference to those other requirements to set parameters for services to be provided. Three examples below show language used in two cases where non-audit (consulting) services are limited to those where independence or objectivity should not be compromised, and for a case where the audit function may be called upon to do work that is normally management's responsibility.*

- *Where the audit function will be limiting non-audit (consulting) services to those that do not compromise objectivity or independence:*

  "The auditor may also assist the mayor, the City Council, and management staff in carrying out their responsibilities by providing them with objective and timely information on the conduct of city operations or advising on appropriate management controls, in accordance with [title of applicable] Auditing Standards."

  "The internal audit department may perform other non-audit functions, consistent with other provisions of this Charter, and prepare and submit such other reports as may be assigned by the Commission."

- *Where the audit function will be providing a full range of non-audit services, even if certain such services may threaten objectivity or independence for audit work:*

  "The auditor may from time to time be called upon to participate in non-audit activities of the Agency, to assist the Executive Director and managers in carrying out their responsibilities, as authorized by the Audit Committee."

Policies and procedures limiting type, nature, and/or level of participation in non-audit (consulting) projects; or establishing controls that minimize future threats to objectivity or independence from participation in non-audit engagements. *If auditors do perform management functions for the organization, the audit unit should establish relevant policies and procedures. Specifically, policies should prohibit those individuals from planning, conducting, or reviewing future audits of the subject matter involving the non-audit (consulting) service. Moreover, if the audit function performs a non-audit (consulting) engagement that will impair the entire audit function's independence or objectivity, the audit function's oversight entity (e.g., the audit committee) should be notified before the engagement begins that audit independence will be impaired on any future audit work performed within the area. Should the audit function proceed to conduct an audit in the activity where the impairment exists, this impairment should be identified in the audit report.*

These prohibitions can be relaxed if there are significant changes to the subject matter area after the assistance work was performed or if the assistance work involved some established de minimums standard, such as "under 40 hours."

The example policy and procedure below describes non-audit (consulting) services, and includes language (see underlined text) that limits the services to within parameters that minimize threats to objectivity and independence of the auditors.

> ***Policy:*** *In addition to audit services, the Auditor's Office provides three other types of services to managers in the jurisdiction, or at the request of the Commission—Quality Assurance for projects in process, Consulting and Training, and Control Self Assessment facilitated workshops.*

Parameters for each type of service are detailed below.

Quality Assurance Services:

In providing quality assurance services, the Office of City Auditor will monitor and assist ongoing projects by assessing if:

- *project objectives will be achieved and are reasonable;*
- *all options have been identified and thoroughly analyzed;*
- *quantitative and qualitative analyses are complete and accurate;*
- *a project plan has been established and project staff are adhering to the plan; and*
- *best practices used by other jurisdictions to accomplish project objectives might be adopted in the City.*

Consulting Services and Training:

Audit staff is available to provide assistance and training to City staff in designing management accountability systems and re-engineering operations. Audit staff is advisory only and management must accept responsibility for implementing any suggestions.

Control Self Assessment Facilitated Workshops:

In this audit process, an employee team meets with auditors to hold structured discussions on how to achieve its objectives in the most efficient and effective way. Action plans, rather than a formal audit report, are developed to address any obstacles to the objective(s). Employee team members are responsible for implementing action plan steps.

The example procedures on the next page contain language that clarifies actions to be taken by the audit function when non-audit (consulting) engagements are accepted that threaten independence and objectivity on future assurance (audit) engagements:

When the audit function is requested by the Audit Committee to conduct non-audit engagements that are determined by the CAE to impair the audit function's independence or an individual auditor's objectivity for conducting subsequent audit work, the following procedures will be carried out:

1. *Prior to commencing the non-audit engagement, the CAE will communicate in writing with the Audit Committee that the requested engagement will impair independence or objectivity; describe the nature of the impairment; and indicate the consequences of the impairment for future audit engagements (e.g., that the audit function must decline future audits in the area, or the Audit Committee will need to contract with a third-party provider to conduct future audits). The CAE should request a response in writing from the Audit Committee, directing the audit function either to proceed with the non-audit engagement, or to decline it.*
2. *If the Audit Committee directs the audit function to proceed with the non-audit engagement, the CAE will document the impairment in:*
   - *The non-audit engagement's documentation, with a copy to management responsible for the non-audit engagement;*
   - *The audit function's annual project planning procedures; and*
   - *The audit function's communications with external quality assurance providers at its next quality assurance review.*

If the Audit Committee directs the audit function to conduct an audit that includes in its scope activities or operations that were part of a prior non-audit engagement conducted by the audit function, about which the CAE previously determined that the non-audit engagement would create an impairment for future audit work, the following procedures should be carried out:

1. *Prior to commencing the audit engagement, the CAE will communicate in writing with the Audit Committee, provide notice and description of the impairment, and indicate options for carrying out the work with a maximum of objectivity (e.g., contracting with a third-party provider, or requesting the assistance of auditors from partner or regulatory entities).*
2. *If the Audit Committee directs the audit function to proceed with the audit engagement, the CAE will document the impairment in:*
   - *The audit engagement's planning documentation; and*
   - *The audit engagement's final report.*
3. *In addition, the CAE shall disclose the occurrence and provide full documentation to the audit function's external quality assurance providers at its next quality assurance review.*

Screening process for non-audit (consulting) projects. *When accepting and performing consulting work, auditors should document their rationale for providing consulting services and demonstrate their judgment that the services do not violate the core elements of the audit role. This information should be disclosed to external quality assurance reviewers. One example policy for screening is below:*

1. *Upon receipt of a request for non-audit (consulting) services, the Internal Audit Department will consider whether providing such services would create a personal impairment either in fact or appearance that would adversely affect either the assigned auditor's objectivity or to the department's independence for conducting subsequent audits within the same area. If the engagement is determined to constitute an impairment to independence or objectivity, the request should be declined. If declined, the factors and final conclusion will be documented in a memorandum addressed to the requestor of the services.*
2. *Before performing non-audit (consulting) services, the auditor in charge will document an understanding with the requestor(s) that the requestor(s) are responsible for the outcome of the work; and, therefore, has a responsibility to be in a position in fact and appearance to make an informed judgment on the results of the non-audit (consulting) work. The Internal Audit Department will establish an agreement with the requestor(s) concerning the objective, scope, and limitations imposed on the non-audit (consulting) engagement services.*

PA Summary

- A **government IAA's** provision of consulting services may be limited by local law, audit standards, etc. The parameters of these services should be defined in its **charter** and supported by its **policies and procedures**.
- **Assurance services** help ensure management's **accountability**. These services include an assistance dimension when auditors recommend operational improvements. But auditors jeopardize their **independence and objectivity** by being responsible for implementing or authorizing improvements, even those arising from consulting.
- When consulting, auditors should stay within the bounds of the **core elements** of the audit function. These give credibility to the auditors' attestation to management assertions. Core elements support the principle that an **objective third party** is providing assurance about the assertions. The core elements that protect auditors' ability to give assurance are (1) independence, (2) objectivity, (3) not auditing one's own work, and (4) not performing functions or making decisions that are managerial.
- Other **threats to auditor independence** include consulting work that (1) creates a mutuality of interest or (2) positions auditors as advocates for the organization.
- **Governing rules** may restrict the IAA's consulting services. These rules may apply to external auditors or all auditors. They may be based on law, regulation, a code of ethics, or audit standards. The CAE should ensure that the IAA's charter, policies, and procedures **comply** with the governing rules.
- Even if restrictive governing rules do not apply, the **quality assurance system** should minimize **threats to auditor independence or objectivity** posed by consulting. Otherwise, the IAA's assurance role and the ability of other auditors to rely on its work may be compromised. **Avoiding these threats** depends in part on distinguishing between (1) merely advising and (2) assuming management responsibilities.
- The IAA should have **documented** procedures for review of threats to independence and objectivity. The documentation should be available to external quality control reviewers.
- The IAA should implement **controls** to reduce the potential threats to auditor independence or objectivity posed by consulting. These controls may include
  - Charter language defining consulting service parameters
  - Policies and procedures limiting type, nature, or level of participation in consulting
  - Screening consulting projects, with limits on engagements threatening objectivity
  - Segregation of consulting units from assurance units in the audit function
  - Rotation of auditors
  - Employing outside providers for (1) consulting or (2) assurance engagements involving activities subject to prior consulting work that impaired objectivity or independence
  - Disclosure in audit reports when objectivity was impaired by participation in a prior consulting project

5. The following is an outline of an example **charter** provided by The IIA:
   a. The **mission** of the internal audit activity (IAA) is stated in terms of the definition of internal auditing.
   b. The **scope of work** of the IAA is to determine whether risk management, control, and governance processes are adequate and functioning to ensure that
      1) Risks are appropriately identified and managed.
      2) Interaction with governance groups occurs as needed.
      3) Significant information is accurate, reliable, and timely.
      4) Employees' actions comply with applicable requirements.
      5) Resources are acquired economically, used efficiently, and adequately protected.
      6) Programs, plans, and objectives are achieved.
      7) Quality and continuous improvement are fostered in control processes.
      8) Significant regulatory issues are recognized and addressed.
   c. Internal auditors may identify **opportunities for improvement** of management control, profitability, and the organization's image. They should be communicated to appropriate management.
   d. The chief audit executive is **accountable** to management and the audit committee to
      1) Provide an annual assessment of the adequacy and effectiveness of the organization's risk management and control processes.
      2) Report significant control issues, including potential improvements, and report on such issues through resolution.
      3) Periodically report on the status and results of the annual audit plan and the sufficiency of IAA resources.
      4) Coordinate and oversee other control and monitoring functions.
   e. To provide for the **independence** of the IAA, its personnel should report to the chief audit executive, who reports functionally to the audit committee and administratively to the CEO. Reports to the audit committee should include a regular report on internal audit personnel.
   f. The **responsibility** of the IAA is to
      1) Develop a risk-based, flexible annual audit plan that includes management's concerns. It should be submitted to the audit committee for review and approval and periodic updates.
      2) Implement the annual audit plan, including any special tasks or projects requested by management and the audit committee.
      3) Maintain a professional audit staff with sufficient knowledge, skills, experience, and professional certifications.
      4) Assess significant merging/consolidating functions and new or changing services, processes, operations, and control processes at the time of their development, implementation, or expansion.
      5) Issue periodic reports to the audit committee and management summarizing results of audit activities.
      6) Inform the audit committee of emerging trends and practices in auditing.
      7) Provide a list of significant measurement goals and results of audit activities to the audit committee.
      8) Assist in the investigation of significant suspected fraud and report the results.
      9) Consider the scope of work of the external auditors and regulators to provide optimal audit coverage at a reasonable cost.

g. The chief audit executive and staff of the IAA are **authorized** to

1) Have unrestricted access to all functions, records, property, and personnel.
2) Have full and free access to the audit committee.
3) Allocate resources, set frequencies, select subjects, determine scopes of work, and apply the techniques required to accomplish audit objectives.
4) Obtain the necessary assistance of auditee personnel and other specialized services from within or outside the organization.

h. The chief audit executive and staff of the IAA are **not authorized** to

1) Perform any operational duties for the organization or its affiliates.
2) Initiate or approve accounting transactions external to the IAA.
3) Direct the activities of any organization employee not employed by the IAA or assigned to assist the internal auditors.

i. The IAA should meet or exceed the **International Standards for the Professional Practice of Internal Auditing**.

6. An alternative to staffing an internal audit activity is to outsource internal auditing functions.

a. To a large organization, the primary advantage of **outsourcing** is that large outside service providers ordinarily have offices in various locations. Thus, engagement requirements in distant locations are more easily accommodated.

b. The disadvantages are that internal auditors tend to be more familiar with the organization, and they are more readily available to the organization because they are unaffected by other priorities, such as other clients.

1) Another disadvantage is that legal requirements may prevent the external audit firm from providing internal audit services.

c. **Cosourcing** is an approach in which the internal audit activity obtains external aid in performing certain activities.

7. Stop and review! You have completed the outline for this subunit. Study multiple-choice questions 1 through 13 beginning on page 88.

2.2 INDEPENDENCE

1. Independence and objectivity are closely related. This subunit primarily addresses the independence attribute of the internal audit activity. It describes the appropriate reporting level of the internal audit activity and states that it should be free from interference. These subjects are covered in one General Attribute Standard, one Specific Attribute Standard, one Assurance Implementation Standard, and four Practice Advisories.

2. ***1100*** ***Independence and Objectivity*** – *The internal audit activity should be independent, and internal auditors should be objective in performing their work.*

a. ***PRACTICE ADVISORY 1100-1: INDEPENDENCE AND OBJECTIVITY***

*1. Internal auditors are independent when they can carry out their work freely and objectively. Independence permits internal auditors to render the **impartial and unbiased** judgments essential to the proper conduct of engagements. It is achieved through **organizational status and objectivity**.*

PA Summary

Internal auditors are independent when they can carry out their work freely and objectively. Independence permits internal auditors to render the **impartial and unbiased** judgments essential to the proper conduct of engagements. It is achieved through **organizational status and objectivity**.

3. ***1110*** ***Organizational Independence*** *– The chief audit executive should report to a level within the organization that allows the internal audit activity to fulfill its responsibilities.*

a. ***PRACTICE ADVISORY 1110-1: ORGANIZATIONAL INDEPENDENCE***

1. *Internal auditors should have the **support of senior management and of the board** so that they can gain the cooperation of engagement clients and perform their work free from interference.*
2. *The chief audit executive should be **responsible to an individual** in the organization **with sufficient authority** to promote independence and to ensure broad engagement coverage, adequate consideration of engagement communications, and appropriate action on engagement recommendations.*
3. *Ideally, the chief audit executive should report **functionally to the audit committee**, board of directors, or other appropriate governing authority, and **administratively to the chief executive officer** of the organization.*
4. *The chief audit executive should have **direct communication with the board**, audit committee, or other appropriate governing authority. Regular communication with the board helps assure independence and provides a means for the board and the chief audit executive to keep each other informed on matters of mutual interest.*
5. ***Direct communication** occurs when the chief audit executive regularly attends and participates in **meetings** of the board, audit committee, or other appropriate governing authority that relate to its oversight responsibilities for auditing, financial reporting, organizational governance, and control. The chief audit executive's attendance and participation at these meetings provide an opportunity to exchange information concerning the plans and activities of the internal audit activity. The chief audit executive should meet privately with the board, audit committee, or other appropriate governing authority at least annually.*
6. *Independence is enhanced when the board concurs in the **appointment or removal** of the chief audit executive.*

PA Summary

- The IAA should be supported by **senior management and the board** to gain the cooperation of clients and work free from interference.
- The CAE should be **responsible to an individual** with sufficient authority to promote independence and to ensure broad coverage, consideration of communications, and appropriate action on recommendations.
- The CAE should report **functionally** to the governing authority and **administratively** to the CEO.
- The CAE should **communicate** directly and regularly with the governing authority. Direct communication involves attendance at meetings of the governing authority relating to its oversight of auditing, financial reporting, governance, and control. The CAE should meet privately with the governing authority **at least annually**.
- The board should concur in **appointment or removal** of the CAE.

b. ***PRACTICE ADVISORY 1110-2: CHIEF AUDIT EXECUTIVE (CAE) REPORTING LINES***

1. *The IIA's* ***International Standards for the Professional Practice of Internal Auditing (Standards)*** *require that the chief audit executive (CAE) report to a level within the organization that allows the internal audit activity to fulfill its responsibilities. The Institute believes strongly that to achieve necessary independence, the CAE should report functionally to the audit committee or its equivalent. For administrative purposes, in most circumstances, the CAE should report directly to the chief executive officer of the organization. The following descriptions of what The IIA considers "functional reporting" and "administrative reporting" are provided to help focus the discussion in this practice advisory.*

   - ***Functional Reporting*** *– The functional reporting line for the internal audit function is the ultimate source of its* ***independence and authority****. As such, The IIA recommends that the CAE report functionally to the audit committee, board of directors, or other appropriate governing authority. In this context, report functionally means that the governing authority should*
     - *approve the overall charter of the internal audit function.*
     - *approve the internal audit risk assessment and related audit plan.*
     - *receive communications from the CAE on the results of the internal audit activities or other matters that the CAE determines are necessary, including private meetings with the CAE without management present.*
     - *approve all decisions regarding the appointment or removal of the CAE.*
     - *approve the annual compensation and salary adjustment of the CAE.*
     - *make appropriate inquiries of management and the CAE to determine whether there are scope or budgetary limitations that impede the ability of the internal audit function to execute its responsibilities.*
   - ***Administrative Reporting*** *– Administrative reporting is the reporting relationship within the organization's management structure that* ***facilitates the day-to-day operations*** *of the internal audit function. Administrative reporting typically includes:*
     - *budgeting and management accounting.*
     - *human resource administration including personnel evaluations and compensation.*
     - *internal communications and information flows.*
     - *administration of the organization's internal policies and procedures.*

2. *This advisory focuses on considerations in establishing or evaluating CAE* ***reporting lines****. Appropriate reporting lines are critical to achieve the* ***independence, objectivity, and organizational stature*** *for an internal audit function necessary to effectively fulfill its obligations. CAE reporting lines are also critical to ensuring the appropriate* ***flow of information*** *and* ***access to key executives*** *and managers that are the foundations of risk assessment and reporting of results of audit activities. Conversely, any reporting relationship that impedes the independence and effective operations of the internal audit function should be viewed by the CAE as a serious* ***scope limitation****, which should be brought to the attention of the audit committee or its equivalent.*

3. *This advisory also recognizes that CAE reporting lines are affected by the nature of the organization (public or private as well as relative size); common practices of each country; growing complexity of organizations (joint ventures, multinational corporations with subsidiaries); and the trend towards internal audit groups providing value-added services with increased collaboration on priorities and scope with their clients. Accordingly, while The IIA believes that there is an ideal reporting structure with functional reporting to the Audit Committee and administrative reporting to the CEO,* ***other relationships can be effective*** *if there are* ***clear distinctions between the functional and administrative reporting lines*** *and* ***appropriate activities*** *are in each line to ensure that the independence and scope of activities is maintained. Internal auditors are expected to use professional judgment to determine the extent to which the guidance provided in this advisory should be applied in each given situation.*

4. *The* ***Standards*** *stress the importance of the chief audit executive reporting to an individual with sufficient authority to promote independence and to ensure broad audit coverage. The Standards are purposely somewhat generic about reporting relationships, however, because they are designed to be applicable at all organizations regardless of size or any other factors. Factors that make "one size fits all" unattainable include organization size and type of organization (private, governmental, corporate). Accordingly, the CAE should consider the following* ***attributes*** *in* ***evaluating the appropriateness of the administrative reporting line****.*
   - *Does the individual have sufficient authority and stature to ensure the effectiveness of the function?*
   - *Does the individual have an appropriate control and governance mindset to assist the CAE in their role?*
   - *Does the individual have the time and interest to actively support the CAE on audit issues?*
   - *Does the individual understand the functional reporting relationship and support it?*

5. *The individual responsible for the administrative reporting line* ***also may be responsible for other activities*** *in the organization that are subject to internal audit. For example, some CAEs report administratively to the Chief Financial Officer, who is also responsible for the organization's accounting functions. In such a case, the CAE should ensure that independence is maintained. Moreover, the internal audit function should be free to audit and report on any activity, assuming that engagement provides coverage the CAE deems to be appropriate for the audit plan. This principle applies even when the activity reports to the same administrator as the internal audit function. Any* ***limitation in scope or reporting*** *of results of these activities should be brought to the attention of the audit committee.*

6. *Under the recent move to a* ***stricter legislative and regulatory climate*** *regarding financial reporting around the globe, the CAE's reporting lines should be appropriate to enable the internal audit activity to meet any* ***increased needs of the audit committee or other significant stakeholders****. Increasingly, the CAE is being asked to take a more significant role in the organization's governance and risk management activities. The reporting lines of the CAE should facilitate the ability of the internal audit activity to meet these expectations.*

7. *Regardless of which reporting relationship the organization chooses, several **key actions** can help assure that the reporting lines support and enable the effectiveness and independence of the internal auditing activity.*
   - ***Functional Reporting:***
     - *The functional reporting line should go directly to the **Audit Committee** or its equivalent to ensure the appropriate level of independence and communication.*
     - *The **CAE should meet privately with the audit committee** or its equivalent, without management present, to reinforce the independence and nature of this reporting relationship.*
     - *The audit committee should have the **final authority** to review and approve the annual audit plan and all major changes to the plan.*
     - *At all times, the **CAE** should have **open and direct access** to the chair of the audit committee and its members; or the chair of the board or full board if appropriate.*
     - ***At least once a year**, the audit committee should review the performance of the CAE and approve the annual compensation and salary adjustment.*
     - *The **charter** for the internal audit function should clearly articulate both the functional and administrative reporting lines for the function as well as the principle activities directed up each line.*
   - ***Administrative Reporting:***
     - *The administrative reporting line of the CAE should be to the **CEO or another executive** with sufficient authority to afford the internal audit function appropriate support to accomplish its day-to-day activities. This support should include positioning the function and the CAE in the organization's structure in a manner that affords appropriate stature for the function within the organization. Reporting too low in an organization can negatively impact the stature and effectiveness of the internal audit function.*
     - *The administrative reporting line should **not have ultimate authority** over the scope or reporting of results of the internal audit activity.*
     - *The administrative reporting line should **facilitate open and direct communications** with executive and line management. The CAE should be able to communicate directly with any level of management including the CEO.*
     - *The administrative reporting line should enable adequate communications and information flow so that the CAE and the internal audit function have an **adequate and timely flow of information** concerning the activities, plans, and business initiatives of the organization.*
     - ***Budgetary controls** and considerations imposed by the administrative reporting line should not impede the ability of the internal audit function to accomplish its mission.*
8. *CAEs should also consider their relationships with **other control and monitoring functions** (risk management, compliance, security, legal, ethics, environmental, external audit) and **facilitate the reporting** of material risk and control issues to the audit committee.*

PA Summary

- To achieve necessary **independence**, the CAE should report functionally to the audit committee or its equivalent. For administrative purposes, the CAE should report directly to the CEO. The **functional reporting line** is the ultimate source of the IAA's independence and authority. Thus, the governing authority should (1) approve the IAA's charter and its risk assessment and related audit plan; (2) receive communications on the results of IAA activities or other necessary matters, including private meetings with the CAE without management; (3) approve decisions about appointing, removing, and compensating the CAE; and (4) inquire of management and the CAE about scope or budgetary limits on the IAA's ability to do its job.
- **Administrative reporting** facilitates daily operations of the IAA. It typically concerns budgeting, management accounting, managing human resources, internal communications, and administration of internal policies and procedures.
- **CAE reporting lines** are critical to establishing the IAA's independence, objectivity, status, information flow, and access to key persons. Reporting relationships impairing independence and effective operations are serious **scope limitations**.
- Reporting lines are affected by the size of the entity, local practices, greater complexity of organizations, and the trend toward IAA collaboration with clients. Lines other than the ideal may be effective, given clear distinctions between the functional and administrative, with appropriate activities in each line. Internal auditors must use professional judgment about such matters.
- The CAE considers various **attributes** in evaluating the **administrative line**, including whether the individual (1) has sufficient authority to ensure the effectiveness of the IAA, (2) has an appropriate control and governance mindset, (3) actively supports the CAE, and (4) understands and supports the functional reporting relationship.
- **Independence** may be threatened if the individual responsible for the administrative line also is responsible for audited activities. In such a case, the CAE should ensure that independence is maintained. Moreover, the IAA should be free to audit and report on any activity, assuming engagement coverage is appropriate for the audit plan. This principle applies even when the activity reports to the same administrator. Any **limitation on scope or reporting** should be reported to the audit committee.
- CAE reporting lines should support the greater **regulatory needs** of the audit committee and other stakeholders and the greater involvement of the CAE in **governance and risk management**.
- Certain **key actions regarding functional reporting** support the IAA's effectiveness, for example, (1) audit committee authority to approve the final audit plan and review the CAE's performance, (2) CAE access to the audit committee or board, (3) annual audit committee review of CAE performance and approval of CAE compensation, and (4) stating reporting lines in the IAA charter.
- Administrative reporting should include positioning the IAA and the CAE in the organization's structure to afford it appropriate **status**. The administrative reporting line also should **not have ultimate authority** over the scope or reporting of results. Moreover, it should **facilitate open and direct communications** with executive and line management and enable **adequate and timely flow of information** about the organization. Finally, **budgetary controls** and considerations imposed by the administrative reporting line should not impede the ability of the IAA to accomplish its mission.
- The CAE considers relationships with **other control functions** and **facilitates reporting** of material issues.

4. ***1110.A1*** – *The internal audit activity should be free from interference in determining the scope of internal auditing, performing work, and communicating results.*

   a. ***PRACTICE ADVISORY 1110.A1-1: DISCLOSING REASONS FOR INFORMATION REQUESTS***

      1. *At times, an internal auditor may be asked by the engagement client or other parties to explain why a document is relevant to an engagement. Disclosure or nondisclosure **during the engagement** of the reasons documents are needed should be **determined based on the circumstances**. Significant irregularities may dictate a less open environment than would normally be conducive to a cooperative engagement. However, that is a judgment that should be made by the chief audit executive in light of the specific circumstances.*

PA Summary

The specific circumstances determine whether the auditor should disclose **during the engagement** the reasons for a document request. Significant irregularities may dictate a less open environment than would normally be conducive to a cooperative engagement.

5. Stop and review! You have completed the outline for this subunit. Study multiple-choice questions 14 through 29 beginning on page 93.

2.3 OBJECTIVITY

1. This subunit addresses objectivity, which is covered in one General Attribute Standard, one Specific Attribute Standard, and two Practice Advisories.
2. ***1100*** ***Independence and Objectivity*** – *The internal audit activity should be independent, and internal auditors should be objective in performing their work.*

   a. **Practice Advisory 1100-1** (see Subunit 2.2) states that independence is achieved through objectivity as well as organizational status.
3. ***1120*** ***Individual Objectivity*** – *Internal auditors should have an impartial, unbiased attitude and avoid conflicts of interest.*

   a. ***PRACTICE ADVISORY 1120-1: INDIVIDUAL OBJECTIVITY***

      1. *Objectivity is an **independent mental attitude** that internal auditors should maintain in performing engagements. Internal auditors are **not** to **subordinate their judgment** on engagement matters to that of others.*
      2. *Objectivity requires internal auditors to perform engagements in such a manner that they have an **honest belief in their work product** and that **no significant quality compromises** are made. Internal auditors are not to be placed in situations in which they feel unable to make objective professional judgments.*
      3. ***Staff assignments** should be made so that potential and actual **conflicts of interest and bias** are avoided. The chief audit executive should periodically obtain from the internal auditing staff information concerning potential conflicts of interest and bias. Staff assignments of internal auditors should be **rotated** periodically whenever it is practicable to do so.*
      4. *The results of internal auditing **work should be reviewed** before the related engagement communications are released to provide **reasonable assurance** that the work was performed **objectively**.*

5. *It is **unethical** for an internal auditor to **accept a fee or gift** from an employee, client, customer, supplier, or business associate. Accepting a fee or gift may create an **appearance** that the auditor's **objectivity has been impaired**. The appearance that objectivity has been impaired may apply to current and future engagements conducted by the auditor. The status of engagements should not be considered as justification for receiving fees or gifts. The receipt of promotional items (such as pens, calendars, or samples) that are available to the general public and have minimal value should not hinder internal auditors' professional judgments. Internal auditors should **report the offer** of all material fees or gifts immediately to their supervisors.*

PA Summary

- Objectivity is an **independent mental attitude**. Auditors must **not subordinate their judgments** on engagement matters. They must have an **honest belief in their work product** and make no significant quality compromises.
- **Staff assignments** should be made to avoid **conflicts of interest and bias**. Staff assignments should be **rotated** periodically whenever it is practicable.
- Work should be **reviewed** before release of communications to give reasonable assurance of objective performance.
- **Accepting a fee or gift** from an employee, client, customer, supplier, or business associate is unethical. It may create an **appearance** that **objectivity has been impaired** in current and future engagements. But the receipt of low-value promotional items that are available to the public should not hinder professional judgments. Internal auditors should **report the offer** of all material items immediately.

4. Stop and review! You have completed the outline for this subunit. Study multiple-choice questions 30 and 31 on page 99.

2.4 INDEPENDENCE AND OBJECTIVITY

1. Most of the materials in this subunit apply to the independence of the internal audit activity and the objectivity of the individual internal auditor. These pronouncements consist of one Specific Attribute Standard, two Assurance Implementation Standards, two Consulting Implementation Standards, and four Practice Advisories.
2. ***1130*** *__Impairments to Independence or Objectivity__ – If independence or objectivity is impaired in fact or appearance, the details of the impairment should be disclosed to appropriate parties. The nature of the disclosure will depend upon the impairment.*

   a. ***__PRACTICE ADVISORY 1130-1: IMPAIRMENTS TO INDEPENDENCE OR OBJECTIVITY__***

      1. *Internal auditors should **report to the chief audit executive** any situations in which a **conflict of interest or bias** is present or may reasonably be inferred. The chief audit executive should then reassign such auditors.*

2. *A **scope limitation** is a restriction placed upon the internal audit activity that precludes the audit activity from accomplishing its objectives and plans. Among other things, a scope limitation may restrict the:*
   - *Scope defined in the charter.*
   - *Internal audit activity's access to records, personnel, and physical properties relevant to the performance of engagements.*
   - *Approved engagement work schedule.*
   - *Performance of necessary engagement procedures.*
   - *Approved staffing plan and financial budget.*
3. *A scope limitation along with its potential effect **should be communicated**, preferably in writing, to the board, audit committee, or other appropriate governing authority.*
4. *The chief audit executive should consider whether it is appropriate to inform the board, audit committee, or other appropriate governing authority regarding **scope limitations** that were **previously communicated to and accepted** by the board, audit committee, or other appropriate governing authority. This may be necessary, particularly when there have been organization, board, senior management, or other changes.*

PA Summary

- Any **conflict of interest or bias** should be reported. The **CAE** should then reassign such auditors.
- A **scope limitation** on the IAA precludes it from accomplishing its objectives and plans. A scope limitation may restrict the (1) scope defined in the **charter**; (2) IAA's **access** to records, personnel, and physical properties; (3) approved **work schedule**; (4) performance of **procedures**; and (5) approved **staffing plan** and **financial budget**. A scope limitation should be reported, preferably in writing, to the governing authority.
- The CAE must consider whether to report scope limitations **previously accepted** by the governing authority.

3. ***1130.A1*** *– Internal auditors should refrain from assessing specific operations for which they were previously responsible. Objectivity is presumed to be impaired if an internal auditor provides assurance services for an activity for which the internal auditor had responsibility within the previous year.*
   a. ***PRACTICE ADVISORY 1130.A1-1: ASSESSING OPERATIONS FOR WHICH INTERNAL AUDITORS WERE PREVIOUSLY RESPONSIBLE***
      1. ***Internal auditors should not assume operating responsibilities.*** *If senior management directs internal auditors to perform nonaudit work, it should be understood that they are not functioning as internal auditors. Moreover, **objectivity** is presumed to be impaired when internal auditors perform an **assurance review** of any activity for which they had authority or responsibility within the past year. This impairment should be considered when **communicating audit engagement results**.*

- *If internal auditors are directed to perform nonaudit duties that may impair objectivity, such as preparation of bank reconciliations, the chief audit executive should inform senior management and the board that this activity is not an assurance audit activity; and, therefore, audit-related conclusions should not be drawn.*
- *In addition, when operating responsibilities are assigned to the internal audit activity, special attention must be given to ensure objectivity when a subsequent assurance engagement in the related operating area is undertaken. Objectivity is presumed to be impaired when internal auditors audit any activity for which they had authority or responsibility within the past year. These facts should be clearly stated when communicating the results of an audit engagement relating to an area where an auditor had operating responsibilities.*

2. *At any point that assigned activities involve the assumption of operating authority, audit objectivity would be presumed to be impaired with respect to that activity.*
3. ***Persons transferred to or temporarily engaged by the internal audit activity** should not be assigned to audit those activities they previously performed until a reasonable period of time (at least one year) has elapsed. Such assignments are presumed to impair objectivity, and additional consideration should be exercised when supervising the engagement work and communicating engagement results.*
4. *The internal auditor's objectivity is not adversely affected when the auditor **recommends standards of control for systems or reviews procedures** before they are implemented. The auditor's objectivity is considered to be impaired if the auditor **designs, installs, drafts procedures for, or operates such systems.***
5. *The **occasional performance of nonaudit work** by the internal auditor, with full disclosure in the reporting process, would not necessarily impair **independence**. However, it would require careful consideration by management and the internal auditor to avoid adversely affecting the internal auditor's objectivity.*

PA Summary

- **Internal auditors should not assume operating responsibilities.** If senior management directs internal auditors to perform nonaudit work, they are not functioning as internal auditors. **Objectivity** is impaired when they perform an **assurance review** of an activity for which they were responsible within the past year. This impairment should be considered when **communicating audit engagement results**.
- **Persons transferred to or temporarily engaged by the IAA** should not be assigned to audit activities they previously performed until a reasonable period (at least one year) has elapsed. This circumstance should be considered when supervising the work and communicating results.
- Internal auditors may **recommend control standards** or **review procedures** before they are implemented without impairing objectivity.
- Occasional nonaudit work, with disclosure, does not necessarily impair **independence**. But careful consideration is needed to avoid impairing **objectivity**.

b. ***PRACTICE ADVISORY 1130.A1-2: INTERNAL AUDIT RESPONSIBILITY FOR OTHER (NON-AUDIT) FUNCTIONS***

1. *Some internal auditors have been assigned or accepted non-audit duties because of a variety of business reasons that make sense to management of the organization. Internal auditors are more frequently being asked to perform roles and responsibilities that may impair independence or objectivity. Given the increasing demand on organizations, both public and private, to develop more efficient and effective operations with fewer resources, some internal audit activities are being directed to assume **responsibility for operations that are subject to periodic internal auditing assessments**.*
2. *When the internal audit activity or individual internal auditor is responsible for, or management is considering assigning, an operation that it might audit, the internal auditor's independence and objectivity may be impaired. The internal auditor should consider the following **factors in assessing the impact on independence and objectivity**:*
   - *The requirements of The IIA **Code of Ethics** and International Standards for the Professional Practice of Internal Auditing **(Standards)**;*
   - *Expectations of **stakeholders** that may include the shareholders, board of directors, audit committee, management, legislative bodies, public entities, regulatory bodies, and public interest groups;*
   - *Allowances or restrictions contained in the internal audit activity **charter**;*
   - ***Disclosures** required by the Standards; and*
   - *Subsequent **audit coverage** of the activities or responsibilities accepted by the internal auditor.*
3. *Internal auditors should consider the following factors to determine an **appropriate course of action** when presented with the opportunity of accepting responsibility for a non-audit function:*
   - *The IIA **Code of Ethics** and **Standards** require the internal audit activity to be independent and internal auditors to be objective in performing their work.*
     - *If possible, internal auditors should **avoid accepting responsibility for non-audit functions** or duties that are subject to periodic internal auditing assessments. If this is not possible, then;*
     - *Impairment to **independence and objectivity** are required to be **disclosed** to appropriate parties, and the nature of the disclosure depends upon the impairment.*
     - ***Objectivity** is presumed to be impaired if an auditor provides assurance services for an activity for which the auditor had **responsibility within the previous year**.*
     - *If on occasion management directs internal auditors to perform non-audit work, it should be understood that they are **not functioning as internal auditors**.*
   - *Expectations of **stakeholders**, including regulatory or legal requirements, should be evaluated and assessed in relation to the potential impairment.*

- *If the internal audit activity **charter** contains specific restrictions or limiting language regarding the assignment of non-audit functions to the internal auditor, then these restrictions should be **disclosed and discussed with management**. If management insists on such an assignment, the auditor should disclose and discuss this matter with the audit committee or appropriate governing body. If the charter is silent on this matter, the guidance noted in the following points should be considered. All the points noted below are subordinated to the language of the charter.*
- ***Assessment** – The results of the assessment should be discussed with management, the audit committee, or other appropriate stakeholders. A determination should be made regarding a number of issues, some of which affect one another:*
  - *The **significance of the operational function** to the organization (in terms of revenue, expenses, reputation, and influence) should be evaluated.*
  - *The length or duration of the assignment and **scope of responsibility** should be evaluated.*
  - *Adequacy of **separation of duties** should be evaluated.*
  - *The **potential impairment** to objectivity or independence or the appearance of such impairment should be considered when reporting audit results.*
- ***Audit of the Function and Disclosure** – Given that the internal audit activity has operational responsibilities and that operation is part of the audit plan, there are several avenues for the auditor to consider.*
  - *The audit may be performed by a **contracted, third party entity**; by **external auditors**; or by the **internal audit function**. In the first two situations, impairment of objectivity is minimized by the use of auditors outside of the organization. In the latter case, objectivity would be impaired.*
  - *Individual auditors with **operational responsibility** should not participate in the audit of the operation. If possible, auditors conducting the assessment should be supervised by, and report the results of the assessment to, those whose independence or objectivity is not impaired.*
  - ***Disclosure** should be made regarding the operational responsibilities of the auditor for the function, the significance of the operation to the organization (in terms of revenue, expenses, or other pertinent information), and the relationship of those who audited the function.*
  - *Disclosure of the internal auditor's operational responsibilities should be made in the related **engagement communication** and in the auditor's **standard communication to the audit committee** or other governing body.*

PA Summary

- Some IAAs increasingly are being directed to assume **responsibility for operations that are subject to periodic internal auditing assessments**. Internal auditors should assess the effect on **independence** and **objectivity** of taking responsibility for an operation subject to audit. The assessment requires consideration of the Code of Ethics, the Standards (including disclosures), the charter, stakeholder expectations, and future audit coverage.
- If possible, internal auditors should **avoid accepting responsibility for nonaudit duties** subject to periodic internal auditing assessments. If this is not possible, **disclosure** of any impairment to appropriate parties is required.
- Expectations of **stakeholders**, including regulatory or legal requirements, should be assessed in relation to the impairment.
- If the IAA **charter** contains specific restrictions on assignment of nonaudit duties, they should be **disclosed and discussed with management**. If management insists on the assignment, the auditor should discuss the matter with the governing body.
- If the **charter is silent** about its responsibility for nonaudit functions, the **assessment** of the effect on independence and objectivity should address the (1) significance of the function, (2) scope of responsibility, (3) separation of duties, and (4) potential impairment.
- If the IAA charter is silent about its responsibility for an audited function, the following are additional considerations: (1) who will perform the audit, (2) exclusion of responsible individuals from the audit, (3) disclosures to be made, and (4) the ways in which disclosures should be communicated.

4. ***1130.A2*** *– Assurance engagements for functions over which the chief audit executive has responsibility should be overseen by a party outside the internal audit activity.*
5. ***1130.C1*** *– Internal auditors may provide consulting services relating to operations for which they had previous responsibilities.*
6. ***1130.C2*** *– If internal auditors have potential impairments to independence or objectivity relating to proposed consulting services, disclosure should be made to the engagement client prior to accepting the engagement.*

   a. ***PRACTICE ADVISORY 1000.C1-2: ADDITIONAL CONSIDERATIONS FOR FORMAL CONSULTING ENGAGEMENTS***

   The following is the portion of this comprehensive Practice Advisory relevant to Standards 1130.C1 and 1130.C2:

   Independence and Objectivity in Consulting Engagements

   5. *Internal auditors are sometimes requested to provide consulting services relating to* ***operations for which they had previous responsibilities or had conducted assurance services****. Prior to offering consulting services, the Chief Audit Executive should confirm that* ***the board*** *understands and approves the concept of providing consulting services. Once approved, the internal audit* ***charter*** *should be amended to include authority and responsibilities for consulting activities, and the internal audit activity should develop appropriate* ***policies*** *and* ***procedures*** *for conducting such engagements.*

6. *Internal auditors should maintain their **objectivity** when drawing conclusions and offering advice to management. If **impairments to independence or objectivity** exist prior to commencement of the consulting engagement, or subsequently develop during the engagement, **disclosure** should be made immediately to management.*
7. *Independence and objectivity may be impaired if **assurance services** are provided **within one year after a formal consulting engagement**. Steps can be taken to minimize the effects of impairment by assigning different auditors to perform each of the services, establishing independent management and supervision, defining separate accountability for the results of the projects, and disclosing the presumed impairment. **Management should be responsible** for accepting and implementing recommendations.*
8. *Care should be taken, particularly involving consulting engagements that are ongoing or continuous in nature, so that internal auditors do not inappropriately or unintentionally **assume management responsibilities** that were not intended in the original objectives and scope of the engagement.*

PA Summary

- The **board** should approve, and the **charter** should provide authority for, consulting services relating to operations for which internal auditors had (1) previous responsibility or (2) performed assurance services. The IAA should have **policies and procedures** for these services.
- **Objectivity** should be maintained, and **impairment** of objectivity or **independence** should be **disclosed**. Impairment may occur if an **assurance service** is performed within a year. Steps should be taken to minimize the effects of impairment, and **management** should be responsible for implementing recommendations.
- Internal auditors should not **inappropriately assume management responsibilities**.

7. Stop and review! You have completed the outline for this subunit. Study multiple-choice questions 32 through 45 beginning on page 99.

2.5 STUDY UNIT 2 SUMMARY

1. The purpose, authority, and responsibility of the internal audit activity should be formally defined in a charter, consistent with the Standards, and approved by the board.
2. The nature of assurance services provided to the organization should be defined in the audit charter. If assurances are to be provided to parties outside the organization, the nature of these assurances should also be defined in the charter. The nature of consulting services also should be defined in the charter.
3. The Glossary in the Standards defines "consulting services" as follows: "Advisory and related client service activities, the nature and scope of which are agreed with the client and which are intended to add value and improve an organization's governance, risk management, and control processes without the internal auditor assuming management responsibility. Examples include counsel, advice, facilitation, and training."
4. The internal audit activity should be independent, and internal auditors should be objective in performing their work.

5. The chief audit executive should report to a level within the organization that allows the internal audit activity to fulfill its responsibilities.
6. The internal audit activity should be free from interference in determining the scope of internal auditing, performing work, and communicating results.
7. Internal auditors should have an impartial, unbiased attitude and avoid conflicts of interest.
8. *Internal auditors should refrain from assessing specific operations for which they were previously responsible. Objectivity is presumed to be impaired if an internal auditor provides assurance services for an activity for which the internal auditor had responsibility within the previous year.*
9. Assurance engagements for functions over which the chief audit executive has responsibility should be overseen by a party outside the internal audit activity.
10. Internal auditors may provide consulting services relating to operations for which they had previous responsibilities.
11. If internal auditors have potential impairments to independence or objectivity relating to proposed consulting services, disclosure should be made to the engagement client prior to accepting the engagement.

QUESTIONS

2.1 Charter

1. During an engagement to evaluate the organization's accounts payable function, an internal auditor plans to confirm balances with suppliers. What is the source of authority for such contacts with units outside the organization?

A. Internal audit activity policies and procedures.

B. The Standards.

C. The Code of Ethics.

D. The internal audit activity's charter.

Answer (D) is correct. *(CIA, adapted)*

REQUIRED: The source of authority for an internal auditor to contact units outside the organization.

DISCUSSION: The purpose, authority, and responsibility of the internal audit activity should be formally defined in a charter, consistent with the Standards, and approved by the board (Standard 1000). Approval of these reporting lines by the board should help to avoid conflict between senior management and the audit committee. The charter should establish the internal audit activity's position within the organization; authorize access to records, personnel, and physical properties relevant to the performance of engagements; and define the scope of internal audit activities (PA 1000-1). Thus, the charter should prescribe the internal audit activity's relationships with other units within the organization and with those outside.

Answer (A) is incorrect because policies and procedures guide the internal auditors in their consistent compliance with the internal audit activity's standards of performance. Answer (B) is incorrect because the IAA's authority is defined in a charter approved by the board. Answer (C) is incorrect because the purpose of the Code of Ethics is to promote an ethical culture in the profession of internal auditing.

2. An element of authority that should be included in the charter of the internal audit activity is

A. Identification of the organizational units where engagements are to be performed.

B. Identification of the types of disclosures that should be made to the audit committee.

C. Access to records, personnel, and physical properties relevant to the performance of engagements.

D. Access to the external auditor's engagement records.

Answer (C) is correct. *(CIA, adapted)*

REQUIRED: The element of authority that should be included in the charter of the internal audit activity.

DISCUSSION: The purpose, authority, and responsibility of the internal audit activity should be defined in a charter, consistent with the Standards, and approved by the board (Standard 1000). The charter should establish the internal audit activity's position within the organization; authorize access to records, personnel, and physical properties relevant to the performance of engagements; and define the scope of internal audit activities (PA 1000-1).

Answer (A) is incorrect because the charter should not specifically identify the subjects of engagements. Answer (B) is incorrect because disclosure to the audit committee is an obligation, not an element of authority. Answer (D) is incorrect because access to the external auditor's engagement records cannot be guaranteed.

3. The audit committee of an organization has charged the chief audit executive (CAE) with upgrading the internal audit activity. The CAE's first task is to develop a charter. What item should be included in the statement of objectives?

A. Report all engagement results to the audit committee every quarter.

B. Notify governmental regulatory agencies of unethical business practices by organization management.

C. Evaluate the adequacy and effectiveness of the organization's controls.

D. Submit budget variance reports to management every month.

Answer (C) is correct. *(CIA, adapted)*

REQUIRED: The item included in the statement of objectives of the charter.

DISCUSSION: The purpose, authority, and responsibility of the internal audit activity should be formally defined in a charter, consistent with the Standards, and approved by the board (Standard 1000). The charter should establish the internal audit activity's position within the organization; authorize access to records, personnel, and physical properties relevant to the performance of engagements; and define the scope of internal audit activities (PA 1000-1). The scope of work of the IAA is to determine whether risk management, control, and governance processes are adequate and functioning.

Answer (A) is incorrect because only significant engagement results should be discussed with the audit committee. Answer (B) is incorrect because internal auditors ordinarily are not required to report deficiencies in regulatory compliance to the appropriate agencies. However, they must observe the law and make disclosures expected by the law and profession (Rule of Conduct 1.2). Answer (D) is incorrect because submission of budgetary variance reports is not a primary objective of internal auditing. It is a budgetary control that management may require on a periodic basis.

4. The authority of the internal audit activity is limited to that granted by

A. The board and the controller.

B. Senior management and the Standards.

C. Management and the board.

D. The audit committee and the chief financial officer.

Answer (C) is correct. *(CIA, adapted)*

REQUIRED: The source of authority of the internal audit activity.

DISCUSSION: The purpose, authority, and responsibility of the internal audit activity should be formally defined in a charter, consistent with the Standards, and approved by the board (Standard 1000). Furthermore, the CAE should seek approval of the charter by senior management. The charter should establish the internal audit activity's position within the organization; authorize access to records, personnel, and physical properties relevant to the performance of engagements; and define the scope of internal audit activities (PA 1000-1).

Answer (A) is incorrect because the controller is not the only member of management. Answer (B) is incorrect because the Standards provide no actual authority to the IAA. Answer (D) is incorrect because management and the board, not a committee of the board and a particular manager, endow the IAA with its authority.

5. Is it appropriate for an internal auditor to conduct an engagement that combines elements of consulting and assurance services?

A. Yes, in all circumstances.

B. Yes, in some circumstances.

C. No, unless the audit committee gives permission.

D. In no circumstances.

Answer (B) is correct. *(Publisher, adapted)*

REQUIRED: The propriety of conducting an engagement that incorporates elements of consulting and assurance activities.

DISCUSSION: In some circumstances, it may be appropriate to conduct an engagement that incorporates elements of both consulting and assurance activities into one consolidated approach. These engagements are referred to as "blended engagements." In other cases, it may be appropriate to distinguish between the assurance and consulting components of the engagement (PA 1000.CI-2).

Answer (A) is incorrect because it may be appropriate to distinguish between the assurance and consulting components of an engagement in some circumstances. Answer (C) is incorrect because it is appropriate to incorporate elements of both consulting and assurance activities into one consolidated approach in some circumstances, but permission of the audit committee is not necessarily required. Answer (D) is incorrect because combining assurance and consulting services is appropriate in some circumstances.

6. Participation on a system conversion team falls into which possible category of consulting engagements?

A. Formal consulting engagements.

B. Special consulting engagements.

C. Informal consulting engagements.

D. Emergency consulting engagements.

Answer (B) is correct. *(Publisher, adapted)*

REQUIRED: The category of consulting engagement that best encompasses participation on a system conversion team.

DISCUSSION: Each organization should consider the type of consulting activities to be offered and determine whether specific policies and procedures should be developed for each type of activity. The four possible categories of consulting engagement are formal, informal, special, and emergency. Special consulting engagements include activities such as participation on a merger and acquisition team or system conversion team (PA 1000.C1-2).

Answer (A) is incorrect because formal consulting engagements are planned and subject to written agreement. Answer (C) is incorrect because informal consulting engagements include routine activities, such as participation on standing committees, limited-life projects, ad-hoc meetings, and routine information exchange. Answer (D) is incorrect because emergency consulting engagements encompass activities like participation on a team established for recovery or maintenance of operations after a disaster or other extraordinary business event, or a team assembled to supply temporary help to meet a special request or unusual deadline.

7. A charter is one of the more important factors positively affecting the internal audit activity's independence. Which of the following is least likely to be part of the charter?

A. Access to records within the organization.

B. The scope of internal audit activities.

C. The length of tenure of the chief audit executive.

D. Access to personnel within the organization.

Answer (C) is correct. *(CIA, adapted)*

REQUIRED: The item not included in the IAA's charter.

DISCUSSION: The independence of the IAA is enhanced when the board concurs in the appointment or removal of the CAE (PA 1110-1), but the length of the CAE's employment is less significant than defining the purpose, authority, and responsibility of the IAA (Standard 1000). The charter establishes the IAA's position within the organization; authorizes access to records, personnel, and physical properties; and defines the scope of internal audit activities (PA 1000-1).

8. Internal auditing has planned an engagement to evaluate the effectiveness of the quality assurance function as it affects the receipt of goods, the transfer of the goods into production, and the scrap costs related to defective items. The engagement client argues that such an engagement is not within the scope of the internal audit activity and should come under the purview of the quality assurance department only. What is the most appropriate response?

A. Refer to the internal audit activity's charter and the approved engagement plan that includes the area designated for evaluation in the current time period.

B. Because quality assurance is a new function, seek the approval of management as a mediator to set the scope of the engagement.

C. Indicate that the engagement will evaluate the function only in accordance with the standards set by, and approved by, the quality assurance function before beginning the engagement.

D. Terminate the engagement because it will not be productive without the client's cooperation.

Answer (A) is correct. *(CIA, adapted)*

REQUIRED: The most appropriate response to an assertion that an engagement to evaluate the effectiveness of the quality assurance function is beyond the scope of the IAA.

DISCUSSION: The charter should define the purpose, authority, and responsibility of the IAA (Standard 1000). Among other matters, it should define the scope of internal audit activities. Furthermore, the CAE should submit annually to senior management for approval, and to the board for its information, a summary of the IAA's work schedule, staffing plan, and financial budget (PA 2020-1).

Answer (B) is incorrect because the engagement client does not determine the scope of this type of assurance engagement. A scope limitation imposed by the client might prevent the IAA from achieving its objectives. Answer (C) is incorrect because other objectives may be established by management and the internal auditors. The engagement should not be limited to the specific standards set by the quality assurance department, but it should consider such standards in the development of the engagement program. Answer (D) is incorrect because the internal auditors should conduct the engagement and communicate any scope limitations to management and the board.

9. The chief audit executive has assigned an internal auditor to perform a year-end engagement to evaluate payroll records. The internal auditor has contacted the director of compensation and has been refused access to necessary documents. To avoid this problem,

A. Access to records relevant to performance of engagements should be specified in the internal audit activity's charter.

B. Internal auditing should be required to report to the CEO of the organization.

C. By following the long-range planning process, access to all relevant records should be guaranteed.

D. Audit committee approval should be required for all scope limitations.

Answer (A) is correct. *(CIA, adapted)*

REQUIRED: The means of avoiding an engagement client's refusal to permit access to necessary documents.

DISCUSSION: The IAA should have the support of management and the board in gaining cooperation from all engagement clients (PA 1110-1). Specific guidelines should be written in its charter authorizing access to records, personnel, and physical properties relevant to the performance of engagements (PA 1000-1). Such provisions reduce the likelihood of scope limitations.

Answer (B) is incorrect because the IAA need not report to a specific individual in the organization, although reporting administratively to the CEO is desirable. Answer (C) is incorrect because following the long-range planning process provides no guarantee of access. Answer (D) is incorrect because the IAA should inform the board of any scope limitations, but its approval is not required.

10. A charter is being drafted for a newly formed internal audit activity. Which of the following best describes the appropriate organizational status that should be incorporated into the charter?

A. The chief audit executive should report to the chief executive officer but have access to the board of directors.

B. The chief audit executive should be a member of the audit committee of the board of directors.

C. The chief audit executive should be a staff officer reporting to the chief financial officer.

D. The chief audit executive should report to an administrative vice president.

Answer (A) is correct. *(CIA, adapted)*

REQUIRED: The appropriate organizational status that should be incorporated into the charter.

DISCUSSION: The CAE should be responsible to an individual in the organization with sufficient authority to promote independence and to ensure broad engagement coverage, adequate consideration of engagement communications, and appropriate action on engagement recommendations. The higher the level to which the IAA reports, the more likely that independence will be assured. Ideally, the CAE should report functionally to the audit committee, board of directors, or other appropriate governing authority and administratively to the CEO (PA 1110-1).

11. The status of the internal audit activity should be free from the effects of irresponsible policy changes by management. The most effective way to assure that freedom is to

A. Have the internal audit charter approved by the board.

B. Adopt policies for the functioning of the internal audit activity.

C. Establish an audit committee within the board.

D. Develop written policies and procedures to serve as standards of performance for the internal audit activity.

Answer (A) is correct. *(CIA, adapted)*

REQUIRED: The most effective way to assure that internal auditing is free from irresponsible policy changes.

DISCUSSION: The purpose, authority, and responsibility of the internal audit activity should be formally defined in a charter, consistent with the Standards, and approved by the board (Standard 1000). The charter should establish the IAA's position within the organization; authorize access to records, personnel, and physical properties relevant to the performance of engagements; and define the scope of internal audit activities. If questions arise, the charter also provides a formal, written agreement with management about the role of the IAA (PA 1000-1).

Answer (B) is incorrect because adoption of policies for the functioning of the IAA does not protect its status. Answer (C) is incorrect because the establishment of an audit committee does not ensure the status of the IAA without its involvement in matters such as acceptance of the charter. Answer (D) is incorrect because written policies and procedures serve to guide the internal auditing staff but have little effect on management.

12. In some organizations, internal auditing functions are outsourced. Management in a large organization should recognize that the external auditor may have an advantage, compared with the internal auditor, because of the external auditor's

A. Familiarity with the organization. Its annual audits provide an in-depth knowledge of the organization.

B. Size. It can hire experienced, knowledgeable, and certified staff.

C. Size. It is able to offer continuous availability of staff unaffected by other priorities.

D. Structure. It may more easily accommodate engagement requirements in distant locations.

Answer (D) is correct. *(CIA, adapted)*

REQUIRED: The advantage of outsourcing internal auditing functions.

DISCUSSION: Large organizations that are geographically dispersed may find outsourcing internal auditing functions to external auditors to be effective. A major public accounting firm ordinarily has operations that are national or worldwide in scope.

Answer (A) is incorrect because the internal auditing staff is likely to be more familiar with the organization than the external auditor given the continuous nature of its responsibilities. Answer (B) is incorrect because the internal auditor can also hire experienced, knowledgeable, and certified staff. Answer (C) is incorrect because the internal auditing staff is more likely to be continuously available. The external auditor has responsibilities to many other clients.

13. Internal auditors may provide consulting services that add value and improve an organization's operations. The performance of these services

A. Impairs internal auditors' objectivity with respect to an assurance service involving the same engagement client.

B. Precludes generation of assurance from a consulting engagement.

C. Should be consistent with the internal audit activity's empowerment reflected in the charter.

D. Imposes no responsibility to communicate information other than to the engagement client.

Answer (C) is correct. *(Publisher, adapted)*

REQUIRED: The internal auditors' responsibility regarding consulting services.

DISCUSSION: The nature of consulting services should be defined in the charter (Standard 1000.C1). Internal auditors have traditionally performed many types of consulting services, including the analysis of controls built into developing systems, analysis of security products, serving on task forces to analyze operations and make recommendations, and so forth. The board (or audit committee) should empower the internal audit activity to perform additional services if they do not represent a conflict of interest or detract from its obligations to the committee. That empowerment should be reflected in the internal audit charter (PA 1000.C1-1).

Answer (A) is incorrect because consulting services do not necessarily impair objectivity. Decisions to implement recommendations made as a result of a consulting service should be made by management. Thus, decision-making by management does not impair the internal auditors' objectivity. Answer (B) is incorrect because assurance and consulting services are not mutually exclusive. One type of service may be generated from the other. Answer (D) is incorrect because a primary internal auditing value is to provide assurance to senior management and audit committee directors. Consulting engagements cannot be rendered in a manner that masks information that in the judgment of the chief audit executive (CAE) should be presented to senior executives and board members (PA 1000.C1-1).

2.2 Independence

Question 14 is based on the following information. The charter of the internal audit activity (IAA) of a large public entity has not yet been approved by the board. However, the board is chaired by the chief executive officer (CEO) and includes the controller and one outside board member. The chief audit executive (CAE) reports directly to the controller who approves the IAA's work schedule. The previous CAE was recently dismissed following a dispute between the CAE and a major engagement client. Within the first month, the new CAE encountered substantial resistance from an engagement client regarding the nature of the work and the IAA's access to records. Moreover, the CEO accused the CAE of not operating "in the best interests of the organization."

14. From the perspective of the internal audit activity, which of the following facts, by themselves, could contribute to a lack of independence?

I. The CEO accused the new auditor of not operating "in the best interests of the organization."

II. The majority of audit committee members come from within the organization.

III. The IAA's charter has not been approved by the board.

A. I only.

B. II only.

C. II and III only.

D. I, II, and III.

Answer (D) is correct. *(CIA, adapted)*

REQUIRED: The factor(s) contributing to a lack of independence.

DISCUSSION: The CEO's statement suggests that the IAA lacks the support of management and the board. Furthermore, the lack of outside audit committee members may contribute to a loss of independence. The failure to approve the charter may have the same effect. The charter enhances the independence of the IAA because, by specifying the purpose, authority, and responsibility of the IAA, it establishes the position of the IAA in the organization (PA 1000-1). Independence is achieved through organizational status and objectivity (PA 1100-1).

Answer (A) is incorrect because lack of a charter and lack of outside auditors weaken the IAA's position. Answer (B) is incorrect because lack of support by the CEO and lack of a charter weaken the IAA's position. Answer (C) is incorrect because lack of support by the CEO weakens the IAA's position.

15. To avoid being the apparent cause of conflict between an organization's senior management and the audit committee, the chief audit executive should

A. Communicate all engagement results to both senior management and the audit committee.

B. Strengthen the independence of the internal audit activity through organizational status.

C. Discuss all reports to senior management with the audit committee first.

D. Request board approval of policies that include IAA relationships with the audit committee.

Answer (D) is correct. *(CIA, adapted)*

REQUIRED: The step taken to prevent the IAA from being the apparent cause of conflict between senior management and the audit committee.

DISCUSSION: The purpose, authority, and responsibility of the internal audit activity should be formally defined in a charter, consistent with the Standards, and approved by the board (Standard 1000). The charter should establish the internal audit activity's position within the organization; authorize access to records, personnel, and physical properties relevant to the performance of engagements; and define the scope of internal audit activities (PA 1000-1). Establishing the IAA's position within the organization (organizational status) is important because, among other things, it helps the IAA to achieve independence. For this purpose, the ideal functional reporting line is from the CAE to the governing authority (for example, the audit committee). The ideal administrative reporting line is from the CAE to the CEO (PA 1110-1). Approval of these reporting lines by the board should help to avoid conflict between senior management and the audit committee.

Answer (A) is incorrect because receipt of all engagement results by senior management and the audit committee is unnecessary and inefficient. Answer (B) is incorrect because organizational status helps the IAA to achieve independence but is not, by itself, enough to avoid conflict. Answer (C) is incorrect because the audit committee essentially has an oversight rather than an operational role.

16. The CAE has relationships with control and monitoring functions other than those in the functional and administrative reporting lines. With respect to these other functions, the CAE should facilitate the reporting of material risk and control issues to

A. The chief executive officer.

B. The external auditor.

C. The audit committee.

D. The board.

Answer (C) is correct. *(Publisher, adapted)*

REQUIRED: The individual or group to whom the CAE should facilitate the reporting.

DISCUSSION: CAEs should consider their relationships with other control and monitoring functions (risk management, compliance, security, legal, ethics, environmental, external audit) and facilitate the reporting of material risk and control issues to the audit committee (PA 1110-2).

17. An organization is in the process of establishing its new internal audit activity. The controller has no previous experience with internal auditors. Due to this lack of experience, the controller advised the applicants that the CAE will be reporting to the external auditors. However, the new chief audit executive will have free access to the controller to report anything important. The controller will then convey the CAE's concerns to the board of directors. The IAA will

A. Be independent because the CAE has direct access to the board.

B. Not be independent because the CAE reports to the external auditors.

C. Not be independent because the controller has no experience with internal auditors.

D. Not be independent because the organization did not specify that the applicants must be certified internal auditors.

Answer (B) is correct. *(CIA, adapted)*

REQUIRED: The true statement about a requirement that the IAA report to the external auditors and the controller.

DISCUSSION: The CAE should be responsible to an individual in the organization with sufficient authority to promote independence (PA 1110-1). External auditors are not individuals in the organization.

Answer (A) is incorrect because the IAA will not have direct access to the board. The access is indirect via the controller. Answer (C) is incorrect because whether the controller has experience with internal auditors does not affect the IAA's independence. Answer (D) is incorrect because, although desirable, the CIA designation is not mandatory for a person to become an internal auditor. A CIA should insist on IAA independence.

18. A medium-sized publicly owned organization operating in Country X has grown to a size that the governing authority believes warrants the establishment of an internal audit activity. Country X has legislated internal auditing requirements for government-owned organizations. The organization changed the bylaws to reflect the establishment of the internal audit activity. The governing authority decided that the chief audit executive (CAE) must be a certified internal auditor and will report directly to the newly established audit committee. Which of the items discussed above will contribute the most to the new CAE's independence?

A. The establishment of the internal audit activity is documented in the bylaws.

B. Country X has legislated internal auditing requirements.

C. The CAE will report to the audit committee.

D. The CAE is to be a certified internal auditor.

Answer (C) is correct. *(CIA, adapted)*

REQUIRED: The item that contributes most to a CAE's independence.

DISCUSSION: Independence is achieved through organizational status and objectivity. The CAE should be responsible to an individual with sufficient authority to promote independence (PA 1110-1). The board (and by extension, the audit committee) is the highest authority in the organization.

Answer (A) is incorrect because documentation in the by-laws does little to promote independence. Answer (B) is incorrect because legislated internal auditing requirements in Country X do not promote independence. Answer (D) is incorrect because independence is achieved through organizational status and objectivity.

19. The CAE should report functionally to a governing authority (audit committee or board of directors). This authority is responsible for which of the following activities?

I. Internal communication and information flows
II. Approval of the internal audit risk assessment and related audit plan
III. Approval of annual compensation and salary adjustment for the CAE

A. I and II.
B. II and III.
C. I and III.
D. I, II, and III.

Answer (B) is correct. *(Publisher, adapted)*
REQUIRED: The activities for which the governing authority is responsible.
DISCUSSION: The IIA recommends that the CAE report functionally to the audit committee, board of directors, or other appropriate governing authority. In this context, report functionally means that the governing authority should

- Approve the overall charter of the internal audit function.
- Approve the internal audit risk assessment and related audit plan.
- Receive communications from the CAE on the results of the internal audit activities or other matters that the CAE determines are necessary, including private meetings with the CAE without management present.
- Approve all decisions regarding the appointment or removal of the CAE.
- Approve the annual compensation and salary adjustment of the CAE.
- Make appropriate inquiries of management and the CAE to determine whether there are scope or budgetary limitations that impede the ability of the internal audit function to execute its responsibilities (PA 1110-2).

Answer (A) is incorrect because internal communication and information flows are administrative reporting items. Answer (C) is incorrect because internal communication and information flows are administrative reporting items. Answer (D) is incorrect because internal communication and information flows are administrative reporting items.

20. The reporting relationship within the organization's management structure that facilitates the day-to-day operations of the internal audit function is referred to as which of the following?

A. Administrative reporting.
B. Financial reporting.
C. Management reporting.
D. Functional reporting.

Answer (A) is correct. *(Publisher, adapted)*
REQUIRED: The type of reporting that facilitates the day-to-day operations of the internal audit function.
DISCUSSION: Administrative reporting is the reporting relationship within the organization's management structure that facilitates the day-to-day operations of the internal audit function (PA 1110-2). Administrative reporting typically includes

- Budgeting and management accounting
- Human resource administration, including personnel evaluations and compensation
- Internal communications and information flows
- Administration of the organization's internal policies and procedures

Answer (B) is incorrect because financial reporting focuses primarily on reporting information about an enterprise's performance provided by measures of earnings and its components. Answer (C) is incorrect because a form of management reporting is the financial statements, which report on the organization's performance to external parties. Answer (D) is incorrect because functional reporting deals with reporting to the audit committee or board of directors in order to achieve independence and authority.

21. An external quality assessment team was evaluating the independence of an internal audit activity. The internal audit activity performs engagements concerning all of the elements included in its scope. Which of the following reporting responsibilities is most likely to threaten the internal audit activity's independence? Reporting to the

A. President.

B. Treasurer.

C. Executive vice president.

D. Audit committee.

Answer (B) is correct. *(CIA, adapted)*

REQUIRED: The reporting responsibility that most likely threatens independence.

DISCUSSION: The CAE should report to an individual in the organization that has sufficient authority to promote independence and to ensure broad engagement coverage, adequate consideration of engagement communications, and appropriate action on engagement recommendations (PA 1110-1). The higher the level to which the IAA reports, the more likely that independence will be assured. The highest level to which it might report is the audit committee, which includes outside members of the board of directors. The next highest is the chief executive officer. Reporting to the treasurer limits the influence and independence of the IAA.

Answer (A) is incorrect because being responsible to the president helps preserve the IAA's independence by enhancing its status. Answer (C) is incorrect because the executive vice president is higher ranking than the treasurer. Answer (D) is incorrect because the audit committee is higher ranking than the treasurer.

22. During the performance of an engagement to evaluate a division's controls over purchasing, the chief purchasing agent asked why the internal auditor had requested documents pertaining to transactions with a particular supplier. The internal auditor's proper response is to

A. Treat the inquiry as a scope limitation.

B. Explain the reasons for the information request to promote cooperation with the engagement client.

C. Refuse to explain the information request to preserve the integrity of the engagement process.

D. Consider the specific circumstances before deciding whether to disclose the reasons for the information request.

Answer (D) is correct. *(Publisher, adapted)*

REQUIRED: The internal auditor's proper response to an engagement client's information request.

DISCUSSION: At times, an internal auditor may be asked by the engagement client or other parties to explain why a document that has been requested is relevant to an engagement. Disclosure or nondisclosure during the engagement of the reasons documents are needed should be determined based on the circumstances. Significant irregularities may dictate a less open environment than would normally be conducive to a cooperative engagement. However, that is a judgment that should be made by the chief audit executive in light of the specific circumstances (PA 1110.A1-1).

Answer (A) is incorrect because a scope limitation is a restriction placed upon the IAA that precludes it from accomplishing its objectives and plans (PA 1130-1). Answer (B) is incorrect because the CAE should consider the specific circumstances before deciding whether to disclose the reasons for the information request. Answer (C) is incorrect because it is not always necessary or desirable to refuse to explain an information request.

23. Independence permits internal auditors to render impartial and unbiased judgments. The best way to achieve independence is through

A. Individual knowledge and skills.

B. Organizational status and objectivity.

C. Supervision within the organization.

D. Organizational knowledge and skills.

Answer (B) is correct. *(CIA, adapted)*

REQUIRED: The best way to achieve independence.

DISCUSSION: The IAA should be independent (Standard 1100). Internal auditors are independent when they can carry out their work freely and objectively. Independence permits internal auditors to render the impartial and unbiased judgments essential to the proper conduct of engagements. It is achieved through organizational status and objectivity (PA 1100-1).

Answer (A) is incorrect because individual knowledge and skills allow individual auditors to achieve professional proficiency. Answer (C) is incorrect because supervision ensures that engagement objectives are achieved, quality is assured, and staff is developed (Standard 2340). Answer (D) is incorrect because organizational knowledge and skills allow the IAA collectively to achieve professional proficiency.

24. The internal audit function should be free to audit and report on any activity that also reports to its administrative head if it considers such coverage to be appropriate for its audit plan. Any limitation in scope or reporting of results of these activities should be brought to the attention of whom?

A. Chief Executive Officer.

B. Chief Financial Officer.

C. External Auditor.

D. Audit Committee.

Answer (D) is correct. *(Publisher, adapted)*

REQUIRED: The person or group to be notified when a scope or reporting limitation exists.

DISCUSSION: The CAE should ensure that appropriate independence is maintained if the individual responsible for the administrative reporting line is also responsible for other activities in the organization that are subject to internal audit. For example, some CAEs report administratively to the Chief Financial Officer, who is also responsible for the organization's accounting functions. The internal audit activity should be free to audit and report on any activity that also reports to its administrative head if it considers such coverage to be appropriate for its audit plan. Any limitation in scope or reporting of results of these activities should be brought to the attention of the audit committee (PA 1110-2).

Answer (A) is incorrect because the CEO is not independent from the organization. Answer (B) is incorrect because the CFO is also responsible for the organization's accounting functions, such that when a scope or reporting limitation exists, the CFO may be responsible for it. Therefore, the CAE should report these limitations to the independent audit committee. Answer (C) is incorrect because the external auditor should not be notified unless the audit committee believes it is necessary.

25. When evaluating the independence of an internal audit activity, a quality assurance review team performing an external assessment considers several factors. Which of the following factors has the least amount of influence when judging an internal audit activity's independence?

A. Criteria used in making internal auditors' assignments.

B. The extent of internal auditor training in communications skills.

C. Relationship between engagement records and engagement communications.

D. Impartial and unbiased judgments.

Answer (B) is correct. *(CIA, adapted)*

REQUIRED: The factor that least influences independence.

DISCUSSION: The IAA should be independent (Standard 1100). Internal auditors are independent when they can carry out their work freely and objectively. Independence permits internal auditors to render the impartial and unbiased judgments essential to the proper conduct of engagements. It is achieved through organizational status and objectivity (PA 1100-1). However, training in communication relates to the knowledge, skills, and other competencies needed to perform engagements, not to independence.

Answer (A) is incorrect because how individual internal auditors are assigned relates to independence. The auditor's personal relationships with operating personnel, work experience with the engagement client, etc., affect independence. Answer (C) is incorrect because, if significant engagement observations found in the engagement records are omitted from the engagement communications, independence is brought into question. Answer (D) is incorrect because unbiased judgment is an aspect of independence.

26. The administrative reporting line of the CAE should be to

A. The audit committee.

B. Line management.

C. Board of directors.

D. CEO or equivalent.

Answer (D) is correct. *(Publisher, adapted)*

REQUIRED: The individual or group to whom the CAE should report administratively.

DISCUSSION: The administrative reporting line of the CAE should be to the CEO or another executive with sufficient authority to provide appropriate support to accomplish its day-to-day activities. This support should include positioning the function and the CAE in the organization's structure in a manner that affords appropriate stature for the function within the organization. Reporting too low a level in an organization can negatively affect the status and effectiveness of the IAA function.

Answer (A) is incorrect because the functional reporting line should go directly to the audit committee. Answer (B) is incorrect because the administrative reporting line should facilitate open and direct communications with line management. Answer (C) is incorrect because the board of directors is a group that the CAE should have open and direct communications with at all times for functional reporting issues.

27. Regardless of which reporting relationship the organization chooses, several key actions can help ensure that the reporting lines support and enable the effectiveness and independence of the internal auditing activity. Which key action will not achieve its functional reporting purpose?

A. The functional reporting line should go directly to the Audit Committee or its equivalent to ensure the appropriate level of independence and communication.

B. The CAE should meet with the audit committee or its equivalent, with management present, to reinforce the independence and nature of this reporting relationship.

C. The audit committee should have the final authority to review and approve the annual audit plan and all major changes to the plan.

D. At all times, the CAE should have open and direct access to the chair of the audit committee and its members; or the chair of the board or full board if appropriate.

Answer (B) is correct. *(Publisher, adapted)*
REQUIRED: The key action that will not achieve its functional reporting purpose.
DISCUSSION: The key actions for functional reporting are:

- The functional reporting line should go directly to the Audit Committee or its equivalent to ensure the appropriate level of independence and communication.
- The CAE should meet privately with the audit committee or its equivalent, without management present, to reinforce the independence and nature of this reporting relationship.
- The audit committee should have the final authority to review and approve the annual audit plan and all major changes to the plan.
- At all times, the CAE should have open and direct access to the chair of the audit committee and its members; or the chair of the board or full board if appropriate.
- At least once a year, the audit committee should review the performance of the CAE and approve the annual compensation and salary adjustment.
- The charter for the internal audit function should clearly articulate both the functional and administrative reporting lines for the function as well as the principle activities directed up each line (PA 1110-2).

The purpose of helping to ensure that the reporting lines are effective and independent will not be achieved if management is present during all the CAE's meetings with the audit committee or its equivalent.

28. A written charter approved by the board that formally defines the internal audit activity's purpose, authority, and responsibility enhances its

A. Exercise of due professional care.

B. Proficiency.

C. Relationship with management.

D. Independence.

Answer (D) is correct. *(CIA, adapted)*
REQUIRED: The purpose of a charter.
DISCUSSION: The charter should (a) establish the IAA's position within the organization; (b) authorize access to records, personnel, and physical properties relevant to the performance of engagements; and (c) define the scope of internal audit activities (PA 1000-1). Thus, the charter helps establish the IAA's organizational status. Objectivity and organizational status are the means of achieving independence (PA 1100-1).
Answer (A) is incorrect because due professional care is an attribute of work performed. Answer (B) is incorrect because proficiency is an attribute of the knowledge, skills, and other competencies possessed by internal auditors. Answer (C) is incorrect because the IAA's relationship with management is a function of professionalism. The charter establishes independence, not a working relationship.

29. Independence permits internal auditors to render the impartial and unbiased judgments essential to the proper conduct of engagements. Which of the following best promotes independence?

A. A policy that requires internal auditors to report to the chief audit executive any situations in which a conflict of interest or bias on the part of the individual internal auditor is present or may reasonably be inferred.

B. A policy that prevents the internal audit activity from recommending standards of control for systems that it evaluates.

C. An organizational policy that allows engagements concerning sensitive operations to be outsourced.

D. An organizational policy that prevents personnel transfers from operating activities to the internal audit activity.

Answer (A) is correct. *(CIA, adapted)*
REQUIRED: The policy best promoting independence.
DISCUSSION: Staff assignments should be made so that potential and actual conflicts of interest and bias are avoided. Moreover, staff assignments of internal auditors should be rotated periodically whenever it is practicable to do so. The CAE should periodically obtain from the internal auditing staff information concerning potential conflicts of interest and bias, and internal auditors should report to the CAE any situations in which a conflict of interest or bias is present or may reasonably be inferred. The CAE should then reassign such auditors (PA 1120-1 and PA 1130-1).
Answer (B) is incorrect because internal auditing may recommend standards of control for systems that it evaluates. Answer (C) is incorrect because outsourcing certain engagements does not promote the independence of the IAA. Answer (D) is incorrect because transfers from operating activities to the IAA usually are permitted. However, transferees should not be assigned to engagements concerning activities they previously performed until a reasonable period of time has elapsed.

2.3 Objectivity

30. An internal auditor has recently received an offer from the manager of the marketing department of a weekend's free use of his beachfront condominium. No engagement is currently being conducted in the marketing department, and none is scheduled. The internal auditor

A. Should reject the offer and report it to the appropriate supervisor.

B. May accept the offer because its value is immaterial.

C. May accept the offer because no engagement is being conducted or planned.

D. May accept the offer if approved by the appropriate supervisor.

Answer (A) is correct. *(Publisher, adapted)*

REQUIRED: The true statement about the offer of a gift by a nonclient member of the organization.

DISCUSSION: It is unethical for an internal auditor to accept a fee or gift from an employee, client, customer, supplier, or business associate. Accepting a fee or gift may imply that the auditor's objectivity has been impaired. Even though an engagement is not being conducted in the applicable area at that time, a future engagement may result in the appearance of impairment of objectivity. Thus, no consideration should be given to the engagement status as justification for receiving fees or gifts. The receipt of promotional items (such as pens, calendars, or samples) that are available to the general public and have minimal value should not hinder internal auditors' professional judgments. Internal auditors should report the offer of all material fees or gifts immediately to their supervisors (PA 1120-1).

Answer (B) is incorrect because the value of a weekend vacation is not immaterial. Answer (C) is incorrect because the status of engagements should not be considered as justification for receiving fees or gifts. Answer (D) is incorrect because a supervisor may not approve unethical behavior.

31. Internal auditors must be objective in performing their work. Assume that the chief audit executive received an annual bonus as part of that individual's compensation package. The bonus may impair the CAE's objectivity if

A. The bonus is administered by the board of directors or its salary administration committee.

B. The bonus is based on monetary amounts recovered or recommended future savings as a result of engagements.

C. The scope of internal auditing work is evaluating control rather than account balances.

D. All of the answers are correct.

Answer (B) is correct. *(CIA, adapted)*

REQUIRED: The conditions under which a bonus may impair the CAE's objectivity.

DISCUSSION: Internal auditors are not to be placed in situations in which they feel unable to make objective professional judgments (PA 1120-1). Thus, objectivity may be impaired if the bonus is based on monetary amounts recovered or recommended future savings as a result of engagements. A bonus based on either of these criteria could unduly influence the type of engagements performed or the recommendations made.

Answer (A) is incorrect because the board of directors should determine the CAE's compensation. Answer (C) is incorrect because the IAA's scope of work includes evaluating and contributing to the improvement of risk management, control, and governance processes. Answer (D) is incorrect because objectivity is not impaired if the board determines the director's compensation or if the scope of work is evaluating control rather than account balances.

2.4 Independence and Objectivity

32. George is the new internal auditor for XYZ Corporation. George was in charge of payroll for XYZ just 10 months ago. Performing what services in regard to payroll is considered an impairment of independence or objectivity if performed by George?

A. Consulting services.

B. Assurance services.

C. Assurance or consulting services.

D. Neither assurance nor consulting services.

Answer (B) is correct. *(Publisher, adapted)*

REQUIRED: The services that will impair independence or objectivity.

DISCUSSION: Internal auditors should refrain from assessing specific operations for which they were previously responsible. Objectivity is presumed to be impaired if an internal auditor provides assurance services for an activity for which the internal auditor had responsibility within the previous year (Standard 1130.A1). Thus, if George provides assurance services for payroll, his objectivity is presumed to be impaired. Internal auditors may provide consulting services relating to operations for which they had previous responsibilities (Standard 1130.C1).

Answer (A) is incorrect because providing consulting services regarding payroll will not impair the independence or objectivity of George (Standard 1130.C1). Answer (C) is incorrect because providing consulting services regarding payroll will not impair the independence or objectivity of George. Answer (D) is incorrect because providing assurance services regarding payroll will impair the objectivity of George (Standard 1130.A1).

33. Independence is most likely impaired by an internal auditor's

A. Continuation on an engagement at a division for which (s)he will soon be responsible as the result of a promotion.

B. Reduction of the scope of an engagement due to budget restrictions.

C. Participation on a task force that recommends standards for control of a new distribution system.

D. Review of a purchasing agent's contract drafts prior to their execution.

Answer (A) is correct. *(CIA, adapted)*

REQUIRED: The action most likely impairing independence.

DISCUSSION: When the IAA or an individual internal auditor is responsible for, or management is considering assigning, an operation that might be the subject of an engagement, independence and objectivity may be impaired. The internal auditor should consider the following factors in assessing the effect on independence and objectivity: The IIA Code of Ethics, the SPPIA, the expectations of the stakeholders, the IAA's charter, required disclosures, and subsequent coverage of the activities or responsibilities accepted (PA 1130.A1-2).

Answer (B) is incorrect because budget restrictions do not constitute an impairment of independence. Answer (C) is incorrect because an internal auditor may recommend standards of control. However, designing, installing, drafting procedures for, or operating systems might impair objectivity (PA 1130.A1-1). Answer (D) is incorrect because an internal auditor may review contracts prior to their execution.

34. Management has requested the internal audit activity to perform an engagement to recommend procedures and policies for improving management control over the telephone marketing operations of a major division. The chief audit executive should

A. Not accept the engagement because recommending controls would impair future objectivity regarding this operation.

B. Not accept the engagement because internal audit activities are presumed to have expertise regarding accounting controls, not marketing controls.

C. Accept the engagement, but indicate to management that, because recommending controls impairs independence, future engagements in the area will be impaired.

D. Accept the engagement because objectivity will not be impaired.

Answer (D) is correct. *(CIA, adapted)*

REQUIRED: The acceptability of an engagement to recommend standards of control.

DISCUSSION: The CAE should accept the engagement; assign staff with the knowledge, skills, and other competencies essential to its performance; and make appropriate recommendations. Recommending standards of control for systems or reviewing procedures prior to implementation does not impair objectivity (PA 1130.A1-1). Moreover, if this engagement is deemed to involve consulting services, objectivity is not required provided that any impairment thereof is disclosed to the client prior to acceptance of the engagement (Standard 1130.C2).

Answer (A) is incorrect because the CAE should accept the engagement. Recommending controls is not considered to impair independence or objectivity. Answer (B) is incorrect because the engagement should be accepted. The IAA should be able to evaluate the adequacy and effectiveness of controls encompassing the organization's governance, operations, and information systems (Standard 2120.A1). Answer (C) is incorrect because independence is not impaired by making control recommendations.

35. When faced with an imposed scope limitation, the chief audit executive should

A. Refuse to perform the engagement until the scope limitation is removed.

B. Communicate the potential effects of the scope limitation to the audit committee of the board of directors.

C. Increase the frequency of engagements concerning the activity in question.

D. Assign more experienced personnel to the engagement.

Answer (B) is correct. *(CIA, adapted)*

REQUIRED: The appropriate response to an imposed scope limitation.

DISCUSSION: A scope limitation is a restriction placed upon the IAA that precludes the accomplishment of its objectives and plans. Among other things, a scope limitation may restrict (a) the scope defined in the charter; (b) the IAA's access to records, personnel, and physical properties relevant to the performance of engagements; (c) the approved engagement work schedule; (d) necessary engagement procedures; and (e) the approved staffing plan and financial budget. A scope limitation along with its potential effect should be communicated, preferably in writing, to the board, audit committee, or other appropriate governing authority (PA 1130-1).

Answer (A) is incorrect because the engagement may be conducted under a scope limitation. Answer (C) is incorrect because a scope limitation does not necessarily require more frequent engagements. Answer (D) is incorrect because a scope limitation does not necessarily require more experienced personnel.

36. In which of the following situations does an internal auditor potentially lack objectivity?

A. An internal auditor reviews the procedures for a new electronic data interchange (EDI) connection to a major customer before it is implemented.

B. A former purchasing assistant performs a review of internal controls over purchasing 4 months after being transferred to the internal auditing department.

C. An internal auditor recommends standards of control and performance measures for a contract with a service organization for the processing of payroll and employee benefits.

D. A payroll accounting employee assists an internal auditor in verifying the physical inventory of small motors.

Answer (B) is correct. *(CIA, adapted)*

REQUIRED: The situation in which the internal auditor may lack objectivity.

DISCUSSION: Persons transferred to or temporarily engaged by the internal audit activity should not be assigned to engagements involving those activities they previously performed until a reasonable period of time (at least one year) has elapsed. Such assignments are presumed to impair objectivity. Additional consideration is required when such persons are supervising the engagement work and communicating engagement results (PA 1130-A1-1). However, internal auditors may provide consulting services relating to operations for which they had previous responsibilities (Standard 1130.C1), provided that prior disclosure is made to the client of any potential impairments of independence or objectivity (Standard 1130.C2). Objectivity is not adversely affected when the internal auditor recommends standards of control for systems or reviews procedures before they are implemented. Designing, installing, drafting procedures for, or operating systems is presumed to impair objectivity. Use of staff from other areas to assist the internal auditor does not impair objectivity, especially when the staff is from outside of the area where the engagement is being performed.

37. Which of the following activities is not presumed to impair the objectivity of an internal auditor?

I. Recommending standards of control for a new information system application

II. Drafting procedures for running a new computer application to ensure that proper controls are installed

III. Performing reviews of procedures for a new computer application before it is installed

A. I only.

B. II only.

C. III only.

D. I and III.

Answer (D) is correct. *(CIA, adapted)*

REQUIRED: The activity(ies) not presumed to impair objectivity.

DISCUSSION: The internal auditor's objectivity is not adversely affected when (s)he recommends standards of control for systems or reviews procedures before they are implemented. Designing, installing, or drafting procedures for operating systems is presumed to impair objectivity (PA 1130.A1-1).

38. The internal auditors must be able to distinguish carefully between a scope limitation and other limitations. Which of the following is not considered a scope limitation?

A. The divisional management of an engagement client has indicated that the division is in the process of converting a major computer system and has indicated that the information systems portion of the planned engagement will have to be postponed until next year.

B. The audit committee reviews the engagement work schedule for the year and deletes an engagement that the chief audit executive thought was important to conduct.

C. The engagement client has indicated that certain customers cannot be contacted because the organization is in the process of negotiating a long-term contract with the customers and they do not want to upset the customers.

D. None of the answers are correct.

Answer (B) is correct. *(CIA, adapted)*

REQUIRED: The item that is not a scope limitation.

DISCUSSION: The audit committee's decision to delete an engagement from the annual engagement work schedule is not a scope limitation. Its responsibility is to review and approve the planned scope of activities for the year.

Answer (A) is incorrect because postponing the portion of an engagement concerning a major computer system is a scope limitation. This delay restricts the performance of the engagement. Scope limitations are reported to senior management and the board for their determination as to whether the limitations are justified. Answer (C) is incorrect because prohibiting contact with certain customers is a scope limitation. This prohibition restricts the performance of specific procedures. Answer (D) is incorrect because other answer choices state scope limitations.

39. Which of the following combinations best illustrates a scope limitation and the appropriate response by the CAE?

	Nature of Limitation	Internal Auditing Action
A.	Engagement client limits scope based upon proprietary information	Report only to the controller
B.	Engagement client will not provide access to records needed for approved work schedule	Report to the board
C.	Engagement client requests that the engagement be delayed for 2 weeks to allow it to close its books	Report directly to the CEO and controller
D.	Engagement client will not allow internal auditor to contact major customers as part of an engagement to evaluate the efficiency of operations	No reporting needed because the operational engagement concerns operational efficiency

Answer (B) is correct. *(CIA, adapted)*

REQUIRED: The combination best illustrating a scope limitation.

DISCUSSION: A scope limitation is a restriction placed on the internal audit activity that precludes the IAA from accomplishing its objectives and plans. Among other things, a scope limitation may restrict the IAA's access to records, personnel, and physical properties relevant to the performance of engagements. A scope limitation and its potential effect should be communicated, preferably in writing, to the board, audit committee, or other appropriate governing authority (PA 1130-1).

Answer (A) is incorrect because a scope limitation should be reported to the board, audit committee, or other appropriate governing authority. Answer (C) is incorrect because merely delaying the engagement to permit closing the books is not usually considered a scope limitation. Answer (D) is incorrect because reporting is necessary.

40. Prior to performing consulting services, the Chief Audit Executive should obtain approval from

A. The audit committee.

B. The board of directors.

C. The chief executive officer.

D. The external auditor.

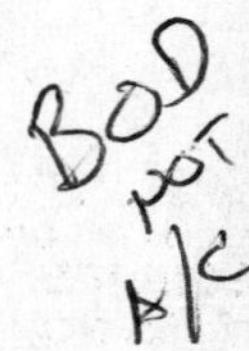

Answer (B) is correct. *(Publisher, adapted)*

REQUIRED: The individual or group who should approve consulting services.

DISCUSSION: Internal auditors are sometimes requested to provide consulting services relating to operations for which they had previous responsibilities or had conducted assurance services. Prior to offering consulting services, the Chief Audit Executive should confirm that the board understands and approves the concept of providing consulting services (PA 1000.C1-2).

41. Independence and objectivity may be impaired if assurance services are provided within one year after a formal consulting engagement. What steps can be taken to minimize the effects of this kind of impairment?

I. Assigning different auditors to perform each of the services

II. Establishing independent management and supervision

III. Defining separate accountability for the results of projects

IV. Disclosing the presumed impairment

A. I and III only.

B. I, III, and IV only.

C. II, III, and IV only.

D. I, II, III, and IV.

Answer (D) is correct. *(Publisher, adapted)*

REQUIRED: The steps that can be taken to minimize the effects of impairment.

DISCUSSION: Independence and objectivity may be impaired if assurance services are provided within one year after a formal consulting engagement. Steps can be taken to minimize the effects of impairment by assigning different auditors to perform each of the services, establishing independent management and supervision, defining separate accountability for the results of the projects, and disclosing the presumed impairment. Management should be responsible for accepting and implementing recommendations (PA 1000.C1-2).

42. During the course of an engagement, an internal auditor makes a preliminary determination that a major division has been inappropriately capitalizing research and development expense. The engagement is not yet completed, and the internal auditor has not documented the problem or determined that it really is a problem. However, the internal auditor is informed that the chief audit executive has received the following communication from the president of the organization:

"The controller of Division B informs me that you have discovered a questionable account classification dealing with research and development expense. We are aware of the issue. You are directed to discontinue any further investigation of this matter until informed by me to proceed. Under the confidentiality standard of your profession, I also direct you not to communicate with the outside auditors regarding this issue."

Which of the following is an appropriate action for the CAE to take regarding the questionable item?

A. Immediately report the communication to The Institute of Internal Auditors and ask for an ethical interpretation and guidance.

B. Inform the president that this scope limitation will need to be reported to the board.

C. Continue to investigate the area until all the facts are determined and document all the relevant facts in the engagement records.

D. Immediately notify the external auditors of the problem to avoid aiding and abetting a potential crime by the organization.

Answer (B) is correct. *(CIA, adapted)*

REQUIRED: The action by the CAE after senior management imposes a scope limitation.

DISCUSSION: A scope limitation along with its potential effect should be communicated, preferably in writing, to the board, audit committee, or other appropriate governing authority (PA 1130-1).

Answer (A) is incorrect because The IIA has no authority in this matter. Answer (C) is incorrect because the CAE should first consult the board. The CAE adds value by serving the organization, and the board may, in fact, be fully aware of the problem and may not want to incur additional costs. Answer (D) is incorrect because the engagement work is preliminary, and the internal auditor has not yet formed a basis for an opinion. Thus, contacting the external auditors is premature. However, if an inquiry is made by the external auditors, the internal auditors should share the work done to date.

43. Which of the following statements is an appropriate reason for the internal audit activity not to participate in the systems development process?

A. Recommendations prior to implementation will affect independence, and the internal auditors will not be able to perform an objective evaluation after the system is implemented.

B. Participation will delay implementation of the project.

C. Participation will cause the internal auditors to be labeled as partial owners of the application, and they will then have to share the blame for any problems that remain in the system.

D. None of the answers are correct.

Answer (D) is correct. *(CIA, adapted)*

REQUIRED: The reason for the IAA not to participate in systems development.

DISCUSSION: Objectivity is not adversely affected when the internal auditors recommend standards of control for systems or review procedures before they are implemented. Designing, installing, drafting procedures for, or operating systems is presumed to impair objectivity (PA 1130.A1-1). Moreover, if this engagement is deemed to involve consulting services, objectivity is not required provided that any impairment thereof is disclosed to the client prior to acceptance of the engagement (Standard 1130.C2).

Answer (A) is incorrect because IAA independence should not be affected by recommending control standards or reviewing procedures before implementation. Answer (B) is incorrect because IAA participation will not delay the project unless needed controls were absent. Answer (C) is incorrect because the internal auditors should participate in systems development but should not draft procedures or design, install, or operate the system.

44. An internal auditor who had been supervisor of the accounts payable section should not perform an assurance review of that section

A. Because there is no way to measure a reasonable period of time in which to establish independence.

B. Until a reasonable period of time has elapsed.

C. Until after the next annual review by the external auditors.

D. Until it is clear that the new supervisor has assumed the responsibilities.

Answer (B) is correct. *(CIA, adapted)*

REQUIRED: The appropriate time for an internal auditor to review an operating activity for which (s)he had responsibility.

DISCUSSION: Persons transferred to, or temporarily engaged by, the internal audit activity should not be assigned to engagements involving assurance reviews of activities they previously performed until a reasonable period of time (at least 1 year) has elapsed. Such assignments are presumed to impair objectivity (PA 1130.A1-1).

Answer (A) is incorrect because a "reasonable period" is ordinarily determinable. Answer (C) is incorrect because the external review does not bear any relation to restoring the internal auditor's objectivity. Answer (D) is incorrect because the new supervisor presumably would have assumed his/her responsibilities immediately. Hence, a reasonable time could not have elapsed.

45. Assuming that the internal auditing staff possesses the necessary experience and training, which of the following services is most appropriate for a staff internal auditor to undertake?

A. Substitute for the accounts payable supervisor while (s)he is on sick leave.

B. Determine the profitability of alternative investment acquisitions and select the best alternative.

C. As part of an evaluation team, review vendor accounting software internal controls and rank according to exposures.

D. Participate in an internal audit of the accounting department shortly after transferring from the accounting department.

Answer (C) is correct. *(CIA, adapted)*

REQUIRED: The service most appropriate for an internal auditor to undertake.

DISCUSSION: An internal auditor's objectivity is not impaired when (s)he recommends standards of control for systems or reviews procedures before they are implemented (PA 1130.A1-1). Moreover, if this engagement is deemed to involve consulting services, objectivity is not required provided that any impairment thereof is disclosed to the client prior to acceptance of the engagement (Standard 1130.C2).

Answer (A) is incorrect because an internal auditor's objectivity is presumed to be impaired for a reasonable period of time with respect to activities (s)he previously performed. Answer (B) is incorrect because investment decisions are the prerogative of management. Answer (D) is incorrect because an internal auditor should not be assigned to engagements concerning activities (s)he previously performed until a reasonable time has elapsed.

STUDY UNIT THREE
INTERNAL AUDIT ROLES I

(20 pages of outline)

This study unit is the first of two that address the **scope of work** of internal auditors. The scope of work is defined in the pronouncements of The IIA. They elaborate on the description of the services performed by the internal audit activity provided in the **definition of internal auditing**. The definition stresses the improvement of risk management, control, and governance processes. However, the internal auditors' work regarding **control** is such a vital part of their responsibilities that it is treated separately in Study Units 5 and 6.

Core Concepts

- The IAA's work focuses on the risk management, control, and governance processes of the organization.
- The IAA appraises the overall management process.
- Governance is the structure implemented by the board to inform, direct, manage, and monitor the activities of the organization toward the achievement of its objectives.
- The CAE establishes and maintains a system to monitor the disposition of results communicated to management.
- Compliance is conformity and adherence to policies, plans, procedures, laws, regulations, contracts, or other requirements.

3.1 NATURE OF WORK

1. This subunit is brief but important. It consists of one General Performance Standard and one Practice Advisory. Standard 2100 reflects the scope of work described in the definition of internal auditing. PA 2100-1 provides frequently tested guidance regarding the management process and its relationship to internal auditing.

2. ***2100*** *__Nature of Work__ – The internal audit activity evaluates and contributes to the improvement of risk management, control, and governance processes using a systematic and disciplined approach.*

   a. ***__PRACTICE ADVISORY 2100-1: NATURE OF WORK__***

      *1. The scope of internal auditing work encompasses a systematic, disciplined approach to evaluating and improving the adequacy and effectiveness of risk management, control, and governance processes and the **quality of performance** in carrying out assigned responsibilities. The **purpose of evaluating the adequacy** of the organization's existing risk management, control, and governance processes is to provide reasonable assurance that these processes are functioning as intended and will enable the organization's objectives and goals to be met. They also **provide recommendations** for improving the organization's operations, in terms of both efficient and effective performance. Senior management and the board might also provide general direction as to the scope of work and the activities to be audited.*

      *2. **Adequacy** of risk management, control, and governance **processes** is present if management has **planned and designed** them to provide reasonable assurance that the organization's objectives and goals will be achieved efficiently and economically. **Efficient performance** accomplishes objectives and goals in an accurate, timely, and economical fashion. **Economical performance** accomplishes objectives and goals with minimal use of resources (i.e., cost) commensurate with the risk exposure. **Reasonable assurance** is provided if the most cost-effective measures are taken in the design and implementation stages to reduce risks and restrict expected deviations to a tolerable level. Thus, the **design process** begins with the establishment of objectives and goals. This is followed by connecting or interrelating concepts, parts, activities, and people to operate together to achieve the established objectives and goals.*

      *3. **Effectiveness** of risk management, control, and governance **processes** is present if management **directs** processes to provide reasonable assurance that the organization's **objectives and goals will be achieved.** In addition to accomplishing the objectives and planned activities, **management directs** by authorizing activities and transactions, monitoring resulting performance, and verifying that the organization's processes are operating as designed.*

4. *Broadly, management is responsible for the* ***sustainability*** *of the whole organization and* ***accountability*** *for the organization's actions, conduct, and performance to the owners, other stakeholders, regulators, and general public. Specifically, the primary objectives of the* ***overall management process*** *are to achieve:*
   - *Relevant, reliable, and credible financial and operating information.*
   - *Effective and efficient use of the organization's resources.*
   - *Safeguarding of the organization's assets.*
   - *Compliance with laws, regulations, ethical and business norms, and contracts.*
   - *Identification of risk exposures and use of effective strategies to control them.*
   - *Established objectives and goals for operations or programs.*
5. ***Management plans, organizes, and directs*** *performance to provide reasonable assurance that objectives and goals will be achieved. Management periodically* ***reviews*** *its objectives and goals and* ***modifies its processes*** *to accommodate changes in internal and external conditions. Management also establishes and maintains an* ***organizational culture****, including an* ***ethical climate*** *that fosters control.*
6. ***Control*** *is any action taken by management to enhance the likelihood that established objectives and goals will be achieved. Controls may be* ***preventive*** *(to deter undesirable events from occurring),* ***detective*** *(to detect and correct undesirable events which have occurred), or* ***directive*** *(to cause or encourage a desirable event to occur). A* ***system of control*** *is the integrated collection of control components and activities that are used by an organization to achieve its objectives and goals.*
7. ***Internal auditors*** *evaluate the* ***whole management process*** *of planning, organizing, and directing to determine whether reasonable assurance exists that objectives and goals will be achieved. Internal auditors should be alert to* ***actual or potential changes*** *in internal or external conditions that affect the ability to provide assurance from a forward-looking perspective. In those cases, internal auditors should address the risk that performance may deteriorate.*
8. *These internal auditing evaluations, in the aggregate, provide information to* ***appraise the overall management process****. All business systems, processes, operations, functions, and activities within the organization are subject to the internal auditors' evaluations. The* ***comprehensive scope of work of internal auditing*** *should provide reasonable assurance that management's*
   - *Risk management system is effective.*
   - *System of internal control is effective and efficient.*
   - *Governance process is effective by establishing and preserving values, setting goals, monitoring activities and performance, and defining the measures of accountability.*

PA Summary

- The **scope of internal auditing** encompasses a systematic, disciplined approach to evaluating and improving the adequacy and effectiveness of **risk management, control, and governance processes (RCG)** and the **quality of performance**. The purpose of evaluating the **adequacy** of RCG is to provide reasonable assurance that they are functioning as intended and will enable objectives to be met. Internal auditors also **provide recommendations** for improving operations. Senior management and the board also might provide general direction about the scope of work.
- **Adequacy** of RCG is present if management has **planned and designed** them to provide reasonable assurance that objectives will be achieved efficiently and economically. **Efficient** means accomplishing objectives in an accurate, timely, and economical fashion. **Economical** means accomplishing objectives with minimal resource use (cost) in proportion to the risk. **Reasonable assurance** is taking the most cost-effective measures to reduce risk and restrict deviations to a tolerable level. **Design** begins with objectives. It is followed by connecting concepts, parts, activities, and people to achieve the objectives.
- **Effectiveness** of RCG is present if management **directs** processes to provide reasonable assurance that **objectives will be achieved**. **Management also directs** by authorizing activities and transactions, monitoring performance, and verifying that processes are operating as designed.
- Management is responsible for the **sustainability** of the organization and its **accountability** to stakeholders. The objectives of the **overall management process** are to achieve (1) relevant, reliable, and credible financial and operating information; (2) effective and efficient use of resources; (3) safeguarding of assets; (4) compliance with laws, regulations, ethical and business norms, and contracts; (5) identification of risks and use of effective control strategies; and (6) established objectives for operations or programs.
- Management periodically **reviews** its objectives and **modifies its processes** as conditions change. It also maintains an **organizational culture**.
- **Control** is any action by management to enhance the likelihood that objectives will be achieved. Controls may be **preventive** (to deter undesirable events), **detective** (to detect and correct undesirable events), or **directive** (to cause or encourage a desirable event). A **system of control** is the integrated set of components and activities used to achieve organizational objectives.
- **Internal auditors** evaluate the **management process** of planning, organizing, and directing. Internal auditors should be alert to **changes** in conditions that affect the ability to provide forward-looking assurance. In those cases, internal auditors should address the risk that performance may deteriorate.
- Internal auditing evaluations provide information to **appraise the overall management process**. The **scope of work of internal auditing** should provide reasonable assurance that management's (1) risk management system is effective; (2) system of internal control is effective and efficient; and (3) governance process is effective by establishing and preserving values, setting goals, monitoring activities and performance, and defining accountability.

3. Stop and review! You have completed the outline for this subunit. Study multiple-choice questions 1 through 6 beginning on page 125.

3.2 GOVERNANCE

1. **Governance** is "the combination of processes and structures implemented by the board to inform, direct, manage, and monitor the activities of the organization toward the achievement of its objectives" (Glossary). It is a fundamental element of the definition of internal auditing. This subject is covered in two General Performance Standards, one Specific Performance Standard, two Assurance Implementation Standards, two Consulting Implementation Standards, and five Practice Advisories.

2. ***2130*** ***Governance*** *– The internal audit activity should assess and make appropriate recommendations for improving the governance process in its accomplishment of the following objectives:*
   - *Promoting appropriate ethics and values within the organization.*
   - *Ensuring effective organizational performance management and accountability.*
   - *Effectively communicating risk and control information to appropriate areas of the organization.*
   - *Effectively coordinating the activities of and communicating information among the board, external and internal auditors, and management.*

   a. ***PRACTICE ADVISORY 2130-1: ROLE OF THE INTERNAL AUDIT ACTIVITY AND INTERNAL AUDITOR IN THE ETHICAL CULTURE OF AN ORGANIZATION***

      1. *This Practice Advisory* ***underscores the importance of organizational culture*** *in establishing the ethical climate of an enterprise and suggests the role that internal auditors could play in improving that ethical climate. Specifically, the Practice Advisory*
         - *Describes the nature of the* ***governance process****.*
         - *Links it to the* ***ethical culture*** *of the organization.*
         - *States that all people associated with the organization, and specifically internal auditors, should assume the role of* ***ethics advocates****.*
         - *Lists the characteristics of an* ***enhanced ethical culture****.*

      2. ***Responsibilities.*** *An organization uses various legal forms, structures, strategies, and procedures to ensure that it*
         - *Complies with society's legal and regulatory* ***rules****.*
         - *Satisfies the* ***generally accepted*** *business norms, ethical precepts, and social expectations of society.*
         - *Provides* ***overall benefit to society*** *and enhances the interests of the specific stakeholders in both the long- and short-term.*
         - *Reports fully and truthfully to its owners, regulators, other stakeholders, and general public to ensure* ***accountability*** *for its decisions, actions, conduct, and performance.*

         The way in which an organization chooses to conduct its affairs to meet those four responsibilities is commonly referred to as its governance process. *The organization's governing body (such as a board of directors or trustees or a managing board) and its senior management are accountable for the effectiveness of the governance process.*

3. *An organization's **governance practices** reflect a unique and ever-changing **culture** that affects roles, specifies behavior, sets goals and strategies, measures performance, and defines the terms of accountability. That culture affects the **values, roles, and behavior** that will be articulated and tolerated by the organization and determines how sensitive -- thoughtful or indifferent -- the enterprise is in meeting its responsibilities to society. Thus, how effective the overall governance process is in performing its expected function largely depends on the organization's culture.*

4. ***All people** associated with the organization share some **responsibility** for the state of its ethical culture. Because of the complexity and dispersion of decision-making processes in most enterprises, each individual should be encouraged to be an **ethics advocate**, whether the role is delegated officially or merely conveyed informally. **Codes of conduct** and **statements of vision and policy** are important declarations of the organization's values and goals, the behavior expected of its people, and the strategies for maintaining a culture that aligns with its legal, ethical, and societal responsibilities. A growing number of organizations have designated a **chief ethics officer** as counselor of executives, managers, and others and as champion within the organization for "doing the right thing."*

5. ***Internal auditors and the internal audit activity** should take an active role in support of the organization's ethical culture. They possess a high level of trust and integrity within the organization and the skills to be effective advocates of ethical conduct. They have the competence and capacity to appeal to the enterprise's leaders, managers, and other employees to comply with the legal, ethical, and societal responsibilities of the organization.*

6. *The internal audit activity may assume one of several different **roles as an ethics advocate**. Those roles include chief ethics officer (ombudsperson, compliance officer, management ethics counselor, or ethics expert), member of an internal ethics council, or assessor of the organization's ethical climate. In some circumstances, the role of chief ethics officer may conflict with the independence attribute of the internal audit activity.*

7. ***At a minimum**, the internal audit activity should **periodically assess** the state of the ethical climate of the organization and the effectiveness of its strategies, tactics, communications, and other processes in achieving the desired level of **legal and ethical compliance**. Internal auditors should evaluate the effectiveness of the following features of an enhanced, highly effective ethical culture:*

   - ***Formal Code of Conduct**, which is clear and understandable, and related statements, policies (including procedures covering fraud and corruption), and other expressions of aspiration.*
   - *Frequent communications and demonstrations of expected ethical attitudes and behavior by the **influential leaders** of the organization.*
   - ***Explicit strategies** to support and enhance the ethical culture with regular programs to update and renew the organization's commitment to an ethical culture.*
   - *Several easily accessible ways for people to **confidentially report** alleged violations of the Code, policies, and other acts of misconduct.*
   - ***Regular declarations** by employees, suppliers, and customers that they are aware of the requirements for ethical behavior in transacting the organization's affairs.*

- ***Clear delegation of responsibilities** to ensure that ethical consequences are evaluated, confidential counseling is provided, allegations of misconduct are investigated, and case findings are properly reported.*
- ***Easy access to learning** opportunities to enable all employees to be ethics advocates.*
- ***Positive personnel practices** that encourage every employee to contribute to the ethical climate of the organization.*
- ***Regular surveys** of employees, suppliers, and customers to determine the state of the ethical climate in the organization.*
- ***Regular reviews** of the formal and informal processes within the organization that could potentially create pressures and biases that would undermine the ethical culture.*
- ***Regular reference and background checks** as part of hiring procedures, including integrity tests, drug screening, and similar measures.*

PA Summary

- This PA (1) describes the **governance process**, (2) links it to the **ethical culture**, (3) states that everyone in the organization should be an **ethics advocate**, and (4) describes an **enhanced ethical culture**.
- The **governance process** consists of the way in which four **responsibilities** are met: (1) **compliance** with legal and regulatory rules, (2) satisfaction of generally accepted norms and social expectations, (3) providing **benefits to society** and specific stakeholders, and (4) reporting fully and truthfully to ensure **accountability**. The organization's governing body and senior management are accountable for the process.
- **Governance practices** reflect the organization's unique, dynamic culture and largely depend on it for effectiveness. The culture sets values, objectives, and strategies; defines roles and behaviors; measures performance; and specifies accountability. Thus, the culture determines the degree of sensitivity to social responsibility.
- All individuals should be **ethics advocates**, codes of conduct and vision statements are often issued, and a chief ethics officer may be appointed.
- Because of their skills and position in the organization, auditors should actively support the ethical culture. **Roles** may include chief ethics officer, member of an ethics council, or assessor of the ethical climate.
- The **minimum IAA role** is assessor of the ethical climate and the effectiveness of processes to achieve legal and ethical compliance. Internal auditors should evaluate the effectiveness of the following features of an enhanced, highly effective ethical culture: (1) a **formal Code of Conduct**; (2) frequent communications by **influential leaders**; (3) **explicit strategies** to enhance the ethical culture with regular programs; (4) easily accessible ways to **confidentially report** alleged violations; (5) **regular declarations** by employees, suppliers, and customers about the requirements for ethical behavior; (6) **clear delegation of responsibilities** for providing counsel, investigation, and reporting; (7) **easy access to learning** opportunities; (8) **positive personnel practices** that encourage every employee to contribute; (9) **regular surveys** to determine the state of the ethical climate; (10) **regular reviews** of the processes that undermine the ethical culture; and (11) **regular reference and background checks**.

3. ***2130.A1*** *– The internal audit activity should evaluate the design, implementation, and effectiveness of the organization's ethics-related objectives, programs, and activities.*
4. ***2130.C1*** *– Consulting engagement objectives should be consistent with the overall values and goals of the organization.*
   a. ***PRACTICE ADVISORY 1000.C1-2: ADDITIONAL CONSIDERATIONS FOR FORMAL CONSULTING ENGAGEMENTS***

   The following is the portion of this comprehensive Practice Advisory relevant to **Standard 2130.C1**:

   9. The internal auditor should exercise ***due professional care*** *in conducting a formal consulting engagement by understanding the following:*

   - ***Needs of management*** *officials, including the nature, timing, and* ***communication*** *of engagement* ***results****.*
   - *Possible* ***motivations and reasons*** *of those requesting the service.*
   - ***Extent of work*** *needed to achieve the engagement's objectives.*
   - ***Skills and resources*** *needed to conduct the engagement.*
   - *Effect on the* ***scope of the audit plan*** *previously approved by the audit committee.*
   - ***Potential impact*** *on future audit assignments and engagements.*
   - *Potential organizational* ***benefits*** *to be derived from the engagement.*

   10. ***Other considerations.*** *In addition to the independence and objectivity evaluation and due professional care considerations, the internal auditor should*

   - *Conduct appropriate meetings and gather necessary information to* ***assess the nature and extent of the service*** *to be provided.*
   - *Confirm that* ***those receiving the service*** *understand and* ***agree with the relevant guidance*** *contained in the internal audit charter, internal audit activity's policies and procedures, and other related guidance governing the conduct of consulting engagements. The internal auditor should* ***decline to perform consulting*** *engagements that are prohibited by the terms of the internal audit charter, conflict with the policies and procedures of the internal audit activity, or do not add value and promote the best interests of the organization.*
   - ***Evaluate*** *the consulting engagement for* ***compatibility*** *with the internal audit activity's* ***overall plan*** *of engagements. The internal audit activity's risk-based plan of engagements may incorporate and rely on consulting engagements, to the extent deemed appropriate, to provide necessary audit coverage to the organization.*
   - ***Document*** *general terms, understandings, deliverables, and other key factors of the* ***formal consulting engagement*** *in a* ***written*** *agreement or plan. It is essential that both the internal auditor and those receiving the consulting engagement understand and agree with the reporting and communication requirements.*

PA Summary

- **Due professional care** for a **formal consulting engagement** requires an understanding of the (1) needs of management, (2) reasons for the service, (3) extent of work, (4) resources required, (5) effect on the audit plan, (6) effect on future engagements, and (7) engagement benefits.
- The auditor should assess the **nature and extent of the service**.
- The auditor should confirm that service recipients **agree with related guidance** (e.g., the IAA's charter, policies, and procedures). Engagements should not be performed when they (1) are prohibited by the charter, (2) conflict with policy, or (3) do not add value.
- An engagement should be compatible with the IAA's **overall plan of engagements**. In appropriate circumstances, consulting engagements may provide necessary audit coverage.
- **Key engagement factors** should be **documented** in a **written agreement**.

5. ***2500*** *Monitoring Progress – The chief audit executive should establish and maintain a system to monitor the disposition of results communicated to management.*

a. ***PRACTICE ADVISORY 2500-1: MONITORING PROGRESS***

1. *The chief audit executive should establish* ***procedures*** *to include the following:*
   - *A time frame within which management's response to the engagement observations and recommendations is required.*
   - *An evaluation of* ***management's response.***
   - *A* ***verification*** *of the response (if appropriate).*
   - *A* ***follow-up*** *engagement (if appropriate).*
   - *A* ***communications procedure*** *that escalates unsatisfactory responses/ actions, including the assumption of risk, to the appropriate levels of management.*

2. *Certain reported observations and recommendations may be so significant as to require immediate action by management. These conditions should be* ***monitored*** *by the internal audit activity* ***until corrected*** *because of the effect they may have on the organization.*

3. ***Techniques used to monitor progress*** *effectively include:*
   - *Addressing engagement observations and recommendations to the* ***appropriate levels of management*** *responsible for taking corrective action.*
   - *Receiving and evaluating management* ***responses*** *to engagement observations and recommendations* ***during the engagement*** *or* ***within a reasonable time*** *period after the engagement results are communicated. Responses are more useful if they include sufficient information for the chief audit executive to evaluate the* ***adequacy and timeliness of corrective action****.*
   - *Receiving* ***periodic updates*** *from management in order to evaluate the status of management's efforts to correct previously communicated conditions.*

- *Receiving and evaluating information from **other organizational units** assigned responsibility for procedures of a follow-up or corrective nature.*
- *Reporting to senior management or the board on the **status of responses** to engagement observations and recommendations.*

PA Summary

- The CAE establishes **procedures** to monitor the disposition of reported results. They include (1) a time frame for **management's response**, (2) an evaluation and **verification** of the response (if appropriate), (3) a **follow-up** (if appropriate), and (4) a **communications procedure** for dealing with unsatisfactory responses.
- Observations and recommendations needing **immediate action** should be monitored **until corrected**.
- Observations and recommendations should be addressed to managers **responsible for corrective action**.
- **Management responses** should be received and evaluated during the engagement or within a reasonable time afterward. Responses should be sufficient for the CAE to evaluate the **adequacy and timeliness of corrective action**.
- Management should give **periodic updates**.
- Information should be received and evaluated from **other units** involved in follow-up or correction.
- The **status of responses** should be reported to senior management or the board.

6. ***2500.A1*** *– The chief audit executive should establish a follow-up process to monitor and ensure that management actions have been effectively implemented or that senior management has accepted the risk of not taking action.*

   a. ***PRACTICE ADVISORY 2500.A1-1: FOLLOW-UP PROCESS***

      1. *Internal auditors should determine that **corrective action was taken** and is achieving the desired results or that senior management or the board has **assumed the risk** of not taking corrective action on reported observations.*
      2. ***Follow-up** by internal auditors is defined as a process by which they determine the adequacy, effectiveness, and timeliness of actions taken by management on reported engagement observations and recommendations, including those made by **external auditors and others**.*
      3. ***Responsibility for follow-up** should be defined in the internal audit activity's written **charter**. The **nature, timing, and extent** of follow-up should be determined by the chief audit executive. Factors that should be considered in determining appropriate follow-up procedures are:*
         - *The significance of the reported observation or recommendation.*
         - *The degree of effort and cost needed to correct the reported condition.*
         - *The impacts that may result should the corrective action fail.*
         - *The complexity of the corrective action.*
         - *The time period involved.*

4. *In some instances, the chief audit executive may judge that management's oral or written* ***response shows that action already taken is sufficient*** *when weighed against the relative importance of the engagement observation or recommendation. On such occasions, follow-up may be performed as part of the next engagement.*

5. *Internal auditors should ascertain that* ***actions taken*** *on engagement observations and recommendations* ***remedy*** *the underlying* ***conditions****.*

6. *The chief audit executive is responsible for* ***scheduling follow-up*** *activities as part of developing engagement* ***work schedules****. Scheduling of follow-up should be based on the* ***risk*** *and exposure involved, as well as the degree of* ***difficulty*** *and the significance of* ***timing*** *in implementing corrective action.*

PA Summary

- Auditors follow up by determining whether (1) effective **corrective action** has been taken or (2) senior management or the board has **assumed the risk** of not taking action.
- **Follow-up** should address the adequacy, effectiveness, and timeliness of actions on reported observations and recommendations, including those by other auditors.
- The **IAA's charter** defines **responsibility for follow-up**. The CAE defines its nature, timing, and extent after considering (1) the significance of what is reported, (2) the effort and cost of correction, (3) the effect of failure of correction, (4) the complexity of correction, and (5) the time involved.
- If **action already taken suffices**, follow-up may be part of the next engagement.
- Auditors should verify that actions **remedy** underlying conditions.
- The CAE includes follow-up as part of the **work schedule**. Scheduling depends on the **risk** involved and the difficulty and timing of corrective action.

7. ***2500.C1*** *– The internal audit activity should monitor the disposition of results of consulting engagements to the extent agreed upon with the client.*

   a. ***PRACTICE ADVISORY 1000.C1-2: ADDITIONAL CONSIDERATIONS FOR FORMAL CONSULTING ENGAGEMENTS***

   The following is the portion of this Practice Advisory relevant to Standard 2500.C1:

   20. *The internal audit activity should* ***monitor the results of consulting engagements*** *to the extent agreed upon with the client. Varying types of monitoring may be appropriate for differing types of consulting engagements. The monitoring effort may depend on various factors, such as management's explicit interest in the engagement or the internal auditor's assessment of the project's risks or value to the organization.*

PA Summary

- The IAA monitors results of consulting as agreed with the client. The type of monitoring may depend on factors such as management's interest in the engagement or the assessment of risk.

8. ***2600*** ***<u>Resolution of Management's Acceptance of Risks</u>*** *– When the chief audit executive believes that senior management has accepted a level of residual risk that may be unacceptable to the organization, the chief audit executive should discuss the matter with senior management. If the decision regarding residual risk is not resolved, the chief audit executive and senior management should report the matter to the board for resolution.*

   a. ***<u>PRACTICE ADVISORY 2600-1: MANAGEMENT'S ACCEPTANCE OF RISKS</u>***

      1. ***Management*** *is responsible for deciding the* ***appropriate action*** *to be taken in response to reported engagement observations and recommendations. The chief audit executive is responsible for* ***assessing*** *such management action for the* ***timely resolution*** *of the matters reported as engagement observations and recommendations. In deciding the extent of follow-up, internal auditors should consider procedures of a* ***follow-up*** *nature* ***performed by others*** *in the organization.*

      2. *As stated in Section 2060 of the Standards, paragraph 3 of Practice Advisory 2060-1, senior management may decide to assume the risk of not correcting the reported condition because of cost or other considerations. The board should be informed of senior management's decision on* ***all significant engagement observations and recommendations****.*

PA Summary

- Management decides the **action taken** in response to engagement results. The CAE assesses this action for **timely resolution**. The extent of follow-up also is a function of follow-up work **done by others**.
- Senior management **may assume** the risk of noncorrection. The decisions on **all significant engagement observations and recommendations** should be reported to the board.

9. **Follow-up**

   a. The **internal auditor** should

      1) Receive all replies by the engagement client to the engagement communications
      2) Evaluate the adequacy of those replies
      3) Be convinced that the action taken will cure the defects

   b. The internal auditor is in the **best position** to carry out this responsibility. (S)he is

      1) Better acquainted with the **facts** than senior management or other control centers in the organization.
      2) More **objective** than the operating manager who must take the corrective action.

   c. The responsibility for determining whether corrective **action is adequate** should be coupled with the **authority** to evaluate the adequacy of replies to engagement communications. The internal auditor should

      1) Report to management when corrective actions are **not timely or effective**.
      2) Submit **periodic reports** to management on open engagement observations and recommendations.

d. The **adequacy of a response** depends on the circumstances in each case. In general, a satisfactory response

1) Addresses itself to the **complete problem**, not just to specific items included in the internal auditor's sample.
2) Shows that action also has been taken to **prevent a recurrence** of the deficient condition.

e. In **evaluating the reply**, the internal auditor should be satisfied that the action promised is actually taken. The auditor should

1) Obtain **copies of revised procedures** issued to correct conditions.
2) Make any **field tests** needed to provide assurance that the condition has been corrected.

f. A **formal system** should be designed to **keep engagements open** until adequate corrective action is assured. For example,

1) Provisions should be made for **formal opening and closing** of engagements.
2) The internal auditors should issue a **formal statement of closure**, supported by copies of replies to engagement communications and explanations of the action taken to ensure the adequacy and effectiveness of corrective measures.
   a) **Closure reports** are directed to the chief audit executive.
3) Engagements should not be removed from the IAA's **open engagements listing** until all required corrective actions have been taken and evaluated.

10. Stop and review! You have completed the outline for this subunit. Study multiple-choice questions 7 through 15 beginning on page 127.

3.3 REGULATORY COMPLIANCE

1. Internal auditors should **assess compliance in specific areas** as part of their role in organizational governance. They also should conduct follow-up and report on management's response to regulatory body reviews. Given the ever-expanding scope of governmental regulation, these duties of internal auditors have assumed increased importance.

   Caution – *Internal auditors are encouraged to consult legal counsel in all matters involving legal issues as requirements may vary significantly in different jurisdictions.*

2. The **Glossary** provides the following definition of **Compliance**:

   Conformity and adherence to policies, plans, procedures, laws, regulations, contracts, or other requirements.

3. ***2100*** ***Nature of Work*** – *The internal audit activity evaluates and contributes to the improvement of risk management, control, and governance processes using a systematic and disciplined approach.*

NOTE: The following Practice Advisory has been slightly modified to eliminate any implication that it applies only to a specific country.

a. ***PRACTICE ADVISORY 2100-5: LEGAL CONSIDERATIONS IN EVALUATING REGULATORY COMPLIANCE PROGRAMS***

   1. ***Compliance programs*** *assist organizations in preventing inadvertent employee violations, detecting illegal activities, and discouraging intentional employee violations. They can also help prove insurance claims, determine director and officer liability, create or enhance corporate identity, and decide the appropriateness of punitive damages. Internal auditors should* ***evaluate an organization's regulatory compliance programs*** *in light of the following suggested steps for effective compliance programs.*

2. *The organization should **establish compliance standards and procedures** to be followed by its employees and other agents who are reasonably capable of reducing the prospect of criminal conduct.*
   - *The organization should develop a **written business code of conduct** that clearly identifies prohibited activities. This code should be written in language that all employees can understand, avoiding legalese.*
   - *A good code provides **guidance to employees on relevant issues.** Checklists, a question and answer section, and reference to additional sources for further information all help make the code user-friendly.*
   - *The organization should create an **organizational chart** identifying board members, senior officers, senior compliance officer, and department personnel who are responsible for implementing compliance programs.*
   - *Codes of conduct that are viewed as legalistic and "one-sided" by employees may increase the risk that employees will engage in unethical or illegal behavior, but codes that are viewed as **straightforward and fair** tend to decrease the risk that employees will engage in such activity.*
   - *Organizations using reward systems that attach financial **incentives** to apparently **unethical or illegal behavior** can expect a poor compliance environment.*
   - *Organizations with international operations should institute a compliance program on a **global basis**, not just for selected geographic locations. Such programs should reflect appropriate local conditions, laws, and regulations.*
3. ***Specific** individual(s) within **high-level personnel** of the organization should be assigned **overall responsibility** to oversee regulatory compliance with standards and procedures.*
   - *High-level personnel of the organization means individuals who have **substantial control** of the organization or who have a **substantial role in the making of policy** within the organization.*
   - *High-level personnel of the organization include a director; an executive officer; an individual in charge of a major business or functional unit of the organization, such as sales, administration, or finance; and an individual with a substantial ownership interest.*
   - *To be fully effective, the **CEO and other senior management** must have **significant involvement** in the program.*
   - *In some organizations, assigning chief compliance responsibilities to the organization's **general counsel** may convince employees that management is not committed to the program, that the program is important to the legal department only and not the organization as a whole. In other organizations, the opposite may be true.*
   - *In a large organization with several business units, compliance responsibilities should be assigned to high-level personnel **in each unit**.*
   - *It is not enough for the organization to create the position of chief compliance officer and to select the rest of the compliance unit. The organization should also ensure that those personnel are **appropriately empowered and supplied** with the resources necessary for carrying out their mission. Compliance personnel should have adequate access to senior management. The chief compliance officer should report directly to the CEO.*

4. *The organization should use **due care** not to delegate substantial discretionary authority to individuals the organization knows, or should know through the exercise of **due diligence**, have a **propensity to engage in illegal activities**.*
   - *Organizations should **screen applicants** for employment at all levels for evidence of past wrongdoing, especially wrongdoing within the organization's industry.*
   - *Employment **applications** should inquire as to past criminal convictions. Professionals should be asked about any history of discipline by licensing boards.*

     NOTE: Disciplinary actions by licensing boards may be a matter of public record.
   - *Care should be taken to ensure that the organization does not infringe upon employees' and applicants' **privacy rights under any applicable laws**. Many jurisdictions have laws limiting the amount of information an organization can obtain in performing background checks on employees.*
5. *The organization should take steps to **communicate effectively its standards and procedures** to all employees and other agents, e.g., by requiring participation in training programs or by disseminating publications that explain in a practical manner what is required.*
   - *The effectiveness of a compliance program will depend upon the ways in which it is communicated to employees. Generally, an **interactive format** works better than a lecture. Programs communicated in person tend to work better than programs communicated entirely through video or game formats. Programs that are **periodically repeated** work better than one-time presentations.*
   - *The best programs include **employee training** that allows employees to practice new techniques and use new information. Such activities are particularly appropriate with regard to management training but are effective with regard to employees at all levels.*
   - *The **language** used by an organization's code of conduct and employee manual should be **easy to understand**. Alternative methods of communicating the code and the employee manual to employees lacking more formal education must be found and implemented.*
   - *Compliance tips, statements, and warnings should be disseminated to employees through a **variety of available media**: newsletters, posters, e-mail, questionnaires, and presentations.*
   - *Organizations should present the program on **multiple occasions** to different sets of employees, targeting the information presented to the areas important to each functional group of employees. The **information should be tailored** to that group's job requirements. For example, environmental compliance information should be directed to those departments, such as manufacturing or real property management, that have an increased likelihood of violating or detecting violations of such laws and regulations. On the other hand, providing such training to a department with no such responsibilities could be detrimental, inspiring employee apathy or a belief that the program was not well constructed.*
   - ***New employees** should receive **basic compliance training** as part of their orientation. Later, they can be incorporated into ongoing compliance efforts in their departments.*

- ***Agents*** *of the organization should be asked to attend a presentation specifically geared toward them. It is important that an organization inform its agents of the* ***organization's core values****, and that the actions of its agents that are attributable to the organization will be* ***monitored*** *in connection with the compliance program. The organization should be prepared to cease doing business with agents who fail to adhere to the organization's compliance standards.*
- *Organizations should* ***require employees to periodically certify*** *that they have read, understood, and complied with the company's code of conduct. This information should be related annually to senior management and the board of directors.*
- *All* ***ethics-related documents*** *– codes of conduct, human resources policies/manuals, etc. – should be* ***readily available*** *to all employees. Continuous access availability, such as through the organization's* ***intranet****, is strongly encouraged.*

6. *The organization should take reasonable steps to achieve compliance with its standards, e.g., by using* ***monitoring and auditing systems*** *reasonably designed to detect criminal conduct by its employees and other agents and by having in place and publicizing a* ***reporting system*** *whereby employees and other agents could report criminal conduct by others within the organization without fear of retribution.*
   - *The organization should devote an amount of resources to the* ***internal audit plan*** *that is appropriate given the size of the company and the difficulty of the audit task. The audit plan should concentrate on the organization's* ***activities in each of its businesses****.*
   - *The audit plan should also include a* ***review of the organization's compliance program and its procedures****, including reviews to determine whether written materials are effective, communications have been received by employees, detected violations have been appropriately handled, discipline has been even-handed, any protections afforded to informants by local law have not been violated, and the compliance unit has fulfilled its responsibilities. The auditors should review the compliance program to determine whether it can be improved and should solicit employee input in that regard.*
   - *Each program should have a* ***"hotline" or other reporting system*** *under which employees can report activity that they believe to be unethical, illegal, or against the organization's code of conduct. Employees must be free to report such behavior without fear of reprisal.*
   - *In some countries, attorney-client and attorney work-product privileges may be legally recognized. These privileges protect certain information disclosed to (or produced by) an attorney from being used by an adverse party in a legal proceeding. In these countries, an* ***attorney*** *monitoring the hotline is best able to protect the privileges. However, one study observed that employees have little confidence in hotlines answered by the legal department or by an outside service. The same study showed that employees have even less confidence in write-in reports or an off-site ombudsperson, but have the most confidence in* ***hotlines answered by an in-house representative and backed by a nonretaliation policy****.*

- *Use of an on-site ombudsperson is more effective if the **ombudsperson reports directly** to the chief compliance officer or the board of directors, if the ombudsperson can **keep the names of informants secret**, if the ombudsperson provides **guidance** to informants, and if the ombudsperson undertakes **follow-up** review to ensure that retaliation has not occurred. Additionally, some jurisdictions now recognize a **limited ombudsperson privilege** under which the ombudsperson is protected from disclosing confidential communications made by informants to the ombudsperson.*
- *An effective tool for uncovering unethical or illegal activity is the **ethics questionnaire**. Each employee of the organization should receive a questionnaire, which asks whether the employee is aware of kickbacks, bribes, or other wrongdoing. To **protect any available privileges**, the questionnaire should be sent by organization counsel; contain a statement that the questionnaire is protected by privilege; require the employee to complete, sign, and return the questionnaire without making a copy; and contain a statement that the organization retains the right to disclose information provided to it to government agencies or in litigation. But a privilege may be lost if the questionnaire is disclosed to outside parties.*

7. *The standards should be **consistently enforced** through appropriate disciplinary mechanisms, including, as appropriate, discipline of individuals responsible for the failure to detect an offense. **Adequate discipline** of individuals responsible for an offense is a necessary component of enforcement; however, the form of discipline that will be appropriate will be case specific.*
   - *The compliance program should contain a disciplinary system under which those who violate the organization's code of conduct receive **punishment appropriate to the offense**, such as warning, loss of pay, suspension, transfer, or termination. If an employee is found to have committed some illegal act, the organization might have to terminate that employee, in keeping with the organization's obligation to use "due care not to delegate substantial discretionary authority to individuals whom the organization knew, or should have known through the exercise of due diligence, had a propensity to engage in illegal activities"* (see paragraph 4).
   - *Discipline under the program must be **fair**. The program has slight chance of succeeding if unethical or illegal activity goes unpunished, especially if tied to the activities of senior management or big producers. Ignored wrongdoing by such persons will encourage such behavior in the rest of the workforce.*
   - *Termination or other **discipline of employees may be limited** by whistle-blower laws, exceptions to the employee-at-will doctrine, employee or union contracts, and employer responsibilities with regard to discrimination, wrongful discharge, and employer bad faith laws/doctrines.*
   - *The program should provide for the **discipline of managers and other responsible persons** who knew or should have known of misconduct and did not report it. Failure of the program to do so may cause a court to find that the program is not effective.*

8. *Organizations should be scrupulous and thorough in **documenting employee discipline**. The organization should be able to prove that it made its best efforts to collect information with regard to any incident and took appropriate action based upon the information available.*

9. *After an offense has been detected, the organization should take all reasonable steps to* ***respond appropriately*** *to the offense and to* ***prevent further similar offenses*** *-- including any necessary modifications to its program to prevent and detect violations of law.*
   - *The organization should respond appropriately to each offense detected by the compliance program. Appropriate responses include* ***disciplinary action*** *taken with regard to those who engaged in misconduct.*
   - *In some circumstances, an appropriate response could require* ***self-reporting*** *the violation to the government,* ***cooperation*** *with governmental investigations, and the* ***acceptance of responsibility*** *for the violation. Note that maintaining an effective compliance program and making appropriate responses could result in more lenient punishment after violations of the law.*
   - ***Failure to detect or prevent a serious violation*** *could indicate that the compliance program needs a major overhaul. At a minimum, after any violation is detected, compliance personnel should examine the program to determine whether changes need to be made.*
   - *One change that may be required in light of a violation could be the* ***replacement or shuffling of compliance personnel****. In fact, the organization may need to discipline or replace any manager who fails to detect or prevent misconduct in the areas under the manager's supervision, especially if the violation is one that the manager should have detected.*

PA Summary

- **Compliance programs** help to prevent unintentional violations, detect illegality, deter intentional violations, prove insurance claims, determine liability, enhance corporate identity, and decide the appropriateness of punitive damages. Internal auditors **evaluate** these programs.
- **Compliance standards and procedures** should be established, including a **clearly written, straightforward, and fair business code of conduct** that provides **guidance to employees on relevant issues** and is user-friendly. Also, an **organizational chart** should identify personnel responsible for compliance programs. Moreover, **financial incentives** should not reward misconduct, and international organizations should have a compliance program on a **global basis** that reflects local conditions and laws.
- **Specific high-level personnel** who are properly empowered and supplied with necessary resources should have overall responsibility for the compliance program. Senior management also should be involved. High-level personnel have **substantial control** of the entity or a **substantial role** in making policy. Furthermore, compliance personnel should have adequate access to senior management, and the chief compliance officer should report directly to the CEO.
- **Due care** should be used not to delegate authority to those with a tendency to **illegality**. **Applications** should inquire about criminal convictions or discipline by licensing boards, and applicants should be **screened** in a lawful manner that does not infringe upon **privacy rights**.

- Standards and procedures, including readily available **ethics-related documents**, should be **communicated effectively**, preferably in an interactive format and on multiple occasions. Training programs and publications are typical methods. The best training allows employees to practice new techniques and use new information. Compliance information should be conveyed through a **variety of available media**. Moreover, the program should be presented to different sets of employees, **targeting the information** to the areas important to each functional group and its job requirements. **New employees** should receive **basic compliance training** as part of their orientation, and **agents** of the entity should be given a presentation specifically for them. Agents should understand the entity's **core values** and that their actions will be **monitored**. Organizations also should **require employees to certify periodically** that they have read, understood, and complied with the code of conduct. This information should be relayed annually to senior management and the board.
- **Monitoring and auditing systems** for detecting illegality and employee "hotline" **reporting systems** should be used. For example, the **internal audit plan** should be given appropriate resources and apply to all of the entity's businesses. Also, it should include a **review of the compliance program**. The review considers effectiveness of written materials, employee receipt of communications; handling of **violations**, fairness of discipline, observance of any protections afforded to informants, and fulfillment of compliance unit responsibilities.
- **Attorney-client and attorney work-product privileges** protect certain information disclosed to (or produced by) an attorney from being used by an adverse party in a legal proceeding. An **attorney** monitoring the hotline is best able to protect the privileges. However, employees may have little confidence in such hotlines or in write-in reports or an off-site ombudsperson. But they may have confidence in **hotlines answered by an in-house representative and backed by a nonretaliation policy**.
- An **on-site ombudsperson** is more effective if (s)he (1) **reports directly** to the chief compliance officer or the board, (2) can **keep the names of informants secret**, (3) provides **guidance** to informants, and (4) undertakes **follow-up** to ensure that retaliation has not occurred.
- An **ethics questionnaire** should be sent to each employee asking whether the employee is aware of kickbacks, bribes, or other wrongdoing.
- Compliance standards should be **consistently enforced** by adequate, fair, case-specific discipline. **Punishment should be appropriate to the offense**, such as a warning, loss of pay, suspension, transfer, or termination. Furthermore, the program should provide for the **discipline of managers and other responsible persons** who knew or should have known of misconduct and did not report it. Failure to do so may cause a court to find that the program is not effective.
- Employee discipline should be thoroughly **documented** so that the entity will be able to prove that it made its best effort to collect information and took appropriate action.
- After detection, the response should be appropriate and designed to **prevent other similar offenses**. In some circumstances, an appropriate response could require **self-reporting** the violation to the government, **cooperation** with investigations, and the **acceptance of responsibility**. But an effective compliance program and appropriate responses could result in more lenient punishment.
- **Failure to detect or prevent a serious violation** could indicate that the compliance program needs a major overhaul. One change that may be required could be the **replacement or transfer of compliance personnel**.

4. Stop and review! You have completed the outline for this subunit. Study multiple-choice questions 16 through 29 beginning on page 130.

3.4 STUDY UNIT 3 SUMMARY

1. The internal audit activity evaluates and contributes to the improvement of risk management, control, and governance processes using a systematic and disciplined approach.
2. The IAA evaluates the adequacy and effectiveness of risk management, control, and governance processes. These processes should provide reasonable assurance that objectives will be met.
3. Management is responsible for the sustainability of the organization and is accountable to stakeholders. Thus, it plans, organizes, and directs and establishes an organizational culture.
4. Because the IAA evaluates the whole management process, its scope of work extends to all systems, processes, operations, functions, and activities.
5. The internal audit activity should assess and make appropriate recommendations for improving the governance process in its accomplishment of the following objectives:
   a. Promoting appropriate ethics and values within the organization.
   b. Ensuring effective organizational performance management and accountability.
   c. Effectively communicating risk and control information to appropriate areas of the organization.
   d. Effectively coordinating the activities of and communicating information among the board, external and internal auditors, and management.
6. The chief audit executive should establish and maintain a system to monitor the disposition of results communicated to management. Thus, the chief audit executive should establish a follow-up process to monitor and ensure that management actions have been effectively implemented or that senior management has accepted the risk of not taking action.
7. Internal auditors should assess compliance in specific areas as part of their role in organizational governance. They also should conduct follow-up and report on management's response to regulatory body reviews.

QUESTIONS

3.1 Nature of Work

1. The scope of internal auditing work encompasses a systematic, disciplined approach to evaluating and improving the adequacy and effectiveness of all of the following processes except

A. Risk management.

B. Control.

C. Financial statements.

D. Governance.

Answer (C) is correct. *(Publisher, adapted)*

REQUIRED: The scope of internal auditing.

DISCUSSION: Financial statements are the responsibility of management, and evaluating the adequacy of the statements is a role of the external auditor. The internal auditor evaluates and contributes to the improvement of risk management, control, and governance processes using a systematic and disciplined approach (Standard 2100). The comprehensive scope of work of internal auditing should provide reasonable assurance that:

- The risk management system is effective.
- The system of internal control is effective and efficient.
- The governance process is effective by establishing and preserving values, setting goals, monitoring activities and performance, and defining the measures of accountability.

2. Adequacy of risk management, control, and governance processes is present if management has planned and designed these processes in a manner that provides reasonable assurance that the organization's objectives and goals will be achieved efficiently and economically. Which of the following statements is not true regarding the efficient and economical achievement of the organization's objectives and goals?

A. Economical performance accomplishes objectives and goals with minimal use of resources with no regard to risk exposure.

B. Efficient performance accomplishes objectives and goals in a timely manner.

C. Economical performance accomplishes objectives and goals with minimal use of resources commensurate with the risk exposure.

D. Efficient performance accomplishes objectives and goals in an accurate and economical manner.

Answer (A) is correct. *(Publisher, adapted)*

REQUIRED: The meaning of efficient and economic performance of an organization's objectives and goals.

DISCUSSION: Efficient performance accomplishes objectives and goals in an accurate, timely, and economical fashion. Economical performance accomplishes objectives and goals with minimal use of resources (i.e., cost) commensurate with risk exposure (PA 2100-1). Thus, in order to achieve economical performance when accomplishing objectives and goals, the minimal cost should correspond to the degree of risk exposure.

3. All of the following are primary objectives of the overall management process except

A. Improving the effectiveness of risk management, control, and governance processes.

B. Compliance with laws, regulations, ethical and business norms, and contracts.

C. Identification of risk exposures and use of effective strategies to control them.

D. Safeguarding of the organization's assets.

Answer (A) is correct. *(Publisher, adapted)*

REQUIRED: The primary objectives of the overall management process.

DISCUSSION: Improving the effectiveness of risk management, control, and governance processes is the scope of internal auditing work. Broadly, management is responsible for the sustainability of the whole organization and accountability for the organization's actions, conduct, and performance to the owners, other stakeholders, regulators, and general public. Specifically, the primary objectives of the overall management process are to achieve (PA 2100-1):

- Relevant, reliable, and credible financial and operating information.
- Effective and efficient use of the organization's resources.
- Safeguarding of the organization's assets.
- Compliance with laws, regulations, ethical and business norms, and contracts.
- Identification of risk exposures and use of effective strategies to control them.
- Established objectives and goals for operations or programs.

4. Which of the following is subject to the internal auditors' evaluations?

I. The human resources function.

II. The purchasing process.

III. The manufacturing and production database system.

A. I only.

B. II only.

C. I, II, and III.

D. None of the answers are correct.

Answer (C) is correct. *(Publisher, adapted)*

REQUIRED: The organizational systems, processes, operations, functions, and activities that are subject to internal auditor evaluations.

DISCUSSION: The internal auditing evaluations, in the aggregate, provide information to appraise the overall management process. Thus, all business systems, processes, operations, functions, and activities within the organization are subject to the internal auditors' evaluations (PA 2100-1).

5. Which of the following is not a type of control?

A. Preventive.

B. Reactive.

C. Detective.

D. Directive.

Answer (B) is correct. *(Publisher, adapted)*

REQUIRED: The types of controls.

DISCUSSION: Control is any action taken by management to enhance the likelihood that established objectives and goals will be achieved (PA 2100-1). Controls may be preventive (to deter undesirable events from occurring), detective (to detect and correct undesirable events which have occurred), or directive (to cause or encourage a desirable event to occur). "Reactive" is not a specified type of control. However, controls may be reactive in the sense that they detect an undesirable event and react to it or correct it.

6. Directors, management, external auditors, and internal auditors all play important roles in creating proper control processes. Senior management is primarily responsible for

A. Establishing and maintaining an organizational culture.

B. Reviewing the reliability and integrity of financial and operational information.

C. Ensuring that external and internal auditors oversee the administration of the system of risk management and control processes.

D. Implementing and monitoring controls designed by the board of directors.

Answer (A) is correct. *(CIA, adapted)*

REQUIRED: The best description of senior management's responsibility.

DISCUSSION: Management plans, organizes, and directs the performance of sufficient actions to provide reasonable assurance that goals and objectives will be achieved. Management periodically reviews its objectives and goals and modifies its processes to accommodate changes in internal and external conditions. Management also establishes and maintains an organizational culture, including an ethical climate that fosters control (PA 2100-1).

Answer (B) is incorrect because internal auditors are responsible for evaluating the adequacy and effectiveness of controls, including those relating to the reliability and integrity of financial and operational information (Standard 2120.A1). Answer (C) is incorrect because senior management's role is to oversee the establishment, administration, and assessment of the system of risk management and control processes (PA 2120.A1-1). Answer (D) is incorrect because the board has oversight responsibilities but ordinarily does not become involved in the details of operations.

3.2 Governance

7. The governance process is also referred to as the way in which an organization chooses to conduct its affairs to meet four key responsibilities. Which of the following is a part of those responsibilities?

I. Complying with society's legal and regulatory rules.
II. Satisfying the generally accepted business norms of society.
III. Providing overall benefit to society and enhancing the interests of the specific stakeholders.
IV. Reporting fully and truthfully to its owners, regulators, other stakeholders, and the general public.

A. I and II only.
B. II and IV only.
C. I, III, and IV only.
D. I, II, III, and IV.

Answer (D) is correct. *(Publisher, adapted)*
REQUIRED: The four key responsibilities of an organization that make up its governance process.
DISCUSSION: An organization uses various legal forms, structures, strategies, and procedures to ensure that it

- Complies with society's legal and regulatory rules.
- Satisfies the generally accepted business norms, ethical precepts, and social expectations of society.
- Provides overall benefit to society and enhances the interests of the specific stakeholders in both the long- and short-term.
- Reports fully and truthfully to its owners, regulators, other stakeholders, and general public to ensure accountability for its decisions, actions, conduct, and performance.

The way in which an organization chooses to conduct its affairs to meet those four responsibilities is commonly referred to as its governance process.

8. Follow-up activity may be required to ensure that corrective action has taken place for certain observations made in an assurance engagement. The internal audit activity's responsibility to perform follow-up activities as required should be defined in the

A. Internal audit activity's written charter.
B. Mission statement of the audit committee.
C. Engagement memo issued prior to each engagement.
D. Purpose statement within applicable engagement communications.

Answer (A) is correct. *(CIA, adapted)*
REQUIRED: The authoritative source defining the IAA's responsibility to perform follow-up activities.
DISCUSSION: Follow-up is a process by which internal auditors determine the adequacy, effectiveness, and timeliness of actions taken by management on reported engagement observations and recommendations, including those made by external auditors and others. Responsibility for follow-up in an assurance engagement should be defined in the IAA's written charter (PA 2500.A1-1). In a consulting engagement, the extent of monitoring of the disposition of results depends upon the agreement with the client.
Answer (B) is incorrect because follow-up is not specified in the content of the audit committee's mission statement. Answer (C) is incorrect because the engagement memo may contain a statement about responsibility for follow-up, but it should be based on the wording and authority of the IAA's charter. Answer (D) is incorrect because follow-up authority and responsibility may be cited in applicable engagement communications, but the definition should be stated first in the IAA's charter.

9. Internal auditors realize that, at times, corrective action is not taken even when agreed to by the appropriate parties. Thus, in an assurance engagement, internal auditors should

A. Decide the extent of necessary follow-up work.
B. Allow management to decide when to follow up because it is management's ultimate responsibility.
C. Decide to conduct follow-up work only if management requests the internal auditor's assistance.
D. Write a follow-up engagement communication with all observations and recommendations and their significance to the operations.

Answer (A) is correct. *(CIA, adapted)*
REQUIRED: The auditor's responsibility to follow up.
DISCUSSION: The nature, timing, and extent of follow-up in an assurance engagement should be determined by the chief audit executive (PA 2500.A1-1).
Answer (B) is incorrect because determining the timing of follow-up is not management's responsibility; it is the responsibility of the CAE. Answer (C) is incorrect because determining the nature and extent of follow-up is the CAE's responsibility. Management's responsibility is to decide the appropriate action to be taken in response to reported engagement observations and recommendations. Answer (D) is incorrect because the internal auditors must decide the extent of follow-up before submitting a follow-up engagement communication.

10. Why should organizations require assurance engagement clients to reply promptly and outline the corrective action that has been implemented on reported observations?

A. To remove items from the pending list as soon as possible.

B. To effect savings or to institute compliance as early as possible.

C. To indicate concurrence with the engagement observations.

D. To ensure that the engagement work schedule is kept up to date.

Answer (B) is correct. *(CIA, adapted)*
REQUIRED: The reason clients should promptly reply and outline the corrective action that has been implemented on reported observations.
DISCUSSION: The internal auditors should determine that corrective action being taken has the desired results (such as cost savings or compliance) or that senior management or the board has assumed the risk of not taking corrective action (PA 2500.A1-1). Consequently, it follows that the objectives of engagements and the timely reporting of observations and recommendations would be defeated if engagement clients do not promptly implement and report on corrective action.
Answer (A) is incorrect because removing items from the pending list concerns a mechanical and immaterial aspect of the communication process. Answer (C) is incorrect because the client may not concur with the observations and recommendations. This dispute may or may not be considered in closing the engagement. Answer (D) is incorrect because ensuring that the engagement work schedule is kept up to date is an administrative function of the IAA.

11. Assume that the internal auditors' observations are so serious that, in their view, they require immediate action by management. Which of the following statements regarding the internal auditors' responsibility with respect to communicating results and follow-up are true?

I. The conditions should be actively monitored by the internal auditors until corrected.

II. The initial observations should be communicated to senior management and the audit committee, even if the engagement is not complete.

III. The internal auditors should test the actions implemented by management to determine if they remedy the problem.

A. I only.

B. II only.

C. II and III only.

D. I, II, and III.

Answer (D) is correct. *(CIA, adapted)*
REQUIRED: The true statement(s) regarding the internal auditors' responsibility for communicating results and following up observations requiring immediate action.
DISCUSSION: Certain reported observations and recommendations may be so significant as to require immediate action by management. These conditions should be monitored by the IAA until corrected because of the effect they may have on the organization. The CAE should establish procedures to determine a time frame within which management's response to the observations is required, to evaluate the response, to verify the response, to conduct a follow-up engagement, and to transmit unsatisfactory responses or actions to the appropriate management levels (PA 2500-1).

12. Upon reviewing the final communication of engagement results, senior management decided to assume the risk of not implementing corrective action on certain engagement observations. Evaluate the following and select the best alternative for the chief audit executive:

A. Notify regulatory authorities of management's decision.

B. Perform additional engagement procedures to further identify the policy violations.

C. Conduct a follow-up engagement to determine whether corrective action was taken.

D. Discuss the matter with senior management and possibly the board if the residual risk accepted is excessive.

Answer (D) is correct. *(CIA, adapted)*
REQUIRED: The best choice when management agrees to assume the risk of not implementing corrective action.
DISCUSSION: According to Standard 2600, "When the chief audit executive believes that senior management has accepted a level of residual risk that may be unacceptable to the organization, the chief audit executive should discuss the matter with senior management. If the decision regarding residual risk is not resolved, the chief audit executive and senior management should report the matter to the board for resolution."
Answer (A) is incorrect because regulatory authorities do not need to be notified. Management has decided to assume responsibility, and no regulatory violations were mentioned. Answer (B) is incorrect because additional procedures are not required unless the CAE believes that the residual risk assumed is too great. Answer (C) is incorrect because a follow-up engagement is not required unless the CAE believes that the residual risk assumed is too great.

13. The preliminary survey discloses that corrective action was never taken on a prior reported assurance engagement observation. Subsequent fieldwork confirms that the condition still exists. Which of the following courses of action should the internal auditors pursue?

A. Take no action. To do otherwise would be an exercise of operational control.

B. Discuss the issue with the chief audit executive. The problem requires an ad hoc solution.

C. Discuss the issue with the person(s) responsible for the problem. (S)he or they should know how to solve the problem.

D. Order the person(s) responsible to correct the problem. (S)he or they have had long enough to do so.

Answer (C) is correct. *(CIA, adapted)*

REQUIRED: The internal auditors' course of action indicated when a prior engagement observation did not result in corrective action.

DISCUSSION: Internal auditors should follow up to ascertain that appropriate action is taken on reported observations and recommendations. Internal auditors should determine that corrective action was taken and is achieving the desired results or that senior management or the board has assumed the risk of not taking corrective action on reported observations (PA 2500.A1-1). Also, discussion of conclusions and recommendations should occur at appropriate levels of management before issuing final engagement communications (PA 2440-1). Client management is at "an appropriate" level. Obtaining client cooperation (or at least understanding) is a vital part of the solution of any problem.

Answer (A) is incorrect because the condition observed may place the organization at risk until the situation changes or the condition is corrected. Answer (B) is incorrect because conditions that have not been corrected are not unique and do not require ad hoc solutions. Answer (D) is incorrect because the internal auditors have no line authority over the client. To exercise such authority impairs objectivity.

14. An organization's internal auditors have conducted a series of assurance engagements. The resulting recommendations have been readily accepted by engagement clients because of the potential cost savings. Given the acceptance of the cost savings engagements and the scarcity of internal auditing resources, the manager in charge of these engagements also decided that follow-up action was not needed. The manager reasoned that cost savings should be sufficient to motivate the client to implement the engagement recommendations. Thus, follow-up was not scheduled as a regular part of the engagement plan. Was the manager's decision appropriate?

A. Yes. Follow-up is not customary.

B. No. The internal auditors should determine whether the client has appropriately implemented all of the engagement recommendations.

C. No. Scarcity of resources is not a sufficient reason to omit follow-up.

D. Yes. Given sufficient evidence of motivation by the client, follow-up is not needed.

Answer (C) is correct. *(CIA, adapted)*

REQUIRED: The propriety of the manager's decision to omit follow-up from the engagement plan.

DISCUSSION: The CAE should establish and maintain a system to monitor the disposition of results communicated to management (Standard 2500). Accordingly, follow-up is required. Cost (lack of resources) is a factor in determining the nature, timing, and extent of follow-up, not in determining whether to follow up. For example, in some instances, the CAE may judge that management's oral or written response shows that action already taken is sufficient when weighed against the relative importance of the engagement observation or recommendation. On such occasions, follow-up may be performed as part of the next engagement (PA 2500.A1-1). In these circumstances, follow-up is delayed, not omitted.

15. What action should the chief audit executive take when (s)he believes that senior management has accepted a level of residual risk that is unacceptable to the organization?

A. Report the matter to the board for resolution.

B. Report the matter to an external authority.

C. Discuss the matter with external auditors.

D. Discuss the matter with senior management.

Answer (D) is correct. *(Publisher, adapted)*

REQUIRED: The action that the CAE should take when (s)he believes that senior management has accepted a level of residual risk that is unacceptable to the organization.

DISCUSSION: When the CAE believes that senior management has accepted a level of residual risk that is unacceptable to the organization, the chief audit executive should discuss the matter with senior management. If the decision regarding residual risk is not resolved, the chief audit executive and senior management should report the matter to the board for resolution (Standard 2600).

Answer (A) is incorrect because the CAE should report the matter to the board for resolution when a decision is not resolved after a discussion with senior management. Answer (B) is incorrect because the matter should be discussed with senior management. Answer (C) is incorrect because the CAE would not discuss the matter with senior management.

3.3 Regulatory Compliance

16. Compliance programs assist organizations by doing which of the following?

I. Evaluating business continuity.
II. Determining director and officer liability.
III. Evaluating disaster recovery plans.

A. I only.

B. II only.

C. I and II only.

D. I, II, and III.

Answer (B) is correct. *(Publisher, adapted)*
REQUIRED: The way(s) in which compliance programs help organizations.
DISCUSSION: Compliance programs assist organizations in preventing inadvertent employee violations, detecting illegal activities, and discouraging intentional employee violations. They can also help prove insurance claims, determine director and officer liability, create or enhance corporate identity, and decide the appropriateness of punitive damages. Evaluating the business continuity and evaluating the disaster recovery plans are both major components of auditing e-commerce activities.

17. An organization should establish compliance standards and procedures and should develop a written business code of conduct to be followed by its employees. Which of the following is true concerning business codes of conduct and the compliance standards?

A. Compliance standards should be straightforward and reasonably capable of reducing the prospect of criminal conduct.

B. The compliance standards should be codified in the charters of the audit committee.

C. Companies with international operations should institute various compliance programs, based on selective geographic locations, that reflect appropriate local regulations.

D. In order to prevent future legal liability, the code should consist of legal terms and definitions.

Answer (A) is correct. *(Publisher, adapted)*
REQUIRED: The true statement regarding the code of conduct and compliance standards.
DISCUSSION: The code of conduct should clearly identify prohibited activities, making compliance standards reasonably capable of reducing the prospect of criminal conduct (i.e., discouraging intentional employee violations). In addition, codes that are straightforward and fair tend to decrease the risk that employees will engage in unethical or illegal behavior (PA 2100-5).
Answer (B) is incorrect because the compliance standards need only be codified in the code of conduct. The item that should be codified in the charters of the audit committee is the chief audit executive's understanding of the expectations of management and the board for the internal audit activity in the organization's risk management process (PA 2100-3). Answer (C) is incorrect because companies with international operations should institute a compliance program on a global basis, not just for selective geographic locations. Such programs should reflect appropriate local conditions, laws, and regulations (PA 2100-5). Answer (D) is incorrect because the code should be written in a language that all employees can understand, avoiding legalese (PA 2100-5).

18. Which of the following is least likely to exemplify a good compliance environment?

A. An international company that institutes a global compliance program that reflects local conditions, laws, and regulations.

B. A company that creates an organizational chart, identifying personnel who are responsible for implementing compliance programs.

C. A company whose code of conduct provides guidance to employees on relevant issues.

D. A company that rewards employees for charging travel hours in order to take advantage of the tax benefits.

Answer (D) is correct. *(Publisher, adapted)*
REQUIRED: The entity with the poorest compliance environment.
DISCUSSION: Companies using reward systems that attach financial incentives to apparently unethical or illegal behavior can expect a poor compliance environment. For instance, a company rewarding its employees for charging travel hours makes itself vulnerable to fraud. Employees may start charging false travel hours to receive additional rewards. Thus, the tax benefit that the company is trying to take advantage of by offering such an incentive may be negated by fraudulent employee practices. A good compliance environment is created when an organization does the following:

- Develops a written, straightforward business code of conduct that clearly identifies prohibited activities, provides guidance to employees on relevant issues, and decreases the risk that employees will engage in unethical or illegal behavior (PA 2100-5).
- Creates an organizational chart identifying board members, senior officers, senior compliance officer, and department personnel who are responsible for implementing compliance programs (PA 2100-5).
- Institutes a compliance program on a global basis, not just for selective geographic locations, which reflects appropriate local conditions, laws, and regulations (PA 2100-5).

19. Environmental compliance information and training is most applicable, and should be provided, to which of the following departments?

A. Sales.

B. Human resources.

C. Manufacturing.

D. Information technology.

Answer (C) is correct. *(Publisher, adapted)*

REQUIRED: The department to which environmental compliance information and training most applies.

DISCUSSION: When presenting compliance information and training, different sets of employees should be targeted based on areas important to each functional group, and the information should be tailored to that group's job requirements (PA 2100-5). Environmental compliance, in this case, is not in reference to the market or information technology environment, but the physical environment. Thus, information regarding environmental compliance is most applicable to the manufacturing department, since this department has an increased likelihood of violating or detecting violations of such laws and regulations.

20. The chief compliance officer of an organization should report to

A. The chief executive officer.

B. The chief general counsel.

C. The chief operating officer.

D. The chief audit executive.

Answer (A) is correct. *(Publisher, adapted)*

REQUIRED: The supervisor to whom the chief compliance officer reports.

DISCUSSION: It is not enough for a company to create the position of chief compliance officer and to select the rest of the compliance unit. The company should also ensure that these personnel are appropriately empowered and supplied with the resources necessary for carrying out their mission. Furthermore, compliance personnel should have adequate access to senior management. A reporting structure in which the chief compliance officer reports directly to the chief executive officer (CEO) is indicative of this access (PA 2100-5).

Answer (B) is incorrect because the chief general counsel, in many organizations, is assigned chief compliance responsibilities. In many companies, however, such a structure may convince employees that management is not committed to the program and that the program is important only to the legal department. Anyone assigned chief compliance responsibilities should report to the CEO. Answer (C) is incorrect because the chief compliance officer should report to the CEO, not the COO. Answer (D) is incorrect because the chief compliance officer should report to the CEO, not the chief audit executive.

21. An organization should use due care not to delegate substantial discretionary authority to individuals the organization knows have a propensity to engage in illegal activities. Which of the following are steps an organization can take to ensure that such individuals are detected?

I. Screening of applicants for employment at all levels for evidence of past wrongdoing, especially past criminal convictions within the company's industry.

II. Asking professionals about any history of discipline in front of licensing boards.

III. Performing non-consensual background checks on employees' or applicants' credit reports to ensure that they are financially sound and are unlikely to commit theft or fraud.

A. I only.

B. III only.

C. I and II only.

D. I, II, and III.

Answer (C) is correct. *(Publisher, adapted)*

REQUIRED: The due diligence steps an organization can take when hiring individuals.

DISCUSSION: As part of the exercise of due diligence, an organization can take a number of steps to protect itself against individuals who have a propensity to engage in illegal activities. For instance, a company can screen applicants for employment at all levels for evidence of past wrongdoing, especially wrongdoing within the company's industry. Furthermore, it may inquire as to past criminal convictions, and professionals may be asked about any history of discipline in front of licensing boards. Care should be taken, however, to ensure that the company does not infringe upon employees' and applicants' privacy rights under applicable laws, since many jurisdictions have laws limiting the amount of information a company may obtain in performing background checks on employees (PA 2100-5).

22. An ombudsperson is most effective when (s)he:

I. Is located on-site.

II. Reports to the chief compliance officer or the board of directors.

III. Is located off-site.

IV. Reports to no one, thus ensuring a whistle-blower's secrecy.

A. II only.

B. I and II only.

C. I and IV only.

D. III and IV only.

Answer (B) is correct. *(Publisher, adapted)*

REQUIRED: The characteristic(s) of an effective ombudsperson.

DISCUSSION: Use of an ombudsperson is more effective if the ombudsperson is located on-site, reports directory to the chief compliance officer or the board of directors, keeps the names of whistle-blowers secret, provides guidance to whistle-blowers, and undertakes follow-up review to ensure that retaliation has not occurred. An ombudsperson must report to someone at a high level in the organization who is empowered to initiate a change in organization policies based on the ombudsperson's findings; thus, reporting to no one is not an option. In addition, an ombudsperson's location on-site promotes employee confidence in the ombudsperson.

23. Employees have the most confidence in a hotline monitored by which of the following?

A. An expert from the legal department, backed by a non-retaliation policy.

B. An in-house representative, backed by a retaliation policy.

C. An on-site ombudsperson, backed by a non-retaliation policy.

D. An off-site attorney who can better protect attorney-client privilege.

Answer (C) is correct. *(Publisher, adapted)*

REQUIRED: The hotline monitor that employees have the most confidence in.

DISCUSSION: Although an attorney monitoring the hotline is better able to protect attorney-client and work-product privileges, one study observed that employees have little confidence in hotlines answered by the legal department or by an outside service. The same study showed that employees have even less confidence in write-in reports or an off-site ombudsperson, but have the most confidence in hotlines answered by an in-house representative (or an on-site ombudsperson) and backed by a non-retaliation policy.

Answer (A) is incorrect because employees have little confidence in hotlines answered by the legal department. Answer (B) is incorrect because a retaliation policy would dissuade whistle-blowers from coming forth due to concern of possible backlash. Answer (D) is incorrect because employees have little confidence in hotlines monitored by the legal department or by an outside service. Thus, they would have even less confidence in an outside attorney.

24. An internal audit plan should include a review of the organization's compliance program and its procedures, including reviews to determine all but which of the following?

A. The effectiveness of written materials.

B. The receipt of communications by employees.

C. The appropriate handling of detected violations.

D. The performance of full background checks on employees and new hires.

Answer (D) is correct. *(Publisher, adapted)*

REQUIRED: The review that is not included in an internal audit plan, with regard to the organization's compliance program.

DISCUSSION: The audit plan should include a review of the organization's compliance program and its procedures, including reviews to determine whether: written materials are effective, communications have been received by employees, detected violations have been appropriately handled, discipline has been even-handed, whistle-blowers have not been retaliated against, and the compliance unit has fulfilled its responsibilities. The auditors should review the compliance program to determine whether it can be improved and should solicit employee input. Moreover, companies should screen applicants for employment at all levels and should inquire as to past criminal convictions, taking care not to infringe upon employees' and applicants' privacy rights. However, a review of the performance of full background checks is not included in an audit plan as part of the review of an organization's compliance program.

25. Which of the following is an effective tool for uncovering unethical or illegal activity in an organization?

A. The screening of applicants.

B. The ethics interview.

C. The background check.

D. The ethics questionnaire.

Answer (D) is correct. *(Publisher, adapted)*

REQUIRED: The tool used to uncover unethical or illegal activity.

DISCUSSION: An effective tool for uncovering unethical or illegal activity is the ethics questionnaire. Each employee of the organization should receive a questionnaire that asks whether the employee is aware of kickbacks, bribes, or other wrongdoing. To protect privilege, the questionnaire should (1) be sent by organization counsel; (2) contain a statement that the questionnaire is protected by privilege; (3) require the employee to complete, sign, and return the questionnaire without making a copy; and (4) contain a statement that the organization retains the right to disclose information provided to the company to government agencies or in litigation. The questionnaire's instructions should also note that privilege will be lost if the questionnaire is disclosed to outside parties.

Answer (A) is incorrect because screening applicants for employment is a way to detect past criminal activity and wrongdoing. Thus, it is of no use in uncovering unethical or illegal activity currently ongoing in an organization. Answer (B) is incorrect because an ethics interview may cause discomfort to an employee, and an employee may not believe that the interview is protected by privilege or as confidential as an ethics questionnaire. Answer (C) is incorrect because the background check is a way to detect past wrongdoing, not ongoing or current unethical or illegal activities.

26. Which of the following are forms of punishment for those who violate an organization's code of conduct?

I. A warning.
II. Loss of pay.
III. Suspension.
IV. Termination.

A. I and II only.

B. I, III, and IV only.

C. I, II, and III only.

D. I, II, III, and IV.

Answer (D) is correct. *(Publisher, adapted)*

REQUIRED: The forms of punishment for a violation of an organization's code of conduct

DISCUSSION: Those who violate the organization's code of conduct should receive punishment appropriate to the offense, such as warning, loss of pay, suspension, transfer, or termination. Nevertheless, if an employee is found to have committed some illegal act, the organization might have to terminate that employee, in keeping with the organization's obligation to use "due care not to delegate substantial discretionary authority to individuals whom the organization knew, or should have known through the exercise of due diligence, had a propensity to engage in illegal activities."

27. Termination or other discipline of employees may be limited by all of the following except

A. Whistle-blower laws.

B. Employer responsibilities with regard to employer good faith doctrines.

C. Union contracts.

D. Exceptions to the employee-at-will doctrine.

Answer (B) is correct. *(Publisher, adapted)*

REQUIRED: The item that does not limit the termination or other discipline of employees.

DISCUSSION: Termination or other discipline of employees may be limited by whistle-blower laws, exceptions to the employee-at-will doctrine, employee or union contracts, and employer responsibilities with regard to discrimination, wrongful discharge, and employer bad faith laws/doctrines.

28. An organization with an effective regulatory compliance program displays which of the following characteristics?

A. It punishes unethical or illegal activity based on seniority.

B. It disciplines those who knew of the misconduct and did not report it, and holds harmless those who should have known, but did not know.

C. After an offense is detected, the organization takes the necessary steps – short of modifying its entire program – to prevent further similar offenses.

D. It is scrupulous in documenting employee discipline.

Answer (D) is correct. *(Publisher, adapted)*

REQUIRED: The characteristics of an organization with an effective regulatory compliance program.

DISCUSSION: Organizations should be scrupulous and thorough in documenting employee discipline. The organization should be able to prove that it made its best efforts to collect information with regard to any incident and took appropriate action based upon the information available.

Answer (A) is incorrect because discipline under the program must be fair. The program has slight chance of succeeding if unethical or illegal activity goes unpunished, especially if tied to the activities of senior management or big producers. Ignored wrongdoing by such persons will encourage wrongful behavior in the rest of the workforce. Answer (B) is incorrect because the program should provide for the discipline of managers and other responsible persons who knew or should have known of misconduct and did not report it. Answer (C) is incorrect because, after an offense has been detected, the organization should take all reasonable steps to respond appropriately to the offense and to prevent further similar offenses, including any necessary modifications to its program to prevent and detect violations of law.

29. Which of the following is true regarding appropriate responses to an offense detected by an organization's compliance program?

I. Disciplinary action taken against those engaged in misconduct is an appropriate response.

II. Self-reporting the violation to the government is an appropriate response.

III. Acceptance of responsibility for the violation is an appropriate response.

IV. An appropriate response can lower the amount of an organization's court fines.

A. I and II only.

B. I and III only.

C. I, II, and III only.

D. I, II, III, and IV.

Answer (D) is correct. *(Publisher, adapted)*

REQUIRED: The true statement(s) regarding appropriate responses to an offense detected by an organization's compliance program.

DISCUSSION: An organization should respond appropriately to each offense detected by the compliance program. Appropriate responses include disciplinary action taken with regard to those who engaged in misconduct. In some circumstances, an appropriate response could require self-reporting the violation to the government, cooperation with governmental investigations, and the acceptance of responsibility for the violation. Similar to the existence of an effective compliance program, making these responses could result in a court lowering the amount of the organization's fine.

STUDY UNIT FOUR
INTERNAL AUDIT ROLES II

(20 pages of outline)

This study unit is the second of two that address the **scope of work** of internal auditors. The scope of work is defined in the pronouncements of The IIA. These pronouncements elaborate on the description of the services performed by the internal audit activity provided in the **definition of internal auditing**. It stresses the improvement of risk management, control, and governance processes. However, the internal auditors' work regarding **control** is such a vital part of their responsibilities that it is treated separately in Study Units 5 and 6.

Core Concepts

- The risk management process identifies, assesses, manages, and controls potential risk exposures.
- Executive management and the audit committee determine the role of the IAA in risk management.
- Information security is a management responsibility.
- The IAA periodically assesses information security practices and makes recommendations.
- The IAA evaluates compliance with laws and regulations concerning privacy.

4.1 RISK MANAGEMENT

1. **Risk management** is "a process to identify, assess, manage, and control potential events or situations to provide reasonable assurance regarding the achievement of the organization's objectives" (Glossary). It is a fundamental element of the definition of internal auditing. This subject is covered in one General Performance Standard, one Specific Performance Standard, two Assurance Implementation Standards, two Consulting Implementation Standards, and six Practice Advisories.
2. ***2100*** ***Nature of Work*** *– The internal audit activity evaluates and contributes to the improvement of risk management, control, and governance processes using a systematic and disciplined approach.*
   a. ***PRACTICE ADVISORY 2100-3: INTERNAL AUDIT'S ROLE IN THE RISK MANAGEMENT PROCESS***
      1. Risk management is a key ***responsibility of management****. To achieve its business objectives, management should ensure that sound risk management* ***processes are in place and functioning****. Boards and audit committees have an* ***oversight role*** *to determine that appropriate risk management processes are* ***in place*** *and that these processes are* ***adequate and effective****.* ***Internal auditors*** *should assist both management and the audit committee by* ***examining, evaluating, reporting, and recommending improvements*** *on the adequacy and effectiveness of management's risk processes. Management and the board are responsible for their organization's risk management and control processes. However, internal auditors acting in a* ***consulting role*** *can assist the organization in identifying, evaluating, and implementing risk management methodologies and controls to address those risks.*

2. *Developing **assessments and reports** on the organization's risk management processes is normally a high audit priority. Evaluating management's risk processes is different from the requirement that auditors use risk analysis to plan audits. However, information from a **comprehensive risk management process**, including the identification of management and board concerns, can assist the internal auditor in **planning audit activities**.*

3. *The chief audit executive should obtain an **understanding** of management's and the board's **expectations of the internal audit activity** in the organization's risk management process. This understanding should be **codified** in the charters of the internal audit activity and audit committee.*

4. ***Responsibilities and activities** should be **coordinated** among all groups and individuals with a role in the organization's risk management process. These responsibilities and activities should be appropriately **documented** in the organization's strategic plans, board policies, management directives, operating procedures, and other governance-type instruments. **Examples** of some of the activities and responsibilities that should be documented include:*
   - *Setting strategic direction may reside with the board or a committee;*
   - *Ownership of risks may be assigned at the senior management level;*
   - *Acceptance of residual risk may reside at the executive management level;*
   - *Identifying, assessing, mitigating, and monitoring activities on a continuous basis may be assigned at the operating level; and*
   - *Periodic assessment and assurance to others should reside with the internal audit activity.*

5. *Internal auditors are expected to **identify and evaluate significant risk exposures** in the **normal course** of their duties.*

6. *The **internal audit activity's role** in the risk management process of an organization can change over time and may be found at some **point along a continuum** that ranges from*
   - *No role, to*
   - *Auditing the risk management process as part of the internal audit plan, to*
   - *Active, continuous support and involvement in the risk management process, such as participation on oversight committees, monitoring activities, and status reporting, to*
   - *Managing and coordinating the risk management process.*

7. *Ultimately, it is the role of **executive management and the audit committee** to **determine the role of internal audit** in the risk management process. Management's view on internal audit's role is likely to be determined by such factors as the culture of the organization, ability of the internal auditing staff, and local conditions and customs of the country.*

8. ***Additional guidance** can be found in the following Practice Advisories:*
   - *PA 2100-4 Internal Audit's Role in Organizations without a Risk Management Process*
   - *PA 1130.A1-2 Internal Audit Responsibility for Other (Non-Audit) Functions (Study Unit 2)*
   - *PA 2110-1 Assessing the Adequacy of Risk Management Processes*
   - *PA 2010-2 Linking the Audit Plan to Risk and Exposures (Study Unit 8)*

PA Summary

- Risk management is the **responsibility** of management. **Management** should ensure that a sound risk management process (RMP) is in place and functioning. **Oversight bodies** ensure that processes are in place, adequate, and effective. **Internal auditors** examine, evaluate, report, and recommend improvements. They also play a **consulting** role in identifying, evaluating, and implementing risk management methods and controls.
- **Assessing and reporting** on the RMP has a high priority. Evaluating these processes differs from using risk analysis to plan audits. But, information from a **comprehensive RMP** aids in planning audits.
- The CAE must understand management's and the board's **expectations** of the IAA in risk management. The understanding should be codified in the **charters** of the IAA and the audit committee.
- **Responsibilities and activities** should be coordinated and documented. For example, (1) setting strategy may reside with the board; (2) ownership of risks may be assigned to senior management; (3) acceptance of residual risk may reside at the executive management level; (4) identifying, assessing, mitigating, and monitoring activities continuously may be assigned at the operating level; and (5) periodic assessment and assurance to others should reside with the IAA.
- Internal auditors normally **identify and evaluate** significant risk exposures.
- Executive management and the audit committee determine **internal audit's role** in risk management. That role may range from no role, to auditing the process as part of the audit plan, to active, continuous support and involvement in the process, to managing and coordinating the process.

b. ***PRACTICE ADVISORY 2100-4: INTERNAL AUDIT'S ROLE IN ORGANIZATIONS WITHOUT A RISK MANAGEMENT PROCESS***

1.-3. *Same as PA 2100-3, paragraphs 1. through 3.*

4. *If an organization has not established a risk management process,* ***the internal auditor should bring this to management's attention*** *along with suggestions for establishing such a process. The internal auditor should seek direction from management and the board as to the* ***internal audit activity's role*** *in the risk management process. The charters for the internal audit activity and audit committee should* ***document*** *the role of each in the risk management process.*

5. *If requested, internal auditors can play a* ***proactive role in assisting with the initial establishment*** *of a risk management process for the organization. A more proactive role supplements traditional assurance activities with a* ***consultative approach*** *to improving fundamental processes. If such assistance exceeds normal assurance and consulting activities conducted by internal auditors,* ***independence*** *could be impaired. In these situations, internal auditors should comply with the* ***disclosure*** *requirements of the Standards. Additional guidance can also be found in Practice Advisory 1130.A1-2: Internal Audit Responsibility for Other (Non-Audit) Functions (Study Unit 2).*

6. *A proactive role in developing and managing a risk management process is not the same as an "ownership of risks" role. To avoid an "ownership of risk" role, internal auditors should seek confirmation from* ***management*** *as to its* ***responsibility*** *for identification, mitigation, monitoring, and "ownership" of risks.*

7. *In summary, internal auditors can facilitate or enable risk management processes, but they should not "own" or be responsible for the management of the risks identified.*

PA Summary

- The internal auditor should provide **suggestions** for establishing the RMP and seek direction from management and the board as to the IAA's role.
- A **proactive auditor role** in establishing the process may include a **consultative** as well as an **assurance** function. If such assistance exceeds normal assurance and consulting activities by internal auditors, **independence** could be impaired. In these situations, internal auditors should comply with the **disclosure** requirements of the Standards.
- A proactive auditor role is **not** an ownership-of-risk role. Internal auditors should seek confirmation from **management** as to its **responsibility** for identification, mitigation, monitoring, and "ownership" of risks.

c. ***PRACTICE ADVISORY 2100-7: THE INTERNAL AUDITOR'S ROLE IN IDENTIFYING AND REPORTING ENVIRONMENTAL RISKS***

Potential Risks

1. *The Chief Audit Executive (CAE) should include the **environmental, health, and safety (EH&S) risks** in any entity-wide risk management assessment and assess the activities in a balanced manner relative to other types of risk associated with an entity's operations. Among the **risk exposures that should be evaluated** are: organizational reporting structures; likelihood of causing environmental harm, fines, and penalties; expenditures mandated by governmental agencies; history of injuries and deaths; record of losses of customers, and episodes of negative publicity and loss of public image and reputation.*
2. *The majority of environmental audit functions report to their organization's environmental component or general counsel, not to the CAE. The **typical organizational models for environmental auditing** fall into one of the following scenarios:*
   - *The CAE and environmental audit chief are in separate functional units with little contact with each other.*
   - *The CAE and environmental audit chief are in separate functional units and coordinate their activities.*
   - *The CAE has responsibility for auditing environmental issues.*
3. *If the CAE finds that the management of the EH&S risks largely depends on an **environmental audit function, the CAE needs to consider the implications** of that organizational structure and its effects on operations and the reporting mechanisms. If the CAE finds that the exposures are not adequately managed and residual risks exist, that conclusion would normally result in changes to the internal audit activity's plan of engagements and further investigations.*
4. *According to an IIA flash **report on environmental auditing issues**:*
   - *About one-half of the environmental auditors seldom meet with a committee of the governing board and only 40 percent have some contact with the CAE.*

- *Seventy percent of the organizations reported that environmental issues are not regularly included on the agenda of the governing board.*
- *About 40 percent of the organizations reported that they had paid fines or penalties for environmental violations in the past three years. Two-thirds of the respondents described their environmental risks as material.*

5. *The Environmental, Health and Safety Auditing Roundtable (new name is The Auditing Roundtable) commissioned Richard L. Ratliff of Utah State University and a group of researchers to perform a study of environmental, health, and safety auditing. The* ***researchers' findings*** *related to the* ***risk and independence*** *issues are as follows:*

   - *The EH&S audit function is somewhat* ***isolated from other organizational auditing activities****. It is organized separately from internal auditing, only tangentially related to external audits of financial statements, and* ***reports to an EH&S executive****, rather than to the governing board or to senior management. This structure suggests that management believes EH&S auditing to be a technical field that is best placed within the EH&S function of the organization.*
   - *With that organizational placement, EH&S auditors could be* ***unable to maintain their independence****, which is considered one of the principal requirements of an effective audit function. EH&S audit managers typically report administratively to the executives who are responsible for the physical facilities being audited. Thus, poor EH&S performance would reflect badly on the* ***facilities management team****, who would therefore try to exercise their authority and influence over what is reported in audit findings, how audits are conducted, or what is included in the audit plan. This potential subordination of the auditors' professional judgment, even when only apparent, violates auditor* ***independence and objectivity****.*
   - *It is also common for* ***written audit reports*** *to be distributed no higher in the organization than to* ***senior environmental executives****. Those executives may have a potential conflict of interest, and they may curtail further distribution of EH&S audit findings to senior management and the governing board.*
   - *Audit information is often classified as (a) subject to the attorney-client privilege or the attorney-work-product privilege (in countries where such privileges are recognized), (b) secret and confidential, or (c), if not confidential, then closely held. These classifications severely restrict access to EH&S audit information.*

Suggestions for the Chief Audit Executive

6. *The CAE should foster a* ***close working relationship with the chief environmental officer*** *and* ***coordinate activities*** *with the plan for environmental auditing. When the environmental audit function reports to someone other than the CAE, the CAE should offer to* ***review the audit plan and the performance of engagements****. Periodically, the CAE should schedule a* ***quality assurance review*** *of the environmental audit function if it is organizationally independent of the internal audit activity. That review should determine if the environmental risks are being adequately addressed. An* ***EH&S audit program*** *could be either (a) compliance-focused (i.e., verifying compliance with laws, regulations, and the entity's own EH&S policies, procedures, and performance objectives) or (b) management-systems-focused (i.e., providing assessments of management systems intended to ensure compliance with legal and internal requirements and the mitigation of risks), or (c) a combination of both approaches.*

7. *The CAE should* ***evaluate whether the environmental auditors****, who are not part of the CAE's organization, are in* ***compliance*** *with recognized professional* ***auditing standards*** *and a recognized* ***code of ethics****. For example, The IIA publishes practice standards and ethical codes.*
8. *The CAE should* ***evaluate the organizational placement and independence of the environmental audit function*** *to ensure that significant matters resulting from serious risks to the enterprise are reported up the chain of command to the audit or other committee of the governing board. The CAE should also* ***facilitate*** *the* ***reporting*** *of significant* ***EH&S risk and control issues*** *to the audit (or other board) committee.*

PA Summary

- The entity-wide risk management assessment includes **environmental, health, and safety (EH&S) risks**. Risk exposures to be evaluated are (1) faulty reporting structures; (2) likelihood of causing environmental harm, fines, and penalties; (3) expenditures mandated by regulators; (4) history of injuries and deaths; (5) loss of customers; and (6) negative publicity and loss of public reputation.
- The **typical organization model for environmental auditing** is one of the following: (1) the CAE and environmental audit chief are in separate functions and have little contact, (2) they are in separate functions and coordinate their activities, or (3) the CAE has responsibility for auditing environmental issues.
- Given an **environmental audit function**, the CAE considers the **implications** for organizational structure, operations, reporting, and the audit plan.
- Researchers' findings related to **risk and independence** for the EH&S audit function include the following:
  1) It is **isolated from other organizational auditing activities** and usually **reports to an EH&S executive**, not the board or senior management.
  2) Thus, EH&S auditors could be **unable to maintain their independence**. EH&S audit managers typically report administratively to executives responsible for the facilities audited. Poor EH&S performance would reflect badly on the **facilities management team**, who might influence audit findings, how audits are conducted, or the audit plan.
  3) **Written audit reports** are commonly distributed no higher than to **senior environmental executives**. Those executives may have a conflict of interest and curtail further distribution of findings.
  4) Access to EH&S audit information is restricted when classified as (a) subject to the attorney-client privilege or the attorney-work-product privilege (where such privileges are recognized); (b) secret and confidential; or (c) if not confidential, then closely held.
- The CAE should have a **close relationship** with the chief environmental officer and **coordinate activities**. The CAE may offer to **review** the environmental audit function's **plan and performance**. The CAE also should schedule a **quality assurance** review of the function and evaluate its organizational placement and **independence** and compliance with **standards**.
  1) An **EH&S audit program** could be (a) compliance-focused, (b) management-systems-focused, or (c) a combination of both approaches.
  2) The CAE should **facilitate** the **reporting** of significant **EH&S risk and control issues** to the audit (or other board) committee.

3. ***2110*** ***Risk Management*** *– The internal audit activity should assist the organization by identifying and evaluating significant exposures to risk and contributing to the improvement of risk management and control systems.*

a. ***PRACTICE ADVISORY 2110-1: ASSESSING THE ADEQUACY OF RISK MANAGEMENT PROCESSES***

1.-2. Same as PA 2100-3, paragraphs 1. and 2. (see pages 135 and 136)

*3. Each organization may choose a **particular methodology to implement its risk management process**. The internal auditor should determine that the methodology is **understood by key groups or individuals** involved in corporate governance, including the board and audit committee. Internal auditors must satisfy themselves that the organization's risk management processes address key objectives to formulate an opinion on the overall adequacy of the risk management processes. The **key objectives** of a risk management process are:*

- ***Risks** arising from business strategies and activities are **identified** and **prioritized**.*
- *Management and the board have determined the **level of risks acceptable to the organization**, including the acceptance of risks designed to accomplish the organization's strategic plans.*
- ***Risk mitigation activities** are designed and implemented to reduce or otherwise manage **risk at levels** that were determined to be **acceptable** to management and the board.*
- ***Ongoing monitoring activities** are conducted to periodically reassess risk and the effectiveness of controls to manage risk. The board and management receive **periodic reports of the results** of the risk management processes. The corporate governance processes of the organization should provide periodic communication of risks, risk strategies, and controls to stakeholders.*

*4. Internal auditors should recognize that there could be significant variations in the techniques used by various organizations for their risk management practices. Risk management **processes should be designed for the nature of an organization's activities**. Depending on the size and complexity of the organization's business activities, risk management processes may be*

- *Formal or informal*
- *Quantitative or subjective*
- *Embedded in the business units or centralized at a corporate level*

*The specific process used by an organization must fit that organization's **culture, management style, and business objectives**. For example, the use of **derivatives** or other sophisticated capital markets products by the organization would require the use of **quantitative risk management tools**. Smaller, less complex organizations may use an informal risk committee to discuss the organization's risk profile and to initiate periodic actions. The auditor should determine that the methodology chosen is both comprehensive and appropriate for the nature of the organization's activities.*

5. *Internal auditors should obtain **sufficient information** to satisfy themselves that the key objectives of the risk management processes are being met in order to form an **opinion on the adequacy of risk management processes**. In gathering such information, the internal auditor should consider the following types of engagement procedures:*

   - *Research and review **reference materials and background information on risk management methodologies** as a basis to assess whether or not the process used by the organization is appropriate and represents best practices for the industry.*
   - *Research and review current developments, trends, industry information, and other **appropriate sources of information** to **determine risks and exposures** that may affect the organization and related **control procedures** used to address, monitor, and reassess those risks.*
   - *Review **corporate policies and minutes of board and audit committee meetings** to determine the organization's business strategies, risk management philosophy and methodology, appetite for risk, and acceptance of risks.*
   - *Review **previous risk evaluation reports** by management, internal auditors, external auditors, and any other sources that may have issued such reports.*
   - *Conduct **interviews with line and executive management** to determine business unit objectives, related risks, and management's risk mitigation and control monitoring activities.*
   - *Assimilate information to **independently evaluate** the **effectiveness** of risk mitigation, monitoring, and communication of risks and associated control activities.*
   - *Assess the **appropriateness of reporting lines** for risk monitoring activities.*
   - *Review the **adequacy and timeliness of reporting** on risk management results.*
   - *Review the completeness of management's **risk analysis, actions taken** to remedy issues raised by risk management processes, and suggest **improvements**.*
   - *Determine the effectiveness of management's **self-assessment processes** through observations, direct tests of control and monitoring procedures, testing the accuracy of information used in monitoring activities, and other appropriate techniques.*
   - *Review risk-related issues that may indicate **weakness in risk management practices** and, as appropriate, discuss with management, the audit committee, and the board of directors. If the auditor believes that management has accepted a level of risk that is inconsistent with the organization's risk management strategy and policies or that is deemed unacceptable to the organization, the auditor should refer to **Standard 2600**, Management's Acceptance of Risks, and any related guidance for additional direction (see Subunit 3.2).*

PA Summary

- To form an **opinion** on the **adequacy** of the risk management process (RMP), the internal auditor must determine that (1) its implementation is understood by key stakeholders and (2) **key objectives** are addressed:
  1) Risks are **identified** and **prioritized**,
  2) Management and the board have determined the **level of risks acceptable to the organization**,
  3) **Risk mitigation activities** are designed and implemented to reduce or manage **risk at acceptable levels**,
  4) **Ongoing monitoring** is conducted to periodically reassess risk and the effectiveness of controls, and
  5) Stakeholders receive **periodic reports of the results** of the RMP.
- The RMP **should be designed for the nature of an organization's activities**. It may be formal or informal, quantitative or subjective; or embedded in business units or centralized. Specific processes should be designed to fit the organization's **culture, management style, and objectives**.
- Sufficient information on the key objectives should be obtained to form an opinion on the adequacy of the RMP. The internal auditor should consider the following:
  1) **Reference materials and background information** to assess whether the RMP represents best practices.
  2) **Current developments, trends, and industry information** to determine risks and exposures and related control procedures.
  3) **Corporate policies and minutes of board and audit committee meetings** to determine philosophy and methods, appetite for risk, and acceptance of risks.
  4) **Previous risk evaluation reports** by management, auditors, and others.
  5) **Interviews with line and executive management** to determine objectives, related risks, and risk mitigation and control monitoring activities.
  6) Information to **independently evaluate** the **effectiveness** of risk mitigation, monitoring, and communication of risks and controls.
  7) Assessment of the **appropriateness of reporting lines**.
  8) Review of the **adequacy and timeliness of reporting** on results.
  9) Review of the completeness of management's **risk analysis and actions taken** to remedy problems.
  10) Suggesting **improvements**.
  11) Determining the effectiveness of management's **self-assessment processes**, e.g., through observation, direct tests of control and monitoring procedures, and testing information used in monitoring.
  12) Reviewing risk-related indications of **weakness in risk management practices** and, as appropriate, discussing them with management, the audit committee, and the board. (Also, see **Standard 2600**, *Management's Acceptance of Risks*, in Subunit 3.2.)

b. ***PRACTICE ADVISORY 2110-2: THE INTERNAL AUDITOR'S ROLE IN THE BUSINESS CONTINUITY PROCESS***

1. ***Business interruption*** *can result from natural occurrences and accidental or deliberate criminal acts. Those interruptions can have significant financial and operational ramifications. Auditors should evaluate the organization's readiness to deal with business interruptions. A* ***comprehensive plan*** *would provide for emergency response procedures, alternative communication systems and site facilities, information systems backup, disaster recovery, business impact assessments and resumption plans, procedures for restoring utility services, and maintenance procedures for ensuring the readiness of the organization in the event of an emergency or disaster.*

2. *Internal auditing activity should assess the organization's* ***business continuity planning*** *process on a regular basis to ensure that senior management is aware of the state of disaster preparedness.*

3. *Many organizations do not expect to experience an interruption or lengthy delay of normal business processes and operations due to a disaster or other unforeseen event. Many business experts say that it is not* ***if*** *a disaster will occur, but* ***when*** *it will occur. Over time, an organization will experience an event that will result in the loss of information, access to properties (tangible or intangible), or the services of personnel. Exposure to those types of risks and the planning for business continuity is an integral part of an organization's risk management process. Advance planning is necessary to minimize the loss and ensure continuity of an organization's* ***critical business functions****. It may enable the organization to maintain an* ***acceptable level of service*** *to its stakeholders.*

4. *A crucial element of business recovery is the existence of a comprehensive and current* ***disaster recovery plan****. The internal auditors can play a role in the organization's planning for disaster recovery. The internal audit activity can (a) assist with the risk analysis, (b) evaluate the design and comprehensiveness of the plan after it has been drawn up, and (c) perform periodic assurance engagements to verify that the plan is kept up to date.*

Planning

5. *Organizations rely upon internal auditors for analysis of operations and assessment of risk management and control processes. Internal auditors acquire an understanding of the overall business operations and the individual functions and how they interrelate with one another. This positions the internal audit activity as a valuable resource in* ***evaluating the disaster recovery plan during its formulation*** *process.*

6. *The internal audit activity can help with an assessment of an organization's* ***internal and external environment****. Internal factors that may be considered include the turnover of management and changes in information systems, controls, and major projects and programs. External factors may include changes in outside regulatory and business environment and changes in markets and competitive conditions, international financial and economic conditions, and technologies. Internal auditors can help* ***identify risks*** *involving critical business activities and* ***prioritize functions*** *for recovery purposes.*

Evaluation

7. *Internal auditors can make a contribution as objective participants when they* ***review*** *the proposed business continuity and disaster recovery plan for* ***design, completeness, and overall adequacy****. The auditor can examine the plan to determine that it reflects the operations that have been included and evaluated in the risk assessment process and contains sufficient internal control concerns and prescriptions. The internal auditor's comprehensive knowledge of the organization's business operations and applications enables it to assist during the* ***development phase*** *of the business continuity plan by evaluating its organization, comprehensiveness, and recommended actions to manage risks and maintain effective controls during a recovery period.*

Periodic Assurance Engagements

8. *Internal auditors should periodically audit the organization's business continuity and disaster recovery plans. The audit objective is to verify that the* ***plans are adequate*** *to ensure the timely resumption of operations and processes after adverse circumstances and that they reflect the* ***current business operating environment****.*

9. *Business continuity and disaster recovery plans can become outdated very quickly. Coping with and responding to changes is an inevitable part of the task of management. Turnover of managers and executives and changes in system configurations, interfaces, and software can have a major impact on these plans. The internal audit activity should examine the recovery plan to determine whether (a) it is structured to* ***incorporate important changes*** *that could take place over time and (b) the revised plan will be* ***communicated to the appropriate people*** *inside and outside the organization.*

10. ***During the audit****, internal auditors should consider:*

    - *Are all plans up to date? Do procedures exist for updating the plans?*
    - *Are all critical business functions and systems covered by the plans? If not, are the reasons for omissions documented?*
    - *Are the plans based on the risks and potential consequences of business interruptions?*
    - *Are the plans fully documented and in accordance with organizational policies and procedures? Have functional responsibilities been assigned?*
    - *Is the organization capable of and prepared to implement the plans?*
    - *Are the plans tested and revised based on the results?*
    - *Are the plans stored properly and safely? Is the location of and access to the plans known to management?*
    - *Are the locations of alternate facilities (backup sites) known to employees?*
    - *Do the plans call for coordination with local emergency services?*

Internal Audit's Role After a Disaster

11. *There is an important role for the internal auditors to play immediately after a disaster occurs. An organization is more vulnerable after a disaster has occurred, and it is trying to recover. During that* ***recovery period****, internal auditors should* ***monitor*** *the* ***effectiveness*** *of the recovery and control of operations. The internal audit activity should identify areas where internal controls and mitigating actions should be improved and* ***recommend improvements*** *to the entity's business continuity plan. The internal audit activity can also provide support during the recovery activities.*

12. *After the disaster, usually within several months, internal auditors can assist in* ***identifying the lessons learned*** *from the disaster and the recovery operations. Those observations and recommendations may enhance activities to recover resources and update the next version of the business continuity plan.*

13. *In the final analysis, it is* ***senior management*** *who will determine the degree of the* ***internal auditor's involvement*** *in the business continuity and disaster recovery processes, considering their knowledge, skills, independence, and objectivity.*

PA Summary

- **Business interruption** can have significant financial and operational effects. The organization should have a **comprehensive disaster recovery plan** to cope with business interruptions. It should provide for emergency response, alternative communications and site facilities, systems backup, disaster recovery, impact assessments, resumption plans, restoration of utility service, and readiness procedures.
- **Auditors** should regularly assess continuity planning.
- Interruptions and losses are inevitable. Thus, **planning** is integral to the RMP so that losses may be minimized, continuity of **critical business functions** ensured, and an **acceptable level of service** maintained.
- Internal auditors analyze operations, assess the RMP and controls, and understand how functions interrelate. Thus, the IAA can help assess an organization's **internal and external environment, identify risks** involving critical business activities, and **prioritize functions** for recovery purposes.
- Internal auditors **review** the proposed plan for **design, completeness, and overall adequacy**. The plan should reflect the operations included and evaluated in the risk assessment and contain sufficient control.
- Internal auditors should perform **periodic assurance engagements** to verify that the **plan is adequate** and reflects the **current business operating environment**. The IAA should examine the plan to determine whether (1) it is structured to **incorporate important changes**, and (2) the revised plan will be **communicated to the appropriate people** inside and outside the organization.

- **During the audit**, internal auditors should consider whether the plan
    1) Is kept up to date.
    2) Covers all critical business functions and systems and documents the reasons for omissions.
    3) Is based on risks and consequences.
    4) Is fully documented in accordance with policies and procedures and assigns functional responsibilities.
    5) Can be implemented.
    6) Is tested and revised based on results.
    7) Is stored properly and safely.
    8) States locations of backup sites that are known to employees.
    9) Calls for coordination with emergency services.
- During the **recovery period**, internal auditors **monitor the effectiveness** of recovery and control of operations and **identify improvements**. Afterward, they may identify **lessons learned**.
- **Senior management** determines **auditor involvement** in the continuity and recovery processes.

4. ***2110.A1*** *– The internal audit activity should monitor and evaluate the effectiveness of the organization's risk management system.*
5. ***2110A.2*** *– The internal audit activity should evaluate risk exposures relating to the organization's governance, operations, and information systems regarding the*
    - *Reliability and integrity of financial and operational information.*
    - *Effectiveness and efficiency of operations.*
    - *Safeguarding of assets.*
    - *Compliance with laws, regulations, and contracts.*
6. ***2110.C1*** *– During consulting engagements, internal auditors should address risk consistent with the engagement's objectives and should be alert to the existence of other significant risks.*
7. ***2110.C2*** *– Internal auditors should incorporate knowledge of risks gained from consulting engagements into the process of identifying and evaluating significant risk exposures of the organization.*
    a. ***PRACTICE ADVISORY 1000.C1-2: ADDITIONAL CONSIDERATIONS FOR FORMAL CONSULTING ENGAGEMENTS***

    The following is the portion of this comprehensive Practice Advisory relevant to **Standards 2110.C1 and 2110.C2**:

    11. *Internal auditors should reach an* ***understanding*** *about the* ***objectives and scope*** *of the consulting engagement with those receiving the service. Any reservations about the value, benefit, or possible negative implications of the consulting engagement should be communicated to those receiving the service. Internal auditors should design the scope of work to ensure that* ***professionalism, integrity, credibility, and reputation*** *of the internal audit activity will be maintained.*

12. *In planning **formal consulting engagements**, internal auditors should design objectives to meet the appropriate needs of management **officials receiving these services**. In the case of **special requests** by management, internal auditors may consider the following actions if they believe that the **objectives** that should be pursued go **beyond those requested** by management:*
    - *Persuade management to include the additional objectives in the consulting engagement; or*
    - *Document the fact that the objectives were not pursued and disclose that observation in the final communication of consulting engagement results; and*
    - *Include the objectives in a separate and subsequent assurance engagement.*
13. ***Work programs** for formal consulting engagements should document the objectives and scope of the engagement, as well as the methodology to be used in satisfying the objectives. The **form and content** of the program may vary depending on the nature of the engagement. In establishing the **scope of the engagement**, internal auditors may expand or limit the scope to satisfy management's request. However, the internal auditor should be satisfied that the projected scope of work will be **adequate to meet the objectives** of the engagement. The objectives, scope, and terms of the engagement should be **periodically reassessed** and adjusted during the course of the work.*
14. *Internal auditors should be observant of the **effectiveness of risk management and control processes** during formal consulting engagements. Substantial risk exposures or material control weaknesses should be brought to the attention of management. In some situations, the auditor's concerns should also be communicated to executive management, the audit committee, or the board of directors. Auditors should (a) determine the **significance** of exposures or weaknesses and the **actions** taken or contemplated to mitigate or correct these exposures or weaknesses and (b) ascertain the **expectations** of executive management, the audit committee, and board in having these matters reported.*

PA Summary

- Internal auditors should have an understanding about the **objectives and scope** of the consulting engagement. They also should communicate reservations about the engagement to the recipients of the service and maintain their professionalism.
- The objectives of **formal engagements** should meet the needs of the recipients of services. For **special request** engagements, internal auditors may consider the following actions if they believe that the **objectives** should go **beyond those requested**:
  1) Persuade management to include the additional objectives, or
  2) Document and disclose in the final communication of results that those objectives were not pursued and include them in a later assurance engagement.

- **Work programs** should document objectives, scope, and methods. The **form and content** of the program may vary. The scope depends on management's request, but it should be adequate to meet the objectives. Moreover, the objectives, scope, and terms of the engagement should be **periodically reassessed**.
- **Substantial risk exposures** or **material control weaknesses** should be reported to management. In some cases, reporting to higher levels also is indicated. Auditors should determine (1) the **significance** of these matters, (2) **actions** taken or considered, and (3) **expectations** of higher authorities about reporting.

8. Stop and review! You have completed the outline for this subunit. Study multiple-choice questions 1 through 14 beginning on page 154.

4.2 INFORMATION SECURITY AND PRIVACY

1. This subunit covers the related topics of security and privacy in two Practice Advisories that interpret the General Performance Standard on the nature of work and one Practice Advisory that interprets the General Performance Standard on performing the engagement.

   NOTE: **Physical security**, such as safeguards against environmental risks and unauthorized access to computer terminals, remains an internal auditing concern even though software controls now provide most protection for information.

2. ***2100*** ***Nature of Work*** *– The internal audit activity evaluates and contributes to the improvement of risk management, control, and governance processes using a systematic and disciplined approach.*

   a. ***PRACTICE ADVISORY 2100-2: INFORMATION SECURITY***

      1. *Internal auditors should determine that management and the board, the audit committee, or other governing body has a clear understanding that information security is a* ***management responsibility****. This responsibility includes* ***all critical information*** *of the organization, regardless of the media in which the information is stored.*

      2. *The chief audit executive should determine that the internal audit activity possesses, or has access to,* ***competent auditing resources*** *to evaluate information security and* ***associated risk exposures****. This includes both* ***internal and external*** *risk exposures, including exposures relating to the organization's relationships with outside entities.*

      3. *Internal auditors should determine that the board, audit committee, or other governing body has sought assurance from management that information security* ***breaches and conditions that might represent a threat*** *to the organization will promptly be made known to those performing the internal auditing activity.*

      4. *Internal auditors should assess the effectiveness of* ***preventive, detective, and mitigative measures*** *against* ***past attacks****, as deemed appropriate, and* ***future attempts*** *or incidents deemed likely to occur. Internal auditors should confirm that the board, audit committee, or other* ***governing body*** *has been* ***appropriately informed*** *of threats, incidents, vulnerabilities exploited, and corrective measures.*

5. *Internal auditors should **periodically assess** the organization's information security practices and **recommend**, as appropriate, enhancements to or implementation of new controls and safeguards. Following an assessment, an **assurance report** should be provided to the board, audit committee, or other appropriate governing body. Such assessments can either be conducted as **separate stand-alone engagements** or as **multiple engagements** integrated into other audits or engagements conducted as part of the approved audit plan.*

PA Summary

- Information security is a **management responsibility** for all critical information regardless of its form.
- The IAA should have **competent auditing resources** for evaluating internal and external risks to information security.
- Internal auditors should determine that the governing body has sought assurance from management that the IAA will be promptly notified about security **breaches and conditions that might represent a threat**.
- Internal auditors assess the effectiveness of **preventive, detective, and mitigative measures** against past and future attacks. The governing body should be appropriately informed.
- Internal auditors also should **periodically assess** security practices, **recommend** new or improved controls, and provide an **assurance report**. Such assessments can be made as **separate engagements** or as **multiple engagements** integrated with other elements of the audit plan.

b. Another aspect of internal auditing's role regarding information security is to evaluate compliance with laws and regulations concerning **privacy**. Thus, internal auditors determine the existence and content of requirements relating to privacy (after consulting with legal counsel). They also determine that systems are designed in accordance with those requirements, compliance is achieved, and compliance is documented.

PRACTICE ADVISORY 2100-8: THE INTERNAL AUDITOR'S ROLE IN EVALUATING AN ORGANIZATION'S PRIVACY FRAMEWORK

1. *Concerns relating to the protection of personal privacy are becoming more apparent, focused, and global as advancements in **information technology and communications** continually introduce new risks and threats to privacy. **Privacy controls are legal requirements** for doing business in most of the world.*

2. *__Privacy definitions vary widely__ depending upon country, culture, political environment, and legal framework. Privacy can encompass **personal** privacy (physical and psychological); privacy of **space** (freedom from surveillance); privacy of **communication** (freedom from monitoring); and privacy of **information** (collection, use, and disclosure of personal information by others). **Personal information** generally refers to information that can be associated with a specific individual or that has identifying characteristics that might be combined with other information to do so. It can include any factual or subjective information, recorded or not, in any form or medium. Personal information might include, for example:*

- *Name, address, identification numbers, income, or blood type;*
- *Evaluations, comments, social status, or disciplinary actions; and*
- *Employee files, credit records, loan records.*

3. *Privacy is a* ***risk management issue****. Failure to protect privacy and personal information with the appropriate controls can have* ***significant consequences*** *for an organization. For example, it can damage the reputation of individuals and the organization, lead to legal liability issues, and contribute to consumer and employee mistrust.*

4. *There are a variety of laws and regulations developing worldwide relating to the protection of personal information. As well, there are generally accepted policies and practices that can be applied to the privacy issue.*

5. *It is clear that good privacy practices contribute to* ***good governance*** *and accountability. The* ***governing body*** *(e.g., the board of directors, head of an agency, or legislative body)* ***is ultimately accountable*** *for ensuring that the principal risks of the organization have been identified and the appropriate systems have been implemented to mitigate those risks. This includes establishing the necessary* ***privacy framework*** *for the organization and monitoring its implementation.*

6. *The internal auditor can contribute to ensuring good governance and accountability by playing a role in helping an organization meet its privacy objectives. The internal auditor is uniquely positioned to* ***evaluate the privacy framework*** *in the organization and* ***identify the significant risks*** *along with the appropriate* ***recommendations*** *for their mitigation.*

7. *In an evaluation of the privacy framework, the internal auditors should consider the following:*
   - *The various* ***laws, regulations, and policies*** *relating to privacy in their respective jurisdictions (including any jurisdiction where the organization conducts business);*
   - *Liaison with* ***in-house legal counsel*** *to determine the exact nature of such laws, regulations, and other standards and practices applicable to the organization and the country/countries in which it does business;*
   - *Liaison with* ***information technology specialists*** *to ensure information security and data protection controls are in place and regularly reviewed and assessed for appropriateness;*
   - *The level or maturity of the organization's* ***privacy practices****. Depending upon the level, the* ***internal auditor may have differing roles****. The auditor may* ***facilitate*** *the development and implementation of the* ***privacy program****, conduct a* ***privacy risk assessment*** *to determine the needs and risk exposures of the organization, or may review and provide* ***assurance*** *on the effectiveness of the privacy policies, practices, and controls across the organization. If the internal auditor assumes a portion of the responsibility for developing and implementing a privacy program, the auditor's* ***independence*** *may be impaired.*

8. *Typically, the internal auditors could be expected to* ***identify*** *the types and appropriateness of* ***information gathered*** *by the organization that is deemed personal or private, the* ***collection methodology*** *used, and whether the organization's use of the information so collected is in accordance with its* ***intended use*** *and the* ***laws****.*

9. *Given the* ***highly technical and legal nature of the topic****, the internal auditor should ensure that the appropriate in-depth* ***knowledge and capacity*** *to conduct any such evaluation of the privacy framework is available, using third-party experts, if necessary.*

PA Summary

- Privacy controls are **legally required** in most countries because advances in **IT and communications** continually create new threats.
- **Privacy definitions** vary: (1) **personal** privacy (physical and psychological); (2) privacy of **space** (freedom from surveillance); (3) privacy of **communication** (freedom from monitoring); and (4) privacy of **information** (collection, use, and disclosure of personal information by others).
  1) **Personal information** is any information that can be associated with a specific individual or that might be combined with other information to do so.
- Privacy is a **risk management issue**. Failing to protect privacy and personal information has significant legal and business consequences for an organization.
- Good privacy practices contribute to **good governance** and accountability. The **governing body** of an organization is **ultimately accountable** for managing privacy risk, e.g., by establishing and monitoring a **privacy framework**.
- The internal auditor **evaluates the privacy framework**, identifies significant risks, and makes recommendations. The internal auditor also considers (1) laws, regulations, and practices in relevant jurisdictions; (2) the advice of legal counsel; and (3) the security efforts of IT specialists.
- Depending on the level or maturity of the organization's **privacy practices**, the role of the internal auditor may be to (1) facilitate the privacy program, (2) do a privacy risk assessment, or (3) perform an assurance service. However, assumption of responsibility may impair **independence**.
- The internal auditor identifies (1) personal **information gathered**, (2) **collection methods**, and (3) whether use of the information is in accordance with its **intended use** and **applicable law**.
- Given the difficulty of the technical and legal issues, the internal auditor should have or obtain the **knowledge and capacity** to evaluate the privacy framework, using outside service providers if needed.

3. *2300* ***<u>Performing the Engagement</u>*** *– Internal auditors should identify, analyze, evaluate, and record sufficient information to achieve the engagement's objectives.*
   a. Laws and regulations concerning privacy also apply to internal auditors.
   b. ***<u>PRACTICE ADVISORY 2300-1: THE INTERNAL AUDITOR'S USE OF PERSONAL INFORMATION IN CONDUCTING AUDITS</u>***
      1. *Concerns relating to the protection of **personal privacy and information** are becoming more apparent, focused, and global as advancements in information technology and communications continually introduce new risks and threats to privacy. **Privacy controls** are legal requirements for doing business in most of the world.*
      2. *Personal information generally refers to information that can be associated with a **specific individual**, or that has identifying characteristics that might be combined with other information to do so. It can include any factual or subjective information, recorded or not, in any form or media. Personal information might include, for example:*
         - *Name, address, identification numbers, income, or blood type;*
         - *Evaluations, comments, social status, or disciplinary actions; and*
         - *Employee files, credit records, loan records.*

3. *For the most part,* ***laws*** *require organizations to* ***identify the purposes*** *for which personal information is collected, at or before the time the information is collected; and that personal information not be used or disclosed for purposes other than those for which it was collected, except with the consent of the individual or as required by law.*
4. *It is important that the internal auditor* ***understands and complies with all laws*** *regarding the use of personal information in the auditor's jurisdiction and those jurisdictions where the organization conducts business.*
5. *The internal auditor must understand that it may be* ***inappropriate****, and in some cases illegal, to access, retrieve, review, manipulate, or use personal information in conducting* ***certain internal audit engagements****.*
6. *The internal auditor should* ***investigate issues*** *before initiating audit effort and seek advice from in-house legal counsel if there are any questions or concerns in this respect.*

PA Summary

- Threats to **personal privacy and information** have increased because of IT and communications advances. Thus, laws require **privacy controls**.
- Personal information identifies a **specific individual**. Examples are identification numbers, income, blood type, evaluations, disciplinary actions, employee files, credit records, and loan records.
- The law usually requires organizations to **identify the purposes** for which personal information is collected, at or before the time it is collected. Its use or disclosure for other purposes is generally prohibited, except with consent or as required by law.
- The internal auditor must **understand and comply with all laws** regarding the use of personal information.
- Access to or use of personal information may be inappropriate or illegal in **certain engagements**.
- The internal auditor should **investigate issues** before initiating audit effort and seek advice from counsel if issues arise regarding use of personal information.

4. Stop and review! You have completed the outline for this subunit. Study multiple-choice questions 15 through 20 beginning on page 159.

4.3 STUDY UNIT 4 SUMMARY

1. Risk management is the responsibility of management. Oversight bodies ensure that processes are in place, adequate, and effective. Internal auditors examine, evaluate, report, and recommend improvements. They also play a consulting role.
2. The entity-wide risk management assessment includes EH&S risks. Given an environmental audit function, the CAE considers the implications for organizational structure, operations, reporting, and the audit plan.
3. The internal audit activity should assist the organization by identifying and evaluating significant exposures to risk and contributing to the improvement of risk management and control systems.
   a. To form an opinion on the adequacy of the process, the internal auditor must determine that (1) the implementation method is understood by key stakeholders and (2) five key objectives are addressed.
4. The organization should have a comprehensive plan to cope with business interruptions. Auditors should assess continuity planning.
5. Information security is a management responsibility for all critical information. The IAA should have competent auditing resources for evaluating internal and external risks to information security.
6. Privacy controls are legally required in most of the world. The governing body of an organization is ultimately accountable for managing privacy risk, e.g., by establishing and monitoring a privacy framework. The internal auditor evaluates the framework, identifies risks, and makes recommendations. The internal auditor considers laws, regulations, and practices; the advice of legal counsel; and the security efforts of IT specialists.
7. Internal auditors must understand and comply with laws protecting personal information.

QUESTIONS

4.1 Risk Management

1. In the risk management process, management's view of the internal audit activity's role is likely to be determined by all of the following factors except

A. Organizational culture.

B. Preferences of the independent auditor.

C. Ability of the internal auditing staff.

D. Local conditions and customs of the country.

Answer (B) is correct. *(Publisher, adapted)*

REQUIRED: The factors influencing management's view on the role of internal audit.

DISCUSSION: It is the role of executive management and the audit committee to determine the role of internal audit in the risk management process. Management's view on internal audit's role is likely to be determined by factors such as the culture of the organization, ability of the internal auditing staff, and local conditions and customs of the country (PA 2100-3).

Answer (A) is incorrect because organizational culture is a factor that influences management's view of the role of internal audit. Answer (C) is incorrect because the ability of the internal auditing staff is a factor that influences management's view of the role of internal audit. Answer (D) is incorrect because local conditions and customs of the country influence management's view of the role of internal audit.

2. Internal auditors can play a more proactive role in assisting with the initial establishment of a risk management process for the organization. However, if such assistance exceeds normal assurance and consulting activities conducted by internal auditors, independence may be impaired. Which of the following impairs the independence of an internal auditor who had participated in the initial establishment of a risk management process?

A. Developing assessments and reports on the risk management process.

B. Managing the identified risks.

C. Evaluating the adequacy and effectiveness of management's risk processes.

D. Implementing controls to address the risks identified.

Answer (B) is correct. *(Publisher, adapted)*

REQUIRED: The activity that impairs independence.

DISCUSSION: A more proactive role in the initial establishment of a risk management process supplements traditional assurance activities with a consultative approach to improving fundamental processes. However, a proactive role in developing a risk management process is not the same as an "ownership of risks" role, which is a role of management (PA 2100-4). The internal auditor cannot assume this role, or any other management, board, or audit committee role in the risk management process, without impairing independence. Boards and audit committees have an oversight role to determine that adequate and effective processes are in place, and managers have the responsibility for the management of the risks identified and for ensuring that sound risk management processes are in place and functioning (PA 2100-3). By managing the identified risks, the internal auditor impairs his/her independence by assuming management's role.

Answer (A) is incorrect because developing assessments and reports on the organization's risk management processes is not only an internal auditing role, but it is normally also a high audit priority. Answer (C) is incorrect because internal auditors should assist both management and the audit committee by examining, evaluating, reporting, and recommending improvements on the adequacy and effectiveness of management's risk processes. Answer (D) is incorrect because internal auditors acting in a consulting role may assist the organization in identifying, evaluating, and implementing risk management methodologies and controls to address those risks (PA 2100-3).

3. Which of the following are key objectives of a risk management process?

I. Risks arising from business strategies and activities are identified and prioritized.

II. Ongoing monitoring activities are conducted to periodically reassess risk and the effectiveness of controls to manage risk.

III. Review of previous risk evaluation reports by management, internal auditors, external auditors, and any other sources that may have issued such reports.

A. I and II only.

B. I and III only.

C. II and III only.

D. I, II, and III.

Answer (A) is correct. *(Publisher, adapted)*

REQUIRED: The items that are key objectives of a risk management process.

DISCUSSION: Internal auditors must determine that the organization's risk management processes address five key objectives to formulate an opinion on the overall adequacy of the risk management processes. The five key objectives of a risk management process are:

- Risks arising from business strategies and activities are identified and prioritized.
- Management and the board have determined the level of risks acceptable to the organization, including the acceptance of risks designed to accomplish the organization's strategic plans.
- Risk mitigation activities are designed and implemented to reduce or otherwise manage risk at levels that were determined to be acceptable to management and the board.
- Ongoing monitoring activities are conducted to periodically reassess risk and the effectiveness of controls to manage risk.
- The board and management receive periodic reports of the results of the risk management processes. The corporate governance processes of the organization should provide periodic communication of risks, risk strategies, and controls to stakeholders.

4. Access to EH&S audit information is severely restricted by all but which of the following classifications?

A. Attorney-client privilege.

B. Accountant-client privilege.

C. Attorney work product.

D. Closely held.

Answer (B) is correct. *(Publisher, adapted)*

REQUIRED: The item that limits access to EH&S audit information.

DISCUSSION: Audit information is often classified as either (a) attorney-client privilege or attorney work product, (b) secret and confidential, or (c) if not confidential, then closely held. This results in severely restricted access to EH&S audit information. The accountant-client privilege, which is not one of the aforementioned classifications, does not limit access to EH&S audit information.

5. Which of the following carries the least environmental, health, and safety risk?

A. A malfunction at a nuclear plant that causes a blackout and results in a loss of public confidence.

B. A chemical plant that disposes of waste in a nearby river.

C. A hydroelectric power plant that is located several miles from a small town.

D. A skyscraper construction site that has had several mishaps, including injuries and death.

Answer (C) is correct. *(Publisher, adapted)*

REQUIRED: The item that poses the least environmental, health, and safety risk.

DISCUSSION: The chief audit executive (CAE) should include the environmental, health, and safety (EH&S) risks in any entity-wide risk management assessment and assess the activities in a balanced manner relative to other types of risk associated with an entity's operations. Among the risk exposures that should be evaluated are: organizational reporting structures; likelihood of causing environmental harm, fines and penalties; expenditures mandated by the Environmental Protection Agency (EPA) or other governmental agencies; history of injuries and deaths; record of losses of customers, and episodes of negative publicity and loss of public image and reputation. As such, based on the risk exposures mentioned, a hydroelectric plant that is located several miles from a small town poses the least EH&S risk.

Answer (A) is incorrect because the blackout risks exposing the plant to negative publicity and a loss of public image and reputation. Answer (B) is incorrect because the disposal of chemical waste into a river increases the likelihood of causing environmental harm, fines, and penalties. Answer (D) is incorrect because the construction site is exposed to risk due to its history of injuries and death.

6. A comprehensive plan to deal with business interruptions will provide for all but which of the following?

A. Segregation of duties.

B. Alternative site facilities.

C. Business impact assessments.

D. Procedures for restoring utility services.

Answer (A) is correct. *(Publisher, adapted)*

REQUIRED: The item that is not included in a comprehensive plan to deal with business interruptions.

DISCUSSION: Auditors should evaluate the organization's readiness to deal with business interruptions. A comprehensive plan would provide for emergency response procedures, alternative communication systems and site facilities, information systems backup, disaster recovery, business impact assessments and resumption plans, procedures for restoring utility services, and maintenance procedures for ensuring the readiness of the organization in the event of an emergency or disaster. Segregation of duties, however, is an audit protocol item in the authentication key area of an audit program.

7. Internal auditors can play a role in an organization's planning for business continuity and disaster recovery. Which of the following is a way in which the internal audit activity helps with the planning phase of a business continuity or disaster recovery plan?

A. Assessing an organization's internal and external environment during the plan formulation process, including the turnover of management, changes in market conditions, and changes in controls.

B. Examining the plan to determine that it reflects the operations that have been included and evaluated in the risk assessment process and contains sufficient internal control concerns and prescriptions.

C. Verifying the adequacy of the plan to ensure the timely resumption of operations and processes after adverse circumstances.

D. Examining the plan to determine whether it is structured to incorporate important changes that could take place over time.

Answer (A) is correct. *(Publisher, adapted)*

REQUIRED: The item that is an internal audit activity in the planning phase of a business continuity or disaster recovery plan.

DISCUSSION: Organizations rely upon internal auditors for analysis of operations and assessment of risk management and control processes. Internal auditors acquire an understanding of the overall business operations, the individual functions, and how they interrelate with one another. This positions the internal audit activity as a valuable resource in evaluating the disaster recovery plan during its formulation process. Internal audit activity can help with an assessment of an organization's internal and external environment. Internal factors that may be considered include the turnover of management and changes in information systems, controls, and major projects and programs. External factors may include changes in outside regulatory and business environment and changes in markets and competitive conditions, international financial and economic conditions, and technologies.

Answer (B) is incorrect because it is an internal audit activity in the evaluation phase of a business continuity or disaster recovery plan. Answer (C) is incorrect because this is part of the internal audit activity's periodic assurance engagements phase of a business continuity or disaster recovery plan. Answer (D) is incorrect because this is part of the internal audit activity's periodic assurance engagements phase of a business continuity or disaster recovery plan.

8. The board's expectations of the internal audit activity regarding the risk management process should be

A. Noted in the work programs for formal consulting engagements.

B. Included in the business continuity plan.

C. Codified in the charters of the internal audit activity and audit committee.

D. Reviewed by the internal auditors immediately following a disaster.

Answer (C) is correct. *(Publisher, adapted)*

REQUIRED: The treatment of the board's expectations of the internal audit activity regarding the risk management process.

DISCUSSION: PA 2100-3 explains that the chief audit executive (CAE) should obtain an understanding of management's and the board's expectations of the internal audit activity in the organization's risk management process. This understanding should be codified in the charters of the internal audit activity and audit committee.

Answer (A) is incorrect because a work program is a listing of specific procedures. Answer (B) is incorrect because business continuity planning is just one element of risk management. Answer (D) is incorrect because the IAA's role should be understood before a crisis.

9. Which of the following is a true statement about the activities of the chief audit executive (CAE) and the chief environmental officer?

A. The chief environmental officer should evaluate whether the environmental auditors are in compliance with recognized professional auditing standards.

B. The CAE should facilitate the reporting of significant environmental risk issues to the audit committee.

C. The CAE does not review the performance of environmental audits when the environmental audit function reports to someone other than the CAE.

D. The activities of the CAE and the chief environmental officer should be completely independent.

Answer (B) is correct. *(Publisher, adapted)*

REQUIRED: The true statement about the activities of the CAE and the chief environmental officer.

DISCUSSION: The following are some suggestions for the CAE (PA 2100-7):

- Foster a close working relationship with the chief environmental officer and coordinate activities with the plan for environmental auditing.
- When the environmental audit function reports to someone other than the CAE, the CAE should review the audit plan and the performance of engagements.
- The CAE should evaluate whether the environmental auditors, who are not part of the CAE's organization, are in compliance with recognized professional auditing standards and a recognized code of ethics.
- The CAE should facilitate the reporting of significant environmental health and safety (EH&S) risk and control issues to the audit (or other board) committee.

Answer (A) is incorrect because the CAE evaluates whether the environmental auditors, who are not part of the CAE's organization, are in compliance with recognized professional auditing standards and code of ethics. Answer (C) is incorrect because the CAE reviews the EH&S audit plan and the performance of engagements when the environmental audit function reports to someone other than the CAE. Answer (D) is incorrect because the CAE should foster a close working relationship with the chief environmental officer and coordinate activities with the plan for environmental auditing.

10. Risk management processes may be all of the following except

A. Quantitative or subjective.

B. Embedded in business units or centralized.

C. Formalized even in small organizations.

D. Formal or informal.

Answer (C) is correct. *(Publisher, adapted)*

REQUIRED: The technique that cannot be used for risk management.

DISCUSSION: Risk management processes should be designed for the nature of an organization's activities. Depending on the size and complexity of the organization's business activities, risk management processes may be formal or informal, quantitative or subjective, or embedded in the business units or centralized at a corporate level. For example, smaller, less complex organizations may use an informal risk committee (PA 2110-1).

11. In forming an opinion on the adequacy of risk management processes, an internal auditor should consider

I. Interviewing line and executive management.
II. Reviewing previous risk evaluation reports.
III. Reviewing corporate policies.
IV. Assessing the appropriateness of reporting lines for risk monitoring activities.

A. I and III only.
B. II and IV only.
C. III only.
D. I, II, III, and IV.

Answer (D) is correct. *(Publisher, adapted)*
REQUIRED: The appropriate procedures for evaluating the adequacy of risk management.
DISCUSSION: Internal auditors must obtain sufficient information to satisfy themselves that the key objectives of the risk management processes are being met. One engagement procedure is interviewing line and executive management to determine business unit objectives, related risks, and management's risk mitigation and control monitoring activities. Another procedure is reviewing previous risk evaluation reports by management, internal auditors, external auditors, and any other sources that may have issued such reports. A third procedure is reviewing corporate policies and minutes of board and audit committee meetings. This procedure helps to determine the organization's business strategies, risk management philosophy and methodology, appetite for risk, and acceptance of risks. A fourth procedure is assessing the appropriateness of reporting lines for risk monitoring activities (PA 2110-1).

12. The review by the internal auditors for design and completeness is part of which of their roles in the creation of a business continuity and disaster recovery plan?

A. Risk analysis.
B. Execution.
C. Evaluation.
D. Performance of assurance engagements.

Answer (C) is correct. *(Publisher, adapted)*
REQUIRED: The audit role in the creation of a business continuity and disaster recovery plan that includes reviewing for design and completeness.
DISCUSSION: Internal auditors are objective participants in the creation of business continuity and disaster recovery plans when they initially review the proposed plans for design, completeness, and overall adequacy. The auditors examine the plan to determine that it reflects the operations that have been included and evaluated in the risk assessment process and contains sufficient internal control concerns and prescriptions (PA 2110-2).
Answer (A) is incorrect because the risk analysis role involves analyzing operations and assessing risk management and control processes to be covered in the business continuity and disaster recovery plan. Answer (B) is incorrect because execution of the business continuity and disaster recovery plan is not part of its creation. Answer (D) is incorrect because the periodic assurance engagements are performed after the plan has been developed and evaluated. The purpose of the engagements is to ensure that the plan does not become outdated.

13. During development of a company's business continuity and flood disaster recovery plan, the internal auditors arranged to meet to identify lessons learned from a disaster and the recovery operations. Which of the following time frames is usually best for this meeting?

A. At least one year following the disaster.
B. During the disaster (for real-time input).
C. Within several months following the disaster.
D. Immediately after the disaster.

Answer (C) is correct. *(Publisher, adapted)*
REQUIRED: The appropriate time for internal auditors to meet to identify lessons learned from a disaster.
DISCUSSION: After a disaster, usually within several months, internal auditors can assist in identifying the lessons learned from the disaster and the recovery operations. Those observations and recommendations may enhance activities to recover resources and update the next version of the business continuity plan (PA 2110-2).
Answer (A) is incorrect because the meeting will be less useful if it occurs too long after the event. For example, memories may have faded and personnel may have changed. Answer (B) is incorrect because efforts are focused on prevention of damage and executing the business continuity plan during the disaster. Answer (D) is incorrect because the internal auditors monitor the effectiveness of the recovery plan immediately after the disaster occurs. They identify improvements in controls and mitigating actions and recommend changes in the plan.

14. What actions may internal auditors consider in a formal consulting engagement if they believe the objectives that should be pursued exceed those requested by management?

I. Document the fact that the objectives were not pursued.

II. Include the objectives in a separate assurance engagement.

A. I only.

B. I or II but not both.

C. Neither I nor II.

D. Both I and II.

Answer (D) is correct. *(Publisher, adapted)*
REQUIRED: The actions internal auditors may consider if the appropriate objectives exceed those requested.
DISCUSSION: In planning formal consulting engagements, internal auditors should design objectives to meet the appropriate needs of management officials receiving those services. Internal auditors may consider the following actions if they believe that the objectives that should be pursued go beyond those requested by management:

- Persuade management to include the additional objectives in the consulting engagement; or
- Document the fact that the objectives were not pursued and disclose that observation in the final communication of consulting engagement results; and
- Include the objectives in a separate and subsequent assurance engagement.

4.2 Information Security and Privacy

15. Security of all critical information of an organization, regardless of the media in which the information is stored, is the responsibility of

A. Shareholders.

B. IT department.

C. Management.

D. All employees.

Answer (C) is correct. *(Publisher, adapted)*
REQUIRED: The responsibility for information security.
DISCUSSION: PA 2100-2 states that internal auditors should determine that management and the board, the audit committee, or other governing body has a clear understanding that information security is a management responsibility.

16. Who determines whether the internal audit activity has access to resources sufficient to evaluate the security of information?

A. The chief executive officer.

B. The chief audit executive.

C. The external auditor.

D. The chief operating officer.

Answer (B) is correct. *(Publisher, adapted)*
REQUIRED: The person responsible for assuring that the IAA has sufficient resources to evaluate information security.
DISCUSSION: The chief audit executive should determine that the internal audit activity possesses, or has access to, competent auditing resources to evaluate information security and associated risk exposures. This includes both internal and external risk exposures, including exposures relating to the organization's relationships with outside entities.

17. Which of the following is part of an organization's governing body's role in protecting against privacy threats?

A. Establishing a privacy framework.

B. Identifying the information gathered by the organization that is deemed personal or private.

C. Identifying the methods used to collect information.

D. Determining whether the use of the information collected is in accordance with its intended use and the laws.

Answer (A) is correct. *(Publisher, adapted)*
REQUIRED: The appropriate role of an organization's governing body in relation to privacy protection.
DISCUSSION: The governing body (e.g., the board of directors, head of an agency, or legislative body) is ultimately accountable for ensuring that the principal risks of the organization have been identified, and the appropriate systems have been implemented to mitigate those risks. This includes establishing the necessary privacy framework for the organization and monitoring its implementation (PA 2100-8).
Answer (B) is incorrect because identification of the information gathered by the organization that is deemed personal or private is a duty of the internal auditors. Answer (C) is incorrect because identification of the collection method used is a duty of the internal auditors. Answer (D) is incorrect because determining whether the use of the information collected is in accordance with its intended use and the laws is a duty of the internal auditors.

18. Freedom from monitoring best describes

A. Personal privacy.

B. Privacy of space.

C. Privacy of communication.

D. Privacy of information.

Answer (C) is correct. *(Publisher, adapted)*

REQUIRED: The type of privacy best described as freedom from monitoring.

DISCUSSION: Privacy can encompass (1) personal privacy (physical and psychological); (2) privacy of space (freedom from surveillance); (3) privacy of communication (freedom from monitoring); and (4) privacy of information (collection, use, and disclosure of personal information by others) (PA 2100-8).

Answer (A) is incorrect because personal privacy is physical and psychological. Answer (B) is incorrect because privacy of space is freedom from surveillance. Answer (D) is incorrect because privacy of information is freedom from collection, use, and disclosure of personal information by others.

19. What should the internal auditor consider to ensure that information security and data protection controls are in place?

A. The applicable laws, regulations, and policies relating to privacy.

B. Liaison with in-house legal counsel.

C. Liaison with information technology specialists.

D. All of the answers are considerations for information security and data protection controls.

Answer (D) is correct. *(Publisher, adapted)*

REQUIRED: The auditor consideration for ensuring that information security and data protection controls are in place.

DISCUSSION: In an evaluation of the privacy framework, PA 2100-8 states that the internal auditor should consider the following:

- The various laws, regulations, and policies relating to privacy in their respective jurisdictions.
- Liaison with in-house legal counsel to determine the exact nature of such laws, regulations, and other standards and practices applicable to the organization and the countries in which it does business.
- Liaison with information technology specialists to ensure information security and data protection controls are in place and regularly reviewed and assessed for appropriateness.

Answer (A) is incorrect because the auditor should also consider liaisons with in-house counsel and information technology specialists. Answer (B) is incorrect because the auditor should also consider the applicable laws, regulations, and policies relating to privacy and liaison with information technology specialists. Answer (C) is incorrect because the auditor should also consider the applicable laws, regulations, and policies relating to privacy and liaison with in-house legal counsel.

20. Personal information may include

I. Blood type
II. Social status
III. Loan records
IV. Disciplinary actions

A. I, II, and IV only.

B. I only.

C. I and II only.

D. I, II, III, and IV.

Answer (D) is correct. *(Publisher, adapted)*

REQUIRED: The item(s) that may be personal information.

DISCUSSION: PA 2300-1 gives the following examples of information that may be personal: (1) blood type, (2) social status, (3) loan records, (4) disciplinary actions, (5) name, (6) address, (7) identification numbers, (8) income, (9) evaluations, (10) comments, (11) employee files, and (12) credit records.

Answer (A) is incorrect because loan records are considered personal information. Answer (B) is incorrect because social status, loan records, and disciplinary actions are considered personal information. Answer (C) is incorrect because loan records and disciplinary actions are considered personal information.

STUDY UNIT FIVE
CONTROL I

(20 pages of outline)

This is the first of two study units on control. It emphasizes pronouncements of The IIA and certain theoretical considerations. Study Unit 6 enlarges upon these considerations, especially with regard to control frameworks. It also extends to the implications of organizational structures and leadership styles and the management of change and conflict.

Governance, risk, and control are interrelated concepts that are fundamental to the field of internal auditing and the work of internal auditors. Study Unit 3 primarily addressed their role in governance. Study Unit 4 primarily addressed the role of internal auditors in risk management. Study Units 5 and 6 relate to control.

According to the **definition of internal auditing**, internal auditors help an organization accomplish its objectives by bringing a systematic, disciplined approach to evaluating and improving the effectiveness of risk management, control, and governance processes. The **Glossary** appended to the Standards defines **control** as follows:

> *Any action taken by management, the board, and other parties to enhance risk management and increase the likelihood that established objectives and goals will be achieved. Management plans, organizes, and directs the performance of sufficient actions to provide reasonable assurance that objectives and goals will be achieved.*

Practice Advisory 2100-1 provides another definition of control:

> *Control is any action taken by management to enhance the likelihood that established objectives and goals will be achieved. Controls may be **preventive** (to deter undesirable events from occurring), **detective** (to detect and correct undesirable events that have occurred), or **directive** (to cause or encourage a desirable event to occur). The concept of a system of control is the integrated collection of control components and activities that are used by an organization to achieve its objectives and goals.*

The definition in Practice Advisory 2100-1 describes three categories of controls. When such controls are absent or are too costly relative to their benefits, **mitigating (compensating) controls** should be in place. Examples are supervisory review when segregation of duties (a preventive control) is not feasible or monitoring of budget variances in the absence of transaction processing controls.

One General Performance Standard and one Specific Performance Standard are relevant to all subunits in this study unit.

2100 ***<u>Nature of Work</u>*** *– The internal audit activity evaluates and contributes to the improvement of risk management, control, and governance processes using a systematic and disciplined approach.*

> ***2120*** ***<u>Control</u>*** *– The internal audit activity should assist the organization in maintaining effective controls by evaluating their effectiveness and efficiency and by promoting continuous improvement.*

One Implementation Standard is relevant to the first four subunits.

2120.A1 – *Based on the results of the risk assessment, the internal audit activity should evaluate the adequacy and effectiveness of controls encompassing the organization's governance, operations, and information systems. This should include:*

- *Reliability and integrity of financial and operational information*
- *Effectiveness and efficiency of operations*
- *Safeguarding of assets*
- *Compliance with laws, regulations, and contracts*

Core Concepts

- Control is any action to enhance risk management and increase the probability of achieving objectives. The management functions of planning, organizing, and directing should provide reasonable assurance of achieving objectives.
- Controls may be preventive, detective, directive, or mitigating.
- The IAA evaluates the effectiveness and efficiency of controls and promotes continuous improvement.
- In assurance engagements, the IAA evaluates the adequacy and effectiveness of controls over governance, operations, and IS. The evaluation extends to reliability and integrity of information, effectiveness and efficiency of operations, safeguarding of assets, and compliance.
- The board is responsible for governance processes and obtaining assurance about risk management and control.
- The board relies on management to maintain effective control but reinforces that reliance with independent oversight.
- Internal auditors should determine the extent to which adequate criteria have been established to evaluate controls.

5.1 ASSESSING CONTROL

1. The following Practice Advisory addresses the role of the internal audit activity in evaluating the organization's control systems.
   a. ***PRACTICE ADVISORY 2120.A1-1: ASSESSING AND REPORTING ON CONTROL PROCESSES***
      1. *One of the tasks of a* ***board*** *of directors is to establish and maintain the organization's* ***governance processes*** *and obtain assurances concerning the effectiveness of the* ***risk management and control processes****.* ***Senior management's role*** *is to oversee the establishment, administration, and assessment of that system of risk management and control processes. The purpose of that multifaceted system of control processes is to support people of the organization in the management of risks and the achievement of the established and communicated* ***objectives*** *of the enterprise. More specifically, those* ***control processes*** *are expected to ensure, among other things, that the following conditions exist:*
         - *Financial and operational information is reliable and possesses integrity.*
         - *Operations are performed efficiently and achieve effective results.*
         - *Assets are safeguarded.*
         - *Actions and decisions of the organization are in compliance with laws, regulations, and contracts.*

2. *Among the responsibilities of the organization's **managers** is the **assessment** of the **control processes in their respective areas**. Internal and external **auditors** provide varying degrees of assurance about the state of effectiveness of the risk management and control processes in select activities and functions of the organization.*
3. *Senior management and the audit committee normally expect that the **chief audit executive** will perform sufficient engagement work and gather other available information during the year so as to form a judgment about the **adequacy and effectiveness of the control processes**. The chief audit executive should communicate that overall judgment about the organization's system of controls to senior management and the audit committee. A growing number of organizations have included a **management's report** on the system of internal controls in their annual or periodic reports to external stakeholders.*
4. *The chief audit executive should develop a **proposed engagement plan** for the coming year that ensures that sufficient information will be obtained to evaluate the effectiveness of the control processes. The plan should call for engagements or other procedures to gather relevant information about **all major operating units and business functions**. The engagement plan should also give special consideration to those operations most affected by **recent or expected changes**. Those changes in circumstances may result from marketplace or investment conditions, acquisitions and divestitures, or restructures and new ventures. The proposed plan should be **flexible** so that adjustments may be made during the year as a result of changes in management strategies, external conditions, or revised expectations about achieving the organization's objectives.*
5. *In determining the proposed engagement plan, the chief audit executive should consider **relevant work** that will be performed **by others**. To minimize duplication and inefficiencies, the work planned or recently completed by **management** in its assessments of controls and quality improvement processes as well as the work planned by the **external auditors** should be considered in determining the expected coverage of the audit plan for the coming year.*
6. *Finally, the chief audit executive should evaluate the **coverage of the proposed plan** from two viewpoints: **adequacy** across organizational entities and **inclusion** of a variety of transaction and business-process types. If the **scope** of the proposed engagement plan is insufficient to enable the expression of assurance about the organization's control processes, the chief audit executive should inform senior management and the audit committee of the expected deficiency, its causes, and the probable consequences.*
7. *The challenge for the internal audit activity is to evaluate the effectiveness of the organization's system of controls based on the aggregation of **many individual assessments**. Those assessments are largely gained from internal auditing engagements, management's self-assessments, and external auditor's work. As the engagements progress, internal auditors should **communicate, on a timely basis**, the observations to the appropriate levels of management so that prompt action can be taken to correct or mitigate the consequences of discovered control discrepancies or weaknesses.*

8. Three key **considerations in reaching an evaluation** of the overall effectiveness of the organization's control processes are
   - Were **significant discrepancies or weaknesses** discovered from the audit work performed and other assessment information gathered?
   - If so, were **corrections or improvements** made after the discoveries?
   - Do the discoveries and their consequences lead to the conclusion that a **pervasive condition** exists, resulting in an unacceptable level of business risk?

   The **temporary existence** of a significant control discrepancy or weakness does not necessarily lead to the judgment that it is pervasive and poses an unacceptable residual risk. The pattern of discoveries, degree of intrusion, and level of consequences and exposures are **factors to be considered** in determining whether the effectiveness of the whole system of controls is jeopardized and unacceptable risks exist. The **report of the chief audit executive** on the state of the organization's control processes should be presented, usually once a year, to senior management and the audit committee.
9. **The report** should emphasize the critical role played by the control processes in the quest to achieve the organization's objectives, and it should refer to major work performed by internal audit and to other important sources of information that were used to formulate the overall assurance judgment. The **opinion section** of the report is normally expressed in terms of **negative assurance**; that is, the engagement work performed for the period and other information gathered did not disclose any significant weaknesses in the control processes that have a pervasive effect. If the control deficiencies or weaknesses are **significant and pervasive**, the assurance section of the report may be a **qualified or adverse opinion**, depending on the projected increase in the level of residual risk and its impact on the organization's objectives.
10. **The target audiences for the annual report** are senior executives and audit committee members. Because these readers have divergent understandings of auditing and business, the chief audit executive's annual report should be clear, concise, and informative. It should be composed and edited to be understandable by them and targeted to meet their **informational needs**. Its value to these readers can be enhanced by including **major recommendations** for improvement and information about current control issues and trends, such as technology and information security exposures, patterns of control discrepancies or weaknesses across business units, and potential difficulties in complying with laws or regulations.
11. Ample evidence exists of an **"expectation gap"** surrounding the internal audit activity's work in evaluating and providing assurance about the state of control processes. One such gap exists between management and the audit committee's normally high expectations about the value of internal auditing services and the internal auditor's more modest expectations that derive from knowledge of practical limitations on audit coverage and from self-doubt about generating sufficient evidence to support an informed and objective judgment. The chief audit executive should be mindful of the possible gap between what is presumed by the report reader and what actually happened during the year. He or she should use the report as another way to address different mental models and to suggest improving the capacity of the function or reducing the constraints to access and audit effectiveness.

PA Summary

- The **board** is responsible for **governance processes** and obtaining assurance about risk **management and control.** **Senior management** oversees the establishment, administration, and assessment of risk management and control processes. The purpose of control is to support risk management and achievement of objectives. Control ensures (1) the reliability and integrity of information; (2) efficient and effective performance; (3) safeguarding of assets; and (4) compliance with laws, regulations, contracts.
- **Each manager** assesses control in his/her area. **Auditors** provide assurance about the effectiveness of risk management and control.
- **The CAE** should gather sufficient information to judge the **adequacy and effectiveness** of control. This judgment should be communicated to senior management and the board. Also, a **management report on control** may be included in annual or periodic reports to external parties.
- The IAA's **proposed engagement plan** should provide sufficient information to evaluate control. The plan should be flexible enough to permit adjustments during the year and should cover all major operations and functions. It also should give special consideration to operations most affected by **recent or expected changes**. Furthermore, the plan should consider **relevant work** that will be performed **by others**, including (1) management's assessments of control and quality processes and (2) the work planned by external auditors.
- The plan's **coverage** should be adequate across organizational entities and inclusive of transaction and business-process types. If the **scope** of the plan is insufficient to give assurance about control, the CAE should inform senior management and the audit committee about causes and probable consequences of the insufficiency.
- The evaluation of control combines **many individual assessments**. Communication of engagement **observations** should be timely.
- The **overall evaluation** of control considers whether (1) significant weaknesses or discrepancies exist, (2) corrections or improvements were made, and (3) a pervasive condition leading to unacceptable risk exists.
- Whether **unacceptable risk** exists because the effectiveness of the whole system of controls is jeopardized depends on the (1) pattern of discoveries, (2) degree of intrusion, and (3) level of consequences.
- The CAE's report on the organization's control processes should be presented, usually once a year, to senior management and the audit committee. The **opinion section** usually expresses **negative assurance**. But, a qualified or adverse opinion is expressed if the control deficiencies or weaknesses are **significant and pervasive.**
- The report should be clear, concise, and informative and targeted to the **needs** of senior management and the audit committee. It should contain **major recommendations** about current control issues and trends.
- The CAE should be aware of the "**expectation gap.**" One such gap is between high expectations about the value of internal auditing and the auditor's more modest expectations based on limitations on audit coverage and doubt about generating sufficient evidence to support an informed judgment. Another gap lies between what is presumed by the report reader and what actually happened. Thus, the CAE should use the report to suggest improving the capacity of the audit function or reducing the limits on access and audit effectiveness.

2. Stop and review! You have completed the outline for this subunit. Study multiple-choice questions 1 through 11 beginning on page 181.

5.2 CONTROL SELF-ASSESSMENT (CSA)

1. The following Practice Advisory describes self-assessment methods and the role of the internal auditors in the process.

   a. ***PRACTICE ADVISORY 2120.A1-2: USING CONTROL SELF-ASSESSMENT FOR ASSESSING THE ADEQUACY OF CONTROL PROCESSES***

      1. ***Senior management*** *is charged with overseeing the establishment, administration, and evaluation of the processes of risk management and control.* ***Operating managers'*** *responsibilities include assessment of the risks and controls in their units. Internal and external* ***auditors*** *provide varying degrees of assurance about the state of effectiveness of the risk management and control processes of the organization. Both managers and auditors have an interest in using techniques and tools that* ***sharpen the focus and expand the efforts to assess risk management and control*** *processes that are in place and to identify ways to improve their effectiveness.*

      2. *A methodology encompassing* ***self-assessment surveys*** *and* ***facilitated workshops*** *called CSA is a useful and efficient approach for managers and internal auditors to collaborate in assessing and evaluating control procedures. In its purest form, CSA* ***integrates business objectives and risks with control processes****. Control self-assessment is also referred to as "control/risk self-assessment" or "CRSA." Although CSA practitioners use a number of differing techniques and formats, most implemented programs* ***share some key features and goals****. An organization that uses self-assessment will have a* ***formal, documented process*** *that allows management and work teams, who are directly involved in a business unit, function, or process, to participate in a structured manner for the* ***purpose*** *of*

         - *Identifying risks and exposures*
         - *Assessing the control processes that mitigate or manage those risks*
         - *Developing action plans to reduce risks to acceptable levels*
         - *Determining the likelihood of achieving the business objectives*

      3. ***The outcomes*** *that may be derived from self-assessment methodologies are*

         - *People in the business units become* ***trained*** *and experienced in* ***assessing risks*** *and* ***associating control processes*** *with managing those risks and improving the chances of achieving business objectives.*
         - ***Informal, "soft" controls*** *are more easily identified and evaluated.*
         - *People are motivated to take* ***"ownership"*** *of the control processes in their units, and corrective actions taken by the work teams are often more effective and timely.*
         - *The entire objectives-risks-controls infrastructure of an organization is subject to greater* ***monitoring and continuous improvement****.*
         - ***Internal auditors*** *become involved in and knowledgeable about the self-assessment process by serving as facilitators, scribes, and reporters for the work teams and as trainers of risk and control concepts supporting the CSA program.*

- *Internal audit activity acquires **more information** about the control processes within the organization and can leverage that additional information in allocating their scarce resources so as to spend a greater effort in investigating and performing tests of business units or functions that have significant control weaknesses or high residual risks.*
- ***Management's responsibility** for the risk management and control processes of the organization is reinforced, and managers will be less tempted to abdicate those activities to specialists, such as auditors.*
- *The primary role of the internal audit activity will continue to include the **validation of the evaluation process** by performing tests and the expression of its professional judgment on the adequacy and effectiveness of the whole risk management and control systems.*

4. *The wide **variety of approaches** used for CSA processes in organizations reflects the differences in industry, geography, structure, organizational culture, degree of employee empowerment, dominant management style, and the manner of formulating strategies and policies. That observation suggests that the success of a particular type of CSA program in one enterprise may not be replicated in another organization. The **CSA process should be customized** to fit the unique characteristics of each organization. Also, it suggests that a CSA approach needs to be **dynamic** and change with the continual development of the organization.*
5. *The **three primary forms of CSA** programs are facilitated team workshops, surveys, and management-produced analysis. Organizations often combine more than one approach.*
6. ***Facilitated team workshops** gather information from work teams representing different levels in the business unit or function. The format of the workshop may be based on objectives, risks, controls, or processes.*
   - ***Objective-based format** focuses on the best way to accomplish a business objective. The workshop begins by **identifying the controls presently in place** to support the objective and then determining the residual risks remaining. The aim of the workshop is to decide whether the control procedures are working effectively and are resulting in residual risks within an acceptable level.*
   - ***Risk-based format** focuses on **listing the risks** to achieving an objective. The workshop begins by listing all possible barriers, obstacles, threats, and exposures that might prevent achieving an objective and then examining the control procedures to determine if they are sufficient to manage the key risks. The aim of the workshop is to determine significant residual risks. This format takes the work team through the **entire objective-risks-controls** formula.*
   - ***Control-based format** focuses on how well the **controls in place are working**. This format is different from the two above because **the facilitator identifies the key risks and controls** before the beginning of the workshop. During the workshop, the work team assesses how well the controls mitigate risks and promote the achievement of objectives. The aim of the workshop is to produce an analysis of the gap between how controls are working and how well management expects those controls to work.*

- ***Process-based format*** *focuses on selected activities that are elements of a chain of processes. The processes are usually a series of related activities that go from some beginning point to an end, such as the various steps in purchasing, product development, or revenue generation. This type of workshop usually covers the identification of the* ***objectives of the whole process and the various intermediate steps****. The aim of the workshop is to evaluate, update, validate, improve, and even streamline the whole process and its component activities. This workshop format may have a greater breadth of analysis than a control-based approach by covering multiple objectives within the process and by supporting concurrent management efforts, such as reengineering, quality improvement, and continuous improvement initiatives.*

7. *The* ***survey form of CSA*** *uses a questionnaire that tends to ask mostly simple "Yes/No" or "Have/Have Not" questions that are carefully written to be understood by the target recipients. Surveys are often used if the desired respondents are too numerous or widely dispersed to participate in a workshop. They are also preferred if the culture in the organization may hinder open, candid discussions in workshop settings or if management desires to minimize the time spent and costs incurred in gathering the information.*

8. *The form of self-assessment called* ***"management-produced analyses"*** *covers most other approaches by management groups to produce information about selected business processes, risk management activities, and control procedures. The analysis is often intended to reach an informed and timely judgment about* ***specific characteristics of control*** *procedures and is commonly* ***prepared by a team in a staff or support role****. The internal auditor may synthesize this analysis with other information to enhance the understanding about controls and to share the knowledge with managers in business or functional units as part of the organization's CSA program.*

9. *All self-assessment programs assume that managers and members of the work teams possess an* ***understanding of risks and control concepts*** *and use those concepts in communications. For training sessions, to facilitate the orderly flow of workshop discussions and as a check on the completeness of the overall process,* ***organizations often use a control framework****, such as the* ***COSO*** *(Committee of Sponsoring Organizations) and* ***CoCo*** *(Canadian Criteria of Control Board) models.*

10. *In the typical CSA* ***facilitated workshop****, a report will be largely created during the deliberations. A group consensus will be recorded for the various segments of the discussions, and the group will review the* ***proposed final report*** *before the end of the final session. Some programs will use anonymous voting techniques to ensure the free flow of information and viewpoints during the workshops and to aid in negotiating differences between viewpoints and interest groups.*

11. ***Internal audit's investment in some CSA programs*** *is fairly significant. It may sponsor, design, implement and, in effect, own the process; conduct the training; supply the facilitators, scribes, and reporters; and orchestrate the participation of management and work teams.* ***In other CSA programs, internal audit's involvement is minimal****, serving as interested party and consultant of the whole process and as ultimate verifier of the evaluations produced by the teams. In most programs, internal audit's investment in the organization's CSA efforts is somewhere between the two extremes described on the previous page. As the level of internal audit's involvement in the CSA program and individual workshop deliberations increases, the* ***chief audit executive should monitor the objectivity of the internal audit staff****, take steps to* ***manage that objectivity*** *(if necessary), and* ***augment internal audit testing*** *to ensure that bias or partiality do not affect the final judgments of the staff.* ***Standard 1120*** *states: "Internal auditors should have an impartial, unbiased attitude and avoid conflicts of interest."*
12. *A CSA program* ***augments the traditional role of the internal audit activity*** *by assisting management in fulfilling its responsibilities to establish and maintain risk management and control processes and to evaluate the adequacy of that system. Through a CSA program, the internal audit activity and the business units and functions* ***collaborate to produce better information*** *about how well the* ***control processes are working*** *and how significant the* ***residual risks*** *are.*
13. *Although providing staff support for the CSA program as facilitator and specialist, the internal audit activity often finds that it* ***may reduce the effort spent in gathering information about control procedures and eliminate some testing****. A CSA program should increase the coverage of assessing control processes across the organization, improve the quality of corrective actions made by the process owners, and focus internal audit's work on* ***reviewing high-risk processes and unusual situations****. It can focus on validating the evaluation conclusions produced by the CSA process, synthesizing the information gathered from the components of the organization, and expressing its overall judgment about the effectiveness of controls to senior management and the audit committee.*

PA Summary

- **Senior management** oversees the processes of risk management and control **(RMC)**. **Operating managers** assess risks and controls in their units. **Auditors** provide assurance about the effectiveness of RMC processes. All want to (1) **sharpen the focus of, and expand efforts to assess**, RMC processes and (2) improve their effectiveness.
- **Control self-assessment (CSA)** is a collaboration between managers and auditors to **evaluate control**. CSA **integrates business objectives and risks with control processes**. Programs vary but share key features. A **formal, documented** process allows those directly involved to participate in (1) identifying risks and exposures, (2) assessing relevant controls, (3) developing plans, and (4) estimating the probability of achieving objectives.
- **Outcomes** of CSA may include (1) **training** in assessment of the objectives-risks-controls infrastructure, (2) recognition of **soft** controls, (3) willingness to take **ownership** of control that results in more effective and timely **corrective action**, (4) greater monitoring and continuous improvement, (5) greater **internal auditor** knowledge of CSA, (6) **more information** about control and better **allocation of resources** to audits of control, (7) reinforcement of **management's responsibility** for control, and (8) continuation of the IAA's primary role in **validation of the evaluation process** by testing and expressing judgment on the adequacy and effectiveness of the RMC process.
- The **variety of approaches** used for CSA reflects the differences among organizations. Accordingly, the CSA process should be customized to fit the organization. CSA also should change as the organization develops.
- The **facilitated team workshop** form of CSA may be based on (1) objectives, (2) risks, (3) controls, or (4) processes. A **final report** should reflect the group consensus.
- **Objective-based format** focuses on the best way to accomplish an objective. It **identifies relevant controls** and determines the **residual risks**. The aim is to decide whether controls are effective and result in acceptable residual risks.
- **Risk-based format** focuses on **listing the risks** of achieving an objective and examining the controls to determine whether they suffice to manage the key risks. The aim is to determine significant residual risks.
- **Control-based format** differs because **the facilitator identifies the key risks and controls** before the workshop begins. The work team assesses how well the controls mitigate risks and promote the achievement of objectives. The aim is to analyze the gap between actual and expected performance of controls.
- **Process-based format** focuses on selected activities in a chain of processes. The processes are a series of related activities from a beginning to an end, such as the steps in purchasing. This workshop format identifies the **objectives of the whole process and the intermediate steps**. The aim is to improve the whole process and its activities. This format may have greater breadth than a control-based approach. It covers multiple objectives within the process and supports such efforts as reengineering, quality improvement, and continuous improvement.
- The **survey** form of CSA uses a simple questionnaire. Surveys are often used when a workshop is impracticable, the culture may hinder open discussions, or the time spent and costs incurred must be minimized.
- The **management analysis** form of CSA often addresses specific aspects of control and is prepared by support staff. The internal auditor may combine this and other information to better understand controls and to share knowledge with managers.

- CSA programs assume an **understanding of risk and control concepts**. Thus, CSA often uses a **control framework**, e.g., COSO or CoCo, that facilitates training and discussion and serves as a check on the completeness of the process.
- **Internal audit's involvement** in CSA may range from ownership of the process to service as a consultant. As involvement in the CSA program and workshop deliberations increases, the CAE **should monitor the objectivity of the internal audit staff**, **manage that objectivity** (if necessary), and **augment testing** to ensure that bias does not affect final judgments.
- The IAA and business units collaborate in CSA to produce **better information** about the effectiveness of controls and the significance of residual risks.
- A CSA program may **reduce the audit effort** devoted to control. It should increase the coverage of control assessments, improve the quality of corrective action, and focus audit work on **reviewing high-risk processes and unusual situations**.

2. Stop and review! You have completed the outline for this subunit. Study multiple-choice questions 12 through 24 beginning on page 184.

5.3 INTERIM REPORTS, DISCLOSURE, AND CERTIFICATION

1. The following is adapted from a Practice Advisory. It covers the role of internal auditors with respect to certain legislative and regulatory requirements. These enactments are responses to scandals that have undermined investor confidence.
   a. *The strength of all financial markets depends on **investor confidence**. Events involving allegations of misdeeds by business executives, independent auditors, and other market participants have undermined that confidence. In response to this threat, a growing number of **legislative bodies and regulatory agencies** in various countries have passed legislation and regulations affecting **disclosures** and **financial reporting**.*
   b. ***Recommended actions for internal auditors.** The following actions and considerations are offered to internal auditors as value-added services that can be provided regarding **interim financial reports, disclosures, and management certifications**.*
      1) *The **internal auditor's role** in such processes may range from initial designer of the process to participant on a disclosure committee, to coordinator or liaison between management and its auditors, or to independent assessor of the process.*
      2) *All internal auditors involved in interim reporting and disclosure processes should have a clearly defined role and evaluate responsibilities with appropriate IIA **Consulting and Assurance Standards** and with guidance contained in related **Practice Advisories**.*
      3) *Internal auditors should ensure that organizations have a **formal policy** and **documented procedures** to govern processes for interim financial reports, related disclosures, and regulatory reporting requirements. Appropriate **review** of any policies and procedures by attorneys, external auditors, and other **experts** can offer additional comfort that policies and procedures are comprehensive and accurately reflect applicable requirements.*

4) Internal auditors should encourage organizations to establish a **"disclosure committee"** to coordinate the process and provide oversight to participants. Representatives from **key areas of the organization** should be represented on the committee, including key financial managers, legal counsel, risk management, internal audit, and any area providing input or data for the regulatory filings and disclosures. Normally the chief audit executive (CAE) should be a member of the disclosure committee. Consideration should be given to the CAE's status on the committee. CAEs who serve as committee chairs or regular or "voting" members need to be aware of **independence considerations** and are advised to review IIA Standards and related Practice Advisories for guidance and required disclosures. Status as an "ex-officio" member normally would not create independence problems.

5) Internal auditors should **periodically review and evaluate** interim reporting and disclosure processes, disclosure committee activities, and related documentation and provide management and the audit committee with an **assessment of the process and assurance concerning overall operations and compliance with policies and procedures**. Internal auditors whose independence may be impaired due to their assigned role in the process should ensure that management and the audit committee are able to obtain appropriate assurance about the process from **other sources**. Other sources can include internal self-assessments as well as third parties such as external auditors and consultants.

6) Internal auditors should **recommend appropriate improvements** to the policies, procedures, and process for interim reporting and related disclosures based on the results of an assessment of related activities. **Recommended best practices** for such activities may include all, or components of, the following tools and procedures, depending on the specific process used by each organization:

a) Properly documented policies, procedures, controls, and monitoring reports
b) Interim period checklist of procedures and key control elements
c) Standardized control reports on key disclosure controls
d) Management self-assessments (such as CSA)
e) Sign-offs or representation statements from key managers
f) Review of draft regulatory filings prior to submission
g) Process maps to document the source of data elements for regulatory filings, key controls, and responsible parties for each element
h) Follow-up on previously reported outstanding items
i) Consideration of internal audit reports issued during the period
j) Special or specifically targeted reviews of high-risk, complex, and problem areas, including material accounting estimates, reserve valuations, off-balance sheet activities, major subsidiaries, joint ventures, and special-purpose entities
k) Observation of the "closing process" for the financial statements and related adjusting entries, including waived adjustments
l) Conference calls with key management from remote locations to ensure appropriate consideration of and participation by all major components of the organization
m) Review of potential and pending litigation and contingent liabilities
n) CAE report on internal control, issued at least annually and possibly more frequently
o) Regularly scheduled disclosure and audit committee meetings

7) *Internal auditors should compare processes for complying with legal or regulatory requirements for interim reporting and disclosures with those for assessing and publicly reporting on **internal controls**. Processes designed to be similar or compatible will contribute to operational efficiencies and reduce the likelihood or risk for problems and errors to occur or go undetected. **While processes and procedures may be similar, it is possible that the internal auditor's role may vary.** In some organizations, the work of internal auditors may form the basis for **management's assertions** about internal control. But in other organizations internal auditors may be called upon to **evaluate a required assessment by management**.*

a) *The nature of internal audit's work, and of its use, can potentially affect the treatment or degree of **reliance** placed upon the internal auditor's work by the **external auditor**. Internal auditors should ensure that each participant's role is clarified and activities are coordinated and agreed upon with management and the external auditors.*

b) *In organizations in which **management conducts its own assessment** of controls as the basis for an opinion, internal auditors should evaluate management's assessment and supporting documentation.*

c) *Internal auditors should evaluate how internal audit report comments are classified and ensure that **comments that may be subject to disclosure** in interim reports or an annual report on internal controls are **appropriately communicated** to management and the audit committee. Extra care should be taken to ensure such comments are adequately resolved in a timely manner.*

2. Stop and review! You have completed the outline for this subunit. Study multiple-choice questions 25 through 27 beginning on page 188.

5.4 AUDITING FINANCIAL REPORTING

1. The Practice Advisory in this subunit complements the material in the prior subunit. It too addresses the internal auditor's role in responding to requirements for organizations to improve their governance and financial reporting processes.

a. ***PRACTICE ADVISORY 2120.A1-4: AUDITING THE FINANCIAL REPORTING PROCESS***

1. *The published reports of **corporate governance failures** in various countries underscore the need for change to achieve greater **accountability and transparency** by all organizations -- profit-making, nonprofit, and governmental. Senior management, boards of directors, internal auditors, and external auditors are the cornerstones of the foundation on which effective organizational governance is built. The **internal audit activity** plays a key role in support of good organizational governance; it has a unique position to assist in improving an organization's operations by evaluating and improving the effectiveness of risk management, control, and governance processes. Recent initiatives have put the spotlight on the need for **senior management** to be more **accountable** for the information contained in an organization's financial reports. Senior management and the audit committee of many organizations are requesting additional services from the internal audit activity to **improve the governance and financial reporting processes**. These requests include evaluations of the organization's internal controls over financial reporting and the reliability and integrity of its financial report.*

Reporting on Internal Control

2. *An organization's audit or other board committee and internal audit activity have **interlocking goals**. The core role of the chief audit executive (CAE) is to ensure that the audit committee receives the **support and assurance services** it needs and requests. One of the primary objectives of the audit committee is **oversight** of the organization's **financial reporting processes** to ensure their reliability and fairness. The committee and senior management typically request that the internal audit activity perform sufficient audit work and gather other available information during the year to **form an opinion on the adequacy and effectiveness of the internal control processes**. The CAE normally communicates that overall evaluation, on a timely basis, to the committee. The committee will evaluate the coverage and adequacy of the CAE's report and may incorporate its conclusion in the committee's report to the governing board.*

3. *The internal audit activity's **work plans and specific assurance engagements** begin with a careful **identification of the exposures** facing the organization, and internal audit's work plan is based on the risks and the **assessment of the risk management and control processes** maintained by management to mitigate those risks. Among the events and transactions included in the identification of risks are*

   - *New businesses, including mergers and acquisitions*
   - *New products and systems*
   - *Joint ventures and partnerships*
   - *Restructuring*
   - *Management estimates, budgets, and forecasts*
   - *Environmental matters*
   - *Regulatory compliance*

A Framework for Internal Control

4. *The assessment of a system of internal control of an organization should employ a broad definition of control. The IIA believes that the most effective internal control guidance available today is the report **Internal Control – Integrated Framework**, published in 1992 and 1994 by the Committee of Sponsoring Organizations (COSO) of the Treadway Commission. While use of the COSO model is widely accepted, it may be appropriate to use some **other recognized and credible model**. Sometimes, regulatory or legal requirements will specify the use of a particular model or control design for an organization or industry within a country*

5. *Several **conclusions** in the Internal Control – Integrated Framework report are relevant to this discussion.*

   - *Internal control is **defined broadly**; it is not limited to accounting controls and is not narrowly restricted to financial reporting.*
   - *While accounting and financial reports are important issues, there are **other important aspects of the business**, such as resource protection, operational efficiency and effectiveness, and compliance with rules, regulations, and organization policies. These factors also have an impact on financial reporting.*
   - *Internal control is **management's responsibility** and requires the participation of all persons within an organization if it is to be effective.*
   - *The control framework is tied to the **business objectives** and is **flexible** enough to be adaptable.*

Reporting on the Effectiveness of Internal Control

6. *The CAE should provide to the audit committee internal audit's* ***assessment of the effectiveness of the organization's system of controls****, including its judgment on the* ***adequacy of the control model or design****. A governing board must rely on management to maintain an adequate and effective internal control system. It will reinforce that reliance with* ***independent oversight****. The board or its audit (or other designated) committee should ask the following questions, and the CAE may be expected to assist in answering them.*

   (a) ***Is there a strong ethical environment and culture?***

   - *Do board members and senior executives set examples of high integrity?*
   - *Are performance and incentive targets realistic, or do they create the excessive pressure for short-term results?*
   - *Is the organization's code of conduct reinforced with training and top-down communication? Does the message reach the employees in the field?*
   - *Are the organization's communication channels open? Do all levels of management get the information they need?*
   - *Is there zero tolerance for fraudulent financial reporting at any level?*

   (b) ***How does the organization identify and manage risks?***

   - *Is there a risk management process, and is it effective?*
   - *Is risk managed throughout the organization?*
   - *Are major risks candidly discussed with the board?*

   (c) ***Is the control system effective?***

   - *Are the organization's controls over the financial reporting process comprehensive, including preparation of financial statements, related notes, and the other required and discretionary disclosures that are an integral part of the financial reports?*
   - *Do senior and line management demonstrate that they accept control responsibility?*
   - *Is there an increasing frequency of "surprises" occurring at the senior management, board, or public levels from the organization's reported financial results or in the accompanying financial disclosures?*
   - *Is there good communication and reporting throughout the organization?*
   - *Are controls seen as enhancing the achievement of objectives or as a "necessary evil?"*
   - *Are qualified people hired promptly, and do they receive adequate training?*
   - *Are problem areas fixed quickly and completely?*

(d) ***Is there strong monitoring?***

- *Is the board independent of management, free of conflicts of interest, well informed, and inquisitive?*
- *Does internal audit have the support of senior management and the audit committee?*
- *Do the internal and external auditors have and use open lines of communication and private access to all members of senior management and the audit committee?*
- *Is line management monitoring the control process?*
- *Is there a program to monitor outsourced processes?*

7. ***Internal controls cannot ensure success***. *Bad decisions, poor managers, or environmental factors can negate controls. Also, dishonest management may* ***override controls*** *and ignore or stifle communications from subordinates. An active and independent governing board that is coupled with open and truthful communications from all components of management and is assisted by capable financial, legal, and internal audit functions is capable of identifying problems and providing effective oversight.*

Roles for the Internal Auditor

8. *The CAE needs to review internal audit's risk assessment and audit plans for the year if* ***adequate resources*** *have not been committed to helping senior management, the audit committee, and the external auditor with their responsibilities in the upcoming year's financial reporting regimen. The* ***financial reporting process*** *encompasses the steps to create the information and prepare financial statements, related notes, and other accompanying disclosures in the organization's financial reports.*

9. ***The CAE should allocate internal audit's resources to the financial reporting, governance, and control processes consistent with the organization's risk assessment***. *The CAE should perform procedures that provide a* ***level of assurance*** *to senior management and the audit committee that the controls surrounding the processes supporting the development of financial reports are* ***adequately designed and effectively executed***. *The controls should be adequate to ensure the prevention and detection of significant errors, irregularities, incorrect assumptions and estimates, and other events that could result in inaccurate or misleading financial statements, related notes, or other disclosures.*

10. *The following lists suggest topics that the CAE may consider in supporting the organization's* ***governance process and the oversight responsibilities*** *of the governing board and its audit committee (or other designated committee) to ensure the reliability and integrity of financial reports.*

(a) ***Financial Reporting***

- *Providing information relevant to the appointment of the independent accountants.*
- *Coordinating audit plans, coverage, and scheduling with the external auditors.*
- *Sharing audit results with the external auditors.*

- *Communicating pertinent observations with the external auditors and audit committee about accounting policies and policy decisions (including accounting decisions for discretionary items and off-balance-sheet transactions), specific components of the financial reporting process, and unusual or complex financial transactions and events (e.g., related-party transactions, mergers and acquisitions, joint ventures, and partnership transactions).*
- *Participating in the financial reports and disclosures review process with the audit committee, external auditors, and senior management; evaluating the quality of the financial reports, including those filed with regulatory agencies.*
- *Assessing the adequacy and effectiveness of the organization's internal controls, specifically those controls over the financial reporting process; this assessment should consider the organization's susceptibility to fraud and the effectiveness of programs and controls to mitigate or eliminate those exposures.*
- *Monitoring management's compliance with the organization's code of conduct and ensuring that ethical policies and other procedures promoting ethical behavior are being followed; an important factor in establishing an effective ethical culture in the organization is when members of senior management set a good example of ethical behavior and provide open and truthful communications to employees, the board, and outside stakeholders.*

(b) ***Corporate Governance***

- *Reviewing corporate policies relating to compliance with laws and regulations, ethics, conflicts of interest, and the timely and thorough investigation of misconduct and fraud allegations.*
- *Reviewing pending litigation or regulatory proceedings bearing on organizational risk and governance.*
- *Providing information on employee conflicts of interest, misconduct, fraud, and other outcomes of the organization's ethical procedures and reporting mechanisms.*

(c) ***Corporate Control***

- *Reviewing the reliability and integrity of the organization's operating and financial information compiled and reported by the organization.*
- *Performing an analysis of the controls for critical accounting policies and comparing them with preferred practices (e.g., transactions in which questions are raised about revenue recognition or off-balance-sheet accounting treatment should be reviewed for compliance with appropriate generally accepted accounting standards).*
- *Evaluating the reasonableness of estimates and assumptions used in preparing operating and financial reports.*
- *Ensuring that estimates and assumptions included in disclosures or comments are in line with underlying organizational information and practices and with similar items reported by other companies, if appropriate.*
- *Evaluating the process of preparing, reviewing, approving, and posting journal entries.*
- *Evaluating the adequacy of controls in the accounting function.*

PA Summary

- **Corporate governance failures** underscore the need for greater **accountability and transparency** by all organizations. Senior management, boards, and auditors are the basis for effective governance. Many organizations are requesting additional services from the IAA to **improve the governance and financial reporting processes**, including evaluations of controls over financial reporting and the reliability and integrity of financial reports.
- The core role of the CAE is to ensure that the audit committee receives the **support and assurance services** it needs and requests. One of its primary objectives is **oversight** of **financial reporting** to ensure reliability and fairness. The IAA typically performs sufficient work and gathers other information to **form an opinion on the adequacy and effectiveness of control**. The CAE communicates that evaluation to the committee, which evaluates the report and may incorporate its conclusion in its report to the governing board.
- The IAA's **work plans and specific assurance engagements** begin **with identification of risk exposures** and its work plan is based on the risks and the **assessment of the RMC processes** that mitigate those risks. Among the matters considered are (1) new businesses, products, and systems; (2) joint ventures and partnerships; (3) restructurings; (4) estimates, budgets, and forecasts; (5) environmental issues; and (6) compliance.
- The most effective control guidance is the **Internal Control – Integrated Framework**, by the Committee of Sponsoring Organizations (COSO). But another **recognized and credible model** may be used unless the law requires otherwise. Control is **defined broadly**. It is not limited to accounting control and financial reporting. **Other aspects of the business** are important, such as resource protection, efficiency and effectiveness, and compliance. These factors also affect financial reporting. Control is **management's responsibility** and requires everyone's participation. The framework is tied to **business objectives** and should be **adaptable**.
- The IAA's report on control assesses effectiveness but also includes a judgment on the **adequacy of the control model or design**. The board relies on management to maintain effective control but reinforces that reliance with **independent oversight**. The board should ask, and the CAE assist in answering, questions about (1) the ethical environment and culture, (2) how risks are identified and managed, (3) the effectiveness of control, and (4) the strength of monitoring.
- **Internal controls cannot ensure success** because bad decisions, poor or dishonest managers, or environmental factors can negate controls. The CAE must review the risk assessment and audit plans for the year if **adequate resources** have not been committed to the financial reporting regimen. The **financial reporting process** involves creating information and preparing statements, notes, and disclosures in financial reports. **IAA resources** should be allocated to financial reporting, governance, and control processes in accordance with the risk **assessment**.
- Audit procedures should provide **assurance** that controls over financial reporting are adequately designed and effectively executed. Controls should ensure the prevention and detection of significant errors, irregularities, incorrect assumptions and estimates, and other events that could misstate financial statements, notes, or disclosures.
- The CAE considers many factors related to financial reporting, corporate governance, and corporate control when supporting the governance process. The purpose is to ensure the reliability of financial reports.

2. Stop and review! You have completed the outline for this subunit. Study multiple-choice questions 28 through 36 beginning on page 189.

5.5 CONTROL CRITERIA

1. This subunit addresses the first element of the control process: establishing standards for the program or operation to be controlled. The topic is covered in three Assurance Implementation Standards, two Consulting Implementation Standards, and two Practice Advisories.
2. ***2120.A2*** *– Internal auditors should ascertain the extent to which operating and program goals and objectives have been established and conform to those of the organization.*
3. ***2120.A3*** *– Internal auditors should review operations and programs to ascertain the extent to which results are consistent with established goals and objectives to determine whether operations and programs are being implemented or performed as intended.*
4. ***2120.A4*** *– Adequate criteria are needed to evaluate controls. Internal auditors should ascertain the extent to which management has established adequate criteria to determine whether objectives and goals have been accomplished. If adequate, internal auditors should use such criteria in their evaluation. If inadequate, internal auditors should work with management to develop appropriate evaluation criteria.*
   a. ***PRACTICE ADVISORY 2120.A4-1: CONTROL CRITERIA***
      1. *Internal auditors should evaluate the established operating targets and expectations and should determine whether those operating standards are acceptable and are being met. When such management targets and criteria are vague,* ***authoritative interpretations*** *should be sought. If internal auditors are required to interpret or select operating standards, they should seek* ***agreement with engagement clients*** *as to the criteria needed to measure operating performance.*

PA Summary

- Internal auditors should evaluate **operating targets and expectations** and whether they are acceptable and being met. If operating criteria are vague, the IAA seeks **authoritative guidance**. If the IAA must interpret or select criteria, agreement with the client should be sought.

5. ***2120.C1*** *– During consulting engagements, internal auditors should address controls consistent with the engagement's objectives and should be alert to the existence of any significant control weaknesses.*

6. ***2120.C2*** *– Internal auditors should incorporate knowledge of controls gained from consulting engagements into the process of identifying and evaluating significant risk exposures of the organization.*

   a. ***PRACTICE ADVISORY 1000.C1-2: ADDITIONAL CONSIDERATIONS FOR FORMAL CONSULTING ENGAGEMENTS***

      The following is the portion of this comprehensive Practice Advisory relevant to Standards 2120.C1 and 2120.C2:

      14. Internal auditors should be observant of the effectiveness of risk management and control processes during formal consulting engagements. ***Substantial risk exposures*** *or* ***material control weaknesses*** *should be brought to the attention of management. In some situations, the auditor's concerns should also be* ***communicated to executive management, the audit committee, or the board*** *of directors. Auditors should use professional judgment (a) to determine the significance of exposures or weaknesses and the actions taken or contemplated to mitigate or correct these exposures or weaknesses and (b) to ascertain the expectations of executive management, the audit committee, and board in having these matters reported.*

PA Summary

- In formal consulting engagements, **material risk exposures and control weaknesses** observed should be reported, in some cases, **to executive management, the audit committee, or the board.**

7. Stop and review! You have completed the outline for this subunit. Study multiple-choice questions 37 through 42 beginning on page 192.

5.6 STUDY UNIT 5 SUMMARY

1. The board establishes the governance process and obtains assurance about the system of risk management and controls. Senior management oversees establishment, administration, and assessment of that system. Each manager assesses control in his/her area. Auditors provide assurance about the effectiveness of risk management and control. The CAE should gather sufficient information to judge the adequacy and effectiveness of control. This judgment should be communicated to management and the board. Also, management may report on control to external parties.
2. CSA is a collaboration between managers and internal auditors to evaluate control. Programs vary but share key features. A formal, documented process allows those directly involved to participate in (a) identifying risks and exposures, (b) assessing relevant controls, (c) developing plans, and (d) estimating the probability of achieving objectives.
3. An organization may be subject to legal and regulatory requirements for interim reports, disclosures, and management certifications. Applicable laws or regulations also may require management to report on controls. The internal auditors' roles in these processes may vary from designer of the process to an assessor of the process.
4. The IIA's favored control framework is the COSO model, but other frameworks may be appropriate. It (a) defines control broadly, (b) stresses all important aspects of the business, (c) states that management is responsible for control, and (d) ties the framework to business objectives.
5. If operating criteria are vague, the IAA seeks authoritative guidance. If the IAA must interpret or select criteria, agreement with clients should be sought.

QUESTIONS

5.1 Assessing Control

1. An internal auditor fails to discover an employee fraud during an assurance engagement. The nondiscovery is most likely to suggest a violation of the Professional Practices Framework if it was the result of a

A. Failure to perform a detailed review of all transactions in the area.

B. Determination that any possible fraud in the area would not involve a material amount.

C. Determination that the cost of extending procedures in the area would exceed the potential benefits.

D. Presumption that the internal controls in the area were adequate and effective.

Answer (D) is correct. *(CIA, adapted)*

REQUIRED: The most likely reason failure to detect fraud is a violation of the Standards.

DISCUSSION: The IAA evaluates the adequacy and effectiveness of controls encompassing the organization's governance, operations, and information systems (Standard 2120.A1). Moreover, the IAA should assist the organization in maintaining effective controls by evaluating their effectiveness and efficiency and by promoting continuous improvement (Standard 2120). Thus, an internal auditor must not simply assume that controls are adequate and effective.

Answer (A) is incorrect because due professional care does not require detailed reviews of all transactions (PA 1220-1). Answer (B) is incorrect because the relative complexity, materiality, or significance of matters to which assurance procedures are applied should be considered. Answer (C) is incorrect because the internal auditor should consider the cost of assurance in relation to potential benefits.

2. From a modern internal auditing perspective, which one of the following statements represents the most important benefit of an internal auditing activity to management?

A. Assurance that published financial statements are correct.

B. Assurance that fraudulent activities will be detected.

C. Assurance that the organization is complying with legal requirements.

D. Assurance that there is reasonable control over day-to-day operations.

Answer (D) is correct. *(CMA, adapted)*

REQUIRED: The most important benefit of an IAA.

DISCUSSION: According to the definition of internal auditing, "Internal auditing is an independent, objective assurance and consulting activity designed to add value and improve an organization's operations. It helps an organization accomplish its objectives by bringing a systematic, disciplined approach to evaluate and improve the effectiveness of risk management, control, and governance processes." Thus, it helps the organization to maintain effective controls by evaluating their effectiveness and efficiency and by promoting continuous improvement (Standard 2120).

Answer (A) is incorrect because published financial statements are only required to be fairly presented. Internal audit activities cannot assure correctness. Answer (B) is incorrect because internal auditing's responsibility with respect to fraud detection is to examine and evaluate the adequacy and effectiveness of internal control. Answer (C) is incorrect because internal auditing evaluates and contributes to the improvement of risk management, control, and governance processes, but it cannot assure compliance with legal requirements.

3. The chief audit executive's responsibility for assessing and reporting on control processes includes

A. Communicating to senior management and the audit committee an annual judgment about internal control.

B. Overseeing the establishment of internal control processes.

C. Maintaining the organization's governance processes.

D. Arriving at a single assessment based solely on the work of the internal audit activity.

Answer (A) is correct. *(Publisher, adapted)*

REQUIRED: The chief audit executive's responsibility for assessing and reporting on control processes.

DISCUSSION: Senior management and the audit committee normally expect that the chief audit executive will perform sufficient engagement work and gather other available information during the year so as to form a judgment about the adequacy and effectiveness of the control processes. The chief audit executive should communicate that overall judgment about the organization's system of controls to senior management and the audit committee. A growing number of organizations have included a management's report on the system of internal controls in their annual or periodic reports to external stakeholders. The report of the chief audit executive should therefore be presented, usually once a year, to senior management and the audit committee (PA 2120.A1-1).

Answer (B) is incorrect because senior management is responsible for overseeing the establishment of internal control processes. Answer (C) is incorrect because the board is responsible for establishing and maintaining the organization's governance processes. Answer (D) is incorrect because the challenge for the internal audit activity is to evaluate the effectiveness of the organization's system of controls based on the aggregation of many individual assessments. Those assessments are largely gained from internal auditing engagements, management's self assessments, and external auditor's work (PA 2120.A1-1).

4. The primary responsibility for overseeing the establishment and administration of internal control rests with

A. The external auditor.

B. Senior management.

C. The controller.

D. The treasurer.

Answer (B) is correct. *(CMA, adapted)*
REQUIRED: The person(s) primarily responsible for establishing and administering internal control.
DISCUSSION: The board establishes and maintains governance processes and obtains assurances about the effectiveness of the risk management and control processes. Senior management's role is to oversee the establishment, administration, and assessment of that system of processes (PA 2120.A1-1).
Answer (A) is incorrect because external auditors must consider internal control, but they do not establish and maintain it. Answer (C) is incorrect because the controller is responsible only to the extent that (s)he is a part of the management team. Answer (D) is incorrect because the treasurer is responsible only to the extent that (s)he is a part of the management team.

5. Which of the following is most likely to be regarded as a strength in internal control in a traditional external audit?

A. The performance of financial audits by the internal audit activity.

B. The performance of operational engagements by internal auditors.

C. The routine supervisory review of production planning.

D. The existence of a preventive maintenance program.

Answer (A) is correct. *(CMA, adapted)*
REQUIRED: The activity most likely regarded as a strong internal control in a traditional external audit.
DISCUSSION: The external auditor's traditional role is to perform an audit to determine whether the externally reported financial statements are fairly presented. Thus, a financial audit by the IAA is relevant to the traditional external audit because it is an engagement in which the reliability and integrity of financial information is evaluated. Such an engagement is consistent with the Standards. According to Standard 2120.A1, based on the results of the risk assessment, the internal audit activity should evaluate the adequacy and effectiveness of controls encompassing the organization's governance, operations, and information systems. This evaluation should extend to the reliability and integrity of financial and operational information; effectiveness and efficiency of operations; safeguarding of assets; and compliance with laws, regulations, and contracts.
Answer (B) is incorrect because operational engagements are concerned with operational efficiency and effectiveness, matters that are not the primary focus of an external audit of financial statements. Answer (C) is incorrect because routine supervisory review of production planning is a concern of management but does not directly affect the fair presentation of the financial statements. Answer (D) is incorrect because the existence of a preventive maintenance program is not directly relevant to a financial statement audit.

6. Controls should be designed to ensure that

A. Operations are performed efficiently.

B. Management's plans have not been circumvented by worker collusion.

C. The internal audit activity's guidance and oversight of management's performance is accomplished economically and efficiently.

D. Management's planning, organizing, and directing processes are properly evaluated.

Answer (A) is correct. *(CIA, adapted)*
REQUIRED: The purpose of controls.
DISCUSSION: The purpose of the multifaceted system of control processes is to support people of the organization in the management of risks and the achievement of the established and communicated objectives of the enterprise. Control processes are expected to ensure operations are performed efficiently and achieve effective results (PA 2120.A1-1).
Answer (B) is incorrect because collusion is an inherent limitation of internal control. Answer (C) is incorrect because representatives of the organization's stakeholders (e.g., the board) provide oversight of risk and control processes administered by management (Glossary). Answer (D) is incorrect because internal auditors evaluate management processes to determine whether reasonable assurance exists that objectives and goals will be achieved (PA 2100-1).

7. Which of the following best defines control?

A. Control is the result of proper planning, organizing, and directing by management.

B. Controls are statements of what the organization chooses to accomplish.

C. Control is provided when cost-effective measures are taken to restrict deviations to a tolerable level.

D. Control accomplishes objectives and goals in an accurate, timely, and economical fashion.

Answer (A) is correct. *(CIA, adapted)*

REQUIRED: The best definition of control.

DISCUSSION: According to the Glossary appended to the Standards, a control is "any action taken by management, the board, and other parties to enhance risk management and increase the likelihood that established objectives and goals will be achieved. Management plans, organizes, and directs the performance of sufficient actions to provide reasonable assurance that objectives and goals will be achieved." Thus, control is the result of proper planning, organizing, and directing by management.

Answer (B) is incorrect because established objectives and goals are what the organization chooses to accomplish. Answer (C) is incorrect because, during the development of risk management, control, and governance processes, reasonable assurance of achieving objectives and goals efficiently and economically is provided when the most cost-effective measures are taken in the design and implementation stages to reduce risks and restrict deviations to a tolerable level (PA 2100-1). Answer (D) is incorrect because efficient performance accomplishes objectives and goals in an accurate, timely, and economical fashion (PA 2100-1).

8. Controls that are designed to provide management with assurance of the realization of specified minimum gross margins on sales are

A. Directive controls.

B. Preventive controls.

C. Detective controls.

D. Output controls.

Answer (A) is correct. *(CIA, adapted)*

REQUIRED: The control that provide assurance of the realization of specified minimum gross margins on sales.

DISCUSSION: A control is any action taken by management, the board, and other parties to enhance the likelihood that established objectives and goals will be achieved (Glossary). The objective of directive controls is to cause or encourage desirable events to occur (PA 2100-1), e.g., providing management with assurance of the realization of specified minimum gross margins on sales.

Answer (B) is incorrect because preventive controls deter undesirable events from occurring. Answer (C) is incorrect because detective controls detect and correct undesirable events that have occurred. Answer (D) is incorrect because output controls relate to the accuracy and reasonableness of information processed by a system, not to operating controls.

9. The procedure requiring preparation of a prelisting of incoming cash receipts, with copies of the prelist going to the cashier and to accounting, is an example of which type of control?

A. Preventive.

B. Corrective.

C. Detective.

D. Directive.

Answer (A) is correct. *(CIA, adapted)*

REQUIRED: The kind of control exemplified by a pre-list of cash receipts.

DISCUSSION: A prelisting of cash receipts in the form of checks is a preventive control. It is intended to deter undesirable events from occurring (PA 2100-1). Because irregularities involving cash are most likely before receipts are recorded, either remittance advices or a prelisting of checks should be prepared in the mailroom so as to establish recorded accountability for cash as soon as possible. A cash register tape is a form of prelisting for cash received over the counter. One copy of a prelisting will go to accounting for posting to the cash receipts journal, and another is sent to the cashier for reconciliation with checks and currency received.

Answer (B) is incorrect because a corrective control rectifies an error or irregularity. Answer (C) is incorrect because a detective control uncovers an error or irregularity that has already occurred. Answer (D) is incorrect because a directive control causes or encourages a desirable event.

10. Controls may be classified according to the function they are intended to perform, for example, as detective, preventive, or directive. Which of the following is a directive control?

A. Monthly bank statement reconciliations.

B. Dual signatures on all disbursements over a specific amount.

C. Recording every transaction on the day it occurs.

D. Requiring all members of the internal audit activity to be CIAs.

Answer (D) is correct. *(CIA, adapted)*

REQUIRED: The directive control.

DISCUSSION: Requiring all members of the internal audit activity to be CIAs is a directive control. The control is designed to cause or encourage a desirable event to occur (PA 2100-1). The requirement enhances the professionalism and level of expertise of the internal audit activity.

Answer (A) is incorrect because monthly bank statement reconciliation is a detective control. The events under scrutiny have already occurred. Answer (B) is incorrect because dual signatures on all disbursements over a specific amount is a preventive control. The control is designed to deter an undesirable event. Answer (C) is incorrect because recording every transaction on the day it occurs is a preventive control. The control is designed to deter an undesirable event.

11. Internal auditors regularly evaluate controls. Which of the following best describes the concept of control as recognized by internal auditors?

A. Management regularly discharges personnel who do not perform up to expectations.

B. Management takes action to enhance the likelihood that established goals and objectives will be achieved.

C. Control represents specific procedures that accountants and internal auditors design to ensure the correctness of processing.

D. Control procedures should be designed from the "bottom up" to ensure attention to detail.

Answer (B) is correct. *(CIA, adapted)*

REQUIRED: The best description of the concept of control as recognized by internal auditors.

DISCUSSION: A control is any action taken by management to enhance the likelihood that established goals and objectives will be achieved. Management plans, organizes, and directs the performance of sufficient actions to provide reasonable assurance that objectives and goals will be achieved (PA 2100-1). Thus, control is the result of proper planning, organizing, and directing by management.

Answer (A) is incorrect because termination of employees who perform unsatisfactorily is not a comprehensive definition of control. Answer (C) is incorrect because control is not limited to processing. Moreover, it is instituted by management, not internal auditors. Answer (D) is incorrect because some control procedures may be designed from the bottom up, but the concept of control flows from management down through the organization.

5.2 Control Self-Assessment (CSA)

12. Which group is charged with overseeing the establishment, administration, and evaluation of the processes of risk management and control?

A. Operating managers.

B. Internal auditors.

C. External auditors.

D. Senior management.

Answer (D) is correct. *(Publisher, adapted)*

REQUIRED: The group charged with overseeing the establishment, administration, and evaluation of the processes of risk management and control.

DISCUSSION: Senior management is charged with overseeing the establishment, administration, and evaluation of the processes of risk management and control. Operating managers' responsibilities include assessment of the risks and controls in their units. Internal and external auditors provide varying degrees of assurance about the state of effectiveness of the risk management and control processes of the organization. (PA 2120.A1-2)

Answer (A) is incorrect because operating managers' responsibilities include assessment of the risk management and control. Answer (B) is incorrect because internal auditors provide varying degrees of assurance about the state of effectiveness of the risk management and control processes of the organization. Answer (C) is incorrect because external auditors provide varying degrees of assurance about the state of effectiveness of the risk management and control processes of the organization.

13. Control self-assessment (CSA) is a process that involves employees in assessing the adequacy of controls and identifying opportunities for improvement within an organization. Which of the following are reasons to involve employees in this process?

I. Employees become more motivated to do their jobs right.

II. Employees are objective about their jobs.

III. Employees can provide an independent assessment of internal controls.

IV. Managers want feedback from their employees.

A. I and II only.

B. III and IV only.

C. I and IV only.

D. II and IV only.

Answer (C) is correct. *(CIA, adapted)*

REQUIRED: The reasons to involve employees in control self-assessment.

DISCUSSION: An organization that uses self-assessment will have a formal, documented process that allows management and work teams, who are directly involved in a business unit, function, or process to participate in a structured manner of the purpose of (1) identifying risks and exposures, (2) assessing the control processes that mitigate, (3) developing action plans to reduce risks to acceptable levels, and (4) determining the likelihood of achieving the business objective. Thus, CSA is a process that involves substantial employee feed back. Among the outcomes that may be derived from self-assessment methodologies are that people are motivated to take "ownership" of the control processes in their unit, and corrective actions taken by the work teams are often more effective and timely.

Answer (A) is incorrect because employees often lack the perspective required to be objective about their jobs or performance. Answer (B) is incorrect because, although employees can be involved in assessing internal controls, their assessments are not independent. Answer (D) is incorrect because employees often lack the perspective required to be objective about their jobs or performance.

14. Which of the following is an outcome that can be derived from control self-assessment (CSA) methodologies?

A. Formal, "hard" controls are more easily identified and evaluated.

B. Management will become involved in and knowledgeable about the self-assessment process by serving as facilitators, scribes, and reporters for the work teams.

C. Auditor's responsibility for the risk management and control processes of the organization will be reinforced.

D. People are motivated to take "ownership" of the control processes in their units and corrective actions taken by work teams are often more effective and timely.

Answer (D) is correct. *(Publisher, adapted)*

REQUIRED: The outcome that can be derived from control self-assessment methodologies.

DISCUSSION: According to PA 2120.A1-2, one of the possible outcomes that may be derived from self-assessment methodologies is that people are motivated to take "ownership" of the control processes in their units and corrective actions taken by work teams are often more effective and timely.

Answer (A) is incorrect because informal, "soft" controls are more easily identified and evaluated. Answer (B) is incorrect because internal auditors will become involved in and knowledgeable about the self-assessment process by serving as facilitators, scribes, and reporters for the work teams and as trainers of risk and control concepts supporting the CSA program. Answer (C) is incorrect because management's responsibility for the risk management and control processes of the organization is reinforced, and managers will be less tempted to abdicate those activities to specialists, such as auditors.

15. Of the three primary forms of CSA programs, which one is designed to gather information from work teams representing different levels in the business unit or function?

A. Auditor-produced analysis.

B. Facilitated team workshops.

C. Surveys.

D. Management-produced analysis.

Answer (B) is correct. *(Publisher, adapted)*

REQUIRED: The form of CSA program that is designed to gather information from work teams representing different levels in the business unit of function.

DISCUSSION: The three primary forms of CSA programs are facilitated team workshops, surveys, and management-produced analysis. Facilitated team workshops gather information from work teams representing different levels in the business unit or function. The format of the workshop may be based on objectives, risks, controls, or processes.

16. CSA may be conducted using a facilitated team workshop approach. Which team workshop format begins by listing all possible barriers, obstacles, threats, and exposures that might prevent achieving an objective?

A. Objective-based format.

B. Control-based format.

C. Process-based format.

D. Risk-based format.

Answer (D) is correct. *(Publisher, adapted)*

REQUIRED: The team workshop format that begins by listing all possible barriers, obstacles, threats, and exposures that might prevent achieving an objective.

DISCUSSION: The risk-based format focuses on listing the risks to achieving an objective. The workshop begins by listing all possible barriers, obstacles, threats, and exposures that might prevent achieving an objective and, then, examining the control procedures to determine whether they are sufficient to manage the key risks. The aim of the workshop is to determine significant residual risks. This format takes the work team through the entire objective-risks-controls formula.

17. The element(s) of control self-assessment (CSA) based on a facilitated team workshop approach include

I. Treating participating employees as process owners

II. Taking surveys of employees regarding risks and controls

III. Interviewing employees separately in the field

A. I only.

B. II only.

C. II and III only.

D. I, II, and III.

Answer (A) is correct. *(Publisher, adapted)*

REQUIRED: The element(s) of CSA.

DISCUSSION: Among the outcomes of self-assessment are that people are motivated to take "ownership" of the control processes in their units (PA 2120.A1-2). The participants are 'process owners' -- management and staff who are involved with the particular issues under examination, who know them best, and who are critical to the implementation of appropriate process controls.

Answer (B) is incorrect because the facilitated team workshop approach to CSA should be contrasted with an approach that merely surveys employees regarding risks and controls. Answer (C) is incorrect because the facilitated team workshop approach to CSA should be contrasted with an approach that merely surveys employees regarding risks and controls or performs separate interviews in the field. Answer (D) is incorrect because the facilitated team workshop approach to CSA should be contrasted with an approach that merely surveys employees regarding risks and controls or performs separate interviews in the field.

18. Which of the following statements about CSA is false?

A. CSA is usually an informal and undocumented process.

B. In its purest form, CSA integrates business objectives and risks with control processes.

C. CSA is also referred to as control/risk self-assessment or CRSA.

D. Most implemented CSA programs share some key features and goals.

Answer (A) is correct. *(Publisher, adapted)*

REQUIRED: The false statement regarding control self-assessment.

DISCUSSION: A methodology encompassing self-assessment surveys and facilitated-workshops called CSA is a useful and efficient approach for managers and internal auditors to collaborate in assessing and evaluating control procedures. In its purest form, CSA integrates business objectives and risks with control processes. Control self-assessment is also referred to as "control/risk self-assessment" or "CRSA." Although CSA practitioners use a number of differing techniques and formats, most implemented programs share some key features and goals. The process is a formal and documented way of allowing participation by those who are directly involved in the business unit, function, or process (PA 2120.A1-2).

19. CSA may be conducted using a facilitated team workshop approach. In which team workshop format does the facilitator identify the key risks and controls before the beginning of the workshop?

A. Control-based format.

B. Objective-based format.

C. Risk-based format.

D. Process-based format.

Answer (A) is correct. *(Publisher, adapted)*

REQUIRED: The format in which the facilitator identifies key risks and controls prior to the workshop.

DISCUSSION: The control-based format focuses on how well the controls in place are working. In this format, the facilitator identifies the key risks and controls before the beginning of the workshop. During the workshop, the work team assesses how well the controls mitigate risks and promote the achievement of objectives. The aim of the workshop is to produce an analysis of the gap between how controls are working and how well management expects those controls to work.

20. CSA may be conducted using a facilitated team workshop format approach. The aim of which team workshop format is to decide whether the control procedures are working effectively and are resulting in residual risks within an acceptable level?

A. Control-based format.

B. Objective-based format.

C. Process-based format.

D. Risk-based format.

Answer (B) is correct. *(Publisher, adapted)*

REQUIRED: The format used to decide whether the control procedures are working effectively and are resulting in residual risks within an acceptable level.

DISCUSSION: The objective-based format focuses on the best way to accomplish a business objective. The workshop begins by identifying the controls presently in place to support the objective and, then, determining the residual risks remaining. The aim of the workshop is to decide whether the control procedures are working effectively and are resulting in residual risks within an acceptable level.

Answer (A) is incorrect because the aim of a control-based format is to produce an analysis of the gap between how controls are working and how well management expects those controls to work. Answer (C) is incorrect because the aim of a process-based format is to evaluate, update, validate, improve, and even streamline the whole process and its component activities. Answer (D) is incorrect because the aim of a risk-based format is to determine significant residual risks.

21. Which of the three primary forms of CSA programs should be used if management wants to minimize the time spent and costs incurred in gathering the information?

A. Management-produced analysis.

B. Facilitated team workshop.

C. Auditor-produced analysis.

D. Survey.

Answer (D) is correct. *(Publisher, adapted)*

REQUIRED: The form of CSA that minimizes the time spent or costs of gathering information.

DISCUSSION: The survey form of CSA uses a questionnaire that tends to ask mostly simple "Yes/No" or "Have/Have Not" questions that are carefully written to be understood by the target recipients. They are preferred if the culture in the organization may hinder open, candid discussions in workshop settings or if management desires to minimize the time spent and costs incurred in gathering the information. (PA 2120.A1-2)

Answer (A) is incorrect because management-produced analysis is not designed to minimize time spent and costs incurred in gathering the information. Answer (B) is incorrect because facilitated team workshop is not designed to minimize time spent and costs incurred in gathering the information. Answer (C) is incorrect because auditor-produced analysis is not one of the three primary forms of CSA programs.

22. Which one of the three primary types of CSA programs allows for internal auditor involvement to synthesize this analysis with other information to enhance the understanding about controls and to share the knowledge?

A. Facilitated team workshop.

B. Management-produced analysis.

C. Survey.

D. Auditor-produced analysis.

Answer (B) is correct. *(Publisher, adapted)*

REQUIRED: The form of CSA program that allows for internal auditor involvement to synthesize this analysis with other information.

DISCUSSION: The form of self-assessment called "management-produced analysis" covers most approaches by management groups to produce information about selected business processes, risk management activities, and control procedures. The internal auditor may synthesize this analysis with other information to enhance the understanding about controls and to share the knowledge with managers in business or functional units as part of the organization's CSA program. (PA 2120.A1-2)

Answer (A) is incorrect because facilitated team workshops gather information from work teams representing different levels in the business unit or function. Answer (C) is incorrect because the survey form of CSA uses a questionnaire that tends to ask mostly simple "Yes/No" or "Have/Have Not" questions that are carefully written to be understood by the target recipients. Answer (D) is incorrect because auditor-produced analysis is not one of the three primary forms of CSA programs.

23. In most programs, the internal audit's investment in the organization's CSA efforts is how large?

I. Internal audit sponsors, designs, implements, and in effect owns the process; conducts the training; supplies the facilitators, scribes, and reporters; and orchestrates the participation of management and work teams.

II. Internal audit serves as an interested party and consultant to the whole process and as ultimate verifier of evaluations produced by the teams.

A. I only.

B. II only.

C. Usually somewhere between I and II.

D. Never more than II, and sometimes less.

Answer (C) is correct. *(Publisher, adapted)*

REQUIRED: The most common investment in an organization's CSA efforts by internal audit.

DISCUSSION: Internal audit's investment in some CSA programs is fairly significant. It may sponsor, design, implement and, in effect, own the process; conduct the training; supply the facilitators, scribes, and reporters; and orchestrate the participation of management and work teams. In other CSA programs, internal audit's involvement is minimal, serving as interested party and consultant of the whole process and as ultimate verifier of the evaluations produced by the teams. In most programs, internal audit's investment in the organization's CSA efforts is somewhere between the two extremes described above. (PA 2120.A1-2)

Answer (A) is incorrect because the typical investment is less than the largest investment that internal audit may have in an organization's CSA efforts. Answer (B) is incorrect because the typical investment is greater than the smallest investment that internal audit may have in an organization's CSA efforts. Answer (D) is incorrect because, in most programs, internal audit's investment is larger than described in II.

24. Which form(s) of CSA program(s) assumes that managers and members of the work teams possess an understanding of risks and controls concepts?

A. The management-produced analysis form.

B. The management-produced analysis and facilitated team workshop forms.

C. The management-produced analysis and survey forms.

D. All self-assessment programs.

Answer (D) is correct. *(Publisher, adapted)*

REQUIRED: The form(s) of CSA program(s) assuming that managers and members of the work teams possess an understanding of risks and controls concepts.

DISCUSSION: All self-assessment programs assume that managers and members of the work teams possess an understanding of risks and controls concepts and use those concepts in communications. For training sessions, to facilitate the orderly flow of workshop discussions and as a check on the completeness of the overall process, organizations often use a control framework, such as the COSO (Committee of Sponsoring Organizations) and CoCo (Canadian Criteria of Control Board) models.

5.3 Interim Reports, Disclosure, and Certification

25. In accordance with the applicable law, management conducts its own assessment of controls as the basis for a public report. What is the internal auditor's role with respect to internal controls?

A. Internal auditors have no responsibility for internal control assessment.

B. Internal auditors should form their opinion based on their assessment of controls.

C. Internal auditors should evaluate management's assessment and supporting documentation.

D. Internal auditors should evaluate management's assessment and supporting documentation against their own assessment and discuss any differences with management.

Answer (C) is correct. *(Publisher, adapted)*

REQUIRED: The role of an internal auditor when management conducts its own assessment of controls as the basis for a public report.

DISCUSSION: Internal auditors should compare processes for complying with legal or regulatory requirements for interim reporting and disclosures with those for assessing and publicly reporting on internal controls. Processes designed to be similar or compatible will contribute to operational efficiencies and reduce the likelihood or risk for problems and errors to occur or go undetected. While processes and procedures may be similar, it is possible that the internal auditor's role may vary. In some organizations the work of internal auditors may form the basis for management's assertions about internal control, while in other organizations internal auditors may be called upon to evaluate management's assessment.

Answer (A) is incorrect because internal auditors have a responsibility with respect to internal controls regardless of whether management conducts its own assessment of controls. Answer (B) is incorrect because internal auditors should evaluate management's assessment and supporting documentation. Answer (D) is incorrect because separate assessments by management and the internal auditors would be time consuming, costly, and unnecessary.

26. Which of the following is the role that the internal auditor most likely cannot accept with respect to processes over interim financial reporting?

A. Initial designer of the required process.

B. Independent assessor of the process.

C. Certifier of the financial statements.

D. Coordinator or liaison between management and its auditors.

Answer (C) is correct. *(Publisher, adapted)*

REQUIRED: The role that the internal auditor most likely cannot accept with respect to processes over interim financial reporting.

DISCUSSION: The IIA recommends a range of actions for internal auditors. The actions are value-added services that can be provided regarding interim financial reports, disclosures, and management certifications. The internal auditors' role in such processes may range from initial designer of the process, participant on a disclosure committee, coordinator or liaison between management and its auditors, to independent assessor of the process. The internal auditor cannot certify the financial statements. This certification is a management function if required by the applicable statutory or regulatory enactment.

Answer (A) is incorrect because being the initial designer of the required process is an action that an internal auditor most likely can perform with respect to processes over interim financial reporting. Answer (B) is incorrect because being the independent assessor of the process is an action that an internal auditor most likely can perform with respect to processes over interim financial reporting. Answer (D) is incorrect because being the coordinator or liaison between management and its auditors is an action that an internal auditor most likely can perform with respect to processes over interim financial reporting.

27. Status as an "ex-officio" or unofficial member of the "disclosure committee" normally avoids which kind of problems for the CAE?

A. Disclosure problems.

B. Internal control problems.

C. Independence problems.

D. Audit committee problems.

Answer (C) is correct. *(Publisher, adapted)*

REQUIRED: The problem that is avoided by the CAE when (s)he has a status as an "ex-officio" member of the "disclosure committee."

DISCUSSION: Normally, the chief audit executive (CAE) should be a member of the disclosure committee. Consideration should be given to the CAE's status on the committee. CAEs who serve as committee chairs or regular or "voting" members need to be aware of independence considerations and are advised to review IIA Standards and related Practice Advisories for guidance and required disclosures. Status as an "ex-officio" member normally would not create independence problems (PA 2120.A1-3).

Answer (A) is incorrect because allowing the CAE to have a status as an "ex-officio" member of the disclosure committee does not have any effect on disclosure. Answer (B) is incorrect because allowing the CAE to have a status as an "ex-officio" member of the disclosure committee does not affect internal controls of an organization. Answer (D) is incorrect because allowing the CAE to have a status as an "ex-officio" member of the disclosure committee does not have any effect on the audit committee.

5.4 Auditing Financial Reporting

28. The chief audit executive (CAE) typically provides which of the following to the audit committee?

A. Overall evaluation of the adequacy and effectiveness of the internal control processes.

B. A conclusion about the coverage and adequacy of the internal auditing report.

C. The internal audit activity's working papers.

D. The committee's report to the governing board.

Answer (A) is correct. *(Publisher, adapted)*

REQUIRED: The information typically provided to the audit committee by the chief audit executive (CAE).

DISCUSSION: The audit committee and senior management typically request that the internal audit activity perform sufficient audit work and gather other available information during the year to form an opinion on the adequacy and effectiveness of the internal control processes. The CAE normally communicates that overall evaluation, on a timely basis, to the committee.

Answer (B) is incorrect because a conclusion about the coverage and adequacy of the internal auditing report is not typically provided by the CAE to the audit committee. Answer (C) is incorrect because the audit committee receives reports, not working papers. Answer (D) is incorrect because the committee's report to the governing board is not drafted by the CAE.

29. Because of the increase in published reports of corporate governance failures, senior management and the audit committee are requesting additional services from internal auditors. These most likely include evaluation of the

A. Reliability of external auditors.

B. Integrity of senior management.

C. Internal controls.

D. Accountability of senior management.

Answer (C) is correct. *(Publisher, adapted)*

REQUIRED: The most likely additional service to be requested of internal auditors.

DISCUSSION: Recent initiatives have put the spotlight on the need for senior management to be more accountable for the information contained in an organization's financial reports. Thus, senior management and the audit committee of many organizations are requesting additional services from the internal audit activity to improve the governance and financial reporting processes. These requests include evaluations of the organization's internal controls over financial reporting and the reliability and integrity of its financial report.

Answer (A) is incorrect because evaluation of the reliability of external auditors is a service internal auditors are less likely to perform than an assessment of controls. For example, management might be required to issue a public report that assesses the controls over financial reporting. Answer (B) is incorrect because the integrity of senior management is not an additional service internal auditors would likely be asked to evaluate. Answer (D) is incorrect because the assessment of controls improves management's accountability. The internal auditors are not likely to be asked to evaluate directly the accountability of senior management.

30. The most effective internal control guidance available today is the COSO's Internal Control – Integrated Framework. Which of the following is one of its conclusions?

A. Only management's participation is needed for control to be effective.

B. The control framework is tied to the business objectives, so it is not flexible enough to be adapted without a major undertaking.

C. Internal control is limited to accounting controls.

D. Operational efficiency and effectiveness are important aspects of the business.

Answer (D) is correct. *(Publisher, adapted)*

REQUIRED: The conclusion of the COSO about internal control.

DISCUSSION: Internal control is defined broadly. It is not limited to accounting controls and is not narrowly restricted to financial reporting. Accounting and financial reports are important issues, but a business has other important aspects, such as resource protection; operational efficiency and effectiveness; and compliance with rules, regulations, and organizational policies. These factors also have an impact on financial reporting.

Answer (A) is incorrect because, according to the COSO model, internal control is management's responsibility but requires the participation of all persons within an organization if it is to be effective. Answer (B) is incorrect because the control framework is tied to the business objectives and is flexible enough to be adaptable. Answer (C) is incorrect because the COSO model defines internal control broadly. It is not limited to accounting controls.

31. The internal audit activity's work plans and specific assurance engagements begin with

A. A careful identification of the exposures facing the organization.

B. Identification of potential lack of goal congruence in the organization.

C. Interpretation of accounting pronouncements.

D. Assessment of internal control over the accounting function.

Answer (A) is correct. *(Publisher, adapted)*

REQUIRED: The beginning of the internal audit activity's work plans and specific assurance engagements.

DISCUSSION: The internal audit activity's work plans and specific assurance engagements begin with a careful identification of the exposures facing the organization. Thus, its work plan is based on the risks and assessment of the risk management and control processes maintained by management to mitigate those risks.

Answer (B) is incorrect because lack of goal congruence is just one of the exposures facing the organization. Answer (C) is incorrect because misapplication of accounting pronouncements is just one of the exposures facing the organization. Answer (D) is incorrect because the IAA must consider all the risk factors that affect financial reporting before devising work plans.

32. The chief audit executive's (CAE) assessment of the effectiveness of the organization's system of controls must include an evaluation of whether it has a strong ethical environment and culture. To complete this task, the CAE most likely must

A. Examine whether board members have engaged in related-party transactions with the organization.

B. Assess whether performance and incentive targets create excessive pressure for short-term results.

C. Determine whether the organization has successfully implemented ISO 9000 standards.

D. Determine whether the organization has a three-strikes-and-out policy concerning fraudulent financial reporting.

Answer (B) is correct. *(Publisher, adapted)*

REQUIRED: The procedure most likely performed to assess the strength of an organization's ethical environment and culture.

DISCUSSION: The CAE should provide the audit committee with internal audit's assessment of the effectiveness of the organization's system of controls, including its judgment on the adequacy of the control model or design. The board or its audit (or other designated) committee should ask certain questions, and the CAE may be expected to assist in answering them. In determining whether a strong ethical environment and culture exist, the following questions should be asked:

- Do board members and senior executives set examples of high integrity?
- Are performance and incentive targets realistic or do they create excessive pressure for short-term results?
- Is the organization's code of conduct reinforced with training and top-down communication? Does the message reach the employees in the field?
- Are the organization's communication channels open? Do all levels of management get the information they need?
- Is there zero tolerance for fraudulent financial reporting at any level?

Answer (A) is incorrect because the issue is not whether board members have engaged in related-party transactions with the organization but whether any such transactions are within ethical and legal guidelines. Answer (C) is incorrect because ISO 9000 standards pertain directly to quality, not the ethical culture. Answer (D) is incorrect because a strong ethical culture requires zero tolerance for any fraudulent financial reporting.

33. The most likely role of the chief audit executive (CAE) with regard to the financial reporting process is to

A. Ensure that adequate resources have been committed to helping others with their responsibilities for financial reporting.

B. Assess the reliability of the external auditor's work and report these conclusions to the relevant regulatory body.

C. Provide explanations of the company's implementation of GAAP to the external auditor.

D. Work closely with the external auditor during the field audit stage.

Answer (A) is correct. *(Publisher, adapted)*

REQUIRED: The role of the CAE in financial reporting.

DISCUSSION: The CAE needs to review internal audit's risk assessment and audit plans for the year if adequate resources have not been committed to helping senior management, the audit committee, and the external auditor with their responsibilities in the upcoming year's financial reporting regimen.

Answer (B) is incorrect because assessing the external auditor's work is a role of the CAE, but conclusions are communicated to senior management and the board. Answer (C) is incorrect because providing explanations of the company's implementation of GAAP is a role of the accounting function. Answer (D) is incorrect because the CAE is unlikely to work closely with the external auditor in the field audit.

34. The CAE should provide to senior management and the audit committee assurance that

A. The external auditors adequately designed and effectively executed their audit.

B. All events in the financial report are accurate.

C. All significant errors are prevented from occurring in the financial report.

D. All incorrect assumptions and estimates are prevented from occurring in the financial report.

Answer (C) is correct. *(Publisher, adapted)*

REQUIRED: The assurance about financial reporting provided to senior management and the audit committee.

DISCUSSION: The CAE should perform procedures that provide a level of assurance to senior management and the audit committee that the controls surrounding the processes supporting the development of financial reports are adequately designed and effectively executed. The controls should be adequate to ensure the prevention and detection of significant errors, irregularities, incorrect assumptions and estimates, and other events that could result in inaccurate or misleading financial statements, related notes, or other disclosures.

Answer (A) is incorrect because the CAE does not normally perform procedures that provide assurance that the external auditors adequately designed and effectively executed their audit. Answer (B) is incorrect because no assurance is provided about immaterial matters. Answer (D) is incorrect because no assurance is provided about immaterial matters.

35. The CAE should consider many factors in supporting the organizations' governance process and the oversight responsibilities of the governing board and its audit committee regarding the reliability of financial reporting, corporate governance, and corporate control. Which consideration directly relates to governance?

A. Evaluating the adequacy of controls over the accounting function.

B. Evaluating the process of preparing journal entries.

C. Ensuring the reasonableness of estimates.

D. Reviewing pending litigation.

Answer (D) is correct. *(Publisher, adapted)*

REQUIRED: The consideration directly related to governance.

DISCUSSION: The following are matters considered with regard to corporate governance:

- Reviewing corporate policies relating to compliance with laws and regulations, ethics, conflicts of interest, and the timely and thorough investigation of misconduct and fraud allegations.
- Reviewing pending litigation or regulatory proceedings bearing on organizational risk and governance.
- Providing information on employee conflicts of interest, misconduct, fraud, and other outcomes of the organization's ethical procedures and reporting mechanisms.

Answer (A) is incorrect because evaluating the adequacy of controls over the accounting function is a corporate control issue. Answer (B) is incorrect because evaluating the process of preparing journal entries is a corporate control issue. Answer (C) is incorrect because ensuring the reasonableness of estimates is a corporate control issue.

36. The chief audit executive assesses the organization's system of controls to determine whether it is effective. For this purpose, the CAE most likely must

A. Examine the budget to ensure that all unfavorable variances are reasonable.

B. Examine the hiring process to determine whether qualified people are hired promptly and new hires are adequately trained.

C. Examine problems and come to a conclusion on how to resolve them.

D. Audit the e-mail interactions of senior managers to assess whether communication is effective among them.

Answer (B) is correct. *(Publisher, adapted)*

REQUIRED: The procedure most likely performed to assess the effectiveness of an organization's system of controls.

DISCUSSION: The CAE may be expected to assist in answering the following questions in determining the effectiveness of an organization's system of controls:

- Are the organization's controls over the financial reporting process comprehensive, including the preparation of financial statements, related notes, and other required discretionary disclosures that are in integral part of the financial reports?
- Do senior and line management demonstrate that they accept control responsibility?
- Is there an increasing frequency of "surprises" occurring at the senior management, board, or public levels from the organization's reported financial results or in the accompanying disclosures?
- Is there good communication and reporting throughout the organization?
- Are controls seen as enhancing the achievement of objectives or as a "necessary evil"?
- Are qualified people hired promptly, and do they receive adequate training?
- Are problem areas fixed quickly and completely?

Answer (A) is incorrect because unfavorable budget variances are not in themselves indicative of ineffective control. Moreover, merely identifying variances does not determine whether they are reasonable. Answer (C) is incorrect because operational problem solving is unrelated to assessing control effectiveness. Answer (D) is incorrect because auditing the e-mail interactions of senior management is an impermissible procedure.

5.5 Control Criteria

37. If an engagement client's operating standards are vague and thus subject to interpretation, the internal auditor should

A. Seek agreement with the engagement client as to the criteria to be used to measure operating performance.

B. Determine best practices in this area and use them as the standard.

C. Interpret the standards in their strictest sense because standards are otherwise only minimum measures of acceptance.

D. Omit any comments on standards and the engagement client's performance in relationship to those standards because such an analysis would be meaningless.

Answer (A) is correct. *(CIA, adapted)*

REQUIRED: The internal auditor's action if an engagement client's operating standards are vague.

DISCUSSION: Management is responsible for establishing adequate criteria for determining whether objectives and goals have been accomplished (Standard 2120.A4). However, established internal auditors should evaluate the operating targets and expectations and should determine whether those operating standards are acceptable and are being met. When such management targets and criteria are vague, authoritative interpretations should be sought. If internal auditors are required to interpret or select operating standards, they should seek agreement with engagement clients as to the criteria needed to measure operating performance (PA 2120.A4-1).

Answer (B) is incorrect because the internal auditor need not apply the principles of competitive benchmarking. Answer (C) is incorrect because circumstances will dictate the interpretation of vague operating standards. Answer (D) is incorrect because the internal auditor must interpret or select standards if an engagement client's operating standards are vague.

38. During a formal consulting engagement, the internal auditor should always bring substantial risk exposures or material control weaknesses to the attention of

A. Executive management.

B. Management.

C. Audit committee.

D. Board of directors.

Answer (B) is correct. *(Publisher, adapted)*

REQUIRED: The group to whom the internal auditor should always communicate substantial risk exposures or material control weaknesses during a formal consulting engagement.

DISCUSSION: Internal auditors should be observant of the effectiveness of risk management and control processes during formal consulting engagements. Substantial risk exposures or material control weaknesses should be brought to the attention of management. In some situations the auditor's concerns should also be communicated to executive management, the audit committee, or the board of directors.

39. An internal auditor should exercise due professional care in performing engagements. Due professional care includes

A. Establishing direct communication between the chief audit executive and the board of directors.

B. Evaluating established operating standards and determining whether those standards are acceptable and are being met.

C. Accumulating sufficient information so that the internal auditor can give absolute assurance that irregularities do not exist.

D. Establishing suitable criteria of education and experience for filling internal auditing positions.

Answer (B) is correct. *(CIA, adapted)*

REQUIRED: The internal auditor's action consistent with due professional care.

DISCUSSION: In the exercise of due professional care, an internal auditor should, among other things, consider the adequacy and effectiveness of risk management, control, and governance processes (Standard 1220.A1). Furthermore, adequate criteria are needed to evaluate controls. Thus, internal auditors should ascertain the extent to which management has established adequate criteria to determine whether objectives and goals have been accomplished (Standard 2120.A4). Internal auditors should evaluate the established operating targets and expectations and should determine whether those operating standards are acceptable and are being met (PA 2120.A4-1).

Answer (A) is incorrect because such communication promotes the independence of the internal audit activity rather than the performance of engagements with due professional care. Answer (C) is incorrect because assurance procedures alone, even when performed with due professional care, cannot guarantee that all significant risks will be identified (Standard 1220.A2). Answer (D) is incorrect because establishing suitable criteria of education and experience for filling internal auditing positions pertains to proficiency, not due professional care.

40. An internal auditor's role with respect to operating objectives and goals includes

A. Approving the operating objectives or goals to be met.

B. Seeking authoritative interpretations when management's targets and criteria are vague.

C. Developing and implementing control procedures.

D. Accomplishing desired operating program results.

Answer (B) is correct. *(CIA, adapted)*

REQUIRED: The internal auditor's role regarding operating objectives and goals.

DISCUSSION: "Internal auditors should evaluate the established operating targets and expectations and should determine whether those operating standards are acceptable and are being met. When such management targets and criteria are vague, authoritative interpretations should be sought. If internal auditors are required to interpret or select operating standards, they should seek agreement with engagement clients as to the criteria needed to measure operating performance" (PA 2120.A4-1). Operational matters are the responsibility of management. "Internal auditors should not assume operating responsibilities" (PA 1130.A1-1).

41. Internal auditors need to ascertain the extent to which management has established adequate criteria to determine whether goals and objectives have been accomplished. Which of the following actions may be appropriate?

I. Determining whether operating and program goals and objectives conform with those of the organization.

II. Reviewing operations to ascertain the extent to which results are consistent with established goals and objectives.

III. Working with management to develop appropriate control evaluation criteria.

A. I only.

B. I and II only.

C. I, II, and III.

D. II only.

Answer (C) is correct. *(Publisher, adapted)*

REQUIRED: The action(s) that may be taken if management has not established criteria for achievement of goals and objectives.

DISCUSSION: "Internal auditors should ascertain the extent to which operating and program goals and objectives have been established and conform to those of the organization" (Standard 2120.A2). Internal auditors also "should review operations and programs to ascertain the extent to which results are consistent with established goals and objectives to determine whether operations and programs are being implemented or performed as intended" (Standard 2120.A3). Furthermore, "Adequate criteria are needed to evaluate controls. Internal auditors should ascertain the extent to which management has established adequate criteria to determine whether objectives and goals have been accomplished. If adequate, internal auditors should use such criteria in their evaluation. If inadequate, internal auditors should work with management to develop appropriate evaluation criteria" (Standard 2120.A4).

42. In evaluating the effectiveness and efficiency with which resources are employed, an internal auditor is responsible for

A. Determining the extent to which adequate operating criteria have been established.

B. Verifying the existence of assets.

C. Reviewing the reliability of operating information.

D. Verifying the accuracy of asset valuation.

Answer (A) is correct. *(CIA, adapted)*

REQUIRED: The internal auditor's responsibility for evaluating economic and efficient use of resources.

DISCUSSION: The internal audit activity evaluates the controls encompassing governance, operations, and information systems. This evaluation includes the effectiveness and efficiency of operations (Standard 2120.A1). Moreover, the internal auditors should "ascertain the extent to which management has established adequate criteria to determine whether objectives and goals have been accomplished" (Standard 2120.A4). They should also "evaluate the established operating targets and expectations and should determine whether those operating standards are acceptable and are being met" (PA 2120.A4-1). Verifying existence relates to the safeguarding of assets. The reliability of operating information and the accuracy of asset valuation concern the reliability and integrity of information.

STUDY UNIT SIX
CONTROL II

(35 pages of outline)

This study unit is the second of two devoted to control. Study Unit 5 emphasized authoritative pronouncements and certain theoretical considerations. Study Unit 6 enlarges upon those considerations, especially with regard to control frameworks. It also extends to related subjects such as the implications of organizational structures and leadership styles and the management of change and conflict.

Core Concepts

- The essence of control is ensuring that plans achieve desired objectives.
- Control measures performance against a standard and takes corrective action if indicated by that measurement.
- The internal control framework developed by the Committee of Sponsoring Organizations (COSO) treats control as a process effected by the board, management, and others. This process should provide reasonable assurance of achieving objectives related to (a) reliability of reporting, (b) effectiveness and efficiency of operations, and (c) compliance with laws and regulations.
  a. The COSO has extended the framework to the broader area of enterprise risk management (ERM). It has also developed guidance for smaller public companies.
- Management control techniques include (a) organization, (b) policies, (c) procedures, (d) personnel, (e) accounting, (f) budgeting, and (g) reporting.
- The elements of organizations are coordination of effort, a common purpose, division of labor, and a hierarchy of authority.
- Leadership is the act or process of influencing, inspiring, and guiding people so they will strive willingly toward the achievement of group objectives through common effort.
- Effective change management is important because an appropriate balance between stability and change is necessary if an organization is to thrive.
- According to Dean Tjosvold, conflict involves "incompatible behaviors; one person interfering, disrupting, or in some other way making actions less effective." However, conflict may be cooperative as well as competitive.

6.1 OVERVIEW OF CONTROL

1. The **essence of control** is ensuring that plans achieve the desired objectives.
   a. Control requires **feedback** on the results of organizational activities for the purposes of measurement and correction.
   b. Control requires **performance** to be
      1) Measured against a **standard**
      2) **Corrected** (if necessary) in accordance with that measurement
         a) Thus, the **timeliness** of feedback is important.
2. **PA 2100-1** classifies controls as preventive, detective, and directive. Controls also are often classified as follows:
   a. **Feedback controls** obtain information about completed activities. They permit improvement in future performance by learning from past mistakes. Thus, corrective action occurs after the fact. Inspection of completed goods is an example.
   b. **Concurrent controls** adjust ongoing processes. These real-time controls monitor activities in the present to prevent them from deviating too far from standards. An example is close supervision of production-line workers.
   c. **Feedforward controls** anticipate and prevent problems. These controls require a long-term perspective. Organizational policies and procedures are examples.
3. Sawyer describes controls as **financial** and **operating** (nonfinancial). Both should be related to objectives and criteria.
   a. Financial controls should be based on relevant established accounting principles. Objectives of financial controls may include (1) proper authorization; (2) appropriate accounting; (3) safeguarding of assets; and (4) compliance with laws, regulations, and contracts.
   b. Operating controls applicable to production and support activities may lack established criteria or standards. Thus, they should be based on management principles and methods and determined with regard to the management functions of planning, organizing, directing, and controlling.
4. Control may be viewed from a **systems perspective**. A **system** is a set of related elements with a purpose.
   a. In every **operating system**, a process transforms an input to an output:

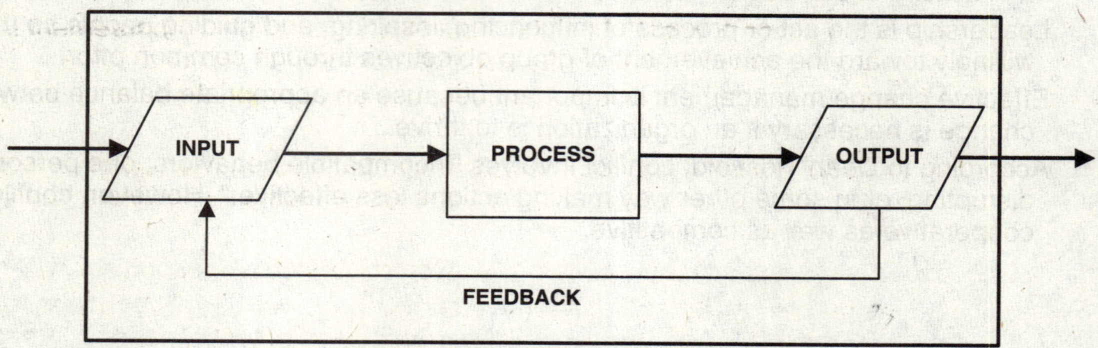

   b. **Feedback** provides information as to whether the desired state has been attained or maintained. This function is control.
   c. The **system boundary** determines what variables are internal or external to the system. They are internal if they are part of the system.

d. **Subsystems** may extend the system's boundaries.
e. Systems are open or closed.
    1) **Open** systems accept uncontrolled inputs that may affect the system.
    2) **Closed** systems do not accept uncontrolled inputs.
        a) Closed systems may be ineffective in rapidly changing environments.

5. A typical **sequence of control functions** includes
    a. Selecting strategic **control points** at which to gather information about the activities being performed
    b. **Observing** the work or collecting samples or other significant data as a basis for **measurement**
    c. Accumulating, classifying, and recording this **information**
    d. **Comparing** it with predetermined quality, schedule, and cost **standards**
    e. Determining whether **performance** is satisfactory
    f. **Reporting** significant deviations to managers concerned
    g. Determining, by repeating the steps, whether action taken is effective in correcting reported deviations **(follow-up)**
        1) Correction should occur before deviations become serious.
    h. Reviewing and revising **standards**
6. **Planning and control** overlap, and some common managerial tools apply to both.
    a. Comprehensive planning includes creation of control mechanisms, i.e., measurement and follow-up.
    b. Budgets and breakeven charts are examples of systematically combining planning with control.
7. Controls may be either **quantitative** or **qualitative**.
    a. Budgets, schedules, quotas, charts, etc., are quantitative.
    b. Job instructions, quality-control standards, and employment criteria are qualitative.
8. Effective control should be
    a. **Timely.** Detection should permit early correction of deviations.
    b. **Economical.** Controls should give reasonable assurance of obtaining expected results within the **cost-benefit** constraint.
    c. **Well-placed.** Control points should be those where measurement is most likely to identify critical deviations from organizational objectives.
    d. **Flexible.** Controls should allow for operational changes. An example is a flexible budget.
    e. **Appropriate.** Controls should satisfy the needs of management and fit within the organizational structure. They also should fairly reflect what they are designed to measure.
    f. Consistent with **accountability**. Controls establish responsibility for results.
    g. Able to **identify causes**. Rapid correction is more likely if responses have been planned for deviations resulting from known potential causes. Variance analysis in cost accounting is a cause-identifying control.

9. **Control standards** may take many forms, depending on the functions and levels where they are applied. They should assist in implementing **plans** and be applied at those points that significantly influence subsequent progress.
   a. Standards must be **accepted** by those whose work will be measured if they are to have maximum effectiveness.
      1) Subordinates should believe that standards are **fair and achievable**, or they will tend to sabotage, ignore, or circumvent them.
      2) **Participation** in the standard-setting process will encourage acceptance of standards. It will increase understanding of their meanings, measures, and purposes by those affected.
   b. Standards should be **flexible** and **reviewed** periodically.
   c. The degree of difficulty in meeting a standard is **tightness**. The more difficult a standard is to achieve, the tighter it is said to be.
      1) Tight standards can have positive **behavioral implications** if they motivate employees to strive for excellence.
         a) They can have negative effects if they are difficult or impossible to attain.
10. **Measurement. Behavioral considerations** are important factors in selecting who does the measuring, as well as what is measured and what standards are used.
   a. **Self-measurement** may create confidence and trust. Moreover, feedback, correction, and learning may occur more quickly.
      1) It also may lead to distortion, concealment, and delay in reporting when goals and measurement criteria are unclear.
      2) It forces clear definition and open communication of organizational objectives because employees must know the standards and measures.
   b. **Second-party measurement** may create hostility, concern, rebellion, and other negative reactions.
      1) It also may minimize bias, influence, and suspicion.
11. **Reengineering.** Control has been facilitated by **improvements in information technology** and reductions in its cost, which have made real-time information common, e.g., airline reservation systems, retail point-of-sale systems, and production-line status systems.
   a. Technological advances also have increased the popularity of reengineering. **Reengineering** (also called **business process reengineering**) entails process innovation and core process redesign. Instead of improving existing procedures, it finds new ways of doing things. Its emphasis is on simplification and elimination of nonvalue-adding activities.
   b. **Downsizing** as well as reengineering have led to the **outsourcing** of traditional functions, e.g., inventory management, accounts payable, and accounts receivable. In the resulting **virtual organization**, responsibility and accountability are transferred to other entities.
   c. Consequently, technology change, reengineering, and downsizing have eliminated many **traditional controls**. They exploit modern technology to improve productivity and decrease the number of clerical workers.
      1) Thus, organizations develop controls that are **automated** and **self-correcting** and require minimal human intervention.

d. The emphasis therefore shifts to **monitoring** internal control so management can determine when an operation may be out of control and corrective action is needed.

1) Most reengineering techniques also assume that humans will be motivated to work actively in improving operations when they are full participants.

2) Monitoring assesses the **quality of internal control over time**. Management considers whether internal control is properly designed and operating as intended and modifies it to reflect changing conditions. Monitoring may be in the form of separate, periodic evaluations, for example, as part of an annual audit. It also may be ongoing.

a) **Ongoing monitoring** occurs as part of routine operations. It includes management and supervisory review, comparisons, reconciliations, and other actions by personnel as part of their regular activities.

12. Stop and review! You have completed the outline for this subunit. Study multiple-choice questions 1 through 11 beginning on page 230.

6.2 CONTROL FRAMEWORKS

1. The Committee of Sponsoring Organizations **(COSO)**, a group that includes The IIA and the AICPA, among others, published *Internal Control - Integrated Framework*. It describes a model (the COSO model) that is the basis for control frameworks developed by other organizations. For example, the AICPA's control pronouncements closely follow the COSO model. The IIA has expressed a preference for the COSO model but states that "it may be appropriate to use some other recognized and credible model" (PA 2120.A1-4).

a. **Definition of control.** The COSO model treats internal control as a **process** – effected by an entity's board of directors, management, and other **personnel** – designed to provide **reasonable assurance** regarding the achievement of **objectives** related to

1) **Reliability** of financial reporting, e.g., published financial information;
2) **Effectiveness and efficiency** of operations, e.g., achievement of performance and profit goals and the safeguarding of resources; and
3) **Compliance** with applicable laws and regulations.

b. Internal control is composed of five interrelated **components**.

1) The **control environment** reflects the attitude and actions of the board and management regarding the significance of control within the organization. It sets the organization's tone and influences the control consciousness of its personnel. Moreover, the control environment provides discipline and structure for the achievement of the primary objectives of internal control. The control environment includes the following elements:

a) **Integrity and ethical values.** Standards should be effectively communicated, e.g., by management example. Management also should remove incentives and temptations for dishonest or unethical acts.

b) **Commitment to competence.** Management must consider the competence levels required for particular jobs.

c) **Board of directors or audit committee participation.** Their independence, experience, stature, and other attributes affect the priority assigned to control by members of the organization.

d) **Management's philosophy and operating style.** This element includes management's

i) Approach to taking and monitoring business **risks**

ii) Attitudes and actions related to financial reporting

iii) Attitudes toward information processing and accounting functions and personnel

e) **Organizational structure.** Key areas of authority and responsibility and appropriate lines of reporting should be considered.

f) **Assignment of authority and responsibility.** How authority over and responsibility for operating activities are assigned and how reporting relationships and authorization hierarchies are established are important factors.

g) **Human resource policies and practices.** Hiring, orientation, training, evaluation, counseling, promoting, compensating, and remedial actions must be considered by management. Training policies should communicate roles and responsibilities and expected levels of performance and behavior.

2) **Risk assessment** is based on a set of complementary **operational, financial reporting, and compliance objectives** linked across all levels of the organization. Risk assessment identifies and analyzes external or internal risks affecting achievement of the objectives at the activity level and the entity level. The assessment provides a foundation for **managing change** in the economy, the industry and regulatory environments, and other operating conditions. The following factors affecting risk should be given special attention:

a) **Changes in the operating environment.** A shift in the regulatory or operating environment may require reconsideration of risks.

b) **New personnel.** New employees may have a different focus on control issues.

c) **New or revamped information systems.** Significant and rapid changes in information systems can affect **control risk**, but IT is important to the risk assessment process because it provides timely information for identifying and managing risks.

d) **Rapid growth.** Expansion can strain controls and increase risk.

e) **New technology.** Integrating new technology into production or information processes may change risk.

f) **New business lines, products, or activities.** New business areas may change risk.

g) **Corporate restructurings.** Staffing changes can cause changes in risk.

h) **Expanded foreign operations.** Expansion to foreign markets may result in changes in risk.

3) **Control activities** are the policies and procedures applied to ensure that management directives are executed and actions are taken to address risks affecting achievement of objectives. Whether **automated or manual**, they have various objectives and are applied at all levels and functions of the organization.

a) **Performance reviews** by top managers include reviews of actual performance versus budgets, forecasts, prior performance, and competitors' results.

b) **Performance reviews at the functional or activity level** involve reviews of performance reports, such as a sales manager's review of results by retail outlet.

c) **Analysis of performance indicators**, that is, comparison of different sets of operating or financial data, may reveal unexpected results or trends that should be investigated.

d) **Information processing** requires checks of accuracy, completeness, and authorization of transactions. These controls include **application controls** and **general controls**. Application controls apply to the execution of specific tasks. General controls include controls over data center operations, system software, access security, and applications development and maintenance.

e) **Physical controls** involve the security of assets and records and periodic counts and reconciliations.

f) **Segregation of duties** involves the separation of the functions of authorization, record keeping, and asset custody so as to minimize the opportunities for a person to be able to perpetrate and conceal errors or fraud in the normal course of his/her duties. For example, a payroll department has a record keeping function, the personnel department authorizes payroll transactions, and the treasurer has custody of cash.

4) **Information and communication.** Relevant internal and external information should be identified, captured, and communicated in a timely manner and in appropriate forms.

a) An **information system** may be formal or informal. It uses internal and external information to generate reports on financial, operational, and compliance matters.

i) These reports facilitate (a) the operation and control of the organization, (b) decision making, and (c) external communications.

ii) An information system may perform a routine **monitoring function** or be used for special tasks.

iii) Information systems should be **integrated** with operations, the financial reporting process, and the **strategic objectives** of the enterprise.

iv) Information should be appropriate, timely, current, accurate, and accessible.

b) **Communication** of information within the organization may take many forms and should be two-way, both vertically and horizontally.

i) Communication of information allows people in the organization to perform their duties regarding financial reporting, operations, and compliance.

ii) Communication also functions in a more general way. Thus, individuals in the organization should understand their obligations regarding **control** and how their work relates to the efforts of others.

iii) Communication channels should be clear, and all parties should have good **listening** skills.

iv) Effective communication between managers and directors is vital.

v) Communication with such **external parties** as customers, suppliers, regulators, and shareholders should be open and effective.

5) **Monitoring** is "a process that assesses the quality of the system's performance over time."

a) It consists of **ongoing activities** built into normal operations to ensure that they continue to be performed effectively. Supervision and other ordinary management functions, consideration of communications with external parties, and the actions of internal and external auditors are examples.

b) Monitoring also involves **separate evaluations**. The need for this form of monitoring depends on the effectiveness of the ongoing monitoring activities and the risk assessment.

i) Separate evaluation may consist of **control self-assessment** or formal evaluations by internal or external **auditors**. Laws and regulations may require that an external assessment of internal control be performed periodically.

ii) **Deficiencies** in internal control should be reported, with the most serious matters being communicated to senior management and the board.

c. Because of the **inherent limitations of control**, it can be designed and implemented to provide only **reasonable assurance** that control objectives are met.

1) **Inherent Limitations**

a) **Human judgment** is faulty, and controls may fail because of simple errors or mistakes.

b) Manual or automated controls can be circumvented by **collusion**.

c) Management may inappropriately **override** internal control.

d) Custom, culture, the corporate governance system, and an effective control environment are not absolute deterrents to **fraud**. For example, if the nature of management incentives increases the risk of material misstatements, the effectiveness of controls may be diminished.

e) **Costs should not exceed the benefits of control.** Although this relationship is a primary design criterion for control, the precise measurement of costs and benefits is not feasible.

d. **Responsibility** for internal control resides with (is "owned" by) the chief executive, but all people in the organization share this responsibility.

1) Parties with significant roles are (a) the financial and accounting officers, (b) other managers, (c) the internal auditors (who nevertheless do not have primary responsibility for establishing or maintaining internal control), (d) the board and the audit committee, and (e) external parties (e.g., the external auditors).

2. The Committee of Sponsoring Organizations (COSO) has published *Enterprise Risk Management - Integrated Framework*. It describes a model that **incorporates** the earlier **COSO control framework** while extending it to the broader area of enterprise risk management **(ERM)**.

a. The **definition of ERM** broadly states key concepts applicable to many types of organizations. The emphasis is on (1) the objectives of a specific entity and (2) establishing a means for evaluating the effectiveness of ERM.

Enterprise risk management is a process, effected by an entity's board of directors, management, and other personnel, applied in strategy setting and across the enterprise, designed to identify potential events that may affect the entity, and manage risk to be within its risk appetite, to provide reasonable assurance regarding the achievement of entity objectives.

b. ERM allows management to optimize **stakeholder value** by coping effectively with **uncertainty** and the **risks** and **opportunities** it presents. ERM helps management to (1) reach objectives, (2) prevent loss of reputation and resources, (3) report effectively, and (4) comply with laws and regulations. The following are the **capabilities** of ERM:

1) **Consideration of risk appetite and strategy.** Risk appetite should be considered in (a) evaluating strategic options, (b) setting objectives, and (c) developing risk management techniques.
2) **Risk response decisions.** ERM permits identification and selection of such responses to risk as (a) avoidance, (b) reduction, (c) sharing, and (d) acceptance.
3) **Reduction of operational surprises and losses.** These are reduced by an improved ability to anticipate potential events and develop responses.
4) **Multiple and cross-enterprise risks.** Risks may affect different parts of the entity. ERM allows (a) effective responses to interrelated effects and (b) integrated responses to multiple risks.
5) **Response to opportunities.** By facilitating the identification of potential events, ERM helps management to respond quickly to opportunities.
6) **Deployment of capital.** The risk information provided by ERM permits (a) assessment of capital needs and (b) better capital allocation.

c. **Events with a negative impact** are risks. **Events with a positive impact** offset risks or create opportunities.

1) An **opportunity** "is the possibility that an event will occur and positively affect the achievement of objectives, supporting value creation or preservation."
2) Management **plans** to exploit opportunities subject to the processes for developing **strategies and objectives**.

d. **Objectives**

1) The following are the four categories of objectives:
   a) **Strategic objectives** align with and support the entity's mission.
   b) **Operations objectives** address effectiveness and efficiency.
   c) **Reporting objectives** concern reliability.
   d) **Compliance objectives** relate to adherence to laws and regulations.
2) These categories overlap but are distinct. They concern different needs, and different managers may be assigned responsibility for them.
   a) The COSO's ERM framework also defines another category – **safeguarding of resources** – that may be appropriate for some organizations.
3) **Strategic and operational** matters are affected by external events that the organization may not control. Hence, ERM should provide reasonable assurance that management and the board receive timely information about whether those objectives are being achieved.
4) **Reporting and compliance** are within the organization's control. Accordingly, ERM should provide reasonable assurance of achieving those objectives.

e. The **components** of ERM are integrated with the **management process** and may mutually influence each other.

   1) The **internal environment** reflects risk management, philosophy, risk appetite, integrity, ethical values, and the overall environment. It sets the tone of the entity.
   2) **Objective setting** precedes event identification. ERM ensures that (a) a process is established and (b) objectives align with the mission and the risk appetite.
   3) **Event identification** relates to internal and external events affecting the organization. It differentiates between opportunities and risks. Opportunities are referred to the strategy or objective-setting processes.
   4) **Risk assessment** considers likelihood and impact (see the definitions of risk in the Glossary) as a basis for risk management. The assessment considers the inherent risk and the residual risk.
   5) **Risk responses** should be consistent with the organization's risk tolerances and appetite.
   6) **Control activities** are policies and procedures to ensure the effectiveness of risk responses.
   7) The **information and communication** component identifies, captures, and communicates relevant and timely information.
   8) **Monitoring** involves ongoing management activities or separate evaluations. The full ERM process is monitored.

f. The **objectives** (the ends) and the **components** (the means) are directly related.

   1) They may be depicted in a **matrix** with eight rows (components) and four columns (categories of objectives).
   2) A third dimension of the matrix consists of the entity's **units** (e.g., entity, division, business unit, and subsidiary levels).

g. **Components** should be **present and functioning effectively**. Consequently, the components are criteria for the effectiveness of ERM.

   1) "Present and functioning effectively" means that (a) no **material weaknesses** exist and (b) **risk** is within the risk appetite.
   2) When ERM is effective regarding all of the **objectives**, the board and management have reasonable assurance that (a) reporting is reliable, (b) compliance is achieved, and (c) they know the extent of achievement of strategic and operations objectives.
   3) The components operate differently in **different organizations**. For example, they may be applied in a less formal way in smaller organizations.

h. **Limitations** of ERM arise from the possibility of (1) faulty human judgment, (2) cost-benefit considerations, (3) simple errors or mistakes, (4) collusion, and (5) management override of ERM decisions.

i. Everyone in the organization bears some **responsibility** for ERM. For example, (1) the CEO has ultimate responsibility, (2) other managers promote compliance with the risk appetite and manage risks consistently with risk tolerances, and (3) internal auditors have supporting roles.

j. According to **The IIA Position Paper**, *The Role of Internal Audit in Enterprise-wide Risk Management*, internal audit has certain core roles and may play certain other legitimate roles.

1) **Core internal audit roles in regard to ERM**
   a) Giving assurance on risk management processes
   b) Giving assurance that risks are correctly evaluated
   c) Evaluating risk management processes
   d) Evaluating the reporting of key risks
   e) Reviewing the management of key risks

2) **Legitimate internal audit roles with safeguards**
   a) Facilitating identification and evaluation of risks
   b) Coaching management in responding to risks
   c) Coordinating ERM activities
   d) Consolidating the reporting on risks
   e) Maintaining and developing the ERM framework
   f) Championing establishment of ERM
   g) Developing risk management strategy for board approval

3) **Roles internal audit should not undertake**
   a) Setting the risk appetite.
   b) Imposing risk management processes.
   c) Managing assurance on risks.
   d) Making decisions on risk responses.
   e) Implementing risk responses on management's behalf.
   f) Accountability for risk management. Thus, an internal auditor should not also be the organization's **chief risk officer (CRO)**. An organization should appoint a CRO who is not part of the internal audit function.
      i) A CRO is a member of management assigned primary responsibility for ERM processes. The CRO is most effective when supported by a specific team with the necessary expertise and experience related to organization-wide risk.

3. Another COSO publication is *Internal Control over Financial Reporting - Guidance for Smaller Public Companies*. It provides guidance to any company on how to apply the COSO control framework "in designing and implementing cost-effective internal control over financial reporting." This guidance is based on **20 basic principles**. These fundamental concepts are derived from the **five components** of the COSO control framework.

a. **Control Environment**

1) **Integrity and ethical values.** Sound values, especially those of senior management, set the standard of conduct.
2) **Board of directors.** The board should understand and oversee financial reporting and related control.
3) **Management's philosophy and operating style.** These support effective control.
4) **Organizational structure.** This supports effective control.
5) **Financial reporting competencies.** Certain employees should be competent in financial reporting and its oversight.
6) **Authority and responsibility.** Appropriate assignment of levels of authority and responsibility should facilitate effective control.
7) **Human resources.** The related policies and practices should be designed and implemented to facilitate effective control.

b. **Risk Assessment**

1) **Financial reporting objectives.** Management should clearly specify the objectives. The criteria should be sufficient to permit identification of risk.
2) **Financial reporting risks.** Risks to achieving the objectives should be analyzed to determine how they should be managed.
3) **Fraud risk.** Material misstatement due to fraud is explicitly considered in the risk assessment.

c. **Control Activities**

1) **Integration with risk assessment.** Control actions should address risks.
2) **Section and development of control activities.** Their cost and potential effectiveness in mitigating risks should be considered.
3) **Policies and procedures.** Policies should be developed and communicated throughout the company. Management directives should be executed using the procedures corresponding to the policies.
4) **Information technology.** IT controls should be designed and implemented to support the achievement of objectives.

d. **Information and Communication**

1) **Financial reporting information.** Relevant information should be identified, captured, and used at all levels and distributed. Its form and timeliness should support the achievement of objectives.
2) **Internal control information.** Information needed by other control components should be identified, captured, and distributed. Its form and timeliness should enable personnel to carry out their responsibilities.
3) **Internal communication.** This supports understanding and execution of control objectives, processes, and responsibilities at all levels.
4) **External communication.** Factors affecting attainment of objectives should be communicated to parties outside the company.

e. **Monitoring**

1) **Ongoing and separate evaluations.** These enable management to determine whether control is present and functioning.
2) **Reporting deficiencies.** These should be identified and communicated on a timely basis to those responsible for corrective action. Management and the board also should be notified as appropriate.

4. The **CoCo model** is an adaptation of the COSO model by the Criteria of Control Board of the Canadian Institute of Chartered Accountants. It is thought to be better designed for internal auditing purposes.

a. The CoCo model consists of **20 criteria** grouped into **four components**. The following listing is from *Sawyer's Internal Auditing*, 5th Ed., L.B. Sawyer, et al., 2003, The Institute of Internal Auditors (pages 68-69):

1) ***Purpose***

a) **Objectives** should be established and communicated.
b) Significant internal and external **risks** should be identified and assessed.
c) **Policies** designed to support the achievement of an organization's objectives and the management of its risks should be established, communicated, and practiced so that people understand what is expected of them and the scope of their freedom to act.
d) **Plans** to achieve the objectives should be established and communicated.
e) Objectives and related plans should include measurable **performance targets and indicators**.

2) ***Commitment***

a) Shared **ethical values**, including integrity, should be established, communicated, and practiced through the organization.

b) **Human resource** policies and practices should be consistent with an organization's ethical values and with achievement of its objectives.

c) **Authority, responsibility, and accountability** should be clearly defined and consistent with an organization's objectives so that decisions and actions are taken by the appropriate people.

d) An atmosphere of **mutual trust** should be fostered to support the flow of information between people and their effective performance toward achieving the organization's objectives.

3) ***Capability***

a) People should have the necessary **knowledge, skills, and tools** to support the achievement of the organization's objectives.

b) **Communication** processes should support the organization's values and the achievement of its objectives.

c) **Sufficient and relevant information** should be identified and communicated in a timely manner to enable people to perform their assigned responsibilities.

d) The decisions and actions of different parts of the organization should be **coordinated**.

e) **Control activities** should be designed as an integral part of the organization, taking into consideration its objectives, the risks to their achievement, and the interrelatedness of control elements.

4) ***Monitoring and Learning***

a) **External and internal environments** should be monitored to obtain information that may signal a need to reevaluate the organization's objectives or controls.

b) **Performance** should be monitored against the targets and indicators identified in the organization's objectives and plans.

c) The **assumptions** behind an organization's objectives and systems should be periodically challenged.

d) **Information** needs and related information systems should be reassessed as objectives change or as reporting deficiencies are identified.

e) **Follow-up** procedures should be established and performed to ensure appropriate change or action occurs.

f) Management should periodically **assess the effectiveness of control** in its organization and communicate the results to those to whom it is accountable.

b. The COSO and CoCo models emphasize **soft controls** (see Roth, "Taking a Hard Look at Soft Controls," *Internal Auditor*, February 1998). For example, the communication of ethical values and the fostering of mutual trust are soft controls in the CoCo model. In the COSO model, soft controls are embodied in the control environment.

1) Soft controls should be distinguished from the **hard controls** represented by compliance with specific policies and procedures imposed upon employees from above.

2) Soft controls have become more necessary as **technology advances** have empowered employees. Technology has given them access to large amounts of critical information and enabled them to make decisions formerly made by those higher in the organizational structure.

   a) In addition to making many hard controls obsolete, technology advances also have permitted the **automation** of hard controls, for example, the embedding of audit modules in computer programs.

3) One approach to auditing soft controls is **control self-assessment**, which is the involvement of management and staff in the assessment of internal controls within their workgroup.

4) Hard and soft controls can be associated with particular risks and measured. The vulnerability (V) addressed can be stated as the product of the probability of occurrence (P) and the significance of the occurrence (S). Accordingly, the formula is

$$PS = V$$

5. The IIA's own **Systems Auditability and Control study** (1991) defined the system of internal controls as follows:

   "Means established to provide reasonable assurance that the overall objectives and goals of the organization are achieved in an efficient, effective, and economical manner. For the purpose of this report, a system of internal control is defined as a set of processes, functions, activities, subsystems, and people who are grouped together or consciously segregated to ensure the effective achievement of objectives."

   a. **Key concepts** are

      1) Reasonable assurance
      2) Objectives as desired accomplishments of the organization
      3) Goals as specific targets that are identifiable, measurable, attainable, and consistent with the objectives

   b. **Components**

      1) **Control environment**

         a) Organizational structure
         b) Control framework

            i) Segregation of incompatible duties
            ii) Competence and integrity of people
            iii) Appropriate levels of authority and responsibility
            iv) Tracing transactions or events to responsible persons
            v) Adequate resources, time, and knowledgeable personnel
            vi) Supervision of staff and review of work

         c) Organizational policies and procedures
         d) External influence

      2) **Manual and automated systems**

         a) Systems software
         b) Application systems

            i) Core business and financial systems
            ii) Specific operational systems

         c) End-user and departmental systems

3) **Control procedures**

a) General controls
b) Application controls
c) Compensating controls

6. See Study Unit 5 for **Practice Advisory 2120.A1-2**: *Using Control Self-Assessment for Assessing the Adequacy of Control Processes.*
7. Stop and review! You have completed the outline for this subunit. Study multiple-choice questions 12 through 33 beginning on page 233.

6.3 MANAGEMENT CONTROL TECHNIQUES

1. Sawyer, Dittenhofer, and Scheiner in *Sawyer's Internal Auditing* (Altamonte Springs, FL: The Institute of Internal Auditors, 5th ed., 2003, pages 63-64; 82-86) provide definitions of control and list the means of achieving control. From an internal auditor's perspective, control may be defined as

> *The employment of all the means devised in an enterprise to promote, direct, restrain, govern, and check upon its various activities for the purpose of seeing that enterprise objectives are met. These means of control include, but are not limited to, form of organization, policies, systems, procedures, instructions, standards, committees, charts of accounts, forecasts, budgets, schedules, reports, records, checklists, methods, devices, and internal auditing.*

2. The means of control are

a. **Organization.** Organization, as a means of control, is an approved **intentional structuring** of roles assigned to people within the entity so that it can achieve its objectives efficiently and economically.

1) Responsibilities should be **divided** so that no one person will control all phases of any transaction. See the discussion of segregation of duties in 6.2.1.b.3).
2) Managers should have the **authority** to take the action necessary to discharge their responsibilities.
3) **Individual** responsibility always should be clearly defined so that it can be neither sidestepped nor exceeded.
4) An official who assigns responsibility and delegates authority to subordinates should have an effective system of **follow-up**. Its purpose is to ensure that tasks assigned are properly carried out.
5) The individuals to whom authority is delegated should be allowed to exercise that authority **without close supervision**. But they should check with their superiors in case of exceptions.
6) People should be required to **account to** their superiors for the manner in which they have discharged their responsibilities.
7) The organization should be **flexible** enough to permit changes in its structure when operating plans, policies, and objectives change.
8) Organizational **structures** should be as simple as possible.
9) Organization **charts and manuals** should be prepared. They help plan and control changes in, as well as provide better understanding of, the organization, chain of authority, and assignment of responsibilities.

b. **Policies.** A policy is any stated principle that requires, guides, or restricts action. Policies should follow certain **principles**.

1) Policies should be clearly stated in **writing** in systematically organized handbooks, manuals, or other publications, and properly approved. But when the organizational culture is strong, the need for formal, written policies is reduced. In a strong culture, substantial training results in a high degree of acceptance of the organization's key values. Thus, such values are intensely held and widely shared.
2) Policies should be systematically **communicated** to all officials and appropriate employees of the organization.
3) Policies must conform with applicable **laws and regulations**. They should be consistent with objectives and general policies prescribed at higher levels.
4) Policies should be designed to promote the conduct of authorized activities in an effective, efficient, and economical manner. They should provide a satisfactory degree of **assurance** that resources are suitably safeguarded.
5) Policies should be periodically **reviewed**. They should be **revised** when circumstances change.

c. **Procedures.** Procedures are methods employed to carry out activities in conformity with prescribed policies. The same principles applicable to policies also are applicable to procedures. In addition,

1) To reduce the possibility of **fraud and error**, procedures should be so **coordinated** that one employee's work is automatically checked by another who is independently performing separate prescribed duties. The extent to which **automatic internal checks** should be built into the system of control depends on many factors. Examples are (a) degree of risk, (b) cost of preventive procedures, (c) availability of personnel, (d) operational impact, and (e) feasibility.
2) For nonmechanical operations, prescribed procedures should **not be so detailed** as to stifle the use of judgment.
3) To promote maximum **efficiency and economy**, prescribed procedures should be as simple and as inexpensive as possible.
4) Procedures should not be **overlapping, conflicting, or duplicative**.
5) Procedures should be periodically **reviewed** and improved as necessary.

d. **Personnel.** People hired or assigned should have the qualifications to do the jobs assigned to them. The best form of control over the performance of individuals is **supervision**. Hence, high standards of supervision should be established. The following practices help improve control.

1) New employees should be investigated as to **honesty and reliability**.
2) Employees should be given **training** that provides the opportunity for improvement and keeps them informed of new policies and procedures.
3) Employees should be given information on the duties and responsibilities of **other segments** of the organization. They will better understand how and where their jobs fit into the organization as a whole.
4) The performance of all employees should be **periodically reviewed** to see whether all essential requirements of their jobs are being met. Superior **performance** should be given appropriate recognition. Shortcomings should be discussed with employees so that they are given an opportunity to improve their performance or upgrade their skills.

e. **Accounting.** Accounting is the indispensable means of **financial control** over activities and resources. It is a framework that can be fitted to assignments of responsibility. Moreover, it is the financial scorekeeper of the organization. The problem lies in what scores to keep. Some basic principles for accounting systems follow:

1) Accounting should fit the **needs of managers** for rational decision making rather than the dictates of a textbook or check list.
2) Accounting should be based on **lines of responsibility**.
3) Financial reports of operating results should parallel the **organizational units** responsible for carrying out operations.
4) Accounting should permit **controllable costs** to be identified.

f. **Budgeting.** A budget is a statement of **expected results** expressed in numerical terms. As a control, it sets a standard for input of resources and what should be achieved as output and outcomes.

1) Those who are responsible for meeting a budget should **participate** in its preparation.
2) Those responsible for meeting a budget should be provided with adequate information that **compares budgets** with actual events and shows reasons for any significant variances.
3) All **subsidiary budgets** should tie into the overall budget.
4) Budgets should set **measurable objectives**. Budgets are meaningless unless managers know why they have a budget.
5) Budgets should help sharpen the **organizational structure**. Objective budgeting standards are difficult to set in a confused combination of subsystems. Budgeting is therefore a form of discipline and coordination.

g. **Reporting.** In most organizations, management functions and makes decisions on the basis of reports it receives. Thus, reports should be timely, accurate, meaningful, and economical. The following are some principles for establishing a satisfactory **internal reporting system**:

1) Reports should be made in accordance with **assigned responsibilities**.
2) Individuals or units should be required to report only on those matters for which they are **responsible**.
3) The **cost** of accumulating data and preparing reports should be weighed against the **benefits** to be obtained from them.
4) Reports should be as **simple** as possible and **consistent** with the nature of the subject matter. They should include only information that serves the **needs** of the readers. Common **classifications and terminology** should be used as much as possible to avoid confusion.
5) When appropriate, **performance reports** should show comparisons with predetermined standards of cost, quality, and quantity. **Controllable costs** should be segregated.
6) When performance cannot be reported in quantitative terms, the reports should be designed to **emphasize exceptions** or other matters requiring management attention.
7) For maximum value, reports should be **timely**. Timely reports based partly on estimates may be more useful than delayed reports that are more precise.
8) Report **recipients should be polled** periodically to see whether they still need the reports they are receiving or whether the reports could be improved.

3. Management control processes can take two approaches.
   a. **Imposed control** is the traditional, mechanical approach, consisting of measuring performance against standards and then taking corrective action through the individual responsible for the function or area being evaluated.
      1) Though common in organizations, it has one striking drawback: Corrective action tends to come **after** the performance has taken place (often resulting in negative disciplinary action).
   b. **Self-control** is an emerging and increasingly important approach. It evaluates the entire process of management and the functions performed. Thus, it attempts to improve that process instead of simply correcting the specific performance of the manager. Management by objectives (MBO) is a good example of this approach.
4. Stop and review! You have completed the outline for this subunit. Study multiple-choice questions 34 through 55 beginning on page 239.

6.4 ORGANIZATIONAL STRUCTURES

1. **Edgar Schein** describes the following **elements** of organizations:
   a. **Coordination of effort** in a cooperative social arrangement
   b. A **common goal or purpose**
   c. **Division of labor** (efficient specialization)
   d. A **hierarchy of authority**
      1) Authority is the right to direct, and to expect performance from, other people. Those people are **accountable** to their superiors in the hierarchy.
2. **Kreitner** (*Management*, 9th ed., Houghton Mifflin, pages 285-287) **classifies organizations** as follows:
   a. **Businesses** are engaged in economic activities with the intent to make a profit.
   b. **Nonprofit service organizations**, such as charities and universities, serve particular groups of clients. Money may come from donations, appropriations, or grants.
   c. **Mutual benefit organizations** are groups that exist to serve their members, e.g., labor unions, political parties, or credit unions.
   d. **Commonweal organizations** provide a standard service to all members of a population. Examples are local police departments and public school systems.
3. A number of **relationships** are present in the structure of an organization, including authority, responsibility, and accountability.
   a. **Authority** is the right to direct and exact performance from others, including the right to prescribe the means and methods by which the work will be done.
   b. **Responsibility** is the obligation to perform.
      1) In the classical view, this obligation is formally imposed by a superior and is inherent in any job.
      2) In the behavioral view, responsibility must and should be delegated. A successive dividing and passing down of responsibility is necessary.
         a) The appropriate amount of authority must be delegated with the responsibility. But a higher position can never rid itself of ultimate responsibility.

c. **Accountability** is the duty to account for the fulfillment of the responsibility. In practice, accountability is

1) The duty to report performance to one's superior

a) The principle of single accountability or **unity of command** means that each subordinate should report to only one superior.

b) Unity of command permits multiple superiors only when coordination of plans is such that no conflicting instructions are given.

2) The physical means for reporting or being able to substantiate performance, i.e., record keeping

4. **Unity of objective.** An organizational structure is effective if it facilitates the contribution of individuals toward the attainment of enterprise objectives. Thus, organizational objectives must be clearly formulated in the planning process.

a. In other words, the purpose of organizing is coordination – ensuring that all individuals in the organization are working toward the same organizational goals.

b. Organizing also allows management to determine when goals are not achieved and where the problems exist within the organization (e.g., monitoring, feedback). Organizing is therefore the beginning of control.

5. **Efficiency.** An organizational structure is efficient if it facilitates the accomplishment of organizational objectives with minimum resources and fewest unsought consequences. An efficient structure maximizes output for a given amount of input and provides inputs of all resources required, whether physical, financial, or human, with minimum waste.

6. **Effectiveness.** An organization that reaches its objectives is effective.

a. Effectiveness can be assessed on a short-, medium-, or long-term basis.

7. **Elements of Organizational Structure**

a. The following are three kinds of differentiation that contribute to **complexity**:

1) **Vertical differentiation** is the depth of the hierarchy. More levels mean more complexity. Thus, information distortion will be more likely, coordination of management activities will be more difficult, and the response to change will be slower and less effective.

2) **Horizontal differentiation** is the extent to which tasks require special skills and knowledge. As these become more diverse, communication and coordination become more difficult.

3) **Spatial differentiation** is the geographical separation of operations.

b. **Formalization** is the extent to which job performance is standardized by job descriptions and clear procedures that define how tasks are to be accomplished. Low formalization enhances worker discretion.

c. **Centralization** is the concentration of authority in an organization and the degree and levels at which it occurs.

8. **Lawrence and Lorsch** addressed the relationship between environmental complexity and the organization's balance between differentiation and integration.

a. **Differentiation** is caused by the division of labor and technical specialization. Thus, specialists in, for example, marketing and IT may have substantial differences in skills, attitudes, and behavior. Differentiation leads to organizational fragmentation because specialists tend to have a narrow focus.

b. **Integration** is the coordination of effort required for achievement of mutual objectives. Typical structural arrangements for achieving integration include a hierarchy of authority, a framework of rules, departmentation, formation of cross-functional groups, computer systems, liaison bodies, and human relations training. For example, a vertically integrated organization unites sources of supply, production, and delivery of products and services.

c. In successful organizations, a **dynamic equilibrium** exists between the tendencies of fragmentation and coordination. Furthermore,

1) Differentiation and integration are related to **environmental complexity**.
2) The higher the differentiation, the greater the obstacles to integration.
3) An unsuccessful organization in a complex environment is likely to be highly differentiated but poorly integrated.

9. **Departmentation** is the grouping of organizational subsystems.

a. **Departmentation by function** is the most widely used method, found in almost every enterprise at some level. The most common departments are selling, production, and finance (though other terms may be used). These often extend upward in the organizational chart to the level below the CEO.

b. **Departmentation by territory** is favored by national or multinational firms and government agencies with scattered offices or plants.

c. **Departmentation by product** is growing in importance for multiline, large-scale enterprises. It is often an outgrowth of functional departmentation and permits extensive authority for a division executive over a given product or product line.

d. **Departmentation by customer** permits service to a customer to be managed by a department head. This form of departmentation is most often found at middle levels (e.g., the loan officer of a large bank who handles one account). It is also often found in the sales department of a firm organized by function.

e. **Project departmentation** is for experimental or onetime activities, e.g., the construction of a ship, a large building, or a major design project (such as a military weapons system).

f. **Matrix organization** has horizontal and vertical lines of authority. It may be a combination of any of the other approaches. For example, a manager for each product may be appointed to supervise personnel who simultaneously report to a manager for each function. This form is used in R&D and in project management.

1) The emphasis of the arrangement is on the result or the product.
2) Parts of the functional organization are temporarily assigned to a project.
3) The project may be to make a product indefinitely or to accomplish a limited but lengthy task, such as construction of a submarine.
4) Matrix design provides the security and accountability of the functional form. However, it also provides expert personnel to the project only when needed and only to the extent required. It allows personnel as well as functions to be most effectively and efficiently used.
5) The technical ability of employees is best appraised by the functional managers. Practical applications skills can be appraised by the project manager on site.
6) Unnecessarily large swings in levels of personnel and equipment are minimized.
7) The **unity of command** is violated. Hence, the authority, responsibility, and accountability of the parties must be clearly defined.
8) Inefficient use of employees is possible. Individuals may be idle while waiting for project assignments.
9) It is difficult for large organizations to use matrix design. They typically have many levels (vertically and horizontally), thus slowing communication.

g. The method of departmentation chosen is contingent upon

1) Organizational plans, programs, policies, and purpose
2) Environmental constraints
3) Training and preferences of available personnel

10. **Mechanistic versus Organic Structures**

a. A **mechanistic structure** is appropriate for organizations focusing on a cost-minimization strategy through tight controls, extensive division of labor, high formalization, and centralization. The information network is limited, and employees rarely participate in decision making.

b. An **organic structure** is decentralized and has low complexity and formalization. It has an extensive information system, and employees participate in decision making. It tends to be flexible and adaptive.

c. Structure is a function of the organization's fundamental strategy.

1) An **innovation strategy** focuses on developing important new products or services. An organic structure provides the flexibility for this strategy.
2) A **cost-minimization strategy** imposes tight controls over expenses and reduces product prices. The mechanistic structure is appropriate.
3) An **imitation strategy** is not adopted by true innovators but rather by organizations that move into new markets only after smaller competitors have demonstrated the potential for success. Imitation strategies are best suited to a structure that combines mechanistic and organic components.

d. Structure is also a function of

1) **Size.** Larger organizations tend to be mechanistic because greater formalization is needed. Strategies also change as size changes. Growing organizations often expand activities within their industry.
2) **Technology.** An organic structure may be best for coping with nonroutine technology because formalization is low.
3) **Environment.** In general, the more stable the environment, the more mechanistic the organization. A mechanistic structure also is appropriate when the environment has little capacity for growth. **Dynamic environments** require an organic structure because of their unpredictability. Moreover, a **complex environment** (e.g., one with numerous and constantly changing competitors) also requires the flexibility and adaptability of an organic structure.

a) The environment has three key dimensions:

i) **Capacity** is the degree of growth an environment can support.
ii) **Volatility** concerns the relative instability in the environment.
iii) **Complexity** is the amount of heterogeneity and concentration in the environment.

Thus, an industry with a few very large firms is homogeneous and concentrated.

b) **Uncertainty** is not a specific environmental factor. The foregoing factors determine the level of uncertainty present in the environment.

11. According to **Henry Mintzberg**, an organization has five components. Depending on which is in control, one of five different structures will evolve.
    a. The five organizational components include the

        1) **Operating core** – workers who perform the basic tasks related to production
        2) **Strategic apex** – top managers
        3) **Middle line** – managers who connect the core to the apex
        4) **Technostructure** – analysts who achieve a certain standardization
        5) **Support staff** – indirect support services
    b. The five structures include the following:
        1) A **simple structure**, such as that of a small retailer, has low complexity and formality, and authority is centralized. Its small size and simplicity usually precludes significant inefficiency in the use of resources. The strategic apex is the dominant component.
        2) A **machine bureaucracy** is a complex, formal, and centralized organization that performs highly routine tasks, groups activities into functional departments, has a strict chain of command, and distinguishes between line and staff relationships. The technostructure dominates.
        3) A **professional bureaucracy** (e.g., a university or library) is a complex and formal but decentralized organization in which highly trained specialists have great autonomy. Duplication of functions is minimized. For example, a university has only one history department. The operating core is in control.
        4) A **divisional structure** is essentially a self-contained organization. Hence, it must perform all or most of the functions of the overall organization of which it is a part. It is characterized by substantial duplication of functions compared with more centralized structures. The middle line dominates.
        5) An **adhocracy** (an organic structure) has low complexity, formality, and centralization. Vertical differentiation is low and horizontal differentiation is high. The emphasis is on flexibility and response. Support staff dominates.

12. **Centralization and Decentralization**
    a. **Centralization** concerns the concentration of authority in an organization and the degree and levels at which it occurs.
    b. **Decentralization** is a philosophy of organizing and managing. Careful selection of which decisions to push down the hierarchy and which to hold at the top is required. The **degree of decentralization** will be greater if
        1) More decisions are made lower in the management hierarchy.
        2) Some important decisions are made lower in the management hierarchy.
        3) More functions are affected by decisions made at lower levels.
        4) Fewer approvals are required before implementation of a decision.
    c. Centralization and decentralization are **relative terms**. Absolute centralization or decentralization is impossible.
    d. The degree of centralization or decentralization depends upon the situation.
        1) **Information.** Decisions cannot be decentralized to those who do not have necessary information, e.g., knowledge of job objectives or measures for evaluation of job performance.
        2) **Ability.** Decisions cannot be decentralized to people who do not have training, experience, knowledge, or the ability to make decisions.
        3) **Timeliness.** The organization should decentralize decisions requiring a quick response to those near the action.

4) **Degree of coordination.** The organization cannot decentralize below the level at which coordination must be maintained.
5) **Significance of decision.** Decisions cannot be decentralized to lower levels if they are of critical importance to the organization.
6) **Morale.** The organization should decentralize, when possible, for the positive influence on morale.

e. Restructuring has been successfully accomplished by setting up **strategic business units (SBUs)**, a means of decentralization.
1) A SBU is an **independent business** that (a) serves a specific market outside the parent, (b) has outside competition, (c) makes key decisions about such matters as strategic planning and product development even though it shares the parent's resources, and (d) constitutes a profit center.
a) A SBU must operate as a **profit center** to provide a measure of its effectiveness independent of the original organization.
2) A SBU allows for entrepreneurial **risk taking**, which might otherwise be limited by the parent's bureaucratic structure and the resulting risk aversion.
a) A SBU is a more appropriately sized unit for coping with **competition**. The larger parent may make decisions more slowly and less competitively.

13. **Span of Control**

a. The number of subordinates who can be effectively and efficiently supervised by one person is limited.
1) Factors to consider in determining the span of control include (a) managers' and employees' preferences, skills, and experience; (b) the organizational culture; (c) tasks to be performed; (d) physical location; and (e) established policies and procedures.

b. **Expansion** of the span of control may be advantageous if it improves morale of individual workers by reducing the extent of supervision. A wider span also is beneficial if it reduces communication and control problems by minimizing the number of organizational levels.

c. **Flat organizational structures** have relatively few levels from top to bottom. **Tall organizational structures** have many levels between top and bottom.
1) Flat structures have the advantages of fast **information flow** from top to bottom of the organization and increased employee satisfaction.
2) Tall structures are faster and more effective at **problem resolution** because of the increased frequency of interaction between superior and subordinate and the greater order imposed by the hierarchy of the tall organizational structure.

d. **Growth** may cause spans of control to become unworkable, necessitating the hiring of more managers. In addition, more formalized policies and procedures must be developed, and the structure tends to become more mechanistic.
1) The **relationship of growth and structure**, however, is linear only within a certain range. For example, adding 100 employees to a company with 100 employees is likely to cause significant structural change. Adding the same number to a workforce of 10,000 is likely to have little structural impact.

14. **New types of organizations** tend to have **flatter structures** (fewer layers), make more use of **teams**, and create **entrepreneurial units**.
    a. An **hourglass organization** has three layers:
        1) The **strategic layer** determines the mission of the organization and ensures that it is successful.
        2) A small group of **middle managers** coordinates a variety of lower-level cross-functional activities. These managers are generalists, not specialists, and they are not simply conduits for operating information. Computer systems can instantly transfer such information directly to the top layer.
        3) Empowered **technical specialists** are most often self-supervised. They lack promotion possibilities but are motivated by lateral transfers, challenging work, training in new skills, and pay-for-performance plans.
    b. A **cluster organization** is in essence a group of teams. Workers are multiskilled and shift among teams as needed. Communication and group skills are vital, requiring special training and team-building exercises. Pay is for knowledge.
    c. **Network organizations**. The relative independence of the various firms in a network differentiates it from a vertically integrated organization.
        1) A network is based on **coordination** through adaptation.
        2) It is a long-term, strategic relationship based on **implicit contracts**.
        3) A network allows member firms to gain a **competitive advantage** against competitors outside the network.
        4) A network may be viewed as a group of activities involving suppliers and customers that add value. Each activity may be performed internally at an **internal cost** or subcontracted at an **external cost**.
            a) When an activity is subcontracted, a **transaction cost** will be incurred.
            b) A technological restriction on the existence of a network is that **external costs must be less than internal costs**. The firms in the network must be able to reduce the transaction costs so that the combination of external and transaction costs is less than internal costs.
            c) The difference between a network and a **normal market** is that transaction costs in the market are low enough for any player. In a network, the participating firms reduce initially high transaction costs through cooperative efforts.
        5) A network is an ultimate expression of **outsourcing**, which entails obtaining goods or services from outside sources that could be acquired internally. For example, a firm may choose to outsource its computer processing or legal work, and a manufacturer may buy rather than make components.
    d. **Virtual organizations** are flexible networks of value-adding subcontractors who communicate via the Internet, email, fax machines, and telephones.
        1) The emphasis is on speed and constant, if not too rapid, change.
        2) Constant learning is essential.
        3) Cross-functional teams are emphasized.
        4) Stress is high.
15. Stop and review! You have completed the outline for this subunit. Study multiple-choice questions 56 through 68 beginning on page 246.

6.5 LEADERSHIP

1. **Leadership** is the act or process of influencing, inspiring, and guiding people so they will strive willingly toward the achievement of group objectives through common effort.

   a. **Formal leadership** pursues the organization's objectives, but **informal leadership** may pursue objectives at variance with the organization's.

      1) Formal leaders ordinarily have formal authority and **legitimate power**. Both kinds of leaders may have any of the other types of power, e.g., expertise, charisma **(referent power)**, or ability to control rewards and punishments **(coercive power)**.

      2) Informal leaders whose objectives are the same as (different from) those of the organization are assets (liabilities).

   b. The **classical position** is that leadership is a characteristic of the individual's personality and cannot be subdivided.

   c. The **traitist approach** attempts to identify traits possessed by leaders. It has produced such a long list of leadership traits that, in effect, it identifies nothing. Nevertheless, a few traits do seem to correlate significantly with a leader's effectiveness: (1) intelligence, (2) scholarship, (3) dependability, (4) social participation and interest, and (5) socioeconomic status (in comparison with nonleaders).

   d. A recent traitist approach to studying leadership is based on the **emotional intelligence** of leaders, that is, their social skills and judgment, maturity, and emotional control. These abilities can be learned, especially when a manager or employee understands that immaturity, erratic behavior, and uncontrolled negative emotions have a bad effect on the workplace. According to Daniel Goleman, a leader can acquire social capital through exhibiting the following **leadership traits**:

      1) **Self-awareness** is knowing oneself.

      2) **Self-management** is the ability to prevent one's mood swings from interfering with positive relationships.

      3) **Social awareness** is understanding the actions and emotions of others. This ability helps a person to adapt in a productive way.

      4) **Relationship management** is an ability possessed by a person who communicates and resolves conflict effectively. Humor and a benign approach are characteristics of people who develop good relationships.

   e. Some writers have argued that **men and women** have different leadership traits. However, the research indicates male and female managers do not match the stereotypes (task orientation versus relationship orientation, respectively).

2. Behavior-oriented researchers examined **leader behavior** to determine whether leaders conduct themselves in certain ways.

   a. **Styles of leadership** are emphasized in behavioral approaches. The personal background of the manager and the personalities and backgrounds of the employees supervised are factors. These styles have been characterized as

      1) **Authoritarian.** The manager dictates all decisions, and communication is downward. Moreover, tasks are clearly defined. This is the classical approach. Employees are not allowed to give input. Authoritarian leaders rely on threats and punishment and do not trust employees. However, such leadership can sometimes be the most effective, given limited time to make a decision or employees who do not respond to any other leadership style. Performance is on time and predictable.

      2) **Democratic (participative).** The leader delegates substantial authority. Employees participate in defining and assigning tasks. Communication is actively upward as well as downward. Thus, employees are more committed.

3) **Laissez faire** (free rein). Employees in a group are given the authority and responsibility to make their own decisions. Communication is mostly horizontal. This style works best when employees show personal initiative, but the group also may flounder without the leader's guidance.

4) **Consultative.** The manager takes the employee's view into account but still makes the decisions.

5) **Bureaucratic.** A manager manages "by the book." Everything must be done according to procedure or policy. If there is no policy to cover a situation, the manager refers to the next level above. Bureaucratic leaders are essentially policemen rather than leaders. Bureaucratic leaders are sometimes necessary when employees are working with dangerous or highly delicate equipment or chemicals. Cash handling functions are sometimes policed by a bureaucratic leader.

b. Two behavior patterns consistently found in leaders are **initiation of structure** and **consideration** (production-centered vs. employee-centered behavior).

1) Initiating structure is directed towards accomplishing tasks. Structure includes
   a) Defining duties
   b) Establishing procedures
   c) Planning and organizing work

2) Consideration behavior is the establishment of a **personal relationship** between the leader and the subordinate. High consideration by the leader includes
   a) Warmth toward the employee as a person
   b) Psychological support for the employee
   c) Helpfulness with problems in the work

3) Both patterns are present in all **job situations**. The relative amounts of each must be appropriate to the situation. For example,
   a) A highly structured situation (e.g., assembly-line work) may respond negatively to further structure initiated by the manager but positively to increased consideration.
   b) A manager of R&D may find the initiation of structure much more productive than increased consideration. Creative personnel working on a disorganized project may find a better-defined project plan much more satisfying than a demonstration of concern by the manager.

4) The following are the four **leadership styles** in this model:
   a) **Low structure and consideration** indicates a passive leader.
   b) **Low structure and high consideration** results from an emphasis on satisfying employee needs.
   c) **High structure and low consideration** results from a primary focus on task accomplishment.
   d) **High structure and high consideration** reflects a strong emphasis on both task accomplishment and satisfying employee needs.

c. The **leadership grid** developed by Robert Blake and Jane Mouton is a trademarked classification scheme. **Concern for production** is on the horizontal axis, and **concern for people** is on the vertical axis.

1) Concern for production emphasizes output, cost control, and profit.

2) Concern for people emphasizes friendship, aiding employees in accomplishing tasks, and addressing employee issues (e.g., compensation).

3) Each axis has a scale of 1 to 9. Thus, the **primary styles** are the following:

   a) **1,1:** Little concern for production or people (impoverished management).

   b) **1,9:** Primary concern for people, little concern for production (country club management).

   c) **9,1:** Primary concern for production, little concern for people (authority-compliance management).

   d) **5,5:** Moderate concern for production and people to maintain status quo (middle-of-the-road management).

   e) **9,9:** Great concern for production and people, trust, teamwork, and commitment (team management). Blake and his associates assert that the 9,9 style is best because it produces the best operating results, health outcomes, and conflict resolutions.

3. **Situational theories** of leadership argue that the appropriate style depends on the situation. The emphasis is on flexibility. No leadership style is best in every situation.

   a. According to Fred E. Fiedler's **contingency theory**, people become leaders not only because of personality attributes, but also because of various situational factors and the interaction between the leaders and the situation.

      1) Thus, the right person at the right time may rise to a position of leadership if his/her personality and the needs of the situation complement each other.

      2) The contingency theory model has **three dimensions**:

         a) **Position power** is a function of the formal authority structure. It is the degree to which the position held enables a leader to evaluate, reward, punish, or promote the group members. It is independent of other sources of power, such as personality or expertise.

         b) **Task structure** is how clearly and carefully members' responsibilities for various tasks are defined. Quality of performance is more easily controlled when tasks are clearly defined.

         c) **Leader-member relations** reflect the extent to which group members like and trust and are willing to follow a leader.

      3) Leaders tend to be task motivated or relationship motivated.

         a) The **task-motivated style** is most effective when the situation is very favorable or very unfavorable.

            i) The situation is **very favorable** when the leader's position of power is high, tasks are well defined, and leader-member relations are good. The situation is **very unfavorable** when the reverse is true.

            ii) In the favorable situation, a leader has little need to address relationships and should concentrate on the work. In the unfavorable situation, the leader emphasizes supervision.

         b) The **relationship-motivated style** is most effective in the middle, less extreme situations, when favorable and unfavorable factors are mixed.

      4) The most effective leadership style is **contingent** upon the degree to which the three dimensions are present in a situation.

      5) Leadership is as much a responsibility of the **placement of leaders** as it is of the leaders themselves. An organization should identify leadership situations and its managers' leadership styles and engineer the job to suit the manager if necessary.

b. According to Hersey and Blanchard's **situational leadership theory**, the appropriate leadership style depends on the **followers' maturity**, i.e., their degree of willingness to be responsible for directing their behavior. Four styles of leadership are described in this model. Its dimensions are task and relationship behaviors.

1) **Selling.** A selling leadership style explains decisions and provides opportunity for clarification (high task and high relationship).
2) **Telling.** A telling leadership style provides specific instructions and closely supervises performance (high task and low relationship).
3) **Participating.** A participating leadership style encourages the sharing of ideas and facilitates decision making (low task and high relationship).
4) **Delegating.** A delegating leadership style turns over responsibility for decisions and implementation (low task and low relationship).

c. **Path-goal theory** emphasizes **motivation**. It combines the research on initiating structure and consideration with expectancy theory.

1) Leaders should motivate employees by clarifying employees' understanding of
   a) Work goals,
   b) The relationship of achievement of those goals with rewards, and
   c) How the goals may be achieved.
2) Leaders should increase payoffs, define the path to success, remove obstacles, and increase the chances of individual satisfaction while the path is being traveled.
3) According to path-goal theory, two groups of contingency factors affect the relationship between leadership behavior and the outcomes of employee performance and satisfaction.
   a) **Environmental factors** are those beyond employees' control (task structure, the formal authority system, and the work group).
   b) **Subordinate factors** include the employees' locus of control, experience, and perceived ability.
4) A leadership style should be chosen that complements but does not duplicate the factors in the environment and is consistent with employees' traits.
   a) The **directive** leader lets employees know what is expected, schedules work to be done, and gives specific guidance on tasks.
      i) A directive style is most effective when the employees are externally controlled, tasks are ambiguous or stressful, and substantial conflict exists in the work group. Thus, a directive style is appropriate when employees do not have high perceived ability or experience.
   b) The **supportive** leader is friendly and shows concern for employee needs.
      i) The supportive style is best when tasks are highly structured and the authority relationships are clear and bureaucratic.
      ii) Employees must want to work, grow, and achieve.
      iii) The supportive style may be best when tasks are unsatisfying.
   c) The **participative** leader consults with employees and uses their suggestions before making a decision.
      i) The participative style is most useful when employees believe they control their own destinies. Such individuals may be resentful if they are not consulted.

d) The **achievement-oriented** leader is a facilitator who sets challenging goals and expects employees to perform at their highest level.

i) Achievement-oriented leadership is appropriate when tasks are nonrepetitive and ambiguous and employee competence is high.

5) In contrast with Fiedler's approach, path-goal theorists believe that managers are able to adapt their styles to the situation.

4. A **transformational leader** combines initiating structure and consideration with such other behaviors as charisma. The transformational leader is able to inspire the members of the organization to aspire to, and to achieve, more than they thought was possible.

   a. Transformational leadership emphasizes vision, development of the individual, empowerment of the worker, and the challenging of traditional assumptions.

   b. Transformational leaders articulate a vision, use nontraditional thinking, encourage individual development, provide workers with regular feedback, use participative decision making, and promote a cooperative and trusting work environment.

   c. The transformational leader normally has charisma, is inspirational, provides intellectual stimulation to workers, and gives individualized consideration.

   d. A **transactional leader** emphasizes monitoring of employees so that they adhere to standards. Thus, the transactional leader ensures that expectations are met, but the transformational leader motivates employees to go beyond expectations.

5. Robert Greenleaf's philosophy of **servant leaders** is founded on the following principles:

   a. They have an instinctive desire to serve others and must therefore consciously decide to become leaders.

   b. They clearly define a vision (goals).

   c. They are trusted by their followers.

   d. They listen first.

   e. They accept people, if not their performance.

   f. They have intuitive foresight that allows them to make sound judgments.

   g. They believe that every problem begins inside themselves. Thus, personal development is their focus.

6. **Mentoring** is systematic development of leadership by providing career counseling and social nurturing. According to Abraham Zalegnick, it requires intensive tutoring, coaching, and guidance.

   a. Some organizations have formal mentoring programs that assign mentors to junior employees. However, some research indicates that a mentoring arrangement that occurs informally and voluntarily may have better results.

   b. According to Kathy Kram's research, mentoring serves career and psychosocial functions.

      1) **Career functions** include sponsorship, visibility, coaching, protection, and assigning challenges.

      2) **Psychosocial functions** include role modeling, acceptance, confirmation, counseling, and friendship.

   c. Mentors also may benefit from intrinsic pleasure in helping others to succeed or from gaining power by transferring values and skills to the people they mentor.

7. Stop and review! You have just completed the outline for this subunit. Study multiple-choice questions 69 through 82 beginning on page 250.

6.6 CHANGE MANAGEMENT

1. Change management is important to all organizations. An appropriate balance between change and stability is necessary if an organization is to thrive. Organizational change is conducted through **change agents**, who may include managers, employees, and consultants hired for the purpose.
   a. Cultural change has been defined as a change in attitudes and mindset, for example, when a total quality management approach is adopted.
   b. A product change is a change in a product's physical attributes and usefulness to customers.
   c. A structural change is a change in an organization's systems or structures.
2. **Nadler and Tushman** have developed a model for categorizing organizational changes.
   a. Change is either **anticipatory or reactive**.
      1) Anticipatory changes are systematically planned changes intended to take advantage of expected situations.
      2) Reactive changes are necessitated by unexpected environmental events or pressures.
   b. The scope of change is either **incremental or strategic**.
      1) Incremental changes involve subsystem adjustments needed to keep the organization on its chosen path.
      2) Strategic changes alter the overall shape or direction of the organization.
   c. **Tuning** is an incremental anticipatory change. Preventive maintenance and continuous improvement (kaizen) are examples.
   d. **Adaptation** is an incremental reactive change. An example is a change in the styling of an automobile to meet competition.
   e. **Reorientation** is a strategic anticipatory change. It is "frame bending" because it is a redirection. For example, some fast-food companies are offering their products in dramatically different locations, such as department stores.
   f. **Re-creation** is a strategic reactive change. It is risky because it is "frame breaking." Moving into an entirely new business is an example.
3. **Employee responses to change** tend to vary with whether they like or fear the change.
   a. If employees **like the change**, their attitude, morale, and desire to make the change work often fluctuate over three stages:
      1) Excessive optimism
      2) Reality check
      3) Constructive adjustment
   b. If employees **fear the change**, their attitude, morale, and desire to make it work often fluctuate over five stages:
      1) Beginning on the wrong track
      2) Joking about the change
      3) Doubt and insecurity
      4) Buying in
      5) Constructive adjustment

c. **Management actions** appropriate to the foregoing stages include

1) Identifying problems and defining the effort and coordination needed while still promoting enthusiasm [stages 3.a.1) and 3.b.2)].
2) Supportive listening, setting reasonable short-term objectives, building confidence, and rewarding positive behavior [stages 3.a.2) and 3.b.3)].
3) Setting longer-term objectives, emphasizing teamwork and learning, and reinforcing achievements [stages 3.a.3) and 3.b.5)].
4) Being a role model for the change and a supportive listener while correcting misperceptions [stage 3.b.1)].
5) Encouraging employees to be forward-looking, building commitment, and rewarding positive behavior [stage 3.b.4)].

4. Organizational and procedural changes often are resisted by the individuals and groups affected. **Resistance** may be caused by simple surprise or by inertia, but it also may arise from

a. Misunderstandings or lack of the needed skills
b. Lack of trust of, or conflicts with, management
c. Emotional reactions when change is forced
d. Bad timing
e. Insensitivity to employees' needs
f. Perceived threats to employees' status or job security
g. Dissolution of tightly knit work groups
h. Interference with achievement of other objectives

5. **Methods of coping with employee resistance** include

a. Prevention through **education and communication**
b. **Participation** in designing and implementing a change
c. **Facilitation and support** through training and counseling
d. **Negotiation** by providing a benefit in exchange for cooperation
e. **Manipulation** of information or events
f. **Co-optation** through allowing some participation but without meaningful input
g. **Coercion**

6. **Organizational development (OD)** is planned fundamental change using behavioral science techniques in a systematic way. It is a top-down approach.

a. OD objectives include (1) inducing employees to share an organizational purpose, (2) improving interpersonal relations (trust, cooperation, etc.), (3) making work more satisfying, (4) promoting problem solving rather than avoidance, (5) creating authority based on knowledge and skill, (6) encouraging personal responsibility, and (7) persuading employees to be willing to change.

b. **Kurt Lewin** described OD as a three-stage process:

1) **Unfreezing** is the diagnosis stage. It involves choosing a change strategy, preparing employees for the change, and offsetting resistance.
2) **Change** is the intervention in (altering of) the status quo.
3) **Refreezing** makes the change relatively permanent so that old habits will not reassert themselves. It is the follow-up stage.

7. **Grassroots change** comes from within the organization.

a. **Tempered radicals** are people who oppose the dominant culture while working for incremental change in accordance with their values.

1) These **change agents** are most likely to succeed by (a) beginning with small changes; (b) taking actions that are thoughtful, well prepared, and consistent with their values; (c) carefully explaining the business rationale for change; and (d) building support groups.

b. The **5P checklist** for change agents applies to all organizations.

1) **Preparation** involves development of definitions of concepts or problems; evaluating assumptions, costs, and benefits; and naming a champion (driver) to lead the process.

2) **Purpose.** This element is the definition of clear and measurable objectives, milestones, and deadlines.

3) **Participation** means refining concepts while recruiting influential supporters and neutralizing opponents.

4) **Progress** relates to meeting milestones and deadlines, shoring up support, and overcoming or avoiding obstacles.

5) **Persistence** is maintaining urgency, avoiding impatience, and keeping expectations realistic.

8. Stop and review! You have completed the outline for this subunit. Study multiple-choice questions 83 through 96 beginning on page 254.

6.7 CONFLICT MANAGEMENT

1. Effective interpersonal relationships and organizational change are closely tied to conflict management.

a. According to Dean Tjosvold, **conflict** involves "incompatible behaviors; one person interfering, disrupting, or in some other way making actions less effective."

1) However, conflict may be cooperative as well as competitive.

b. **Cooperative conflict** is constructive. The existence of cooperative (shared) goals is the basis for treating the conflict as a mutual problem.

1) In this context, the parties may be able to trust each other's motives and believe what the other says.

2) Discussions are productive, the attitude (and the result) is win-win, and the parties move ahead together.

c. **Competitive conflict** is destructive. Opposite goals are pursued, and neither side trusts or believes the other.

1) The parties avoid genuine dialogue, and the attitude is win-lose.

2) Ultimately, the parties take separate paths.

2. **Conflict triggers** raise the probability of conflict between groups or individuals.

a. They should be allowed to exist if they cause **cooperative conflict**. Otherwise, they should be eliminated.

b. Conflict may be triggered by

1) Poorly defined **job descriptions** (jurisdictional boundaries).

a) Reorganization may be the solution.

2) **Scarcity** of people, funds, or other resources.

a) Increasing resources may be the solution.

3) **Failure of communication.**

a) Removing obstacles that hinder effective two-way communication is essential, but the problem is perennial.

4) **Deadlines.**

a) Time pressure may induce better performance (constructive) or anger and frustration (destructive).

5) Policies, procedures, rules, or other standards viewed by employees as **unfair**.
   a) If very unpopular, they should be changed to avoid competitive conflict.
6) Individual **personality differences**.
   a) Reassignment or termination of employees may be the solution.
7) Differences in **status**, an issue in any hierarchical entity.
   a) The remedy is respect for the ideas, values, and concerns of lower-level employees.
8) Not meeting **expectations**.
   a) The problem can be avoided through clarifying in advance the expectations employees have about their jobs.

3. Managers may address **competitive conflicts** in the following ways:
   a. **Problem solving** is a means of resolving the conflict by confronting it and removing its causes. The emphasis is on facts and solutions, not personalities and assignment of blame.
      1) The disadvantage is that problem solving is time consuming.
   b. **Smoothing** is a short-term avoidance approach. The parties in conflict are asked by management to submerge their differences temporarily, e.g., until a project is completed. It does not resolve the conflict.
   c. **Forcing** occurs when a superior uses his/her formal authority to order a particular outcome. It does not resolve the conflict. Indeed, forcing may intensify it.
   d. **Superordinate goals** are the overriding goals of the entity to which subunit and personal goals are subordinate. An appeal to these goals is another short-term solution that does not resolve the conflict.
   e. **Compromise** entails negotiation by the parties in conflict. The conflict is resolved through a process by which each side makes concessions. Thus, the parties both gain and lose.
      1) However, if the negotiators on both sides are not skillful (see the earlier description of cooperative conflict), the conflict is suppressed, not resolved.
      2) The disadvantage of fully negotiating a compromise is that the process is time consuming.
   f. **Expanding resources** resolves conflicts that result from scarcity.
   g. **Avoidance** is nonaction. It withdraws from and suppresses the conflict but does not solve the underlying problem.
   h. **Accommodation** is the willingness of one party to the conflict to place another's needs and concerns above his/her own.
4. **Cooperative conflict** may result in better decision making, a reduction in complacency, more self-criticism, greater creativity, and solutions to problems. Cooperative conflict drives the change processes that all organizations need to survive and prosper.
   a. Thus, **intentional stimulation of conflict** may be desirable. For example, management may intentionally trigger conflict by
      1) Making changes in the organizational structure;
      2) Hiring new employees with different values, managerial styles, attitudes, and backgrounds; or
      3) Designating individuals to oppose the majority views of the group.
5. Stop and review! You have completed the outline for this subunit. Study multiple-choice questions 97 through 103 beginning on page 257.

6.8 STUDY UNIT 6 SUMMARY

1. A control sequence includes (a) selecting strategic control points, (b) gathering information about the work done to permit measurement, (c) classifying and recording the information, (d) comparing the information with standards, (e) determining whether performance is satisfactory, (f) reporting significant deviations, (g) determining whether corrective action is effective, and (h) reviewing and revising standards.
2. Planning and control overlap.
3. Effective control is timely, economical, well placed, flexible, and appropriate. It should identify causes of deviations and be consistent with accountability.
4. Improvements in IT, reductions in cost, the popularity of reengineering, and downsizing are factors that have revolutionized control systems.
5. The IIA's preferred control framework is the COSO model. Its components are (a) the control environment, (b) risk assessment, (c) control activities, (d) the information and communication system, and (e) monitoring.
6. Enterprise risk management (ERM) is a process effected by the board, management, and others. It is applied in strategy setting and across the enterprise. ERM is designed to identify potential events that may affect the entity and to manage risk within its risk appetite. Moreover, ERM should provide reasonable assurance regarding achievement of entity objectives.
7. ERM has six capabilities: (a) consideration of risk appetite and strategy, (b) risk response decisions, (c) reduction of operational surprises and losses, (d) response to multiple and cross-enterprise risks, (e) response to opportunities, and (f) deployment of capital.
8. ERM's categories of objectives are strategic, operational, reporting, and compliance.
9. The components of ERM are (a) the internal environment, (b) objective setting, (c) event identification, (d) risk assessment, (e) risk response, (f) control activities, (g) information and communication, and (h) monitoring.
10. The COSO's guidance for smaller public companies derives 20 basic principles from the five components of the COSO control framework.
11. The CoCo model consists of 20 criteria grouped into four components: (a) purpose, (b) commitment, (c) capability, and (d) monitoring and learning.
12. Sawyer states seven means of control. **Organization** is an intentional structuring of roles assigned to people within the entity so that it can achieve its objectives efficiently and economically. A **policy** is any stated principle that requires, guides, or restricts action. **Procedures** are methods employed to carry out activities in conformity with prescribed policies. **People** hired or assigned should have the qualifications to do the jobs assigned to them. The best form of control over the performance of individuals is supervision. **Accounting** is the indispensable means of financial control over activities and resources. A **budget** is a statement of expected results expressed in numerical terms. As a control, it sets a standard for input of resources and what should be achieved as output and outcomes. In most organizations, management functions and makes decisions on the basis of **reports** it receives. Thus, reports should be timely, accurate, meaningful, and economical.
13. A number of relationships are present in the structure of an organization, including authority, responsibility, and accountability.
14. The elements of structure are differentiation, formalization, and centralization.
15. Departmentation may be by function, customer, territory, product, or project. Matrix organization has horizontal and vertical lines of authority. It may be a combination of any of the other approaches.

16. Structures may be mechanistic or organic depending on the entity's structure. Size, technology, and environment also affect structure.
17. Mintzberg's organizational components are the operating core, strategic apex, middle line, technostructure, and support staff.
18. New types of organizations are the hourglass, cluster, and network.
19. A more recent traitist approach is based on the emotional intelligence of leaders, that is, their social skills and judgment, maturity, and emotional control.
20. Styles of leadership are emphasized in behavioral approaches. The personal background of the manager and the personalities and backgrounds of the employees supervised are factors. These styles have been characterized as (a) authoritarian, (b) democratic, (c) free rein, (d) consultative, and (e) bureaucratic.
21. Two behavior patterns consistently found in leaders are initiation of structure and consideration (production-centered vs. employee-centered behavior).
22. According to Fred E. Fiedler's contingency theory, people become leaders not only because of personality attributes, but also because of various situational factors and the interaction between the leaders and the situation. The contingency theory model has three dimensions: position power, task structure, and leader-member relations.
23. According to Hersey and Blanchard's situational leadership theory, the appropriate leadership style depends on the followers' maturity, i.e., their degree of willingness to be responsible for directing their behavior. Four styles of leadership are described in this model. Its dimensions are task and relationship behaviors.
24. Path-goal theory emphasizes motivation. It combines the research on initiating structure and consideration with expectancy theory.
25. A transformational leader combines initiating structure and consideration with such other behaviors as charisma. The transformational leader is able to inspire the members of the organization to aspire to, and to achieve, more than they thought was possible.
26. According to Nadler and Tushman, organizational change is anticipatory or reactive, and its scope is incremental or strategic. Changes include tuning, adaptation, reorientation, and re-creation.
27. The stages of employee emotional responses to change vary with whether they fear the change. Management actions should vary with each stage.
28. Employee resistance to change has many causes. Management techniques for coping with resistance range from prevention to coercion.
29. OD is planned, fundamental change using behavioral science techniques in a systematic way. The three stages of OD are unfreezing, change, and refreezing.
30. Change also may arise from efforts at the grassroots.
31. Cooperative conflict is constructive. The existence of cooperative (shared) goals is the basis for treating the conflict as a mutual problem. Competitive conflict is destructive. Opposite goals are pursued, and neither side trusts or believes the other.
32. Conflict triggers raise the probability of conflict between groups or individuals.
33. Managers may address competitive conflicts in the following ways: (a) problem solving, (b) smoothing, (c) forcing, (d) appeal to superordinate goals, (e) compromise, (f) expanding resources, (g) avoidance, or (h) accommodation.

QUESTIONS

6.1 Overview of Control

1. Which of the following is an example of a feedback control?

A. Preventive maintenance.

B. Inspection of completed goods.

C. Close supervision of production-line workers.

D. Measuring performance against a standard.

Answer (B) is correct. *(Publisher, adapted)*

REQUIRED: The example of a feedback control.

DISCUSSION: Feedback controls obtain information about completed activities. They permit improvement in future performance by learning from past mistakes. Thus, corrective action occurs after the fact. Inspection of completed goods is an example of a feedback control.

Answer (A) is incorrect because preventive maintenance is a feedforward control. It attempts to anticipate and prevent problems. Answer (C) is incorrect because the close supervision of production-line workers is a concurrent control. It adjusts an ongoing process. Answer (D) is incorrect because measuring performance against a standard is a general aspect of control.

2. An organization's policies and procedures are part of its overall system of internal controls. The control function performed by policies and procedures is

A. Feedforward control.

B. Implementation control.

C. Feedback control.

D. Application control.

Answer (A) is correct. *(CIA, adapted)*

REQUIRED: The control function of policies and procedures.

DISCUSSION: Feedforward control anticipates and prevents problems. Policies and procedures serve as feedforward controls because they provide guidance on how an activity should be performed to best ensure that an objective is achieved.

Answer (B) is incorrect because implementation controls are controls applied during systems development. Answer (C) is incorrect because policies and procedures provide primary guidance before and during the performance of some task rather than give feedback on its accomplishment. Answer (D) is incorrect because application controls apply to specific applications, e.g., payroll or accounts payable.

3. Specific airline ticket information, including fare, class, purchase date, and lowest available fare options, as prescribed in the organization's travel policy, is obtained and reported to department management when employees purchase airline tickets from the organization's authorized travel agency. Such a report provides information for

A. Quality of performance in relation to the organization's travel policy.

B. Identifying costs necessary to process employee business expense report data.

C. Departmental budget-to-actual comparisons.

D. Supporting employer's business expense deductions.

Answer (A) is correct. *(CIA, adapted)*

REQUIRED: The information provided by reporting employee airline ticket information.

DISCUSSION: Feedback is a part of the internal control cycle. It provides a basis for comparing actual performance (purchases of tickets given the available options) with standards (organizational policy).

Answer (B) is incorrect because this ticket information is preliminary; employees may change tickets and routings prior to their trip. Answer (C) is incorrect because departmental budget-to-actual comparisons do not necessarily reflect the actual costs ultimately incurred. Answer (D) is incorrect because supporting expense deductions may not necessarily reflect actual costs.

4. Control devices may be

	Quantitative	Qualitative
A.	Yes	Yes
B.	Yes	No
C.	No	Yes
D.	No	No

Answer (A) is correct. *(Publisher, adapted)*

REQUIRED: The form of control devices.

DISCUSSION: Control devices may be either qualitative or quantitative. Budgets, schedules, quotas, and charts are examples of quantitative control devices. Job instructions, quality-control standards, and employment criteria are qualitative control devices.

5. The steps in a typical control process include

1. Selecting strategic control points at which to gather information about activities being performed
2. Accumulating, classifying, and recording data samples
3. Observing the work or collecting samples of data
4. Determining whether performance is satisfactory
5. Reviewing and revising standards
6. Reporting significant deviations to managers concerned

What is the proper order of these steps?

A. 1, 3, 2, 4, 6, 5

B. 1, 2, 3, 4, 5, 6

C. 1, 3, 4, 2, 6, 5

D. 1, 3, 4, 2, 5, 6

Answer (A) is correct. *(Publisher, adapted)*

REQUIRED: The proper sequence of steps in a typical control process.

DISCUSSION: The proper sequence of steps in a typical control process is as follows:

1. Selecting strategic control points at which to gather information about activities being performed
2. Observing the work or collecting samples of data
3. Accumulating, classifying, and recording data samples
4. Comparing samples with predetermined quality, schedule, and cost standards
5. Determining whether performance is satisfactory
6. Reporting significant deviations to managers concerned
7. Determining, by repeating the above steps, whether action taken is effective in correcting reported deviations (follow-up)
8. Reviewing and revising standards

Answer (B) is incorrect because observation must occur before classifying and recording data samples. Answer (C) is incorrect because data must be recorded before comparisons can occur. Answer (D) is incorrect because data must be recorded before comparisons can occur.

6. Which of the following statements regarding effective control systems is false?

A. Excessive controls are costly in time and money.

B. Outdated information is inappropriate.

C. Controls should measure the performance of all areas.

D. Controls should be simple.

Answer (C) is correct. *(Publisher, adapted)*

REQUIRED: The false statement regarding effective control systems.

DISCUSSION: An effective control system should be meaningful. Thus, controls should be in place to measure performance only in important areas. Excessive controls in minor areas are not economical because the added benefits do not outweigh the loss of time and money.

Answer (A) is incorrect because effective controls should be economical because excessive controls are costly in time and money. Answer (B) is incorrect because effective controls need to be timely because outdated information may be unreliable. Answer (D) is incorrect because effective controls need to be simple enough so that people using the control can understand it.

7. Standards must

A. Fail to assist in implementing plans.

B. Not be applied at those points that significantly influence subsequent progress.

C. Be accepted by those who carry them out if they are to have maximum effectiveness.

D. Not be reviewed periodically for adjustment or elimination because of changed circumstances.

Answer (C) is correct. *(Publisher, adapted)*

REQUIRED: Additional guidelines for standards.

DISCUSSION: Standards must be accepted by those who will carry them out if they are to have maximum effectiveness. Subordinates should believe that standards are both fair and achievable. Participation in the standard-setting process will encourage acceptance of standards.

Answer (A) is incorrect because standards should assist in implementing plans. Answer (B) is incorrect because standards should be applied at those points that significantly influence subsequent progress. Answer (D) is incorrect because standards should be reviewed periodically for adjustment or elimination because of changed circumstances.

Questions 8 and 9 are based on the following information. The marketing department for a major retailer assigns separate product managers for each product line. Product managers are responsible for ordering products and determining retail pricing. Each product manager's purchasing budget is set by the marketing manager. Products are delivered to a central distribution center where goods are segregated for distribution to the company's 52 department stores. Because receipts are recorded at the distribution center, the company does not maintain a receiving function at each store. Product managers are evaluated on a combination of sales and gross profit generated from their product lines. Many products are seasonal and individual store managers can require that seasonal products be removed to make space for the next season's products.

8. Which of the following is a control deficiency in this situation?

A. The store manager can require items to be removed, thus affecting the potential performance evaluation of individual product managers.

B. The product manager negotiates the purchase price and sets the selling price.

C. Evaluating product managers by total gross profit generated by product line will lead to dysfunctional behavior.

D. There is no receiving function located at individual stores.

Answer (D) is correct. *(CIA, adapted)*

REQUIRED: The control deficiency.

DISCUSSION: With no receiving function at the individual stores, the possibility exists that goods could be diverted from the distribution center and not delivered to the appropriate retail stores.

Answer (A) is incorrect because goods are seasonal and store space is limited. This is a constraint that is consistent with maximizing revenue and profitability for the organization. Answer (B) is incorrect because the product manager is evaluated based on sales and gross profit; thus, performing both of these duties is not a conflict. Answer (C) is incorrect because evaluating the product managers on gross profit and budgeted sales holds them accountable for profitability. This approach is consistent with their authority over ordering and pricing.

9. Requests for purchases beyond those initially budgeted must be approved by the marketing manager. This procedure:

I. Should provide for the most efficient allocation of scarce organizational resources.

II. Is a detective control procedure.

III. Is unnecessary because each product manager is evaluated on profit generated.

A. I only.

B. III only.

C. II and III only.

D. I, II, and III.

Answer (A) is correct. *(CIA, adapted)*

REQUIRED: The true statement(s) about unbudgeted purchase requests.

DISCUSSION: The organization has two scarce resources to allocate: (1) its purchasing budget (constrained by financing ability) and (2) space available in retail stores. Thus, there is a need for a mechanism to allocate these two scarce resources to maximize the overall return to the organization. This is the proper mechanism.

Answer (B) is incorrect because the gross profit evaluation is effective in evaluating product managers, but it does not necessarily restrain excess spending. Answer (C) is incorrect because approval by the marketing manager is a preventive control, which deters undesirable events from occurring. A detective control detects and corrects undesirable events that have occurred. Also, the gross profit evaluation is effective only in evaluating the manager. Answer (D) is incorrect because approval by the marketing manager is a preventive control, which deters undesirable events from occurring. A detective control detects and corrects undesirable events that have occurred. Also, the gross profit evaluation is effective only in evaluating the manager.

10. Which of the following would minimize defects in finished goods caused by poor quality raw materials?

A. Documented procedures for the proper handling of work-in-process inventory.

B. Required material specifications for all purchases.

C. Timely follow-up on all unfavorable usage variances.

D. Determination of the amount of spoilage at the end of the manufacturing process.

Answer (B) is correct. *(CIA, adapted)*

REQUIRED: The action to minimize defects in finished goods caused by poor quality materials.

DISCUSSION: Specifications for raw materials purchased are control criteria that provide an objective means of determining that the materials are of the minimum quality required. The control sequence includes comparison of actual performance (e.g., actual purchases) with predetermined quality, scheduling, and cost standards.

Answer (A) is incorrect because documented procedures for handling work-in-process inventory do not ensure that materials are of sufficient quality. Answer (C) is incorrect because follow-up on unfavorable usage variances may lead to detection and correction of use of substandard materials but does not prevent or minimize defects in products already processed. Answer (D) is incorrect because determination of spoilage after raw materials have been used in production is not a preventive control.

11. The requirement that purchases be made from suppliers on an approved vendor list is an example of a:

A. Preventive control.

B. Detective control.

C. Corrective control.

D. Monitoring control.

Answer (A) is correct. *(CIA, adapted)*

REQUIRED: The type of control requiring that purchases be made from suppliers on an approved vendor list.

DISCUSSION: Preventive controls are actions taken prior to the occurrence of transactions with the intent of stopping errors from occurring. Use of an approved vendor list is a control to prevent the use of unacceptable suppliers.

Answer (B) is incorrect because a detective control identifies errors after they have occurred. Answer (C) is incorrect because corrective controls correct the problems identified by detective controls. Answer (D) is incorrect because monitoring controls are designed to ensure the quality of the control system's performance over time.

6.2 Control Frameworks

12. Which of the following are elements included in the control environment?

A. Organizational structure, management philosophy, and planning.

B. Integrity and ethical values, assignment of authority, and human resource policies.

C. Competence of personnel, backup facilities, laws, and regulations.

D. Risk assessment, assignment of responsibility, and human resource practices.

Answer (B) is correct. *(Publisher, adapted)*

REQUIRED: The elements of the control environment.

DISCUSSION: According to the Glossary appended to the Standards, the control environment includes the attitude and actions of the board and management regarding the significance of control within the organization. The control environment provides the discipline and structure for the achievement of the primary objectives of the system of internal control. The control environment includes the following elements:

- Integrity and ethical values
- Management's philosophy and operating style
- Organizational structure
- Assignment of authority and responsibility
- Human resource policies and practices
- Competence of personnel

Answer (A) is incorrect because planning is not an element of the control environment. Answer (C) is incorrect because backup facilities, laws, and regulations are not elements of the control environment. Answer (D) is incorrect because risk assessment is part of planning the internal audit activity and specific engagements.

13. Internal control can provide only reasonable assurance that the organization's objectives and goals will be met efficiently and effectively. One factor limiting the likelihood of achieving those objectives is that

A. The internal auditor's primary responsibility is the detection of fraud.

B. The audit committee is active and independent.

C. The cost of internal control should not exceed its benefits.

D. Management monitors performance.

Answer (C) is correct. *(Publisher, adapted)*

REQUIRED: The true statement about the limitation of internal control.

DISCUSSION: A limiting factor is that the cost of internal control should not exceed the benefits that are expected to be derived. Thus, the potential loss associated with any exposure or risk is weighed against the cost to control it. Although the cost-benefit relationship is a primary criterion that should be considered in designing and implementing internal control, the precise measurement of costs and benefits usually is not possible.

Answer (A) is incorrect because the internal auditor's responsibility regarding internal control is to examine and evaluate the adequacy and effectiveness of the system of internal control. Answer (B) is incorrect because an active audit committee strengthens the control environment. Answer (D) is incorrect because management's directing function includes authorizing activities and transactions, monitoring resulting performance, and verifying that processes are operating as designed (PA 2100-1).

14. An adequate system of internal controls is most likely to detect a fraud perpetrated by a

A. Group of employees in collusion.

B. Single employee.

C. Group of managers in collusion.

D. Single manager.

Answer (B) is correct. *(CIA, adapted)*

REQUIRED: The fraud most likely to be detected by an adequate system of internal controls.

DISCUSSION: Segregation of duties and other control processes serve to prevent or detect a fraud committed by an employee acting alone. One employee may not have the ability to engage in wrongdoing or may be subject to detection by other employees in the course of performing their assigned duties. However, collusion may circumvent controls. For example, comparison of recorded accountability for assets with the assets known to be held may fail to detect fraud if persons having custody of assets collude with record keepers.

Answer (A) is incorrect because a group has a better chance of successfully perpetrating a fraud than does an individual employee. Answer (C) is incorrect because management can override controls. Answer (D) is incorrect because even a single manager may be able to override controls.

15. Two organizations have recently merged. The audit committee has asked the internal auditors from both organizations to assess risks that should be addressed after the merger. One manager has suggested that the engagement teams jointly examine the organizational culture and the "tone at the top" to identify control risks associated with the proposed merger. Which of the following statements is true?

A. The organizational culture is not a part of the control environment and therefore should not be considered for a proposed engagement.

B. Although the organizational culture could be considered part of the control environment, the assessment of such an environment would be highly subjective and therefore not useful.

C. Differences in the organizational culture should be systematically identified because the differences may present major risks to the success of the merger. However, identifying differences is not an appropriate activity because it is political and subjective.

D. None of the answers are correct.

Answer (D) is correct. *(CIA, adapted)*

REQUIRED: The true statement about the corporate culture.

DISCUSSION: The control environment includes the attitude and actions of the board and management regarding the significance of control within the organization. The control environment provides the discipline and structure for the achievement of the primary objectives of the system of internal control. The control environment includes the following elements:

- Integrity and ethical values
- Management's philosophy and operating style
- Organizational structure
- Assignment of authority and responsibility
- Human resource policies and practices
- Competence of personnel

Answer (A) is incorrect because the organizational culture is an integral part of the control environment. Answer (B) is incorrect because subjectivity is a significant factor in engagements. Answer (C) is incorrect because identifying differences in organizational cultures is an appropriate activity. The differences may affect internal control.

16. COSO treats internal control as a process designed to provide reasonable assurance regarding the achievement of objectives related to

A. Reliability of financial reporting.

B. Effectiveness and efficiency of operations.

C. Compliance with applicable laws and regulations.

D. All of the answers are correct.

Answer (D) is correct. *(Publisher, adapted)*

REQUIRED: The true statement regarding COSO's objectives in relation to internal control.

DISCUSSION: The COSO treats internal control as a process designed to provide a reasonable assurance regarding the achievement of objectives related to reliability of financial reporting, effectiveness and efficiency of operations, and compliance with applicable laws and regulations. The reliability of financial reporting concerns published financial information. The effectiveness and efficiency of operations relates to achievement of performance and profit goals and the safeguarding of resources. A final related objective is the compliance with applicable laws and regulations.

17. Which of the following are elements of the control environment?

A. Integrity and ethical value.

B. Organizational structure.

C. Assignment of authority and responsibility.

D. All of the answers are correct.

Answer (D) is correct. *(Publisher, adapted)*

REQUIRED: The elements of the control environment.

DISCUSSION: The elements of the control environment include: integrity and ethical value, commitment to competence, board of directors or audit committee participation, management's philosophy and operating style, organizational structure, assignment of authority and responsibility, and human resource policies and practices.

18. Management has a role in the maintenance of control. In fact, management sometimes is a control. Which of the following involves managerial functions as a control?

A. Monitoring performance.

B. Use of an organizational policies manual.

C. Maintenance of a quality assurance program.

D. Establishment of an internal audit activity.

Answer (A) is correct. *(CIA, adapted)*

REQUIRED: The item that involves managerial functions as a control.

DISCUSSION: Monitoring is a component of the control environment. It is a process that assesses the quality of the system's performance over time. It consists of ongoing activities built into normal operations to ensure that they continue to be performed effectively. Supervision and other ordinary management functions, consideration of communications with external parties, and the actions of internal and external auditors are examples.

Answer (B) is incorrect because the manual advises but does not control. Answer (C) is incorrect because a quality assurance program is a form of internal assessment. The manager of the program should be independent of the operations assessed. Answer (D) is incorrect because an internal audit activity should be independent of the operations reviewed and is not a managerial function.

19. Which of the following is a factor affecting risk?

A. New personnel.

B. New or revamped information systems.

C. Rapid growth.

D. All of the answers are correct.

Answer (D) is correct. *(Publisher, adapted)*

REQUIRED: The item that is a factor affecting risk.

DISCUSSION: New personnel, new or revamped information systems, and rapid growth are all factors that affect risk.

20. The policies and procedures helping to ensure that management directives are executed and actions are taken to address risks to achievement of objectives describes

A. Risk assessments.

B. Control environments.

C. Control activities.

D. Monitoring.

Answer (C) is correct. *(Publisher, adapted)*

REQUIRED: The definition of control activities.

DISCUSSION: Control activities are the policies and procedures helping to ensure that management directives are executed and actions are taken to address risks to achievement of objectives.

Answer (A) is incorrect because risk assessment identifies and analyzes external or internal risks to achievement of the objectives at the activity level as well as the entity level. Answer (B) is incorrect because control environments reflect the attitude and actions of the board and management regarding the significance of control within the organization. Answer (D) is incorrect because monitoring is a process that assesses the quality of the system's performance over time.

21. Which of the following is not a component of the CoCo model?

A. Commitment.

B. Capability.

C. Control environment.

D. Monitoring and learning.

Answer (C) is correct. *(Publisher, adapted)*

REQUIRED: The item that is not a component of the CoCo model.

DISCUSSION: Control environment is not one of the four components of the CoCo model. The four components are commitment, capability, monitoring and learning, and purpose.

22. In regard to The IIA's own Systems Auditability and Control study, what elements are encompassed by the control framework?

A. Segregation of incompatible duties.

B. Appropriate levels of authority and responsibility.

C. Supervision of staff and review of work.

D. All of the answers are correct.

Answer (D) is correct. *(Publisher, adapted)*

REQUIRED: Activities within the control framework of The IIA's Systems Auditability and Control study.

DISCUSSION: The activities under the control framework include (1) segregation of incompatible duties; (2) appropriate levels of authority and responsibility; (3) supervision of staff and review of work; (4) tracing transactions or events to responsible persons; (5) adequate resources, time, and knowledgeable personnel; and (6) competence and integrity of people.

23. Enterprise Risk Management (ERM) helps management achieve all of the following except

A. Reaching objectives.

B. Reporting on a timely basis.

C. Preventing loss of reputation and resources.

D. Complying with laws and regulations.

Answer (B) is correct. *(Publisher, adapted)*

REQUIRED: The item not a purpose of ERM.

DISCUSSION: Enterprise Risk Management (ERM) helps management

1. Reach objectives
2. Prevent loss of reputation and resources
3. Report effectively
4. Comply with laws and regulations

ERM allows management to report effectively, not necessarily on a timely basis.

Answer (A) is incorrect because ERM helps management reach objectives. Answer (C) is incorrect because ERM helps management prevent loss of reputation and resources. Answer (D) is incorrect because ERM helps management comply with laws and regulations.

24. Management considers risk appetite for all of the following reasons except

A. Evaluating strategic options.

B. Setting objectives.

C. Developing risk management techniques.

D. Increasing the net present value of investments.

Answer (D) is correct. *(Publisher, adapted)*

REQUIRED: The item not a reason for considering risk appetite.

DISCUSSION: Risk appetite should be considered in

1. Evaluating strategic options
2. Setting related objectives
3. Developing risk management techniques

Increasing the net present value of investments is an operational objective. It would be determined after consideration of the entity's risk appetite and other strategic factors.

Answer (A) is incorrect because management considers risk appetite when evaluating strategic options. Answer (B) is incorrect because management considers risk appetite when setting objectives. Answer (C) is incorrect because management considers risk appetite when developing risk management techniques.

25. ERM allows management greater capabilities. Which of the following is not a capability of ERM?

A. Reduced operational surprises and losses.

B. Better deployment of capital.

C. Increased productivity.

D. Improved risk response decisions.

Answer (C) is correct. *(Publisher, adapted)*

REQUIRED: The item not a capability of ERM.

DISCUSSION: The following are the categories of the capabilities of ERM:

1. Risk appetite and strategy
2. Risk response decisions
3. Operational surprises and losses
4. Multiple and cross-enterprise risks
5. Opportunities
6. Deployment of capital

While increased productivity may result from ERM, it is not directly a capability provided by ERM.

Answer (A) is incorrect because reduction of operational surprises and losses is a capability of ERM. Answer (B) is incorrect because better deployment of capital is a capability of ERM. Answer (D) is incorrect because improvement of risk response decisions is a capability of ERM.

26. Which of the following is a category of objectives of ERM?

A. Compliance.

B. Control expenses.

C. Planning.

D. Information and communication.

Answer (A) is correct. *(Publisher, adapted)*

REQUIRED: The category of ERM objectives.

DISCUSSION: ERM has four categories of objectives. Strategic objectives align with and support the entity's mission. Operations objectives address effectiveness and efficiency. Reporting objectives concern reliability. Compliance objectives relate to adherence to laws and regulations.

Answer (B) is incorrect because control of expenses is an operations objective of ERM. Answer (C) is incorrect because planning is not a category of objectives for ERM. It is a means of achieving objectives. Answer (D) is incorrect because information and communication is a component of ERM.

27. ERM is **not** expected to provide reasonable assurance of achieving which objectives?

A. Strategic and reporting.

B. Operations and reporting.

C. Strategic and operations.

D. Compliance.

Answer (C) is correct. *(Publisher, adapted)*

REQUIRED: The objectives about which ERM is not expected to provide reasonable assurance of achievement.

DISCUSSION: Strategic and operational matters are affected by external events that the organization may not control. Hence, ERM is expected to provide reasonable assurance only that management and the board receive timely information about whether those objectives are being achieved. It does not provide reasonable assurance the objectives are being achieved.

Answer (A) is incorrect because reporting objectives are within the organization's control. Thus, ERM should provide reasonable assurance of achieving them. Answer (B) is incorrect because reporting objectives are within the organization's control. Thus, ERM should provide reasonable assurance of achieving them. Answer (D) is incorrect because compliance objectives are within the organization's control. Thus, ERM should provide reasonable assurance of achieving them.

28. Components of ERM are integrated with the management process. Which of the following correctly states four components of ERM?

A. Event identification, risk assessment, control activities, and objective setting.

B. Internal environment, objective setting, monitoring, and risk minimization.

C. External environment, risk assessment, monitoring, and event identification.

D. Objective setting, external environment, risk assessment, and control activities.

Answer (A) is correct. *(Publisher, adapted)*

REQUIRED: The item identifying four components of ERM.

DISCUSSION: Event identification, risk assessment, control activities, and objective setting are components of ERM. Event identification relates to internal and external events affecting the organization. It differentiates between opportunities and risks. Opportunities are referred to the strategy or objective-setting processes. Risk assessment considers likelihood and impact (see the definitions of risk in the Glossary) as a basis for risk management. The assessment considers the inherent risk and the residual risk. Control activities are policies and procedures to ensure the effectiveness of risk responses. Objective setting precedes event identification. ERM ensures that (a) a process is established and (b) objectives align with the mission and the risk appetite.

Answer (B) is incorrect because risk assessment, not minimization, is a component of ERM. Answer (C) is incorrect because the internal, not external, environment is a component of ERM. Answer (D) is incorrect because the internal, not external, environment is a component of ERM.

29. Which of the following control models is fully incorporated into the broader integrated framework of ERM?

A. CoCo.

B. COSO.

C. Systems Assurance and Control.

D. COBIT.

Answer (B) is correct. *(Publisher, adapted)*

REQUIRED: The control model incorporated in the ERM framework.

DISCUSSION: The Committee of Sponsoring Organizations published *Enterprise Risk Management – Integrated Framework.* It describes a model that incorporates the earlier COSO control framework while extending it to the broader area of enterprise risk management.

30. The components of ERM should be present and functioning effectively. What does "present and functioning effectively" mean?

I. No material weaknesses exist.
II. Risk is within the risk appetite.

A. I only.

B. II only.

C. Both I and II.

D. Neither I nor II.

Answer (C) is correct. *(Publisher, adapted)*

REQUIRED: The definition of "present and functioning effectively."

DISCUSSION: "Present and functioning effectively" means that (1) no material weaknesses exist and (2) risk is within the risk appetite.

Answer (A) is incorrect because "present and functioning effectively" also means that risk is within the risk appetite. Answer (B) is incorrect because "present and functioning effectively" also means that no material weaknesses exist. Answer (D) is incorrect because "present and functioning effectively" means that (1) no material weaknesses exist and (2) risk is within the risk appetite.

31. Limitations of ERM may arise from

A. Faulty human judgment.

B. Cost-benefit considerations.

C. Collusion.

D. All of the answers are correct.

Answer (D) is correct. *(Publisher, adapted)*

REQUIRED: The limitations of ERM.

DISCUSSION: Limitations of ERM arise from the possibility of (1) faulty human judgment, (2) cost-benefit considerations, (3) simple errors or mistakes, (4) collusion, and (5) management override of ERM decisions.

Answer (A) is incorrect because limitations of ERM can also arise from cost-benefit considerations and collusion. Answer (B) is incorrect because limitations of ERM can also arise from faulty human judgment and collusion. Answer (C) is incorrect because limitations of ERM can also arise from faulty human judgment and cost-benefit considerations.

32. The function of the chief risk officer (CRO) is most effective when the CRO:

A. Manages risk as a member of senior management.

B. Shares the management of risk with line management.

C. Shares the management of risk with the chief audit executive.

D. Monitors risk as part of the enterprise risk management team.

Answer (D) is correct. *(CIA, adapted)*

REQUIRED: The circumstances in which the function of the CRO is most effective.

DISCUSSION: A CRO is a member of management assigned primary responsibility for enterprise risk management processes. The CRO is most effective when supported by a specific team with the necessary expertise and experience related to organization-wide risk.

Answer (A) is incorrect because senior management has an oversight role in risk management. Answer (B) is incorrect because the risk knowledge at the line level is specific only to that area of the organization. Answer (C) is incorrect because the CAE should not be accountable for a management function.

33. Which of the following statements is correct regarding corporate compensation systems and related bonuses?

I. A bonus system should be considered part of the control environment of an organization and should be considered in formulating a report on internal control.

II. Compensation systems are not part of an organization's control system and should not be reported as such.

III. An audit of an organization's compensation system should be performed independently of an audit of the control system over other functions that impact corporate bonuses.

A. I only.

B. II only.

C. III only.

D. II and III only.

Answer (A) is correct. *(CIA, adapted)*

REQUIRED: The correct statement(s) regarding corporate compensation systems and related bonuses.

DISCUSSION: The control environment reflects the attitude and actions of the board and management regarding the significance of control within the organization. It sets the organization's tone and influences the control consciousness of its personnel. Moreover, the control environment provides discipline and structure for the achievement of the primary objectives of internal control. The control environment includes, among other things, the element of human resource policies and practices. Thus, hiring, orientation, training, evaluation, counseling, promotion, compensation, and remedial actions must be considered by management.

Answer (B) is incorrect because compensation systems are part of the organization's control systems. Answer (C) is incorrect because audits of the compensation systems can be combined with an audit over other functions that impact corporate bonuses. Answer (D) is incorrect because compensation systems are part of the organization's control systems, and they may be audited in combination with other functions that affect corporate bonuses.

6.3 Management Control Techniques

34. Budgets are a necessary component of financial decision making because they help provide a(n)

A. Efficient allocation of resources.

B. Means to use all the firm's resources.

C. Automatic corrective mechanism for errors.

D. Means to check managerial discretion.

Answer (A) is correct. *(CIA, adapted)*

REQUIRED: The major benefit of budgets.

DISCUSSION: A budget is a quantitative model of a plan of action developed by management. A budget functions as an aid to planning, coordination, and control. Thus, a budget helps management to allocate resources efficiently.

Answer (B) is incorrect because budgets are designed to use resources efficiently, not just use them. Answer (C) is incorrect because budgets per se provide for no automatic corrections. Answer (D) is incorrect because budgets are a management tool and are not designed to thwart managerial discretion.

35. Which of the following is the principal advantage of budgeting?

A. Employee motivation.

B. Performance evaluation.

C. Forced planning.

D. Communication.

Answer (C) is correct. *(CIA, adapted)*

REQUIRED: The major contribution of budgeting to management.

DISCUSSION: Managers in a formal budget setting are compelled to examine the future and be prepared to respond to future conditions. Without budgets, many operations would fail because of inadequate planning. Budgeting is therefore a form of discipline and coordination.

Answer (A) is incorrect because employee motivation is a significant but secondary purpose of budgets. Answer (B) is incorrect because performance evaluation is a significant but secondary purpose of budgets. Answer (D) is incorrect because communication is a significant but secondary purpose of budgets. Planning is the foundation of other managerial functions, such as communication.

36. Internal control should follow certain basic principles to achieve its objectives. One of these principles is the segregation of functions. Which one of the following examples does not violate the principle of segregation of functions?

A. The treasurer has the authority to sign checks but gives the signature block to the assistant treasurer to run the check-signing machine.

B. The warehouse clerk, who has the custodial responsibility over inventory in the warehouse, may authorize disposal of damaged goods.

C. The sales manager has the responsibility to approve credit and the authority to write off accounts.

D. The department time clerk is given the undistributed payroll checks to mail to absent employees.

Answer (A) is correct. *(CMA, adapted)*

REQUIRED: The situation that does not violate the principle of segregation of functions.

DISCUSSION: Controls include segregation of duties to reduce the risk that any person may be able to perpetrate and conceal errors or fraud in the normal course of his/her duties. Different persons should authorize transactions, record transactions, and maintain custody of assets. The treasurer's department should have custody of assets but should not authorize or record transactions. Because the assistant treasurer reports to the treasurer, the treasurer is merely delegating an assigned duty related to asset custody. The use of the check-signing machine does not conflict with any other duty of the assistant treasurer and does not involve authorization or recording of transactions.

Answer (B) is incorrect because authorization to dispose of damaged goods could be used to cover thefts of inventory for which the warehouse clerk has custodial responsibility. Transaction authorization is inconsistent with asset custody. Answer (C) is incorrect because the sales manager could approve credit to a controlled entity and then write off the account as a bad debt. The sales manager's authorization of credit is inconsistent with his/her indirect access to assets. Answer (D) is incorrect because the time clerk could conceal the termination of an employee and retain that employee's paycheck. Record keeping is inconsistent with asset custody.

37. If internal control is well designed, two tasks that should be performed by different persons are

A. Approval of bad debt write-offs, and reconciliation of the accounts payable subsidiary ledger and controlling account.

B. Distribution of payroll checks and approval of sales returns for credit.

C. Posting of amounts from both the cash receipts journal and cash payments journal to the general ledger.

D. Recording of cash receipts and preparation of bank reconciliations.

Answer (D) is correct. *(CMA, adapted)*

REQUIRED: The tasks that should be performed by different persons if internal control is well designed.

DISCUSSION: Recording of cash establishes accountability for assets. The bank reconciliation compares that recorded accountability with actual assets. The recording of cash receipts and preparation of bank reconciliations should therefore be performed by different individuals because the preparer of a reconciliation could conceal a cash shortage. For example, if a cashier both prepares the bank deposit and performs the reconciliation, (s)he could embezzle cash and conceal the theft by falsifying the reconciliation.

Answer (A) is incorrect because there is no conflict between writing off bad debts (accounts receivable) and reconciling accounts payable, which are liabilities. Answer (B) is incorrect because distribution of payroll checks and approval of sales returns are independent functions. People who perform such disparate tasks are unlikely to be able to perpetrate and conceal a fraud. In fact, some organizations use personnel from an independent function to distribute payroll checks. Answer (C) is incorrect because posting both ledgers would cause no conflict as long as the individual involved did not have access to the actual cash. If a person has access to records but not the assets, no danger exists of embezzlement without collusion.

38. Which one of the following situations represents an internal control weakness in the payroll department?

A. Payroll department personnel are rotated in their duties.

B. Paychecks are distributed by the employees' immediate supervisor.

C. Payroll records are reconciled with quarterly tax reports.

D. The timekeeping function is independent of the payroll department.

Answer (B) is correct. *(CMA, adapted)*

REQUIRED: The internal control weakness in the payroll department.

DISCUSSION: Paychecks should not be distributed by supervisors because an unscrupulous person could terminate an employee and fail to report the termination. The supervisor could then clock in and out for the employee and keep the paycheck. A person unrelated to either payroll record keeping or the operating department should distribute checks.

Answer (A) is incorrect because periodic rotation of payroll personnel inhibits the perpetration and concealment of fraud. Answer (C) is incorrect because this analytical procedure may detect a discrepancy. Answer (D) is incorrect because timekeeping should be independent of asset custody and employee records.

39. Which of the following activities represents both an appropriate personnel department function and a deterrent to payroll fraud?

A. Distribution of paychecks.

B. Authorization of overtime.

C. Authorization of additions and deletions from the payroll.

D. Collection and retention of unclaimed paychecks.

Answer (C) is correct. *(CIA, adapted)*

REQUIRED: The activity that is both a personnel department function and a fraud deterrent.

DISCUSSION: The payroll department is responsible for assembling payroll information (record keeping). The personnel department is responsible for authorizing employee transactions such as hiring, firing, and changes in pay rates and deductions. Segregating the recording and authorization functions helps prevent fraud.

Answer (A) is incorrect because the treasurer should perform the asset custody function regarding payroll. Answer (B) is incorrect because authorizing overtime is a responsibility of operating management. Answer (D) is incorrect because unclaimed checks should be in the custody of the treasurer until they can be deposited in a special bank account.

40. Which of the following describes a control weakness?

A. Purchasing procedures are well designed and are followed unless otherwise directed by the purchasing supervisor.

B. Prenumbered blank purchase orders are secured within the purchasing department.

C. Normal operational purchases fall in the range from $500 to $1,000 with two signatures required for purchases over $1,000.

D. The purchasing agent invests in a publicly traded mutual fund that lists the stock of one of the organization's suppliers in its portfolio.

Answer (A) is correct. *(CIA, adapted)*

REQUIRED: The control weakness.

DISCUSSION: Well-designed procedures that are set aside at management's discretion are not adequate controls. Control procedures must be followed consistently to be effective. However, the possibility of management override is an inherent limitation of internal control.

Answer (B) is incorrect because use of prenumbered blank purchase orders secured within the purchasing department is a common control. Answer (C) is incorrect because requiring a more stringent authorization procedure for larger purchases is an appropriate control as long as documentation supports the purchases. Answer (D) is incorrect because the purchasing agent's mutual fund investment should not be a conflict of interest. The relationship between the return on the investment and any possible action by the agent to favor the supplier is very weak.

41. The most appropriate method to prevent fraud or theft during the frequent movement of trailers loaded with valuable metal scrap from the manufacturing plant to the organization's scrap yard about 10 miles away would be to

A. Perform complete physical inventory of the scrap trailers before leaving the plant and upon arrival at the scrap yard.

B. Require existing security guards to log the time of plant departure and scrap yard arrival. The elapsed time should be reviewed by a supervisor for fraud.

C. Use armed guards to escort the movement of the trailers from the plant to the scrap yard.

D. Contract with an independent hauler for the removal of scrap.

Answer (B) is correct. *(CIA, adapted)*

REQUIRED: The most appropriate method to prevent fraud or theft during the frequent movement of trailers loaded with valuable metal scrap.

DISCUSSION: Having the security guards record the times of departure and arrival is a cost-effective control because it entails no additional expenditures. Comparing the time elapsed with the standard time allowed and investigating material variances may detect a diversion of part of the scrap.

Answer (A) is incorrect because performing a complete physical inventory of the scrap at both locations would not be economically feasible. Answer (C) is incorrect because hiring armed guards to escort the scrap trailers is unlikely to be necessary unless the scrap is extremely valuable. Logging departures and arrivals will be sufficient in most cases. Answer (D) is incorrect because using an independent hauler would provide no additional assurance of prevention or detection of wrongdoing.

42. A utility with a large investment in repair vehicles would most likely implement which internal control to reduce the risk of vehicle theft or loss?

A. Review insurance coverage for adequacy.

B. Systematically account for all repair work orders.

C. Physically inventory vehicles and reconcile the results with the accounting records.

D. Maintain vehicles in a secured location with release and return subject to approval by a custodian.

Answer (D) is correct. *(CIA, adapted)*

REQUIRED: The internal control to reduce the risk of vehicle theft or loss.

DISCUSSION: Physical control of assets is a preventive control that reduces the likelihood of theft or other loss. Keeping the vehicles at a secure location and restricting access establishes accountability by the custodian and allows for proper authorization of their use.

Answer (A) is incorrect because insurance provides for indemnification if loss or theft occurs. It reduces financial exposure but does not prevent the actual loss or theft. Answer (B) is incorrect because an internal control designed to ensure control over repair work performed has no bearing on the risk of loss. Answer (C) is incorrect because taking an inventory is a detective, not a preventive, control.

43. To minimize the risk that agents in the purchasing department will use their positions for personal gain, the organization should

A. Rotate purchasing agent assignments periodically.

B. Request internal auditors to confirm selected purchases and accounts payable.

C. Specify that all items purchased must pass value-per-unit-of-cost reviews.

D. Direct the purchasing department to maintain records on purchase prices paid, with review of such being required each 6 months.

Answer (A) is correct. *(CIA, adapted)*
REQUIRED: The control to minimize the risk that agents in the purchasing department will use their positions for personal gain.
DISCUSSION: The risk of favoritism is increased when buyers have long-term relationships with specific vendors. Periodic rotation of buyer assignments will limit the opportunity to show favoritism. This risk is also reduced if buyers are required to take vacations.
Answer (B) is incorrect because confirmation does not enable internal auditors to detect inappropriate benefits received by purchasing agents or deter long-term relationships. Answer (C) is incorrect because value-per-unit-of-cost reviews could be helpful in assuring value received for price paid but do not directly focus on receipt of inappropriate benefits by purchasing agents. Answer (D) is incorrect because review of records every 6 months does not enable the organization to detect receipt of inappropriate benefits by an agent or deter relationships that could lead to such activity.

44. A system of internal control includes physical controls over access to and use of assets and records. A departure from the purpose of such procedures is that

A. Access to the safe-deposit box requires two officers.

B. Only storeroom personnel and line supervisors have access to the raw materials storeroom.

C. The mailroom compiles a list of the checks received in the incoming mail.

D. Only salespersons and sales supervisors use sales department vehicles.

Answer (B) is correct. *(Publisher, adapted)*
REQUIRED: The departure from the purpose of control activities that limit access to assets.
DISCUSSION: Storeroom personnel have custody of assets, and supervisors are in charge of execution functions. To give supervisors access to the raw materials storeroom is a violation of the essential internal control principle of segregation of functions.
Answer (A) is incorrect because it is appropriate for two officers to be required to open the safe-deposit box. One supervises the other. Answer (C) is incorrect because the mailroom typically compiles a prelisting of cash. The list is sent to the accountant as a control for actual cash sent to the cashier. Answer (D) is incorrect because use of sales department vehicles should be limited to sales personnel unless proper authorization is obtained.

45. Which of the following controls could be used to detect bank deposits that are recorded but never made?

A. Establishing accountability for receipts at the earliest possible time.

B. Linking receipts to other internal accountabilities, for example, collections to either accounts receivable or sales.

C. Consolidating cash receiving points.

D. Having bank reconciliations performed by a third party.

Answer (D) is correct. *(CIA, adapted)*
REQUIRED: The control to detect failure to make recorded bank deposits.
DISCUSSION: Having an independent third party prepare the bank reconciliations would reveal any discrepancies between recorded deposits and the bank statements. A bank reconciliation compares the bank statement with company records and resolves differences caused by deposits in transit, outstanding checks, NSF checks, bank charges, errors, etc.

46. Management can best strengthen internal control over the custody of inventory stored in an off-site warehouse by implementing

A. Reconciliations of transfer slips to/from the warehouse with inventory records.

B. Increases in insurance coverage.

C. Regular reconciliation of physical inventories to accounting records.

D. Regular confirmation of the amount on hand with the custodian of the warehouse.

Answer (C) is correct. *(CIA, adapted)*
REQUIRED: The best method to strengthen control over off-site inventory.
DISCUSSION: The most effective control over off-site inventory is the periodic comparison of the recorded accountability for inventory with the actual physical inventory.
Answer (A) is incorrect because examination of documents is a less effective procedure than actual observation of the inventory. Answer (B) is incorrect because increasing insurance coverage helps protect the business against losses but does not strengthen internal control over the custody of inventory. Answer (D) is incorrect because confirming with the custodian the amount of inventory on hand does not verify that the inventory is actually at the warehouse.

47. Upon receipt of purchased goods, receiving department personnel match the quantity received with the packing slip quantity and mark the retail price on the goods based on a master price list. The annotated packing slip is then forwarded to inventory control and goods are automatically moved to the retail sales area. The most significant control strength of this activity is

A. Immediately pricing goods for retail sale.

B. Matching quantity received with the packing slip.

C. Using a master price list for marking the sale price.

D. Automatically moving goods to the retail sales area.

Answer (C) is correct. *(CIA, adapted)*

REQUIRED: The most significant control strength of the procedure described.

DISCUSSION: Use of the master price list ensures that the correct retail price is marked.

Answer (A) is incorrect because timing is not as important as the accuracy of prices. Answer (B) is incorrect because matching quantity received with the packing slip does not ensure receipt of the quantity ordered. Answer (D) is incorrect because goods may or may not be needed in retail sales.

48. A manufacturer uses large quantities of small, inexpensive items, such as nuts, bolts, washers, and gloves, in the production process. As these goods are purchased, they are recorded in inventory in bulk amounts. Bins are located on the shop floor to provide timely access to these items. When necessary, the bins are refilled from inventory, and the cost of the items is charged to a consumable supplies account, which is part of shop overhead. Which of the following would be an appropriate improvement of controls in this environment?

A. Relocate bins to the inventory warehouse.

B. Require management review of reports on the cost of consumable items used in relation to budget.

C. Lock the bins during normal working hours.

D. None of the above controls are needed for items of minor cost and size.

Answer (B) is correct. *(CIA, adapted)*

REQUIRED: The control over small, inexpensive items used in manufacturing.

DISCUSSION: In accordance with the cost-benefit criterion, control expenditures for manufacturing supplies (nuts, bolts, etc.) should be minimal. Nevertheless, some controls should be implemented. For example, usage should be estimated and compared with stock balances and also with the number of using personnel. Moreover, variances should be calculated for the difference between costs incurred and budgeted amounts.

Answer (A) is incorrect because the bins should be on the shop floor where the nuts, bolts, etc., are needed. Answer (C) is incorrect because locking the bins would limit the efficiency and effectiveness of shop personnel. Answer (D) is incorrect because controls are needed even for items of minor cost and size.

49. When a supplier of office products is unable to fill an order completely, it marks the out-of-stock items as back ordered on the customer's order and enters these items in a back order file that management can view or print. Customers are becoming disgruntled with the supplier because it seems unable to keep track of and ship out-of-stock items as soon as they are available. The best approach for ensuring prompt delivery of out-of-stock items is to

A. Match the back order file to goods received daily.

B. Increase inventory levels to minimize the number of times that out-of-stock conditions occur.

C. Implement electronic data interchange with supply vendors to decrease the time to replenish inventory.

D. Reconcile the sum of filled and back orders with the total of all orders placed daily.

Answer (A) is correct. *(CIA, adapted)*

REQUIRED: The best approach for ensuring prompt delivery of out-of-stock items.

DISCUSSION: The system should be designed automatically to reconcile the back-order file with shipments on a daily basis. The system could therefore identify unfilled orders for appropriate and prompt action.

Answer (B) is incorrect because an increase in inventory minimizes out-of-stock conditions but has no effect on tracking and shipping goods as soon as they are available. Answer (C) is incorrect because the use of EDI has no effect on tracking and shipping goods as soon as they are available. Answer (D) is incorrect because reconciling the sum of filled and back orders with the total of all orders placed daily ensures that orders were either filled or back ordered but will not affect delivery of the items that are out of stock.

50. A restaurant chain has over 680 restaurants. All food orders for each restaurant are required to be entered into an electronic device that records all food orders by food servers and transmits the order to the kitchen for preparation. All food servers are responsible for collecting cash for all their orders and must turn in cash at the end of their shift equal to the sales value of food ordered for their I.D. number. The manager then reconciles the cash received for the day with the computerized record of food orders generated. All differences are investigated immediately by the restaurant. Organizational headquarters has established monitoring controls to determine when an individual restaurant might not be recording all its revenue and transmitting the applicable cash to the corporate headquarters. Which one of the following is the best example of a monitoring control?

A. The restaurant manager reconciles the cash received with the food orders recorded on the computer.

B. All food orders must be entered on the computer, and segregation of duties is maintained between the food servers and the cooks.

C. Management prepares a detailed analysis of gross margin per store and investigates any store that shows a significantly lower gross margin.

D. Cash is transmitted to corporate headquarters on a daily basis.

Answer (C) is correct. *(CIA, adapted)*

REQUIRED: The best example of a monitoring control.

DISCUSSION: Monitoring is a process that assesses the quality of internal control over time. It involves assessment by appropriate personnel of the design and operation of controls and the taking of corrective action. Monitoring can be done through ongoing activities or separate evaluations. Ongoing monitoring procedures are built into the normal recurring activities of an entity and include regular management and supervisory activities. Thus, analysis of gross margin data and investigation of significant deviations is a monitoring process.

Answer (A) is incorrect because the manager's activity is an example of a reconciliation control applied at the store level. Monitoring is an overall control that determines whether other controls are operating effectively. Answer (B) is incorrect because the division of duties is an operational control. Answer (D) is incorrect because daily transmission of cash is an operational control.

51. Insurers may receive hospitalization claims directly from hospitals by computer media; no paper is transmitted from the hospital to the insurer. Which of the following controls is most effective in detecting fraud in such an environment?

A. Use integrated test facilities to test the correctness of processing in a manner that is transparent to data processing.

B. Develop monitoring programs to identify unusual types of claims or an unusual number of claims by demographic classes for investigation by the claims department.

C. Use generalized audit software to match the claimant identification number with a master list of valid policyholders.

D. Develop batch controls over all items received from a particular hospital and process those claims in batches.

Answer (B) is correct. *(CIA, adapted)*

REQUIRED: The most effective preventive control over transmission of insurance claims by computer.

DISCUSSION: Monitoring assesses the quality of internal control over time. Management considers whether internal control is properly designed and operating as intended and modifies it to reflect changing conditions. Monitoring may be in the form of separate periodic evaluations or of ongoing monitoring. Ongoing monitoring occurs as part of routine operations. It includes management and supervisory review, comparisons, reconciliations, and other actions by personnel as part of their regular activities. Thus, monitoring of the number and nature of claims may serve to detect failures of internal control.

Answer (A) is incorrect because an ITF is useful in determining the correctness of processing of validly entered transactions. The issue in this case is the validity of the entered transactions. Answer (C) is incorrect because an edit control should be built into the application to test for valid policy numbers. Answer (D) is incorrect because batch controls are designed to ensure that all items submitted are processed, i.e., that they are not lost or added to. Batch controls serve a control purpose, but the major concern in this situation is the validity of the input.

52. Which of the following controls would prevent the ordering of quantities in excess of an organization's needs?

A. Review of all purchase requisitions by a supervisor in the user department prior to submitting them to the purchasing department.

B. Automatic reorder by the purchasing department when low inventory level is indicated by the system.

C. A policy requiring review of the purchase order before receiving a new shipment.

D. A policy requiring agreement of the receiving report and packing slip before storage of new receipts.

Answer (A) is correct. *(CIA, adapted)*

REQUIRED: The control to prevent the ordering of quantities in excess of an organization's needs.

DISCUSSION: Supervisory review at the originating department level is one means of control over the number of items ordered. This control is an example of the segregation of duties. Authorization should be separate from record keeping and asset custody.

Answer (B) is incorrect because automatic reordering does not consider future plans, which could lead to purchases of excess material. Answer (C) is incorrect because review of the purchase order before receiving a new shipment is a control for the risk of accepting unordered goods. Answer (D) is incorrect because a policy requiring agreement of the receiving report and packing slip before storage of new receipts is a control over the risk of receiving an amount other than that ordered.

53. Which of the following observations by an auditor is most likely to indicate the existence of control weaknesses over safeguarding of assets?

I. A service department's location is not well suited to allow adequate service to other units.

II. Employees hired for sensitive positions are not subjected to background checks.

III. Managers do not have access to reports that profile overall performance in relation to other benchmarked organizations.

IV. Management has not taken corrective action to resolve past engagement observations related to inventory controls.

A. I and II only.

B. I and IV only.

C. II and III only.

D. II and IV only.

Answer (D) is correct. *(CIA, adapted)*

REQUIRED: The auditor observations most likely to indicate the existence of control weaknesses over safeguarding of assets.

DISCUSSION: Internal auditors evaluate risk exposures and the adequacy and effectiveness of controls relating to, among other things, safeguarding of assets (Standards 2110.A2 and 2120.A1). Lack of background checks for employees hired for sensitive positions and failure to take corrective action on past engagement observations relating to safeguarding of assets are red flags signifying control weaknesses. Regular reference and background checks, integrity tests, and drug screening are hiring procedures that may be part of an effective ethical culture (PA 2130-1). Furthermore, internal auditors should follow up on engagement observations to determine what corrective actions have been taken or whether management or the board has assumed the risk of not taking action. If the risk assumed may be unacceptable to the organization, the CAE may need to discuss the matter with senior management and the board (Standards 2500.A1 and 2600).

Answer (A) is incorrect because a service department's location concerns achieving organizational objectives, not safeguarding of assets. Answer (B) is incorrect because a service department's location concerns achieving organizational objectives, not safeguarding of assets. But failure to do background checks is a control weakness related to asset security. Answer (C) is incorrect because managers not having access to reports profiling overall performance concerns achieving organizational objectives.

54. A control likely to prevent purchasing agents from favoring specific suppliers is:

A. Requiring management's review of a monthly report of the totals spent by each buyer.

B. Requiring buyers to adhere to detailed material specifications.

C. Rotating buyer assignments periodically.

D. Monitoring the number of orders placed by each buyer.

Answer (C) is correct. *(CIA, adapted)*

REQUIRED: The control likely to prevent purchasing agents from favoring specific suppliers.

DISCUSSION: The risk of favoritism is increased when buyers have long-term relationships with specific vendors. Periodic rotation of buyer assignments will limit the opportunity for any buyer to show favoritism to a particular supplier.

Answer (A) is incorrect because requiring review of a monthly report of the totals spent by each buyer does not enable the organization to detect receipt of inappropriate benefits by an agent or deter relationships that could lead to such activity. Answer (B) is incorrect because detailed material specifications will not prevent buyer favoritism in placing orders. Answer (D) is incorrect because the number of orders placed is not relevant to preventing favoritism.

55. Appropriate internal control for a multinational corporation's branch office that has a monetary transfer unit requires that:

A. The individual who initiates wire transfers not reconcile the bank statement.

B. The branch manager receive all wire transfers.

C. Foreign currency rates be computed separately by two different employees.

D. Corporate management approve the hiring of monetary transfer unit employees.

Answer (A) is correct. *(CIA, adapted)*

REQUIRED: The appropriate internal control requirement for a multinational corporation's branch office having a monetary transfer unit.

DISCUSSION: A control is any action taken by management to enhance the likelihood that established goals and objectives will be achieved. Controls include segregation of duties to reduce the risk that any person may be able to perpetrate and conceal errors or fraud in the normal course of his/her duties. Different persons should authorize transactions, record transactions, and maintain custody of assets. Independent reconciliation of bank accounts is necessary for good internal control.

Answer (B) is incorrect because having the branch manager receive all wire transfers is not an important internal control consideration. Answer (C) is incorrect because foreign currency translation rates are verified, not computed. Having two employees in the same department perform the same task will not significantly enhance internal control. Answer (D) is incorrect because corporate management approval of hiring monetary transfer unit employees is not an important internal control consideration.

6.4 Organizational Structures

56. In organizations in which new product groups are often created, a structure that combines functional and product departmentation and creates dual lines of authority would be optimal. The best structure for this organization is

A. Professional bureaucracy.

B. Mechanistic.

C. Matrix.

D. Machine bureaucracy.

Answer (C) is correct. *(CIA, adapted)*

REQUIRED: The structure that combines functional and product departmentation and creates dual lines of authority.

DISCUSSION: A matrix organization is characterized by vertical and horizontal lines of authority because the product manager borrows specialists from various functions who continue to report to their functional managers. Thus, the resulting arrangement is a hybrid of functional and product departmentation. The advantage is flexibility and rapidity of response to new conditions. The disadvantage is violation of the unity-of-command concept.

Answer (A) is incorrect because a professional bureaucracy is a structure with high complexity and low formalization in which highly trained specialists have great autonomy. Answer (B) is incorrect because a mechanistic structure is complex, formal, and centralized. It adheres to the unity-of-command concept. Answer (D) is incorrect because a machine bureaucracy is formal and complex.

57. A new manager of a production department has been asked to assess the effectiveness of that department. The organization needs to satisfy both internal and external constituents and takes a broad approach to effectiveness. To complete the assignment successfully, the manager should

A. Measure the daily productivity of the department.

B. Do a survey of employee morale, as it is often a major underlying factor in productivity.

C. Compare the past year's production against annual goals.

D. Consider short-, medium-, and long-term effectiveness.

Answer (D) is correct. *(CIA, adapted)*

REQUIRED: The approach to assessing departmental effectiveness.

DISCUSSION: Kreitner (6th ed., pages 279-80) states, "Organizational effectiveness can be defined as meeting organizational objectives and prevailing societal expectations in the near future, adapting and developing in the intermediate future, and surviving in the distant future. In the near term (about one year), it should be effective in achieving its goals, efficient in its use of resources, and a source of satisfaction to its constituencies (owners, employees, customers, and society). In the intermediate term (2 to 4 years), it should adapt to new possibilities and obstacles and develop its abilities and those of its members. In the long term (5+ years), the organization should be able to survive in an uncertain world."

Answer (A) is incorrect because daily productivity relates to short-term effectiveness only. Answer (B) is incorrect because a survey of employee morale may contribute to assessing effectiveness, but it is not sufficient for assessing overall effectiveness. Answer (C) is incorrect because comparing production against goals is a measure of short-term effectiveness.

58. When an organization depends to a great extent on its environment, which of the following statements best characterizes the relationship among an organization's environment, the level of uncertainty it faces, and its structure? The more dynamic and complex the environment, the

A. More uncertainty the organization will face and the more organic the structure should be.

B. More uncertainty the organization will face and the more mechanistic the structure should be.

C. Less uncertainty the organization will face and the more autocratic the structure should be.

D. Less uncertainty the organization will face and the more organic the structure should be.

Answer (A) is correct. *(CIA, adapted)*

REQUIRED: The statement best characterizing the relationship among an organization's environment, the level of uncertainty it faces, and its structure.

DISCUSSION: A dynamic and complex organizational environment faces constant change, so the level of uncertainty increases. The more uncertainty an organization faces, the more organic the structure should be. Organic organizations tend to be flexible and adaptive to change.

59. In what form of organization does an employee report to multiple managers?

A. Bureaucracy.

B. Matrix.

C. Departmental.

D. Mechanistic.

Answer (B) is correct. *(CIA, adapted)*

REQUIRED: The organization in which an employee reports to multiple managers.

DISCUSSION: A matrix organization (project management) is characterized by vertical and horizontal lines of authority. The project manager borrows specialists from line functions as needed. This manager's authority is limited to the project, and the specialists will otherwise report to the line managers.

Answer (A) is incorrect because, in a bureaucracy, each subordinate reports to a single manager. Answer (C) is incorrect because departmental organization structures represent the typical organization with unified and clear single lines of authority. Answer (D) is incorrect because mechanistic organization structure is another term for a bureaucracy.

60. The relationship between organizational structure and technology suggests that, in an organization using mass production technology (for example, automobile manufacturing), the best structure is

A. Organic, emphasizing loose controls and flexibility.

B. Matrix, in which individuals report to both product and functional area managers.

C. Mechanistic, that is, highly formalized with tight controls.

D. Integrated, emphasizing cooperation among departments.

Answer (C) is correct. *(CIA, adapted)*

REQUIRED: The best structure for an organization using mass production technology.

DISCUSSION: According to Joan Woodward's work on the relationship of technology and structure in manufacturing, companies may be categorized as engaged in unit production (units or small batches), mass production (large batches), or process production (continuous processing). Mass production is most effective if the entity has a mechanistic structure characterized by moderate vertical differentiation, high horizontal differentiation, and high formalization. This structure is one in which tasks are well defined, most communication is downward, and control is tight.

Answer (A) is incorrect because an organic structure is flexible and therefore not suited to mass production. Answer (B) is incorrect because matrix is not a type of structure but rather a type of departmentation. Answer (D) is incorrect because an integrated structure is a nonsense term in this context.

61. As an organization increases the number of employees, its structure becomes more complex. Rules become more formalized and more supervisors are hired to direct the increased numbers of subordinates. What is the nature of the size-structure relationship?

A. The size-structure relationship is linear.

B. The structure becomes fixed once an organization attains a level of about 200 employees.

C. The size-structure relationship is concave.

D. None of the answers are correct.

Answer (D) is correct. *(CIA, adapted)*

REQUIRED: The nature of the size-structure relationship in an increasingly complex organization.

DISCUSSION: As an organization increases in size, its structure tends to become more formal and mechanistic. More policies and procedures are necessary to coordinate the increased number of employees, and more managers must be hired. However, the relationship between size and changes in structure is linear only within a certain range. For example, adding 100 employees to a company with 100 employees is likely to cause significant structural change, but adding the same number to a workforce of 10,000 is likely to have little impact. By the time a company reaches a certain size (1,500 to 2,000 or more), it usually has most of the qualities of a mechanistic structure.

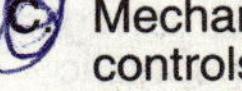

62. Centralization and decentralization are defined according to the relative delegation of decision-making authority by top management. Many managers believe that decentralized organizations have significant advantages over centralized organizations. A major advantage of a decentralized organization is that

A. Decentralized organizations are easier to control.

B. Decentralized structures streamline organizations and eliminate duplication of resources.

C. Decentralized organizations have fewer managers than centralized organizations.

D. Decentralized organizations encourage increased initiative among employees.

Answer (D) is correct. *(CIA, adapted)*

REQUIRED: The major advantage of a decentralized organization.

DISCUSSION: A decentralized organization allows lower-level employees to participate in decision making. This increased involvement encourages initiative and creative thinking and is especially appropriate in complex and rapidly changing environments.

Answer (A) is incorrect because decentralized organizations are more difficult to control. Answer (B) is incorrect because centralized structures streamline organizations and eliminate duplication of resources. Answer (C) is incorrect because the number of managers is not related to the degree of centralization or decentralization but is a function of the span of control.

63. The optimal span of control of a manager is contingent upon several situational variables. For instance, a manager supervising workers within the same work area who are performing identical tasks that are simple and repetitive would best be able to supervise

A. An unlimited number of employees.

B. Only a few workers (a narrow span of control).

C. A relatively large number of employees (a wide span of control).

D. Fewer workers than if the workers were geographically dispersed.

Answer (C) is correct. *(CIA, adapted)*

REQUIRED: The optimal span of control of a manager supervising workers within the same work area who are performing identical tasks that are simple and repetitive.

DISCUSSION: In any situation, there are underlying variables that influence the number of subordinates a manager can supervise. In general, if jobs are similar, procedures are standardized, and physical dispersion is minimized, a wide span of control is most effective.

Answer (A) is incorrect because, although a manager under these conditions would be able to supervise a large number of employees, an upper limit must exist. Answer (B) is incorrect because the conditions described support a wide, rather than a narrow, span. Answer (D) is incorrect because geographical dispersion would decrease rather than increase the span of control.

64. Which type of organization is based upon strategic long-term relationships based upon implicit contracts and coordination through adaptation?

A. Hourglass organization.

B. Cluster organization.

C. Network organization.

D. Virtual organization.

Answer (C) is correct. *(Publisher, adapted)*

REQUIRED: The organization based upon strategic long-term relationship based upon implicit contracts and coordination through adaption.

DISCUSSION: A network organization is a network based upon coordination through adaptation. It also is based upon long-term relationships without specific legal ties.

Answer (A) is incorrect because an hourglass organization has three layers: a strategic layer, a group of middle managers, and lower-level technical specialists. There are also specific legal contracts in the form of employer-employee contracts. Answer (B) is incorrect because a cluster organization is essentially a group of teams. The teams are still part of an organization with explicit contracts, such as employer-employee contracts. Answer (D) is incorrect because a virtual organization is a network of value-adding subcontractors who are linked by electronic mediums.

65. A public university is a

A. Commonweal organization.

B. Business organization.

C. Nonprofit service organization.

D. Mutual benefit organization.

Answer (C) is correct. *(Publisher, adapted)*

REQUIRED: The classification of a university.

DISCUSSION: Nonprofit service organizations include charities and universities. Nonprofit service organizations serve particular groups of clients.

Answer (A) is incorrect because a commonweal organization provides a standard service to all members of the population. Examples include fire stations and police departments. Answer (B) is incorrect because business organizations are engaged in to make a profit. Answer (D) is incorrect because a mutual benefit organization is comprised of groups that serve their members such as labor unions or political parties.

66. Although bureaucracy is often perceived negatively by the public, it is a feature of nearly every large company. Which of the following is a sign that a bureaucracy is dysfunctional?

A. A diversity of jobs.

B. Rules that obscure responsibility.

C. A large number of rules necessary for day to day operations.

D. Obedience to authority.

Answer (B) is correct. *(Publisher, adapted)*

REQUIRED: The symptoms of a dysfunctional bureaucracy.

DISCUSSION: A sign that a bureaucracy is dysfunctional is the development of rules that are meaningless or that obscure accountability. A lack of accountability shows that the bureaucracy is ineffective at identifying the source problems and creating solutions to solve the problems.

Answer (A) is incorrect because a diversity of jobs prevents employees from becoming bored with routine and unchallenging tasks. Answer (C) is incorrect because many bureaucracies have rules to guide day to day operations. As long as the rules have a purpose and are not meaningless, the rules do not create a dysfunctional environment. Answer (D) is incorrect because obedience to authority is required for a corporation's operations to run smoothly. However, obedience at all costs is a sign that the bureaucracy is dysfunctional.

67. Halo Corporation consists of ten groups, each of which is composed of multi-skilled workers. Workers are often transferred between teams as needed and communication between and within groups is emphasized. Halo Corporation is best described as a(n)

A. Hourglass organization.

B. Cluster organization.

C. Network organization.

D. Virtual organization.

Answer (B) is correct. *(Publisher, adapted)*

REQUIRED: The characteristics of a cluster organization.

DISCUSSION: A cluster organization is essentially a group of teams. The workers are often multi-skilled and shift among teams as needed. The workers undergo special training and team-building exercises. The pay also is based upon knowledge.

Answer (A) is incorrect because an hourglass organization has three layers: a strategic layer, a group of middle managers, and lower-level technical specialists. Answer (C) is incorrect because a network organization is a group of members who do not have legal ties but form a strategic relationship to have an advantage over competition. Answer (D) is incorrect because a virtual organization is typically a group of sub- contractors who are linked via the Internet, fax machines, and telephones.

68. The CEO of a rapidly growing high-technology firm has exercised centralized authority over all corporate functions. Because the company now operates in four geographically dispersed locations, the CEO is considering the advisability of decentralizing operational control over production and sales. Which of the following conditions probably will result from and be a valid reason for decentralizing?

A. Greater local control over compliance with governmental regulations.

B. More efficient use of headquarters staff officials and specialists.

C. Lower overall operating costs.

D. Quicker and better operating decisions.

Answer (D) is correct. *(CIA, adapted)*

REQUIRED: The condition that would be a valid reason for decentralizing.

DISCUSSION: Decentralization results in greater speed in making operating decisions because they are made by lower-level managers instead of being referred to top management. The quality of operating decisions should also be enhanced, assuming proper training of managers, because those closest to the problems should be the most knowledgeable about them.

Answer (A) is incorrect because compliance with governmental regulations is probably more easily achieved by centralization. A disadvantage of decentralization is the difficulty of ensuring uniform action by units of the entity that have substantial autonomy. Answer (B) is incorrect because decentralization may result in duplication of efforts, resulting in less efficient use of headquarters staff officials and specialists. Answer (C) is incorrect because decentralization may result in duplication of efforts, thereby increasing overall costs.

6.5 Leadership

69. According to the contingency theory of leadership, a manager will be most effective when (s)he

A. Consistently initiates structure.

B. Adapts his/her style to specific circumstances.

C. Is task oriented.

D. Is relationship oriented.

Answer (B) is correct. *(Publisher, adapted)*

REQUIRED: The most effective management approach according to contingency theory.

DISCUSSION: Fred E. Fiedler's contingency theory of management holds that no single style of directing is best for all occasions. A successful director (leader) must, for each situation, balance his/her formal authority, the task structure, and the leader's relationships with the pertinent group members.

Answer (A) is incorrect because a relationship- (employee-) oriented approach may be preferable when tasks are highly structured. Answer (C) is incorrect because a relationship- (employee-) oriented approach may be preferable when tasks are highly structured. Answer (D) is incorrect because, when tasks are ill-defined, the more effective manager may be one who concentrates on defining and organizing the jobs to be done rather than on motivating employees.

70. Which of the following is true regarding the most recent traitist approach to leadership?

A. It attempts to identify traits possessed by leaders.

B. It has produced such a long list of leadership traits that, in effect, it identifies nothing.

C. It is based on scholarship, dependability, and social participation.

D. It is based on social skills, judgment, maturity, and emotional control.

Answer (D) is correct. *(Publisher, adapted)*

REQUIRED: The true statement regarding the most recent approach to traitist leadership.

DISCUSSION: The most recent traitist approach is based on the emotional intelligence of leaders, that is, their social skills and judgment, maturity, and emotional control. These abilities can be learned, especially when a manager or employee understands that immaturity, erratic behavior, and uncontrolled negative emotions have a bad effect on the workplace.

71. Which of the following leadership types is best known as an agent of change?

A. Participative leader.

B. Traitist leader.

C. Transformational leader.

D. Free-rein leader.

Answer (C) is correct. *(Publisher, adapted)*

REQUIRED: The leadership style that is best used when an agent of change is needed.

DISCUSSION: A transformational leader is an agent of change who attempts to inspire the members of the organization to aspire to, and to achieve, more than they thought possible. Transformational leadership emphasizes vision, development of the individual, empowerment of the worker, and the challenging of traditional assumptions. The transformational leader normally has charisma, is motivational, provides intellectual stimulation to workers, and gives individualized consideration.

Answer (A) is incorrect because a participative leader is simply one who allows employees to have input into the decision-making process. Answer (B) is incorrect because "traitist leader" is essentially a nonsense term as used here; the traitist approach was a field of study that attempted to identify the traits possessed by leaders. Answer (D) is incorrect because a free-rein leader is one who allows employees to make their own decisions.

72. Leadership situations vary with regard to the degree to which the leader can determine what subordinates will do, how they will do it, and what the results will be. According to Fiedler's contingency theory, a leader with a relationship-oriented management style will be most effective when (s)he exerts

A. Great control.

B. Moderate control.

C. Little control.

D. Great or little control.

Answer (B) is correct. *(Publisher, adapted)*

REQUIRED: The situation in which a relationship-oriented management style will be most effective.

DISCUSSION: A relationship-oriented manager is employee centered. His/her self-esteem is strongly affected by personal interactions with subordinates. Fiedler indicated that such a manager is most effective when not faced with the extremes of high- or low-control situations. High control follows from strong position power, a structured task, and good leader-member relations. A low-control situation has just the opposite characteristics. In a high-control environment, a concern for personal relations may be unimportant. In a low-control situation, the relationship-oriented leader may be unable to provide the needed task structuring. Thus, the moderate control situation is best. An example is an assembly-line situation (a structured task) in which leader-member relations are poor.

73. If a supervisor uses a supportive management approach, evidenced by positive feelings and concern for subordinates, a problem might result because

A. An approach based on pure power makes it difficult to motivate staff.

B. This approach depends on material rewards for the worker.

C. This approach depends on people who want to work, grow, and achieve.

D. The manager must believe in the teamwork approach.

Answer (C) is correct. *(CIA, adapted)*

REQUIRED: The problem that could result from using a supportive management approach.

DISCUSSION: Supportive management techniques orient workers toward performance rather than obedience or happiness. The leader should have positive feelings for his/her employees and should attempt to encourage participation and involvement. This approach is effective when used with employees who are motivated to work, improve themselves and their abilities, and accomplish goals.

Answer (A) is incorrect because an approach based on pure power is an autocratic style of leadership, not a supportive approach. Answer (B) is incorrect because the custodial model depends on material rewards for the worker. This model is predicated on the belief that a happy worker is a productive worker. Answer (D) is incorrect because the manager's beliefs are not sufficient. The workers must also believe in the system.

74. Which of the following statements is true regarding authoritarian leadership styles?

A. The manager dictates all decisions to the employees, so communication is downward and tasks are clearly defined in authoritarian leadership.

B. Employees in a group are given the authority and responsibility to make their own decisions in democratic leadership.

C. The leader delegates substantial authority and employees participate in defining and assigning tasks in laissez faire leadership.

D. None of the answers are correct.

Answer (A) is correct. *(Publisher, adapted)*

REQUIRED: The true statement regarding leadership styles.

DISCUSSION: When a manager uses an authoritarian leadership style, he/she dictates all decisions to the employees, so communication is downward. Moreover, tasks are clearly defined. This is considered the classical approach to leadership. Employees are not allowed to give input.

Answer (B) is incorrect because the leader delegates substantial authority in democratic leadership. In addition, employees participate in defining and assigning tasks. Therefore, communication is actively upward as well as downward. Answer (C) is incorrect because employees in a group are given the authority and responsibility to make their own decisions in laissez faire leadership. Answer (D) is incorrect because one of the answer choices is correct.

75. The manager of a team of actuaries has been asked to develop the basic pricing structure for a new health insurance product. The team has successfully designed other pricing structures in recent years. The manager was assigned to the team 6 months ago. What is the best leadership style for the manager of this team?

A. Directive.

B. Supportive.

C. Participative.

D. Achievement-oriented.

Answer (C) is correct. *(CIA, adapted)*

REQUIRED: The best leadership style for a new manager of a team that has successfully completed similar projects.

DISCUSSION: Participative style is most useful when subordinates believe they control their own destinies, that is, when they have an internal locus of control. Such individuals may be resentful if they are not consulted.

Answer (A) is incorrect because directive leadership provides highest subordinate satisfaction when a team encounters substantive internal conflict, when tasks are ambiguous, and when subordinates' locus of control is external. Answer (B) is incorrect because supportive style is best when tasks are highly structured and the authority relationships are clear and bureaucratic. Answer (D) is incorrect because achievement-oriented style will increase subordinates' expectations that high performance will result from their best efforts.

76. The workers in a factory have been told that their machines are obsolete and will be replaced by new, computer-assisted machines. The workers must be retrained and are eager to learn everything about the new machines. The manager was recently hired from a company where the new machines were extensively used and is very familiar with them. In this case, what is the best leadership style for the manager?

A. Directive.

B. Supportive.

C. Participative.

D. Achievement-oriented.

Answer (A) is correct. *(CIA, adapted)*

REQUIRED: The best leadership style for the manager when workers must be retrained and are eager to learn.

DISCUSSION: According to path-goal theory, two groups of contingency factors affect the relationship between leadership behavior and outcomes (performance and satisfaction): environmental factors beyond subordinates' control (task structure, the formal authority system, and the work group) and subordinate factors. The latter include the subordinate's center of control, experience, and perceived ability. A leadership style should be chosen that complements but does not duplicate the factors in the environment and is consistent with subordinates' characteristics. A directive style is most effective when the subordinate's locus of control is external, tasks are ambiguous or stressful, and substantial conflict exists in the work group. Thus, a directive style is appropriate when subordinates do not have high perceived ability or experience.

Answer (B) is incorrect because subordinates who are neither competent nor confident are best led using the directive style. Answer (C) is incorrect because subordinates with an internal locus of control need a leader with a participative style. Answer (D) is incorrect because achievement-oriented leadership is appropriate when tasks are nonrepetitive and ambiguous and employee competence is high.

77. A production team has been together for several years and has worked well together. However, severe arguments have recently occurred between two members of the group, and other members have begun to take sides. This problem has had a negative effect on production performance. The best leadership style for the manager in this situation is

A. Directive.

B. Supportive.

C. Participative.

D. Achievement-oriented.

Answer (A) is correct. *(CIA, adapted)*

REQUIRED: The best leadership style for the manager given substantive internal conflict.

DISCUSSION: Directive leadership provides highest subordinate satisfaction when a team encounters substantive internal conflict. Thus, directive leadership is the appropriate complement to the environmental factors. The leader should intervene to compensate for the stress and strife in the workplace.

Answer (B) is incorrect because supportive style is best when tasks and authority relationships are highly structured. Answer (C) is incorrect because participative style is most useful when subordinates believe they control their own destinies. Answer (D) is incorrect because achievement-oriented leadership is appropriate when tasks are nonrepetitive and ambiguous and employee competence is high.

78. A manager in a government agency supervises a section of clerical employees who review license applications for approval or denial. The clerical jobs are well defined procedurally and are covered by government regulations. In this case, what is the best leadership style for the manager?

A. Directive.

B. Supportive.

C. Participative.

D. Achievement-oriented.

Answer (B) is correct. *(CIA, adapted)*

REQUIRED: The best leadership style for the manager of clerical workers.

DISCUSSION: A supportive style is best when tasks are highly structured and the authority relationships are clear and bureaucratic. This approach depends on people who want to work, grow, and achieve. The supportive style may be best when tasks are unsatisfying.

Answer (A) is incorrect because a directive style is most effective when the employees' locus of control is external, tasks are ambiguous or stressful, and substantial conflict exists in the work group. Thus, a directive style is appropriate when employees do not have high perceived ability or experience. Answer (C) is incorrect because a participative style is most useful when subordinates believe they control their own destinies. Answer (D) is incorrect because achievement-oriented leadership is appropriate when tasks are nonrepetitive and ambiguous and employee competence is high.

79. A leader who explains decisions and provides opportunity for clarification is described as having which leadership style?

A. Selling.

B. Telling.

C. Participating.

D. Delegating.

Answer (A) is correct. *(CIA, adapted)*

REQUIRED: The leadership style that includes explaining decisions and providing an opportunity for clarification.

DISCUSSION: According to Hersey and Blanchard, a selling style of leadership provides a high degree of task orientation and a high degree of relationship orientation. This type of leader explains decisions and provides opportunities for clarification. Thus, upward and downward, two-way communication is active. This approach is more democratic than authoritarian.

Answer (B) is incorrect because a telling leadership style (high task and low relationship) provides specific instructions and closely supervises performance. Answer (C) is incorrect because a participating leadership style (low task and high relationship) encourages the sharing of ideas and facilitates decision-making. Answer (D) is incorrect because a delegating leadership style (low task and low relationship) turns over responsibility for decisions and implementation.

80. Which of the following constitute initiating structure behavior?

I. Defining duties
II. Planning and organizing work
III. Helping with problems in the work

A. I and II only.

B. I and III only.

C. II and III only.

D. I, II, and III.

Answer (A) is correct. *(Publisher, adapted)*

REQUIRED: The initiating structure behavior.

DISCUSSION: Initiating structure behavior is directed towards accomplishing tasks. Structure includes defining duties, establishing procedures, planning and organizing work. Consideration on the other hand, is the establishment of a personal relationship between the leader and the subordinate. High consideration by the leader includes warmth towards the employee as a person, psychological support for the employee, and helpfulness with problems in the work.

Answer (B) is incorrect because helping with problems in the work is consideration behavior. Answer (C) is incorrect because helping with problems in the work is consideration behavior. Answer (D) is incorrect because helping with problems in the work is consideration behavior.

81. In the leadership grid developed by Robert Blake and Jane Mouton, each axis has a scale of 1 to 9. A primary style of 9,9 indicates

A. Little concern for production or people (impoverished management).

B. Moderate concern for production and people to maintain status quo (middle-of-the-road management).

C. Great concern for production and people, trust, teamwork, and commitment (team management).

D. Primary concern for production, little concern for people (authority-compliance management).

Answer (C) is correct. *(Publisher, adapted)*

REQUIRED: The true statement about the leadership grid.

DISCUSSION: A primary style that rates 9,9 on a scale of 1 to 9 indicates that it is at a maximum on both axes. Thus, there is great concern for production and great concern for people. This leadership style emphasizes output, cost control, and profit in addition to friendship, aiding employees, and addressing employee issues.

Answer (A) is incorrect because little concern for production or people is equivalent to 1,1 on the leadership grid. Answer (B) is incorrect because moderate concern for production and people to maintain status quo is equivalent to a 5,5 on the leadership grid. Answer (D) is incorrect because primary concern for production with little concern for people is equivalent to a 9,1 on the leadership grid.

82. Leadership styles differ depending upon the personality type of the individual leader. A risk-averse leader will generally

A. Make decisions more slowly.

B. Require less information than a risk taker.

C. Maintain status differences between themselves and others.

D. Work well in participative efforts where joint responsibility is assumed by several people.

Answer (A) is correct. *(Publisher, adapted)*

REQUIRED: The trait generally attributed to a risk-averse leader.

DISCUSSION: A risk-averse leader will avoid risky situations, make decisions more slowly, and seek more information than a person who is described as a risk taker.

Answer (B) is incorrect because a risk-averse person requires more information than a risk taker. Answer (C) is incorrect because the maintenance of status differences is an aspect of authoritativeness, not of risk aversion. Answer (D) is incorrect because less authoritative individuals work well in participative efforts; this is not related to risk aversion.

6.6 Change Management

83. A major corporation is considering significant organizational changes. Which of the following groups will not be responsible for implementing these changes?

A. Employees.

B. Top management.

C. Common shareholders.

D. Outside consultants.

Answer (C) is correct. *(CIA, adapted)*

REQUIRED: The group not responsible for implementing organizational changes.

DISCUSSION: Common shareholders are not responsible for implementing decisions within the organization. If members of the management team also are common shareholders, they must make decisions consistent with their stewardship function. Thus, they must separate their ownership interests from their managerial responsibilities. Organizational change is conducted through change agents, who may include employees, managers, or outside consultants.

Answer (A) is incorrect because organizational change is conducted through change agents, who may include employees. Answer (B) is incorrect because organizational change is conducted through change agents, who may include managers. Answer (D) is incorrect because organizational change is conducted through change agents, who may include outside consultants. Outsiders can offer an objective, independent view, but they lack knowledge of the organization and do not have to cope with the effects of the changes.

84. Lack of skills, threats to job status and security, and fear of failure have all been identified as reasons that employees often

A. Want to change the culture of their organization.

B. Are dissatisfied with the structure of their organization.

C. Are unable to perform their jobs.

D. Resist organizational change.

Answer (D) is correct. *(CIA, adapted)*

REQUIRED: The result of lack of skills, threats to job security, and fear of failure.

DISCUSSION: Employees resist change for many reasons: surprise, inertia, misunderstanding, ignorance, lack of skills, emotional effects, lack of trust, fear of failure, personality conflicts, poor timing, lack of tact, threats to job status and security, and breakup of the work group. Resistance may be overcome by involving employees to gain feedback and allay fears.

Answer (A) is incorrect because these factors inhibit changes in the culture of the organization. Answer (B) is incorrect because the three factors are not symptoms of dissatisfaction with the structure of the organization. Answer (C) is incorrect because the three factors do not indicate an inability to perform.

85. Organizational development (OD) is one of the major approaches to proactive management of change in organizations. One of the major objectives of OD is to

A. Increase the power of leaders.

B. Align the organization's and the employees' goals.

C. Attract better employees to the organization.

D. Provide the organization and its managers with ways to increase efficiency.

Answer (B) is correct. *(CIA, adapted)*

REQUIRED: The major objective of organizational development.

DISCUSSION: The objectives of OD are to deepen the sense of organizational purpose and align individuals with it; to promote interpersonal trust, communication, cooperation, and support; to encourage a problem-solving approach; to develop a satisfying work experience; to supplement formal authority with authority based on expertise; to increase personal responsibility; and to encourage willingness to change.

Answer (A) is incorrect because OD focuses on participation and power sharing. Answer (C) is incorrect because attracting better applicants to an organization is not a major goal of OD. Answer (D) is incorrect because OD provides an organization and its managers with higher effectiveness.

86. An organization's management perceives the need to make significant changes. Which of the following factors is management least likely to be able to change?

A. The organization's members.

B. The organization's structure.

C. The organization's environment.

D. The organization's technology.

Answer (C) is correct. *(CIA, adapted)*

REQUIRED: The factor management is least likely to be able to change.

DISCUSSION: The environment of an organization consists of external forces outside its direct control that may affect its performance. These forces include competitors, suppliers, customers, regulators, climate, culture, politics, technological change, and many other factors. The organization's members are a factor that managers are clearly able to change.

87. An internal auditor is conducting an operational review that affects several different functional units. The auditor believes that the process under review can be improved, but the operating managers are resistant to suggestions for change. There are several methods the auditor could use to overcome the operating managers' resistance. Identify the technique that will produce the highest probability of success with the fewest negative side effects.

A. Negotiation with the operating managers.

B. Participation by the managers in the decision process.

C. Coercion of the managers through threats.

D. Cooperation by approaching each manager individually.

Answer (B) is correct. *(CIA, adapted)*

REQUIRED: The best method for overcoming resistance to change.

DISCUSSION: Participation by the operating managers in the decision process can improve the overall decision, reduce resistance, and secure their commitment to the change.

Answer (A) is incorrect because negotiation may result in sacrifice by one or both parties. Also, if significant concessions are made to one manager, the others will try to gain a similar advantage. Answer (C) is incorrect because coercion is a temporary solution. Resistance will only be subdued, not eliminated. In addition, future cooperation between the auditor and operating managers will be severely restricted. Answer (D) is incorrect because cooperation of individual managers is not optimal. A manager approached to obtain his/her endorsement may feel that (s)he is being used.

88. Mayan Tech changed its design software to meet competition. According to Nadler and Tushman, this kind of organizational change is a

A. Strategic reactive change.

B. Incremental reactive change.

C. Strategic anticipatory change.

D. Incremental anticipatory change.

Answer (B) is correct. *(Publisher, adapted)*

REQUIRED: The nature of a software change to meet competition.

DISCUSSION: Change is either anticipatory or reactive. Anticipatory changes are systematically planned changes intended to take advantage of expected situations. Reactive changes are due to unexpected environmental events or pressures. Mayan Tech changed its software in reaction to changes by its competition. The scope of a change is either incremental or strategic. Incremental changes are subsystem adjustments needed to keep the organization on its chosen path. Strategic changes alter the overall shape or direction of the organization. Mayan Tech adapted an existing product in order to continue business as usual.

Answer (A) is incorrect because the change was incremental (not strategic). Answer (C) is incorrect because the change kept the organization on its chosen path and was a reaction to changes by the competition. The change was incremental and reactive (not strategic and anticipatory). Answer (D) is incorrect because the change was a reaction to (not anticipation of) changes by the competition.

89. The employees of X Corp. displayed excessive optimism following an announcement by management of major strategic changes soon to be implemented. What stage of change will employees most often experience next?

A. Constructive adjustment.

B. Joking about the change.

C. Lack of needed skills.

D. Reality check.

Answer (D) is correct. *(Publisher, adapted)*

REQUIRED: The second stage of a positive response by employees to change.

DISCUSSION: If employees like the change, their attitude, morale, and desire to make the change work often fluctuate over three stages: (1) excessive optimism, (2) reality check, and (3) constructive adjustment.

Answer (A) is incorrect because constructive adjustment tends to follow excessive optimism and a reality check. Answer (B) is incorrect because joking about the change is the second stage of a negative response by employees who fear the change. Answer (C) is incorrect because lack of needed skills is a cause of resistance to change, not a stage of response to change.

90. Co-optation is a

A. Method of coping with employee resistance.

B. Cause of resistance to change.

C. Model for categorizing organizational changes.

D. Way of allowing meaningful input by resistant employees.

Answer (A) is correct. *(Publisher, adapted)*

REQUIRED: The definition of co-optation.

DISCUSSION: Methods of coping with employee resistance include co-optation through allowing some participation but without meaningful input.

Answer (B) is incorrect because co-optation is a method of coping with employee resistance. Answer (C) is incorrect because co-optation is a method of coping with employee resistance. Answer (D) is incorrect because co-optation is a way of allowing some participation but without meaningful input.

91. Employee resistance to change may be caused

A. Only by simple surprise or by inertia.

B. By manipulation of information or events.

C. By bad timing.

D. Coercion.

Answer (C) is correct. *(Publisher, adapted)*

REQUIRED: The cause of employee resistance to change.

DISCUSSION: Resistance may be caused by simple surprise or by inertia, but it also may arise from (1) misunderstandings or lack of the needed skills; (2) lack of trust of, or conflicts with, management; (3) emotional reactions when change is forced; (4) bad timing; (5) insensitivity to employees' needs; (6) perceived threats to employees' status or job security; (7) dissolution of tightly knit work groups; and (8) interference with achievement of other objectives.

Answer (A) is incorrect because simple surprise and inertia are not the only possible causes of resistance. Answer (B) is incorrect because manipulation of information or events is a method of coping with employee resistance to change. Answer (D) is incorrect because coercion is a method of coping with employee resistance.

92. Which stage of organizational development (OD) is the diagnosis stage?

A. Change.

B. Unfreezing.

C. Refreezing.

D. Liquidation.

Answer (B) is correct. *(Publisher, adapted)*

REQUIRED: The diagnosis stage of OD.

DISCUSSION: Unfreezing is the diagnosis stage. It involves choosing a change strategy, preparing employees for the change, and offsetting resistance.

Answer (A) is incorrect because change is the intervention in (altering of) the status quo. It occurs after unfreezing. Answer (C) is incorrect because refreezing makes the change relatively permanent so that old habits will not reassert themselves. It is the follow-up stage to change. Answer (D) is incorrect because liquidating is not a stage of OD.

93. A small group of employees at Mega Corp. have organized with the purpose of making a few small incremental changes within the company. This group of change agents has been very productive by taking thoughtful, well-prepared actions towards developing definitions of problems, evaluating assumptions, and estimating costs and benefits of solutions. Despite their initial success, these tempered radicals have had trouble carrying their plan forward due to the lack of a champion. This group is at what step in the 5P checklist for change agents?

A. Preliminary.

B. Persistence.

C. Preparation.

D. Progress.

Answer (C) is correct. *(Publisher, adapted)*

REQUIRED: The step in the 5P checklist for change agents related to naming a champion.

DISCUSSION: The employees are still at the preparation step. The 5P checklist for change agents consists of the following:

1. Preparation involves development of definitions of concepts or problems; evaluating assumptions, costs, and benefits; and naming a champion (driver) to lead the process;
2. Purpose is the definition of clear and measurable objectives, milestones, and deadlines;
3. Participation means refining concepts while recruiting influential supporters and neutralizing opponents;
4. Progress relates to meeting milestones and deadlines, shoring up support, and overcoming or avoiding obstacles; and
5. Persistence is maintaining urgency, avoiding impatience, and keeping expectations realistic.

Answer (A) is incorrect because the preliminary step is not part of the 5P checklist. Answer (B) is incorrect because persistence involves maintaining urgency, avoiding impatience, and keeping expectations realistic. Answer (D) is incorrect because preparation (not progress) includes naming a champion.

94. Of the following reasons for employees to resist a major change in organizational processes, which is **least** likely?

A. Threat of loss of jobs.

B. Required attendance at training classes.

C. Breakup of existing work groups.

D. Imposition of new processes by senior management without prior discussion.

Answer (B) is correct. *(CIA, adapted)*

REQUIRED: The least likely reason for employees to resist a major change in organizational processes.

DISCUSSION: Change management is important to all organizations. An appropriate balance between change and stability is necessary if an organization is to thrive. Employee training programs educate employees to perform jobs in a new or different way. Thus, they are a means of coping with employee resistance to change through facilitation and support of the change.

Answer (A) is incorrect because real or imagined loss of jobs is a common reason for employees to resist any change. Answer (C) is incorrect because members of work groups often exert peer pressure on one another to resist change, especially if social relationships are changed. Answer (D) is incorrect because lack of communication and discussion of the need for change threatens the status quo, which fosters employee resistance.

95. An organization is changing to a quality assurance program that incorporates quality throughout the process. This is very different from its years of dependence on quality control at the end of the process. This type of change is a:

A. Cultural change.

B. Product change.

C. Structural change.

D. Organizational change.

Answer (A) is correct. *(CIA, adapted)*

REQUIRED: The type of change effected by emphasizing quality throughout the process instead of at the end of the process.

DISCUSSION: A cultural change involves a change in attitudes and mindset.

Answer (B) is incorrect because product change is change in a product's physical attributes and usefulness to customers. Answer (C) is incorrect because no change to systems and structures is mentioned. Answer (D) is incorrect because no organizational change occurred. The change involves only quality assurance.

96. A chief audit executive plans to make changes that may be perceived negatively by the audit staff. The best way to reduce resistance would be to:

A. Develop the new approach fully before presenting it to the audit staff.

B. Ask the chief executive officer (CEO) to approve the changes and have the CEO attend the departmental staff meeting when they are presented.

C. Approach the staff with the general idea and involve them in the development of the changes.

D. Get the internal audit activity's clients to support the changes.

Answer (C) is correct. *(CIA, adapted)*

REQUIRED: The best way to reduce resistance to changes that may be perceived negatively by the audit staff.

DISCUSSION: Change management is important to all organizations. An appropriate balance between change and stability is necessary. Organizational and procedural changes often are resisted by the individuals and groups affected. Involving the staff in the change from the beginning participation will reduce their resistance to change.

Answer (A) is incorrect because fully developing the plan before presenting it to the audit staff will not help reduce their resistance to change. Answer (B) is incorrect because involving the CEO will not necessarily reduce the audit staff's resistance to change. Answer (D) is incorrect because involving the internal audit activity's clients will not necessarily reduce the audit staff's resistance to change.

6.7 Conflict Management

97. Matthew and Nick are working on similar projects. After a review, Matthew informs Nick that his work contains many errors and is not acceptable. Matthew discusses with Nick ways to improve the quality of his work. Nick acknowledges his mistakes and vows to work harder. He listens to Matthew's suggestions and corrects the errors on the current project. This is an example of

A. Cooperative conflict.

B. Competitive conflict.

C. Destructive conflict.

D. None of the answers are correct.

Answer (A) is correct. *(Publisher, adapted)*

REQUIRED: Nature of the conflict.

DISCUSSION: Matthew's conflict with Nick is productive because dialogue between the two workers is productive. They share the same goals for a high quality project.

Answer (B) is incorrect because the two employees are not competing with each other. Matthew is desiring to help Nick with his project. Answer (C) is incorrect because Matthew and Nick both displayed constructive behavior. Answer (D) is incorrect because the situation is an example of cooperative conflict.

98. Conflict may be

I. Cooperative
II. Competitive

A. I only.

B. II only.

C. Both I and II.

D. Neither I nor II.

Answer (C) is correct. *(Publisher, adapted)*

REQUIRED: The accurate description of conflict.

DISCUSSION: Conflict may be either cooperative or competitive. Cooperative conflict is constructive and competitive conflict is destructive.

Answer (A) is incorrect because conflict may be cooperative or competitive. Answer (B) is incorrect because conflict may also be cooperative. Answer (D) is incorrect because conflict may be both cooperative and competitive.

99. Which of the following conflict triggers is best resolved by reorganization?

A. Scarcity of people, funds, or other resources.

B. Badly defined job descriptions.

C. Failure of communication.

D. Deadlines.

Answer (B) is correct. *(Publisher, adapted)*

REQUIRED: The conflict trigger best resolved by reorganization.

DISCUSSION: If badly designed job descriptions occur, the best resolution is reorganization.

Answer (A) is incorrect because the scarcity of people, funds, or other resources is best resolved by increasing resources. Answer (C) is incorrect because failure of communication is best resolved by removing obstacles to effective two-way communication. Answer (D) is incorrect because deadlines may induce better performance or anger and frustration. Reorganization is not the best solution for conflicts with deadlines.

100. Which of the following conflict resolution techniques has the goal of maintaining harmonious relationships by placing another's needs and concerns above your own?

A. Accommodation.

B. Compromise.

C. Collaboration.

D. Avoidance.

Answer (A) is correct. *(CIA, adapted)*

REQUIRED: The conflict resolution technique with a goal of maintaining harmonious relationships.

DISCUSSION: The goal of accommodation is maintaining harmonious relationships by placing an emphasis on another's needs and concerns.

Answer (B) is incorrect because compromise resolves conflict through a process in which each side makes concessions. Answer (C) is incorrect because collaboration resolves conflict. The parties work together to obtain a solution. Answer (D) is incorrect because avoidance does not resolve conflict. It is nonaction.

101. Time consumption is a disadvantage when managers address conflict by

A. Smoothing.

B. Forcing.

C. Problem solving.

D. None of the answers are correct.

Answer (C) is correct. *(Publisher, adapted)*

REQUIRED: The way in which managers address conflict that uses excessive time.

DISCUSSION: Problem solving is a way managers address conflicts, but it requires a large amount of time to resolve.

Answer (A) is incorrect because smoothing is a short-term avoidance approach. Answer (B) is incorrect because forcing occurs when a superior uses his or her formal authority to order a particular outcome. Answer (D) is incorrect because problem solving takes managers a long time to resolve conflicts.

102. Carling, a manager, resolves a conflict between two employees, Philip and John, by recommending concessions to be made by both employees. The two employees agree to the concessions and the conflict is resolved. Both Philip and John gain and lose. Which of the following describes the way Carling addressed the conflict?

A. Forcing.

B. Smoothing.

C. Compromise.

D. Problem solving.

Answer (C) is correct. *(Publisher, adapted)*

REQUIRED: The ways in which managers address conflicts.

DISCUSSION: Compromise entails negotiation by the parties in conflict. The conflict is resolved through a process by which each side makes concessions. Thus, the parties both gain and lose. Because Philip and John each made concessions, the conflict was resolved through compromise.

Answer (A) is incorrect because forcing occurs when a superior uses his or her formal authority to order a particular outcome. It does not resolve the conflict. Forcing may intensify it. Answer (B) is incorrect because smoothing is a short-term avoidance approach. The parties in conflict are asked by management to submerge their differences temporarily until a project is completed. Answer (D) is incorrect because problem solving is a means of resolving the conflict by confronting it and removing its causes. The emphasis is on facts and solutions, not personalities and assignment of blame.

103. During a meeting of an internal audit project team, two members of the team disagree, and one accuses the other of trying to advance personal interests over the interests of the audit. The audit manager should:

A. Discipline both auditors after the meeting for their lack of professional conduct.

B. Continue the meeting but speak to the accusing auditor later regarding the inappropriate conduct.

C. Meet with both auditors after the meeting to resolve the conflict and the inappropriate behavior.

D. Stop the meeting and refer the matter to the entire team for discussion.

Answer (C) is correct. *(CIA, adapted)*

REQUIRED: The audit manager's action when two members of the audit project team disagree.

DISCUSSION: Effective interpersonal relationships and organizational change are closely tied to conflict management. Meeting with both auditors after the meeting allows both parties to discuss and resolve their differences under the supervision of the audit manager. Moreover, part of the CAE's responsibility for supervision is to adopt suitable policies and procedures for resolving professional differences (PA 2340-1).

Answer (A) is incorrect because the manager should address the behavior and not miss the opportunity for coaching and conflict resolution with both staff members. Answer (B) is incorrect because, although one auditor has behaved improperly, both auditors allowed the situation to occur, and both should be involved in its resolution to protect team morale and effectiveness. Answer (D) is incorrect because this conflict is not a matter for the entire team to address. The team may be advised after the resolution but should not be involved in a disciplinary action by the manager.

STUDY UNIT SEVEN
PLANNING AND SUPERVISING THE ENGAGEMENT

(13 pages of outline) Ch. 6 -

An **engagement** consists of (1) planning, (2) performing the engagement, (3) communicating results, and (4) monitoring progress. The internal auditor's responsibility is to plan and perform the engagement, subject to review and approval by supervisors. This study unit concerns the first phase of the engagement. Supervision is included because it begins with planning.

In this study unit, we present the pronouncements by The IIA that are relevant to the planning phase. This study unit also contains supplementary information about certain aspects of the engagement and the relevant pronouncements on supervision.

Core Concepts

- Internal auditors should develop and document a plan for the engagement. It should include the (a) scope, (b) objectives, (c) timing, and (d) resource allocations.
- Internal auditors should make a preliminary assessment of the relevant risks. Objectives of the engagement should reflect the risk assessment.
- The engagement scope should suffice to meet the engagement objectives.
- Engagement resource allocation depends on the nature and complexity of the engagement, time limitations, and available resources.
- Engagement work programs should meet the engagement objectives, be recorded, and receive prior approval. They consist of the planned engagement procedures.
- The preliminary survey is a process for gathering information to (a) understand the activity reviewed, (b) identify areas for special emphasis, (c) obtain useful information, and (d) determine whether further auditing is needed.
- Engagement supervision ensures that objectives are achieved, quality is assured, and staff is developed.

7.1 PLANNING

1. This subunit describes the planning process and provides criteria for evaluating that process. The engagement planning process is addressed by one General Performance Standard, one Specific Performance Standard, one Assurance Implementation Standard, one Consulting Implementation Standard, and one Practice Advisory.

2. ***2200*** ***Engagement Planning*** *– Internal auditors should develop and record a plan for each engagement, including the scope, objectives, timing, and resource allocations.*

   a. ***PRACTICE ADVISORY 2200-1: ENGAGEMENT PLANNING***

      1. The internal auditor is responsible for planning and conducting the engagement assignment, subject to supervisory review and approval. The ***engagement program*** *should:*

      - ***Document*** *the internal auditor's* ***procedures*** *for collecting, analyzing, interpreting, and documenting information during the engagement.*
      - *State the* ***objectives*** *of the engagement.*
      - *Set forth the* ***scope*** *and degree of testing required to achieve the engagement objectives in each phase of the engagement.*
      - *Identify technical aspects, risks, processes, and transactions that should be examined.*
      - *State the* ***nature and extent of testing*** *required.*
      - *Be prepared* ***prior to*** *the commencement of engagement work and be modified, as appropriate, during the course of the engagement.*

      2. The ***chief audit executive*** *is responsible for determining how, when, and to whom engagement results will be* ***communicated****. This determination should be documented and communicated to management, to the extent deemed practicable, during the* ***planning phase*** *of the engagement.* ***Subsequent changes*** *that affect the timing or reporting of engagement results should also be communicated to management, if appropriate.*

      3. Other requirements of the engagement, such as the engagement ***period covered*** *and estimated* ***completion dates****, should be determined. The final engagement* ***communication format*** *should be considered because proper planning at this stage facilitates preparing the final engagement communication.*

      4. All those in ***management*** *who need to know about the engagement should be informed.* ***Meetings*** *should be held with management responsible for the activity being examined. A* ***summary*** *of matters discussed at meetings and any conclusions reached should be prepared; distributed to individuals, as appropriate; and retained in the engagement working papers.* ***Topics of discussion*** *may include:*

      - *Planned engagement objectives and scope of work*
      - *The timing of engagement work*
      - *Internal auditors assigned to the engagement*
      - *The process of communicating throughout the engagement, including the methods, time frames, and individuals who will be responsible*
      - *Business conditions and operations of the activity being reviewed, including recent changes in management or major systems*
      - *Concerns or any requests of management*
      - *Matters of particular interest or concern to the internal auditor*
      - *Description of the internal auditing activity's reporting procedures and follow-up process*

PA Summary

- The internal auditor plans and conducts the engagement, subject to supervisory review and approval. The **engagement program** (1) documents **procedures**, (2) states the engagement's **objectives and scope**, (3) identifies **risks** and other matters to be examined, and (4) states the **nature and extent** of testing.
- The program is prepared **before** work begins and is modified during the work.
- The **CAE** determines how, when, and to whom results are **communicated**. If appropriate, these documented determinations are communicated to management during **planning**. **Subsequent changes** that affect the timing or reporting of engagement results also should be communicated.
- Other engagement requirements to be determined are the **period** covered, completion dates, and the communication **format**.
- **Managers** should be informed on a need-to-know basis.
- **Meetings** should be held with responsible managers. **Summaries** of discussions and conclusions should be prepared, distributed, and retained. **Topics of discussion** may include: (1) engagement objectives and scope, (2) timing of work, (3) auditors assigned, (4) the process of communicating throughout the engagement, (5) conditions and operations of the activity reviewed, (6) management concerns or requests, (7) matters of particular interest to the auditor, and (8) the IAA's reporting and follow-up process.

3. ***2201*** ***Planning Considerations*** *– In planning the engagement, internal auditors should consider:*
   - *The objectives of the activity being reviewed and the means by which the activity controls its performance.*
   - *The significant risks to the activity, its objectives, resources, and operations and the means by which the potential impact of risk is kept to an acceptable level.*
   - *The adequacy and effectiveness of the activity's risk management and control systems compared to a relevant control framework or model.*
   - *The opportunities for making significant improvements to the activity's risk management and control systems.*
4. ***2201.A1*** *– When planning an engagement for parties outside the organization, internal auditors should establish a written understanding with them about objectives, scope, respective responsibilities and other expectations, including restrictions on distribution of the results of the engagement and access to engagement records.*
5. ***2201.C1*** *– Internal auditors should establish an understanding with consulting engagement clients about objectives, scope, respective responsibilities, and other client expectations. For significant engagements, this understanding should be documented.*
6. Stop and review! You have completed the outline for this subunit. Study multiple-choice questions 1 through 6 beginning on page 274.

7.2 OBJECTIVES, RISK ASSESSMENT, AND SURVEY

1. This subunit defines objectives, procedures, the scope of work, and the purpose of the preliminary risk assessment. These concepts are covered in one Specific Performance Standard, two Assurance Implementation Standards, one Consulting Implementation Standard, and two Practice Advisories.
2. ***2210*** ***Engagement Objectives*** *– Objectives should be established for each engagement.*
   a. ***PRACTICE ADVISORY 2210-1: ENGAGEMENT OBJECTIVES***
      1. *Planning should be documented. Engagement objectives and scope of work should be established.* ***Engagement objectives*** *are broad statements developed by internal auditors and define what the engagement is intended to accomplish.* ***Engagement procedures*** *are the means to attain engagement objectives. Engagement objectives and procedures, taken together, define the scope of the internal auditor's work.*
      2. *Engagement objectives and procedures should address the* ***risks*** *associated with the activity under review. The term risk is the possibility of an event's occurring that could have an impact on the achievement of objectives. Risk is measured in terms of impact and likelihood. The* ***purpose of the risk assessment*** *during the planning phase of the engagement is to identify significant areas of activity that should be examined as potential engagement objectives.*

PA Summary

- **Planning** should be documented. **Engagement objectives** are broad statements of what is to be accomplished. **Engagement procedures** are the means of attaining the objectives. Together, they define the **engagement scope**.
- Objectives and procedures should address the **risks** associated with the activity under review. The preliminary **risk assessment** identifies significant activities to be examined as potential objectives.

3. ***2210.A1*** *– Internal auditors should conduct a preliminary assessment of the risks relevant to the activity under review. Engagement objectives should reflect the results of this assessment.*
   a. ***PRACTICE ADVISORY 2210.A1-1: RISK ASSESSMENT IN ENGAGEMENT PLANNING***
      1. ***Background information*** *should be obtained about the activities to be reviewed. A review of background information should be performed to determine the impact on the engagement. Such items include:*
         - *Objectives and goals*
         - *Policies, plans, procedures, laws, regulations, and contracts that could have a significant impact on operations and reports*

         - ***Organizational information****, e.g., number and names of employees, key employees, job descriptions, and details about recent changes in the organization, including major system changes*
         - *Budget information, operating results, and financial data of the activity to be reviewed*
         - ***Prior*** *engagement* ***working papers***

- ***Results of other engagements***, *including the work of external auditors, completed or in process*
- ***Correspondence*** *files to determine potential significant engagement issues*
- *Authoritative and technical* ***literature*** *appropriate to the activity*

2. *If appropriate, a* ***survey*** *should be conducted to become familiar with the engagement client's activities, risks, and controls; to identify areas for engagement emphasis; and to invite comments and suggestions from engagement clients. A survey is a process for* ***gathering information, without detailed verification***, *on the activity being examined. The main purposes are to:*
   - *Understand the activity under review*
   - *Identify significant areas warranting special emphasis*
   - *Obtain information for use in performing the engagement*
   - *Determine whether further auditing is necessary*
3. *A survey permits an* ***informed approach*** *to planning and carrying out engagement work. It is an effective tool for applying the internal audit activity's resources where they can be used most effectively. The* ***focus of a survey*** *will vary depending upon the nature of the engagement. The scope of work and the time requirements of a survey will vary.* ***Contributing factors*** *include the internal auditor's training and experience, knowledge of the activity being examined, the type of engagement being performed, and whether the survey is part of a recurring or follow-up assignment. Time requirements will also be influenced by the size and complexity of the activity being examined, and by the geographical dispersion of the activity.*
4. *A survey may involve use of the following* ***procedures***:

   - *Discussions with the engagement client*
   - *Interviews with individuals affected by the activity, e.g., users of the activity's output*
   - *On-site observations*
   - *Review of management reports and studies*
   - *Analytical auditing procedures*
   - *Flowcharting*
   - *Functional "walk-through" (tests of specific work activities from beginning to end)*
   - *Documenting key control activities*
5. *A* ***summary of results*** *should be prepared at the conclusion of the survey. The summary should identify:*

   - *Significant engagement* ***issues*** *and reasons for pursuing them in more depth*
   - *Pertinent* ***information developed*** *during the survey*
   - *Engagement* ***objectives***, *engagement* ***procedures***, *and special approaches such as computer-assisted audit techniques (CAATs)*
   - *Potential critical* ***control points***, *control* ***deficiencies***, *or excess controls*
   - *Preliminary estimates of* ***time and resource*** *requirements*
   - ***Revised dates*** *for reporting phases and completing the engagement*
   - *When applicable,* ***reasons for not continuing*** *the engagement*

PA Summary

- The auditor obtains and reviews **background information** about the activities audited. Such items include (1) objectives; (2) policies, plans, procedures, laws, regulations, and contracts; (3) **organizational information**, e.g., details about recent changes; (4) budgets, operating results, and financial data; (5) **prior working papers**; (6) **results of other engagements**; (7) **correspondence**; and (8) **literature** appropriate to the activity.
- A **survey** is usually performed to (1) become familiar with the client's activities, risks, and controls; (2) identify areas of emphasis; and (3) invite comments from the client. A survey **gathers information, without detailed verification**, on the activity being examined. Its purposes are to (1) understand the activity, (2) identify areas for emphasis, (3) obtain information, and (4) determine whether further auditing is necessary.
- A survey permits **informed planning and performance** of the work. Its focus, scope, and time required will vary with the circumstances, including (1) the auditor's training and experience, (2) knowledge of the activity, (3) the type of engagement, (4) size and complexity of the activity, and (5) geographical factors.
- Possible **survey procedures** include (1) client discussions, (2) observations, (3) user interviews, (4) report reviews, (5) analytical tests, (6) flowcharting, (7) a walk-through, and (8) control documentation.
- A **summary of survey results** should be prepared that identifies (1) significant **issues**; (2) **information developed**; (3) **objectives, procedures,** and special approaches (e.g., CAATs); (4) critical **control points, deficiencies**, or excess controls; (5) **time and resource** requirements; (6) **revised reporting dates**; and (7) any **reasons for not continuing** the engagement.

4. The preliminary or **on-site survey** allows for the gathering of information, without detailed verification, about the activities to be reviewed. It is also an opportunity for the internal auditor and the client to begin a **participative engagement**.
5. The survey should result in thorough internal auditor familiarity with the **engagement client's**
   a. Objectives
   b. Organizational structure
   c. Operations
   d. Physical facilities
   e. Risk management, control, and governance systems (including documentation and procedures)
      1) Internal auditors must consider all such policies and procedures, not merely those relevant to a financial statement audit.
   f. Personnel
   g. Information systems
6. The survey should become the basis for an efficient, effective **engagement work program** that
   a. Concentrates on matters of significance.
   b. Reduces the time allocated to areas in which risk appears to be minimal.

7. The survey should set a **cooperative tone** for the field work that follows.
8. The more complex and extensive the activity, the greater the need for the **overview** provided by the preliminary survey.
9. The survey requires certain **abilities**. The internal auditor must
   a. Ask intelligent questions
   b. Prepare suitable questionnaires
   c. Have a **clear understanding** of
      1) The information needed,
      2) Sources of that information, and
      3) How to obtain the information.
   d. Understand and be adept at flowcharting and other **means of documenting** the information obtained
   e. Understand **management's objectives** and be able to identify the objectives of each activity reviewed.
   f. Understand the purposes of **risk management, control, and governance** policies and procedures
   g. Identify the **risks** implicit in the areas under review
10. Defects in risk management and control processes discovered during the survey should be **immediately communicated** to the person who can best take corrective action.
    a. The initial communication should be **oral**. If corrective action is taken, no further steps are needed until the final engagement communication.
    b. If corrective action is not taken, the defect is significant, and, in the internal auditor's opinion, correction cannot be safely delayed, management should be alerted in an **interim or progress communication**.
11. The **overall results** of the survey, if warranted, may be communicated to management in an **oral presentation**.
12. The results should be **documented**.
13. ***2210.A2*** *– The internal auditor should consider the probability of significant errors, irregularities, noncompliance, and other exposures when developing the engagement objectives.*
14. ***2210.C1*** *– Consulting engagement objectives should address risks, controls, and governance processes to the extent agreed upon with the client.*
15. Stop and review! You have completed the outline for this subunit. Study multiple-choice questions 17 through 25 beginning on page 276.

7.3 SCOPE AND RESOURCES

1. This subunit contains the pronouncements on the established engagement scope and resource (especially staffing) allocation. These topics are addressed in two Specific Performance Standards, two Assurance Implementation Standards, one Consulting Implementation Standard, and one Practice Advisory.
2. ***2220*** ***Engagement Scope*** *– The established scope should be sufficient to satisfy the objectives of the engagement.*

   2220.A1 *– The scope of the engagement should include consideration of relevant systems, records, personnel, and physical properties, including those under the control of third parties.*

***2220.A2** – If significant consulting opportunities arise during an assurance engagement, a specific written understanding as to the objectives, scope, respective responsibilities and other expectations should be reached and the results of the consulting engagement communicated in accordance with consulting standards.*

***2220.C1** – In performing consulting engagements, internal auditors should ensure that the scope of the engagement is sufficient to address the agreed-upon objectives. If internal auditors develop reservations about the scope during the engagement, these reservations should be discussed with the client to determine whether to continue with the engagement.*

3. ***2230*** ***Engagement Resource Allocation*** *– Internal auditors should determine appropriate resources to achieve engagement objectives. Staffing should be based on an evaluation of the nature and complexity of each engagement, time constraints, and available resources.*

   a. ***PRACTICE ADVISORY 2230-1: ENGAGEMENT RESOURCE ALLOCATION***

      1. *In determining the resources necessary to perform the engagement, **evaluation** of the following is important:*

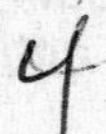

         - *The **number and experience level** of the internal auditing staff required should be based on an evaluation of the nature and complexity of the engagement assignment, time constraints, and available resources.*
         - ***Knowledge, skills, and other competencies** of the internal auditing staff should be considered in selecting internal auditors for the engagement.*
         - ***Training needs** of internal auditors should be considered because each engagement assignment serves as a basis for meeting developmental needs of the internal audit activity.*
         - *Consideration of the use of **external resources** when additional knowledge, skills, and other competencies are needed.*

PA Summary

- **Resource allocation** decisions are based on evaluation of (1) the **number and experience** of staff required; (2) the **knowledge, skills, and competencies** of the staff; (3) **training** needs; and (4) whether **external resources** are needed.

4. Stop and review! You have completed the outline for this subunit. Study multiple-choice questions 26 through 29 beginning on page 282.

7.4 WORK PROGRAMS

1. This subunit is devoted to engagement work programs (also see PA 2200-1 in Subunit 7.1). They are addressed in one Specific Performance Standard, one Assurance Implementation Standard, one Consulting Implementation Standard, and two Practice Advisories.
2. ***2240*** ***Engagement Work Program*** *– Internal auditors should develop work programs that achieve the engagement objectives. These work programs should be recorded.*

   a. ***PRACTICE ADVISORY 2240-1: ENGAGEMENT WORK PROGRAM***

      1. *Engagement procedures, including the testing and sampling techniques employed, should be selected in advance, if practicable, and expanded or altered if circumstances warrant. More detailed guidance is described in **Practice Advisory 2200-1**.*

2. *The process of collecting, analyzing, interpreting, and documenting information should be **supervised** to provide reasonable assurance that the auditor's objectivity is maintained and engagement goals are met.*

PA Summary

- **Procedures** should be **selected** in advance and modified as needed.
- Performance of the engagement should be **supervised** so that objectivity is maintained and goals met.

3. ***2240.A1*** *– Work programs should establish the procedures for identifying, analyzing, evaluating, and recording information during the engagement. The work program should be approved prior to its implementation, and any adjustments approved promptly.*
   a. ***PRACTICE ADVISORY 2240.A1-1: APPROVAL OF WORK PROGRAMS***
      1. *In obtaining approval of the engagement work plan, such plans should be **approved in writing by the chief audit executive** or designee prior to the commencement of engagement work. Adjustments to engagement work plans should be approved in a timely manner. Initially, approval may be obtained orally, if factors preclude obtaining written approval prior to commencing engagement work.*

PA Summary

- **Work programs** should be approved in writing by the CAE. **Adjustments** should be timely approved.

4. ***2240.C1*** *– Work programs for consulting engagements may vary in form and content depending upon the nature of the engagement.*
5. A **pro forma work program** is designed to be used for repeated engagements related to similar operations. It is ordinarily modified over a period of years in response to problems encountered in the field. The "canned" program assures at least minimum coverage, provides comparability, and saves resources when operations at different locations have similar activities, risks, and controls.
   a. However, a pro forma (standard) work program is not appropriate for a complex or changing operating environment. The engagement objectives and related procedures may no longer be relevant.
6. Stop and review! You have completed the outline for this subunit. Study multiple-choice questions 30 through 38 beginning on page 283.

7.5 SUPERVISION

1. This subunit includes the pronouncements relevant to supervision of engagements as well as some supplementary guidance. Engagement supervision is the subject of one Specific Performance Standard and one Practice Advisory.

2. ***2340*** *Engagement Supervision – Engagements should be properly supervised to ensure objectives are achieved, quality is assured, and staff is developed.*

   a. ***PRACTICE ADVISORY 2340-1: ENGAGEMENT SUPERVISION***

      1. *The chief audit executive is responsible for assuring that appropriate engagement supervision is provided. Supervision is a process that* ***begins with planning*** *and continues throughout the examination, evaluation, communication, and follow-up phases of the engagement. Supervision includes:*

         - *Ensuring that the auditors assigned possess the requisite* ***knowledge, skills, and other competencies*** *to perform the engagement.*
         - *Providing appropriate* ***instructions during the planning of the engagement*** *and approving the engagement program.*
         - *Seeing that the* ***approved engagement program*** *is carried out unless changes are both justified and authorized.*

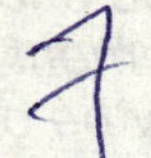

         - *Determining that engagement* ***working papers*** *adequately support the engagement observations, conclusions, and recommendations.*
         - *Ensuring that engagement* ***communications*** *are accurate, objective, clear, concise, constructive, and timely.*
         - *Ensuring that engagement* ***objectives*** *are met.*
         - *Providing opportunities for developing internal auditors' knowledge, skills, and other competencies.*

      2. *Appropriate* ***evidence of supervision*** *should be documented and retained. The extent of supervision required will depend on the* ***proficiency and experience*** *of internal auditors and the complexity of the engagement. The chief audit executive has overall* ***responsibility for review*** *but may designate appropriately experienced members of the internal audit activity to perform the review. Appropriately experienced internal auditors may be used to review the work of other less experienced internal auditors.*

      3. *All internal auditing assignments, whether performed by or for the internal audit activity, remain the responsibility of the chief audit executive. The* ***chief audit executive is responsible for all significant professional judgments*** *made in the planning, examination, evaluation, communication, and follow-up phases of the engagement. The chief audit executive should adopt suitable means to ensure that this responsibility is met.* ***Suitable means*** *include policies and procedures designed to:*

         - *Minimize the risk that professional judgments may be* ***inconsistent with*** *the professional judgment of the chief audit executive resulting in a significant adverse effect on the engagement.*
         - ***Resolve differences in professional judgment*** *between the chief audit executive and internal auditing staff members over significant issues relating to the engagement. Such means may include: (a) discussion of pertinent facts, (b) further inquiry or research, and (c) documentation and disposition of the differing viewpoints in the engagement working papers. In instances of a difference in professional judgment over an ethical issue, resolution may include referral of the issue to those individuals in the organization having responsibility over ethical matters.*

4. *Supervision extends to staff training and development, employee performance evaluation, time and expense control, and similar **administrative areas**.*

5. *All **engagement working papers** should be reviewed to ensure that they properly support the engagement communications and that all necessary procedures have been performed. **Evidence of supervisory review** should consist of the reviewer's initialing and dating each working paper after it is reviewed. Other review techniques that provide evidence of supervisory review include completing an engagement working paper review checklist or preparing a memorandum specifying the nature, extent, and results of the review.*

6. *Reviewers may make a **written record (review notes) of questions** arising from the review process. When clearing review notes, care should be taken to ensure that the working papers provide adequate evidence that questions raised during the review have been resolved. Acceptable alternatives with respect to **disposition of review notes** are:*
   - *Retaining the review notes as a record of the questions raised by the reviewer and the steps taken in their resolution.*
   - *Discarding the review notes after the questions raised have been resolved and the appropriate engagement working papers have been amended to provide the additional information requested.*

PA Summary

- **Supervision** is relevant to all phases of the engagement from planning through the examination, evaluation, communication, and follow-up.
- **Evidence of supervision** should be documented and retained. Its extent depends on the auditor's proficiency and experience and the nature of the engagement.
- The **CAE** may appropriately delegate the responsibility for supervisory review.
- The CAE is responsible for all **significant professional judgments**. The CAE should adopt **suitable means** to (1) minimize the risk of applying inconsistent professional judgments and (2) resolve differences in professional judgment between the CAE and staff members.
- Supervision extends to **administrative areas**.
- All **working papers** should be reviewed to ensure that they support the engagement communications and that all necessary procedures have been performed. Evidence of review should be provided consisting of the reviewer's initialing and dating each working paper after it is reviewed.
- **Written review notes** record questions arising from the review. When clearing review notes, care should be taken to ensure that the working papers provide adequate evidence that questions raised have been resolved.

3. The internal audit activity should maintain the same degree of control over its own activities as it expects from other subunits of the organization.
4. All projects should be **formally assigned**. Each should have
   a. An assignment sheet, i.e., a work order authorizing expenditure of engagement work hours.
   b. An engagement title indicating the activity covered.
   c. A number identifying the engagement and indicating its nature, e.g., a regular or special internal audit, a consulting engagement, or a fraud investigation.
5. The chief audit executive should **review the progress of each engagement** periodically in terms of budgeted employee-days, actual employee-days, and estimated completion date.

6. Schedules for **job completion** should be set early, usually before the midpoint of the assignment.
7. **Requests for budget adjustment** also should be made well before job completion, i.e., as soon as it becomes apparent that the actual project differs significantly from that described in the engagement work schedule.
8. **Adjusted budgets** normally will be carried forward to future budgets and work schedules. Temporary obstacles, e.g., those created by inexperienced assistants and unexpected problems, should not justify budget adjustments.
9. **Projects should be formally closed** upon the issuance of a final engagement communication if no matters are unresolved when it is released. Otherwise, they should be closed by the submission of a closure communication to the CAE. This submission occurs when action on all unresolved matters discussed in the final engagement communication is complete.
10. **Activity reports** should be prepared for senior management and the board at least annually. These activity reports
    a. Highlight significant engagement observations, conclusions, and recommendations.
    b. Explain major deviations from approved engagement work schedules, staffing plans, and financial budgets.
11. All engagements should be kept under **budgetary control**.
    a. **Project budgets** are usually stated in employee-hours or employee-days.
    b. **Financial budgets** should include items other than internal audit activity staff payroll, e.g.,
        1) Administrative and clerical support
        2) Engagement-related and training-related travel
        3) Outside service providers
        4) Telephone
        5) Supplies
        6) Library
        7) Staff professional society membership dues
    c. Budgets for **recurring engagements** should be the same as those shown in the engagement work schedule.
    d. Budgets for engagements for which the IAA has **no prior experience** should be set as soon as possible after the scope of the engagement becomes known.
    e. Because no projects are precisely the same (even those covering the same activity), budgets should be **reevaluated after the preliminary survey**.
        1) Excessive budgets should be reduced.
        2) Insufficient budgets should be expanded or the scope of the engagement reduced.
        3) Adjustments and the reasons for them should be documented for future engagement work schedules.
    f. **Budget adjustments** should be justified. They should be **approved** at a level higher than the engagement supervisor. Requests for budget adjustment should show
        1) The operational activities to be reviewed according to the engagement work schedule
        2) The activities actually being carried on
        3) The employee-days attributable to the difference

12. **Administrative records** should provide the CAE with control over engagements in progress and with sufficient information for useful reports to management on engagement accomplishments.
    a. Staff auditors should **submit time sheets** periodically, showing the employee-days charged against their projects and accounting for all employee-days in the reporting period.
        1) Time should be accumulated in registers by project, including time off, vacations, holidays, etc.
    b. Staff auditors should report weekly to their supervisors on the **time spent and the status of the job**.
    c. The internal audit activity should **maintain records** to gather data for
        1) Status reports on all ongoing engagements
        2) Communication of results
        3) Suggestions adopted
        4) Savings accomplished as a result of recommendations
        5) Time expended by type of engagement in comparison with amounts budgeted
13. Stop and review! You have completed the outline for this subunit. Study multiple-choice questions 39 through 49 beginning on page 286.

7.6 STUDY UNIT 7 SUMMARY

1. Internal auditors consider (a) the objectives, resources, operations, and risks associated with the activities reviewed; (b) the relevant risk management and control systems; and (c) possible improvements in those systems. The internal auditors can then (a) establish the engagement's objectives, (b) determine its scope, (c) allocate resources appropriate to the achievement of the objectives, and (d) develop a work program.
2. The engagement program (a) documents engagement procedures, (b) states the engagement's objectives and scope, (c) identifies risks and other matters to be examined, and (d) states the nature and extent of testing. The program is prepared before work begins and is modified during the work.
3. Engagement objectives are broad statements of what is to be accomplished. Engagement procedures are the means of attaining the objectives. Together, they define the engagement scope.
4. Internal auditors should conduct a preliminary assessment of the risks relevant to the activity under review. Engagement objectives should reflect the results of this assessment.
5. A survey is usually performed to (a) become familiar with the client's activities, risks, and controls; (b) identify areas of emphasis; and (c) invite comments from the client.
6. The established scope should be sufficient to satisfy the objectives of the engagement.
7. Internal auditors should determine appropriate resources to achieve engagement objectives. Staffing should be based on an evaluation of the nature and complexity of each engagement, time constraints, and available resources.

QUESTIONS

7.1 Planning

1. Internal auditors should develop and record a plan for each engagement. The planning process should include all the following except

A. Establishing engagement objectives and scope of work.

B. Obtaining background information about the activities to be reviewed.

C. Identifying sufficient information to achieve engagement objectives.

D. Determining how, when, and to whom the engagement results will be communicated.

Answer (C) is correct. *(CIA, adapted)*

REQUIRED: The item not part of the planning process.

DISCUSSION: Planning should include establishing engagement objectives and scope of work, obtaining background information about the activities to be reviewed, determining the resources necessary to perform the engagement, and informing those in management who need to know about the engagement. It also includes performing, as appropriate, a survey to become familiar with activities, risks, and controls; to identify areas for engagement emphasis; and to invite comments and suggestions from engagement clients. Furthermore, planning extends to developing work programs; determining how, when, and to whom engagement results will be communicated; and obtaining approval of the engagement work program. Identifying sufficient information to achieve engagement objectives is done during field work, not planning.

2. An outside consultant is developing methods for the management of a city's capital facilities. An appropriate scope of an engagement to evaluate the consultant's product is to

A. Review the consultant's contract to determine its propriety.

B. Establish the parameters of the value of the items being managed and controlled.

C. Determine the adequacy of the risk management and control systems for the management of capital facilities.

D. Review the handling of idle equipment.

Answer (C) is correct. *(CIA, adapted)*

REQUIRED: The appropriate scope of an engagement to evaluate a consultant's product.

DISCUSSION: According to Standard 2201, "In planning the engagement, internal auditors should consider:

- The objectives of the activity being reviewed and the means by which the activity controls its performance.
- The significant risks to the activity, its objectives, resources, and operations and the means by which the potential impact of risk is kept to an acceptable level.
- The adequacy and effectiveness of the activity's risk management and control systems compared to a relevant control framework or model.
- The opportunities for making significant improvements to the activity's risk management and control systems."

Answer (A) is incorrect because the review of the consultant's contract to determine its propriety is related to the procurement decision. Answer (B) is incorrect because the establishment of parameters for values of items being managed and controlled is a management responsibility. Answer (D) is incorrect because management must determine policies regarding idle equipment. Some equipment may be retained for emergency use.

3. Documentation required to plan an internal auditing engagement should include information that

A. Resources needed to complete the engagement were considered.

B. Planned engagement work will be completed on a timely basis.

C. Intended engagement observations have been clearly identified.

D. Internal audit activity resources are efficiently and effectively employed.

Answer (A) is correct. *(CIA, adapted)*

REQUIRED: The information included in the documentation required to plan an engagement.

DISCUSSION: Planning should be documented. It includes establishing engagement objectives and scope of work, obtaining background information about activities to be reviewed, determining the resources required for the engagement, and informing those in management who need to know about the engagement. It also includes performing, as appropriate, a survey to become familiar with activities, risks, and controls; to identify areas for engagement emphasis; and to invite comments and suggestions from engagement clients. Furthermore, planning extends to developing work programs; determining how, when, and to whom engagement results will be communicated; and obtaining approval of the engagement work program.

Answer (B) is incorrect because whether the planned work will actually be completed on time cannot be known in the planning phase. Answer (C) is incorrect because observations are what is actually found by performing procedures. Auditors must not anticipate the results of the work. To do so indicates a lack of objectivity. Answer (D) is incorrect because documenting the economic and efficient use of resources can be done only on completion of the engagement.

4. Which of the following is least likely to be placed on the agenda for discussion at a pre-engagement meeting?

A. Purpose and scope of the engagement.

B. Records and client personnel needed.

C. Sampling plan and key criteria.

D. Expected starting and completion dates.

Answer (C) is correct. *(CIA, adapted)*

REQUIRED: The item least likely to be discussed at a pre-engagement meeting.

DISCUSSION: Meetings should be held with management responsible for the activity being examined (PA 2200-1). These pre-engagement meetings between the internal auditor and engagement client are opportunities to discuss planning and housekeeping matters regarding the forthcoming engagement. The sampling plan would probably not be discussed because it is not determined until the preliminary survey and evaluation of controls are completed.

5. One of the primary roles of an engagement work program is to

A. Serve as a tool for planning and conducting engagement work.

B. Document an internal auditor's evaluations of controls.

C. Provide for a standardized approach to the engagement.

D. Assess the risks associated with the activity under review.

Answer (A) is correct. *(CIA, adapted)*

REQUIRED: The item that states one of the primary roles of an engagement work program.

DISCUSSION: Work programs document procedures for collecting, analyzing, interpreting, and documenting information; state engagement objectives; set forth the scope and degree of testing needed to achieve objectives in each phase of the engagement; identify technical aspects, risks, processes, and transactions to be examined; state the nature and extent of testing required, and are prepared before work begins, with appropriate modification during the engagement (PA 2200-1).

Answer (B) is incorrect because engagement working papers include results of control evaluations. Answer (C) is incorrect because the work program should be logical, but it may not be consistent from year to year given the changing conditions to which the engagement client must adapt. The work program should be tailored to the current year's situation; thus, standardization may not be appropriate. Answer (D) is incorrect because the risk assessment in the planning phase helps to identify objectives, a step that must be taken before the work program can be developed.

6. Engagement work programs testing controls should

A. Be tailored for each operation evaluated.

B. Be generalized to fit all situations without regard to departmental lines.

C. Be generalized so as to be usable at all locations of a particular department.

D. Reduce costly duplication of effort by ensuring that every aspect of an operation is examined.

Answer (A) is correct. *(CIA, adapted)*

REQUIRED: The true statement about work programs.

DISCUSSION: Work programs document procedures for collecting, analyzing, interpreting, and documenting information; state engagement objectives; set forth the scope and degree of testing needed to achieve objectives in each phase of the engagement; identify technical aspects, risks, processes, and transactions to be examined; state the nature and extent of testing required, and are prepared before work begins, with appropriate modification during the engagement (PA 2200-1). However, a work program must be adapted to the specific needs of the engagement after the internal auditor establishes the engagement objectives and scope and determines the resources required.

Answer (B) is incorrect because a generalized program allows for variations resulting from changing circumstances and varied conditions. Answer (C) is incorrect because a generalized program cannot consider variations in circumstances and conditions. Answer (D) is incorrect because every aspect of an operation need not be examined, only those aspects likely to conceal problems and difficulties.

7.2 Objectives, Risk Assessment, and Survey

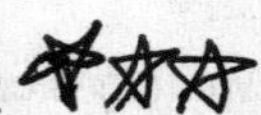

7. The scope of an internal auditing engagement is initially defined by the

A. Engagement objectives.

B. Scheduling and time estimates.

C. Preliminary survey.

D. Engagement work program.

Answer (A) is correct. *(CIA, adapted)*

REQUIRED: The factor initially defining the scope of an internal auditing engagement.

DISCUSSION: According to Standard 2220, "The established scope should be sufficient to satisfy the objectives of the engagement." Moreover, according to PA 2210-1, "Planning should be documented. Engagement objectives and scope of work should be established. Engagement objectives are broad statements developed by internal auditors and define what the engagement is intended to accomplish. Engagement procedures are the means to attain engagement objectives. Engagement objectives and procedures, taken together, define the scope of the internal auditor's work."

Answer (B) is incorrect because the scheduling and time estimates are based on the objectives and scope of the engagement. Answer (C) is incorrect because the preliminary survey is performed before the objectives are determined, but the objectives and procedures define the scope of the engagement. Answer (D) is incorrect because the work program is developed after the preliminary survey and is based on the objectives of the engagement.

8. The established scope of the engagement should be sufficient to satisfy the objectives of the engagement. When developing the objectives of the engagement, the internal auditor should consider the

A. Probability of significant noncompliance.

B. Information included in the engagement work program.

C. Results of engagement procedures.

D. Resources required.

Answer (A) is correct. *(Publisher, adapted)*

REQUIRED: The factor the internal auditor should consider when developing the objectives of the engagement.

DISCUSSION: According to Standard 2210.A2, the internal auditor should consider the probability of significant errors, irregularities, noncompliance, and other exposures when developing assurance engagement objectives. In a consulting engagement, the objectives should address risks, controls, and governance processes to the extent agreed upon with the client (Standard 2210.C1).

Answer (B) is incorrect because engagement objectives must be determined before the engagement work program is written. Answer (C) is incorrect because the objectives determine the procedures to be performed. Answer (D) is incorrect because internal auditors determine the resources required to achieve the engagement objectives.

9. Which of the following is the best explanation of the difference, if any, between engagement objectives and procedures?

A. Procedures establish broad general goals; objectives specify the detailed work to be performed.

B. Objectives are tailor-made for each engagement; procedures are generic in application.

C. Objectives define desired accomplishments; procedures provide the means of achieving objectives.

D. Procedures and objectives are essentially the same.

Answer (C) is correct. *(CIA, adapted)*

REQUIRED: The difference between objectives and procedures.

DISCUSSION: According to PA 2210-1, "Planning should be documented. Engagement objectives and scope of work should be established. Engagement objectives are broad statements developed by internal auditors and define what the engagement is intended to accomplish. Engagement procedures are the means to attain engagement objectives. Engagement objectives and procedures, taken together, define the scope of the internal auditor's work."

Answer (A) is incorrect because objectives are specific goals, and procedures specify the detailed work. Answer (B) is incorrect because both objectives and procedures must be defined specifically for each engagement. Answer (D) is incorrect because procedures are the means of collecting, analyzing, interpreting, and documenting information during the engagement to achieve the objectives.

10. Which of the following statements is an engagement objective?

A. Observe the deposit of the day's cash receipts.

B. Analyze the pattern of any cash shortages.

C. Evaluate whether cash receipts are adequately safeguarded.

D. Recompute each month's bank reconciliation.

Answer (C) is correct. *(CIA, adapted)*

REQUIRED: The engagement objective.

DISCUSSION: Engagement objectives should be established for each engagement (Standard 2210). They are broad statements developed by internal auditors and define what the engagement is intended to accomplish (PA 2210-1). Procedures are the means of achieving the objectives. Evaluating whether cash receipts are adequately safeguarded is an objective because it states what the engagement is to accomplish.

Answer (A) is incorrect because observation is a procedure. Answer (B) is incorrect because analysis is a procedure. Answer (D) is incorrect because recomputation is a procedure.

11. In planning an engagement, the internal auditor should establish objectives and procedures to address the risk associated with the activity. Risk is defined as

A. The possibility that the balance or class of transactions and related assertions contains misstatements that could be material to the financial statements.

B. The uncertainty of the occurrence of an event that could affect the achievement of objectives.

C. The failure to adhere to organizational policies, plans, and procedures or to comply with relevant laws and regulations.

D. The failure to accomplish established objectives and goals for operations or programs.

Answer (B) is correct. *(CIA, adapted)*

REQUIRED: The definition of risk.

DISCUSSION: According to PA 2210-1, "Engagement objectives and procedures should address the risks associated with the activity under review. The term risk is the possibility of an event's occurring that could have an impact on the achievement of objectives. Risk is measured in terms of impact and likelihood. The purpose of the risk assessment during the planning phase of the engagement is to identify significant areas of activity that should be examined as potential engagement objectives."

Answer (A) is incorrect because the risk of material misstatement in financial statement assertions consists of inherent risk, control risk, and detection risk as defined in the AICPA's auditing standards. Answer (C) is incorrect because the failure to adhere to organizational policies, plans, and procedures or to comply with relevant laws and regulations is just one type of adverse effect that can result from unmitigated risk. Answer (D) is incorrect because the failure to accomplish established objectives and goals for operations or programs is just one type of adverse effect that can result from unmitigated risk.

12. Which of the following activities represents the greatest risk to a post-merger manufacturing organization and is therefore most likely to be the subject of an internal auditing engagement?

A. Combining imprest funds.

B. Combining purchasing functions.

C. Combining legal functions.

D. Combining marketing functions.

Answer (B) is correct. *(CIA, adapted)*

REQUIRED: The activity representing the greatest risk.

DISCUSSION: According to Standard 2210.A1, "Internal auditors should conduct a preliminary survey of the risks relevant to the activity under review. Engagement objectives should reflect the results of this assessment." In a consulting engagement, the objectives should address risks, controls, and governance processes to the extent agreed upon with the client (Standard 2210.C1). Purchasing functions ordinarily represent the greatest exposure to loss of the items listed and are therefore most likely to be evaluated. The financial exposure in the purchasing function is ordinarily greater than in, for example, the legal and marketing functions. After a merger, risk is heightened because of the difficulty of combining the disparate systems of the two organizations. Thus, the likelihood of an engagement is increased.

Answer (A) is incorrect because imprest funds are typically immaterial in amount. Answer (C) is incorrect because legal functions do not typically represent a risk of loss as great as the purchasing functions. Answer (D) is incorrect because marketing functions do not typically represent a risk of loss as great as the purchasing functions.

13. In planning an assurance engagement, a survey could assist with all of the following, except

A. Obtaining engagement client comments and suggestions on control problems.

B. Obtaining preliminary information on controls.

C. Identifying areas for engagement emphasis.

D. Evaluating the adequacy and effectiveness of controls.

Answer (D) is correct. *(CIA, adapted)*

REQUIRED: The planning item with which a survey would not assist.

DISCUSSION: A survey is a process for gathering information, without detailed verification, on the activity being examined. A survey may involve discussions with the client, documenting key control activities, and identifying significant engagement issues (PA 2210.A1-1). A survey does not help in evaluating the adequacy and effectiveness of controls except to the extent the internal auditor gains familiarity with the controls. Evaluation requires testing.

14. An assurance engagement in the quality control department is being planned. Which of the following is least likely to be used in the preparation of a preliminary survey questionnaire?

A. An analysis of quality control documents.

B. The permanent engagement file.

C. The prior engagement communications.

D. Management's charter for the quality control department.

Answer (A) is correct. *(CIA, adapted)*

REQUIRED: The document least likely to be included in preparing a preliminary survey questionnaire.

DISCUSSION: A survey is a process for gathering information, without detailed verification, on the activity being examined (PA 2210.A1-1). An analysis of quality control documents is a part of field work, which follows the preliminary survey.

Answer (B) is incorrect because the permanent engagement file probably contains information, such as problems detected in prior years that will help in the development of appropriate questions to ask this year. Answer (C) is incorrect because the prior engagement communications will likely assist in developing the current year's questionnaire. Answer (D) is incorrect because knowing what the department is supposed to do will help the internal auditor develop knowledgeable questions.

15. The internal-auditor-in-charge has just been informed of the next engagement and the assigned engagement team. What is the appropriate phase for finalizing the time budget?

A. During formulation of the internal audit activity's engagement work schedule.

B. After the preliminary survey.

C. During the initial planning meeting.

D. After the completion of all field work.

Answer (B) is correct. *(CIA, adapted)*

REQUIRED: The appropriate phase for finalizing the engagement time budget.

DISCUSSION: A survey is a process for gathering information, without detailed verification, on the activity being examined. Among other things, the summary of results prepared at the end of the survey identifies preliminary estimates of time and resource requirements and revised dates for reporting phases and completing the engagement (PA 2210.A1-1). Thus, if the survey discloses significant differences from the project that was placed in the long-range plan, budget adjustments should be requested and authorized.

Answer (A) is incorrect because an initial budget is determined during formulation of the engagement work schedule (the long-range plan of the IAA), but revisions based on the survey may be required. Answer (C) is incorrect because the project is not sufficiently well defined during the initial planning meeting to complete the time budget. Answer (D) is incorrect because, after the completion of all field work, the bulk of staff hours have been expended, and the usefulness of the time budget as a control and evaluation tool would be negated.

16. An internal auditor has just completed a survey to become familiar with the organization's payroll operations. Which of the following should be performed next?

A. Assign internal audit personnel.

B. Establish initial engagement objectives.

C. Write the engagement work program.

D. Conduct field work.

Answer (C) is correct. *(CIA, adapted)*

REQUIRED: The step following the survey.

DISCUSSION: The work program is normally prepared after the survey. The survey allows the internal auditor to become familiar with the engagement client and therefore provides input to the work program.

Answer (A) is incorrect because internal audit personnel are usually assigned before the survey. Answer (B) is incorrect because initial engagement objectives are established at the beginning of the planning process. They should be specified before the survey. Answer (D) is incorrect because field work can be performed only after the work program has been written. Thus, field work cannot immediately follow the survey.

17. During which phase of the engagement does the internal auditor identify the objectives and related controls of the activity being examined?

A. Preliminary survey.

B. Staff selection.

C. Work program preparation.

D. Final communication of results.

Answer (A) is correct. *(CIA, adapted)*

REQUIRED: The stage of the engagement in which the internal auditor identifies objectives and related controls.

DISCUSSION: Planning should include performing, as appropriate, a survey to become familiar with activities, risks, and controls; to identify areas for engagement emphasis; and to invite client comments and suggestions (PA 2210.A1-1).

Answer (B) is incorrect because staff selection is the process of deciding which internal auditors will work on the engagement. Answer (C) is incorrect because the work program is prepared after the preliminary survey. Answer (D) is incorrect because final communication of results occurs after the completion of the engagement.

18. The preliminary survey indicates that severe staff reductions at the engagement location have resulted in extensive amounts of overtime among accounting staff. Department members are visibly stressed and very vocal about the effects of the cutbacks. Accounting payrolls are nearly equal to prior years, and many key controls, such as segregation of duties, are no longer in place. The accounting supervisor now performs all operations within the cash receipts and posting process and has no time to review and approve transactions generated by the remaining members of the department. Journal entries for the last 6 months since the staff reductions show increasing numbers of prior-month adjustments and corrections, including revenues, cost of sales, and accruals that had been misstated or forgotten during month-end closing activity. The internal auditor should

A. Discuss these observations with management of the internal audit activity to determine whether further work would be an efficient use of internal auditing resources at this time.

B. Proceed with the scheduled engagement but add personnel based on the expected number of observations and anticipated lack of assistance from local accounting management.

C. Research temporary help agencies and evaluate the cost and benefit of outsourcing needed services.

D. Suspend further engagement work because the observations are obvious and make the final communication of results.

Answer (A) is correct. *(CIA, adapted)*

REQUIRED: The internal auditor action given the absence of many key controls.

DISCUSSION: A preliminary survey allows the internal auditor to become familiar with activities, risks, and controls; to identify areas for engagement emphasis; and to invite engagement client comments and suggestions. Among many other matters, the summary of results prepared at the conclusion of the survey should identify, when applicable, reasons for not continuing the engagement (PA 2210.A1-1). In this case, additional planning is necessary to modify the engagement for the difficult circumstances discovered during the preliminary survey and to address the responsibilities of the IAA.

Answer (B) is incorrect because what additional work will be necessary is not clear in these circumstances. Answer (C) is incorrect because management has not accepted this plan of action. Answer (D) is incorrect because a final communication of results would violate the Standards, including those relating to objectivity, due professional care, and performance of the engagement.

19. Which of the following best describes a preliminary survey?

A. A standardized questionnaire used to obtain an understanding of management objectives.

B. A statistical sample of key employee attitudes, skills, and knowledge.

C. A "walk-through" of the financial control system to identify risks and the controls that can address those risks.

D. A process used to become familiar with activities and risks in order to identify areas for engagement emphasis.

Answer (D) is correct. *(CIA, adapted)*

REQUIRED: The best description of a preliminary survey.

DISCUSSION: Planning includes performing, as appropriate, a survey to become familiar with the activities, risks, and controls; to identify areas for engagement emphasis; and to invite engagement client comments and suggestions (PA 2210.A1-1). Detailed procedures performed during a preliminary survey include use of standard questionnaires, statistical sampling, and a walk-through.

20. The internal auditors of a financial institution are performing an engagement to evaluate the institution's investing and lending activities. During the last year, the institution has adopted new policies and procedures for monitoring investments and the loan portfolio. The internal auditors know that the organization has invested in new types of financial instruments during the year and is heavily involved in the use of financial derivatives to appropriately hedge risks. If the internal auditors were to conduct a preliminary review, which of the following procedures should be performed?

A. Review reports of engagements performed by regulatory and external auditors since the last internal auditing engagement.

B. Interview management to identify changes made in policies regarding investments or loans.

C. Review minutes of board meetings to identify changes in policies affecting investments and loans.

D. All of the answers are correct.

Answer (D) is correct. *(CIA, adapted)*

REQUIRED: The procedure performed in a preliminary review of investing and lending activities.

DISCUSSION: Engagement planning should be documented and should include, among other things, obtaining background information, for example, from prior working papers, results of other engagements, budgetary data, financial statements, organizational information (major system changes, etc.), correspondence, and technical literature. Planning also includes performing, as appropriate, a survey to become familiar with the activities, risks, and controls; to identify areas for engagement emphasis; and to invite engagement client comments and suggestions. A survey involves discussions with the client; interviews with individuals affected by the activity, e.g., users of the activity's output; on-site observations; review of management reports and studies; analytical auditing procedures; flowcharting; functional "walk-through" (tests of specific work activities from beginning to end); and documenting key control activities (PA 2210.A1-1).

21. An internal auditor conducts a preliminary survey and identifies a number of significant engagement issues and reasons for pursuing them in more depth. The engagement client informally communicates concurrence with the preliminary survey results and asks that the internal auditor not report on the areas of significant concern until the client has an opportunity to respond to the problem areas. Which of the following engagement responses is not appropriate?

A. Keep the engagement on schedule and discuss with management the need for completing the engagement on a timely basis.

B. Consider the risk involved in the areas involved, and, if the risk is high, proceed with the engagement.

C. Consider the engagement to be terminated with no communication of results needed because the engagement client has already agreed to take constructive action.

D. Work with the engagement client to keep the engagement on schedule and address the significant issues in more depth, as well as the client's responses, during the course of the engagement.

Answer (C) is correct. *(CIA, adapted)*

REQUIRED: The inappropriate response to an engagement client's request not to communicate results.

DISCUSSION: The apparently constructive action by the engagement client may be a delaying tactic intended to conceal more serious problems after the internal auditor has identified significant engagement issues. Moreover, no basis is given for not pursuing the engagement. The internal auditor should always consider the risk associated with the potential observations as a basis for determining the need for more immediate attention.

22. During a preliminary survey, an auditor found that several accounts payable vouchers for major suppliers required adjustments for duplicate payment of prior invoices. This would indicate

A. A need for additional testing to determine related controls and the current exposure to duplicate payments made to suppliers.

B. The possibility of unrecorded liabilities for the amount of the overpayments.

C. Insufficient controls in the receiving area to ensure timely notice to the accounts payable area that goods have been received and inspected.

D. The existence of a sophisticated accounts payable system that correlates overpayments to open invoices and therefore requires no further audit concern.

Answer (A) is correct. *(CIA, adapted)*

REQUIRED: The implication of a finding of duplicate payments to major suppliers.

DISCUSSION: An engagement's objectives and procedures should address the risks associated with the activities under review. Engagement objectives are broad statements of what is to be accomplished. Engagement procedures are the means of attaining the objectives. Together, they define the engagement scope. The purpose of the risk assessment in the planning phase is to identify significant activities requiring examination as potential objectives (PA 2210-1). Accordingly, this preliminary survey information should prompt the auditor to identify the magnitude of duplicate payments.

Answer (B) is incorrect because unrecorded liabilities are not likely to result in the generation of duplicate accounts payable vouchers. Answer (C) is incorrect because the existence of duplicate payments is most likely related to a problem in accounts payable. Answer (D) is incorrect because duplicate payments are not overpayments. They are exceptions and should be handled as such.

23. Which of the following procedures should be performed as part of a preliminary review in an audit of a bank's investing and lending activities?

A. Review reports of audits performed by regulatory and outside auditors since the last internal audit engagement.

B. Interview management to identify changes made in policies regarding investments or loans.

C. Review minutes of the board of directors' meetings to identify changes in policies affecting investments and loans.

D. All of the answers are correct.

Answer (D) is correct. *(CIA, adapted)*

REQUIRED: The procedure performed as part of a preliminary review in an audit of a bank's investing and lending activities.

DISCUSSION: Internal auditors should conduct a preliminary assessment of the relevant risks in the activity under review. Engagement objectives should reflect the results. A survey is usually performed to (1) become familiar with the client's activities, risks, and controls; (2) identify areas of emphasis; and (3) invite comments from the client. Possible survey procedures include (1) observations, (2) interviews, (3) report reviews, (4) analytical tests, (5) flowcharting, (6) a walk-through, and (7) control documentation (PA 2210.A1-1).

Answer (A) is incorrect because reviewing reports is not the only procedure performed as part of a preliminary review. Answer (B) is incorrect because interviewing management is not the only procedure performed as part of a preliminary review. Answer (C) is incorrect because procedures in addition to reviewing the minutes of board meetings are performed in a preliminary review.

24. An auditor, experienced in air-quality issues, discovered a significant lack of knowledge about legal requirements for controlling air emissions while interviewing the manager of the environmental, health, and safety (EHS) department. The auditor should

A. Alter the scope of the engagement to focus on activities associated with air emissions.

B. Share extensive personal knowledge with the EHS manager.

C. Take note of the weakness and direct additional questions to determine the potential effect of the lack of knowledge.

D. Report potential violations in this area to the appropriate regulatory agency.

Answer (C) is correct. *(CIA, adapted)*

REQUIRED: The auditor's action upon discovering the EHS manager's significant lack of knowledge about environmental law.

DISCUSSION: An engagement's objectives and procedures should address the risks associated with the activities under review. The preliminary risk assessment identifies significant activities requiring examination as potential objectives. Thus, the auditor should ensure that the field work is designed to identify potential instances of noncompliance. In the closing conference, the auditor should recommend additional training for the EHS manager.

Answer (A) is incorrect because the scope of the engagement should not be altered too early. Maintaining a broad scope and not reducing the scope prematurely are important considerations in the engagement process. Answer (B) is incorrect because, although the auditor may be able to contribute to the EHS manager's knowledge of pertinent air-quality matters, the auditor should focus on, during this phase of the engagement, learning what the manager does. Answer (D) is incorrect because an auditor should not report violations or potential violations to regulatory agencies. Such matters are the responsibility of company counsel.

25. If an auditor's preliminary evaluation of internal controls results in an observation that controls may be inadequate, the next step would be to

A. Expand audit work prior to the preparation of an engagement final communication.

B. Prepare a flowchart depicting the internal control system.

C. Note an exception in the engagement final communication if losses have occurred.

D. Implement the desired controls.

Answer (A) is correct. *(CIA, adapted)*

REQUIRED: The next step if the preliminary evaluation of internal controls results in an observation that controls may be inadequate.

DISCUSSION: The purpose of the risk assessment during the planning phase is to identify significant areas of activity that should be examined as potential engagement objectives (PA 2210-1). If the preliminary evaluation indicates control problems, the auditor usually decides to apply additional engagement procedures to reach the engagement objectives.

Answer (B) is incorrect because a flowchart is prepared during the preliminary evaluation. Answer (C) is incorrect because the auditor is not ready to report until more work has been performed. Answer (D) is incorrect because managers, not auditors, implement controls.

7.3 Scope and Resources

26. The scope of an internal auditing assurance engagement should include consideration of

A. Only those systems and records under the control of the engagement client.

B. Relevant physical properties under third-party control.

C. Engagement observations, conclusions, and recommendations.

D. Final engagement communications.

Answer (B) is correct. *(Publisher, adapted)*

REQUIRED: The item within the scope of an internal auditing assurance engagement.

DISCUSSION: The scope of the engagement should include consideration of relevant systems, records, personnel, and physical properties, including those under the control of third parties (Standard 2220.A1). Engagement results reported in final engagement communications follow from performing the procedures and achieving the objectives that define the engagement scope.

27. As a particular engagement is being planned in a high-risk area, the chief audit executive determines that the available staff does not have the requisite skills to perform the assignment. The best course of action consistent with engagement planning principles is to

A. Not perform the engagement because the requisite skills are not available.

B. Use the engagement as a training opportunity and let the internal auditors learn as the engagement is performed.

C. Consider using external resources to supplement the needed knowledge, skills, and other competencies and complete the assignment.

D. Perform the engagement but limit the scope in light of the skill deficiency.

Answer (C) is correct. *(CIA, adapted)*

REQUIRED: The course of action when the internal auditing staff does not have adequate skills to perform the engagement.

DISCUSSION: In determining the resources needed to perform the engagement, the CAE should consider the knowledge, skills, and other competencies of the internal auditing staff in selecting internal auditors for the engagement. The CAE should consider the use of external resources when additional knowledge, skills, and other competencies are needed (PA 2230-1).

Answer (A) is incorrect because not performing the engagement is unacceptable, especially for a high-risk area. Answer (B) is incorrect because engagements should be properly supervised. The IAA has no one to provide this supervision. Answer (D) is incorrect because limiting the scope of the engagement should be done only when the requisite skills are not available even from external resources. If the scope is limited, management should be informed of the constraint in an interim report.

28. The chief audit executive of a multinational organization must form an engagement team to examine a newly acquired subsidiary in another country. Consideration should be given to which of the following factors?

I. Local customs
II. Language skills of the internal auditor
III. Experience of the internal auditor
IV. Monetary exchange rate

A. I, II, and III.

B. II, III, and IV.

C. I and III.

D. I and II.

Answer (A) is correct. *(CIA, adapted)*

REQUIRED: The factors considered in forming a team to conduct an engagement in another country.

DISCUSSION: Internal auditors should determine appropriate resources to achieve engagement objectives. Staffing should be based on an evaluation of the nature and complexity of each engagement, time constraints, and available resources (Standard 2230). Thus, the knowledge, skills, and other competencies of the internal auditing staff should be considered in selecting internal auditors for the engagement (PA 2230-1). Thus, in an engagement to be performed in a foreign country, the language skills of the internal auditor and knowledge of local customs must be considered. For example, gender and ethnic issues may be important in some countries because of religious restrictions and incompatibilities. As always, experience levels are relevant in making staff assignments.

Answer (B) is incorrect because the exchange rate is irrelevant to determining the needed traits of the team members. Answer (C) is incorrect because the language skills of the internal auditor must be considered. Answer (D) is incorrect because experience must always be considered.

29. In the preparation of an engagement work program, which of the following items is not essential?

A. The performance of a preliminary survey.

B. A review of material from prior engagement communications.

C. The preparation of a budget identifying the costs of resources needed.

D. A review of criteria established by management to determine whether operating goals and objectives have been accomplished.

Answer (C) is correct. *(CIA, adapted)*

REQUIRED: The item not essential to preparing the work program.

DISCUSSION: Standard 2230 states, "Internal auditors should determine appropriate resources to achieve engagement objectives. Staffing should be based on an evaluation of the nature and complexity of each engagement, time constraints, and available resources." Hence, it is implicit that the work program should state the resources necessary to carry out the detailed tasks specified. However, quantification of costs is not essential to writing the work program.

Answer (A) is incorrect because the preliminary survey provides necessary background information about activities, risks, and controls. Answer (B) is incorrect because engagement communications contain, among other things, information about observations from prior engagements and corrective actions taken. Answer (D) is incorrect because internal auditors should ascertain the extent to which management has established adequate criteria to determine whether objectives and goals have been accomplished (Standard 2120.A4).

7.4 Work Programs

30. Writing an engagement work program occurs at which stage of the engagement?

A. During the planning stage.

B. Subsequent to evaluating risk management and control systems.

C. As the engagement is performed.

D. At the end of each engagement when the standard work program should be revised for the next engagement to ensure coverage of noted problem areas.

Answer (A) is correct. *(CIA, adapted)*

REQUIRED: The stage of the engagement during which the work program is written.

DISCUSSION: Standard 2200 states, "Internal auditors should develop and record a plan for each engagement." Thus, Standard 2240 states, "Internal auditors should develop work programs that achieve the engagement objectives. These work programs should be recorded." Furthermore, work programs should be prepared prior to the commencement of engagement work and modified, as appropriate, during the course of the engagement (PA 2200-1). Accordingly, work programs are prepared during the planning stage.

Answer (B) is incorrect because the work program states the scope, degree, nature, and extent of testing. Hence, it must be written in the planning stage. Answer (C) is incorrect because the internal auditor should write the work program during the planning stage, not as the engagement is performed. However, the work program may be modified during the engagement. Answer (D) is incorrect because, although revising the work program at the end of one engagement for the next engagement is allowed, it should still be written during the planning phase.

31. A work program for a comprehensive assurance engagement to evaluate a purchasing function should include

A. Procedures arranged by relative priority based upon perceived risk.

B. A statement of the engagement objectives for the operation under review with agreement by the engagement client.

C. Procedures to accomplish engagement objectives.

D. A focus on risks affecting the financial statements as opposed to controls.

Answer (C) is correct. *(CIA, adapted)*

REQUIRED: The content of a work program for a comprehensive engagement to evaluate a purchasing function.

DISCUSSION: Work programs are a necessary part of engagement planning. They establish the procedures for identifying, analyzing, evaluating, and recording information during the engagement. Work programs should be approved prior to their implementation, and any adjustments should be approved promptly (Standard 2240.A1).

Answer (A) is incorrect because engagement procedures should normally be arranged in an order that will most efficiently complete the work program. Answer (B) is incorrect because engagement objectives should be stated, but they do not need to be agreed to by the engagement client. Answer (D) is incorrect because the engagement should not be narrowly focused on the reliability and integrity of financial information.

32. Which of the following is not ordinarily considered an essential criterion for developing engagement work programs?

A. Description of the objectives of the engagement client operation to be evaluated.

B. Specificity as to the controls to be tested.

C. Specificity as to procedures to be followed.

D. Specificity as to the methodology to be used for the engagement procedures.

Answer (D) is correct. *(CIA, adapted)*

REQUIRED: The criterion not considered essential for developing engagement work programs.

DISCUSSION: Work programs are a necessary part of engagement planning. They consist of the specific work steps required for the engagement, but they must allow for some latitude for flexibility in carrying out the steps. Thus, they should be expanded or altered if circumstances warrant (PA 2240-1).

Answer (A) is incorrect because the objectives of the operation to be evaluated set the parameters of the engagement work. Answer (B) is incorrect because the work program should include the scope, degree, nature, and extent of testing required. Answer (C) is incorrect because the work program must include the engagement procedures necessary to achieve engagement objectives.

33. The engagement work program should be approved

A. No later than the conclusion of engagement work.

B. By the engagement client or designee.

C. Orally in some circumstances.

D. In writing by the board.

Answer (C) is correct. *(Publisher, adapted)*

REQUIRED: The true statement about approval of an engagement work program.

DISCUSSION: An engagement work program should be approved in writing by the CAE or designee prior to the commencement of engagement work. Adjustments should be approved in a timely manner. Initial approval may be obtained orally if circumstances preclude obtaining written approval prior to commencing engagement work (PA 2240.A1-1).

34. Which of the following is a step in an engagement work program?

A. The engagement will commence in 6 weeks and include tests of compliance with laws, regulations, and contracts.

B. A determination is made concerning whether the manufacturing operations are effective and efficient.

C. Internal auditors may not reveal engagement observations to non-supervisory, operational personnel during the course of this engagement.

D. The methods used to identify defective units produced are observed.

Answer (D) is correct. *(CIA, adapted)*

REQUIRED: The step in an engagement work program.

DISCUSSION: An engagement work program is a document that lists the procedures to be followed during an engagement. These procedures are designed to achieve the engagement objectives. Thus, observing the engagement client's execution of methods for identifying defects is an action performed to achieve the engagement objectives and should be included in the work program.

Answer (A) is incorrect because a partial statement of the scope and the proposed starting time are not engagement procedures. Answer (B) is incorrect because determination of whether operations are effective and efficient is an engagement objective. Answer (C) is incorrect because a prohibition on revealing observations is a rule for the conduct of the internal auditors.

35. The internal audit activity is planning a 3-year effort to perform engagements at all branches of a large international car rental agency. Management is especially concerned with standardized operation of the accounting, car rental, and inventory functions. What type of work program is most appropriate for this project?

A. A pro forma program developed and tested by the internal audit activity.

B. Individual programs developed by the internal auditor-in-charge after a preliminary survey of each branch.

C. A checklist of branch standard operating procedures.

D. An industry-developed engagement guide.

Answer (A) is correct. *(CIA, adapted)*

REQUIRED: The type of work program most appropriate for standardized operations at many locations.

DISCUSSION: A pro forma work program is designed to be used for repeated engagements related to similar operations. It is ordinarily modified over a period of years in response to problems encountered in the field. The "canned" program assures at least minimum coverage, provides comparability, and saves resources when operations at different locations have similar activities, risks, and controls.

Answer (B) is incorrect because use of tailored work programs would conflict with management's desire for standardization. Answer (C) is incorrect because a checklist of branch standard operating procedures is only one input into the development of a work program. Answer (D) is incorrect because an industry guide might not be tailored to the specific needs of the organization.

36. A standard engagement work program is not appropriate for which situation?

A. A stable operating environment undergoing only minimal changes.

B. A complex or changing operating environment.

C. Multiple locations with similar operations.

D. Subsequent engagements to provide assurance about inventory performed at same location.

Answer (B) is correct. *(CIA, adapted)*

REQUIRED: The situation in which a standard work program is not appropriate.

DISCUSSION: A standard work program is not appropriate for a complex or changing operating environment. The engagement objectives and related procedures may no longer be relevant.

Answer (A) is incorrect because a standard work program is appropriate for use in a minimally changing operating environment. It may save effort and provide continuity. Answer (C) is incorrect because a standard work program can be used for engagements at multiple locations with similar operations if the same activities, risks, and controls are present. Answer (D) is incorrect because a standard work program is acceptable for conducting subsequent inventory engagements at the same location if the inventory functions performed have not varied substantially.

37. What action should an internal auditor take upon discovering that an area was omitted from the engagement work program?

A. Document the problem in the engagement working papers and take no further action until instructed to do so.

B. Perform the additional work needed without regard to the added time required to complete the engagement.

C. Continue the engagement as planned and include the unforeseen problem in a subsequent engagement.

D. Evaluate whether completion of the engagement as planned will be adequate.

Answer (D) is correct. *(CIA, adapted)*

REQUIRED: The action to take upon discovering that an area was omitted from the engagement work program.

DISCUSSION: Work programs are necessarily tentative because the internal auditors are likely to encounter unexpected situations while carrying out the detailed work. If they learn that an area is not covered, they must determine whether they can achieve the engagement objectives and satisfy their professional responsibilities without modification of the work program. Modification will necessitate consultation with supervisors to obtain authorization to adjust time and financial budgets.

Answer (A) is incorrect because the internal auditor must determine whether changes in the work program are needed. Answer (B) is incorrect because changes in the engagement budgets should be authorized by appropriate persons. Answer (C) is incorrect because an engagement in the unforeseen area may be necessary to achieve current engagement objectives.

38. An internal auditor has some suspicion of, but no information about, potential misstatement of financial statements. The internal auditor would fail to exercise due professional care by

A. Identifying potential ways in which a misstatement could occur and ranking the items for investigation.

B. Informing the engagement manager of the suspicions and asking for advice on how to proceed.

C. Not testing for possible misstatement because the engagement work program had already been approved by engagement management.

D. Expanding the engagement work program, without the engagement client's approval, to address the highest ranked ways in which a misstatement may have occurred.

Answer (C) is correct. *(CIA, adapted)*

REQUIRED: The act in violation of the due professional care standard.

DISCUSSION: Due professional care requires the exercise of the care and skill expected of a reasonably prudent and competent internal auditor in the same or similar circumstances (PA 1220-1). Because engagement work programs are expected to be modified to reflect changing circumstances, the internal auditor would fail to exercise due professional care by not investigating a suspected misstatement solely because the engagement work program had already been approved.

Answer (A) is incorrect because ranking the ways in which a misstatement could occur is consistent with the due professional care standard. Answer (B) is incorrect because seeking advice is consistent with exercising the standard of due professional care. Answer (D) is incorrect because the internal auditor does not need the engagement client's approval to expand the engagement work program.

7.5 Supervision

39. The purpose of including a time budget in an engagement work program is to

A. Provide an objective means of evaluating the internal auditor's competence.

B. Assure timely completion of the engagement.

C. Provide a means of controlling and evaluating the progress of the engagement.

D. Restrict the scope of the engagement.

Answer (C) is correct. *(CIA, adapted)*

REQUIRED: The purpose of a time budget in an engagement work program.

DISCUSSION: Internal auditors should develop and record work programs to achieve the engagement objectives (Standard 2240). The work program lists the procedures to be followed during the engagement. Accordingly, a work program is a useful tool for scheduling and controlling (supervising) the engagement. Supervision includes, among other things, determining that the approved work program is carried out unless changes are justified and authorized. Moreover, supervision extends to time and expense control (PA 2340-1). For this purpose, a time budget is necessary to evaluate and control the progress of the engagement. It permits comparison of the actual time spent on a procedure with its allotted time.

Answer (A) is incorrect because whether an internal auditor remains within the time budget is affected by many factors other than professional competence. Answer (B) is incorrect because the establishment of a budget cannot assure that work will be completed on a timely basis. Answer (D) is incorrect because a time budget is not intended to limit the scope of the engagement.

40. Which of the following statements is true with respect to a time budget for an internal audit engagement?

A. Requests for time budget adjustments should be approved by the audit committee.

B. Time budgets should be strictly adhered to, regardless of circumstances.

C. Time budgets should be used for financial audits, but not for operational audits.

D. Time budgets should normally be prepared in terms of hours or days.

Answer (D) is correct. *(CIA, adapted)*

REQUIRED: The true statement about a time budget for an internal audit engagement.

DISCUSSION: Supervision extends to time and expense control (PA 2340-1). A budget is a plan that contains a quantitative statement of expected results. It may be defined as a "quantified program." All engagement projects and other assignments should be kept under budgetary control. Time budgets for engagement projects are usually prepared in employee-hours or employee-days.

Answer (A) is incorrect because requests for time budget adjustments should be approved by the CAE, not the audit committee. Answer (B) is incorrect because budgets should be subject to adjustment for unexpected conditions. Answer (C) is incorrect because time budgets are equally applicable to all types of engagements.

41. The best control over the work on which internal auditors' opinions are based is

A. Supervisory review of all engagement work.

B. Preparation of time budgets for internal auditing activities.

C. Preparation of engagement working papers.

D. Staffing of internal audit activities.

Answer (A) is correct. *(CIA, adapted)*

REQUIRED: The best control over the work on which internal auditors' opinions are based.

DISCUSSION: The engagement should be properly supervised to ensure objectives are achieved, quality is assured, and staff is developed (Standard 2340). Supervision includes ensuring that the auditors assigned possess the requisite knowledge, skills, and other competencies to perform the engagement; providing appropriate instructions during the planning of the engagement and approving the engagement work program; seeing that the approved engagement work program is carried out unless changes are both justified and authorized; determining that engagement working papers adequately support the engagement observations, conclusions, and recommendations; ensuring that engagement communications are accurate, objective, clear, concise, constructive, and timely; ensuring that engagement objectives are met; and providing opportunities for developing internal auditors' knowledge, skills, and other competencies. Hence, supervision is a control that encompasses all aspects of engagements (PA 2340-1).

Answer (B) is incorrect because, although useful, time budgets do not ensure the adequacy of work supporting opinions. Answer (C) is incorrect because engagement working papers support the conclusions and engagement results, but supervision is necessary to ensure the adequacy of work. Answer (D) is incorrect because proper staffing is required, but supervision is essential to ensure an adequate basis for opinions.

42. Which of the following activities does not constitute engagement supervision?

A. Preparing a preliminary engagement work program.

B. Providing appropriate instructions to the internal auditors.

C. Reviewing engagement working papers.

D. Ensuring that engagement communications meet appropriate criteria.

Answer (A) is correct. *(CIA, adapted)*

REQUIRED: The activity not constituting supervision.

DISCUSSION: The engagement should be properly supervised to ensure objectives are achieved, quality is assured, and staff is developed (Standard 2340). Supervision includes, among other things, providing appropriate instructions during the planning of the engagement and approving the engagement work program; determining that engagement working papers adequately support the engagement observations, conclusions, and recommendations; and ensuring that engagement communications are accurate, objective, clear, concise, constructive, and timely (PA 2340-1). Preparing a preliminary engagement work program is part of engagement planning but not an aspect of engagement supervision.

43. Which of the following best describes what should determine the extent of supervision required for a particular internal auditing engagement?

A. Whether the engagement involves possible fraud on the part of management.

B. Whether the engagement involves possible violations of laws or governmental regulations.

C. The proficiency of the internal auditors and the complexity of the engagement.

D. The internal audit activity's prior experience in dealing with the particular engagement client.

Answer (C) is correct. *(CIA, adapted)*

REQUIRED: The best description of what should determine the extent of supervision of an engagement.

DISCUSSION: The CAE is responsible for providing appropriate engagement supervision. The extent of supervision required will depend on the proficiency and experience of the internal auditors and the complexity of the engagement (PA 2340-1). The engagement's involvement in possible management fraud or possible violations of laws or governmental regulations and the IAA's prior experience with the engagement client are not the primary determinants of the extent of supervision required.

44. A new staff internal auditor's first assignment is to review the cash management operations of the organization. The staff internal auditor has no background in cash management. Under which of the following conditions would this arrangement be appropriate?

I. The senior internal auditor is skilled in the area and closely supervises the staff internal auditor.

II. The staff internal auditor performs the work and prepares an engagement communication that is reviewed in detail by the chief audit executive.

A. I only.

B. II only.

C. Both I and II.

D. Neither I nor II.

Answer (A) is correct. *(CIA, adapted)*

REQUIRED: The condition(s) in which review by an inexperienced auditor is appropriate.

DISCUSSION: Engagements should be properly supervised to ensure that objectives are achieved, quality is assured, and staff is developed (Standard 2340). Moreover, supervision includes ensuring that the auditors assigned possess the necessary knowledge, skills, and other competencies to perform the engagement. The extent of supervision depends on the proficiency and experience of the internal auditors and the complexity of the engagement. Thus, the skill of the senior auditor and the closeness of the supervision compensate for the new auditor's inexperience regarding cash management.

Answer (B) is incorrect because supervision involves far more than a review of the engagement communication. Answer (C) is incorrect because the internal auditors assigned to the engagement must have or obtain the necessary proficiency, and the staff internal auditor must be closely supervised. Answer (D) is incorrect because the internal auditors assigned to the engagement must have or obtain the necessary proficiency, and the staff internal auditor must be closely supervised.

45. Which of the following best describes engagement supervision?

A. The manager of each engagement has the ultimate responsibility for supervision.

B. Supervision is primarily exercised at the final review stage of an engagement to ensure the accuracy of the engagement communications.

C. Supervision is most important in the planning phase of the engagement to ensure appropriate coverage.

D. Supervision is a continuing process beginning with planning and ending with the conclusion of the engagement.

Answer (D) is correct. *(CIA, adapted)*

REQUIRED: The best description of engagement supervision.

DISCUSSION: The CAE is responsible for ensuring that appropriate engagement supervision is provided. Supervision is a process that begins with planning and continues through the examination, evaluation, communication, and follow-up phases of the engagement (PA 2340-1).

Answer (A) is incorrect because the CAE has the ultimate responsibility for supervision. Answer (B) is incorrect because supervision should begin at the planning phase and continue throughout the engagement. Answer (C) is incorrect because supervision is equally important in all phases of the engagement.

46. When engagements are performed for the internal audit activity by nonstaff members, the chief audit executive is responsible for

A. Ensuring that the engagement communications are accurate, objective, clear, concise, constructive, and timely.

B. Reviewing the engagement work programs for approval.

C. Providing appropriate supervision from the beginning to the conclusion of the engagement.

D. None of the work performed by those outside the internal audit activity.

Answer (C) is correct. *(CIA, adapted)*

REQUIRED: The CAE's responsibility for work performed by nonstaff members.

DISCUSSION: All internal auditing engagements, whether performed by or for the IAA, remain the responsibility of the CAE. The CAE is responsible for all significant professional judgments made in the planning, examination, evaluation, communication, and follow-up phases of the engagement (PA 2340-1).

Answer (A) is incorrect because ensuring that the engagement communications are accurate, objective, clear, concise, constructive, and timely is only one of the responsibilities of supervision. Answer (B) is incorrect because supervision is a continuing process beginning with planning and ending with the follow-up phase of the engagement. Answer (D) is incorrect because the CAE is responsible for all work performed by and for the IAA.

47. Supervision of an internal audit engagement should include

A. Determining that engagement working papers adequately support the engagement observations.

B. Assigning staff members to the particular engagement.

C. Determining the scope of the engagement.

D. Appraising each internal auditor's performance on at least an annual basis.

Answer (A) is correct. *(CIA, adapted)*

REQUIRED: The extent of supervision of an engagement.

DISCUSSION: Supervision includes ensuring that the auditors assigned possess the requisite knowledge, skills, and other competencies to perform the engagement; providing appropriate instructions during the planning of the engagement and approving the engagement work program; seeing that the approved engagement work program is carried out unless changes are both justified and authorized; determining that engagement working papers adequately support the engagement observations, conclusions, and recommendations; ensuring that engagement communications are accurate, objective, clear, concise, constructive, and timely; ensuring that engagement objectives are met; and providing opportunities for developing internal auditors' knowledge, skills, and other competencies (PA 2340-1).

Answer (B) is incorrect because engagement resource allocation is a planning function, not a supervisory function (PA 2230-1). Answer (C) is incorrect because determining the engagement scope is a planning function, not a supervisory function. Answer (D) is incorrect because appraising performance on an annual basis is not a supervisory function of a specific engagement but is part of the management of the human resources of the internal audit activity (PA 2030-1).

48. The chief audit executive is responsible for engagement supervision. The most important form of supervision during the field work phase of engagements involves

A. Seeing that the approved engagement work program is carried out unless changes are both justified and authorized.

B. Providing suitable instructions to subordinates at the outset of the engagement and approving the engagement work program.

C. Appraising each internal auditor's performance at least annually.

D. Making sure that communications are accurate, objective, clear, concise, constructive, and timely.

Answer (A) is correct. *(CIA, adapted)*

REQUIRED: The most important form of supervision during the field work phase.

DISCUSSION: Supervision includes ensuring that the auditors assigned possess the requisite knowledge, skills, and other competencies to perform the engagement; providing appropriate instructions during the planning of the engagement and approving the engagement work program; seeing that the approved engagement work program is carried out unless changes are both justified and authorized; determining that engagement working papers adequately support the engagement observations, conclusions, and recommendations; ensuring that engagement communications are accurate, objective, clear, concise, constructive, and timely; ensuring that engagement objectives are met; and providing opportunities for developing internal auditors' knowledge, skills, and other competencies (PA 2340-1). Execution of the engagement work program requires supervision during field work. The other supervisory tasks are carried out before or after field work.

Answer (B) is incorrect because "at the outset of the engagement" is not during field work. Answer (C) is incorrect because annual performance appraisal is not specific to a particular engagement. Answer (D) is incorrect because engagement communications are prepared at the conclusion of field work.

49. Determining that engagement objectives have been met is part of the overall supervision of an engagement and is the ultimate responsibility of the

A. Staff internal auditor.

B. Audit committee.

C. Engagement supervisor.

D. Chief audit executive.

Answer (D) is correct. *(CIA, adapted)*

REQUIRED: The person(s) with ultimate responsibility for determining that engagement objectives have been met.

DISCUSSION: The chief audit executive is responsible for ensuring that appropriate engagement supervision is provided. Supervision is a process that begins with planning and continues through the examination, evaluation, communication, and follow-up phases of the engagement (PA 2340-1).

STUDY UNIT EIGHT
MANAGING THE INTERNAL AUDIT ACTIVITY I

(24 pages of outline)

Disk 4

This is the first of two study units on management of the internal audit activity (IAA). According to **General Performance Standard 2000 – Managing the Internal Audit Activity**,

> *The chief audit executive should effectively manage the internal audit activity to ensure it adds value to the organization.*

Practice Advisory 2000-1: Managing the Internal Audit Activity elaborates on this responsibility as follows:

> 1. *The chief audit executive is responsible for properly managing the internal audit activity so that:*
>   - *Engagement work fulfills the general purposes and responsibilities described in the charter, approved by senior management, and accepted by the board.*
>   - *Resources of the internal audit activity are efficiently and effectively employed.*
>   - *Engagement work conforms to the International Standards for the Professional Practice of Internal Auditing.*

The **chief audit executive (CAE)** should (1) establish risk-based plans, (2) communicate plans and resource needs to senior management and the board for their approval, (3) develop policies and procedures, (4) coordinate efforts with other service providers, and (5) report periodically to senior management and the board. The CAE also must develop a quality assurance and improvement program for the IAA.

Core Concepts

- The CAE establishes risk-based plans to determine the IAA's priorities. They should be consistent with the goals of the organization.
- Planning involves establishing (a) goals, (b) engagement work schedules, (c) staffing plans and financial budgets, and (d) activity reports.
- Plans should be based on risk assessment.
- The audit universe includes components of the organization's strategic plan.
- The CAE communicates plans and resource requirements to senior management and the board for review and approval.
- The CAE reports to senior management and the board on the IAA's (a) purpose, (b) authority, (c) responsibility, and (d) performance. The CAE also reports on significant risk, control, and governance issues, as well as other matters upon request.
- The audit committee and the IAA have interlocking goals. Thus, a strong working relationship is essential for them to fulfill their responsibilities.
- Sound governance depends on the synergy among (a) the board, (b) management, (c) internal auditing, and (d) external auditing.
- The CAE ensures that the IAA's resources are appropriate, sufficient, and effectively used.
- The CAE establishes policies and procedures to guide the IAA.

8.1 PLANNING

1. This subunit concerns the need for risk-based planning for the IAA. Planning for the management of the IAA is addressed in one Specific Performance Standard, one Assurance Implementation Standard, one Consulting Implementation Standard, and two Practice Advisories.

2. ***2010*** ***Planning*** *– The chief audit executive should establish risk-based plans to determine the priorities of the internal audit activity, consistent with the organization's goals.*

   a. ***PRACTICE ADVISORY 2010-1: PLANNING***

      1. *Planning for the* ***internal audit activity*** *should be consistent with its* ***charter*** *and with the goals of the organization. The planning* ***process*** *involves establishing:*
         - *Goals.*
         - *Engagement work schedules.*
         - *Staffing plans and financial budgets.*
         - *Activity reports.*

      2. *The* ***goals*** *of the internal audit activity should be capable of being accomplished within* ***specified operating plans and budgets*** *and, to the extent possible, should be measurable. They should be accompanied by* ***measurement criteria*** *and targeted* ***dates of accomplishment****.*

      3. ***Engagement work schedules*** *should include the following:*
         - *What activities are to be performed;*
         - *When they will be performed; and*
         - *The estimated time required, taking into account the scope of the engagement work planned and the nature and extent of related work performed by others.*

      4. *Matters to be considered in* ***establishing*** *engagement work schedule* ***priorities*** *should include:*
         - *The dates and results of the last engagement;*
         - *Updated assessments of risks and effectiveness of risk management and control processes;*
         - *Requests by senior management, the audit committee, and the governing body;*

         NOTE: Governmental **regulatory requirements** (for example, an audit of the use of financial assistance provided from public funds) also may be a source of engagements.

         - *Current issues relating to organizational governance;*
         - *Major changes in the enterprise's business, operations, programs, systems, and controls;*
         - *Opportunities to achieve operating benefits; and*
         - *Changes to and capabilities of the audit staff. The work schedules should be sufficiently flexible to cover unanticipated demands on the internal audit activity.*

PA Summary

- **Planning** for the IAA is subject to its **charter** and organizational goals. The process establishes (1) goals, (2) work schedules, (3) staffing plans and financial budgets, and (4) activity reports.
- IAA **goals** should be (1) accomplished within specified **plans** and **budgets**, (2) measurable, and (3) accompanied by **criteria** and accomplishment dates.
- **Work schedules** answer the questions what is to be done, when, and how long (considering work planned and the work performed by others).
- Setting **work schedule priorities** requires consideration of matters ranging from results of prior engagements to changes in the entity's business.

b. ***PRACTICE ADVISORY 2010-2: LINKING THE AUDIT PLAN TO RISK AND EXPOSURES***

1. *The internal audit activity's plan should be designed based on an **assessment of risk and exposures** that may affect the organization. Ultimately, the objective is to provide management with information to mitigate the negative consequences associated with accomplishing the organization's objectives. The degree or materiality of exposure can be viewed as **risk mitigated by establishing control activities**.*

   NOTE: Risk is concerned with the probability rather than the certainty of loss. Assessing the risk of an activity involves analysis of numerous factors, estimation of probabilities and amounts of potential losses, and an appraisal of the costs and benefits of risk reduction. Consequently, in assessing the magnitude of risk associated with any factor in a risk model, the necessity of informed judgment by the internal auditor is implied.

2. *The **audit universe** can include components from the organization's **strategic plan**. By incorporating components of the organization's strategic plan, the audit universe will consider and reflect the **overall business plan objectives**. Strategic plans are also likely to reflect the organization's **attitude toward risk** and the **degree of difficulty in achieving planned objectives**. It is advisable to assess the audit universe on at least an annual basis to reflect the most current strategies and direction of the organization. The audit universe can be influenced by the **results of the risk management process**. When developing plans, the outcomes of the risk management process should be considered.*

3. ***Work schedules** should be based on, among other factors, an **assessment of risk priority and exposure**. Prioritizing is needed to make decisions for applying relative resources based on the significance of risk and exposure. A variety of **risk models** exist to assist the chief audit executive in prioritizing potential engagement subject areas. Most risk models use **risk factors** to establish the priority of engagements, such as dollar materiality, asset liquidity, management competence, quality of internal controls, degree of change or stability, time of last engagement, complexity, and employee and government relations.*

4. ***Changes** in management direction, objectives, emphasis, and focus should be reflected in **updates to the audit universe and related plan**.*

5. *In conducting engagements, methods and techniques for testing and validating exposures should be reflective of the **risk materiality** and **likelihood of occurrence**.*

6. ***Management reporting and communication*** *should convey* ***risk management conclusions and recommendations*** *to reduce exposures. For management to fully understand the degree of exposure, it is critical that reporting identify the criticality and consequence of the risk activity to achieving objectives.*
7. *The chief audit executive should, at least annually, prepare a* ***statement of the adequacy of internal controls to mitigate risks****. This statement should also comment on the significance of unmitigated risk and management's acceptance of such risk.*

PA Summary

- The IAA's **plan** is based on an **assessment of risk and exposure**. The objective is to provide information to help management mitigate the negative consequences of accomplishing the organization's objectives. The degree of exposure is **risk mitigated by control**.
- The **audit universe** may reflect the organization's strategic plan. Thus, it may reflect (1) the overall business objectives, (2) the attitude toward risk, (3) the difficulty of reaching objectives, and (4) the results of risk management. The audit universe should be assessed at least annually to reflect the most current strategies and direction of the organization.
- **Work schedules** are based on an assessment of risk priority and exposure. Various **risk models** may be used to prioritize engagements. Most risk models are based on risk factors, e.g., quality of controls, degree of change, or materiality.
- The audit universe and plan must be updated for changes in management direction.
- Methods of testing exposures should reflect **risk materiality** and **probability**.
- **Management reporting** must state risk management conclusions and recommendations. It also must identify the **criticality and consequence** of the risk activity.
- The CAE should prepare an annual statement of the **adequacy of controls**, the significance of unmitigated risk, and management's acceptance of such risk.

3. ***2010.A1*** *– The internal audit activity's plan of engagements should be based on a risk assessment, undertaken at least annually. The input of senior management and the board should be considered in this process.*
4. ***2010.C1*** *– The chief audit executive should consider accepting proposed consulting engagements based on the engagement's potential to improve management of risks, add value, and improve the organization's operations. Those engagements that have been accepted should be included in the plan.*
5. Stop and review! You have completed the outline for this subunit. Study multiple-choice questions 1 through 25 beginning on page 315.

8.2 COMMUNICATION OF PLANS

1. This subunit concerns communicating the IAA's plans to senior management and the board. The topic is covered in one Specific Performance Standard and one Practice Advisory.
2. ***2020*** ***Communication and Approval*** *– The chief audit executive should communicate the internal audit activity's plans and resource requirements, including significant interim changes, to senior management and to the board for review and approval. The chief audit executive should also communicate the impact of resource limitations.*
   a. ***PRACTICE ADVISORY 2020-1: COMMUNICATION AND APPROVAL***
      1. *The chief audit executive should submit **annually** to **senior management** for approval, and to **the board** for its information, a summary of the internal audit activity's **work schedule, staffing plan, and financial budget**. The chief audit executive should also submit all significant **interim changes** for approval and information. Engagement work schedules, staffing plans, and financial budgets should inform senior management and the board of the **scope of internal auditing work** and of any **limitations** placed on that scope.*
      2. *The approved engagement work schedule, staffing plan, and financial budget, along with all significant interim changes, should contain sufficient information to enable the board to ascertain whether the internal audit activity's **objectives and plans** support those of the organization and the board.*

PA Summary

- The CAE annually submits to senior management for approval and to the board a summary of the IAA's **work schedule, staffing plan, and financial budget**. The CAE also submits all significant **interim changes**. The **scope of work** and any **limitations** on it should be disclosed.
- These communications should allow the board to determine whether the IAA's **objectives and plans** are consistent with the organization's.

3. Stop and review! You have completed the outline for this subunit. Study multiple-choice questions 26 and 27 beginning on page 323.

8.3 REPORTING

1. This subunit addresses reporting of the IAA's accomplishments and other matters. The topic is the subject of one Specific Performance Standard and one Practice Advisory.

2. ***2060*** ***Reporting to the Board and Senior Management*** – *The chief audit executive should report periodically to the board and senior management on the internal audit activity's purpose, authority, responsibility, and performance relative to its plan. Reporting should also include significant risk exposures and control issues, corporate governance issues, and other matters needed or requested by the board and senior management.*

   a. ***PRACTICE ADVISORY 2060-1: REPORTING TO THE BOARD AND SENIOR MANAGEMENT***

      1. *The chief audit executive should submit* ***activity reports*** *to senior management and to the board* ***at least annually****. Activity reports should highlight* ***significant engagement observations and recommendations*** *and should inform senior management and the board of any* ***significant deviations*** *from approved engagement work schedules, staffing plans, and financial budgets, and the reasons for them.*

      2. ***Significant engagement observations*** *are those conditions that, in the judgment of the chief audit executive, could adversely affect the organization. Significant engagement observations may include conditions dealing with irregularities, illegal acts, errors, inefficiency, waste, ineffectiveness, conflicts of interest, and control weaknesses. After reviewing such conditions with* ***senior management****, the chief audit executive should communicate significant engagement observations and recommendations to* ***the board****, whether or not they have been satisfactorily resolved.*

      3. ***Management's responsibility*** *is to make decisions on the appropriate action to be taken regarding significant engagement observations and recommendations. Senior management may decide to* ***assume the risk of not correcting the reported condition*** *because of cost or other considerations. The board should be informed of senior management's decisions on all significant observations and recommendations.*

      4. *The chief audit executive should consider whether it is appropriate to inform the board regarding* ***previously reported****, significant observations and recommendations in those instances when senior management and the board* ***assumed the risk*** *of not correcting the reported condition. This may be particularly necessary when there have been organization, board, senior management, or other changes.*

      5. *In addition to subjects covered above,* ***activity reports*** *should also compare (a) actual* ***performance*** *with the internal audit activity's* ***goals and engagement work schedules****, and (b)* ***expenditures*** *with* ***financial budgets****. Reports should explain the reason for major variances and indicate any action taken or needed.*

   NOTE: Thus, the CAE should report key performance indicators.

PA Summary

- The CAE submits **activity reports at least annually**. They describe (1) significant engagement observations (those adversely affecting the organization) and recommendations and (2) significant deviations from work schedules, staffing plans, and financial budgets, and the reasons for them.
- **Significant observations and recommendations** are reviewed with senior management and then communicated to the board, whether or not resolved.
- **Management** is responsible for making decisions about actions to be taken but may **assume the risk** of not correcting the reported conditions. The **board** should be informed of all decisions regarding significant matters.
- The CAE considers whether the board should be informed about **previously reported** significant matters when senior management and the board **assumed the risk** of not correcting the reported condition.
- **Activity reports** also compare (1) performance with goals and work schedules and (2) expenditures with budgets. Reports explain major variances and indicate action taken or needed.

3. Stop and review! You have completed the outline for this subunit. Study multiple-choice questions 28 and 29 on page 324.

8.4 RELATIONSHIP WITH THE AUDIT COMMITTEE

1. This subunit consists of one Practice Advisory that describes the IAA's roles and responsibilities in its dealings with the governance body commonly known as the audit committee. The PA interprets Standard 2060 (see Subunit 8.3). The subunit also contains additional outlines of the audit committee's characteristics and responsibilities, including a sample charter.

   a. ***PRACTICE ADVISORY 2060-2: RELATIONSHIP WITH THE AUDIT COMMITTEE***

      1. *The term "audit committee," as used in this document, refers to the* ***governance body*** *that is charged with oversight of the organization's* ***audit and control functions****. Although these fiduciary duties are often delegated to an audit committee of the board of directors, the information in this Practice Advisory is also intended to apply to other oversight groups with equivalent authority and responsibility, such as trustees, legislative bodies, owners of an owner-managed entity, internal control committees, or full boards of directors.*

      2. *The Institute of Internal Auditors recognizes that* ***audit committees and internal auditors have interlocking goals****. A* ***strong working relationship*** *with the audit committee is essential for* ***each to fulfill its responsibilities*** *to senior management, board of directors, shareholders, and other outside parties. This Practice Advisory summarizes The Institute's views concerning the aspects and attributes of an appropriate relationship between an audit committee and the internal audit function. The Institute acknowledges that audit committee responsibilities encompass activities that are beyond the scope of this advisory and in no way intends it to be a comprehensive description of audit committee responsibilities.*

3. *There are **three areas of activities** that are key to an effective relationship between the audit committee and the internal audit function, chiefly through the Chief Audit Executive (CAE):*
   - ***Assisting the audit committee** to ensure that its charter, activities, and processes are appropriate to fulfill its responsibilities.*
   - *Ensuring that the **charter, role, and activities of internal audit** are clearly understood and responsive to the needs of the audit committee and the board.*
   - *Maintaining **open and effective communications** with the audit committee and the chairperson.*

Audit Committee Responsibilities

4. *The CAE should assist the committee in ensuring that the charter, role and activities of the committee are appropriate for it to achieve its responsibilities. The CAE can play an important role by **assisting the committee to periodically review its activities and suggesting enhancements**. In this way, the CAE serves as a valued advisor to the committee on audit committee and regulatory practices. Examples of activities that the CAE can undertake are:*
   - ***Reviewing the charter** for the audit committee at least annually and advise the committee whether the charter addresses all responsibilities directed to the committee in any terms of reference or mandates from the board of directors.*
   - ***Reviewing or maintaining a planning agenda** for the audit committee's meeting that details all required activities to ascertain whether they are completed. The agenda assists the committee in reporting to the board annually that it has completed all assigned duties.*
   - ***Drafting the audit committee's meeting agenda** for the chairman's review, facilitating the distribution of the material to the audit committee members, and writing up the minutes of the audit committee meetings.*
   - *Encouraging the audit committee to conduct periodic reviews of its activities and practices **compared with current best practices** to ensure that its activities are consistent with leading practices.*
   - *Meeting periodically with the chairperson to discuss whether the **materials and information** being furnished to the committee are meeting their needs.*
   - *Inquiring of the audit committee whether any **educational or informational sessions or presentations** would be helpful, such as training new committee members on risk and controls.*
   - *Inquiring of the committee whether the **frequency and time** allotted to the committee are sufficient.*

Internal Audit Activity's Role

5. *The CAE's relationship to the audit committee should revolve around a core role of the CAE ensuring that the audit committee understands, supports, and receives all assistance needed from the internal audit function. The IIA supports the concept that sound governance is dependent on the synergy generated among the **four principal components of effective corporate governance** systems: boards of directors, management, internal auditors, and external auditors. In that structure, internal auditors and audit committees are **mutually supportive**. Consideration of the work of internal auditors is essential for the audit committee to gain a complete understanding of an organization's operations. A primary component of the CAE's role with the committee is to ensure this objective is accomplished and the committee views the **CAE as their trusted advisor**. The CAE can perform a number of activities to accomplish this role:*

- *Request that the committee review and approve the* ***internal audit charter*** *on an annual basis.*
- *Review with the audit committee the* ***functional and administrative reporting lines*** *of internal audit to ensure that the organizational structure in place allows adequate independence for internal auditors (Practice Advisory 1110-2: Chief Audit Executive (CAE) Reporting Lines).*
- *Incorporate in the charter for the audit committee the* ***review of hiring decisions****, including appointment, compensation, evaluation, retention, and dismissal of the CAE.*
- *Incorporate in the charter for the audit committee the review and approval of proposals to* ***outsource*** *any internal audit activities.*
- *Assist the audit committee in evaluating the* ***adequacy of the personnel and budget****, and the* ***scope and results*** *of the internal audit activities, to ensure that there are no budgetary or scope limitations that impede the ability of the internal audit function to execute its responsibilities.*
- *Provide information on the* ***coordination with and oversight of other control and monitoring functions*** *(e.g., risk management, compliance, security, business continuity, legal, ethics, environmental, external audit).*
- *Report* ***significant issues related to the processes for controlling*** *the activities of the organization and its affiliates, including potential improvements to those processes, and provide information concerning such issues through resolution.*
- *Provide information on the status and results of the* ***annual audit plan*** *and the* ***sufficiency of department resources*** *to senior management and the audit committee.*
- *Develop a* ***flexible annual audit plan*** *using an appropriate* ***risk-based*** *methodology, including any risks or control concerns identified by management, and submit that plan to the audit committee for review and approval as well as periodic updates.*
- *Report on the* ***implementation of the annual audit plan****, as approved, including as appropriate any special tasks or projects requested by management and the audit committee.*
- *Incorporate into the internal audit charter the responsibility for the internal audit department to report to the audit committee on a timely basis any* ***suspected fraud*** *involving management or employees who are significantly involved in the internal controls of the company,* ***assist in the investigation*** *of significant suspected fraudulent activities within the organization, and notify management and the audit committee of the results.*
- *Inform the audit committee that* ***quality assessment reviews*** *of the internal audit activity should be done every five years to comply with The IIA's* ***International Standards for the Professional Practice of Internal Auditing (Standards).*** *Regular quality assessment reviews will provide assurance to the audit committee and to management that internal auditing activities conform to* ***Standards****.*

Communications with the Audit Committee

6. *To a large degree, the overall effectiveness of the CAE and audit committee relationship will revolve around the communications between the parties. Today's audit committees expect a high level of open and candid communications. If the CAE is to be viewed as a trusted advisor by the committee,* ***communication is the key element****. Internal auditing, by definition, can help the audit committee accomplish its objectives by bringing a systematic, disciplined approach to its activities. However, in the absence of appropriate communication, it is not possible for the committee to determine whether internal auditing has met its objectives. The chief audit executive should consider providing communications to the audit committee in the following areas:*
   - *Discussion of sensitive issues in* ***private meetings*** *on a* ***regular basis****.*
   - ***Annual summary report or assessment*** *of the results of the audit activities relating to the defined mission and scope of audit work.*
   -  ***Periodic reports*** *to the audit committee and management summarizing results of audit activities.*
   - *Information about* ***emerging trends and successful practices*** *in internal auditing.*
   - *Discussion of fulfillment of committee* ***information needs****.*
   - *Review of* ***completeness and accuracy*** *of information submitted.*
   - *Confirmation of* ***coordination of activities between internal and external auditors****. The CAE should determine whether there is any duplication between the work of the internal and external auditors and give the reasons for such duplication.*

PA Summary

- The audit committee or its equivalent is a **governance** body that oversees audit and control.
- The audit committee and the IAA have interlocking goals and must have a **strong relationship** so that both may fulfill their responsibilities.
- The CAE **assists the audit committee** by (1) helping it to review its activities and (2) suggesting enhancements. The CAE may (1) review the audit committee's **charter** to advise whether all of the committee's responsibilities are addressed, (2) review or maintain its **planning agenda** to determine whether all activities are completed, (3) draft its **meeting agenda** for review and write up the minutes of meetings, (4) encourage periodic committee reviews for comparison with **current best practices**, (5) meet with the chair to discuss whether the **information** received by the audit committee is sufficient, (6) inquire about providing **educational presentations**, and (7) inquire about the sufficiency of the **frequency and time** allotted to the audit committee.
- The CAE's **core role** is to ensure that the audit committee understands, supports, and receives all assistance needed from the IAA. The principal components of an **effective governance system** are (1) the board, (2) management, (3) the IAA, and (4) external auditing. Consideration of the **work of the IAA** is essential to the audit committee's understanding of operations. The CAE ensures (1) accomplishment of this objective and (2) that the audit committee views the CAE as a **trusted advisor**.

- The CAE's role as advisor to the audit committee includes suggesting steps to promote the IAA's status and independence, for example, audit committee review of (1) the **IAA charter** annually, (2) **functional and administrative** reporting lines, (3) decisions about the **employment** of the CAE, (4) **outsourcing** of IAA functions, (5) personnel and budgets, and (6) scope and results of IAA functions.
- The CAE also should (1) develop a **risk-based and flexible annual audit plan** to be approved by the audit committee, (2) report on its **implementation**, and (3) provide information about its **results** and the sufficiency of IAA resources.
- The CAE reports on (1) **coordination with and oversight** of other control and monitoring functions and (2) issues related to **control processes**. Moreover, the CAE includes in the IAA charter the responsibility for timely reporting of **suspected fraud** involving anyone significantly involved in internal control, **assisting in the investigation**, and notifying management and the audit committee of the results. The CAE also informs the audit committee that a **quality assessment review** of the IAA should be done every five years to comply with the **Standards**.
- **Communication** is the key element in the relationship of the CAE and the audit committee. Thus, **regular private meetings** should be held. The CAE should consider communications about the following: (1) annual and periodic **reports**, (2) trends and **practices** in auditing, (3) fulfilling the audit committee's **information needs**, (4) reviewing information for **completeness and accuracy**, and (5) confirming **coordination** with external auditors and explaining any duplication of work.

2. **Audit committees.** The audit committee is a subcommittee of **outside directors** who are independent of management. Its purpose is to help keep external and internal auditors independent and to assure that the directors are exercising due care.
   a. The role of an audit committee or an equivalent in strengthening the position of auditors is widely recognized. The audit committee should
      1) Have a **written charter** developed by its governing authority describing its duties and responsibilities.
      2) Review the **independence** of the external auditor.
      3) **Report to stakeholders** (e.g., shareholders). Reports should include a letter from the chair of the audit committee describing its responsibilities and activities.
      4) **Monitor compliance** with codes of conduct and legal and regulatory standards.
      5) Have sufficient **resources**.
      6) Oversee the **regulatory reporting process**.
      7) Monitor instances in which management seeks second opinions on significant **accounting issues**.
   b. Many **stock exchanges** require a listed organization to have an audit committee.
   c. An audit committee composed of nonmanagement directors promotes the **independence** of all auditors, especially when it selects the external audit firm and the chief audit executive. A strong audit committee insulates the auditors from influences that may compromise their independence and objectivity.
      1) An audit committee also may serve as a mediator of disputes between the auditors and management.

d. **Audit Committee Functions**

1) **Select an external auditor** and review the audit fee and the engagement letter
2) Review the external auditor's overall **audit plan**
3) Review **preliminary** annual and interim **financial statements**
4) Review **results of engagements** performed by external auditors, including the management letter (advice and observations not required to be communicated by auditing standards)
5) Approve the **charter** of the internal audit activity (Standard 1000)
6) Review and approve the internal audit activity's **plans and resource requirements** and receive a summary of the IAA's work schedule, staffing plan, and financial budget (Standard 2020 and PA 2020-1)
7) Communicate directly with the **chief audit executive**, who should regularly attend and participate in meetings (PA 1110-1)
8) Review evaluations of **risk management, control, and governance** processes reported by the internal auditors
9) Ensure that engagement results are given due consideration and receive distributions of **final engagement communications** by the internal auditors (PA 2440-1)
10) Review policies on **unethical and illegal** procedures
11) Review financial statements to be transmitted to **regulatory agencies**
12) Participate in the selection of **accounting policies**
13) Review the impact of new or proposed **legislation or regulations**
14) Review the organization's **insurance** program
15) Consider the effectiveness and efficiency of **information systems**
16) Evaluate executive **performance and compensation**

e. **External auditors** have recognized the importance of **reporting to audit committees or comparable governance bodies**. Among the matters that may be communicated are (1) internal-control-related matters, (2) significant accounting policies, (3) management judgments and accounting estimates, (4) significant audit adjustments, (5) disagreements with management, and (6) difficulties encountered during the audit.

1) One of the factors encompassed by the **control environment** component of internal control is participation by the board, audit committee, or other governing authority. The **control consciousness** of the organization is improved if the audit committee is (a) independent of management, (b) composed of experienced and respected people, (c) extensively involved in oversight of organizational activities, (d) willing to raise and pursue difficult questions with management, and (e) in close communication with the internal and external auditors.

2) **Fraud** involving senior management or fraud that materially misstates the financial statements should be reported directly to the audit committee.

a) The external auditors also should obtain assurance that the audit committee is adequately informed about other **illegal acts** coming to the auditors' attention.

f. The following is The IIA's **sample charter for the audit committee** (*Sawyer's Internal Auditing, 5th ed.*, pages 1328-1332):

Audit Committee Charter

PURPOSE

To assist the board of directors in fulfilling its oversight responsibilities for the financial reporting process, the system of internal control, the audit process, and the company's process for monitoring compliance with laws and regulations and the code of conduct.

AUTHORITY

The audit committee has authority to conduct or authorize investigations into any matters within its scope of responsibility. It is empowered to:

Appoint, compensate, and oversee the work of any registered public accounting firm employed by the organization.

Resolve any disagreements between management and the auditor regarding financial reporting.

Pre-approve all auditing and non-audit services.

Retain independent counsel, accountants, or others to advise the committee or assist in the conduct of an investigation.

Seek any information it requires from employees – all of whom are directed to cooperate with the committee's requests – or external parties.

Meet with company officers, external auditors, or outside counsel, as necessary.

COMPOSITION

The audit committee will consist of at least three and no more than six members of the board of directors. The board or its nominating committee will appoint committee members and the committee chair.

Each committee member will be both independent and financially literate. At least one member shall be designated as the "financial expert," as defined by applicable legislation and regulation.

MEETINGS

The committee will meet at least four times a year, with authority to convene additional meetings, as circumstances require. All committee members are expected to attend each meeting, in person or via tele- or video-conference. The committee will invite members of management, auditors, or others to attend meetings and provide pertinent information, as necessary. It will hold private meetings with auditors (see below) and executive sessions. Meeting agendas will be prepared and provided in advance to members, along with appropriate briefing materials. Minutes will be prepared.

RESPONSIBILITIES

The committee will carry out the following responsibilities:

Financial Statements

- *Review significant accounting and reporting issues, including complex or unusual transactions and highly judgmental areas, and recent professional and regulatory pronouncements, and understand their impact on the financial statements.*
- *Review with management and the external auditors the results of the audit, including any difficulties encountered.*
- *Review the annual financial statements, and consider whether they are complete, consistent with information known to committee members, and reflect appropriate accounting principles.*
- *Review other sections of the annual report and related regulatory filings before release and consider the accuracy and completeness of the information.*
- *Review with management and the external auditors all matters required to be communicated to the committee under generally accepted auditing standards.*
- *Understand how management develops interim financial information, and the nature and extent of internal and external auditor involvement.*
- *Review interim financial reports with management and the external auditors before filing with regulators, and consider whether they are complete and consistent with the information known to committee members.*

Internal Control

- *Consider the effectiveness of the company's internal control system, including information technology security and control.*
- *Understand the scope of internal and external auditors' review of internal control over financial reporting, and obtain reports on significant findings and recommendations, together with management's responses.*

Internal Audit

- *Review with management and the chief audit executive the charter, plans, activities, staffing, and organizational structure of the internal audit function.*
- *Ensure there are no unjustified restrictions or limitations, and review and concur in the appointment, replacement, or dismissal of the chief audit executive.*
- *Review the effectiveness of the internal audit function, including compliance with The Institute of Internal Auditors' Standards.*
- *On a regular basis, meet separately with the chief audit executive to discuss any matters that the committee or internal audit believes should be discussed privately.*

External Audit

- *Review the external auditors' proposed audit scope and approach, including coordination of audit effort with internal audit.*
- *Review the performance of the external auditors, and exercise final approval on the appointment or discharge of the auditors.*
- *Review and confirm the independence of the external auditors by obtaining statements from the auditors on relationships between the auditors and the company, including non-audit services, and discussing the relationships with the auditors.*
- *On a regular basis, meet separately with the external auditors to discuss any matters that the committee or auditors believe should be discussed privately.*

Compliance

- *Review the effectiveness of the system for monitoring compliance with laws and regulations and the results of management's investigation and follow-up (including disciplinary action) of any instances of noncompliance.*
- *Review the findings of any examinations by regulatory agencies, and any auditor observations.*
- *Review the process for communicating the code of conduct to company personnel, and for monitoring compliance therewith.*
- *Obtain regular updates from management and company legal counsel regarding compliance matters.*

Reporting Responsibilities

- *Regularly report to the board of directors about committee activities, issues, and related recommendations.*
- *Provide an open avenue of communication between internal audit, the external auditors, and the board of directors.*
- *Report annually to the shareholders, describing the committee's composition, responsibilities and how they were discharged, and any other information required by rule, including approval of non-audit services.*
- *Review any other reports the company issues that relate to committee responsibilities.*

Other Responsibilities

- *Perform other activities related to this charter as requested by the board of directors.*
- *Institute and oversee special investigations as needed.*
- *Review and assess the adequacy of the committee charter annually, requesting board approval for proposed changes and ensure appropriate disclosure as may be required by law or regulation.*
- *Confirm annually that all responsibilities outlines in this chapter have been carried out.*
- *Evaluate the committee's and individual members' performance on a regular basis.*

g. In response to numerous financial reporting scandals involving large businesses, various countries have enacted laws and regulations relating to corporate governance. These laws and regulations often include provisions addressing the role of the audit committee or a comparable governance body. The following are examples of such provisions:

1) Each member of the **audit committee** may be required to be **independent** of the **board**.
2) The audit committee may be required to be directly responsible for **appointing, compensating, and overseeing** the work of the external auditors, who should **report directly** to the audit committee.
3) The audit committee may be required to implement procedures for the receipt, retention, and treatment of **complaints about accounting and auditing matters**.
4) The audit committee also may be required to be **appropriately funded** by the organization and may hire independent counsel or other advisors.

3. Stop and review! You have completed the outline for this subunit. Study multiple-choice questions 30 through 46 beginning on page 325.

8.5 RESOURCE MANAGEMENT

1. This subunit addresses management of human resources of the internal audit activity. It includes one Specific Performance Standard and one Practice Advisory.
2. ***2030*** ***Resource Management*** *– The chief audit executive should ensure that internal audit resources are appropriate, sufficient, and effectively deployed to achieve the approved plan.*

a. ***PRACTICE ADVISORY 2030-1: RESOURCE MANAGEMENT***

1. *The **chief audit executive (CAE)** is primarily responsible for the **sufficiency** and management of the internal audit resources in a manner that ensures the fulfillment of the internal audit's responsibilities as detailed in the internal audit charter. This includes **effective communications** and **reporting of resource needs and status** to senior management and the board. Internal audit **resources** may include employees, external resources, or a combination thereof. Ensuring the adequacy of the internal audit resources is ultimately a responsibility of the organization's **board and senior management,** and the CAE should assist them in discharging this responsibility.*

2. *The **skills, capabilities and technical knowledge** of the internal audit resources must be appropriate for the planned activities. The CAE should conduct a **periodic skills assessment or inventory** to determine the specific skills required to perform the internal audit activities. The skills assessment should be based on and consider the various **needs identified in the risk assessment and audit plan**. The CAE should then determine and assign resources that possess the skills, knowledge, and competencies identified by the skills assessment. This may include assessments of technical skills, language skills, business knowledge, fraud detection and prevention, accounting and auditing expertise. The CAE must ensure that the **skills assessment is driven by the needs of the audit coverage** and that this coverage is not being determined primarily by the capabilities present within the internal audit organization.*

*Recognizing the dynamic nature of risk, the CAE should periodically update the skills assessment. Based on these updates, the CAE may consider **needs to increase the skills, capabilities and knowledge** of the existing staff. The extent and formality of the skills assessment should be appropriate for the size and complexity of the internal audit function.*

3. *Internal audit resources, both staffing and financial, should be sufficient to execute the audit activities in both the* ***depth and timeliness*** *expected by the audit committee and management.* ***Resourcing plans*** *should consider carefully the resultant audit coverage and components such as*
   a. *The amount of the audit universe that is covered over what period of time.*
   b. *The coverage of the higher risk areas in the plan.*
   c. *The geographic coverage.*
   d. *The capacity for unplanned projects, management requests, or other non-audit events.*
   e. *The nature and extent of the work to be performed.*
4. *The CAE must also ensure that resources are effectively* ***deployed****. This includes assigning auditors who are competent and* ***qualified for specific assignments****. It also includes developing a* ***resourcing approach and organizational structure*** *that are appropriate for the business structure, complexity, and geographical dispersion of the organization.*
5. *In considering the* ***sufficiency*** *of resourcing levels,* ***if trade-offs are considered*** *for cost or other reasons, the CAE should ensure that the decision process includes* ***clear communications of the impact*** *on the timing or coverage of the objectives stated in the internal audit plan. If the CAE believes that resourcing levels are* ***insufficient*** *to accomplish the internal audit charter,* ***that view should be clearly communicated*** *to the board and senior management for their final determination.*
6. *From an overall resource management standpoint, the CAE should also consider other aspects such as* ***succession planning, staff evaluation and development programs, and other human resource disciplines****. The CAE must also ensure that the resourcing needs of internal audit are appropriately addressed, whether those skills are present or not within in the internal audit function itself. The CAE should consider* ***other approaches to addressing resource needs*** *including external sourcing arrangements, other company employees, or specialized consultants.*
7. *Because of the critical nature of resources, the CAE should maintain* ***ongoing communications*** *and dialogue with senior management and the board on the adequacy of resources for the internal audit function. At least annually, the CAE should present a* ***detailed summary of status and adequacy of resources*** *to the board. The CAE should ensure that the board is provided with relevant, reliable, and accurate data to demonstrate the adequacy of resources. To that end, the CAE should develop* ***appropriate metrics, goals, and objectives*** *that could be used to* ***monitor*** *the overall adequacy of resources. This can include (a) comparisons of resources to the audit plan, (b) the impacts of temporary shortages or vacancies, (c) educational and training activities, and (d) changes to specific skill needs and requirements as determined by changes in the organization's businesses or risk profiles and third-party arrangements.*

PA Summary

- The **CAE** is primarily responsible for the **sufficiency and management of IAA resources**, including effective communication of needs and status to senior management and the board. These parties ultimately must ensure the adequacy of resources. **Resources** may include employees, external resources, or a combination.
- The CAE conducts a **periodic skills assessment** (inventory) based on the audit coverage needs identified in the risk assessment and audit plan. Audit coverage should **not** be determined primarily by the capabilities present within the IAA. **Updates** of the skills assessment may reveal a need to increase the skills, capabilities, and technical knowledge of the staff.
- Resources should be sufficient for audit activities performed in the ways **expected** by the audit committee and management. **Resourcing plans** address **coverage issues** such as (1) the amount of the audit universe covered in a given period, (2) high-risk areas, (3) geographic coverage, (4) capacity to meet unplanned demands, and (5) nature and extent of work.
- Resources must be effectively **deployed**. The CAE must assign auditors **qualified** for their tasks and develop an appropriate **resourcing approach** and **organizational structure**.
- If cost or other **tradeoffs** are considered in **resource decisions**, the CAE should clearly communicate the effects on the timing or coverage of the audit plan and the accomplishment of the IAA's objectives. If resources are **insufficient**, that view should be **clearly communicated** to the board and senior management.
- The CAE also considers such matters as succession planning, staff evaluation and development, and other **human resource disciplines**. Appropriately addressing **resource needs** may require consideration of the use of external sourcing, specialized consultants, or other employees of the organization.
- The CAE should have **ongoing communication** with senior management and the board about **resource adequacy**. The CAE also should give the board, at least annually, a **detailed summary** of resource status and adequacy. The CAE should provide metrics and objectives appropriate for **monitoring resource adequacy**, for example, (1) comparisons of resources with the audit plan; (2) the effects of temporary shortages; (3) educational and training activities; and (4) changes in skill needs because of changes in businesses, risk profiles, and third-party arrangements.

3. **Job Descriptions**

   a. Facilitate recruiting by stating explicit job requirements
   b. Provide objective promotion criteria
   c. Are used to justify adequate salaries
   d. Express organizational expectations of employees
   e. Compel the internal audit activity to engage in personnel planning
   f. May be prepared for the chief audit executive and other administrators

      1) The internal audit activity's charter is effectively a job description for the CAE.

      NOTE: The descriptions for the positions of manager, supervisor, and senior are presented beginning on the next page (adapted from Sawyer, Dittenhofer, and Scheiner, *Sawyer's Internal Auditing*, pages 846, 847, and 848, respectively).

MANAGER

Purpose

- *To administer the internal audit activity of an assigned location or operation.*
- *To develop a comprehensive, practical program of engagement coverage for the assigned location or operation.*
- *To obtain accomplishment of the program in accordance with acceptable engagement standards and stipulated schedules.*
- *To maintain effective working relations with executive and operating management.*

Authority and Responsibility

Within the general guidelines provided by the chief audit executive:

- *Prepares a comprehensive, long-range program of engagement coverage for the location to which assigned.*
- *Identifies those activities subject to engagement coverage, evaluates their significance, and assesses the degree of risk inherent in the activity in terms of cost, schedule, and quality.*
- *Establishes the related departmental structure.*
- *Obtains and maintains an audit staff capable of accomplishing the internal audit function.*
- *Assigns engagement areas, staff, and budget to supervisors.*
- *Develops a system of cost and schedule control over engagement projects.*
- *Establishes standards of performance and, by review, determines that performance meets the standards.*
- *Provides executive management within the assigned location with reports on engagement coverage and engagement results, and interprets those results so as to improve the engagement program and the engagement coverage.*
- *Establishes and monitors accomplishment of objectives directed toward increasing the internal audit activity's ability to serve management.*

SUPERVISOR

Purpose

- *To develop a comprehensive, practical program of engagement coverage for assigned areas.*
- *To supervise the activities of staff assigned to the review of various organizational and functional activities.*
- *To ensure conformance with acceptable standards, plans, budgets, and schedules.*
- *To maintain effective working relations with operating management.*
- *To provide for and conduct research and develop manuals and training guides.*

Authority and Responsibility

Under the general guidance of a manager:

- *Supervises the work of staff engaged in the reviews of organizational and functional activities.*
- *Provides a comprehensive, practical schedule of annual engagement coverage within general areas assigned by the manager.*
- *Determines areas of risk and appraises their significance in relation to operational factors of cost, schedule, and quality. Classifies engagement projects as to degree of risk and significance and as to frequency of coverage.*
- *Provides for flexibility in engagement schedules so as to be responsive to management's special needs.*
- *Schedules projects and staff assignments so as to comply with management's needs, within the scope of the internal audit activity's overall schedule.*
- *Coordinates the program with the organization's public accountant.*
- *Reviews and approves the purpose, scope, and approach of each engagement project for assigned areas.*
- *Directs engagement projects to see that professional standards are maintained in the planning and execution and in the accumulation of information.*
- *Counsels and guides staff to see that the approved engagement objectives are met and that adequate, practical coverage is achieved.*
- *Reviews and edits engagement communications and, in organizations with the auditor-in-charge for the assigned project, discusses the communications with appropriate management.*
- *Presents oral briefing to branch-level management.*

- *Provides for and performs research on engagement techniques.*
- *Provides formal plans for the recruiting, selecting, training, evaluating, and supervising of staff personnel. Develops manuals and other training aids.*
- *Accumulates data, maintains records, and prepares reports on the administration of engagement projects and other assigned activities.*
- *Identifies factors causing deficient conditions and recommends courses of action to improve the conditions, including special surveys and audits.*
- *Provides for a flow of communication from operating management to the manager and to the chief audit executive. Assists in evaluating overall results of the engagements.*

SENIOR

Purpose

- *To conduct reviews of assigned organizational and functional activities.*
- *To evaluate the adequacy and effectiveness of the management controls over those activities.*
- *To determine whether organizational units are performing their planning, accounting, custodial, risk management, or control activities in compliance with management instructions, applicable statements of policy and procedures, and in a manner consistent with both organizational objectives and high standards of administrative practice.*
- *To plan and execute engagements in accordance with accepted standards.*
- *To report engagement observations and to make recommendations for correcting unsatisfactory conditions, improving operations, and reducing cost.*
- *To perform special reviews at the request of management.*
- *To direct the activities of assistants.*

Authority and Responsibility

Under the general guidance of a supervisor:

- *Surveys functions and activities in assigned areas to determine the nature of operations and the adequacy of the system of control to achieve established objectives.*
- *Determines the direction and thrust of the proposed engagement effort.*
- *Plans the theory and scope of the engagement, and prepares an engagement work program.*
- *Determines the engagement procedures to be used, including statistical sampling and the use of information technology.*
- *Identifies the key control points of the system.*
- *Evaluates a system's effectiveness through the application of a knowledge of business systems, including financial, manufacturing, engineering, procurement, and other operations, and an understanding of engagement techniques.*
- *Recommends necessary staff required to complete the engagement.*
- *Performs the engagement in a professional manner and in accordance with the approved engagement work program.*
- *Obtains, analyzes, and appraises information as a basis for an informed, objective conclusion (opinion) on the adequacy and effectiveness of the system and the efficiency of performance of the activities being reviewed.*
- *Directs, counsels, and instructs staff assistants assigned to the engagement, and reviews their work for sufficiency of scope and for accuracy.*
- *Makes oral or written presentations to management during and at the conclusion of the engagement, discussing observations and recommending corrective action to improve operations and reduce cost.*
- *Prepares formal written communications, expressing opinions on the adequacy and effectiveness of the system and the efficiency with which activities are carried out.*
- *Appraises the adequacy of the corrective action taken to improve deficient conditions.*

4. **Selection of Staff**
   a. Modern internal auditing demands a superior staff.
      1) Staffing provides the personnel necessary to carry on the work of the IAA.
      2) Mediocre personnel are incapable of carrying out progressive programs.
      3) Each internal auditor must have the capacity to expand his/her abilities as management makes increasing demands for modern services.
   b. The CAE should set high standards for the staff.
   c. Professional education, ability, and certain personality traits are needed.
   d. **Source of Staff**
      1) **Promoting from within** has many advantages:
         a) The character, personality, work attitudes, and other personal qualifications of staff members are known.
         b) Internal recruits are familiar with organizational policies and practices and have a broader perspective of operations.
         c) Experience and work qualifications can be closely evaluated.
         d) Internal recruiting can promote staff morale.
      2) **Recruiting experienced personnel** externally also has advantages:
         a) The organization can attract specific skills needed.
         b) The range of possible services is broadened.
         c) New ideas are brought to the organization.
         d) Training costs are reduced.
      3) **Recruiting of university graduates** is another possibility.
         a) The organization must be able to train and develop personnel.
         b) Benefits include updating accounting and auditing skills.
   e. **Interviewing and testing techniques**
      1) The selection of staff is dependent on evaluating applicants.
      2) The interviews should be carefully planned and structured.
      3) Competent interviewers should be assigned.
      4) Supervisors of the new staff should be present at the interviews.
      5) **Appropriate questions and forms** should be prepared in advance to evaluate
         a) Technical qualifications and educational background
         b) Personal appearance
         c) Ability to communicate
         d) Work experience and judgment
         e) Motivation
         f) Potential to contribute to the organization
      6) Applicants who have earned the **CIA designation** have demonstrated qualifications in internal auditing. Other qualities can be examined by a variety of tests that will vary with the job to be filled.
         a) **Writing ability.** Sawyer, Dittenhofer, and Scheiner suggest requiring a written engagement communication from the applicant based on a prescribed format and a hypothetical situation. **Grading criteria** for evaluation of writing ability include correctness, conciseness, clarity, organization, and vocabulary.

b) **Ability to organize thoughts.** Sawyer, Dittenhofer, and Scheiner suggest the applicant arrange a series of 25 statements to describe an engagement observation.

i) The statements are mixed and given identifying numbers. The applicant is asked to arrange them in proper sequence.

c) **Ability to distinguish between fact and speculation.** The applicant must identify the statements of undeniable fact and of mere conjecture in a brief paragraph.

5. **Training of Staff**

a. **Staff orientation.** An adequate orientation program provides reasonable assurance that the new employee will become productive promptly. It promotes employee morale and deters good employees from leaving.

1) The orientation program should be well designed and controlled.
2) Appropriate materials should be devised.
3) Employees should be familiarized with organizational policies.
4) The **technical orientation** may extend to

a) Introductions to staff personnel and other employees
b) Discussion of engagement objectives
c) Copies of internal auditing manuals
d) Discussion of duties and responsibilities
e) Control of work
f) General information on the structure of the organization
g) Literature on modern internal auditing
h) Working paper techniques
i) Development of engagement observations
j) Communication formats
k) Instructor's follow-up and feedback after new staff member has performed actual fieldwork

b. **Objectives of staff training** are to

1) Assist internal auditing to do a better job
2) Add versatility to the IAA
3) Help develop supervisory skill
4) Prepare the staff member for promotion
5) Improve job satisfaction, organizational loyalty, and productivity
6) Improve technical skills
7) Update knowledge of new professional pronouncements and reporting techniques (continuing education)

c. Possible **training formats** include

1) Formal classroom study
2) Self-study
3) Attendance at formal meetings of The IIA and other groups
4) Industry conferences
5) University courses
6) On-the-job training
7) Research projects

d. Required **components of a successful training program**
   1) The trainee's commitment and interest
   2) Sufficient time and resources to permit training objectives to be met
   3) High-quality training materials
   4) Trainee participation
   5) Reinforcement

e. One aspect of a successful, ongoing training program is holding **regular staff meetings** to explain new techniques, discuss new policies, and receive suggestions from staff.

6. **Evaluation of Staff**
   a. A written appraisal of each internal auditor's performance is required **at least annually**.
   b. The evaluation provides a basis for **counseling** subordinates on their strong and weak attributes, opportunities for advancement, and programs for self-improvement.
   c. The evaluation is a basis for promotions, transfers, and compensation adjustments.
   d. The evaluation is done by the person with responsibility for the particular employee.
   e. **Criteria** for evaluation are weighted and applied to performance on specific projects. Personnel whose performance is being appraised should be notified of the criteria and methods at the time they begin employment. The criteria include type of skill required, extent of responsibility, scope of effort, and nature of working conditions.
   f. Each auditor should receive a full explanation of the appraisal and results of his/her evaluation.

7. Stop and review! You have completed the outline for this subunit. Study multiple-choice questions 47 through 56 beginning on page 330.

8.6 POLICIES AND PROCEDURES

1. This subunit concerns the formal guidance to be provided by the chief audit executive. This guidance is discussed in one Specific Performance Standard and in one Practice Advisory.

2. ***2040*** ***Policies and Procedures*** *– The chief audit executive should establish policies and procedures to guide the internal audit activity.*

   a. ***PRACTICE ADVISORY 2040-1: POLICIES AND PROCEDURES***

      1. *The* ***form and content of written policies and procedures*** *should be appropriate to the size and structure of the internal audit activity and the complexity of its work. Formal administrative and technical audit manuals may not be needed by all internal auditing entities. A* ***small internal audit activity*** *may be managed informally. Its audit staff may be directed and controlled through daily, close supervision and written memoranda. In a* ***large internal audit activity****, more formal and comprehensive policies and procedures are essential to guide the audit staff in the consistent compliance with the internal audit activity's standards of performance.*

PA Summary

- **Written policies and procedures** for the IAA should be appropriate to its size, structure, and work. Formal manuals may not be needed for all IAAs. A **small IAA** may be managed informally. A **large IAA** may require more formal and comprehensive policies and procedures.

3. **Personnel manuals** describe the organization and its relationship to employees, including
   a. Objectives and goals (also of divisions, subsidiaries, etc.)
   b. History
   c. Fringe benefits (medical, pension, life insurance, etc.)
   d. Vacation and sick-pay policies
   e. Promotion policies
   f. Development and training programs
4. **Audit (technical) manuals** provide guidance on completing **specific engagements** in compliance with the technical standards and policies of the IAA. They include
   a. **General and specific guidelines** on
      1) Engagement objectives (may classify types of engagements)
      2) Theory and purpose of internal auditing
      3) Scope of engagement, engagement work programs, and time budgets
      4) Working papers
      5) Engagement communications
      6) Internal controls
      7) Internal administration
      8) Performance standards
   b. **Special technical topics**, such as
      1) Information technology auditing
      2) Statistical sampling
      3) Procedures for suspected fraud
      4) Fraud investigations
   c. Matters related to **administration of an individual engagement**, such as
      1) Notification of client about a pending engagement
      2) Preliminary survey and engagement work program
      3) Engagement time budget and changes in it
      4) Application of engagement procedures
      5) Changes in engagement work programs
      6) Working paper preparation, review, and control
      7) Communication draft review with clients
      8) Communication format
      9) Communication review
      10) Client replies to engagement communications
      11) Follow-up on observations and recommendations
5. **Administrative policy and procedure manuals** guide the operation of the IAA. They may contain
   a. The charter
   b. A policy statement of the relationship of the IAA with other subunits
   c. The definition of responsibilities of personnel
   d. An IAA organizational chart
   e. Approvals required for actions
   f. Personnel policies unique to the IAA
   g. Personnel records
   h. Travel instructions
   i. Expense reports
   j. Time reports
   k. Staff evaluations
   l. Descriptions for permanent files, temporary files, and working paper retention

m. Communication preparation and review procedures
n. Engagement research responsibilities
o. Training and education programs
p. The history of the IAA, including the relationship with management and the board, to provide staff auditors with the activity's philosophy and approach to internal auditing.

6. Stop and review! You have completed the outline for this subunit. Study multiple-choice questions 57 through 61 beginning on page 333.

8.7 STUDY UNIT 8 SUMMARY

1. Planning for the IAA is subject to its charter and organizational goals. The process establishes (a) goals, (b) work schedules, (c) staffing plans and financial budgets, and (d) activity reports.
2. The IAA's plan is based on assessment of risk and exposure. The objective is to provide information to mitigate risk. The audit universe may reflect the organization's strategic plan. Thus, it may reflect (a) the overall business objectives, (b) attitude toward risk, (c) the difficulty of reaching objectives, and (d) the results of risk management.
3. The CAE annually submits to senior management and the board a summary of the IAA's work schedule, staffing plan, and financial budget. They should disclose the scope of work and any limitations on it.
4. The CAE submits activity reports at least annually. They (a) highlight significant engagement observations (those adversely affecting the organization) and (b) are informative of significant deviations from work schedules, etc., and the reasons for them. Significant observations and recommendations are reviewed with senior management and then communicated to the board, whether or not resolved.
5. The audit committee oversees audit and control. The audit committee and the IAA must have a strong relationship so that both may fulfill their responsibilities.
6. The principal components of the governance system are (a) the board, (b) management, (c) the IAA, and (d) external auditing. Considering the work of the IAA is essential to the audit committee's understanding of operations. The CAE ensures accomplishment of this objective and that the audit committee views the CAE as a trusted advisor.
7. The CAE's functions include
   a. Assisting the audit committee to ensure that its charter, activities, and processes are appropriate to fulfill its responsibilities.
   b. Ensuring that the charter, role, and activities of internal audit are clearly understood and responsive to the needs of the audit committee and the board.
   c. Maintaining open and effective communication with the audit committee and the chairperson.
8. The CAE is primarily responsible for the sufficiency, appropriateness, and effective deployment of the resources of the IAA consistent with the approved audit plan. Thus, the CAE must (a) conduct a periodic skills assessment, (b) assign auditors qualified for their task, (c) develop an appropriate sourcing approach and organizational structure, (d) clearly communicate the effects of resource decisions, (e) consider staff development and evaluation, (f) consider use of resources external to the IAA, (g) have ongoing communication with senior management and the board about resource adequacy, and (h) provide the board at least annually with a detailed summary of resource status.
9. Written policies and procedures for the IAA should be appropriate to its size, structure, and work. A small IAA may be managed informally.

QUESTIONS

8.1 Planning

1. The chief audit executive should establish goals as part of the planning process for the internal audit activity. What are the traits of internal auditing goals?

A. Measurable and attainable.

B. Budgeted and approved.

C. Planned and attainable.

D. Requested and approved.

Answer (A) is correct. *(CIA, adapted)*

REQUIRED: The traits of internal auditing goals.

DISCUSSION: Goals should be capable of accomplishment within given operating plans and budgets and should be measurable to the extent possible. They should be accompanied by measurement criteria and targeted dates of accomplishment (PA 2010-1).

Answer (B) is incorrect because goals should be attainable within budget constraints. However, approval is not a trait of goals themselves. Answer (C) is incorrect because goals should be measurable. Answer (D) is incorrect because goals are not usually requested. Instead, they are established by the CAE.

2. Which of the following factors serves as a direct input to the internal audit activity's financial budget?

A. Engagement work schedules.

B. Activity reports.

C. Past effectiveness of the internal audit activity in identifying cost savings.

D. Internal audit activity's charter.

Answer (A) is correct. *(CIA, adapted)*

REQUIRED: The direct input to the IAA's financial budget.

DISCUSSION: The IAA's planning process involves establishing goals, engagement work schedules, staffing plans and financial budgets, and activity reports (PA 2010-1). Engagement work schedules include what is to be done, when, and the time required. These factors directly affect the amounts in the financial budget.

Answer (B) is incorrect because activity reports compare actual performance with goals and schedules and actual expenditures with financial budgets. Answer (C) is incorrect because past performance is an indicator of the value of internal auditing, but it will not affect the funds committed to current operations. Answer (D) is incorrect because the charter defines the purpose, authority, and responsibility of the IAA.

3. At a meeting with engagement managers, the chief audit executive is allocating the engagement work schedule for next year's plan. Which of the following methods will ensure that each manager receives an appropriate share of both the work schedule and internal audit activity resources?

A. Work is assigned to each manager based on risk and skill analysis.

B. Each of the managers selects the individual assignments desired, based on preferences for the area and the management personnel involved.

C. Each manager chooses assignment preferences based on the total staff hours that are currently available to each manager.

D. The full list of scheduled engagements is published for the staff, and work assignments are made based on career interests and travel requirements.

Answer (A) is correct. *(CIA, adapted)*

REQUIRED: The method that ensures proper sharing of engagement work and resources.

DISCUSSION: Engagements should be performed with proficiency and due professional care (Standard 1200). Thus, professional care should be commensurate with the complexities of the engagement and should assure that the technical proficiency and educational background of the personnel assigned are appropriate. A skill analysis of tasks to be performed is therefore necessary. Furthermore, matters to be considered in establishing engagement work schedule priorities include (1) updated assessments of risks and effectiveness of risk management and control processes and (2) changes to and capabilities of the staff (PA 2010-1).

Answer (B) is incorrect because choice based on personal preference does not ensure the exercise of due professional care. Answer (C) is incorrect because available staff hours do not correlate with risk or the composite skills necessary for individual assignments. Answer (D) is incorrect because, although career interests and travel requirements are considerations for staffing engagements, these factors do not constitute an objective basis for making assignments.

4. The chief audit executive is preparing the engagement work schedule for the next budget year and has limited resources. In deciding whether to schedule the purchasing or the personnel department for an engagement, which of the following is the least important factor?

A. Major changes in operations have occurred in one of the departments.

B. The internal audit staff has recently added an individual with expertise in one of the areas.

C. More opportunities to achieve operating benefits are available in one of the departments than in the other.

D. Updated assessed risk is significantly greater in one department than the other.

Answer (B) is correct. *(CIA, adapted)*

REQUIRED: The least important factor in deciding whether to schedule the purchasing or the personnel department for an engagement.

DISCUSSION: Matters to be considered in establishing engagement work schedule priorities should include (a) the dates and results of the last engagement; (b) updated assessments of risks and effectiveness of risk management and control processes; (c) requests by senior management, audit committee, and governing body; (d) current issues relating to organizational governance; (e) major changes in the enterprise's business, operations, programs, systems, and controls; (f) opportunities to achieve operating benefits; and (g) changes in and capabilities of the staff. The work schedules should be sufficiently flexible to cover unanticipated demands on the IAA (PA 2010-1). The addition of a new staff member is probably less important than the other factors cited.

Answer (A) is incorrect because a major change in operations is a reason for an engagement. Answer (C) is incorrect because potential operating benefits are a reason for an engagement. Answer (D) is incorrect because updated assessed risk is a reason for an engagement.

5. Which of the following factors is not included in determining the engagement work schedule?

A. Engagement work programs.

B. The effectiveness of risk management and control processes.

C. Workload requirements.

D. Issues relating to organizational governance.

Answer (A) is correct. *(CIA, adapted)*

REQUIRED: The activity not included in developing the engagement work schedule.

DISCUSSION: Engagement work schedules should include (a) what activities are to be performed; (b) when they will be performed; and (c) the estimated time required, taking into account the scope of the engagement work planned and the nature and extent of related work performed by others. Matters to be considered in establishing engagement work schedule priorities should include (a) the dates and results of the last engagement; (b) updated assessments of risks and effectiveness of risk management and control processes; (c) requests by senior management, the audit committee, and the governing body; (d) current issues relating to organizational governance; (e) major changes in the enterprise's business, operations, programs, systems, and controls; (f) opportunities to achieve operating benefits; and (g) changes in and capabilities of the staff. The work schedules should be sufficiently flexible to cover unanticipated demands on the IAA (PA 2010-1). Development of work programs occurs during the planning phase of an individual engagement.

6. During discussions with senior management, the chief audit executive identified several strategic business issues to consider in preparing the annual engagement work schedule. Which of the following does not represent a strategic issue for this purpose?

A. A monthly budgeting process will be implemented.

B. An international marketing campaign will be started to develop product recognition and also to leverage the new organization-based advertising department.

C. Joint venture candidates will be sought to provide manufacturing and sourcing capabilities in European and Asian markets.

D. A human resources database will be established to ensure consistent administration of policies and to improve data retention.

Answer (A) is correct. *(CIA, adapted)*

REQUIRED: The item not a strategic issue to consider in preparing the annual engagement work schedule.

DISCUSSION: The audit universe may include components from the organization's strategic plan. By including components of this plan, the audit universe will consider and reflect the overall business plan objectives (PA 2010-2). However, implementing a monthly budgeting process is an operating decision to facilitate the budgeting process and improve information. It does not constitute a strategic issue, but it does entail a major change in operations, etc.

Answer (B) is incorrect because an international marketing campaign is a strategic issue. The CAE will need to ensure that the new marketing process and the centralized advertising department are recognized and monitored in risk assessment and planning activities. Answer (C) is incorrect because extending operations to European and Asian markets is a strategic issue. The addition of joint-venture partners will add new or additional concerns for risk assessment and planning in the IAA. Answer (D) is incorrect because establishing a human resources database is a strategic issue. The assumptions and ongoing activities related to a human resources database will require consideration in the planning of the IAA.

7. Which of the following is the best source of a chief audit executive's information for planning staffing requirements?

A. Discussions of internal audit needs with senior management and the board.

B. Review of internal audit staff education and training records.

C. Review internal audit staff size and composition of similarly sized organizations in the same industry.

D. Interviews with existing internal audit staff.

Answer (A) is correct. *(CIA, adapted)*

REQUIRED: The best source of a CAE's information for planning staffing requirements.

DISCUSSION: The CAE should establish risk-based plans to determine the priorities of the IAA. These plans should be consistent with the goals of the organization (Standard 2010). The planning process involves establishing goals, engagement work schedules, staffing plans and financial budgets, and activity reports (PA 2010-1). Input from senior management and the board is necessary for developing the IAA's risk-based plan of engagements (Standard 2010.A1).

Answer (B) is incorrect because the scheduled work is the first consideration in determining the number and qualifications of the staff required. Review of staff education and training records is a subsequent step. Answer (C) is incorrect because the staffing plan must consider the unique needs of a particular organization. The review of staff size and composition of similarly sized organizations in the same industry may not satisfy the engagement objectives for a particular organization. Answer (D) is incorrect because the scheduled work is the first consideration in determining the number and qualifications of the staff required. Interviews with existing staff occur later.

8. Which internal audit planning tool is general in nature and is used to ensure adequate engagement coverage over time?

A. The audit plan.

B. The engagement work program.

C. The internal audit activity's budget.

D. The internal audit activity's charter.

Answer (A) is correct. *(CIA, adapted)*

REQUIRED: The internal audit planning tool used to ensure adequate engagement coverage over time.

DISCUSSION: The CAE should establish risk-based plans to determine the priorities of the IAA. These plans should be consistent with the goals of the organization (Standard 2010). The planning process involves establishing goals, engagement work schedules, staffing plans and financial budgets, and activity reports (PA 2010-1). The CAE submits annually to senior management for approval, and to the board for its information, summaries of work schedules, staffing plans, and financial budgets (PA 2020-1). Thus, the planning process involves establishing engagement work schedules. These should include (a) what activities are to be performed; (b) when they will be performed; and (c) the estimated time required, taking into account the scope of the work planned and the nature and extent of related work performed by others (PA 2010-1).

Answer (B) is incorrect because the engagement work program is limited in scope to a particular project. Answer (C) is incorrect because the IAA's budget may be used to justify a head count, but it is not used to ensure adequate engagement coverage over time. Answer (D) is incorrect because the charter is not an engagement planning tool.

9. A chief audit executive may use risk analysis in preparing work schedules. Which of the following is not considered in performing a risk analysis?

A. Issues relating to organizational governance.

B. Skills available on the internal audit staff.

C. Results of prior engagements.

D. Major operating changes.

Answer (B) is correct. *(CIA, adapted)*

REQUIRED: The item not considered in performing a risk analysis.

DISCUSSION: Matters to be considered in establishing engagement work schedule priorities should include (a) the dates and results of the last engagement; (b) updated assessments of risks and effectiveness of risk management and control processes; (c) requests by senior management, audit committee, and governing body; (d) current issues relating to organizational governance; (e) major changes in the enterprise's business, operations, programs, systems, and controls; (f) opportunities to achieve operating benefits; and (g) changes in and capabilities of the staff. The work schedules should be sufficiently flexible to cover unanticipated demands on the IAA (PA 2010-1). The skills of the staff do not affect the risk associated with potential engagement clients.

Answer (A) is incorrect because issues relating to organizational governance are factors that should be considered. Answer (C) is incorrect because results of prior engagements should be considered. Answer (D) is incorrect because major operating changes should be considered.

10. A manager responsible for the supervision and review of other internal auditors needs the necessary skills, knowledge, and other competencies. Which of the following does not describe a skill, knowledge, or other competency necessary to supervise a particular engagement?

A. The ability to review and analyze an engagement work program to determine whether the proposed engagement procedures will result in information relevant to the engagement's objectives.

B. Assuring that an engagement communication is supported and accurate relative to the information documented in the engagement working papers.

C. Using risk assessment and other judgmental processes to develop an engagement work schedule for the internal audit activity and present the schedule to the board.

D. Determining that staff auditors have completed the engagement procedures and that engagement objectives have been met.

Answer (C) is correct. *(CIA, adapted)*

REQUIRED: The skill, knowledge, or other competency not necessary to supervise a particular engagement.

DISCUSSION: The CAE, not a manager, should establish risk-based plans to determine the priorities of the IAA, consistent with the organization's goals (Standard 2010). The planning process involves establishing goals, engagement work schedules, staffing plans and financial budgets, and activity reports (PA 2010-1). The CAE should communicate the IAA's plans and resource requirements, including significant interim changes, to senior management and the board for review and approval (PA 2020-1). Supervision includes approving the engagement work program; determining that the engagement working papers support observations, conclusions, and recommendations; and making certain that engagement objectives have been met (PA 2340-1).

11. The chief audit executive for an organization has just completed a risk assessment process, identified the areas with the highest risks, and assigned an engagement priority to each. Which of the following conclusions most logically follow(s) from such a risk assessment?

I. Items should be quantified as to risk in the rank order of quantifiable monetary exposure to the organization.

II. The risk priorities should be in order of major control deficiencies.

III. The risk assessment process, though quantified, is the result of professional judgments about both exposures and probability of occurrences.

A. I only.

B. III only.

C. II and III only.

D. I, II, and III.

Answer (B) is correct. *(CIA, adapted)*

REQUIRED: The conclusion(s) logically following from a risk assessment process.

DISCUSSION: Risk is the possibility of an event's occurrence that could have an impact on the achievement of objectives. Risk is measured in terms of impact (exposures) and likelihood (probability) (Glossary appended to the Standards). Engagement work schedules should be based on, among other things, an assessment of risk priority and exposure. Prioritizing is needed to make decisions for applying relative resources based on the significance of risk and exposure. A variety of risk models may assist the CAE in prioritizing potential engagement subject areas. Most of these models use risk factors to establish the priority of engagements, for example, monetary materiality, asset liquidity, management competence, quality of internal controls, degree of change or stability, time of last engagement, complexity, or employee and governmental relations (PA 2010-2). Higher priorities are usually assigned to activities with higher risks. However, an "assessment" of risk priority and exposure necessarily implies the exercise of professional judgment. Thus, although risk factors may be weighted to determine their relative significance, a ranking based solely on such specific criteria as monetary exposure or control deficiencies is not always indicated.

12. Which of the following factors is considered the least important in deciding whether existing internal audit resources should be moved from an ongoing compliance engagement to a divisional-level engagement requested by management?

A. A financial audit of the division performed by the external auditor a year ago.

B. The potential for fraud associated with the ongoing engagement.

C. An increase in the level of expenditures experienced by the division for the past year.

D. The potential for significant regulatory fines associated with the ongoing engagement.

Answer (A) is correct. *(CIA, adapted)*

REQUIRED: The least important factor affecting an allocation of internal audit resources.

DISCUSSION: Prioritizing is needed to make decisions about applying relative resources based on the significance of risk and exposure. Most risk models use risk factors to establish engagement priorities (PA 2010-2). One such factor is the potential for fraud. Internal auditors traditionally regard fraud as significant even if the immediate exposure is not significant. Increased expenditures also constitute a significant risk factor because they represent an increase in potential loss. For the same reason, potential regulatory fines may also create an exposure sufficiently great to affect the determination of priorities. Thus, the result of an external financial audit performed a year ago is the least likely to affect the current allocation of internal audit resources. Any adverse engagement observations most probably have been acted upon, and, in any case, may not be germane to the ongoing compliance engagement or the proposed divisional-level engagement.

13. Which of the following comments is(are) true regarding the assessment of risk associated with two projects that are competing for limited internal audit resources?

I. Activities that are requested by the board always should be considered higher risk than those requested by management.

II. Activities with higher financial budgets always should be considered higher risk than those with lower financial budgets.

III. Risk always should be measured by the potential monetary or other adverse exposure to the organization.

A. I only.

B. II only.

C. III only.

D. I and III.

Answer (C) is correct. *(CIA, adapted)*

REQUIRED: The true statement(s) about risk assessment.

DISCUSSION: Risk is the uncertainty of an event's occurrence that could have an impact on the achievement of objectives. Risk is measured in terms of consequences (exposures) and likelihood (probability) (Glossary appended to the Standards). Engagement work schedules should be based on, among other things, an assessment of risk priority and exposure (PA 2010-2). However, a rigid procedure for conducting the risk assessment, including the assignment of engagement priorities, should not be followed. Thus, a ranking based on the source of a request for performance of an engagement or the financial budget of an engagement client is unlikely to reflect a comprehensive assessment based on a sufficient number of risk factors. A criterion based on the degree of adverse exposure to the organization is preferable.

14. Which of the following represent(s) appropriate internal audit action in response to the risk assessment process?

I. The low-risk areas may be delegated to the external auditor, but the high-risk areas should be performed by the internal audit activity.

II. The high-risk areas should be integrated into an engagement work schedule along with the high-priority requests of senior management and the audit committee.

III. The risk analysis should be used in determining an annual engagement work schedule; therefore, the risk analysis should be performed only on an annual basis.

A. I only.

B. II only.

C. III only.

D. I and III only.

Answer (B) is correct. *(CIA, adapted)*

REQUIRED: The appropriate internal audit action in response to a risk assessment.

DISCUSSION: The risk assessment is preliminary to the development of the engagement work schedule. Higher priorities are usually assigned to engagement subject areas with higher risks. Thus, updated assessments of risks and effectiveness of risk management and control processes are considered in establishing engagement work schedule priorities. Other matters to be considered in establishing the engagement work schedule are the dates and results of the last engagement; requests by senior management, the audit committee, and the governing body; current issues relating to organizational governance; major changes; opportunities to achieve operating benefits; and changes in and capabilities of the internal auditor staff (PA 2010-1). Work should be coordinated with the external auditor to avoid duplication of effort and to ensure adequate coverage, but allocation of tasks to the external auditor and the IAA is not necessarily risk-based. Moreover, changing conditions may require updating the risk assessment during the year.

15. The internal auditor is considering making a risk analysis as a basis for determining the areas of the organization where engagements should be performed. Which one of the following statements is true regarding risk analysis?

A. The extent to which management judgments are required in an area could serve as a risk factor in assisting the internal auditor in making a comparative risk analysis.

B. The highest risk assessment should always be assigned to the area with the largest potential loss.

C. The highest risk assessment should always be assigned to the area with highest probability of occurrence.

D. Risk analysis must be reduced to quantitative terms in order to provide meaningful comparisons across an organization.

Answer (A) is correct. *(CIA, adapted)*

REQUIRED: The true statement about risk analysis.

DISCUSSION: Most risk models use risk factors to establish the priority of engagements, for example, monetary materiality, asset liquidity, management competence, quality of internal controls, degree of change or stability, time of last engagement, complexity, or employee or governmental relations (PA 2010-2). Hence, the internal auditor could appropriately consider the extent of management competence, including judgment, as a risk factor.

Answer (B) is incorrect because risk analysis should consider both the potential loss (or damages) and the probability of occurrence. An area with the largest potential loss may have a very low expected loss. Answer (C) is incorrect because a high probability of occurrence may be associated with a small potential loss. Answer (D) is incorrect because the concept of risk analysis is not limited to quantitative measures.

16. The chief audit executive set up a computerized spreadsheet to facilitate the risk assessment process involving a number of different divisions in the organization. The spreadsheet included the following factors:

- Pressure on divisional management to meet profit goals
- Complexity of operations
- Competence of divisional personnel
- The monetary amount of subjectively influenced accounts in the division, such as accounts in which management's judgment can affect the expense, e.g., postretirement benefits

The CAE used a group meeting of internal audit managers to reach a consensus on the competence of divisional personnel. Other factors were assessed as high, medium, or low by either the CAE or an internal audit manager who had performed an engagement at the division. The CAE assigned a weight ranging from 0.5 to 1.0 to each factor and then computed a composite risk score. Which statement is true?

A. The risk analysis is not appropriate because it mixes both quantitative and qualitative factors, thereby making expected values calculation impossible.

B. Assessing factors at discrete levels such as high, medium, and low is inappropriate for the risk assessment process because the ratings are not quantifiable.

C. The weighting is subjective and should have been determined through a process such as multiple-regression analysis.

D. Using a subjective group consensus to assess personnel competence is appropriate.

Answer (D) is correct. *(CIA, adapted)*

REQUIRED: The true statement about the risk assessment.

DISCUSSION: The risk assessment should incorporate information from a variety of sources, such as discussions with the board and management and with internal audit management and staff. Thus, seeking the consensus of experienced internal audit managers regarding personnel matters is appropriate. This method tends to eliminate the extreme judgments that might be made by a single evaluator.

Answer (A) is incorrect because risk analysis should consider all appropriate factors. It need not be limited to quantitative or expected value calculations. Answer (B) is incorrect because high, medium, and low may be the most precise measures available. Answer (C) is incorrect because subjective analysis is acceptable. Use of multiple-regression analysis to determine a weighted average for the risk-weighting model is not feasible because no criteria exist to determine the weightings.

17. A chief audit executive (CAE) uses a risk assessment model to establish the annual audit plan. Which of the following would be an appropriate action by the CAE?

I. Maintain ongoing dialogue with management and the audit committee

II. Ensure that the schedule of audit priorities remains unchanged

III. Employ only quantitative methods to determine risk weightings

IV. Revise the risk assessment and audit priorities as warranted

A. III only.

B. I and II only.

C. I and IV only.

D. III and IV only.

Answer (C) is correct. *(CIA, adapted)*

REQUIRED: The appropriate action(s) when the CAE uses a risk assessment model to establish the annual audit plan.

DISCUSSION: The CAE should establish risk-based plans to determine the priorities of the internal audit activity, consistent with the organization's goals (Standard 2010). It is a best practice for risk assessment to be a dynamic process, changing over time and as new information, business strategies, and risks are identified. Ongoing consultation with members of management and the audit committee is a way for the internal audit activity to obtain such information and stay attuned to organizational developments that may affect existing audit priorities. To accommodate such emerging priorities, the work schedule may need to be altered.

Answer (A) is incorrect because the weighting of risk is both a quantitative and a qualitative (judgment) exercise. Answer (B) is incorrect because audit schedules will likely change regularly to meet the needs of the organization, particularly if based on an effective risk assessment process. Answer (D) is incorrect because the weighting of risk is both a quantitative and a qualitative (judgment) exercise. Furthermore, the CAE should engage in ongoing consultation with members of management and the audit committee.

18. When a risk assessment process has been used to construct an audit engagement schedule, which of the following should receive attention first?

A. The external auditors have requested assistance for their upcoming annual audit.

B. A new accounts payable system is currently undergoing testing by the information technology department.

C. Management has requested an investigation of possible lapping in receivables.

D. The existing accounts payable system has not been audited over the past year.

Answer (C) is correct. *(CIA, adapted)*

REQUIRED: The item that should receive attention first when a risk assessment process has been used to construct an audit engagement schedule.

DISCUSSION: Prioritizing is needed to make decisions about applying resources to engagements based on the relative significance of their risk and exposure estimates. Most risk models use risk factors to establish engagement priorities (PA 2010-2). Internal auditors traditionally regard fraud as significant even if the immediate exposure is not. Thus, management's request to investigate a possible fraud in the accounts receivable unit must take precedence.

Answer (A) is incorrect because external audit requests for assistance should be subordinate to fraud investigations. Answer (B) is incorrect because, given that the new system is not yet in production, it need not receive immediate attention. Answer (D) is incorrect because a management request involving a fraud should take priority over a system that has not been audited over the past year.

19. A chief audit executive is reviewing the following enterprise-wide risk map:

IMPACT		LIKELIHOOD		
		Remote	Possible	Likely
	Critical	Risk A	Risk B	
	Major			Risk D
	Minor		Risk C	

Which of the following is the correct prioritization of risks, considering limited resources in the internal audit activity?

A. Risk B, Risk C, Risk A, Risk D.

B. Risk A, Risk B, Risk C, Risk D.

C. Risk D, Risk B, Risk C, Risk A.

D. Risk B, Risk C, Risk D, Risk A.

Answer (C) is correct. *(CIA, adapted)*

REQUIRED: The correct prioritization of risks, given the enterprise-wide risk map.

DISCUSSION: Risk is the possibility of an event's occurrence that could have an impact on the achievement of objectives. Risk is measured in terms of impact (exposures) and likelihood (probability). Prioritizing is needed to make decisions for applying resources to engagements based on the relative significance of their risk and exposure estimates. The best order of priority listed (highest to lowest) is (1) Risk D (likely-major), (2) Risk B (possible-critical), (3) Risk C (possible-minor), and (4) Risk A (remote-critical). However, it is not entirely clear that Risk D and Risk C should have higher priorities than Risks B and A, respectively. For example, depending on the values assigned to the variables, a possible-critical impact (B) might have a higher priority than a likely-major impact (D).

Answer (A) is incorrect because Risk D clearly takes precedence over Risk C. It has a higher likelihood and a greater impact. Answer (B) is incorrect because Risk B clearly has a higher priority than Risk A. It has a higher likelihood and the same impact. Answer (D) is incorrect because Risk D has a higher likelihood and a greater impact than Risk C.

20. Which of the following represents the best risk assessment technique?

A. Assessment of the risk levels for future events based on the extent of uncertainty of those events and their impact on achievement of long-term organizational goals.

B. Assessment of inherent and control risks and their impact on the extent of financial misstatements.

C. Assessment of the risk levels of current and future events, their effect on achievement of the organization's objectives, and their underlying causes.

D. Assessment of the risk levels of current and future events, their impact on the organization's mission, and the potential for elimination of existing or possible risk factors.

Answer (C) is correct. *(CIA, adapted)*

REQUIRED: The best risk assessment technique.

DISCUSSION: Risk is the possibility of an event's occurrence that could have an impact on the achievement of objectives. Risk is measured in terms of impact (exposures) and likelihood (probability). Most risk models use risk factors to establish engagement priorities (PA 2010-2). This is the best response because it takes a comprehensive approach to risk assessment. It considers not only the event and the impact but also the causes.

Answer (A) is incorrect because causation also should be considered. Answer (B) is incorrect because risk events include more than those classified as inherent and control risks (terms used in the audit risk model used in financial statement audits). Moreover, a comprehensive approach should be adopted. Answer (D) is incorrect because elimination of risks is less likely than mitigation.

Questions 21 and 22 are based on the following information. During the planning phase, a chief audit executive (CAE) is evaluating four audit engagements based on the following factors: the engagement's ability to reduce risk to the organization, the engagement's ability to save the organization money, and the extent of change in the area since the last engagement. The CAE has scored the engagements for each factor from low to high, assigned points, and calculated an overall ranking. The results are shown below with the points in parentheses:

Audit	Risk Reduction	Cost Savings	Changes
1	High (3)	Medium (2)	Low (1)
2	High (3)	Low (1)	High (3)
3	Low (1)	High (3)	Medium (2)
4	Medium (2)	Medium (2)	High (3)

21. Which audit engagements should the CAE pursue if all factors are weighed equally?

A. 1 and 2 only.

B. 1 and 3 only.

C. 2 and 4 only.

D. 3 and 4 only.

Answer (C) is correct. *(CIA, adapted)*

REQUIRED: The audit engagements the CAE should pursue given information about risk reduction, savings, and changes in the areas to be audited.

DISCUSSION: The CAE establishes risk-based plans to determine the priorities of the IAA, consistent with the organization's goals (Standard 2010). Among the factors considered in setting priorities are (1) updated assessments of risks and the effectiveness of risk management and control; (2) major changes in the organization's business, operations, programs, systems, and controls; and (3) opportunities to achieve operating benefits (PA 2010-1). Accordingly, given that risk reduction, cost savings, and changes in areas to be audited are weighted equally, the CAE should purse audits 2 and 4 because they have the highest total points.

Answer (A) is incorrect because audit 1 has fewer total points than audit 4. Answer (B) is incorrect because audits 1 and 3 have fewer total points than audits 2 and 4. Answer (D) is incorrect because audit 3 has fewer total points than audit 2.

22. If the organization has asked the CAE to consider the cost savings factor to be twice as important as any other factor, which engagements should the CAE pursue?

A. 1 and 2 only.

B. 1 and 3 only.

C. 2 and 4 only.

D. 3 and 4 only.

Answer (D) is correct. *(CIA, adapted)*

REQUIRED: The audits the CAE should pursue if the cost savings factor is twice as important as any other factor.

DISCUSSION: After doubling the cost savings points, audit 3 [$1 + (2 \times 3) + 2 = 9$] and audit 4 [$2 + (2 \times 2) + 3 = 9$] have the highest total points.

Answer (A) is incorrect because audit 1 and audit 2 have 8 total points each. Answer (B) is incorrect because audit 1 has 8 total points. Answer (C) is incorrect because audit 2 has 8 total points.

23. Which of the following is the best reason for the chief audit executive to consider the strategic plan in developing the annual audit plan?

A. To ensure that the internal audit plan supports the overall business objectives.

B. To ensure that the internal audit plan will be approved by senior management.

C. To make recommendations to improve the strategic plan.

D. To emphasize the importance of the internal audit function.

Answer (A) is correct. *(CIA, adapted)*

REQUIRED: The best reason for the chief audit executive to consider the strategic plan in developing the annual audit plan.

DISCUSSION: The chief audit executive should establish risk-based plans to determine the priorities of the internal audit activity, consistent with the organization's goals (Standard 2010). Considering the strategic plan in the development of the internal audit plan will ensure that the audit objectives support the overall business objectives stated in the strategic plan.

Answer (B) is incorrect because making the internal audit plan fit better with the strategic plan may not have an effect on management's approval. Answer (C) is incorrect because recommending improvements to the strategic plan is not the primary purpose of the CAE's review. Answer (D) is incorrect because the importance of the internal audit function depends on the authority granted to it by the board and senior management.

24. In assessing organizational risk in a manufacturing environment, which of the following would have the most long-range impact on the organization?

A. Production scheduling.

B. Inventory policy.

C. Product quality.

D. Advertising budget.

Answer (C) is correct. *(CIA, adapted)*

REQUIRED: The item having the most long-range impact in a manufacturing environment.

DISCUSSION: Product quality has the greatest long-term effect on organizational risk. A decline in product quality poses grave risks to the success (and even the existence) of the organization. Loss of customer satisfaction because of poor quality results in a decline in competitiveness in the organization's markets.

Answer (A) is incorrect because production scheduling is most likely to have short-term effects. Answer (B) is incorrect because an inventory policy is most likely to have short-term effects. Answer (D) is incorrect because an advertising budget may be for an annual or shorter period. Thus, the effect of ineffective or underfunded advertising is more readily reversed than poor quality.

25. A chief audit executive would most likely use risk assessment for audit planning because it provides

A. A systematic process for assessing and integrating professional judgment about probable adverse conditions.

B. A listing of potentially adverse effects on the organization.

C. A list of auditable activities in the organization.

D. The probability that an event or action may adversely affect the organization.

Answer (A) is correct. *(CIA, adapted)*

REQUIRED: The most likely reason a CAE uses risk assessment for audit planning.

DISCUSSION: The chief audit executive should establish risk-based plans to determine the priorities of the internal audit activity, consistent with the organization's goals (Standard 2010). The internal audit activity's plan should be designed based on an assessment of risk and exposures that may affect the organization. Ultimately, the objective is to provide management with information to mitigate the negative consequences associated with accomplishing the organization's objectives (PA 2010-2).

Answer (B) is incorrect because a listing of potentially adverse effects might convince the CAE of the need for risk assessment. But this process is not itself a risk assessment. Answer (C) is incorrect because a list of auditable activities is used in the risk assessment process but is not the rationale for using risk assessment. Answer (D) is incorrect because the probability that an event or action may adversely affect the organization is one definition of risk.

8.2 Communication of Plans

26. Recent criticism of an internal audit activity suggested that engagement coverage was not providing adequate feedback to senior management on the processes used in the organization's key lines of business. The problem was further defined as lack of feedback on the recent implementation of automated support systems. Which two functions does the chief audit executive need to improve?

A. Staffing and communicating.

B. Staffing and decision making.

C. Planning and organizing.

D. Planning and communicating.

Answer (D) is correct. *(CIA, adapted)*

REQUIRED: The functions to be improved.

DISCUSSION: The lack of feedback indicates the CAE has problems in planning and allocating internal audit resources to communicate necessary information to management. The CAE should establish risk-based plans to determine the priorities of the IAA, consistent with the organization's goals (Standard 2010). Moreover, "the chief audit executive should communicate the internal audit activity's plans and resource requirements, including significant interim changes, to senior management and to the board for review and approval. The chief audit executive should also communicate the impact of resource limitations" (Standard 2020). The engagements described are within the scope of the IAA. "Internal auditors should review operations and programs to ascertain the extent to which results are consistent with established goals and objectives to determine whether operations and programs are being implemented or performed as intended" (Standard 2120.A3).

Answer (A) is incorrect because the facts do not indicate the existence of staffing problems. Answer (B) is incorrect because decision making and staffing are not problems. Answer (C) is incorrect because nothing indicates that the structure of the entity is a problem.

27. Which of the following is an appropriate responsibility of an audit committee?

A. Performing a review of the procurement function of the organization.

B. Reviewing the internal audit activity's engagement work schedule submitted by the chief audit executive.

C. Reviewing the engagement records of the public accounting firm to determine the firm's competence.

D. Recommending the assignment of specific internal auditing staff members for specific engagements.

Answer (B) is correct. *(CIA, adapted)*

REQUIRED: The appropriate responsibility for an audit committee.

DISCUSSION: The audit committee consists of outside members of the board of directors (who should be independent of management). Regular communication with this committee helps assure independence and provides a means for the directors and the IAA to keep each other informed. According to Standard 2020, the CAE should communicate the IAA's plans and resource requirements to senior management and the board for review and approval. Moreover, PA 2020-1 states that the CAE should submit to senior management for approval, and to the board for its information, a summary of the IAA's work schedule, staffing plan, and financial budget.

Answer (A) is incorrect because reviewing the procurement function of the organization requires detailed technical ability. Answer (C) is incorrect because reviewing the IAA's engagement work schedule requires detailed technical ability. Answer (D) is incorrect because specific assignments should be made by IAA management.

8.3 Reporting

28. A chief audit executive's activity report should

A. List the material engagement observations of major engagements.

B. List uncorrected reported conditions.

C. Report the weekly activities of the individual internal auditors.

D. Compare engagements completed with engagements planned.

Answer (D) is correct. *(CIA, adapted)*

REQUIRED: The true statement about a CAE's activity report.

DISCUSSION: Activity reports should be submitted periodically to senior management and the board. These reports should compare (a) actual performance with the IAA's goals and engagement work schedules and (b) expenditures with financial budgets. They should explain the reasons for major variances and indicate any action taken or needed (PA 2060-1).

Answer (A) is incorrect because a list of material engagement observations is not an activity report. Answer (B) is incorrect because a list of uncorrected reported conditions is not an activity report. Answer (C) is incorrect because a report of weekly activities is not an activity report.

29. The chief audit executive routinely presents an activity report to the board as part of the board meeting agenda each quarter. Senior management has asked to review this presentation before each board meeting so that any issues or questions can be discussed beforehand. The CAE should

A. Provide the activity report to senior management as requested and discuss any issues that may require action to be taken.

B. Withhold disclosure of the activity report to senior management because such matters are the sole province of the board.

C. Disclose to the board only those matters in the activity report that pertain to expenditures and financial budgets of the internal audit activity.

D. Provide information to senior management that pertains only to completed engagements and observations available in published engagement communications.

Answer (A) is correct. *(CIA, adapted)*

REQUIRED: The action that should be taken regarding the review of internal auditing reports by senior management.

DISCUSSION: The CAE should submit activity reports to senior management and to the board annually or more frequently as necessary. Activity reports should highlight significant engagement observations and recommendations and should inform senior management and the board of any significant deviations from approved engagement work schedules, staffing plans, and financial budgets, and the reasons for them (PA 2060-1).

Answer (B) is incorrect because activity reports should be presented to senior management. Answer (C) is incorrect because the report should not be restricted to expenditures and financial budgets. Information about significant deviations from engagement work schedules and staffing plans should be included. Answer (D) is incorrect because the information need not be limited to completed engagements and observations available in published engagement communications.

8.4 Relationship with the Audit Committee

30. Audit committees have been identified as a major factor in promoting the independence of both internal and external auditors. Which of the following is the most important limitation on the effectiveness of audit committees?

A. Audit committees may be composed of independent directors. However, those directors may have close personal and professional friendships with management.

B. Audit committee members are compensated by the organization and thus favor an owner's view.

C. Audit committees devote most of their efforts to external audit concerns and do not pay much attention to the internal audit activity and the overall control environment.

D. Audit committee members do not normally have degrees in the accounting or auditing fields.

Answer (A) is correct. *(CIA, adapted)*

REQUIRED: The most important limitation on the effectiveness of audit committees.

DISCUSSION: The audit committee is a subcommittee made up of outside directors who are independent of management. Its purpose is to help keep external and internal auditors independent of management and to assure that the directors are exercising due care. However, if independence is impaired by personal and professional friendships, the effectiveness of the audit committee may be limited.

Answer (B) is incorrect because the compensation audit committee members receive is usually minimal. They should be independent and therefore not limited to an owner's perspective. Answer (C) is incorrect because, although audit committees are concerned with external audits, they also devote attention to the internal audit activity. Answer (D) is incorrect because audit committee members do not need degrees in accounting or auditing to understand engagement communications.

31. The audit committee may serve several important purposes, some of which directly benefit the internal audit activity. The most significant benefit provided by the audit committee to the internal audit activity is

A. Protecting the independence of the internal audit activity from undue management influence.

B. Reviewing annual engagement work schedules and monitoring engagement results.

C. Approving engagement work schedules, scheduling, staffing, and meeting with the internal auditors as needed.

D. Reviewing copies of the procedures manuals for selected organizational operations and meeting with organizational officials to discuss them.

Answer (A) is correct. *(CIA, adapted)*

REQUIRED: The most significant benefit provided by the audit committee to the internal auditor.

DISCUSSION: The audit committee is a subcommittee of outside directors who are independent of corporate management. Its purpose is to help keep external and internal auditors independent of management and to assure that the directors are exercising due care. This committee often selects the external auditors, reviews their overall audit plan, and examines the results of external and internal audits.

32. To avoid creating conflict between the chief executive officer (CEO) and the audit committee, the chief audit executive should

A. Submit copies of all engagement communications to the CEO and audit committee.

B. Strengthen independence through organizational status.

C. Discuss all pending engagement communications to the CEO with the audit committee.

D. Request board establishment of policies covering the internal audit activity's relationships with the audit committee.

Answer (D) is correct. *(CIA, adapted)*

REQUIRED: The measure that avoids conflict between the CEO and the audit committee.

DISCUSSION: The charter of the audit committee is developed by its governing authority to describe its responsibilities. For example, The IIA's sample charter states the following responsibilities regarding the IAA: (1) review with management and the CAE the charter, plans, activities, staffing, and organizational structure of the internal audit function; (2) ensure there are no unjustified restrictions or limitations, and review and concur in the appointment, replacement, or dismissal of the CAE; (3) review the effectiveness of the internal audit function, including compliance with the Standards; and (4), on a regular basis, meet separately with the CAE to discuss any matters that the committee or internal audit believes should be discussed privately. The CEO and audit committee most likely should receive summary reports. Senior management and the board ordinarily are not involved in the details of internal audit work. Independence is not sufficient to avert conflict unless reporting relationships are well defined.

33. Which of the following actions is an appropriate response by organizations wishing to improve the public's perception of their financial reporting?

A. Increased adoption of audit committees composed of outside directors.

B. Viewing internal auditing as a transient profession -- a stepping stone to managerial positions.

C. Requiring internal auditors to report all significant observations of illegal activity to the chief executive officer.

D. Keeping external and internal auditing work separated to maintain independence.

Answer (A) is correct. *(CIA, adapted)*

REQUIRED: The appropriate means of improving the public's perception of financial reporting.

DISCUSSION: The audit committee consists of outside directors who are independent of management. Its purpose is to help keep external and internal auditors independent of management and to assure that the directors are exercising due care. This committee selects the external auditors, reviews their overall audit plan, examines the results of external and internal auditing engagements, meets regularly with the CAE, and reviews the IAA's engagement work schedule, staffing plan, and financial budget. These functions should increase public confidence that financial statements are fairly presented.

Answer (B) is incorrect because transience of internal auditors impairs the proficiency of the IAA. Answer (C) is incorrect because, if illegal activities involve senior management, distribution of engagement communications should be to the audit committee, not the CEO. Answer (D) is incorrect because the work of the internal and external auditors should be coordinated to minimize duplicate efforts. Coordination does not impair independence or reduce public confidence.

34. Which of the following is not an appropriate member of an audit committee?

A. The vice president of the local bank used by the organization.

B. An academic specializing in business administration.

C. A retired executive of a firm that had been associated with the organization.

D. The organization's vice president of operations.

Answer (D) is correct. *(CIA, adapted)*

REQUIRED: The person not an appropriate member of an audit committee.

DISCUSSION: The audit committee consists of outside directors who are independent of management. Its purpose is to help keep external and internal auditors independent of management and to assure that the directors are exercising due care. This committee selects the external auditors, reviews their overall audit plan, examines the results of external and internal auditing engagements, meets regularly with the CAE, and reviews the IAA's engagement work schedule, staffing plan, and financial budget. Engagements may be performed in the vice president's area of responsibility. Thus, (s)he is not independent of the IAA. The vice president is also not an outside director. The vice president of the local bank used by the organization, an academic specializing in business administration, and a retired executive of a firm that had been associated with the organization are all external parties who are usually independent of the organization's internal operations.

35. Which of the following audit committee activities is of the greatest benefit to the internal audit activity?

A. Review and approval of engagement work programs.

B. Assurance that the external auditor will rely on the work of the internal audit activity whenever possible.

C. Review and endorsement of all internal auditing engagement communications prior to their release.

D. Support for appropriate monitoring of the disposition of recommendations made by the internal audit activity.

Answer (D) is correct. *(CIA, adapted)*

REQUIRED: The audit committee activity of the greatest benefit to the IAA.

DISCUSSION: The organizational status of the IAA is enhanced when it has the support of management and of the board. Internal auditors can thereby gain the cooperation of engagement clients and perform their work free from interference (PA 1110-1).

Answer (A) is incorrect because review and approval of engagement work programs is the responsibility of internal auditing supervisors. Answer (B) is incorrect because whether the external auditor will make use of the work of internal auditing is not for the audit committee to decide. Answer (C) is incorrect because review and approval of internal auditing engagement communications is the responsibility of the chief audit executive or his/her designee.

36. Which of the following features of a large manufacturer's organizational structure is a control weakness?

A. The information systems department is headed by a vice president who reports directly to the president.

B. The chief financial officer is a vice president who reports to the chief executive officer.

C. The audit committee of the board consists of the chief executive officer, the chief financial officer, and a major shareholder.

D. The controller and treasurer report to the chief financial officer.

Answer (C) is correct. *(CIA, adapted)*

REQUIRED: The control weakness in a large manufacturer's organizational structure.

DISCUSSION: The audit committee has a control function because of its oversight of internal as well as external auditing. It should be made up of directors who are independent of management. The authority and independence of the audit committee strengthen the position of the internal audit activity.

Answer (A) is incorrect because this reporting relationship is a strength. It prevents the information systems operation from being dominated by a user. Answer (B) is incorrect because it is a normal and appropriate reporting relationship. Answer (D) is incorrect because it is a normal and appropriate reporting relationship.

37. The audit committee strengthens the control processes of an organization by

A. Assigning the internal audit activity responsibility for interaction with governmental agencies.

B. Using the chief audit executive as a major resource in selecting the external auditors.

C. Following up on recommendations made by the chief audit executive.

D. Approving internal audit activity policies.

Answer (C) is correct. *(CIA, adapted)*

REQUIRED: The way in which the audit committee strengthens control processes.

DISCUSSION: Internal auditors should have the support of senior management and the board (board of directors, audit committee, board of trustees of a nonprofit organization, etc.) to gain the cooperation of engagement clients and perform their work free from interference. Such support promotes independence and ensures broad engagement coverage, adequate consideration of engagement reports, and appropriate action on engagement recommendations (PA 1110-1). Moreover, among the audit committee's functions are to ensure that engagement results are given due consideration and to receive distributions of final engagement communications by the internal auditors (PA 2440-1). This enhancement of the position of internal auditing in turn strengthens control processes.

38. An audit committee of the board of directors of an organization is being established. Which of the following is normally a responsibility of the committee with regard to the internal audit activity?

A. Approval of the selection and dismissal of the chief audit executive.

B. Development of the annual engagement work schedule.

C. Approval of engagement work programs.

D. Determination of engagement observations appropriate for specific engagement communications.

Answer (A) is correct. *(CIA, adapted)*

REQUIRED: The responsibility of an audit committee.

DISCUSSION: Independence is enhanced when the board concurs in the appointment or removal of the CAE (PA 1110-1). The audit committee is a subcommittee of outside directors who are independent of management. The term "board" includes the audit committee.

Answer (B) is incorrect because development of the annual engagement work schedule is an operational function of the CAE and the IAA staff. The annual engagement work schedule, staffing plan, and financial budget are submitted to senior management and the board (PA 2020-1). Answer (C) is incorrect because approval of engagement work programs is a technical responsibility of the IAA staff. Answer (D) is incorrect because the determination of engagement observations appropriate for specific engagement communications is a field operation of the IAA staff.

39. The review of findings of regulatory agencies is consistent with which audit committee responsibility?

A. Reporting responsibilities.

B. Compliance.

C. Internal audit.

D. External audit.

Answer (B) is correct. *(Publisher, adapted)*

REQUIRED: The audit committee responsibility related to the findings of regulatory agencies or the external auditor.

DISCUSSION: The audit committee's responsibility with regard to compliance involves reviewing the findings of any examinations by regulatory agencies and any auditor observations. Compliance relates to activities that must be addressed by laws and regulations.

Answer (A) is incorrect because reporting responsibilities involve reporting to parties such as the board of directors, management, and the external auditor. Answer (C) is incorrect because the internal audit involves the structure of the organization and the audit committee itself. Answer (D) is incorrect because the external audit function is concerned with the retention of the external auditor and communication with the external auditor.

40. What part of an audit committee charter states that the audit committee is required to assist the board of directors in fulfilling its oversight responsibilities?

A. The audit committee's purpose.

B. The audit committee's authority.

C. The audit committee's composition.

D. The audit committee's responsibilities.

Answer (A) is correct. *(Publisher, adapted)*

REQUIRED: The components of the audit committee charter.

DISCUSSION: The IIA's sample charter for the audit committee includes the following purpose statement:

"... assist the board of directors in fulfilling its oversight responsibilities for the financial reporting process, the system of internal control, the audit process, and the company's process for monitoring compliance with laws and regulations and the code of conduct."

The statement of purpose is typically the first paragraph of the audit committee charter because it outlines the audit committee's intended function.

Answer (B) is incorrect because the audit committee's authority is the scope of its power to oversee the external audit function, seek information, conduct investigations, etc. Answer (C) is incorrect because the audit committee's composition addresses how many members it has and who will be appointed. Answer (D) is incorrect because audit committee responsibilities involve functions related to the financial statements and internal control.

41. Which of the following communication activities should the chief audit executive provide to the audit committee?

I. Keep the audit committee informed of emerging trends and successful practices in internal auditing.

II. Issue periodic reports to the audit committee and management summarizing results of audit activities.

III. Confirm there is effective and efficient work coordination of activities between internal and external auditors.

A. I only.

B. I and II only.

C. II and III only.

D. I, II, and III.

Answer (D) is correct. *(Publisher, adapted)*

REQUIRED: The communication to the audit committee recommended for the chief audit executive.

DISCUSSION: A large part of the effectiveness of the chief audit executive involves communication between the internal audit activity and the audit committee. Therefore, the chief audit executive should keep the audit committee informed of emerging trends and successful practices in internal auditing, issue periodic reports to the audit committee and management summarizing results of audit activities, and confirm there is effective and efficient work coordination of activities between internal and external auditors (PA 2060-2).

42. Who is responsible for assisting the audit committee so that the charter, role, and activities of the committee are appropriate for it to achieve its responsibilities?

A. Management.

B. The board of directors.

C. The chief audit executive.

D. The external auditor.

Answer (C) is correct. *(Publisher, adapted)*

REQUIRED: The person(s) responsible for assisting the audit committee.

DISCUSSION: The chief audit executive should assist the audit committee because the two parties have interlocking goals. Through helping the audit committee, the chief audit executive reviews the audit committee's activities and makes suggestions for improvements. This creates an environment in which the chief audit executive is considered an advisor to the audit committee (PA 2060).

Answer (A) is incorrect because management should not be involved in determining the audit committee's charter, role, and activities. Answer (B) is incorrect because the board of directors may not have the technical knowledge to ensure the activities of the audit committee are appropriate to achieve its responsibilities. Answer (D) is incorrect because the external auditor is not responsible for the audit committee's charter, role, and activities.

43. How often does The IIA's Standards require audit committees to undergo quality assessment reviews of the internal audit activity?

A. Every year.

B. Every 3 years.

C. Every 5 years.

D. Every 10 years.

Answer (C) is correct. *(Publisher, adapted)*

REQUIRED: The frequency of quality assessment reviews of the internal audit to meet the Standards.

DISCUSSION: The IIA's International Standards for the Professional Practice of Internal Auditing require that quality assessment reviews of the internal audit activity be done every five years.

Answer (A) is incorrect because the quality assessment reviews are supposed to be done every five years. Answer (B) is incorrect because the quality assessment reviews are supposed to be done every five years. Answer (D) is incorrect because the quality assessment reviews are supposed to be done every five years.

44. Which of the following is the primary purpose of the work of the internal auditors with respect to the audit committee?

A. To review information submitted to the audit committee for completeness and accuracy.

B. To gain a complete understanding of the organization's operations.

C. To provide a summary report of the results or assessments on the results of the audit activities relating to the defined mission and scope of audit work.

D. To keep the audit committee informed of emerging trends and successful practices in internal auditing.

Answer (B) is correct. *(Publisher, adapted)*

REQUIRED: The relationship between the internal auditors and the audit committee.

DISCUSSION: Synergy among the board of directors, management, internal auditors, and external auditors is supportive of sound governance. Thus, the roles of internal auditors and the audit committee are mutually supportive. The work of the internal auditors is essential for the audit committee to gain a complete understanding of an organization's operations (PA 2060-2).

Answer (A) is incorrect because the review of information is a communications function of the chief audit executive and the audit committee and not the primary purpose of the internal auditor's work. Answer (C) is incorrect because summary reports involve communications between the chief audit executive and the audit committee. Answer (D) is incorrect because the chief audit executive is responsible for keeping the audit committee informed of emerging trends and successful practices in internal auditing.

45. Who has primary responsibility for providing information to the audit committee on the professional and organizational benefits of coordinating internal audit assurance and consulting activities with other assurance and consulting activities?

A. The external auditor.

B. The chief audit executive.

C. The chief executive officer.

D. Each assurance and consulting function.

Answer (B) is correct. *(CIA, adapted)*

REQUIRED: The source of primary responsibility for providing information to the audit committee about the benefits of coordination of internal audit activities with those of other providers of assurance and consulting services.

DISCUSSION: The CAE's relationship to the audit committee should revolve around a core role of ensuring that the audit committee understands, supports, and receives all assistance needed from the internal audit function. In this role, the CAE provides the audit committee with information on the coordination with, and oversight of, other control and monitoring functions (PA 2060-2).

Answer (A) is incorrect because the CAE is responsible for ensuring that the internal audit activity's work maximizes the benefits achievable from coordination with other assurance and consulting activities. Comments on this function should always form part of any activity reports by the chief audit executive, not the external auditor, to the audit committee. Answer (C) is incorrect because the chief executive officer normally is not responsible for planning, work, and coordination related to internal audit assurance and consulting engagements or coordination with other assurance and consulting activities. Answer (D) is incorrect because not all other assurance and consulting activities are organizationally responsible to the audit committee for their work. Moreover, they may not have the opportunity to report information directly to the audit committee.

46. During a review of contracts, a chief audit executive (CAE) suspects that a supplier was given an unfair advantage in bidding on a contract. After learning that the chief executive officer (CEO) of the company is a member of the supplier's board of directors, how should the CAE proceed?

A. Submit a draft report to senior management, excluding the CEO.

B. Contact the organization's external auditors for assistance.

C. Obtain supporting documentation and present the finding to the chairperson of the audit committee.

D. Immediately notify the board of directors.

Answer (C) is correct. *(CIA, adapted)*

REQUIRED: The CAE's action after learning the CEO is a member of the supplier's board of directors.

DISCUSSION: The CAE's relationship to the audit committee should revolve around a core role of the CAE ensuring that the audit committee understands, supports, and receives all assistance needed from the internal audit function. In this role, the CAE should incorporate into the internal audit charter the responsibility for the internal audit department to (1) report to the audit committee on a timely basis any suspected fraud involving management or employees who are significantly involved in the internal controls of the company, (2) assist in the investigation of significant fraudulent activities within the organization, and (3) notify management and the audit committee of the results.

Regarding the information the CAE learned about the CEO, a draft of the proposed report on fraud or conflict-of-interest situations should be submitted to the chairman of the audit committee as a next step in light of the CEO's position in the company.

Answer (A) is incorrect because the CEO is a member of senior management. Other members of senior management may receive a final report that has been reviewed and approved by legal counsel. Answer (B) is incorrect because external auditors should not be contacted. External auditors may be given a final report that has been reviewed and approved by legal counsel. Answer (D) is incorrect because the CAE should obtain supporting documentation before informing the audit committee or the board.

8.5 Resource Management

47. The capabilities of individual staff members are key features in the effectiveness of an internal audit activity. What is the primary consideration used when staffing an internal audit activity?

A. Background checks.

B. Job descriptions.

C. Continuing education.

D. Organizational orientation.

Answer (B) is correct. *(CIA, adapted)*

REQUIRED: The primary consideration used when staffing an IAA.

DISCUSSION: The skills, capabilities, and technical knowledge of internal audit resources must be appropriate for planned activities (PA 2030-1). Properly formulated job descriptions provide a basis for identifying job qualifications (including training and experience). Hence, they facilitate recruiting human resources with the necessary attributes.

Answer (A) is incorrect because background checks help assure that statements made by prospective employees are accurate. However, they are not the primary requisite. Answer (C) is incorrect because continuing education occurs after the proper people are hired. Answer (D) is incorrect because a thorough orientation helps the new employee become productive more rapidly. However, it will not compensate for hiring the wrong person.

48. Having been given the task of developing a performance appraisal system for evaluating the performance of a large internal auditing staff, you should

A. Provide for an explanation of the appraisal criteria and methods at the time the appraisal results are discussed with the internal auditor.

B. Provide general information concerning the frequency of evaluations and the way evaluations will be performed without specifying their timing and uses.

C. Provide primarily for the evaluation of criteria such as diligence, initiative, and tact.

D. Provide primarily for the evaluation of specific accomplishments directly related to the performance of the engagement work program.

Answer (D) is correct. *(CIA, adapted)*

REQUIRED: The characteristic of a performance appraisal system.

DISCUSSION: An effective evaluation system should be based on relevant, reliable, and objective measures closely related to actual job performance on specific projects (e.g., execution of the engagement work program).

Answer (A) is incorrect because the personnel whose performance is being appraised should be notified of the criteria and methods at the time they begin employment. Answer (B) is incorrect because the timing and uses of evaluations are important matters that should be clearly communicated. Answer (C) is incorrect because the criteria listed are traits, not accomplishments. Although traits are important, an evaluation system for internal audit performance should primarily focus on specific accomplishments.

49. Which of the following aspects of evaluating the performance of staff members is considered to be a violation of good human resources management techniques?

A. The evaluator should justify very high and very low evaluations because of their impact on the employee.

B. Evaluations should be made annually or more frequently to provide the employee feedback about competence.

C. The first evaluation should be made shortly after commencing work to serve as an early guide to the new employee.

D. Because there are so many employees whose performance is completely satisfactory, it is preferable to use standard evaluation comments.

Answer (D) is correct. *(CIA, adapted)*

REQUIRED: The aspect of evaluating the performance of staff members considered a violation of good management techniques.

DISCUSSION: The evaluation provides a basis for counseling subordinates on their strong and weak attributes, opportunities for advancement, and programs for self-improvement. It also is a basis for promotions, transfers, and compensation adjustments. Thus, individualized attention is clearly desirable.

Answer (A) is incorrect because a very high or very low evaluation has behavioral and other implications that require special consideration. Answer (B) is incorrect because evaluations should be made at least annually. Answer (C) is incorrect because prompt feedback serves to provide the employee with early advice as to the acceptability of performed work.

50. Which of the following statements most accurately reflects the chief audit executive's responsibilities for internal audit resources?

A. The CAE is responsible for ensuring that audit coverage is based on the periodic skills assessment.

B. The CAE is responsible for evaluating the detailed summary of audit resources presented by management to the board.

C. The CAE is not responsible for such human resource functions as evaluation and development.

D. The CAE is responsible for communicating resource needs to the board but has no explicit responsibility for administering the organization's compensation program.

Answer (D) is correct. *(CIA, adapted)*

REQUIRED: The CAE's responsibilities for internal audit resources.

DISCUSSION: The CAE has primary responsibility for the sufficiency, appropriateness, and effective deployment of internal audit resources. This includes effective communication of resource needs and status to senior management and the board (PA 2030-1). Responsibility for administering the organization's compensation program normally resides in the human resources (personnel) area.

Answer (A) is incorrect because the CAE has responsibility for ensuring that the skills assessment is driven by the needs of the audit coverage, not by the capabilities already present in the IAA. Answer (B) is incorrect because the CAE has responsibility for presenting, at least annually, a detailed summary of the status and adequacy of internal audit resources to the board. Answer (C) is incorrect because the CAE has responsibility for considering human resource disciplines, such as succession planning and staff evaluation and development programs.

51. In most organizations, the rapidly expanding scope of internal auditing responsibilities requires continual training. What is the main purpose of such a training program?

A. To comply with continuing education requirements of professional organizations.

B. To use slack periods in engagement scheduling.

C. To help individuals to achieve personal career goals.

D. To achieve both individual and organizational goals.

Answer (D) is correct. *(CIA, adapted)*

REQUIRED: The main purpose of a training program.

DISCUSSION: By being informed and up to date, internal auditors are better prepared to reach their personal goals. In addition, IAA responsibilities are more readily discharged by auditors having the required knowledge, skills, and other competencies.

Answer (A) is incorrect because the CAE should establish a program for selecting and developing human resources, but compliance with continuing education requirements of professional organizations is not the primary purpose. Answer (B) is incorrect because training can be conducted during slack periods, but this is not the primary objective. Answer (C) is incorrect because both personal and IAA goals should be achieved.

52. The key factor in the success of an internal audit activity's human resources program is

A. An informal program for developing and counseling staff.

B. A compensation plan based on years of experience.

C. A well-developed set of selection criteria.

D. A program for recognizing the special interests of individual staff members.

Answer (C) is correct. *(CIA, adapted)*

REQUIRED: The key factor in the success of an IAA's human resources program.

DISCUSSION: Internal auditors should be qualified and competent. Because the selection of a superior staff is dependent on the ability to evaluate applicants, selection criteria must be well-developed. Appropriate questions and forms should be prepared in advance to evaluate, among other things, the applicant's technical qualifications, educational background, personal appearance, ability to communicate, maturity, persuasiveness, self-confidence, intelligence, motivation, and potential to contribute to the organization.

Answer (A) is incorrect because the human resources program should be formal. Answer (B) is incorrect because the quality of the human resources is more significant than compensation. Answer (D) is incorrect because the quality of the human resources is more significant than special interests of the staff.

53. What is the most appropriate preventive measure for staff communication problems with engagement clients?

A. Provide staff with sufficient training to enhance communication skills.

B. Avoid unnecessary communication with engagement clients.

C. Discuss communication problems with staff auditors.

D. Meet with engagement clients to resolve communication problems.

Answer (A) is correct. *(CIA, adapted)*

REQUIRED: The most appropriate solution to resolve staff communication problems with engagement clients.

DISCUSSION: Internal auditors should be skilled in oral and written communications so that they can clearly and effectively convey such matters as engagement objectives, evaluations, conclusions, and recommendations (PA 1219-1).

Answer (B) is incorrect because the issue is the quality rather than the quantity of communication. Answer (C) is incorrect because communication problems should be resolved through effective training. Answer (D) is incorrect because meeting with engagement clients will not resolve problems caused by poor staff communication skills.

54. In selecting an instructional strategy for developing internal audit staff, a chief audit executive should begin by reviewing

A. Organizational objectives.

B. Learning content.

C. Learners' readiness.

D. Budget constraints.

Answer (A) is correct. *(CIA, adapted)*

REQUIRED: The item a chief audit executive should first review in selecting an instructional strategy for developing an internal audit staff.

DISCUSSION: The chief audit executive should ensure that internal audit resources are appropriate, sufficient, and effectively deployed to achieve the approved plan (Standard 2030). The approved plan should be consistent with the goals of the organization.

Answer (B) is incorrect because the learning content cannot be prepared without first reviewing the organizational objectives. Answer (C) is incorrect because learners' readiness should be considered later in the program development process. Answer (D) is incorrect because budget constraints should be considered later in the process.

55. The most important reason for the chief audit executive to ensure that the internal audit department has adequate and sufficient resources is to

A. Ensure that the function is adequately protected from outsourcing.

B. Demonstrate sufficient capability to meet the audit plan requirements.

C. Establish credibility with the audit committee and management.

D. Fulfill the need for effective succession planning.

Answer (B) is correct. *(CIA, adapted)*

REQUIRED: The most important reason for the chief audit executive to ensure that the internal audit department has adequate and sufficient resources.

DISCUSSION: Standard 2030 requires that internal audit resources be appropriate, sufficient, and effectively deployed to achieve the approved plan of engagements.

Answer (A) is incorrect because the decision to outsource the internal audit function is not primarily based on existing resources. Answer (C) is incorrect because the amount of resources is not a significant factor in establishing credibility. Answer (D) is incorrect because succession planning is not related to the amount of audit resources.

56. The internal audit activity has recently experienced the departure of two internal auditors who cannot be immediately replaced due to budget constraints. Which of the following is the **least** desirable option for efficiently completing future engagements, given this reduction in resources?

A. Using self-assessment questionnaires to address audit objectives.

B. Employing information technology in audit planning, sampling, and documentation.

C. Eliminating consulting engagements from the engagement work schedule.

D. Filling vacancies with personnel from operating departments that are not being audited.

Answer (C) is correct. *(CIA, adapted)*

REQUIRED: The least desirable option for efficiently completing future engagements given the reduction in resources.

DISCUSSION: The chief audit executive should ensure that internal audit resources are appropriate, sufficient, and effectively deployed to achieve the approved plan (Standard 2030). The audit schedule should only be reduced as a last resort once all other viable alternatives have been explored, including the request for additional resources.

Answer (A) is incorrect because using self-assessment questionnaires are an efficient means of addressing the objectives of certain internal audits. Answer (B) is incorrect because use of technology is an appropriate means of achieving efficiencies in audit execution. Answer (D) is incorrect because using operating personnel with internal audit expertise and corporate experience is an appropriate way to enhance internal audit resources.

8.6 Policies and Procedures

57. In most cases, an internal audit activity should document policies and procedures to ensure the consistency and quality of its work. The exception to this principle is directly related to

A. Departmentation.

B. Division of labor.

C. Size of the internal audit activity.

D. Authority.

Answer (C) is correct. *(CIA, adapted)*

REQUIRED: The exception to documentation of policies and procedures.

DISCUSSION: Formal administrative and technical manuals may not be needed by all internal audit entities. A small IAA may be managed informally. Its staff may be directed and controlled through daily, close supervision and written memoranda. In a large IAA, more formal and comprehensive policies and procedures are essential to guide the staff in the consistent compliance with the IAA's standards of performance (PA 2040-1).

Answer (A) is incorrect because departmentation can improve communications among team members, but sufficient direct supervision may be lacking if spans of control are large. Answer (B) is incorrect because division of labor produces highly specialized individuals, but formalized guidance is necessary for newer employees if the IAA is large. Answer (D) is incorrect because, regardless of the degree of authority wielded by the chief audit executive, formal policies are needed in a large IAA.

58. Which of the following is most essential for guiding the internal audit staff in maintaining daily compliance with the internal audit activity's standards of performance?

A. Quality program assessments.

B. Position descriptions.

C. Performance appraisals.

D. Policies and procedures.

Answer (D) is correct. *(CIA, adapted)*

REQUIRED: The item most essential for guiding the internal audit staff in maintaining daily compliance with the IAA's standards.

DISCUSSION: The chief audit executive should establish policies and procedures to guide the IAA (Standard 2040). The form and content of written policies and procedures should be appropriate to the size and structure of the IAA and the complexity of its work. Formal administrative and technical manuals may not be needed by all IAAs. A small IAA may be managed informally. Its staff may be directed and controlled through daily, close supervision and written memoranda. In a large IAA, more formal and comprehensive policies and procedures are essential to guide the staff in the consistent compliance with the IAA's standards of performance (PA 2040-1) Quality program assessments, position descriptions, and performance appraisals do not provide specific daily guidance to the staff with respect to performance standards.

59. Policies and procedures should be established to guide the internal audit activity. Which of the following statements is false with respect to this requirement?

A. The form and content of written policies and procedures should be appropriate to the size of the internal audit activity.

B. All internal audit activities should have a detailed policies and procedures manual.

C. Formal administrative and technical manuals may not be needed by all internal auditing activities.

D. A small internal audit activity may be managed informally through close supervision and written memos.

Answer (B) is correct. *(CIA, adapted)*

REQUIRED: The false statement about written policies and procedures to guide the IAA.

DISCUSSION: The form and content of written policies and procedures should be appropriate to the size and structure of the IAA and the complexity of its work. A small IAA may be managed informally (PA 2040-1).

Answer (A) is incorrect because the form and content of written policies and procedures should be appropriate to the size of the IAA. Answer (C) is incorrect because formal administrative and technical manuals may not be needed by all IAAs. Answer (D) is incorrect because a small IAA may be managed informally through close supervision and written memos.

60. Which of the items below most likely reflects differences between the policies of a relatively large and a relatively small internal audit activity? The policies for the large activity should

A. Define the scope and status of internal auditing.

B. Contain the authority to carry out engagements.

C. Be specific as to activities to be carried out.

D. Be in considerable detail.

Answer (D) is correct. *(CIA, adapted)*

REQUIRED: The item that most likely reflects differences between the policies of relatively large and small IAAs.

DISCUSSION: The chief audit executive should establish policies and procedures to guide the IAA (Standard 2040). The form and content of written policies and procedures should be appropriate to the size and structure of the IAA and the complexity of its work. Formal administrative and technical manuals may not be needed by all IAAs. A small IAA may be managed informally. Its staff may be directed and controlled through daily, close supervision and written memoranda. In a large IAA, more formal and comprehensive policies and procedures are essential to guide the staff in the consistent compliance with the IAA's standards of performance (PA 2040-1).

Answer (A) is incorrect because the scope and status of internal auditing are covered in the charter. Answer (B) is incorrect because the authority to carry out engagements is covered in the charter. Answer (C) is incorrect because, whether the IAA is large or small, it must have policies that specifically state its functions.

61. Policies and procedures relative to managing the internal audit activity should

A. Ensure compliance with its performance standards.

B. Give consideration to its structure and the complexity of the work performed.

C. Result in consistent job performance.

D. Prescribe the format and distribution of engagement communications and the classification of engagement observations.

Answer (B) is correct. *(CIA, adapted)*

REQUIRED: The true statement about policies and procedures for managing the IAA.

DISCUSSION: The CAE should establish policies and procedures to guide the IAA (Standard 2040). The form and content of written policies and procedures should be appropriate to the size and structure of the IAA and the complexity of its work (PA 2040-1).

Answer (A) is incorrect because engagements should be properly supervised to ensure objectives are achieved, quality is assured, and staff is developed (Standard 2340). Compliance with performance standards is a quality issue, and ensuring quality requires more than establishing policies and procedures. Answer (C) is incorrect because whether policies and procedures are required depends on the size and structure of the IAA. Moreover, these measures alone do not ensure consistent performance. Answer (D) is incorrect because prescribing the format and distribution of engagement communications and the classification of engagement observations is a discretionary measure that depends on the size and structure of the IAA and the complexity of work performed.

STUDY UNIT NINE
MANAGING THE INTERNAL AUDIT ACTIVITY II

(33 pages of outline)

This is the second study unit covering management of the internal audit activity. The subject of the first two subunits is the relationship of the IAA with external providers of assurance and consulting services, including regulators. The subject of the next five subunits is the IAA's quality assurance and improvement program. These subunits address internal and external assessments, including benchmarking.

The first two subunits contain Practice Advisories interpreting the following Specific Performance Standard:

2050 ***Coordination*** – *The chief audit executive should share information and coordinate activities with other internal and external providers of relevant assurance and consulting services to ensure proper coverage and minimize duplication of efforts.*

NOTE: This Standard applies not only to external auditors but also to other "providers," such as regulatory bodies (e.g., governmental auditors) and certain of the organization's other subunits (e.g., a health and safety department).

The subunits on quality assurance contain Specific Attribute Standards and Practice Advisories relating to the General Attribute Standard on quality assurance and improvement programs.

Subunit 9.7 provides a brief outline of benchmarking, a common quality management tool useful for periodic internal assessments of the IAA.

Core Concepts

- The CAE shares information and coordinates activities with other providers of relevant assurance and consulting services to ensure proper coverage and minimize duplication of effort.
- Internal auditors should have some role in the selection or retention of the external auditors.
- The CAE should maintain a quality assurance and improvement program that covers all aspects of the IAA, continuously monitors its effectiveness, and provides assurance of its compliance with the Standards and Code of Ethics.
- The IAA should have a process to monitor and assess the quality program.
- Internal assessments include ongoing reviews of the IAA and periodic reviews performed through self-assessment or by other qualified persons in the organization.
- External assessments should be performed at least once every five years by qualified, independent reviewers from outside the organization. The CAE communicates the results to the board.
- Internal auditors should report that their activities are in accordance with the Standards, provided that assessments demonstrate that the IAA is in compliance with the Standards.

9.1 COORDINATION

1. Issues include avoiding duplication of effort, work done for external providers, assessment of their performance, and other matters relevant to coordination of efforts. These issues are addressed in one Practice Advisory.

   a. ***PRACTICE ADVISORY 2050-1: COORDINATION***

      1. *Internal and external auditing work should be coordinated to ensure adequate audit coverage and to minimize duplicate efforts. The scope of internal auditing work encompasses a systematic, disciplined approach to evaluate and improve the effectiveness of risk management, control, and governance processes. The **scope of internal auditing work** is described within Section 2100 of the Standards. On the other hand, the **external auditors' ordinary examination** is designed to obtain sufficient evidential matter to support an opinion on the overall fairness of the annual financial statements. The **scope of the work of external auditors** is determined by their professional standards, and they are responsible for judging the **adequacy of procedures performed and evidence obtained** for purposes of expressing their opinion on the annual financial statements.*

      2. ***Oversight of the work of external auditors**, including coordination with the internal audit activity, is generally the responsibility of the board. **Actual coordination** should be the responsibility of the chief audit executive. The chief audit executive will require the support of the board to achieve effective coordination of audit work.*

      3. *In coordinating the work of internal auditors with the work of external auditors, the chief audit executive should ensure that work to be performed by internal auditors in fulfillment of Section 2100 of the Standards does **not duplicate the work of external auditors** that can be relied on for purposes of internal auditing coverage. To the extent that professional and organizational reporting responsibilities allow, internal auditors should conduct engagements in a manner that allows for **maximum audit coordination and efficiency**.*

      4. *The chief audit executive may agree to **perform work for external auditors** in connection with their annual audit of the financial statements. Work performed by internal auditors to assist external auditors in fulfilling their responsibility is subject to all relevant provisions of the International Standards for the Professional Practice of Internal Auditing.*

      5. *The chief audit executive should make **regular evaluations of the coordination** between internal and external auditors. Such evaluations may also include assessments of the overall efficiency and effectiveness of internal and external auditing functions, including **aggregate audit cost**.*

      6. *In exercising its oversight role, the board may request the chief audit executive to **assess the performance of external auditors**. Such assessments should ordinarily be made in the context of the chief audit executive's **role of coordinating** internal and external auditing activities and should extend to other performance matters only at the specific request of senior management or the board. Assessments of the performance of external auditors should be based on **sufficient information** to support the conclusions reached. Assessments of the external auditors' performance with respect to the coordination of internal and external auditing activities should reflect the **criteria described in this Practice Advisory**.*

7. *Assessments of the performance of external auditors extending to **matters beyond coordination** with the internal auditors may address additional factors, such as:*
   - *Professional knowledge and experience*
   - *Knowledge of the organization's industry*
   - *Independence*
   - *Availability of specialized services*
   - *Anticipation of and responsiveness to the needs of the organization*
   - *Reasonable continuity of key engagement personnel*
   - *Maintenance of appropriate working relationships*
   - *Achievement of contract commitments*
   - *Delivery of overall value to the organization*
8. *The chief audit executive should **communicate the results of evaluations of coordination** between internal and external auditors to senior management and the board along with, as appropriate, any relevant comments about the performance of external auditors.*
9. ***External auditors** may be required by their professional standards to ensure that **certain matters are communicated to the board**. The chief audit executive should communicate with external auditors regarding these matters so as to have an understanding of the issues. These matters may include:*
   - *Issues that may affect the independence of the external auditors*
   - *Significant control weaknesses*
   - *Errors and irregularities*
   - *Illegal acts*
   - *Management judgments and accounting estimates*
   - *Significant audit adjustments*
   - *Disagreements with management*
   - *Difficulties encountered in performing the audit*
10. *Coordination of audit efforts involves **periodic meetings** to discuss matters of mutual interest.*
    - ***Audit coverage**. Planned audit activities of internal and external auditors should be discussed to ensure that audit coverage is coordinated and duplicate efforts are minimized. Sufficient meetings should be scheduled during the audit process to ensure coordination of audit work and efficient and timely completion of audit activities and to determine whether **observations and recommendations** from work performed to date require that the **scope of planned work be adjusted**.*
    - ***Access to each other's audit programs and working papers.** Access to the external auditors' programs and working papers may be important in order for internal auditors to be satisfied as to the **propriety for internal audit purposes of relying on the external auditors' work**. Such access carries with it the responsibility for internal auditors to respect the **confidentiality** of those programs and working papers. Similarly, access to the internal auditors' programs and working papers should be given to external auditors in order for external auditors to be satisfied as to the **propriety, for external audit purposes, of relying on the internal auditors' work**.*

- ***Exchange of audit reports and management letters.*** *Internal audit* ***final communications****, management's* ***responses*** *to those communications, and subsequent internal audit activity* ***follow-up reviews*** *should be made available to external auditors. These communications assist external auditors in determining and adjusting the scope of work. In addition, the internal auditors need access to the external auditors' management letters. Matters discussed in* ***management letters assist internal auditors in planning*** *the areas to emphasize in future internal audit work. After review of management letters and initiation of any needed corrective action by appropriate members of management and the board, the chief audit executive should ensure that appropriate* ***follow-up and corrective action*** *have been taken.*
- ***Common understanding of audit techniques, methods, and terminology.*** *First, the chief audit executive should understand the* ***scope of work planned by external auditors*** *and should be satisfied that the external auditors' planned work, in conjunction with the internal auditors' planned work, satisfies the requirements of Section 2100 of the Standards. Such satisfaction requires an understanding of the* ***level of materiality*** *used by external auditors for planning and the nature and extent of the external auditors' planned procedures.*

  Second, the chief audit executive should ensure that the ***external auditors'*** *techniques, methods, and terminology are sufficiently understood by internal auditors to enable the chief audit executive to (1)* ***coordinate*** *internal and external auditing work; (2)* ***evaluate****, for purposes of reliance, the external auditors' work; and (3) ensure that internal auditors who are to perform work to fulfill the external auditors' objectives can* ***communicate*** *effectively with external auditors.*

  Finally, the chief audit executive should provide sufficient information to enable external auditors to understand the ***internal auditors'*** *techniques, methods, and terminology to facilitate reliance by external auditors on work performed using such techniques, methods, and terminology. It may be more efficient for internal and external auditors to use* ***similar techniques, methods, and terminology*** *to effectively coordinate their work and to rely on the work of one another.*

PA Summary

- Internal and external auditing work should be **coordinated** to ensure adequate audit coverage and to minimize duplicate efforts. **Internal auditors** evaluate and improve **risk management, control, and governance**. However, **external auditors** ordinarily perform an examination sufficient to express an opinion on the financial statements. Their scope of work is determined by their professional standards, and they judge the adequacy of procedures and evidence.
- The **board** oversees the work of external auditors, but the CAE **actually** coordinates the work with that of the IAA. The work of internal auditors should not be duplicative. The objective is maximum coordination and efficiency consistent with reporting responsibilities.
- Work done for external auditors is subject to the **Standards**.
- The CAE **regularly evaluates** coordination and may assess the overall efficiency and effectiveness of auditing functions, including aggregate audit cost.
- The board may request the CAE to **assess the work of the external auditors**. The CAE's assessment ordinarily is in the context of the **coordination role** and should reflect the criteria in this PA. Assessments should be based on **sufficient information** to support the conclusions reached.
- Management or the board also may specifically request an assessment of the external audit work extending to **matters beyond coordination**, such as (1) responsiveness to the organization's needs, (2) reasonable continuity of key personnel, (3) maintenance of working relationships, (4) achievement of commitments, and (5) delivery of overall value.
- The **results of evaluations** of coordination should be communicated with relevant comments to senior management and the board.
- The CAE should obtain an understanding of matters **required to be communicated** to the board by the **external auditors**, for example, independence issues, control weaknesses, and illegal acts.
- Internal and external auditors should have **periodic meetings** to discuss (1) audit coverage, including whether **observations and recommendations** from work performed require that the **scope of work be adjusted**; (2) access to audit programs and working papers to determine the propriety of using each others' work; (3) exchange of audit reports and management letters, such as those that assist internal auditors in planning future work and external auditors in determining the scope of work, including: internal audit **final communications**, management's **responses**, and **follow-up reviews**; and (4) common understanding of audit techniques, methods, and terminology.
- Furthermore, the CAE should understand the **scope of work of the external auditors** and should be satisfied that their work, together with the internal auditors' work, complies with the Standards. Satisfaction requires an understanding of the **level of materiality** used by the external auditors.
- Also, the CAE must (1) ensure that the **external auditors'** techniques, etc., are sufficiently understood by internal auditors, and (2) provide sufficient information to enable external auditors to understand the **internal auditors'** techniques.

2. Stop and review! You have completed the outline for this subunit. Study multiple-choice questions 1 through 8 beginning on page 367.

9.2 EXTERNAL AUDIT SERVICES

1. Internal auditors should have some role in the selection or retention of the external auditors. This topic is covered in one Practice Advisory.

   a. ***PRACTICE ADVISORY 2050-2: ACQUISITION OF EXTERNAL AUDIT SERVICES***

      1. *The **internal auditor's participation** in the selection, evaluation, or retention of the organization's external auditors **may vary** from no role in the process, to advising management or the audit committee, assistance or participation in the process, management of the process, or auditing the process. Because the Standards require internal auditors to "share information and coordinate activities with other internal and external providers of relevant assurance and consulting services," it is advisable for internal auditors to have **some role or involvement in the selection or retention** of the external auditors and in the **definition of scope of work**.*

      2. *A board or audit committee **approved policy** can facilitate the **periodic request for external audit services** and position such exercises as normal business activities so that the present service providers do not view a decision to request proposals as a signal that the organization is dissatisfied with present services. If a specific policy does not exist, the internal auditor should determine if such services are subject to any **other existing procurement policies** of the organization. In the absence of appropriate policies, the internal auditor should consider **facilitating development** of appropriate policies.*

      3. ***Appropriate policies** for selection or retention of external audit services should consider addressing the following **attributes**:*

         - *Board or audit committee approval of the policy*
         - *Nature and type of services covered by the policy*
         - *Duration of contract, frequency of the formal request for services, or determination to retain the existing service providers*
         - *Participants or members of the selection and evaluation team*
         - *Any critical or primary criteria that should be considered in the evaluation*
         - *Limitations on service fees and procedures for approving exceptions to the policy*
         - *Regulatory or other governing requirements unique to specific industries or countries*

      4. *A board policy may also address the acquisition of **services other than just financial statement audits** that may be offered by **external audit firms**. Those may include:*

         - *Tax services*
         - *Consulting and other non-audit services*
         - *Internal audit outsourcing or co-sourcing services*

           NOTE: Organizations subject to securities regulation may need to consider external auditor independence requirements for providing internal audit services. These may be contained in the rules of the regulatory body with jurisdiction.

         - *Other outsourced or co-sourced services*
         - *Special services, such as agreed-upon service engagements*
         - *Valuation, appraisal, and actuarial services*
         - *Temporary services such as recruiting, bookkeeping, technology services*
         - *Legal services provided by external audit firms*

5. ***Appropriate documentation*** *should be retained concerning a periodic,* ***formal decision to retain*** *the existing service providers and forgo or delay requests to other potential service providers.*

6. *A* ***plan*** *should be developed for the* ***selection process*** *that identifies the selection committee participants, key deliverables and target dates for each phase of the process, candidates from whom to request proposals, nature and extent of services to be requested, and how information will be communicated to potential candidates. Often, at the start of the selection process, an organization may conduct a* ***comprehensive meeting*** *with all potential candidates in which management makes a formal presentation to cover pertinent information for the service request and supplies the candidates with a formal information package or report describing the services being requested. This general meeting can be* ***followed with individual, onsite meetings*** *for each candidate and include appropriate management representatives. Other combinations of meetings and information packages are also practical or appropriate for special situations.*

7. *A* ***two-phased request*** *may be necessary to facilitate a* ***screening process*** *to narrow or reduce the field of potential service providers to a reasonable number of final candidates.* ***Initial information requests*** *should be focused on obtaining appropriate statements of qualifications, including background and other general information about the potential candidates. Information should be obtained, such as history of the firm, size of the firm, resources available, firm philosophy and audit approach, special expertise, local or servicing office that would handle the engagement, related industry experience, and biographies of key team members that would be assigned to the engagement.*

8. *After the initial screening process, those candidates selected to advance to the next phase should be sent a* ***second request for information that provides more specifics*** *about the services requested. A detailed service request that itemizes deliverables expected and key target dates should be developed. Candidates should be requested to provide specific details, including* ***pricing for the services****. A timetable for the remainder of the process can be supplied that schedules dates for delivery of the additional information requested, meetings for presentations by the candidates to the selection committee, and a date for the final selection. The detailed service request should be specific for* ***each of the services requested*** *and should indicate whether the services may be awarded as one package or split between multiple candidates.*

9. *It may be appropriate to* ***compare and summarize the attributes of the candidates by key criteria*** *and provide it in a format that facilitates consistent evaluation of all the service providers.* ***Questions*** *may be supplied that stimulate thought processes and focus the evaluation on key criteria. An* ***evaluation form*** *can facilitate collection of each participant's analysis and conclusions about each of the candidates.* ***Background information****, such as the organization's past history with the various candidates, type of services previously provided, and fee history, can provide the selection team with an appropriate perspective to begin the evaluation.*

10. ***Service arrangements*** *for external audit engagements should be* ***documented*** *in a written agreement signed by both the service provider and the engagement client.*

11. *If the selection process results in a* ***change in the service providers****, appropriate* ***transition plans*** *should be developed to facilitate a smooth and orderly change.* ***Notifications*** *to appropriate parties, including regulatory bodies if required, should be communicated in a timely manner.*

12. *Internal auditors should determine how the organization **monitors** ongoing service activities from external auditors. Compliance with the terms of service contracts and other agreements should be assessed on a periodic basis. Assessment of the **independence** of the external auditors should include internal audit participation, be performed at least annually, and be communicated to the audit committee.*

PA Summary

- Internal auditors should have some involvement in **selecting or retaining the external auditors** and in defining the scope of work.
- A board or audit committee **policy** should establish that the **periodic request** for external audit services is a **normal activity**, not a sign of dissatisfaction. Absent such a policy, the internal auditor should facilitate development of appropriate procurement policies.
- **Attributes of a policy** may include (1) board approval, (2) a description of the services, (3) contract duration, (4) criteria, (5) members of the evaluation team, (6) fee limits, and (7) regulatory requirements.
- **Services provided by external auditors** other than financial statement audits may be sought. Examples are (1) internal audit outsourcing or co-sourcing, (2) consulting, (3) tax or legal services, and (4) temporary or special services.
- The formal retention decision should be **documented**.
- A plan should be developed for the **selection process** that identifies the participants, key deliverables and target dates, candidates, nature and extent of services, and how information will be communicated. A **comprehensive meeting** with all candidates and **individual onsite meetings** should be held.
- A **two-phased request** to facilitate **screening** begins with an **initial information request** statements of qualifications, including background and other general information about the potential candidates. The **detailed service request** seeks pricing and other information. It itemizes deliverables expected and key target dates and should be specific for **each of the services requested** and indicate whether the services may be awarded as one package or split.
- **Candidate attributes** may be compared and summarized using key criteria to facilitate consistent evaluation.
- A written, signed agreement should document the **service arrangement**.
- A **change in service providers** requires a transition plan. Timely notifications should be made to appropriate parties, including regulatory bodies.
- Internal auditors (1) determine how external auditors are **monitored** and (2) assess their (a) compliance with agreements periodically and (b) **independence** at least annually.

2. Stop and review! You have completed the outline for this subunit. Study multiple-choice questions 9 through 13 beginning on page 370.

9.3 QUALITY ASSURANCE AND IMPROVEMENT PROGRAMS (QAIP)

1. The QAIP should provide reasonable assurance that the IAA's work conforms with applicable standards. The relevant pronouncements include one General Attribute Standard, one Specific Attribute Standard, and two Practice Advisories.
2. ***1300*** ***Quality Assurance and Improvement Programs*** *– The chief audit executive should develop and maintain a quality assurance and improvement program that covers all aspects of the internal audit activity and continuously monitors its effectiveness. This program includes periodic internal and external quality assessments and ongoing internal monitoring. Each part of the program should be designed to help the internal auditing activity add value to and improve the organization's operations and to provide assurance that the internal audit activity is in conformity with the Standards and the Code of Ethics.*

   a. ***PRACTICE ADVISORY 1300-1: QUALITY ASSURANCE AND IMPROVEMENT PROGRAM***

      1. ***Overview of a Quality Assurance and Improvement Program (QAIP)*** *– The chief audit executive (CAE) is responsible for establishing an internal audit activity whose scope of work includes all the activities in the International Standards for the Professional Practice of Internal Auditing (Standards) and in The Institute of Internal Auditor's (IIA) definition of internal auditing. To ensure that this occurs, Standard 1300 requires that the CAE develop and maintain a quality assurance and improvement program (QAIP).*

      2. ***Implementing a QAIP*** *– The CAE should be accountable for implementing processes that are designed to provide* ***reasonable assurance*** *to the various* ***stakeholders*** *of the internal audit activity that it:*

      - *Performs in accordance with its* ***charter****, which should be consistent with the Standards and* ***Code of Ethics****,*
      - *Operates in an effective and efficient manner, and*
      - *Is perceived by those stakeholders as adding value and improving the organization's operations.*

      These processes should include appropriate ***supervision****,* *periodic* ***internal assessments*** *and ongoing* ***monitoring*** *of quality assurance, and periodic* ***external assessments****.*

      3. ***Nature and Scope of a QAIP*** *– The QAIP should be sufficiently comprehensive to encompass* ***all aspects of operation and management*** *of an internal audit activity, as found in the Standards and* ***best practices*** *of the profession. The QAIP processes should be performed by or under* ***direct supervision*** *of the CAE. Except in small internal audit activities, the CAE would usually delegate most QAIP responsibilities to subordinates. In large or complex environments (e.g., numerous business units or locations), the CAE should establish a* ***formal QAIP function*** *independent of the audit and consulting segments of the internal audit activity. This* ***independent*** *function should be headed by an* ***audit executive****. This executive (and limited staff) would not normally perform all of the QAIP responsibilities, but would administer and monitor these activities.*

4. ***Key Elements of a QAIP*** – *The QAIP should be structured to achieve an optimum level of* ***professional competence****. Its reviews should be administered, to the extent practicable, independently of the functions and activities being reviewed. The following key elements of the internal audit activity – performed or administered by a person or functional unit under the direction of the CAE – should be considered for the QAIP function:*
   - *Oversee the development and implementation of* ***internal audit policies/procedures****; administer/maintain the internal audit activity's policy/procedure manual.*
   - *Assist the CAE and audit management with* ***budgeting and financial administration*** *for the internal audit activity.*
   - *Maintain and update the comprehensive* ***audit risk universe****, including gathering and incorporating new information impacting the universe; overseeing the* ***division of responsibilities*** *among internal audit, external audit, and other evaluation and investigation functions.*
   - *Administer the general operation of the* ***system for evaluation of audit risk and long-range planning*** *– assisting the CAE and audit management in this area.*
   - *Assist with the overall* ***scheduling*** *process for audit and consulting engagements and the associated* ***time tracking****.*
   - *Assist internal audit management in the acquisition, maintenance, and employment of* ***audit tools*** *and other use of technology.*
   - *Administer* ***external recruitment*** *and the internal audit activity's participation in the organization's internal* ***staff rotation*** *and* ***management development*** *programs.*
   - *Oversee the* ***training/development of staff*** *– e.g., selection or development of training courses and administration of the related* ***career planning*** *and* ***performance evaluation*** *processes, including the tracking system for professional development of individual staff members.*
   - *Oversee the system(s) for internal* ***audit statistics/metrics*** *and for post-audit and other surveys (e.g., of the customers and other stakeholders of the internal audit activity).*
   - *Administer/monitor quality assurance and process improvement activities, including formal internal and external* ***quality assessments****.*
   - *Oversee/administer information gathering and preparation of the* ***periodic summary reports*** *by the internal audit activity to senior management and the audit committee (including reports of the results of internal and external quality assessments).*
   - *Administer/maintain the comprehensive* ***follow-up database*** *for recommendations and action plans resulting from internal audit engagements and the work of external auditors and other internal evaluation and investigation functions.*
   - *Assist the CAE, audit management, and internal audit staff in keeping current with the* ***Standards, other changes and emerging best practices*** *of the internal audit profession, regulatory matters, and other emerging issues and opportunities – under the direction of internal audit management.*
   - *The words "assist, administer, oversee, monitor, and maintain" are intended to indicate that the person(s) working in the QAIP function would not necessarily perform much of this work. It would be assigned – either ad-hoc for particular tasks or on a longer-term basis – to other internal audit executives and staff, but would be overseen, administered, etc., through the QAIP.*

PA Summary

- The CAE implements processes of a Quality Assurance and Improvement Program (QAIP) to give **reasonable assurance** to stakeholders that the IAA (1) performs in accordance with its charter, the Standards, and the Code of Ethics; (2) operates efficiently and effectively; and (3) is perceived as adding value and improving operations. These **processes** include (1) supervision, (2) periodic internal and external assessments, and (3) ongoing monitoring of quality assurance.
- The QAIP embraces all facets of the IAA as reflected in the Standards and **best practices** of the profession. Its processes are performed or supervised by the CAE. A large entity should have a **formal, independent** QAIP administered and monitored by an **audit executive**.
- The **key elements** of an IAA's QAIP function should be structured to achieve optimal **professional competence**. The reviews performed should be independent of what is reviewed to the extent feasible. The key elements may involve assistance, administration, oversight, monitoring, or maintenance duties relating to the following: (1) policies and procedures, (2) budgeting and financial management, (3) the audit risk universe, (4) division of auditors' responsibilities, (5) evaluation of audit risk and long-range planning, (6) scheduling and time tracking, (7) audit technology, (8) personnel matters (external recruitment, staff rotation, training/development of staff, career, planning, and performance evaluations), (9) audit statistics, (10) quality assessments, (11) summary reporting, (12) the follow-up database, and (13) keeping current with changes in professional standards and practices.

3. ***1310*** ***Quality Program Assessments*** *– The internal audit activity should adopt a process to monitor and assess the overall effectiveness of the quality program. The process should include both internal and external assessments.*

   a. ***PRACTICE ADVISORY 1310-1: QUALITY PROGRAM ASSESSMENTS***

      1. ***Monitoring quality programs*** *is defined as* ***ongoing and periodic assessments of the entire spectrum of audit and consulting work*** *performed by the internal audit activity and is not limited to assessing its Quality Assurance and Improvement Program (QAIP) – see Practice Advisory 1300-1. These ongoing and periodic assessments should be composed of rigorous, comprehensive processes; continuous* ***supervision and testing*** *of performance of audit and consulting work; and* ***periodic validations of compliance*** *with the Standards. Monitoring should also include ongoing measurements and analyses of* ***performance metrics*** *(e.g., audit plan accomplishment, cycle time, recommendations accepted, and customer satisfaction). If the results of these assessments indicate areas for improvement by the internal audit activity, the improvements should be implemented by the chief audit executive (CAE) through the QAIP.*

2. ***Definition and Timing of Assessments***

- ***Ongoing internal assessments*** *(the term is synonymous with the terms "internal review" and "self-assessment" used elsewhere in the Practice Advisories) should be an integral* ***part of the day-to-day supervision, review, and measurement*** *of the internal audit activity, as set forth in Practice Advisory 1311-1, paragraphs two and three.*
- ***Periodic internal assessments*** *should be completed as set forth in Practice Advisory 1311-1.*
- *There are* ***two approaches to external assessments****. The first approach is a* ***full external assessment*** *conducted by a qualified, independent external reviewer or review team. This approach involves an outside team of competent professionals under the leadership of an experienced and professional project manager (see qualifications of external reviewers in Practice Advisory 1312-1.) The second approach involves the use of a qualified, independent external reviewer or review team to conduct an* ***independent validation of the internal self-assessment and report*** *completed by the internal audit activity. This alternative approach brings in a qualified, independent reviewer or review team who is well versed in quality assessment methodology to validate the aforementioned self-assessment of the internal audit activity. Independent external reviewers should be well versed in leading internal audit practices.*
- *While there may be circumstances when a full external review is not deemed appropriate or necessary (see Practice Advisory 1312-2), the full external assessment by a qualified, independent external reviewer or review team gives maximum benefit and accountability to internal auditors and their various stakeholders. The CAE should involve senior management and the board in determining the approach.*
- *External assessments of the internal audit activity should be performed in accordance with Practice Advisories 1312-1 and 1312-2.*

3. ***Assessing Quality Programs*** *–* ***Assessments should evaluate and conclude on the quality*** *of the internal audit activity and lead to* ***recommendations*** *for appropriate improvements. Assessments of quality programs should include evaluation of:*

- ***Compliance*** *with the Standards and Code of Ethics, including timely corrective actions to remedy any significant instances of noncompliance*
- ***Adequacy*** *of the internal audit activity's charter, goals, objectives, policies, and procedures*
- *Contribution to the organization's* ***governance, risk management, and control*** *processes*
- ***Compliance*** *with applicable laws, regulations, and government or industry standards*
- *Effectiveness of* ***continuous improvement*** *activities and adoption of* ***best practices***
- *The extent to which the auditing activity* ***adds value*** *and* ***improves the organization's operations***

4. ***Continuous Improvement*** *– All QAIP efforts should include appropriate and* ***timely modification*** *of resources, technology, processes, and procedures as indicated by monitoring and assessment activities.*

5. ***Communicating Results*** *– To provide accountability and transparency, the CAE should communicate the results of external, and, as appropriate, internal quality program assessments with the various* ***stakeholders*** *of the activity (such as senior management, the board, and external auditors).* ***At least annually****, the CAE should report to the board on the quality program efforts and results.*

PA Summary

- **Monitoring of quality programs** extends to **ongoing and periodic assessments** of **all work** done by the IAA. It is not limited to assessing the QAIP. These assessments include (1) routine supervision and testing of performance and (2) periodic validation of compliance with the Standards. Monitoring also includes measuring and analyzing performance. Indicated improvements should be implemented by the CAE through the QAIP.
- **Ongoing internal assessment** should be part of daily supervision, review, and measurement of the IAA.
- An **external assessment** is conducted by a qualified, independent external reviewer or review team. It may be a **full external assessment** led by an experienced and professional project manager or an **independent validation** of the internal self-assessment and report by the IAA. A full external review provides the maximum benefit and accountability. But in certain cases it may not be appropriate or necessary.
- An assessment evaluates and states conclusions about the **quality of the IAA** and produces **recommendations**. An assessment evaluates (1) compliance with the Standards, Code of Ethics, other standards, laws, and regulations; (2) adequacy of the IAA's charter, objectives, policies, and procedures; (3) the contribution to risk management, control, and governance; (4) continuous improvement and adoption of best practices; and (5) whether the IAA adds value and improves operations.
- QAIP efforts include the **timely modifications** indicated by monitoring and assessment.
- The **results** of assessments should be **communicated** to stakeholders. The CAE should report to the board on the QAIP **at least annually**.

4. Stop and review! You have completed the outline for this subunit. Study multiple-choice questions 14 and 15 on page 372.

9.4 INTERNAL ASSESSMENTS

1. Ongoing and periodic internal assessments cover all the work of the IAA. They are not limited to assessing the QAIP. Recall that **internal assessment** means the same as **internal review** or **self-assessment**. This subunit consists of one Specific Attribute Standard and two Practice Advisories.
2. ***1311*** ***Internal Assessments*** *– Internal assessments should include:*
   - *Ongoing reviews of the performance of the internal audit activity; and*
   - *Periodic reviews performed through self-assessment or by other persons within the organization, with knowledge of internal auditing practices and the Standards.*

a. ***PRACTICE ADVISORY 1311-1: INTERNAL ASSESSMENTS***

1. ***Overview*** – *The chief audit executive (CAE) is responsible for establishing an internal audit activity whose scope of work includes all the activities in the Standards. To ensure this occurs, Standard 1300 requires that the CAE develop and maintain a Quality Assurance and Improvement Program (QAIP). The QAIP should include both ongoing and periodic internal assessments (the term is synonymous with the terms "internal review" and "self-assessment" used elsewhere in the Practice Advisories). These assessments should cover the entire spectrum of audit and consulting work performed by the internal audit activity and should not be limited to assessing its QAIP – see Practice Advisory 1300-1.*

2. ***Ongoing internal assessments*** *are usually incorporated into the routine policies and practices used to manage the internal audit activity and should be conducted by means of such processes and tools as:*

   - ***Engagement supervision*** *as described in Practice Advisory 2340-1, Engagement Supervision*
   - ***Checklists*** *and other means to give assurance that processes adopted by the internal audit activity (e.g., in an audit and procedures manual) are being followed*
   - ***Feedback*** *from audit customers and other stakeholders*
   - *Selective* ***peer reviews*** *of workpapers by staff not involved in the respective audits*
   - ***Project budgets****, timekeeping systems, audit plan completion, and cost recoveries*
   - ***Analyses of other performance metrics*** *(such as cycle time and recommendations accepted)*

3. ***Conclusions*** *should be developed as to the quality of* ***ongoing performance****, and* ***follow-up*** *action should be taken to ensure appropriate improvements are implemented.*

4. ***Periodic internal assessments*** *usually represent nonroutine, special-purpose reviews and compliance testing. They should be designed to assess (a)* ***compliance*** *with the internal audit activity's charter, the Standards, and The IIA's Code of Ethics, and (b) the* ***efficiency and effectiveness*** *of the activity in meeting the needs of its various stakeholders. The IIA's Quality Assessment Manual, or a comparable set of guidance and tools, should serve as the basis for periodic internal assessments.*

5. *Periodic internal assessments may:*

   - *Include more in-depth* ***interviews and surveys*** *of stakeholder groups*
   - *Be performed by members of the internal audit activity* ***(self-assessment)***
   - *Be performed by* ***Certified Internal Auditors*** *(CIAs) or other competent audit professionals currently assigned elsewhere in the organization*
   - *Encompass a* ***combination of self-assessment and preparation of materials*** *subsequently reviewed by CIAs or other competent audit professionals*
   - *Include* ***benchmarking*** *of the internal audit activity's practices and performance metrics against relevant* ***best practices*** *of the internal audit profession*

6. *A periodic internal assessment performed within a short time before an external assessment can serve to **facilitate and reduce the cost of the external assessment**. If the periodic internal assessment is performed by a qualified, independent external reviewer or review team, the assessment results should **not communicate any assurances** on the outcome of the subsequent external quality assessment. The report may offer suggestions and recommendations to enhance the internal audit activities' practices. If the external assessment takes the form of a "self-assessment with independent validation" (Practice Advisory 1312-2), the periodic internal assessment can serve as the **self-assessment portion** of this process.*
7. ***Conclusions** should be developed as to the quality of **performance** and the appropriate action initiated to achieve **improvements and conformity to the Standards**, as necessary.*
8. *__Communicating Results__ – The CAE should establish a **structure for reporting results** of internal assessments that maintains appropriate credibility and objectivity. Generally, those assigned responsibility for conducting ongoing and periodic reviews should report to the CAE while performing the reviews and should communicate results directly to the CAE.*
9. *At least annually, the CAE should report the results of **internal assessments**, necessary **action plans**, and their successful **implementation** to the board and also share information with appropriate persons outside the activity (such as senior management and external auditors).*

PA Summary

- **Ongoing internal assessments** are part of the IAA's routine activities. They are reflected in, for example, (1) engagement supervision; (2) checklists and other assurance processes; (3) feedback; (4) peer reviews of working papers; (5) budgets, timekeeping, and tracking of audit plan completion and cost recoveries; and (6) analyses of other performance metrics.
- **Periodic internal assessments** are nonroutine reviews and tests of (1) the IAA's compliance with its charter, the Standards, and The IIA's Code of Ethics; and (2) the IAA's **efficiency and effectiveness** in meeting the needs of stakeholders.
- Periodic internal assessment may involve (1) more thorough feedback from stakeholders (via **interviews and surveys**) than in an ongoing assessment, (2) **self-assessment**, (3) assessment by **audit professionals** (e.g., CIAs), (4) a **combination of self-assessment** and preparation of materials to be reviewed by audit professionals, and (5) **benchmarking** against best practices.
- A periodic internal assessment may facilitate and reduce the **cost of an external assessment** performed shortly afterward. But the results should not communicate assurances about the outcome of the external assessment, although the report may give recommendations to enhance IAA practices. Moreover, the periodic internal assessment may be the self-assessment part of a **self-assessment with independent validation**.
- After an ongoing or periodic internal assessment, **conclusions** about **performance** should be drawn and **follow-up** should ensure improvements are made.
- Those conducting internal assessments generally should report directly to the CAE, who should establish a **structure for reporting results** that maintains credibility and objectivity.
- **At least annually**, the CAE reports results, action plans, and implementation information to the board and **shares information** with appropriate parties outside The IIA, e.g., senior management and external auditors.

b. ***PRACTICE ADVISORY 1311-2: ESTABLISHING MEASURES (QUANTITATIVE METRICS AND QUALITATIVE ASSESSMENTS) TO SUPPORT REVIEWS OF INTERNAL AUDIT ACTIVITY PERFORMANCE***

1. *Introduction – Standard 1310 provides that internal audit activities should adopt a **process to monitor and assess the overall effectiveness of its quality program**. The process should include both internal and external assessments. PA 1311-1 suggests using the **analysis of performance measures** as an element in conducting these internal reviews.*

   *In addition to **compliance** with the Standards, audit activity **performance measures** may include the following: level of contribution to the improvement of risk management and control and governance processes, achievement of key goals and objectives assigned, evaluation of progress against audit activity plan, improved staff productivity, increased cost efficiency of the audit process, increased number of action plans for process improvements, adequate engagement planning and supervision, effectiveness in meeting the needs of stakeholders, sufficiency of quality assurance reviews, etc.*

2. *Establishing the Performance Measurement Process – To establish effective performance measures, the CAE should **establish a process** that:*
   - ***Identifies critical performance categories** (e.g., internal stakeholder satisfaction). This advisory suggests the use of the following categories:*
     - *Stakeholder satisfaction*
     - *Internal audit processes*
     - *Innovation and capabilities*
   - *Identifies performance category **strategies and measurements.** Strategies should be pursued in a manner that complies with the Standards, other appropriate professional standards, and applicable laws and regulations, as well as ensuring stakeholder satisfaction. The use of performance measures can be an element of the internal audit activity's **internal assessment process** to comply with the Standards.*
   - *Provides a process for performance **measures** to be routinely **monitored, analyzed, and reported**.*

   *The CAE should ensure that the **measures used are appropriate** for their activity's size and their applicable industry, country, national laws and regulations, and operating environment. Performance measures should be **specific to the organization**, and the CAE is cautioned against relying on general measures that are not meaningful to the specific audit activity. Examples of measurements that could be considered important to the CAEs are listed in Exhibit A at the end of this practice advisory.*

3. *Identifying Critical Performance Categories – As noted above, the CAE should identify key performance measurement categories such as stakeholder satisfaction, audit processes, and innovation and capabilities of internal audit.*

   ***Stakeholders** could include the audit committee, executive management, external government bodies and regulators, and the external auditors. **Audit processes** could include risk assessment, planning, and audit methodologies. **Innovation and capabilities** could include effective use of technology, training, and industry knowledge.*

4. ***Identifying Performance Category Strategies and Measurements*** – *The IIA Standards, other applicable professional standards, the corporate and internal audit activity strategic plans, laws and regulations, and the internal audit activity charter and mission will provide an effective* ***foundation for determining the appropriate strategies*** *for each category of performance. Performance category strategies and measurements are based on this foundation and an analysis of stakeholder satisfaction.*

   The figure below provides a pictorial representation that outlines performance category examples:

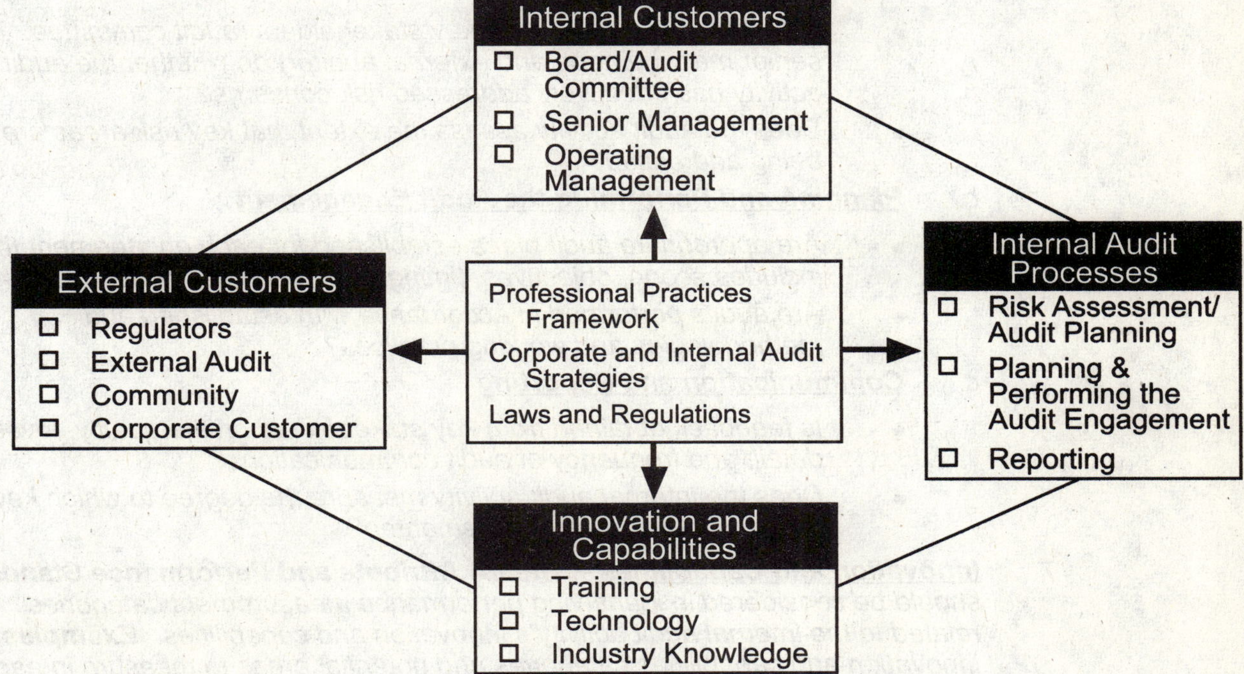

5. ***Internal and External Stakeholders*** – *Typically, the* ***key stakeholders (customers)*** *for the internal audit activity are divided into internal and external stakeholders.*

   - ***Internal stakeholders*** *may include the board/audit committee and senior and operating management.*
   - ***External stakeholders*** *may include regulators and the external audit.*

   The CAE should identify all ***relevant stakeholders*** *and the products and services that are important or should be important to each stakeholder. The CAE should perform an assessment of their* ***current level of satisfaction*** *(and corresponding priorities) and any* ***identified gaps****. Assessments can be performed via interviews, facilitated sessions, and/or questionnaires. As gaps are identified, the CAE is encouraged to develop an appropriate* ***action plan****. The satisfaction among stakeholders may need to be reconciled and validated.*

   Considerations in identifying relevant stakeholders and their satisfaction include:

   - *The* ***extent of regulation*** *for the organization and/or audit activity*
   - *The* ***relationship*** *with the key internal and external stakeholders*
   - *The* ***nature of the organization*** *(publicly vs. privately held, for example)*

6. ***Internal Audit Processes*** – ***The IIA Performance Standards*** *should be considered in identifying performance measurement categories in internal audit processes. Additionally, key deliverables required by the* ***internal audit charter*** *should be considered. The feedback and measurement mechanisms could be customized to gather information relating to management consulting engagements (which may not necessarily follow the same 'processes' as audits) and for fraud investigation services, if these are included in the internal audit department's charter.* ***Examples*** *of internal audit process categories and potential areas to measure in each category are*

   a. ***Risk Assessment/Audit Planning***

      - *Is feedback obtained from key stakeholders (audit committee, senior management, and external auditor) on whether the audit activity has effectively addressed risk concerns?*
      - *Does the audit activity assess the extent that key risk areas are being addressed?*

   b. ***Planning and Performing the Audit Engagement***

      - *Are appropriate audit plans established for each engagement that includes scope, objectives, timing, and resource allocations?*
      - *Are audits performed in accordance with established audit methodologies and working practices?*

   c. ***Communication and Reporting***

      - *Is feedback obtained from key stakeholders on the quality, level of detail, and frequency of audit communications?*
      - *Does the internal audit activity measure the degree to which key recommendations are implemented?*

7. ***Innovation and Capabilities*** – ***The IIA Attribute and Performance Standards*** *should be considered in identifying performance measurement categories related to the internal audit activity's innovation and capabilities.* ***Examples*** *of innovation and capabilities categories and potential areas to measure in each category are*

   a. ***Training***

      - *Are measurements in place to ensure that audit staff receives sufficient training (hours of training per staff, completion by staff of critical training subjects, etc.)?*
      - *Is audit staff satisfaction with training measured?*
      - *Is the number of staff certifications measured?*

   b. ***Use of Technology***

      - *Have goals been established for staff training in the use of technology? Are measures in place to ensure these goals are achieved?*
      - *Have goals been established for using technology to effectively support audit testing and analysis? Are measures in place to ensure these goals are achieved?*

   c. ***Industry Knowledge***

      - *Are measures in place to ensure that the staff has sufficient knowledge of industry, business, operations, and key functions (for example, measuring the completion of orientation sessions, audit projects in key areas, working in the operations)?*

8. ***Implementing an Effective Performance Measurement and Reporting Process*** – *The CAE should establish a measurement process that drives behavior that supports* ***established audit activity goals/objectives*** *and that provides an appropriate* ***assessment of achievement*** *of those goals/objectives. An effective ongoing process would include:*

- ***Performance measures*** *that are aligned with the Standards, key strategic objectives, and applicable laws and regulations. These measures can be both* ***qualitative and quantitative****. Measurement points should be clear, measurable, achievable, realistic goals and/or standards.*
- ***Consistent processes*** *for gathering, summarizing, and analyzing measurement data and providing timely feedback.*
- ***Processes to ensure measures are kept current*** *with changing expectations, conditions, priorities, and objectives.*
- ***Reporting of the results*** *of the measurement process to department management and key stakeholders.*
- ***Annual reporting*** *on the effectiveness of the internal audit activity to the audit committee.*

The figure below provides a visual example of how the performance measurement process could be applied. This example shows performance measurements for the innovation and capability category, including linkage between corporate strategy and audit strategy.

Corporate Strategy

Leverage capability of key systems for key financial and management reporting as well as automating internal controls.

↓

Internal Audit Strategy

Leverage reporting within key systems for auditing applications that support key processes audited.

↓

Performance Category: Innovation and Capability

Category Strategy: Recruit and train staff in systems reporting and audit capabilities.

Measurements:
- Training hours per auditor on related systems
- Number of staff with systems audit experience

For ***additional guidance, resources, and examples****, please see the list of related IIA Standards and Practice Advisories and other resources that follow.*

Related Practice Advisories and Other Resources

Practice Advisory 2100-3: Internal Auditing's Role in the Risk Management Process

Practice Advisory 2140-4: Internal Auditing's Role in Organizations without a Risk Management Process

Other Practice Advisories in this study unit

Additional Resources:

- *The Quality Assessment Manual published by The Institute of Internal Auditors.*
- *Committee of Sponsoring Organizations of the Treadway Commission (COSO), Enterprise Risk Management – Integrated Framework*
- *"20 Questions Directors Should Ask About Internal Audit" by John Fraser and Hugh Lindsay. This paper is available from The IIA. It was sponsored by The IIA Research Foundation, the Canadian Institute of Chartered Accountants, and the Institute of Corporate Directors.*
- *The IIA's Global Auditing Information Network (GAIN). The network enables an organization to compare its audit department's size, experience, expertise, and other metrics against the aggregated averages of similar-sized organizations in its industry.*
- *"A Balanced Scorecard Framework for Internal Auditing Departments" by Mark L. Frigo, Ph.D., CPA, CMA. This book was sponsored by The IIA Research Foundation.*

*The **exhibit** below was extracted and adapted from "A Balanced Scorecard Framework for Internal Auditing Departments." This exhibit provides a point-in-time snapshot of performance measurements that were considered important to a limited number of CAEs. Specific performance measures should be selected that meet the unique needs of the IAA.*

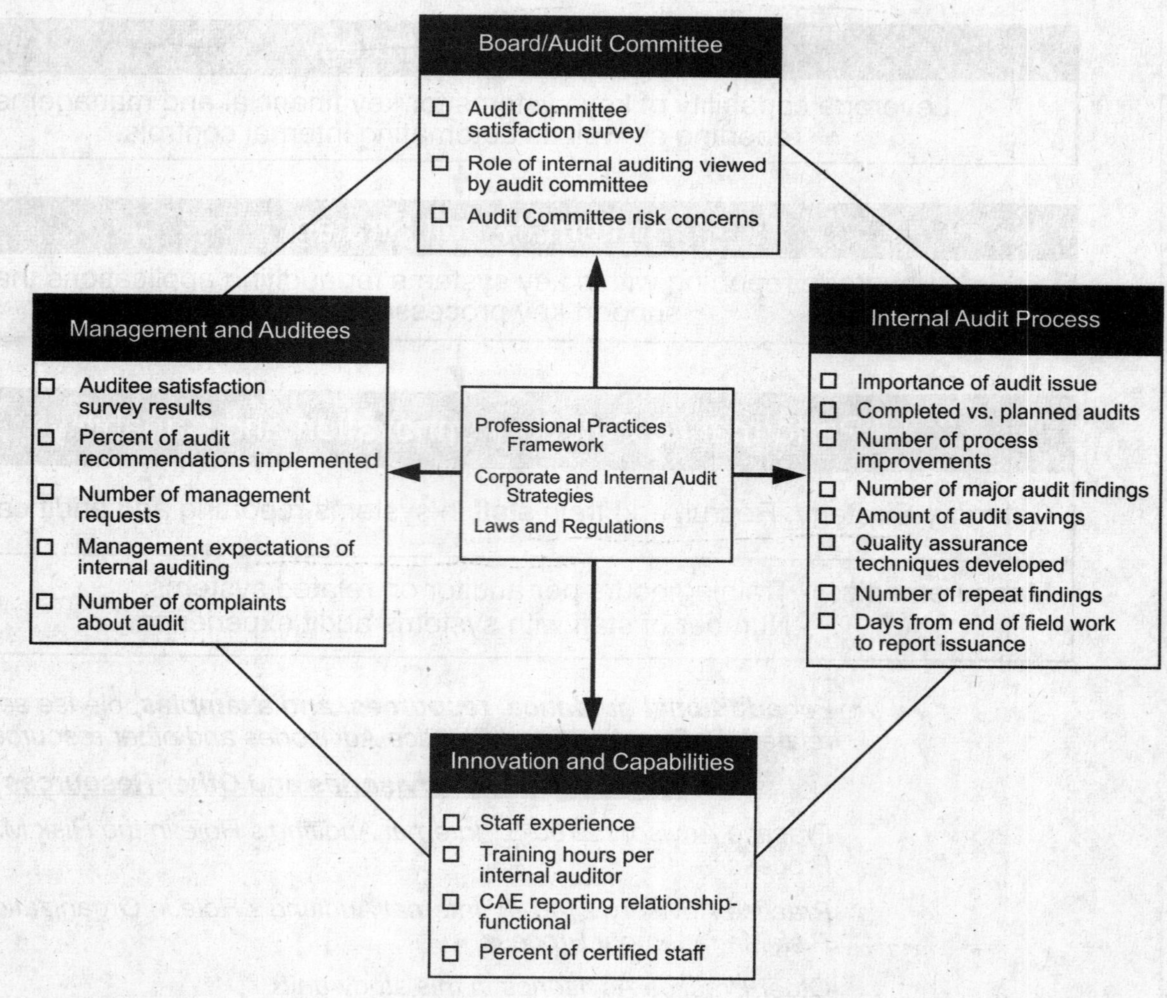

PA Summary

- The **analysis of performance measures** is an element in conducting internal reviews. These measures may include (1) contribution to improving risk management, control, and governance; (2) achievement of key objectives; (3) evaluation of progress against the audit plan; (4) improvement in productivity; (5) cost efficiency of the audit process; (6) number of action plans for process improvements; (7) adequacy of planning and supervision; (8) effectiveness in meeting stakeholder's needs; and (9) sufficiency of quality assurance reviews.
- The **performance measurement process** (1) identifies **critical performance categories**, e.g., (a) stakeholder satisfaction, (b) internal audit processes, and (c) innovation and capabilities; (2) identifies performance category **strategies and measures**; and (3) provides a process for **monitoring, analysis, and reporting** of performance measures. Use of such measures is an element of the **internal assessment**. Strategies should comply with the Standards, other professional standards, and law and regulations, and they should satisfy stakeholders.
- Performance measures should be **appropriate** to the IAA's size, industry, etc., and specific to the organization.
- **Stakeholders** include the audit committee, senior managers, governments, and external auditors. **Audit processes** include risk assessment, planning, and audit methods. **Innovation and capabilities** include effective use of technology, training, and industry knowledge.
- The **foundation for determining strategies and measures** consists of (1) professional standards, (2) strategic plans of the organization and the IAA, (3) laws, (4) regulations, and (5) the IAA's mission and charter. Analysis of stakeholder satisfaction also is a basis for determining strategies and measures for each performance category.
- **Key stakeholders (customers)** are (1) internal (the board, senior managers, and operating managers), and (2) external (regulators, external auditors, the community, and corporations).
- The CAE identifies **relevant stakeholders** and the products and services that should be important to them. The CAE then assesses their **current satisfaction** levels. **Identified satisfaction gaps** lead to developing **action plans**. Considerations relevant to this process are (1) relationships with key stakeholders, (2) nature of the organization, and (3) degree of regulation.
- Considerations for identifying performance measurement categories for **internal audit processes** are The IIA Performance Standards and the IAA's charter. Examples are (1) risk assessment/audit planning, (2) planning and performing the engagement, and (3) communication and reporting.
- The Attribute and Performance Standards are considered in determining performance measurement categories for **innovation and capabilities**. Examples are (1) training, (2) use of technology, and (3) industry knowledge.
- The **measurement process** should motivate behavior supporting established objectives and provide appropriate assessments of achievement.
- **Performance measures** should be consistent with the Standards, strategic objectives, laws, and regulations. They may be qualitative or quantitative.
- The processes for (1) data gathering, summarization, and analysis and (2) providing timely feedback should be **consistent**. Measures also should be kept **current**.
- Results should be **reported** to key stakeholders, and an annual report should be made to the audit committee.

3. Stop and review! You have completed the outline for this subunit. Study multiple-choice question 16 on page 372.

9.5 EXTERNAL ASSESSMENTS

1. A periodic external assessment should cover all of the work of the IAA. It is not limited to assessing the QAIP. This subunit contains one Specific Attribute Standard and two Practice Advisories.
2. ***1312*** ***External Assessments*** *– External assessments should be conducted at least once every five years by a qualified, independent reviewer or review team from outside the organization. The potential need for more frequent external assessments as well as the qualifications and independence of the external reviewer or review team, including any potential conflict of interest, should be discussed by the CAE with the board. Such discussions should also consider the size, complexity, and industry of the organization in relation to the experience of the reviewer or review team.*
   a. ***PRACTICE ADVISORY 1312-1: EXTERNAL ASSESSMENTS***
      1. ***Overview*** *– The CAE is responsible for establishing an internal audit activity whose scope of work includes all activities in the Standards. To ensure this occurs, Standard 1300 requires the CAE to develop and maintain a Quality Assurance and Improvement Program (QAIP). The QAIP should include a periodic external assessment conducted at least once every five years by a qualified, independent reviewer or review team. External assessments may take the form of a comprehensive self-assessment with independent validation (Practice Advisory 1312-2). External assessments should also cover the entire spectrum of audit and consulting work performed by the internal audit activity and should not be limited to assessing its QAIP – see Practice Advisory 1300-1. To achieve optimum benefits from an external assessment, the scope of work should include benchmarking, identification, and reporting of leading practices that could assist the internal audit activity in becoming more efficient and/or effective. This can be accomplished through either an independent review by a qualified, independent reviewer or review team or a self-assessment with independent validation. Nonetheless, the CAE should ensure the scope clearly states the expected deliverables of the external assessment in each case.*
      2. ***General Considerations*** *– External assessments of an internal audit activity should appraise (and may express an* ***opinion*** *as to) the internal audit activity's compliance with the Standards and, as appropriate, should include* ***recommendations*** *for improvement. These reviews can have considerable value to the chief audit executive (CAE) and other members of the internal audit activity, especially when benchmarking and best practices are shared. Only qualified, independent reviewers (Paragraph seven, below) should perform such reviews.*
      3. *On completion of the review, a* ***formal communication*** *should be given to the board (as defined in the Glossary to the Standards) and to senior management.*
      4. ***General Qualifications for External Reviewers*** *– External reviewers, including those who validate self-assessments (Practice Advisory 1312-2), should be* ***independent*** *of the organization and of the internal audit activity. The review team should consist of individuals who are competent in the* ***professional practice of internal auditing*** *and the* ***external assessment process****.*

5. ***Independence*** *– The* ***individual or organization*** *that performs the external assessment, the* ***members of the assessment team****, and any* ***other individuals who participate*** *in the external assessment should be free from any obligation to, or interest in, the organization whose internal audit activity is the subject of the external assessment or the personnel of such organization. Particular matters relating to independence, which should be considered by the CAE, in consultation with the board, in selecting a qualified, independent external reviewer or review team, include:*

   - *Any* ***real or apparent conflicts of interest of firms that provide:***
     - *The audit of the financial statements.*
     - *Significant consulting services in the areas of governance, risk management, financial reporting, internal control, and other related areas.*
     - *Assistance to the internal audit activity. The significance and amount of work performed by the professional service provider should be considered in the deliberation.*
   - *Any real or apparent conflicts of interest of* ***former employees*** *of the organization who would perform the assessment. Consideration should be given to the length of time the individual has been independent of the organization.*
   - *Individuals who perform the assessment must be* ***independent of the organization*** *whose internal audit activity is the subject of the assessment and must not have either a real or an apparent conflict of interest. "Independent of the organization" means not a part of, or under the control of, the organization to which the internal auditing activity belongs. In the selection of a* ***qualified, independent external reviewer or review team,*** *consideration should be given to a possible real or apparent conflict of interest the reviewer may have due to* ***present or past relationships*** *with the organization or its internal auditing activity, including the reviewer's participation in internal quality assessments.*
   - *Individuals in* ***another department*** *of the subject organization or in a* ***related organization****, although organizationally separate from the internal audit activity, are not considered independent for purposes of conducting an external assessment. A "related organization" may be a parent organization; an affiliate in the same group of entities; or an entity with regular oversight, supervision, or quality assurance responsibilities with respect to the subject organization.*
   - ***Real or apparent conflicts involving peer review arrangements.*** *Peer review arrangements between* ***three or more organizations*** *(e.g., within an industry or other affinity group, regional association, or other group of organizations – except as precluded by the "related organization" definition in the previous point) may be structured in a manner that alleviates independence concerns, but care must be taken to ensure that the issue of independence does not arise. Peer reviews* ***between two organizations*** *would not pass the independence test.*
   - *To overcome concerns that there may be an appearance or reality of impairment of independence in instances such as those discussed in this section,* ***one or more independent individuals*** *could be part of the external assessment team – or scheduled to participate subsequently – to* ***independently validate the work*** *of that external assessment team.*

6. **Integrity and Objectivity** – Integrity requires the reviewer(s) to be **honest and candid** within the constraints of confidentiality. Service and the public trust should not be subordinated to personal gain and advantage. Objectivity is a state of mind and a quality that lends value to a reviewer's services. The principle of objectivity imposes the obligation to be **impartial, intellectually honest, and free of conflicts of interest**.

7. **Competence** – Performing and communicating the results of an external assessment require the exercise of **professional judgment**. Accordingly, an individual serving as an external reviewer should:

   - Be a **competent, certified audit professional** – which would enable him/her to provide a qualified assessment – who possesses current, in-depth knowledge of the Standards
   - Be well versed in the **best practices** of the profession
   - Have at least **three years of recent experience** in the practice of internal auditing or related consulting at a management level

   Leaders of independent review teams and external reviewers who independently validate the results of the self-assessment (Practice Advisory 1312-2) should have an **additional level of competence and experience** gained from working previously as a team member on an external quality assessment, successful completion of The IIA's quality assessment training course or similar training, and CAE or comparable senior internal audit management experience.

8. The reviewer(s) should possess **information technology expertise** and relevant **industry experience**. Individuals with expertise in **other specialized areas** may assist the team. For example, specialists in enterprise risk management, statistical sampling, operations monitoring systems, or control self-assessment may participate in certain segments of the assessment.

9. **Senior Management and the Board** – The CAE should involve senior management and the board in selecting the approach and selection of an external quality assessment provider.

10. **Scope of External Assessments** – The external assessment should consist of a broad scope of coverage that includes the following elements of the internal audit activity:

    - **Compliance with** the Standards, The IIA's Code of Ethics, and the internal audit activity's charter, plans, policies, procedures, practices, and applicable legislative and regulatory requirements,
    - **Expectations** of the internal audit activity expressed by the board, executive management, and operational managers,
    - **Integration** of the internal audit activity into the organization's **governance process**, including the attendant relationships between and among the key groups involved in that process,
    - **Tools and techniques** employed by the internal audit activity,
    - Mix of **knowledge, experience, and disciplines** within the staff, including staff focus on process improvement, and
    - Determination as to whether or not the audit activity **adds value** and **improves** the organization's **operations**.

11. **Communicating Results** – The **preliminary results** of the review should be discussed with the CAE during and at the conclusion of the assessment process. **Final results** should be communicated to the CAE or other official who authorized the review for the organization, preferably with copies sent directly to appropriate members of senior management and the board.

12. *The communication* ***may include:***
    - *An* ***opinion*** *on the internal audit activity's* ***compliance with the Standards*** *based on a structured rating process. The term "compliance" means the practices of the internal audit activity, taken as a whole, satisfy the requirements of the Standards. Similarly, "noncompliance" means that the impact and severity of the deficiencies in the practices of the internal audit activity are so significant that they impair the internal audit activity's ability to discharge its responsibilities. The degree of "partial compliance" with individual Standards, if relevant to the overall opinion, should also be expressed in the report on the independent assessment. The expression of an opinion on the results of the external assessment requires the application of* ***sound business judgment, integrity, and due professional care.***
    - *An assessment and evaluation of the use of* ***best practices****, both those observed during the assessment and others potentially applicable to the activity.*
    - ***Recommendations*** *for improvement, if appropriate.*
    - ***Responses from the CAE*** *that include an action plan and implementation dates.*
13. *To provide* ***accountability and transparency****, the CAE should communicate the results of* ***external quality assessments*** *– including specifics of planned remedial actions for significant issues and subsequent information as to accomplishment of those planned actions – to the various stakeholders of the activity, such as senior management, the board, and external auditors.*

PA Summary

- The QAIP should include a **periodic external assessment** conducted at least once every **five years**. An external assessment may be (1) an independent review by a qualified, independent reviewer or review team or (2) a comprehensive **self-assessment with independent validation**. An external assessment also should cover all work by the IAA and is not limited to assessing the QAIP. To achieve optimal benefits, the scope of work should include benchmarking, identification, and reporting of leading practices that could improve the IAA's efficiency or effectiveness. Moreover, the scope must clearly state the **expected deliverables** of any external assessments.
- An external assessment should **appraise** (and may express an **opinion** on) the IAA's **compliance** with the Standards and include **recommendations**.
- **External reviewers** should be **independent** of the organization and the IAA. They should be **competent** in internal auditing and external assessment.
- External reviewers (individual or organizational participants) must not have a **real or an apparent conflict of interest** due to current or past **relationships** with the organization. Matters relating to independence that should be considered include conflicts of **former employees** or of **firms** providing (1) the financial statement audit, (2) significant consulting services, or (3) assistance to the IAA. An individual in another part of the IAA's organization (e.g., a parent or an affiliate) or in a related organization is not independent. Independence means not a part of, or under the control of, the organization.
- **Peer review arrangements** among three organizations (but not between two) may satisfy the independence requirement.
- Given concerns about independence, one or more **independent individuals** could provide separate validation.

PA Summary continued on next page

PA Summary continued

- **Integrity** means honesty and candor limited by confidentiality, with no subordination of service and the public trust to personal gain. **Objectivity** is impartiality, intellectual honesty, and freedom from conflicts of interest.
- Because of the need for **professional judgment**, an external assessor should be a competent, certified, and experienced audit professional who is well versed in best practices. Leaders of independent review teams and external reviewers who independently validate a self-assessment must have an **additional level of competence and experience** gained from prior assessment work, training, and service as a senior internal auditor.
- The reviewer(s) should have **IT and industry experience**, and other **specialists** may be needed.
- **Senior management and the board** should be involved in selecting (1) the approach and (2) the external quality assessment provider.
- The **broad scope** of the review extends to **compliance** with the Standards and Code of Ethics, the IAA's charter, laws, etc. It also extends to (1) the **expectations** of management and the board, (2) integration of the IAA with **the governance process**, (3) tools and techniques, (4) competence (mix of the staff's knowledge, experience and disciplines), and (5) whether the IAA **adds value** and **improves operations**.
- **Preliminary results** of the review are discussed with the CAE. **Final results** are communicated to the CAE, preferably with copies sent directly to appropriate members of senior management and the board.
- The communication **includes an opinion** on **compliance with the Standards**. Compliance means the practices of the IAA, as a whole, satisfy the Standards. Noncompliance means that deficiencies are so significant that they impair the IAA's ability to discharge its responsibilities. The degree of **partial compliance** is expressed if relevant. Expression of an opinion requires **sound business judgment, integrity, and due professional care**. The communication also includes (1) an evaluation of the use of **best practices**, (2) recommendations, and (3) **CAE responses** regarding action plans and implementation dates.
- The **results** of external quality assessments, including specific planned remediation and accomplishment of those actions, should be communicated to stakeholders of the IAA (e.g., senior management, the board, and external auditors) to provide **accountability and transparency**.

b. ***PRACTICE ADVISORY 1312-2: EXTERNAL ASSESSMENT – SELF-ASSESSMENT WITH INDEPENDENT VALIDATION***

1. ***Overview*** *– The CAE is responsible for establishing an internal audit activity whose scope of work includes all activities in the Standards. To ensure that this occurs, Standard 1300 requires that the CAE develop and maintain a Quality Assurance and Improvement Program. The QAIP should include a periodic external assessment, conducted at least once every five years by a qualified, independent reviewer or review team. The external assessment may take the form of a comprehensive self-assessment with independent validation. These external assessments should cover the entire spectrum of audit and consulting work performed by the internal audit activity and should not be limited to assessing its QAIP – see Practice Advisory 1300-1.*

2. ***Self-assessment with Independent Validation*** – *The IIA has taken into account concerns that an external assessment by a* ***qualified, independent reviewer or review team*** *may be troublesome for* ***smaller internal audit activities*** *or that there may be circumstances in other organizations where a full external assessment by an independent team is* ***not deemed appropriate or necessary****. For example, the internal audit activity may (a) be in an industry subject to extensive regulation and/or supervision, (b) be otherwise subject to extensive external oversight and direction relating to governance and internal controls, (c) have been recently subjected to external review(s) and/or consulting services in which there was extensive benchmarking with best practices, or (d) in the judgment of the CAE, the benefits of self-assessment for staff development and the strength of the internal QAIP currently outweigh the benefits of a quality assessment by an external team. In consideration of such circumstances, The IIA has provided an alternative process, a "self-assessment with independent [external] validation," that features*
   - *A* ***comprehensive and fully documented*** *self-assessment process, which should emulate the external assessment process, at least with respect to evaluation of* ***compliance with the Standards****.*
   - *An* ***independent on-site validation*** *by a qualified, independent reviewer.*
   - ***Economical time and resource requirements****; e.g., the primary focus would be on compliance with the Standards.*
   - ***Attention to other areas*** *– such as benchmarking, review, and consultation as to employment of best practices – and interviews with senior and operating management* ***may be reduced****. However, this information is one of the optimum benefits of an external assessment.*
   - *Otherwise, the* ***same requirements and criteria*** *as set forth in Practice Advisory 1312-1 would apply for:*
     - *General considerations*
     - *Qualifications of the external reviewer or review team*
     - *Independence, integrity and objectivity, competence, approval by management and the board, and scope (except for areas such as employment of tools, techniques, other best practices, career development, and value-adding activities)*
     - *Communication of results (including remedial actions and their accomplishment)*
3. ***Senior Management and the Board*** *– The CAE should involve senior management and the board in determining the approach and the selection of the qualified, independent external reviewer or review team who will independently validate the results of the self-assessment.*
4. ***Validation Process*** *– A* ***team under the direction of the CAE*** *should perform and fully document the self-assessment process. The IIA's Quality Assessment Manual contains an outline of the process, including guidance and tools for the self-assessment. A draft report, similar to that for an external assessment, should be prepared including the* ***CAE's judgment on compliance with*** *the Standards.*
5. *A* ***qualified, independent reviewer or review team*** *should perform* ***limited tests of the self-assessment*** *so as to validate the results and express an opinion on the indicated level of the activity's conformity to the Standards. The independent validation should follow the process outlined in The IIA's Quality Assessment Manual or a similar comprehensive process.*
6. *Upon completion of the independent validation, including a rigorous review of the self-assessment team's evaluation of compliance with the Standards and the Code of Ethics:*

- *The qualified, independent external reviewer(s) should* ***review the draft report*** *mentioned in Paragraph four, above, and attempt to reconcile unresolved issues (if any).*
- ***If in agreement*** *with the opinion on compliance with the Standards and Code of Ethics, the qualified, independent external reviewer(s) should* ***add wording*** *(as needed) to the report,* ***concurring*** *with the self-assessment process and opinion and, to the extent deemed appropriate, in the report's findings, conclusions, and recommendations.*
- ***If not in agreement*** *with the evaluation, the qualified independent external reviewer(s) should* ***add dissenting wording*** *to the report, specifying the points of disagreement with it and, to the extent deemed appropriate, with the significant findings, conclusions, recommendations, and opinions in the report.*
- *Alternatively, the qualified, independent external reviewer(s) may prepare a* ***separate independent validation report****, concurring or expressing disagreement as outlined above, to accompany the report of the self-assessment.*
- *The* ***final report(s)*** *of the self-assessment with independent validation should then be signed by the self-assessment team and the qualified, independent external reviewer(s) and issued by the CAE to senior management and the board.*

PA Summary

- **Self-assessment with independent, external validation** is an alternative to full external assessment. It is used when the IAA is small or such an assessment is not appropriate or necessary, for example, if the IAA is in a regulated industry, is otherwise subject to extensive oversight, or has been recently reviewed. This alternative should be comprehensive and fully documented and similar to the **external assessment**, especially regarding compliance with the Standards. Moreover, an **independent, onsite validation** by a qualified, independent reviewer is required. However, the process has more **economical time and resource requirements**, and attention to certain **other areas** (e.g., best practices and interviews with management) may be reduced. Otherwise, the guidance in **PA 1312-1** applies.
- **Senior management and the board** should be involved in determining the approach and selecting the external validator.
- A **team directed by the CAE** performs the self assessment. A key resource is The IIA's Quality Resource Manual.
- A **draft report** should be prepared. It should be similar to that for an external assessment and include the **CAE's judgment on compliance with the Standards**.
- The qualified, independent reviewer (or team) performs **limited tests** to (1) validate the self-assessment results and (2) **express an opinion** on compliance with the Standards. The validation process should follow that in The IIA's Quality Assessment Manual or a similar one.
- After completing the validation process, the qualified, independent external reviewer(s) **reviews the draft report** and reconciles unresolved issues (if any). The reviewer then adds concurring or dissenting language or prepares a separate report. The **final report(s)** should be signed by the appropriate parties and issued to senior management and the board.

3. Stop and review! You have completed the outline for this subunit. Study multiple-choice questions 17 through 19 on page 373.

9.6 REPORTING

1. The final step in the external assessment process is reporting results and responding to them. This subunit contain three Specific Attribute Standards and two Practice Advisories.
2. ***1320*** ***Reporting on the Quality Program*** – *The chief audit executive should communicate the results of external assessments to the board.*
   a. ***PRACTICE ADVISORY 1320-1: REPORTING ON THE QUALITY PROGRAM***
      1. *Upon completion of an external assessment, the review team should issue a **formal report** containing an opinion on the internal audit activity's **compliance** with the International Standards for the Professional Practice of Internal Auditing (Standards) (see Practice Advisory 1312-1). The report should also address compliance with the internal audit activity's **charter and other applicable standards** and include appropriate **recommendations** for improvement. The report should be addressed to the person or organization requesting the assessment. The chief audit executive should prepare a **written action plan** in response to the significant comments and recommendations contained in the report of external assessment. Appropriate **follow-up** is also the chief audit executive's responsibility.*
      2. *The evaluation of compliance with the Standards is a critical component of an external assessment. The review team should acknowledge the Standards in order to evaluate and opine on the internal audit activity's compliance. However, as noted in Practice Advisory 1310-1, there are **additional criteria** that should be considered in evaluating the performance of an internal audit activity.*

PA Summary

- The result of the external assessment is a **formal report** expressing an opinion on **compliance with the Standards**. The report also addresses compliance with the charter and other applicable standards and states recommendations. The CAE's responsibility is to prepare a **written action plan** in response and to follow up.

3. ***1330*** ***Use of "Conducted in Accordance with the Standards"*** – *Internal auditors are encouraged to report that their activities are "conducted in accordance with the International Standards for the Professional Practice of Internal Auditing." However, internal auditors may use the statement only if assessments of the quality improvement program demonstrate that the internal audit activity is in compliance with the Standards.*
   a. ***PRACTICE ADVISORY 1330-1: USE OF "CONDUCTED IN ACCORDANCE WITH THE STANDARDS"***
      1. ***General Considerations*** – *External and internal assessments of an internal audit activity should be performed to appraise and **express an opinion** as to the internal audit activity's compliance with the International Standards for the Professional Practice of Internal Auditing (Standards), and the Code of Ethics and, as appropriate, should include **recommendations** for improvement.*

2. ***Use of Compliance Phrase*** – *The compliance phrase to be used may be: "in compliance with the Standards," or "in conformity to the Standards," or "in accordance with the Standards." Use of the compliance phrase requires an external assessment* ***at least once*** *during* ***each five-year period****, along with* ***periodic internal assessments****, which have concluded that the internal audit activity is in compliance with the Standards and Code of Ethics. Initial use of the compliance phrase is not appropriate until an* ***external review****, performed within the past five years, has demonstrated that the internal audit activity is in compliance with the Standards and the Code of Ethics. Instances of noncompliance that affect the overall scope or operation of the internal audit activity, including failure to obtain an external assessment by January 1, 2007, should be* ***disclosed to senior management and the board.***
3. *Prior to the internal audit activity's use of the compliance phrase, any instances of* ***noncompliance*** *that have been disclosed by a* ***quality assessment*** *(internal or external), which impair the internal audit activity's ability to discharge its responsibilities*
   - *Should be adequately remedied,*
   - *The* ***remedial actions*** *should be documented and reported to the relevant assessor(s), to obtain* ***concurrence*** *that the noncompliance has been adequately remedied, and*
   - *The remedial actions and agreement of the relevant assessor(s) therewith should be reported to* ***senior management and the board.***

PA Summary

- Assessments of the IAA are performed to **express an opinion** on compliance with the Standards and Code of Ethics and to make **recommendations**.
- **Use of the compliance phrase** requires an **external assessment** at least once every five years and **periodic internal assessments** that have concluded that the IAA is in compliance. Initial use of the phrase is not appropriate until an **external review** within the past five years has demonstrated compliance. **Noncompliance** affecting the overall scope or operation of the IAA should be disclosed to the board and senior management.
- Prior to the use of the phrase, **noncompliance** disclosed by a quality assessment that impairs the IAA's ability to perform its duties should be remedied. **Remedial action** should be documented, the **assessor's** concurrence should be obtained, and the action and concurrence should be reported to **senior management and the board**.

4. ***1340*** ***Disclosure of Noncompliance*** – *Although the internal audit activity should achieve full compliance with the Standards and internal auditors with the Code of Ethics, there may be instances in which full compliance is not achieved. When noncompliance impacts the overall scope or operation of the internal audit activity, disclosure should be made to senior management and the board.*
5. Stop and review! You have completed the outline for this subunit. Study multiple-choice questions 20 through 24 beginning on page 374.

9.7 BENCHMARKING

1. **Benchmarking** is a tool used in the implementation of a **total quality management approach**. This approach applies to the business or operating processes of an organization and to other activities, such as internal or external assessments of the internal audit activity. The following outline describes techniques for improving the effectiveness of benchmarking, which is a means of helping organizations with productivity management and business process reengineering.

   a. **Best practices.** Benchmarking is a continuous evaluation of the practices of the best organizations in their class, and the adaptation of processes to reflect the best of these practices. It entails analysis and measurement of key outputs against those of the best organizations. This procedure also involves identifying the underlying key actions and causes that contribute to the **performance difference**.

      1) Benchmarking is an ongoing process that entails **quantitative and qualitative measurement** of the difference between the performance of an activity and the performance by the best in the world. The benchmark organization need not be a competitor. It may even be another activity in the same organization.

   b. The first phase in the benchmarking process is to **select and prioritize benchmarking projects**.

      1) An organization must understand its **critical success factors** and **business environment** to identify key business processes and drivers and to develop parameters defining what processes to benchmark.

         a) The **criteria for selecting what to benchmark** arise from the reasons for a process and its importance to the entity's mission, values, and strategy. These reasons relate to satisfaction of end users or customer needs.

   c. The next phase is to organize **benchmarking teams**. A team organization permits an equitable division of labor, participation by those responsible for implementing changes, and inclusion of a variety of functional expertise and work experience.

      1) **Team members** should have (a) knowledge of the function to be benchmarked, (b) respected positions in the organization, (c) good communication skills, (d) teaming skills, (e) motivation to innovate and to support cross-functional problem solving, and (f) project management skills.

   d. The benchmarking team must thoroughly investigate and document the organization's **internal processes**. The organization is a series of processes, not a fixed structure.

      1) A **process** is a network of related and independent activities joined by their outputs. One way to determine the primary characteristics of a process is to trace the path a request for a product or service takes through the organization.

      2) The team also must develop a **family of measures** that are true indicators of process performance. It also develops a **process taxonomy**, a set of process elements, measures, and phrases that describes the process to be benchmarked.

   e. **Researching and identifying** best-in-class performance is often the most difficult phase. The critical steps are (1) setting up databases, (2) choosing information-gathering methods (internal sources, external public domain sources, and original research are the possible approaches), (3) formatting questionnaires (lists of questions prepared in advance), and (4) selecting benchmarking partners.

f. The **data analysis** phase entails (1) identifying performance gaps, (2) understanding the reasons they exist, and (3) prioritizing the key activities that will facilitate the behavioral and process changes needed to implement recommendations.

1) Sophisticated statistical and other methods may be needed when the study involves many variables, testing of assumptions, or presentation of quantified results.

g. Leadership is most important in the **implementation** phase of the benchmarking process because the team must be able to justify its recommendations. Moreover, the process improvement teams must manage the implementation of approved changes.

2. A study cited in *Sawyer's Internal Auditing* (5th ed.), page 278, describes **best practices for an internal auditing activity**:

a. Obtaining an understanding of customers (auditees) so as to satisfy their needs
b. Treating the IAA as if it were on a service line of a for-profit entity
c. Applying quality principles and developing performance measures
d. Auditing operations as well as controls to improve entity performance
e. Serving as an agent for change in the organization
f. Communicating regularly within the IAA and with customers (auditees) and shareholders
g. Integrating information technology and auditing
h. Emphasizing the professional satisfaction of the internal auditors

3. Stop and review! You have completed the outline for this subunit. Study multiple-choice questions 25 through 28 beginning on page 375.

9.8 STUDY UNIT 9 SUMMARY

1. Internal auditors evaluate and improve risk management, control, and governance. External auditors ordinarily perform an examination sufficient to express an opinion on the financial statements. They judge the adequacy of procedures and evidence. The board oversees the work of external auditors, but the CAE actually coordinates the work with that of the IAA. The work of internal auditors should not be duplicative. The objective is maximum coordination and efficiency.

2. Internal auditors should have some involvement in selecting or retaining the external auditors and in defining the scope of work. A policy should establish that the periodic request for external audit services is a normal activity, not a sign of dissatisfaction. Absent such a policy, the internal auditor should facilitate development of appropriate procurement policies.

3. The CAE implements processes (a QAIP) to give reasonable assurance to stakeholders that the IAA (a) performs in accordance with its charter, the Standards, and the Code of Ethics; (b) operates efficiently and effectively; and (c) is perceived as adding value and improving operations. These processes include (a) supervision, (b) internal and external assessments, and (c) monitoring of quality assurance. The QAIP embraces all facets of the IAA. Its processes are performed or supervised by the CAE. A large entity should have a formal, independent QAIP headed by an audit executive.

4. Monitoring of quality programs extends to assessments of all work done by the IAA. These assessments include (a) routine supervision and testing or performance and (b) periodic validation of compliance with the Standards. Monitoring also includes measuring and analyzing performance. Internal assessment should be part of daily supervision, review, and measurement of the IAA. At least one external assessment should be performed every five years. When an external assessment is performed, no periodic assessment is required.

5. Ongoing internal assessments are reported of routine activities. They are reflected in, for example, (a) supervision, (b) checklists, (c) feedback, and (d) budgets. Periodic internal assessments are nonroutine reviews and tests of compliance, efficiency, and effectiveness.
6. The performance measurement process (a) identifies critical performance categories, e.g., (1) stakeholder satisfaction, (2) audit processes, and (3) innovation and capabilities; (b) identifies performance category strategies and measures; and (c) provides a process for monitoring, analysis, and reporting of performance measures. Use of such measures is an element of the internal assessment. Performance measures should be appropriate to the IAA's size, industry, etc., and specific to the organization.
7. An external assessment should express an opinion on compliance with the Standards and include recommendations. External reviewers should be independent. They should be competent in internal auditing and the external assessment process. External reviewers must not have a real or an apparent conflict of interest. An individual in another part of the IAA's organization or in related organizations is not independent.
8. The result of the external assessment is a formal report expressing an opinion on compliance with the Standards. The report also addresses compliance with the charter and other standards and states recommendations. The CAE's responsibility is to prepare a written action plan in response and to follow up.
9. Use of the compliance phrase requires an external assessment at least once every five years and periodic internal assessments that have demonstrated compliance. Noncompliance affecting the overall scope or operation of the IAA should be disclosed to the board and senior management.
10. Benchmarking is a continuous evaluation of the practices of the best organizations in their class, and the adaptation of processes to reflect the best of these practices. It entails analysis and measurement of key outputs against those of the best organizations. This procedure also involves identifying the underlying key actions and causes that contribute to the performance difference.

QUESTIONS

9.1 Coordination

1. Which of the following is a false statement about the relationship between internal auditors and external auditors?

A. Oversight of the work of external auditors is the responsibility of the chief audit executive.

B. Sufficient meetings should be scheduled between internal and external auditors to assure timely and efficient completion of the work.

C. Internal and external auditors may exchange engagement communications and management letters.

D. Internal auditors may provide engagement work programs and working papers to external auditors.

Answer (A) is correct. *(CIA, adapted)*

REQUIRED: The false statement about the relationship between internal and external auditors.

DISCUSSION: Oversight of the work of the independent outside auditor, including coordination with the IAA, is generally the responsibility of the board. Actual coordination should be the responsibility of the CAE. However, the board in the exercise of its oversight role may request that the CAE assess the performance of the external auditors. Ordinarily, this assessment is made in the context of the CAE's function of coordinating internal and external auditing activities (PA 2050-1).

Answer (B) is incorrect because coordination between internal and external auditors involves, among other things, sufficient meetings to ensure coordination of engagement work and efficient and timely completion of engagement activities and to determine whether observations and recommendations from work performed to date require that the scope of planned work be adjusted. Answer (C) is incorrect because coordination between internal and external auditors involves, among other things, exchange of internal audit communications and external auditors' management letters. Answer (D) is incorrect because coordination between internal and external auditors involves, among other things, access to each other's work programs and working papers.

2. In recent years, which two factors have changed the relationship between internal auditors and external auditors so that internal auditors are partners rather than subordinates?

A. The increasing liability of external auditors and the increasing professionalism of internal auditors.

B. The increasing professionalism of internal auditors and the evolving economics of external auditing.

C. The use of computerized accounting systems and the evolving economics of external auditing.

D. The globalization of audit entities and the increased reliance on computerized accounting systems.

Answer (B) is correct. *(CIA, adapted)*

REQUIRED: The two factors that have changed the relationship between internal and external auditors.

DISCUSSION: An external auditor may decide that the internal auditors' work will have an effect on audit procedures if (1) that work is relevant, (2) it is efficient to consider how the work may affect the audit, and (3) the external auditor determines that the internal auditors are sufficiently competent and objective. Hence, internal auditors may be viewed as partners in the audit because of their increasing professionalism. Moreover, the evolving economics of external auditing creates an imperative to control audit fees by eliminating duplication of effort and monitoring more closely the hours worked by external auditors.

Answer (A) is incorrect because increasing liability makes external auditors less likely to determine that the work of the internal auditors has an effect on the external audit procedures. Answer (C) is incorrect because the use of computerized accounting systems would have no significant effect on the relative roles of external and internal auditors. Answer (D) is incorrect because the globalization of audit entities would have no significant effect on the relative roles of external and internal auditors.

Questions 3 and 4 are based on the following information. You are the chief audit executive of a parent organization that has foreign subsidiaries. Independent external audits performed for the parent are not conducted by the same firm that conducts the foreign subsidiary audits. Because the internal audit activity occasionally provides direct assistance to both external firms, you have copies of audit programs and selected working papers produced by each firm.

---

3. The foreign subsidiary's auditors would like to rely on some of the work performed by the parent organization's audit firm, but they need to review the working papers first. They have asked you for copies of the working papers of the parent organization's audit firm. What is the most appropriate response to the foreign subsidiary's auditors?

A. Provide copies of the working papers without notifying the parent's audit firm.

B. Notify the parent's auditors of the situation and request that they either provide the working papers or authorize you to do so.

C. Provide copies of the working papers and notify the parent's audit firm that you have done so.

D. Refuse to provide the working papers under any circumstances.

Answer (B) is correct. *(CIA, adapted)*

REQUIRED: The proper response to a request by one external audit firm for another external audit firm's working papers held by the internal auditors.

DISCUSSION: Coordination of internal and external auditing efforts involves access to each other's work programs and working papers. However, such access carries with it the responsibility to respect the confidentiality of those programs and working papers (PA 2050-1). Hence, the internal auditors should seek the approval of the parent's external auditors before granting access to their working papers to the external auditors of the subsidiaries.

Answer (A) is incorrect because the working papers are the property of the parent's external auditors, and their confidentiality should be respected. Answer (C) is incorrect because the external auditors should give prior authorization for the release of their working papers. Answer (D) is incorrect because the CAE has the responsibility to ensure proper coordination with external auditors.

4. The foreign subsidiary's external audit firm wants to rely on an audit of a function at the parent organization. The audit was conducted by the internal audit activity. To place reliance on the work performed, the foreign subsidiary's auditors have requested copies of the working papers. What is the most appropriate response to the foreign subsidiary's auditors?

A. Provide copies of the working papers.

B. Ask the parent's audit firm if it is appropriate to release the working papers.

C. Ask the board for permission to release the working papers.

D. Refuse to provide the working papers under any circumstances.

Answer (A) is correct. *(CIA, adapted)*

REQUIRED: The proper response to a request by external auditors for the internal auditors' working papers.

DISCUSSION: Internal and external auditing efforts should be coordinated to ensure adequate coverage and to minimize duplication of effort. Coordination involves access to each other's work programs and working papers. Access to the internal auditors' work programs and working papers should be given to the external auditors in order for them to be satisfied as to the propriety, for external audit purposes, of relying on the internal auditors' work (PA 2050-1).

Answer (B) is incorrect because the working papers are the property of the organization. The responsibility of the CAE is to maintain the security of the working papers and to coordinate efforts with the external auditors. Thus, the decision belongs not to the parent's external auditors but to the CAE. Answer (C) is incorrect because access to working papers by external auditors should be subject to the approval of the CAE (PA 2330.A1-1). Answer (D) is incorrect because the CAE should ensure proper coordination with external auditors by, among other things, granting the external auditors access to the internal auditors' working papers.

5. To improve their efficiency, internal auditors may rely upon the work of external auditors if it is

A. Performed after the internal auditing work.

B. Primarily concerned with operational objectives and activities.

C. Coordinated with internal auditing work.

D. Conducted in accordance with the Code of Ethics.

Answer (C) is correct. *(CIA, adapted)*

REQUIRED: The circumstances in which internal auditors may rely upon the work of external auditors.

DISCUSSION: In coordinating the work of internal auditors with the work of external auditors, the CAE should ensure that work to be performed by internal auditors does not duplicate the work of the external auditors that can be relied upon for purposes of internal auditing coverage. To the extent that professional and organizational reporting responsibilities allow, internal auditors should perform services in a manner that allows for maximum coordination and efficiency (PA 2050-1).

Answer (A) is incorrect because duplication of effort may result if the external audit is performed after the internal auditing engagement. Answer (B) is incorrect because internal auditing encompasses both financial and operational objectives and activities. Thus, internal auditing coverage could also be provided by external audit work that included primarily financial objectives and activities. Answer (D) is incorrect because external auditing work is conducted in accordance with auditing standards generally accepted in the host country.

6. Which of the following is not a true statement about the relationship between internal auditors and external auditors?

A. External auditors must assess the competence and objectivity of internal auditors.

B. There may be periodic meetings between internal and external auditors to discuss matters of mutual interest.

C. There may be an exchange of engagement communications and management letters.

D. Internal auditors may provide engagement work programs and working papers to external auditors.

Answer (A) is correct. *(CIA, adapted)*

REQUIRED: The true statement about the relationship between internal auditors and external auditors.

DISCUSSION: The external auditor assesses the objectivity and competence of the internal auditors if their activities are relevant to the external audit and it is efficient to consider how that work may affect the nature, timing, and extent of external audit procedures. If the internal auditors are found to be sufficiently competent and objective, the external auditor then considers how their work will affect the external audit. Thus, external auditors are not required to assess the competence and objectivity of internal auditors.

Answer (B) is incorrect because the relationship should involve a sufficient number of meetings (PA 2050-1). Answer (C) is incorrect because the relationship should involve reasonable mutual access to engagement communications and management letters (PA 2050-1). Answer (D) is incorrect because the relationship should involve reasonable mutual access to engagement work programs and working papers (PA 2050-1).

7. If a department outside of the internal audit activity is responsible for reviewing a function or process, the internal auditors should:

A. Consider the work of the other department when assessing the function or process.

B. Ignore the work of the other department and proceed with an independent audit.

C. Reduce the scope of the audit since the work has already been performed by the other department.

D. Yield the responsibility for assessing the function or process to the other department.

Answer (A) is correct. *(CIA, adapted)*

REQUIRED: The response of the internal auditors if a department outside of the IAA reviews a function or process.

DISCUSSION: The chief audit executive should share information and coordinate activities with other internal and external providers of relevant assurance and consulting services to ensure proper coverage and minimize duplication of efforts (Standard 2220). This standard applies not only to external auditors but also to other "providers," such as regulatory bodies (e.g., governmental auditors) and certain of the organization's other subunits (e.g., a health and safety department). Review and testing of the other department's work may reduce necessary audit coverage of the function or process.

Answer (B) is incorrect because concentrating on the function or process might lead to a duplication of efforts. Answer (C) is incorrect because the internal auditor cannot rely on the work of others without verifying the results. Answer (D) is incorrect because the internal audit activity's overall responsibility for assessing the function or process is not affected by the other department's coverage.

8. Assessments of the independence of an organization's external auditors should:

A. Be carried out only when the external auditor is appointed.

B. Not include any participation by the internal audit activity.

C. Include the internal audit activity only when the external auditor is appointed.

D. Include the internal audit activity at the time of appointment and regularly thereafter.

Answer (D) is correct. *(CIA, adapted)*

REQUIRED: The true statement about assessments of the independence of an organization's external auditors.

DISCUSSION: The internal auditor's participation in the selection, evaluation, or retention of the organization's external auditors may vary from no role in the process to advising management or the audit committee, assistance or participation in the process, management of the process, or auditing the process. Because internal auditors must "share information and coordinate activities with other internal and external providers of relevant assurance and consulting services," it is advisable for internal auditors to have some role or involvement in the selection or retention of the external auditors and in the definition of scope of work (PA 2050-2). Internal auditors (1) determine how external auditors are monitored and (2) assess their (a) compliance with agreements and (b) independence.

Answer (A) is incorrect because the independence assessment should be carried out at least annually. Answer (B) is incorrect because the internal audit activity should have some involvement in selecting and retaining the external auditors and in defining the scope of work. Answer (C) is incorrect because the internal audit activity should have been involved in the selection process prior to the external auditor's appointment.

9.2 External Audit Services

9. Appropriate policies for selection or retention of external audit services should consider addressing the following attributes except

A. Nature and type of services covered by the policy.

B. The need to limit negotiations to the current external auditor.

C. Regulatory or other governing requirements unique to specific industries or countries.

D. Participants or members of the selection and evaluation team.

Answer (B) is correct. *(Publisher, adapted)*

REQUIRED: The attribute not addressed in policies for the selection or retention of external audit services.

DISCUSSION: Policies for selection or retention of external audit services should not limit such procurement to the current external auditor. A decision to request proposals is not necessarily a signal of dissatisfaction with the current service providers. In addition to the other answers listed, the procurement policy should address whether board or audit committee approval is required, duration of the contract, frequency of request for services or decision to retain existing service providers, critical or primary criteria that should be considered, and limitations on service fees and procedures (PA 2050-2).

Answer (A) is incorrect because the nature and type of services covered should be addressed. Answer (C) is incorrect because regulatory or other governing requirements unique to specific industries or countries should be addressed. Answer (D) is incorrect because participants or members of the selection and evaluation team should be addressed.

10. Why should internal auditors help develop policies for the selection, evaluation, or retention of external auditor services other than for an external audit?

A. So that the present external audit service providers do not view a decision to request proposals as a signal that the organization is dissatisfied with present services.

B. Such services cannot be subject to any other existing procurement policies of the organization.

C. Internal auditors must coordinate activities with external providers of assurance services.

D. It is required in the charter of the internal audit function.

Answer (C) is correct. *(Publisher, adapted)*

REQUIRED: The reason internal auditors help to develop policies to acquire external auditor services.

DISCUSSION: PA 2050-2 covers acquisition of external audit services. External nonaudit services consist of tax services; consulting services; outsourcing or cosourcing services; valuation, appraisal, and actuarial services; temporary services such as recruiting, bookkeeping, and technology services; special services, such as agreed-upon service engagements; and legal services provided by external audit firms. Because the Standards require internal auditors to "share information and coordinate activities with other internal and external providers of relevant assurance and consulting services," it is advisable for internal auditors to have some role or involvement in the selection or retention of the external auditors and in the definition of scope of work.

Answer (A) is incorrect because a decision to request proposals is not necessarily a signal of dissatisfaction with the current service providers. Answer (B) is incorrect because general procurement policies may affect all procurement within an organization. Answer (D) is incorrect because the internal audit charter usually does not specify detailed policies.

11. Services other than financial statement audits may be offered by external audit firms (e.g., tax services, external legal services). Acquisition of these other services is addressed in

A. Board policies.

B. Preliminary survey.

C. Administrative policy and procedure manuals.

D. Policies of the internal audit activity.

Answer (A) is correct. *(Publisher, adapted)*

REQUIRED: The source of guidance for acquisition of external audit services other than financial statement audits.

DISCUSSION: In addition to external financial statement audit services, board policies also may address the acquisition of other services offered by external audit firms. Those services may include (1) tax services, (2) consulting services, (3) internal audit outsourcing services, (4) valuation services, (5) temporary services, and (6) legal services provided by external audit firms (PA 2050-2).

Answer (B) is incorrect because the preliminary survey is a stage of an audit engagement. Answer (C) is incorrect because administrative policy and procedure manuals provide guidelines and standards for the operation of the internal audit activity. Answer (D) is incorrect because the CAE does not make decisions about acquisition of external audit services.

12. Written agreements for external audit engagements are to be signed by the

A. Chief audit executive and internal auditors.

B. Service provider and engagement client.

C. Audit committee and chief audit executive.

D. Board of directors and chief audit executive.

Answer (B) is correct. *(Publisher, adapted)*

REQUIRED: The parties who sign the written agreement for external audit engagements.

DISCUSSION: PA 2050-2 addresses the acquisition of external audit services. It states that service arrangements for external auditing should be documented in a written agreement signed by both the service provider and the engagement client.

Answer (A) is incorrect because the CAE and internal auditors represent the engagement client. The agreement should be signed by representatives of the engagement client and the service provider. Answer (C) is incorrect because the audit committee and the CAE represent the engagement client. The agreement should be signed by representatives of the engagement client and the service provider. Answer (D) is incorrect because the board of directors and the CAE represent the engagement client. The agreement should be signed by representatives of the engagement client and the service provider.

13. During a two-phased screening process for selecting a service provider for external auditing, the second request for information is most likely to ask for

A. The firm's special expertise.

B. Pricing for services.

C. Industry experience.

D. Office handling the engagement.

Answer (B) is correct. *(Publisher, adapted)*

REQUIRED: The information most likely sought in a second request.

DISCUSSION: A two-phased request consists of the initial information request and a second request for information that is more specific. The initial request is for general information, including history of the firm, size of the firm, resources available, firm philosophy and audit approach, special expertise, local or servicing office that would handle the engagement, related industry experience, and biographies of key team members that would be assigned to the engagement. The second request includes detailed itemization of deliverables expected and key target dates, pricing for services, and meetings for presentations by the candidates to the selection committee (PA 2050-2).

Answer (A) is incorrect because the firm's special expertise is information normally sought in a first request. Answer (C) is incorrect because industry experience is information normally sought in a first request. Answer (D) is incorrect because the office handling the engagement is information normally sought in a first request.

9.3 Quality Assurance and Improvement Programs

14. A quality assurance and improvement program of an internal audit activity provides reasonable assurance that internal auditing work is performed in accordance with its charter. Which of the following are designed to provide feedback on the effectiveness of an internal audit activity?

I. Proper supervision
II. Proper training
III. Internal reviews
IV. External reviews

A. I, II, and III only.
B. II, III, and IV only.
C. I, III, and IV only.
D. I, II, III, and IV.

Answer (C) is correct. *(CIA, adapted)*
REQUIRED: The elements designed to provide feedback on the effectiveness of an IAA.
DISCUSSION: A quality assurance and improvement program should be designed to provide reasonable assurance to the various stakeholders of the IAA that it (1) performs in accordance with its charter, which should be consistent with the Standards and the Code of Ethics; (2) operates effectively and efficiently; and (3) is perceived by the stakeholders as adding value and improving operations. The program should include appropriate supervision, periodic internal assessment and ongoing monitoring of quality assurance, and periodic external assessments (PA 1300-1).

15. Which of the following is part of an internal audit activity's quality assurance program, rather than being included as part of other responsibilities of the chief audit executive (CAE)?

A. The CAE provides information about and access to internal audit workpapers to the external auditors to enable them to understand and determine the degree to which they may rely on the internal auditors' work.
B. Management approves a formal charter establishing the purpose, authority, and responsibility of the internal audit activity.
C. Each individual internal auditor's performance is appraised at least annually.
D. Supervision of an internal auditor's work is performed throughout each audit engagement.

Answer (D) is correct. *(CIA, adapted)*
REQUIRED: The item that is part of an internal audit activity's quality assurance program.
DISCUSSION: The CAE develops and maintains a quality assurance and improvement program (QAIP) that includes ongoing and periodic internal assessments. Ongoing internal assessments are usually incorporated into the routine policies and practices used to manage the IAA. They include such processes and tools as engagement supervision, checklists, feedback from stakeholders, peer reviews of working papers, project budgets, timekeeping systems, audit plan completion, cost recoveries, and analyses of other performance metrics.
Answer (A) is incorrect because providing working papers to the external auditors relates to the responsibility of the CAE to coordinate with external auditors. Answer (B) is incorrect because a CAE's responsibility to seek approval of a charter to establish the authority, purpose, and responsibility of the IAA is not part of a quality assurance program. Answer (C) is incorrect because individual performance appraisals are part of a CAE's responsibility for personnel management and development.

9.4 Internal Assessments

16. Ordinarily, those conducting internal quality program assessments should report to

A. The board.
B. The chief audit executive.
C. Senior management.
D. The internal auditing staff.

Answer (B) is correct. *(CIA, adapted)*
REQUIRED: The person(s) to whom those conducting internal quality program assessments should report.
DISCUSSION: "The CAE should establish a structure for reporting results of internal assessments that maintains appropriate credibility and objectivity. Generally, those assigned responsibility for conducting ongoing and periodic reviews should report to the CAE while performing the reviews and should communicate results directly to the CAE" (PA 1311-1).
Answer (A) is incorrect because the CAE should at least annually report the results of internal assessments to the board. Answer (C) is incorrect because the CAE should share information about internal assessments with appropriate persons outside the IAA, such as senior management. Answer (D) is incorrect because results ordinarily should be communicated directly to the CAE. Given a self-assessment, reporting to the internal auditing staff essentially involves having the staff report to itself.

9.5 External Assessments

17. Quality program assessments may be performed internally or externally. A distinguishing feature of an external assessment is its objective to

A. Identify tasks that can be performed better.

B. Determine whether internal auditing services meet professional standards.

C. Set forth the recommendations for improvement.

D. Provide independent assurance.

Answer (D) is correct. *(CIA, adapted)*

REQUIRED: The distinguishing feature of an external assessment.

DISCUSSION: External assessments should be conducted at least once every 5 years by a qualified, independent reviewer or review team from outside the organization (Standard 1312). Participants in the external assessment should be free of any obligation, or interest in, the organization whose IAA is assessed. (PA 1312-1).

Answer (A) is incorrect because an internal assessment will identify tasks that can be performed better. Answer (B) is incorrect because an internal assessment will determine whether internal auditing services meet professional standards. Answer (C) is incorrect because an internal assessment will set forth recommendations for improvement.

18. External assessment of an internal audit activity is not likely to evaluate

A. Adherence to the internal audit activity's charter.

B. Compliance with the Standards for the Professional Practice of Internal Auditing.

C. Detailed cost-benefit analysis of the internal audit activity.

D. The tools and techniques employed by the internal audit activity.

Answer (C) is correct. *(CIA, adapted)*

REQUIRED: The purpose not served by external assessment of an IAA.

DISCUSSION: The external assessment has a broad scope of coverage that includes (1) compliance with the Standards, the Code of Ethics, and the IAA's charter, plans, policies, procedures, practices, and applicable legislative and regulatory requirements; (2) the expectations of the IAA expressed by the board, senior management, and operational managers; (3) the integration of the IAA into the governance process; (4) the tools and techniques employed by the IAA; (5) the mix of knowledge, experience, and disciplines within the staff, including staff focus on process improvement; and (6) the determination whether the audit activity adds value and improves operations (PA 1312-1). However, the costs and benefits of internal auditing are neither easily quantifiable nor the subject of an external assessment.

Answer (A) is incorrect because adherence to the IAA's charter is within the broad scope of coverage of the external assessment. Answer (B) is incorrect because compliance with the Standards is within the broad scope of coverage of the external assessment. Answer (D) is incorrect because the tools and techniques of the IAA are within the broad scope of coverage of the external assessment.

19. The final results of an external assessment review of an internal audit activity (IAA) should be communicated to the chief audit executive (CAE) or other appropriate authorizing official. This communication may include

A. The reviewer's statement of an action plan in response to the recommendations.

B. An opinion on whether the practices of the IAA as a whole comply with the Standards.

C. An opinion on the IAA's compliance with its charter.

D. The reviewer's assessment of the use of best practices, other recommendations, and statement of implementation dates for responses to the review.

Answer (B) is correct. *(Publisher, adapted)*

REQUIRED: The content of a communication of the final results of an external assessment.

DISCUSSION: The communication may include an opinion on the IAA's compliance with the Standards based on a structured rating process. Compliance means that the practices of the IAA, taken as a whole, satisfy the requirements of the Standards (PA 1312-1). (But PA 1320-1 states that the review team should issue a formal report containing an opinion on compliance with the Standards.)

Answer (A) is incorrect because the communication may include responses from the CAE that include an action plan and implementation dates. Answer (C) is incorrect because an opinion on compliance with the Standards may be expressed. Answer (D) is incorrect because the communication may include the CAE's responses that describe an action plan and state implementation dates for the plan.

9.6 Reporting

20. According to Standard 1340, disclosure should be made to senior management and the board whenever

A. The internal audit activity does not comply with the Standards.

B. The internal auditors do not comply with the Code of Ethics.

C. The internal audit activity does not comply with the Standards, or the internal auditors do not comply with the Code of Ethics.

D. Noncompliance with the Standards or the Code of Ethics affects the overall operation of the internal audit activity.

Answer (D) is correct. *(Publisher, adapted)*

REQUIRED: The circumstance in which disclosure should be made to senior management and the board.

DISCUSSION: Although the internal audit activity should achieve full compliance with the Standards and internal auditors with the Code of Ethics, there may be instances in which full compliance is not achieved. When noncompliance affects the overall scope or operation of the internal audit activity, disclosure should be made to senior management and the board (Standard 1340).

21. Internal auditors may report that their activities are conducted in accordance with the Standards. They may use this statement only if

A. They demonstrate compliance with the Standards.

B. An independent external assessment of the internal audit activity is conducted annually.

C. Senior management or the board is accountable for implementing a quality program.

D. External assessments of the internal audit activity are made by external auditors.

Answer (A) is correct. *(Publisher, adapted)*

REQUIRED: The condition permitting internal auditors to report that their activities are in accordance with the Standards.

DISCUSSION: Standard 1330 states internal auditors are encouraged to report that their activities are "conducted in accordance with the International Standards for the Professional Practice of Internal Auditing." However, internal auditors may use the statement only if assessments of the quality improvement program demonstrate that the internal audit activity is in compliance with the Standards. Internal auditors are encouraged to use the compliance phrase in formal communications with stakeholder groups to demonstrate commitment to quality and to provide assurance to those who rely on the results of such communications (PA 1330-1).

Answer (B) is incorrect because an independent external assessment of the IAA should be conducted at least once every 5 years (Standard 1312). Answer (C) is incorrect because the IAA should adopt a process to monitor and assess the overall effectiveness of the quality program. The process should include internal and external assessments (Standard 1310). Answer (D) is incorrect because assessments also may be made by others who are (1) independent and (2) competent in the professional practice of internal auditing and the external assessment process (PA 1312-1).

22. When is initial use of the compliance phrase by internal auditors appropriate?

A. After an internal review completed within the past five years shows compliance.

B. After an external review completed within the past ten years.

C. After an internal review completed within the past ten years.

D. After an external review completed within the past five years shows compliance.

Answer (D) is correct. *(Publisher, adapted)*

REQUIRED: The time when the use of the compliance phrase is appropriate.

DISCUSSION: PA 1330-1 covers the use of the phrase "conducted in accordance with the standards" and the requirements for initial use. Use of the compliance phrase requires periodic internal assessments. These must have concluded that the IAA is in compliance with the Standards and Code of Ethics. Initial use of the compliance phrase is not appropriate until an external review, performed within the past five years, has demonstrated that the internal audit activity is in compliance.

Answer (A) is incorrect because initial use of the compliance phrase requires the completion of an external review. Answer (B) is incorrect because initial use of the compliance phrase requires the completion of a review within the past five years showing compliance. Answer (C) is incorrect because initial use of the compliance phrase requires the completion of an external review within the past five years showing compliance.

23. Following an external assessment of the internal audit activity, who is (are) responsible for communicating the results to the board?

A. Internal auditors.

B. Audit committee.

C. Chief audit executive.

D. External auditors.

Answer (C) is correct. *(Publisher, adapted)*

REQUIRED: The individual or group responsible for communicating the results of external assessments to the board.

DISCUSSION: The chief audit executive should communicate the results of external assessments to the board (Standard 1320).

Answer (A) is incorrect because the chief audit executive (not internal auditors) is responsible for communicating the results of external assessments to the board. Answer (B) is incorrect because the chief audit executive (not the audit committee) is responsible for communicating the results of external assessments to the board. Answer (D) is incorrect because the chief audit executive (not external auditors) is responsible for communicating the results of external assessments to the board.

24. Reporting on the internal audit activity's quality program by the external review team should include a formal report. It should contain an opinion on

A. The IAA's compliance with the IAA's charter.

B. The IAA's compliance with the Standards.

C. The IAA's recommendations for improvement.

D. The chief audit executive's written action plan.

Answer (B) is correct. *(Publisher, adapted)*

REQUIRED: The content of the review team's formal report on an external assessment.

DISCUSSION: The report should include an opinion on the IAA's compliance with the Standards. The report also should address compliance with the IAA's charter and other applicable standards and include appropriate recommendations for improvement. The chief audit executive should prepare a written action plan in response to significant comments and recommendations contained in the report of external assessment (PA 1320-1).

Answer (A) is incorrect because the report should address, but not express an opinion on, compliance with the charter. Answer (C) is incorrect because the report should address, but not express an opinion on, the IAA's recommendations for improvement. Answer (D) is incorrect because the final communication may include, but does not express an opinion on, a response from the CAE in the form of an action plan.

9.7 Benchmarking

25. Which of the following statements regarding benchmarking is false?

A. Benchmarking involves continuously evaluating the practices of best-in-class organizations and adapting company processes to incorporate the best of these practices.

B. Benchmarking, in practice, usually involves a company's formation of benchmarking teams.

C. Benchmarking is an ongoing process that entails quantitative and qualitative measurement of the difference between the company's performance of an activity and the performance by the best in the world or the best in the industry.

D. The benchmarking organization against which a firm is comparing itself must be a direct competitor.

Answer (D) is correct. *(Publisher, adapted)*

REQUIRED: The false statement about benchmarking.

DISCUSSION: Benchmarking is an ongoing process that entails quantitative and qualitative measurement of the difference between the company's performance of an activity and the performance by a best-in-class organization. The benchmarking organization against which a firm is comparing itself need not be a direct competitor. The important consideration is that the benchmarking organization be an outstanding performer in its industry.

26. An example of an internal nonfinancial benchmark is

A. The labor rate of comparably skilled employees at a major competitor's plant.

B. The average actual cost per pound of a specific product at the company's most efficient plant.

C. A $50,000 limit on the cost of employee training programs at each of the company's plants.

D. The percentage of customer orders delivered on time at the company's most efficient plant.

Answer (D) is correct. *(CIA, adapted)*

REQUIRED: The internal nonfinancial benchmark.

DISCUSSION: Benchmarking is a continuous evaluation of the practices of the best organizations in their class and the adoption of processes to reflect the best of these practices. It entails analysis and measurement of key outputs against those of the best organizations. This procedure also involves identifying the underlying key actions and causes that contribute to the performance difference. The percentage of orders delivered on time at the company's most efficient plant is an example of an internal nonfinancial benchmark.

Answer (A) is incorrect because the labor rate of a competitor is a financial benchmark. Answer (B) is incorrect because the cost per pound at the company's most efficient plant is a financial benchmark. Answer (C) is incorrect because the cost of a training program is a financial benchmark.

27. In a benchmarking activity, the critical steps for researching and identifying best-in-class performance are

A. Setting up databases, identifying performance gaps, understanding the reasons they exist, and prioritizing the key activities that will facilitate changes needed to implement recommendations.

B. Setting up databases, choosing information-gathering methods, formatting questionnaires, and selecting benchmarking partners.

C. Setting up databases, applying quality principles, integrating information technology and auditing, and developing performance measures.

D. Identifying performance gaps, understanding the reasons they exist, choosing information-gathering methods, and prioritizing the key activities that will facilitate changes needed to implement recommendations.

Answer (B) is correct. *(Publisher, adapted)*

REQUIRED: The critical steps for researching and identifying best-in-class performance.

DISCUSSION: Benchmarking consists of six phases. Researching and identifying best-in-class performance is often the most difficult phase. It consists of four critical steps: (1) setting up databases, (2) choosing information-gathering methods (internal sources, external public domain sources, and original research are the possible approaches), (3) formatting questionnaires, and (4) selecting benchmarking partners.

Answer (A) is incorrect because identifying performance gaps, understanding the reasons they exist, and prioritizing the key activities that will facilitate the behavioral and process changes needed to implement recommendations are part of the data analysis phase. Answer (C) is incorrect because applying quality principles, integrating information technology and auditing, and developing performance measures are all "best practices for an internal auditing activity" as cited in *Sawyer's Internal Auditing* (5th ed.), page 278. Answer (D) is incorrect because identifying performance gaps, understanding the reasons they exist, and prioritizing the key activities that will facilitate the behavioral and process changes needed to implement recommendations are part of the data analysis phase.

28. Which of the following are phases in the benchmarking process?

A. Organization of benchmarking teams and data analysis.

B. Setting up databases and implementation.

C. Data analysis and identifying performance gaps

D. Develop a family of measures indicating process performance and develop a process taxonomy.

Answer (A) is correct. *(Publisher, adapted)*

REQUIRED: The phases in the benchmarking process.

DISCUSSION: Benchmarking is a tool used in the implementation of a total quality management approach. Benchmarking is a continuous evaluation of the practices of the best organizations in an organization's class and consists of six phases: (1) selecting and prioritizing benchmarking projects, (2) organizing benchmarking teams, (3) investigating and documenting the organization's internal processes, (4) researching and identifying best-in-class performance, (5) data analysis, and (6) implementation.

Answer (B) is incorrect because setting up databases is only one of four steps in the fourth phase (research and identify best-in-class performance). Answer (C) is incorrect because identifying performance gaps is part of the data analysis phase (not a separate phase in benchmarking). Answer (D) is incorrect because developing (1) a family of measures indicating process performance and (2) a process taxonomy are tasks performed by the benchmarking team during the investigation and documentation of internal processes. Another task in that phase is tracing the path a request for a product or service takes through the organization.

STUDY UNIT TEN
ENGAGEMENT PROCEDURES, ETHICS, AND FRAUD

(30 pages of outline)

The CIA exam contains questions that ask for the best, most effective, least appropriate, etc., procedures to achieve engagement objectives. The purpose of this study unit is to provide guidance for determining the most (or least) effective procedure under given circumstances. If the question asks for the best, the most effective, etc., it will have one good answer and three incorrect answers. If the question asks for the least effective procedure, it will state three effective procedures and one inappropriate procedure.

This study unit also addresses the consideration of fraud in planning an engagement.

Core Concepts

- Internal auditors apply engagement (audit) procedures to obtain sufficient, competent, relevant, and useful information (evidence) to achieve the internal audit engagement's objectives.
- Auditors should be proficient in the highest levels of comprehension when selecting procedures: analysis, synthesis, and evaluation.
- Categories of procedures include (a) observing, (b) questioning, (c) analysis, (d) verifying, (e) investigating, and (f) evaluating.
- An organization's code of ethics is the established general value system the organization wishes to apply to its members' activities by communicating organizational purposes and beliefs and establishing uniform ethical guidelines for members.
- The purpose of The IIA Code of Ethics is to promote an ethical culture in the profession of internal auditing.
- Internal auditors must uphold four principles:
  a. Integrity
  b. Objectivity
  c. Confidentiality
  d. Competency
- Fraud is characterized by intentional deception. It may be perpetuated for the benefit, or to the detriment, of the organization. The perpetrators may be persons outside or inside the organization.
- Internal auditors should be able to identify opportunities for fraud, understand fraud schemes and how to prevent them, and recognize fraud signs.
- The degree of fraud exposure depends on inherent risk, the effectiveness of controls, and the honesty and integrity of people.
- Fraud risk assessment should be based on an enterprise risk management (ERM) model if one is in use.
- Control is the principal method of preventing fraud. Internal auditors assist in fraud prevention by evaluating the adequacy and effectiveness of control.
- Management is responsible for establishing and maintaining effective control to detect fraud.

- With regard to fraud detection, auditors must exercise due professional care. However, exercise of due professional care does not guarantee detection.
- The fraud investigation is begun when a concern about control failures or a suspicion of wrongdoing is raised within the organization.
- Management should develop controls over the investigation process.
- The role of internal audit in fraud investigations should be defined in the charter. Moreover, fraud investigation teams must be proficient regarding fraud schemes, investigatory methods, and the law.
- An investigation plan should be developed.
- Internal audit must report immediately any incident of significant fraud or erosion of trust to senior management and the board.
- Management is responsible for resolving fraud incidents.
- Internal auditors should include procedures in routine audit programs or design specific programs for detecting fraud.
- The internal auditor may give advice about designing a communication strategy and tactical plan.

10.1 ENGAGEMENT PROCEDURES

1. Internal auditors apply **engagement (audit) procedures** to obtain sufficient, competent, relevant, and useful **information (evidence)** to achieve the internal audit engagement's **objectives**.
   a. For example, internal auditors may perform **assurance engagements** in which they must evaluate the reliability of the output of an accounting information system. Such an engagement involves **substantive testing** of the balances and transactions. It also involves **tests** of the adequacy and effectiveness of **controls** to determine the effectiveness of accounting and control systems and procedures.
   b. **Consulting engagements** also require the gathering, analysis, synthesis, and evaluation of information relevant to the engagement objectives.
2. **Levels of comprehension.** Internal auditors should be **proficient** in analysis, synthesis, and evaluation. This principle applies not only in selecting procedures but also in every other aspect of engagement work. These are higher levels of comprehension than rote memorization, concept learning, and problem solving.
   a. **Analysis** results in an understanding of a situation, set of circumstances, or process. This understanding should apply both to the elements AND to the relationship of the elements of a situation, set of circumstances, or process. Thus, analysis is a means of understanding a **whole** by studying its **parts** and their relationships to each other and to the whole. It requires deductive reasoning.
      1) EXAMPLE: In an engagement to evaluate the effectiveness and efficiency of the use of production capacity, the internal auditor must determine whether customer orders should be accepted at a lower-than-usual price. Variables to consider include contribution margin generated, available production capacity, and psychological and economic effects on other customers.
   b. **Synthesis** involves developing standards and generalizations for a situation, set of circumstances, or a process. It is a means of combining individual components or parts to produce a whole. Synthesis requires inductive reasoning.

1) EXAMPLE: The development of an engagement work program is the documentation of the procedures for identifying, analyzing, evaluating, and recording information. For this purpose, the internal auditors must synthesize many factors, including (a) the engagement objectives, (b) prior results, (c) organizational changes, (d) legal and regulatory issues, (e) identified risks, (f) technical aspects of the engagement, (g) information obtained during the preliminary survey, (h) budgetary and other resource limits, and (i) many other matters.

c. **Evaluation** is relating a situation, set of circumstances, or process to predetermined or synthesized standards. Evaluation usually includes both analysis and synthesis.

1) EXAMPLE: Internal auditors rely on their training, experience, understanding, and seasoned judgment (if not intuition) to assess the quality of a situation, set of circumstances, or process (or its elements).

2) EXAMPLE: Multiple-choice questions consist of a series of either true or false statements with one exception (the correct answer). If the question is evaluative, all of the answer choices will be true or false, but one answer will be better than the others. "The most important nonfinancial issue that a company should consider is . . ." requires evaluation of qualitative variables.

3. The following **questions and answers** are helpful in selecting engagement procedures.

a. What are engagement (audit) procedures?

1) Engagement procedures are designed to gather information that corroborates and documents evidence that specified **risk management, control, and governance** processes are effective.

b. How do procedures relate to the information to be gathered?

1) Engagement procedures produce **information (evidence)** about the underlying activity. Both the procedures and the resulting evidence should be documented in the internal auditor's working papers.

c. How is the underlying activity relevant to the procedure(s)?

1) To account for or audit any activity (or to account for inactivity), the internal auditor must obtain an **understanding of the activity** by asking questions about what, why, when, how, and by whom.

d. How are the organization's systems, processes, and procedures related to the engagement procedures?

1) Engagement procedures may be applied to an accounting or other information system, its processes, and its procedures to develop evidence regarding the **reliability and integrity** of the information.

e. What is risk?

1) **Risk** is the possibility that an event will occur having an impact on the achievement of objectives. It is measured in terms of impact and likelihood. Examples of such events are asset loss, incurring a liability, financial statement misstatement, or incorrect analysis, synthesis and evaluation of a situation, set of circumstances, or process. The risk for internal auditors is that the information gathered (or its evaluation) may not reflect the true status of the subject of the engagement.

f. Why is the **assertions model** useful in selecting procedures for financial audits?

1) In **financial audits**, the primary concern is with the **assertions** explicitly or implicitly made by the information or its presentation, e.g., amounts of revenue or expense and the balances of assets and liabilities. Thus, internal auditors must develop and use engagement procedures to test the assertions.

2) EXAMPLE: The following assertions model is from a pronouncement of the American Institute of Certified Public Accountants:

a) **Transactions and Events for a Period**

i) **Occurrence.** Recorded items relate to the entity and have occurred.
ii) **Completeness.** Items that should be recorded were recorded.
iii) **Accuracy.** Data related to recorded items were recorded properly.
iv) **Cutoff.** Items were recorded in the proper period.
v) **Classification.** Items were recorded in the proper accounts.

b) **Balances at Period-end**

i) **Existence.** The items exist.
ii) **Rights and obligations.** The rights to assets are held or controlled, and the liabilities are obligations.
iii) **Completeness.** Items that should be recorded were recorded.
iv) **Valuation and allocation.** Amounts are proper, and resulting adjustments are proper.

c) **Presentation and Disclosure**

i) The (a) occurrence, (b) rights and obligations, (c) completeness, (d) accuracy, (e) classification, and (f) valuation assertions also apply to disclosures.
ii) **Understandability.** Items are clearly expressed.

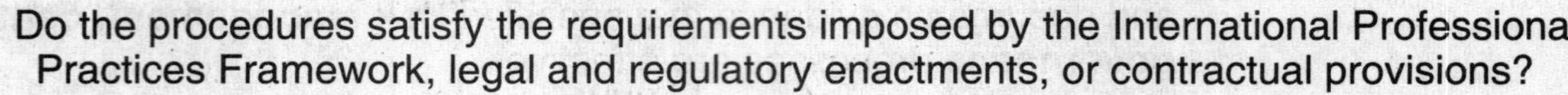

g. Do the procedures satisfy the requirements imposed by the International Professional Practices Framework, legal and regulatory enactments, or contractual provisions?

1) The IIA's **International Professional Practices Framework** is covered throughout Parts I and II of the CIA exam and the Gleim CIA books, CD-ROM, online course, and audios. Your thorough understanding of these pronouncements will make you a more effective internal auditor and prepare you for success on the CIA exam.

h. What do you need to do to become more proficient in evaluating procedures?

1) To improve your performance on procedure questions, analyze, synthesize, and evaluate how you respond to practice questions that are provided here. It is imperative to answer practice questions and learn from your experience.

4. **Categories of procedures.** Sawyer (*Sawyer's Internal Auditing*, 5th ed., The IIA, pp. 282-295) describes six categories of procedures. These procedures are used by internal auditors in their field work to examine, measure, and evaluate selected "documents, transactions, conditions, and processes." The first five categories relate to measurement and the sixth to evaluation.

a. **Observing** is a purposeful visual examination involving a mental comparison with standards and an evaluation of what is seen.

1) Observations should be **documented**.
2) The quality of observations is dependent upon the **experience and training** of the internal auditor. The greater the experience and the better the training, the more likely that variances from the desirable conditions will be observed.
3) Observation is usually preliminary to **confirmation** by other procedures, i.e., analysis and investigation. Confirmation by other procedures prevents observations from being successfully challenged.

4) Observation occurs during the **preliminary survey** of the physical plant and work flows. It may also occur when questioning.
5) Observation may detect **risk exposures** such as ineffective controls, idle resources, security breaches, or environmental and safety hazards.

b. **Questioning** may be done orally or in writing. It is the most pervasive procedure in reviews of operations.

1) **Oral questioning** is the most common form of this procedure. It is also the most difficult. It requires skill in human relations and in phrasing questions so as to elicit the most useful information.
2) An internal auditor must be able to avoid needlessly antagonizing or intimidating the people interviewed. However, (s)he must not waver from **the objective** of finding the truth.
3) Oral information should be **confirmed** by asking at least one other person.
4) **Quality of service** is normally best determined by inquiring of people who use the service, especially when it involves technical matters that only user-technicians understand.
5) A **standard operating procedure questionnaire** helps not only the internal auditor but also clients. Clients may find it more comprehensible than a procedures manual. They also may find it to be an educational device. Thus, a crucial internal audit function is to appraise written operating procedures to determine whether they are current, valid, relevant, and in use.
6) **Questionnaires** should be limited to material concerns, updated, and cleared with client management. Moreover, an issue may arise as to whether certain sensitive matters should be addressed in questionnaires.

c. **Analysis** means understanding a whole by studying its parts and their relationships to each other and to the whole. Analytical procedures are performed to discover "qualities, causes, effects, motives, and possibilities" as a basis for judgment or further examination.

1) **Analytical procedures** are valuable whether the subject is an account balance, an operating function, or a process. They are also useful for understanding policy statements, contracts, statutes, the work of committees related to a multifaceted program, and anything else capable of being examined in terms of its significant elements.
2) Analysis involves making **comparisons**, noting **trends**, and identifying **variances** from expectations. Accordingly, internal auditors must establish standards or benchmarks as a basis for comparisons, investigate variances, and perform any necessary additional tests.

d. **Verifying** is a process of **corroboration and comparison**, for example, of

1) One document or oral statement with another;
2) A general ledger balance with the detail in the subsidiary ledger;
3) A manager's approval with an authorizing directive issued by a higher level of management; or
4) A purchase with a purchase requisition, an allowed amount (such as a bill of materials), production schedule, or receiving report.

e. **Investigating** is a systematic search for hidden facts when wrongdoing or otherwise **suspect conditions** exist.

1) Investigating should be distinguished from **analyzing and verifying**, methods that are applied to information that is not (or not yet) suspect.

2) A **probe** is a type of investigation specifically related to **wrongdoing**. An example is a fraud investigation. Internal auditors must be cautious in such matters. An improperly conducted probe may have unfortunate legal and criminal ramifications, including injury to the organization because of violations of employees' rights.

f. **Evaluating** is appraisal or estimation of work, i.e., the making of a judgment. This conclusion is a determination of the adequacy, efficiency, and effectiveness of the subject matter.

1) Evaluating is based on **professional judgment**, which affects all aspects of the engagement. Typical evaluations include whether
   - a) The risks of not reviewing an activity exceed the costs of procedures,
   - b) Detailed procedures are necessary or a simple walk-through will suffice, or
   - c) Sample results are sufficient for the internal auditor's purposes given the risk assessments of the activity being reviewed.

2) Evaluating determines the **significance of results** and possibly indicates the corrective action to be taken.

3) Evaluating is a step beyond **analyzing and verifying** (the conclusion of the measurement or fact-finding process). It is the ultimate result of the internal auditor's consulting responsibility because it gives meaning to the facts found in light of engagement objectives and standards.

4) Even an experienced internal auditor should adopt a structured approach to the **evaluation of findings**. For example, Sawyer suggests that the following should be considered when an internal auditor evaluates deviations from standards:
   - a) The significance of the deviations
   - b) Who or what has been damaged
   - c) The degree of damage or possible damage
   - d) Whether the deviations prevented the organization from reaching its objectives
   - e) Whether the deviations are likely to recur in the absence of corrective action
   - f) Why and how the deviations occurred
   - g) What caused the deviations
   - h) Whether the cause has been precisely described and explains all aspects of the deviations

5) Internal auditors have a duty to recommend **corrective action**. Recommendations should be based on, among other things, the following considerations:
   - a) The most economical methods of solving the problem
   - b) The objectives of the recommendations
   - c) What management should be trying to achieve
   - d) The choices available and how they match the objectives
   - e) The tentative choice selected and its possible negative effects
   - f) The best choice with the least negative effects
   - g) Methods of control over the corrective action, e.g., to ensure that it is actually and fully implemented and that future deviations will be reported

5. Stop and review! You have completed the outline for this subunit. Study multiple-choice questions 1 through 20 beginning on page 406.

10.2 PERSPECTIVE ON ETHICS

1. **Definitions**
   a. **Business ethics** are an organization's policies and standards established to ensure certain kinds of behavior by its members.
   b. **Individual ethics** are the moral principles and standards of conduct adhered to by an individual.
2. **Issues in Business Ethics**
   a. General business understanding of ethical issues
   b. Compliance with laws (tax, securities, antitrust, environmental, privacy, labor, etc.)
   c. External financial reporting
   d. Conflicts of interest
   e. Entertainment and gift expenses
   f. Relations with customers and suppliers (Should gifts or kickbacks be given or accepted?)
   g. Social responsibility
3. **Factors That May Lead to Unethical Behavior**
   a. In any normal population, some people behave unethically. If these people hold leadership positions, they may have a bad influence on subordinates.
   b. **Organizational Factors**
      1) Pressures to improve short-run performance may promote unethical behavior.
      2) Emphasis on strict adherence to chain-of-command authority may provide excuses for ignoring ethics when following orders.
      3) Informal work-group loyalties may subvert ethical behavior.
      4) Committee decision processes may make it possible to abstain from or avoid ethical obligations.
   c. **External Factors**
      1) Pressure of competition may compromise ethics in the interest of survival.
      2) Wrongful behavior of others may force a compromise of ethics.
      3) Definitions of ethical behavior may vary from one culture to another. For instance, bribes to officials or buyers may be consistent with some countries' customary business practices.
4. **General Guides to Ethics**
   a. The **Golden Rule** states, "Do unto others as you would have them do unto you."
   b. **Fairness.** Individuals and businesses should act in ways that are fair or just to all.
   c. **General respect.** Individuals and businesses should act to respect the planet and the rights of others because business decisions have widespread effects.
   d. **Law.** Another view is that adherence to legal codes satisfies ethical obligations.
   e. However, most people believe that law embodies **ethical precepts** but is not synonymous with them. Thus, what is unethical may not be illegal, and nonlegal sources of ethical guidance must be considered.
      1) For example, the philosopher Immanuel Kant devised the **categorical imperative**. It is an approach to any ethical decision that asks what the consequences would be if all persons in the same circumstances (category) behaved similarly.

2) **Natural law** concepts are a source of ethical standards because they assert that certain human rights are fundamental, such as the life, liberty, and pursuit of happiness rights mentioned in the U.S. Declaration of Independence. Under this view, a business decision should be evaluated based on how it affects the rights of groups, e.g., consumers or employees.

3) According to **utilitarian ethics**, a decision is good if it maximizes social utility, that is, provides the greatest good for the greatest number of people.

4) Various concepts of the **social responsibility** of business have evolved from a greater awareness of ethical obligations.

a) The economist **Milton Friedman** took a limited view. He argued that a business must stay "within the rules of the game." Thus, it should engage in "open and free competition without deception or fraud," but it is otherwise obligated only to earn profits.

b) A second view is that businesses must consider the interests of all **stakeholders**. In a given situation, some may have interests superior to the interest of shareholders.

c) A third view is that major corporations have **citizenship** responsibilities, for example, to protect the environment or promote human rights.

5. **Simplified Criteria for Evaluating Ethical Behavior**

a. "Would this behavior be acceptable if people I respect knew I was doing this?"

b. "What are the consequences of this behavior for myself, other employees, customers, and society?"

6. Ethics are **individual and personal**, influenced by

a. Life experiences (rewards for doing right, punishment for doing wrong)
b. Friendship groups (professional associations, informal groups)
c. Organizational pressures (responsibilities to superiors and the organization)

7. **Codes of Ethics**

a. An organization's code of ethics is the **established general value system** the organization wishes to apply to its members' activities by

1) Communicating organizational purposes and beliefs and
2) Establishing uniform ethical guidelines for members.

a) This guidance extends to decision making.

b. Because laws and specific rules cannot cover all situations, organizations benefit from having an established code of ethics. The code effectively **communicates acceptable values** to all members, including recruits and subcontractors. For example, a code may

1) Require compliance with the law.

2) Prohibit conflicts of interest, such as accepting anything from customers and vendors, using organizational information for personal gain, or having financial dealings with those who also deal with the organization.

3) Provide a method of **policing and disciplining members** for violations through

a) Formal review panels.
b) Group pressure (informal).

4) Set high **standards** against which individuals can measure their own performance.

5) Communicate to those **outside the organization** the value system from which its members must not be asked to deviate.

c. A typical code for auditors or accountants in an organization requires

1) **Independence** from conflicts of economic or professional interest

a) They are responsible for **presenting information fairly** to shareholders or owners rather than protecting management.

b) They are responsible for presenting appropriate information to **all managers**. They should not favor certain managers or conceal unfavorable information.

c) They are responsible for **maintaining an ethical presence** in the conduct of professional activities.

i) They should do what they can to ensure organizational **compliance** with the spirit as well as the letter of pertinent laws and regulations.

ii) They should conduct themselves according to the highest moral and legal **standards**.

iii) They should report to appropriate internal or external authority any **illegal or fraudulent** organizational act.

2) **Integrity** and a refusal to compromise professional values for the sake of personal goals

3) **Objectivity** in presenting information, preparing reports, and making analyses

8. **Role of the Internal Auditor**

a. ***2130*** *Governance – The internal audit activity should assess and make appropriate recommendations for improving the governance process in its accomplishment of the following objectives:*

- *Promoting appropriate ethics and values within the organization.*
- *Ensuring effective organizational performance management and accountability.*
- *Effectively communicating risk and control information to appropriate areas of the organization.*
- *Effectively coordinating the activities of and communicating information among the board, external and internal auditors and management.*

2130.A1 *– The internal audit activity should evaluate the design, implementation, and effectiveness of the organization's ethics-related objectives, programs, and activities.*

2130.C1 *– Consulting engagement objectives should be consistent with the overall values and goals of the organization.*

b. For related guidance in Study Unit 3, see ***Practice Advisory 2130-1: Role of the Internal Audit Activity and Internal Auditor in the Ethical Culture of an Organization***.

9. Stop and review! You have completed the outline for this subunit. Study multiple-choice questions 21 through 27 beginning on page 414.

10.3 THE IIA CODE OF ETHICS

1. CIA examination candidates should know the four **Principles** and twelve **Rules of Conduct**. The full text, including the Introduction and Applicability and Enforcement sections, appears at the end of this subunit.
2. The IIA Code of Ethics should be read with the **International Standards for the Professional Practice of Internal Auditing**.
3. The IIA Code of Ethics applies to **individuals and entities**, including members of The Institute, CIAs, and candidates for certification. However, it also furnishes guidance to **anyone who provides internal auditing services**.

THE INSTITUTE OF INTERNAL AUDITORS CODE OF ETHICS

INTRODUCTION: *The purpose of The Institute's Code of Ethics is to promote an ethical culture in the profession of internal auditing.*

Internal auditing is an independent, objective assurance and consulting activity designed to add value and improve an organization's operations. It helps an organization accomplish its objectives by bringing a systematic, disciplined approach to evaluate and improve the effectiveness of risk management, control, and governance processes.

A code of ethics is necessary and appropriate for the profession of internal auditing, founded as it is on the trust placed in its objective assurance about risk management, control, and governance. The Institute's Code of Ethics extends beyond the definition of internal auditing to include two essential components:

1. *Principles that are relevant to the profession and practice of internal auditing.*
2. *Rules of Conduct that describe behavior norms expected of internal auditors. These rules are an aid to interpreting the Principles into practical applications and are intended to guide the ethical conduct of internal auditors.*

The Code of Ethics together with The Institute's International Professional Practices Framework and other relevant Institute pronouncements provide guidance to internal auditors serving others. "Internal auditors" refers to Institute members, recipients of or candidates for IIA professional certifications, and those who provide internal auditing services within the definition of internal auditing.

APPLICABILITY AND ENFORCEMENT: *This Code of Ethics applies to both individuals and entities that provide internal auditing services.*

For Institute members and recipients of or candidates for IIA professional certifications, breaches of the Code of Ethics will be evaluated and administered according to The Institute's Bylaws and Administrative Guidelines. The fact that a particular conduct is not mentioned in the Rules of Conduct does not prevent it from being unacceptable or discreditable, and therefore, the member, certification holder, or candidate can be liable for disciplinary action.

Principles

Internal auditors are expected to apply and uphold the following principles:

Integrity

The integrity of internal auditors establishes trust and thus provides the basis for reliance on their judgment.

Objectivity

Internal auditors exhibit the highest level of professional objectivity in gathering, evaluating, and communicating information about the activity or process being examined. Internal auditors make a balanced assessment of all the relevant circumstances and are not unduly influenced by their own interests or by others in forming judgments.

Confidentiality

Internal auditors respect the value and ownership of information they receive and do not disclose information without appropriate authority unless there is a legal or professional obligation to do so.

Competency

Internal auditors apply the knowledge, skills, and experience needed in the performance of internal auditing services.

RULES OF CONDUCT

1. ***Integrity***
   Internal auditors:
   - *1.1 Shall perform their work with honesty, diligence, and responsibility.*
   - *1.2 Shall observe the law and make disclosures expected by the law and the profession.*
   - *1.3 Shall not knowingly be a party to any illegal activity, or engage in acts that are discreditable to the profession of internal auditing or to the organization.*
   - *1.4 Shall respect and contribute to the legitimate and ethical objectives of the organization.*
2. ***Objectivity***
   Internal auditors:
   - *2.1 Shall not participate in any activity or relationship that may impair or be presumed to impair their unbiased assessment. This participation includes those activities or relationships that may be in conflict with the interests of the organization.*
   - *2.2 Shall not accept anything that may impair or be presumed to impair their professional judgment.*
   - *2.3 Shall disclose all material facts known to them that, if not disclosed, may distort the reporting of activities under review.*
3. ***Confidentiality***
   Internal auditors:
   - *3.1 Shall be prudent in the use and protection of information acquired in the course of their duties.*
   - *3.2 Shall not use information for any personal gain or in any manner that would be contrary to the law or detrimental to the legitimate and ethical objectives of the organization.*
4. ***Competency***
   Internal auditors:
   - *4.1 Shall engage only in those services for which they have the necessary knowledge, skills, and experience.*
   - *4.2 Shall perform internal auditing services in accordance with the International Standards for the Professional Practice of Internal Auditing.*
   - *4.3 Shall continually improve their proficiency and the effectiveness and quality of their services.*

4. Stop and review! You have completed the outline for this subunit. Study multiple-choice questions 28 through 62 beginning on page 417.

10.4 FRAUD RESPONSIBILITIES OF INTERNAL AUDITORS

1. This subunit concerns the duty of internal auditors to deter, detect, investigate, and communicate information about fraud. Fraud is a form of **white-collar crime**, a term that applies to numerous nonviolent offenses that have cheating and dishonesty as their main characteristic. Other examples are insider trading, embezzlement, and forgery. These matters are covered in one Assurance Implementation Standard and two Practice Advisories. The foregoing pronouncements are related to the specific Attribute Standard on proficiency.
2. ***1210.A2*** – *The internal auditor should have sufficient knowledge to identify the indicators of fraud but is not expected to have the expertise of a person whose primary responsibility is detecting and investigating fraud.*

a. ***PRACTICE ADVISORY 1210.A2-1: AUDITOR'S RESPONSIBILITIES RELATING TO FRAUD RISK ASSESSMENT, PREVENTION, and DETECTION***

WHAT IS FRAUD?

Fraud encompasses a range of irregularities and illegal acts characterized by intentional deception or misrepresentation*, which an individual knows to be false or does not believe to be true. Throughout this practice advisory, and in PA 1210.A.2-2, the guidance may refer to certain actions as "fraud," which may also be legally defined and/or commonly known as corruption. Fraud is perpetrated by a person knowing that it could result in some unauthorized benefit to him or her, to the organization, or to another person, and can be perpetrated by persons outside and inside the organization.*

1. ***Fraud perpetrated to the detriment of the organization*** *is conducted generally for the direct or indirect benefit of an employee, outside individual, or another organization. Some examples are*
   - *Acceptance of bribes or kickbacks*
   - *Diversion to an employee or outsider of a potentially profitable transaction that would normally generate profits for the organization*
   - *Embezzlement, as typified by the misappropriation of money or property, and falsification of financial records to cover up an act, thus making detection difficult*
   - *Intentional concealment or misrepresentation of events, transactions, or data*
   - *Claims submitted for services or goods not actually provided to the organization*
   - *Intentional failure to act in circumstances where action is required by the company or by law*
   - *Unauthorized or illegal use of confidential or proprietary information*
   - *Unauthorized or illegal manipulation of information technology networks or operating systems*
   - *Theft*
2. ***Fraud designed to benefit the organization*** *generally produces such benefit by exploiting an unfair or dishonest advantage that also may deceive an outside party. Perpetrators of such acts usually accrue an indirect personal benefit, such as management bonus payments or promotions. Examples of fraud designed to benefit the organization include*
   - *Improper payments, such as illegal political contributions, bribes, and kickbacks, as well as payoffs to government officials, intermediaries of government officials, customers, or suppliers*
   - *Intentional and improper representation or valuation of transactions, assets, liabilities, and income, among others*
   - *Intentional and improper transfer pricing (e.g., valuation of goods exchanged between related organizations). By purposely structuring pricing techniques improperly, management can improve their operating results to the detriment of the other organization*
   - *Intentional and improper related-party activities in which one party receives some benefit not obtainable in an arm's-length transaction*
   - *Intentional failure to record or disclose significant information accurately or completely, which may present an enhanced picture of the organization to outside parties*
   - *Sale or assignment of fictitious or misrepresented assets*

- *Intentional failure to act in circumstances where action is required by the company or by law*
- *Intentional errors in tax compliance activities to reduce taxes owed*
- *Prohibited business activities, such as those that violate government statutes, rules, regulations, or contracts*

In addition to the above, different ways of classifying or categorizing fraud exist. The auditor may want to explore information published by professional accounting or fraud investigation firms and associations to determine which classification method is most appropriate for their organization.

WHY DOES FRAUD OCCUR?

There are generally three factors that influence the commission of fraud. These are opportunity, motive, and rationalization.

1. ***Opportunity***
   - *A process may be designed properly for typical conditions. However, a window of opportunity may arise for something to go wrong or create circumstances for the control to fail.*
   - *An opportunity for fraud may exist due to poor control design or lack of controls. For example, a system can be developed that appears to protect assets, but which is missing an important control. Anyone aware of the gap can take what they want without much effort.*
   - *Persons in positions of authority can create opportunities to override existing controls, because subordinates or weak controls allow them to circumvent the rules.*
2. ***Motive** (also called incentive or pressure)*
   - *While people can rationalize their acts, there needs to be a motive to make them behave that way.*
   - *Power is a great motivator. Power can be simply gaining esteem in the eyes of family or coworkers. For instance, many computer frauds are done to show the hacker has the power to do it rather than to cause intentional harm.*
   - *Another motivator is the gratification of a desire, such as greed, or an addiction.*
   - *The third motivator is pressure, either from physical stresses or from outside parties.*
3. ***Rationalization***
   - *Most individuals consider themselves good persons, even if they occasionally do something bad. To convince themselves they are still good persons, they may rationalize or deny their acts. For example, these individuals might consider that they were entitled to the stolen item or that if executives break the rules, it must be alright for others to do so as well.*
   - *Some people will do things that are defined as unacceptable behavior by the organization, yet are commonplace in their culture or were accepted by previous employers. As a result, these individuals will not comply with rules that don't make sense to them.*
   - *Some people may have periods of financial difficulty in their lives, have succumbed to a costly addiction, or are facing other pressures. Consequently, they will rationalize that they are just borrowing the money and, when their lives improve, they will pay it back. Others may feel that stealing from an organization is not bad, thereby depersonalizing the act.*

*Although auditors may not be able to know the exact motive or rationalization leading to fraud, they are expected to understand enough about internal controls to **identify opportunities for fraud**. Auditors also should understand fraud schemes and scenarios, as well as be aware of the **signs that point to fraud and how to prevent them**. Information available from The IIA and other professional associations or organizations should be reviewed to ensure that the auditor's knowledge is current.*

FRAUD AND MISCONDUCT RISK ASSESSMENT

*All organizations are exposed to a degree of fraud risk in any process where human input is required. The degree to which an organization is exposed relates to the **fraud risks inherent in the business**, the extent to which effective **internal controls** are present either to prevent or detect fraud, and the **honesty and integrity** of those involved in the process.*

***Fraud risk** is the **probability** that fraud will occur and the potential severity or **consequences** to the organization when it occurs. The probability of a fraudulent activity is based, typically, on how easy it is to commit fraud, the motivational factors leading to fraud, and the organization's fraud history. **Fraud management** includes limiting or eliminating consequences, which is more than limiting or eliminating financial loss. For example, for some organizations, loss of reputation may have considerable impact on the ability to attract and retain skilled employees or customers for their products, as well as to obtain facilities and licenses necessary for the business' growth and sustainability.*

***To assess fraud risk**, internal auditors should use the organization's **enterprise risk management model** if one is in use. Otherwise, auditors could use the following guidelines:*

1. *Understand the **specific fraud schemes** that could threaten the organization. Use a **risk model** to map and assess the organization's vulnerability to these fraud schemes, which covers all inherent risks to the organization. The risk model also should use **consistent categories** (i.e., there should be no overlap between risk areas) and be detailed enough for a risk assessment to identify and cover anticipated high-risk areas.*

   *The **Committee of Sponsoring Organizations** of the Treadway Commission's (COSO's) Enterprise Risk Management framework provides a useful model that includes sections on:*

   - ***Event identification**, such as brainstorming activities, interviews, focus groups, surveys, industry research, and event inventories*
   - ***Risk assessments** that include probabilities and consequences*
   - ***Risk response strategies**, such as treating, transferring, tolerating, or terminating risk*
   - ***Control activities**, such as linking risks to existing anti-fraud programs and control activities, and validating their effectiveness*
   - ***Monitoring**, including audit plans and programs that consider residual fraud and risk due to misconduct*

2. *When evaluating controls to prevent or reduce fraud risks to an organization, **cost and benefit considerations** should be made. The evaluation should consider whether fraud could be committed by an individual or requires **collusion**. In practice, 100 percent fraud prevention is neither possible nor cost effective. Considerations also should be made regarding the negative effects of unjustly suspecting employees or giving the appearance that employees are not trusted.*

ELEMENTS OF FRAUD PREVENTION OR DETERRENCE

*Fraud prevention involves those actions taken to discourage the commission of fraud and limit fraud exposure when it occurs. The principal mechanism for preventing fraud is **internal control**. Primary responsibility for establishing and maintaining internal control should rest with **management**.*

*The following are some control elements of a **fraud prevention program** presented within the **COSO control framework** as an example. Each element would be a valid consideration, regardless of which control framework the auditor uses.*

1. ***Control environment.*** *Organizations must establish an appropriate control environment that includes*
   - *A code of conduct, ethics policy, or fraud policy to set the appropriate tone at the top*
   - *Ethics and whistleblower hotline programs to report concerns*
   - *Hiring and promotion guidelines and practices*
   - *Oversight by the audit committee, board, or other oversight body*
   - *Investigation of reported issues and remediation of confirmed violations*
2. ***Fraud risk assessment.*** *Organizations should identify and assess fraud-related risks, including assessing the potential for fraudulent financial reporting, asset misappropriations, improper receipts and expenditures, or financial misconduct by management and others. Companies also should assess whether adequate segregation of duties exists.*
3. ***Control activities.*** *Organizations should establish and implement effective control practices, including actions taken by management to identify, prevent, and mitigate fraudulent financial reporting or misuse of the organization's assets, as well as prevent override of controls by management. In addition, organizations should establish an affirmation or certification process to confirm employees have read and understood corporate policies and are in compliance with them.*
4. ***Information and communication.*** *Organizations must establish effective fraud-related information and communication practices, including documentation and dissemination of policies, guidance, and results; opportunities to discuss ethical dilemmas; communication channels; training for personnel; and considerations of the impact and use of technology for fraud deterrence, such as the use of continuous monitoring software.*
5. ***Monitoring.*** *Organizations should conduct ongoing and periodic performance assessments and identify the impact and use of computer technology for fraud deterrence.*

Internal Auditor's Role

*Internal auditors are responsible for assisting organizations to prevent fraud by examining and evaluating the **adequacy and effectiveness of their internal controls' system**, commensurate with the extent of a potential exposure within the organization. When meeting their responsibilities, internal auditors should consider the following elements:*

1. ***Control environment.*** *Assess aspects of the control environment, conduct proactive fraud audits and investigations, communicate results of fraud audits, and provide support for remediation efforts. In some cases, internal auditors also may own the whistleblower hotline.*

2. ***Fraud risk assessment.*** *Evaluate management's fraud risk assessment, in particular, their processes for identifying, assessing, and testing potential fraud and misconduct schemes and scenarios, including those that could involve suppliers, contractors, and other parties.*
3. ***Control activities.*** *Assess the design and operating effectiveness of fraud-related controls; ensure that audit plans and programs address residual risk and incorporate fraud audits; evaluate the design of facilities from a fraud or theft perspective; and review proposed changes to laws, regulations, or systems, and their impacts on controls.*
4. ***Information and communication.*** *Assess the operating effectiveness of information and communication systems and practices, as well as provide support to fraud-related training initiatives.*
5. ***Monitoring.*** *Assess monitoring activities and related computer software; conduct investigations; support the audit committee's oversight related to control and fraud matters; support the development of fraud indicators; and hire and train employees so they can have the appropriate fraud audit or investigative experience.*

FRAUD DETECTION

Management and the internal audit activity have different roles with respect to fraud detection. Here is a description of each:

Management's Role in Fraud Detection

Management is responsible for ***establishing and maintaining an effective control system*** *at a reasonable cost. This includes designing some controls to indicate when other controls are not working effectively. Following up on these indicators may result in the determination that fraud may have occurred.*

One example of a ***monitoring control*** *is the establishment and communication of a hotline or similar system customers or employees can use to make complaints or identify concerns. Other monitoring and detection controls include*

- *Installing alarm systems on facility doors and windows*
- *Installing surveillance cameras*
- *Designing edit checks into information systems*
- *Performing inventory counts*
- *Auditing*
- *Reviewing and approving invoices and cost center charges*
- *Reconciling accounts*

Internal Auditor's Role in Fraud Detection

To the degree that fraud may be present in activities covered in the normal course of audit work, internal auditors have a responsibility to exercise ***due professional care*** *as specifically defined in Standard 1220 of the* International Standards for the Professional Practice of Internal Auditing *with respect to fraud detection.*

However, most internal auditors are not expected to have knowledge equivalent to that of a ***person whose primary responsibility is detecting and investigating fraud****. Also, audit procedures alone, even when carried out with due professional care, do not guarantee that fraud will be detected.*

A well-designed internal control system should not be conducive to fraud. Tests conducted by auditors improve the likelihood that any existing fraud indicators will be detected and considered for further investigation.

*In conducting engagements, the **internal auditor's responsibilities for detecting fraud** are to*

- *Consider fraud risks in the assessment of control design and determination of audit steps to perform. While internal auditors are not expected to detect fraud and irregularities, internal auditors are expected to obtain reasonable assurance that business objectives for the process under review are being achieved and material control deficiencies – whether through simple error or intentional effort – are detected.*
- *Have **sufficient knowledge of fraud to identify red flags** indicating fraud may have been committed. This knowledge includes the characteristics of fraud, the techniques used to commit fraud, and the various fraud schemes and scenarios associated with the activities reviewed.*
- ***Be alert to opportunities that could allow fraud**, such as control weaknesses. If significant control weaknesses are detected, additional tests conducted by internal auditors should be directed at identifying other fraud indicators. Some examples of indicators are unauthorized transactions, sudden fluctuations in the volume or value of transactions, control overrides, unexplained pricing exceptions, and unusually large product losses. Internal auditors should recognize that the presence of more than one indicator at any one time increases the probability that fraud has occurred.*
- ***Evaluate the indicators of fraud** and decide whether any further action is necessary or whether an investigation should be recommended.*
- ***Notify the appropriate authorities** within the organization to recommend an investigation if a determination is made that fraud has occurred.*

PA Summary

- **Fraud encompasses an array of irregularities and illegal acts characterized by intentional deception or misrepresentation.** It can be perpetrated for the benefit, or to the detriment, of the organization and by persons outside or inside the organization. Fraud perpetrated to the **detriment of the organization** generally is for the direct or indirect benefit of an employee, outside individual, or another organization. Fraud designed to **benefit the organization** generally produces such benefit by exploiting an unfair or dishonest advantage that also may deceive an outside party.
- The **factors** that influence the commission of fraud are **opportunity, motive (incentive or pressure), and rationalization**. Internal auditors should know enough about **internal control** to identify opportunities, understand fraud schemes and how to prevent them, and recognize fraud signs. An **opportunity** for fraud may exist due to (1) occurrence of abnormal conditions, (2) poor control design, (3) lack of controls, or (4) override of existing controls by persons in positions of authority. **Motives** are (1) power, (2) gratification of a desire, and (3) pressure. **Rationalization** is finding some justification for fraudulent actions.
- The **degree of fraud exposure** depends on inherent risk, the effectiveness of controls (detective or preventive), and the honesty and integrity of the people involved.
- **Fraud risk** has two elements: (1) the probability of fraud and (2) the consequences if it occurs. Probability is based on how easy it is to commit fraud, motives leading to fraud, and the entity's fraud history.
- **Fraud management** limits or eliminates financial and nonfinancial consequences.

PA Summary continued on next page

PA Summary continued

- **Fraud risk assessment** should be based on an **ERM model** if one is in use. Otherwise, auditors should understand specific schemes and use a **risk model** to assess vulnerability. This model should cover all inherent risks, use **consistent categories**, and be detailed enough for a risk assessment to identify high-risk areas. The **COSO's model** has sections on (1) event identification, (2) risk assessments, (3) risk response strategies, (4) control activities, and (5) monitoring. An **evaluation of controls** considers the **costs and benefits** of prevention and whether fraud requires **collusion**. Complete fraud prevention is neither possible nor cost effective.
- **Fraud prevention** discourages the commission of fraud and limits exposure when it occurs. The principal mechanism for preventing fraud is **control**. Primary responsibility for establishing and maintaining control rests with **management**.
- The **elements** of the **COSO control framework** provide an example of the control elements of a **fraud prevention program**: (1) control environment, (2) fraud risk assessment, (3) control activities, (4) information and communication, and (5) monitoring.
- **Internal auditors** are responsible for assisting in the **prevention** of fraud by examining and evaluating the **adequacy and effectiveness** of the system of internal control, in proportion to the extent of the potential exposure in the organization. To meet their responsibilities, internal auditors consider their specific duties with respect to the five elements of the fraud prevention program in the COSO control framework.
- **Management's responsibility** for **fraud detection** is to establish and maintain effective control at a reasonable cost.
- The internal auditor's role in **fraud detection** includes exercising **due professional care**. The exercise of due professional care does **not** guarantee detection of fraud.
- Auditors need not have the **fraud knowledge** of a specialist.
- **Well-designed controls** are not conducive to fraud. Audit tests improve the likelihood that **fraud indicators** will be detected.
- Internal auditors should consider **fraud risk** when assessing control design and selecting audit procedures. Auditors should obtain reasonable assurance that objectives are achieved and material control deficiencies are detected.
- Internal auditors also must (1) have sufficient **knowledge of fraud** to identify **red flags** (characteristics, techniques used, and schemes), (2) be alert to opportunities (e.g., control weaknesses) that could allow fraud, (3) **evaluate** the indicators, and (4) **notify appropriate authorities** if necessary.

b. ***PRACTICE ADVISORY 1210.A2-2: AUDITOR'S RESPONSIBILITIES RELATING TO FRAUD INVESTIGATION, REPORTING, RESOLUTION, AND COMMUNICATION***

INVESTIGATING FRAUD

This section of the practice advisory does ***not refer to the activity known as "auditing for fraud,"*** *defined as "an audit designed to proactively detect indications of fraud in those processes or transactions where analysis indicates the risk of fraud to be significant." This guidance refers to investigations initiated when a* ***concern over control failures or suspicion of wrongdoing is raised within the organization****. Suspicions can result from a formal complaint process, informal tips, or an audit, including an audit designed to test for fraud.*

*A **fraud investigation** consists of gathering sufficient information about specific details and performing those procedures necessary to determine whether fraud has occurred, the loss or exposures associated with the fraud, who was involved in it, and the fraud scheme (how it happened). An important outcome of investigations is that innocent persons are cleared of suspicion.*

*Investigations should be designed to discover the **full nature and extent of the fraudulent activity**, not just the event that may have initiated the investigation. Investigation work includes preparing workpapers/file documentation sufficient for a legal proceeding.*

*Internal auditors, lawyers, investigators, security personnel, and other **specialists** from inside or outside the organization are the parties that usually conduct or participate in fraud investigations.*

*Investigations and the **related resolution activities** need to be carefully managed in consideration of **local law**. Laws may direct how and where investigations are conducted, disciplinary and recovery practices, and communications. It is in the best interests of an auditor, both professionally and legally, to work effectively with the organization's legal counsel and to become familiar with the relevant laws. The guidance provided here is directed at an international audience and is therefore general in nature.*

Management's Role

*Management is responsible for developing **controls over the investigation process**, including developing policies and procedures for effective investigations and standards for handling the results of investigations, reporting, and communications. Such standards are often documented in a **fraud policy**, and internal audit may be involved in developing the policy.*

*Such policies and procedures must consider the **rights of individuals** involved, the **qualifications** of those authorized to conduct investigations, and the **relevant laws** of the countries and local governments where the frauds occurred or were investigated. The policies should consider the extent to which management will **discipline** employees, suppliers, or customers, including taking legal measures to recover losses and civil or criminal prosecution. It is important for management to clearly define the **authority and responsibilities of various roles** within an investigation, especially the relationship between the investigator and legal counsel. It is also important for management to design and comply with **procedures that minimize internal communications about an ongoing investigation**, especially in the initial phases.*

*The policy should specify the **role the investigator will have in making a determination that fraud has been committed**. Management should consider whether the investigator or management reaches a conclusion of fraud, or whether the company refers the facts to outside authorities for their conclusion. A judgment that fraud has occurred may, in some jurisdictions, only be made by law enforcement or judicial authorities. The investigation may simply result in a conclusion that company policy was violated.*

Internal Audit's Role

*The role of internal audit in investigations should be defined in the **internal audit charter** as well as the fraud policies. For example, internal audit may have the primary responsibility for fraud investigations, may act as a resource for investigations, or must refrain from involving itself in investigations (because it is responsible for assessing the effectiveness of investigations). Any of these roles can be acceptable, as long as the impact of these activities on internal audit's independence is recognized and handled appropriately.*

***To maintain proficiency**, fraud investigation teams have a responsibility to obtain sufficient knowledge of fraud schemes, investigation techniques, and laws. There are national and international programs that provide training and certifications for investigators and forensic specialists.*

***If internal audit is responsible** for ensuring that investigations are conducted, it may conduct an investigation using in-house staff, **outsourcing**, or a combination of both. In some cases, internal audit may also use non-audit employees of the organization to assist.*

*It is often important to assemble the investigation team without delay. If the organization needs **external experts**, the chief audit executive should consider **pre-qualifying the service provider[s]** so that the external resources are available quickly.*

*If the organization has not assigned primary responsibility for the investigation function to internal audit, auditors may still be asked to help **gather information and make recommendations for internal control improvements**.*

NOTE: An internal auditor's engagement to conduct a fraud investigation is an example of **forensic auditing** (see subunit 10.6).

Investigator's Role (whether assigned to internal auditing or elsewhere)

*An **investigation plan** must be developed for each investigation, following the organization's investigation procedures or protocols. The lead investigator should determine the **knowledge, skills, and other competencies** needed to carry out the investigation effectively and assign competent, appropriate people to the team. This process should include assurance that there is no potential **conflict of interest** with those being investigated or with any of the employees of the organization.*

The plan should consider methods to:

- *Gather evidence, such as surveillance, interviews, or written statements*
- *Document the evidence, considering legal rules of evidence and the business uses of the evidence*
- *Determine the extent of the fraud*
- *Determine the scheme (techniques used to perpetrate the fraud)*
- *Evaluate the cause*
- *Identify the perpetrators*

*At any point in this process, the investigator may conclude that the complaint or suspicion was unfounded and follow a process to **close the case**.*

***Activities should be coordinated** with management, legal counsel, and other specialists, such as human resources and insurance risk management, as appropriate throughout the course of the investigation.*

*Investigators must be knowledgeable and cognizant of the **rights of persons** within the scope of the investigation and the **reputation of the organization itself**.*

*The **level and extent of complicity** in the fraud throughout the organization should be assessed. This assessment can be critical to ensuring that crucial evidence is not destroyed or tainted and to avoid obtaining misleading information from persons who may be involved.*

REPORTING ON FRAUD

Fraud reporting consists of the various ***oral or written, interim or final communications*** *to senior management or the board of directors regarding the status and results of fraud investigations. Reports can be preliminary and ongoing throughout the investigation. A written report may follow any oral briefing made to management and the board of directors to document the findings.*

Section 2400 of the International Standards for the Professional Practice of Internal Auditing *provides information applicable to engagement communications. Additional interpretive guidance on fraud reporting internally follows:*

- *A draft of the proposed final communications on fraud should be submitted to* ***legal counsel for review****. If the organization is able to invoke* ***client privilege****, and has chosen to do so, the report must be addressed to legal counsel.*
- *When the* ***incidents of significant fraud, or erosion of trust****, have been established to a reasonable certainty, senior management and the board of directors should be notified immediately.*
- *The* ***results of a fraud investigation*** *may indicate that fraud may have had a previously undiscovered adverse effect on the organization's financial position and its operational results for one or more years for which* ***financial statements*** *have already been issued. Senior management and the board of directors should be informed of such a discovery.*
- *A written report or other* ***formal communication should be issued at the conclusion of the investigation phase****. It should include the basis for beginning an investigation, time frames, observations, conclusions, resolution, and corrective action taken (or recommendations) to improve controls. Depending on how the investigation was resolved, the report may need to be written in a manner that provides* ***confidentiality*** *to some of the people involved. The content of this report is sensitive, and it must meet the needs of the board of directors and management while complying with legal requirements and restrictions and company policies and procedures.*

RESOLUTION OF FRAUD INCIDENTS

Management is responsible for resolving fraud incidents*, not the internal auditor or the investigator. Resolution consists of determining what actions will be taken by the organization once a fraud scheme and perpetrator[s] have been fully investigated and evidence has been reviewed.*

Internal auditors *should assess the facts of investigations and advise management relating to* ***remediation of control weaknesses*** *that lead to the fraud. Auditors should* ***design additional steps in routine audit programs*** *or develop "auditing for fraud" programs to help disclose the existence of similar frauds in the future.*

Management's fraud policies and procedures *(mentioned earlier in the practice advisory) should define who has authority and responsibility for each process.* ***Internal auditors may be involved as advisors*** *in the following processes, as long as the impact of these activities on internal audit's* ***independence*** *is recognized and handled appropriately. Resolution may include all or some of the following:*

- *Providing closure to persons who were initially under suspicion but were found to be innocent*
- *Providing closure to those who reported a concern*
- *Disciplining an employee in accordance with company standards, employment legislation, or employment contracts*
- *Requesting voluntary financial restitution from an employee, customer, or supplier*

- *Terminating contracts with suppliers*
- *Reporting the incident to law enforcement, regulatory bodies, or similar authorities, and cooperating with their investigation*
- *Entering into civil litigation or similar legal processes*
- *Filing an insurance claim*
- *Filing a complaint with the perpetrator's professional association*

In addition to advising clients, internal auditors may become involved in:

- *Monitoring the investigation process to help ensure that the organization follows relevant policies, procedures, and applicable laws and statutes (where internal auditing was not responsible for conducting the investigation)*
- *Locating or securing the misappropriated or related assets*
- *Supporting the organization's legal, insurance, or other recovery actions*
- *Evaluating and monitoring the organization's internal and external post-investigation reporting and communication plans and practices*
- *Monitoring the implementation of recommended control improvements to help ensure timeliness, effectiveness, and efficiency*

COMMUNICATIONS

To limit the risk of the unofficial dissemination of inappropriate or inaccurate information, the internal auditor can advise management in the ***design of a communication strategy and tactical plan*** *as early in the investigation as possible.*

In addition to fraud reporting mentioned above, there are two types of communications that may result from an investigation: ***public communications*** *that may arise and* ***planned internal communications.***

Any ***comments made by management*** *to the press, law enforcement, or other external parties are best coordinated through legal counsel. Comments should be made only by authorized spokespersons.*

Internal communications *are a strategic tool used by management to reinforce its position relating to* ***integrity****, to demonstrate that it takes appropriate action when company* ***policy is violated****, and to show why* ***internal controls*** *are important. Such communications may take the form of a newsletter article or a memo from management, or the situation may be used as an example in the organization's integrity training program. These communications generally take place* ***after the case has been resolved internally****, and they do not specify the names of perpetrators or other specific investigation details that are not necessary for the message or that contravene laws.*

An investigation and its results may cause ***significant stress or morale issues*** *that may disrupt the organization, especially when the fraud becomes public. Management may plan interactive employee sessions and/or team building strategies for this contingency.*

FORMING AN OPINION ON THE SYSTEM OF INTERNAL CONTROL RELATED TO FRAUD

The internal auditor may be asked by management or the board to express an opinion on the organization's system of internal control related to fraud. Auditors should refer to various practice advisories in the 2410 series and other IIA practice aids, such as "Practical Considerations Regarding Internal Auditing Expressing an Opinion on Internal Controls," to determine whether they have sufficiently considered related information before expressing an opinion.

PA Summary

- The **fraud investigation** described in PA 1210.A2-2 (as opposed to an audit for fraud) is begun when (1) concern about **control failures** or (2) suspicion of wrongdoing is raised within the organization. An investigation should be designed to determine whether fraud has occurred, the loss or exposures, who was involved, and the fraud scheme. It should discover the **full nature and extent** of the fraud. The investigation and resolution activities must be in accordance with local law, and the auditor should work effectively with legal counsel and become familiar with the relevant laws.
- **Management** should develop **controls over the investigation process**, including policies, procedures, and standards. Such standards are often documented in a **fraud policy**, and internal audit may be involved in developing the policy. Policies and procedures must consider (1) the rights of individuals, (2) the qualifications of investigators, (3) relevant laws, (4) the extent of discipline, (5) the authority and responsibilities of the persons involved in the investigation, and (6) compliance with procedures for minimizing internal communication about an ongoing investigation. The policy should specify the **role the investigator will have in making a determination that fraud has been committed**.
- The **role of internal audit** should be defined in the **charter**. Moreover, fraud investigation teams must be **proficient** regarding fraud schemes, investigation methods, and the law. If internal audit is responsible for the investigation, use of **external experts** (possibly pre-qualified) or nonaudit employees of the organization may be necessary. If auditors do not have primary responsibility for the investigation, they may be asked to **gather information and make recommendations for control improvements**.
- An **investigation plan** should be developed, and the lead investigator should assign people to the team. **Conflicts of interest** should be avoided. Furthermore, investigators should (1) assess the probable level and extent of **complicity in the fraud**; (2) determine **competencies** required; (3) design procedures; (4) **coordinate activities** with management, counsel, and other specialists; and (5) be aware of the **rights** of all persons and the organization's **reputation**.
- **Reporting of fraud** consists of the various oral or written, interim, or final communications to management or the board regarding the status and results of fraud investigations. A draft of the final communication should be submitted to **legal counsel for review**. To invoke **client privilege**, the report must be addressed to counsel. Internal audit has the responsibility to report immediately any **incident of significant fraud or erosion of trust** to senior management and the board. If the investigation's results indicate that **previously issued financial statements** may have been adversely affected, senior management and the board also should be informed. A formal communication is issued at the **end of the investigation**. The report may need to protect the **confidentiality** of some people and comply with the law and organizational policy.
- Management is responsible for **resolving fraud incidents**. Resolution consists of actions to be taken after completion of the investigation and review of the evidence. **Internal auditors** assess the facts and provide advice about remediation of control weaknesses. In addition, they should include procedures in **routine audit programs** or **design specific programs** for detecting fraud. **Management's fraud policies and procedures** should define who has authority and responsibility for each process. Internal auditors may be **advisors** in many parts of the process, but the effect on internal audit's **independence** should be handled appropriately.

PA Summary continued on next page

PA Summary continued

- The internal auditor may give advice about designing a **communication strategy and tactical plan**. Communications may include public communications and planned internal communications. **Comments by management** are best coordinated through legal counsel and made only by authorized spokespersons.
- An internal auditor asked to **express an opinion** on the system of internal control related to fraud should consult The IIA practice aids.

3. Stop and review! You have completed the outline for this subunit. Study multiple-choice questions 63 through 72 beginning on page 429.

10.5 FRAUD INDICATORS

1. Professional literature has devoted considerable attention to the **red flags** that may signal fraudulent conduct. The internal auditor should be alert to red flags and investigate any conditions that might indicate potential fraud. Red flags do not need to be documented unless the auditor conducts a fraud investigation or the red flags are pertinent to a particular engagement observation.
2. **Opportunities Contributing to or Permitting Fraud**
   a. Ineffective internal control, for example,
      1) Not separating the functional responsibilities of authorization, custodianship, and record keeping, e.g., failing to segregate users and computer functions, such as by access controls, or not segregating duties within the computer function
      2) Unlimited access to assets
      3) Failure to record transactions, resulting in lack of accountability
      4) Not comparing existing assets with recorded amounts
      5) Transaction execution without proper authorizations
      6) Not implementing prescribed controls because of
         a) Lack of personnel
         b) Unqualified personnel
      7) Lack of computer expertise by supervisors
      8) Ability to bypass controls with utility programs
      9) Unrestricted access to computer disks
      10) Location of computer terminals off-site without compensating controls
      11) Use of untested off-the-shelf vendor software
   b. Collusion among employees over whom little control is exercised
   c. Existence of liquid assets, such as cash, bearer securities, or highly marketable merchandise
   d. An employee is trusted so completely that duties are not segregated.
   e. A manager continually handles the organization's most urgent problems.
3. **Rationalizations for fraud.** (For a discussion, see Subunit 10.4.)
4. **Danger Signs Pointing toward the Possibility of Embezzlement** (Sawyer, Dittenhofer, and Scheiner, *Sawyer's Internal Auditing*, 5th ed., p. 1183). The following are some of the many **behavioral document or lifestyle symptoms** of fraud. Moreover, some of these symptoms may themselves create the **situational pressures** leading to fraud, for example, an excessive lifestyle, indebtedness, or gambling problems.
   a. *Borrowing small amounts from fellow employees*
   b. *Placing personal checks in change funds -- undated, postdated -- or requesting others to "hold" checks*

c. *Personal checks cashed and returned for irregular reasons*
d. *Collectors or creditors appearing at the place of business, and excessive use of telephone to "stall off" creditors*
e. *Placing unauthorized IOUs in change funds, or prevailing on others in authority to accept IOUs for small, short-term loans*
f. *Inclination toward covering up inefficiencies by "plugging" figures*
g. *Pronounced criticism of others, so as to divert suspicion*
h. *Replying to questions with unreasonable explanations*
i. *Gambling in any form beyond ability to stand the loss*
j. *Excessive drinking and nightclubbing or associating with questionable characters*
k. *Buying or otherwise acquiring through "business" channels expensive automobiles and extravagant household furnishings*
l. *Explaining a higher standard of living as money left from an estate*
m. *Getting annoyed at reasonable questioning*
n. *Refusing to leave custody of records during the day; working overtime regularly*
o. *Refusing to take vacations and shunning promotions for fear of detection*
p. *Constant association with, and entertainment by, a member of a supplier's staff*
q. *Carrying an unusually large bank balance, or heavy buying of securities*
r. *Extended illness of self or family, usually without a plan of debt liquidation*
s. *Bragging about exploits, and/or carrying unusual amounts of money*
t. *Rewriting records under the guise of neatness in presentation*

5. **Common Forms of Fraud** (Sawyer, Dittenhofer, and Scheiner, *Sawyer's Internal Auditing*, 5th ed., pp. 1181-1182)
   a. *Pilfering stamps*
   b. *Stealing merchandise, tools, supplies, and other items of equipment*
   c. *Removing small amounts from cash funds and registers*
   d. *Failing to record sales of merchandise, and pocketing the cash*
   e. *Creating overages in cash funds and registers by underrecording*
   f. *Overloading expense accounts or diverting advances to personal use*
   g. *Lapping collections on customers' accounts*
   h. *Pocketing payments on customers' accounts, issuing receipts on scraps of paper or in self-designed receipt books*
   i. *Collecting an account, pocketing the money, and charging it off to bad debt expense; collecting charged-off accounts and not reporting*
   j. *Charging customers' accounts with cash stolen*
   k. *Issuing credit for false customer claims and returns*
   l. *Failing to make bank deposits daily, or depositing only part of the money*
   m. *Altering dates on deposit slips to cover stealing*
   n. *Making round sum deposits -- attempting to catch up by end of month*
   o. *Carrying fictitious extra help on payrolls, or increasing rates or hours*
   p. *Carrying employees on payroll beyond actual severance dates*
   q. *Falsifying additions to payrolls; withholding unclaimed wages*
   r. *Destroying, altering, or voiding cash sales tickets and pocketing the cash*
   s. *Withholding cash sales amounts by using false charge accounts*
   t. *Recording unwarranted cash discounts*
   u. *Increasing amounts of petty cash vouchers and/or totals in accounting for disbursements*

v. *Using personal expenditure receipts to support false paid-out items*
w. *Using carbon copies of previously used original vouchers, or using a properly approved voucher of a prior period by changing the date*
x. *Paying false invoices, either self-prepared or obtained through collusion with suppliers*
y. *Increasing the amounts of suppliers' invoices through collusion*
z. *Charging personal purchases to the company through the misuse of purchase orders*
aa. *Billing stolen merchandise to fictitious accounts*
ab. *Shipping stolen merchandise to an employee or relative's home*
ac. *Falsifying inventories to cover thefts or delinquencies*
ad. *Seizing checks payable to the company or to suppliers*
ae. *Raising canceled bank checks to agree with fictitious entries*
af. *Inserting fictitious ledger sheets*
ag. *Causing erroneous footings of cash receipts and disbursements books*
ah. *Deliberately confusing postings to control and detail accounts*
ai. *Selling waste and scrap and pocketing the proceeds*
aj. *"Selling" door keys or combinations to safes or vaults*
ak. *Creating credit balances on ledgers and converting to cash*
al. *Falsifying bills of lading and splitting with carrier*
am. *Obtaining blank checks (unprotected) and forging the signature*
an. *Permitting special prices or privileges to customers, or granting business to favored suppliers, for "kickbacks"*
ao. *Improper use of access cards, such as credit, retail, telephone, and smart cards*

6. **Management fraud** usually occurs because of the ease with which management can circumvent the system of internal control. Sawyer, Dittenhofer, and Scheiner list eight reasons behind management fraud. These are **motives (incentives or situational pressures)**.
   a. *Executives sometimes take rash steps from which they cannot retreat.*
   b. *Profit centers may distort facts to hold off divestment.*
   c. *Incompetent managers may deceive to survive.*
   d. *Performance may be distorted to warrant larger bonuses.*
   e. *The need to succeed can turn managers to deception.*
   f. *Unscrupulous managers may serve interests that conflict.*
   g. *Profits may be inflated to obtain advantages in the market place.*
   h. *The one who controls both the assets and their records is in a perfect position to falsify the latter.*

7. **Fraud Danger Signals.** Even the most effective internal control can sometimes be circumvented -- perhaps by collusion of two or more employees. Thus, an auditor must be sensitive to certain conditions that might indicate the existence of fraud, including
   a. High personnel turnover
   b. Low employee morale
   c. Paperwork supporting adjusting entries not readily available
   d. Bank reconciliations not completed promptly
   e. Increases in the number of customer complaints
   f. Deteriorating income trend when the industry or the organization as a whole is doing well
   g. Numerous audit adjustments of significant size
   h. Write-offs of inventory shortages with no attempt to determine cause
   i. Unrealistic performance expectations

j. Rumors of conflicts of interest
k. Use of duplicate invoices to support payments to suppliers
l. Use of sole-source procurement contracts

8. **Organizational-Level Red Flags** (*Tone at the Top*, The IIA, November 2003)
   a. Abnormally rapid growth or profits, particularly relative to the industry
   b. Financial results excessively better than those of competitors absent significant operational differences
   c. Unexplained changes in trends or financial statement relationships
   d. Accounts or operations located in tax-haven countries without a good business rationale
   e. Decentralized operations coupled with a weak internal reporting system
   f. Earnings growth combined with a lack of cash
   g. Excessively optimistic public statements about future growth
   h. Use of accounting principles that conform with the letter (form) of requirements, not the substance, or that vary from industry practice
   i. A debt ratio that is too high or difficulty in paying debt
   j. Excessive sensitivity to interest rate fluctuations
   k. End-of-period transactions that are complex, unusual, or significant
   l. Nonenforcement of the organization's ethics code
   m. Material related-party transactions not in the ordinary course of business
   n. Potential business failure in the near term
   o. Use of unusual legal entities, many lines of authority, or contracts with no obvious business reason
   p. Business arrangements that are difficult to understand and do not seem to have any practical applicability to the entity.
9. Stop and review! You have completed the outline for this subunit. Study multiple-choice questions 73 through 89 beginning on page 433.

10.6 ENGAGEMENT PROCEDURES RELATED TO FRAUD

1. The nature and extent of the specific procedures performed to detect and investigate fraud depend on the circumstances of the particular engagement, including the unique characteristics of the organization and the internal auditor's risk assessment.
   a. Accordingly, an outline of the many possible procedures relative to fraud is beyond the scope of this text. However, **analytical procedures** are routinely performed in many engagements. They may provide an early indication of fraud.

2. Internal auditors should have an awareness of the circumstances in which their own procedures and expertise may be insufficient. Thus, they may need to make use of **specialists**.
   a. For example, **forensic experts** may supply special knowledge regarding authenticity of documents and signatures, mechanical sources of documents (printers, typewriters, computers, etc.), paper and ink chemistry, and fingerprint analysis.
3. **Forensic auditing** is the use of accounting and auditing knowledge and skills in matters having civil or criminal legal implications. Engagements involving fraud, litigation support, and expert witness testimony are examples.
4. Stop and review! You have completed the outline for this subunit. Study multiple-choice questions 90 through 106 beginning on page 438.

10.7 CONTROLS RELATED TO FRAUD

1. Like engagement procedures, specific controls are too diverse to be within the scope of this text.
2. Study Units 5 and 6 contain extensive guidance on control concepts, vocabulary, and techniques. They apply to the design and implementation of controls that are relevant to, among many other things, the prevention and detection of fraud.
3. Stop and review! You have completed the outline for this subunit. Study multiple-choice questions 107 through 114 beginning on page 445.

10.8 STUDY UNIT 10 SUMMARY

1. Procedures are performed to obtain sufficient, competent, relevant, and useful information to achieve the engagement objectives. Assurance and consulting engagements are within the scope of internal auditing.
2. Auditors must be proficient in the highest levels of comprehension. Analysis results in an understanding of a situation, set of circumstances, or process. This understanding should apply both to the elements AND to the relationship of the elements of a situation, set of circumstances, or process. Synthesis involves developing standards and generalizations for a situation, set of circumstances, or a process. It is a means of combining individual components or parts to produce a whole. Evaluation is relating a situation, set of circumstances, or process to predetermined or synthesized standards. Evaluation usually includes both analysis and synthesis.
3. Engagement procedures are designed to gather information that corroborates and documents evidence that specified risk management, control, and governance processes are effective.
4. Selection of procedures requires understanding how they relate to (a) the information to be gathered; (b) the underlying activity; and (c) the organization's systems, processes, and procedures. An auditor also must understand the nature of risk and determine that procedures meet legal, contractual, and professional requirements.
5. In financial audits, an understanding of an assertions model may be needed.
6. Observing is a purposeful visual examination involving a mental comparison with standards and an evaluation of what is seen.
7. Questioning may be done orally or in writing. It is the most pervasive procedure in reviews of operations.
8. Analysis means understanding a whole by studying its parts. Analytical procedures are performed to discover "qualities, causes, effects, motives, and possibilities" as a basis for judgment or further examination.
9. Verifying is a process of corroboration and comparison.
10. Investigating is a systematic search for hidden facts when wrongdoing or otherwise suspect conditions exist.
11. Evaluating is appraisal or estimation of work, i.e., the making of a judgment. This conclusion is a determination of the adequacy, efficiency, and effectiveness of the subject matter.
12. Codes of ethics may be viewed from an organizational or an individual perspective.
13. Issues in business ethics include compliance, external reporting, conflicts of interest, relations with customers and suppliers, and social responsibility.
14. Many organizational and external factors may lead to unethical behavior.
15. General guides to ethics are diverse: (a) the Golden Rule, (b) fairness, (c) general respect, (d) law, (e) Kant's categorical imperative, (f) natural law, (g) utilitarian ethics, and (h) various concepts of social responsibility.

16. A code of ethics communicates acceptable values to members and people outside the organization, provides a method of policing and disciplining members, and sets high standards.
17. An internal auditor must follow The IIA Code of Ethics. According to its Rules of Conduct, an internal auditor must
    a. Perform work with honesty, diligence, and responsibility
    b. Observe the law and make proper disclosures
    c. Not knowingly be a party to an illegal activity or engage in discreditable acts
    d. Respect and contribute to appropriate organizational objectives
    e. Avoid activities or relationships, including conflicts of interest, that presumably impair unbiased assessment
    f. Accept nothing that impairs professional judgment
    g. Disclose material facts so that reports are not distorted
    h. Use and protect information prudently
    i. Not use information for personal gain or in a way contrary to law or appropriate organizational objectives
    j. Perform services only if (s)he has the needed competencies
    k. Perform services in accordance with the Standards
    l. Improve proficiency continually
18. Fraud encompasses an array of irregularities and illegal acts characterized by intentional deception. It can be perpetrated for the benefit, or to the detriment, of the organization and by persons outside as well as inside the organization. Fraud perpetrated to the detriment of the organization generally is for the direct or indirect benefit of an employee, outside individual, or another organization. Fraud designed to benefit the organization generally produces such benefit by exploiting an unfair or dishonest advantage that also may deceive an outside party.
19. The factors that influence the commission of fraud are opportunity, motive (incentive or pressure), and rationalization.
20. Fraud risk has two elements: (a) the probability of fraud and (b) the consequence if it occurs.
21. The COSO has sections on (a) event identification, (b) risk assessments, (c) risk response strategies, (d) control activities, and (e) monitoring.
22. The elements of the COSO control framework provide an example of the control elements of a fraud prevention program: (a) control environment, (b) fraud risk assessment, (c) control activities, (d) information and communication, and (e) monitoring.
23. Internal auditors should consider fraud risk when assessing control design and selecting audit procedures.
24. An investigation should be designed to discover the full nature and extent of the fraud.
25. Controls over the investigation must consider (a) the rights of individuals, (b) the qualifications of investigators, (c) relevant laws, (d) the extent of discipline, (e) the authority and responsibilities of the persons involved, and (f) compliance with procedures for minimizing internal communication about investigation.
26. Investigators should (a) assess the probable level and extent of complicity in the fraud, (b) determine competencies required, (c) design procedures, (d) coordinate activities, and (e) be aware of the rights of all persons and the organization's reputation.
27. Reporting of fraud consists of the various oral or written, interim, or final communications to management or the board regarding the status and results of fraud investigations.

28. Resolution consists of actions to be taken after completion of the investigation and review of the evidence. Internal auditors assess the facts and provide advice about remediation of control weaknesses.
29. Management's fraud policies and procedures should define who has authority and responsibility for each process.
30. Professional literature has devoted considerable attention to the red flags that may signal fraudulent conduct. The internal auditor should be alert to red flags and investigate any conditions that might indicate potential fraud. Red flags do not need to be documented unless the auditor conducts a fraud investigation or the red flags are pertinent to a particular engagement observation.
31. Forensic auditing is the use of accounting and auditing knowledge and skills in matters having civil or criminal legal implications. Engagements involving fraud, litigation support, and expert witness testimony are examples.

QUESTIONS

10.1 Engagement Procedures

1. Internal auditors must use both inductive and deductive reasoning when gathering information and reaching conclusions. They must also understand the differences between the two types of reasoning in order to assess the strengths and weaknesses of each. Which of the following procedures uses deductive reasoning?

A. The internal auditor uses generalized audit software to select a sample of items for confirmation. Based on the confirmation responses, the auditor concludes that accounts receivable as recorded exist.

B. The internal auditor performs analytical procedures to estimate the accuracy of the sales account balance. No material differences are noted. Based on this, the internal auditor assumes that the underlying record keeping must be correct.

C. The internal auditor observes the client's physical inventory process and records test counts of inventory. Those test counts are traced to the year-end inventory compilation, and no exceptions are noted. The internal auditor concludes that the compiled inventory exists.

D. The internal auditor examines sales transactions recorded during January Year 2 and finds that none of those sales represent Year 1 sales. The internal auditor concludes that Year 1 sales are recorded properly.

Answer (B) is correct. *(CIA, adapted)*

REQUIRED: The audit procedure using deductive reasoning.

DISCUSSION: Deductive reasoning is the inference of a conclusion about particulars from general or universal premises. In contrast, inductive reasoning is the inference of a generalized conclusion from particular instances. Analytical procedures are based on the general premise that plausible relationships among the data may reasonably be expected to continue in the absence of known conditions to the contrary. For example, absent unusual circumstances, the sales balance is relatively predictable given its known relationship to other factors, such as cost of sales. Thus, the process is one of deductive reasoning because a general premise (the known relationship of sales to other data) is applied to draw a conclusion about a particular instance (the sales balance).

Answer (A) is incorrect because sampling receivables is an example of an inductive process. It entails gathering empirical data about particular items and then determining the general principle that the evidence supports. Answer (C) is incorrect because test counting inventory is an example of an inductive process. It entails gathering empirical data about particular items and then determining the general principle that the evidence supports. Answer (D) is incorrect because examining sales recorded after the balance sheet date is an example of an inductive process. It entails gathering empirical data about particular items and then determining the general principle that the evidence supports.

Inductive vs. Deductive

2. The internal auditor is concerned about whether all the debits to the computer security expense account are appropriate expenditures. The most appropriate engagement procedure is to

A. Take an attribute sample of computing invoices and determine whether all invoices are properly classified.

B. Perform an analytical review comparing the amount of expenditures incurred this year with the amounts incurred on a trend line for the past 5 years.

C. Take an attribute sample of employee wage expenses incurred by the outsourcing organization and trace to the proper account classification.

D. Take a sample of all debits to the account and investigate by examining source documents to determine the nature and authority of the expenditure.

Answer (D) is correct. *(CIA, adapted)*

REQUIRED: The most appropriate audit procedure to determine the validity of computer security expenses.

DISCUSSION: The sample should be taken from the population of interest, that is, debits to the expense account. The proper engagement procedure is to vouch the accounting records to the source documents.

Answer (A) is incorrect because the sample would be too broad to be efficient. The auditor is specifically interested in the debits to the account. Answer (B) is incorrect because analytical procedures provide information as to whether the total expense is reasonable. They do not determine whether specific debits are correct. Answer (C) is incorrect because this procedure furnishes some information about the wage component of costs, but it is not relevant to other computer security costs.

3. A production manager for a moderate-sized manufacturer began ordering excessive raw materials and had the materials delivered to a wholesaler the manager runs as a side business. The manager falsified receiving documents and approved the invoices for payment. Which of the following engagement procedures most likely will detect this fraud?

A. Take a sample of cash disbursements; compare purchase orders, receiving reports, invoices, and check copies.

B. Take a sample and confirm the amount purchased, purchase price, and date of shipment with the vendors.

C. Observe the receiving dock and count materials received; compare the counts to receiving reports completed by receiving personnel.

D. Prepare analytical tests comparing production, materials purchased, and raw materials inventory levels and investigate differences.

Answer (D) is correct. *(CIA, adapted)*

REQUIRED: The audit procedure most likely to detect the fraud.

DISCUSSION: Because the materials are shipped to and used in another business, the analytic comparisons (variance analysis) will show an unexplained increase in materials used.

Answer (A) is incorrect because documents have been falsified, and all supporting documents should match for each cash disbursement. Answer (B) is incorrect because all transactions will appear to be valid from the perspective of vendors. Answer (C) is incorrect because fraudulent orders are shipped to another location. Thus, the receiving dock activities will appear to be satisfactory.

4. To determine whether credit controls are inconsistently applied, preventing valid sales to creditworthy customers, the internal auditor should

A. Confirm current accounts receivable.

B. Trace postings on the accounts receivable ledger.

C. Analyze collection rates and credit histories.

D. Compare credit histories for those receiving credit and for those denied credit.

Answer (D) is correct. *(CIA, adapted)*

REQUIRED: The audit procedure to determine whether credit controls are inconsistently applied.

DISCUSSION: Credit policy should maximize profits by balancing bad debt losses and the increase in sales derived from granting credit. One concern in an engagement involving credit management is whether credit policies and procedures are fairly administered.

Answer (A) is incorrect because, if credit is not granted, there would be no balance to confirm. Answer (B) is incorrect because, if credit is not granted, there would be no posting to trace. Answer (C) is incorrect because, if credit is not granted, there would be no receivable to collect.

Question 5 is based on the following information. The internal audit activity has been assigned to perform an engagement involving a division. Based on background review, the internal auditor knows the following about management policies:

- Organizational policy is to rapidly promote divisional managers who show significant success. Thus, successful managers rarely stay at a division for more than 3 years.
- A significant portion of division management's compensation comes in the form of bonuses based on the division's profitability.

The division was identified by senior management as a turnaround opportunity. The division is growing but is not scheduled for a full audit by the external auditors this year. The division has been growing about 7% per year for the past 3 years and uses a standard cost system.

During the preliminary review, the internal auditor notes the following changes in financial data compared with the prior year:

- Sales have increased by 10%.
- Cost of goods sold has increased by 2%.
- Inventory has increased by 15%.
- Divisional net profit has increased by 8%.

5. It is November and the internal auditing manager is finalizing plans for a year-end engagement at the division. Based on the data, the engagement procedure with highest priority is to

A. Select sales transactions and trace shipping documents to entries into cost of goods sold to determine whether all shipments were recorded.

B. Schedule a complete count of inventory at year-end and have the internal auditor observe and test the year-end inventory.

C. Schedule a complete investigation of the standard cost system by preparing cost buildups of a sample of products.

D. Schedule a year-end sales cutoff test.

Answer (B) is correct. *(CIA, adapted)*

REQUIRED: The audit procedure with the highest priority.

DISCUSSION: Given that sales increased by 10% and inventory by 15% while cost of goods sold increased by only 2%, the data indicate that inventory is overstated and cost of goods sold is understated. Inventory might be overstated because of either quantity or cost differences. Because year-end is near, the most appropriate procedure is to begin a physical observation of inventory and extend the engagement to price tests after establishing the existence of inventory.

Answer (A) is incorrect because testing sales is appropriate, but the major problem appears to be the existence of inventory, and the internal auditor should start there. Answer (C) is incorrect because investigating the standard cost system is appropriate, but the major problem appears to be the existence of inventory, and the internal auditor should start there. Answer (D) is incorrect because the problem is occurring during normal operations. Because of the red flags, the internal auditor should schedule a cutoff test, but the existing red flags point primarily to a problem with inventory overstatement.

6. Assume the internal auditor becomes concerned that significant fraud may be taking place by dentists who are billing the health care processor for services that were not provided. For example, employees may have their teeth cleaned, but the dentist charges the processor for pulling teeth and developing dentures. The most effective procedure to determine whether such a fraud exists is to

A. Develop a schedule of payments made to individual dentists. Verify that payments were made to the dentists by confirming the payments with the health care processor.

B. Take a random sample of payments made to dentists and confirm the amounts paid with the dentists' offices to determine that the amounts agree with the amounts billed by the dentists.

C. Take a random sample of claims submitted by dentists and trace through the system to determine whether the claims were paid at the amounts billed.

D. Take a discovery sample of employee claims that were submitted through dentist offices, and confirm the type of service performed by the dentist through direct correspondence with the employee who had the service performed.

Answer (D) is correct. *(CIA, adapted)*

REQUIRED: The most effective audit procedure to reveal overcharging by districts.

DISCUSSION: A discovery sample is used to identify critical errors or irregularities, that is, when a single deviation is critical. This method cannot be used to evaluate the results statistically if deviations are found. Because dentists are suspected of filing fraudulent claims, the auditor should take a discovery sample of employee claims. The internal auditor should then confirm the work done by the dentist according to the claim with the employee. The employee is the best source of information as to whether the service was provided.

Answer (A) is incorrect because developing a schedule of payments and verifying that the payments were made does not reveal whether the claims were proper or fraudulent. Answer (B) is incorrect because verifying that dentists were paid the amounts that they billed does not reveal whether the claims were proper or fraudulent. Answer (C) is incorrect because verifying that claims were paid at the amounts billed does not reveal whether the claims were proper or fraudulent.

7. The internal auditor found that the purchasing department has a policy of setting all purchasing lead times to the highest number of days experienced within each product subassembly, even though some subassemblies required 3 or more months to complete. To address the objective of reducing inventory holding costs related to this policy, the internal auditor should focus on

A. Reviewing production requirements for a sample of products to determine at which point in the production process materials and subassemblies are needed.

B. Evaluating whether product-line assignments were rotated among the members of the purchasing department.

C. Identifying signature approval authority among members of the purchasing department in relation to any computer system controls.

D. Testing those products having the highest sales to determine the average number of days that the completed products were held in inventory.

Answer (A) is correct. *(CIA, adapted)*

REQUIRED: The audit procedure to address the objective of reducing inventory holding costs given that purchasing uses a uniform lead time.

DISCUSSION: The effect of the current policy is to increase inventory holding costs. Using the longest lead time avoids stockout costs but ensures that many items will be delivered long before they are needed.

Answer (B) is incorrect because rotating assignments would not directly affect holding costs. Answer (C) is incorrect because approval requirements would not increase holding costs. Answer (D) is incorrect because this would address holding costs for finished goods, but not for raw materials and subassemblies.

8. A large manufacturer has a transportation division that supplies gasoline for the organization's vehicles. Gasoline is dispensed by an attendant who records the amount issued on a serially prenumbered gasoline disbursement form, which is then given to the accounting department for proper recording. When the quantity of gasoline falls to a certain level, the service station attendant prepares a purchase requisition and sends it to the purchasing department where a purchase order is prepared and recorded in a gasoline purchases journal. Which of the following engagement procedures will best determine whether gasoline disbursements are fully and completely recorded?

A. Compare the gasoline purchase requisitions with the gasoline disbursement records.

B. Select a number of gasoline purchases from the gasoline purchases journal and compare them with their corresponding purchase orders and ascertain that they are serially prenumbered, are matched with purchase requisitions, and are authorized by someone independent of employees of the service station.

C. Perform analytical procedures comparing this period's gasoline consumption with prior periods.

D. Match the quantity of gasoline disbursed according to disbursement forms with an independent reading of quantity disbursed at the pump.

Answer (D) is correct. *(CIA, adapted)*

REQUIRED: The best audit procedure to determine whether gasoline disbursements are fully and completely recorded.

DISCUSSION: Physical information is best obtained through direct observation or inspection by the internal auditor. Because the gasoline disbursement forms are prenumbered, the internal auditor is able to match them with the independent reading of quantity disbursed at the pump to test the completeness of disbursement records.

Answer (A) is incorrect because matching the gasoline purchase requisitions with the gasoline disbursement records is not a meaningful procedure. Temperature-related expansion and contraction can cause significant differences between purchases and disbursements. Answer (B) is incorrect because matching entries from the gasoline purchases journal with the corresponding purchase orders ascertains that purchases are supported by proper source documents but does not assure the completeness of the disbursement records. Answer (C) is incorrect because performing analytical procedures does not provide any information regarding proper controls over gasoline purchases.

9. Which of the following engagement techniques would be most persuasive in determining that significant inventory values on the books of an acquiree are accurately stated?

A. Obtain a management representation letter stating that inventory values are correctly stated.

B. Flowchart the inventory and warehousing cycle and form an opinion based on the quality of internal controls.

C. Conduct a physical inventory and bring in an independent expert if necessary to value inventory items.

D. Interview purchasing and materials control personnel to ascertain the quality of internal controls over inventory.

Answer (C) is correct. *(CIA, adapted)*
REQUIRED: The audit procedure providing the most persuasive evidence that inventory is accurately stated.
DISCUSSION: A physical inventory should almost certainly be requested for an acquisition involving significant inventory values. The internal auditor's direct observation of inventory provides the most reliable information. Appraisal by an outside service provider may be necessary if the internal audit activity lacks the necessary expertise.
Answer (A) is incorrect because management certification as a means of attesting inventory values does not provide sufficient, reliable, relevant, and useful information. Answer (B) is incorrect because flowcharting the internal controls is not an accurate test of inventory value. Answer (D) is incorrect because testimonial information is not sufficient to determine the correctness of inventory values.

10. Cash receipts should be deposited on the day of receipt or the following business day. Select the most appropriate engagement procedure to determine that cash is promptly deposited.

A. Review cash register tapes prepared for each sale.

B. Review the functions of cash handling and maintaining accounting records for proper separation of duties.

C. Compare the daily cash receipts totals with the bank deposits.

D. Review the functions of cash receiving and disbursing for proper separation of duties.

Answer (C) is correct. *(CIA, adapted)*
REQUIRED: The most appropriate audit procedure to determine that cash is promptly deposited.
DISCUSSION: A standard control over the cash receipts function is to require that daily cash receipts be deposited promptly and intact. Hence, the total of cash receipts for a day should equal the bank deposit because no cash disbursements are made from the daily receipts. To determine whether cash receipts are promptly deposited, the internal auditor should compare the daily cash receipts totals with bank deposits.
Answer (A) is incorrect because cash register tapes will not ensure that cash is deposited. Answer (B) is incorrect because separating functions will not ensure that cash is deposited. Answer (D) is incorrect because separate receiving and disbursing functions will not ensure that cash is promptly deposited.

11. One of the engagement objectives of a financial audit of the organization's accounts receivable function is to determine whether prescribed standard procedures are followed when credit is granted. Which of the following engagement procedures will produce the most reliable information?

A. Ask management of the credit department if specific policies and procedures are followed when granting credit.

B. Select a statistical sample of credit applications and test them for conformance with prescribed procedures.

C. Analytically review the relationships between trends in credit sales and bad debts.

D. Review procedures for periodically aging accounts receivable.

Answer (B) is correct. *(CIA, adapted)*
REQUIRED: The audit procedure resulting in the most competent evidence regarding the accounts receivable function.
DISCUSSION: To determine whether the accounts receivable function is following prescribed standards for the granting of credit, the internal auditor should select a statistical sample of credit applications and test them for conformance with prescribed procedures. Detailed testing of actual credit applications produces direct information about the application (or the lack of application) of specific procedures, for example, authorization of credit by an appropriate individual.
Answer (A) is incorrect because interviews with credit department management produce testimonial information that is more useful in gaining an understanding of operations or providing insight into the reasons for exceptions. Answer (C) is incorrect because analytical procedures can be used to isolate unusual or unexplained fluctuations but do not locate the cause. Answer (D) is incorrect because an aged accounts receivable schedule provides information about whether a particular account might be collected, not the application of credit procedures.

12. In a review of the accounting department's bank reconciliation unit, which of the following is an appropriate engagement procedure to test canceled checks for authorized signatures?

A. Compare the check date with the first cancelation date.

B. Determine that all checks are signed by individuals authorized by the board.

C. Examine a representative sample of signed checks and determine that the signatures are authorized in the organization's signature book.

D. Complete the tests of controls over check signatures in 4 hours.

Answer (C) is correct. *(CIA, adapted)*

REQUIRED: The audit procedure step for the review of canceled checks for authorization.

DISCUSSION: Cash disbursements must be properly authorized. The issuance of checks is performed by the treasury function after review of supporting documents, including a payment voucher prepared by the accounts payable department. Proper control procedures require that check-signing responsibility be limited to a few persons whose signatures are kept on file at the financial institutions where the organization has accounts.

Answer (A) is incorrect because comparing the check date with the first cancelation date has no bearing on a review for authorized signatures. Answer (B) is incorrect because a statement of an engagement objective is not an engagement procedure. Answer (D) is incorrect because a time budget goal is not an engagement procedure.

13. During an engagement to review the December 31, Year 2, accounts payable balance of a division, the internal auditor has received from the division controller's office a schedule listing the creditors and the amount owed to each at December 31, Year 2. Which of the following engagement procedures best determines that no individual account payable has been omitted from the schedule?

A. Send confirmation requests to a randomly selected sample of creditors listed on the schedule.

B. Send confirmation requests to creditors listed on the schedule that were not listed on the corresponding December 31, Year 1, schedule.

C. Examine support for selected January Year 3 payments to creditors, ascertaining that those relating to Year 3 are not on the schedule.

D. Examine support for selected January Year 3 payments to creditors, ascertaining that those relating to Year 2 are on the schedule.

Answer (D) is correct. *(CIA, adapted)*

REQUIRED: The best audit procedure to detect unrecorded payables.

DISCUSSION: The greatest danger in an engagement involving accounts payable is that unrecorded liabilities exist. Omission of an entry to record a payable is an irregularity more difficult to detect than an inaccurate or false entry. The search for unrecorded payables should include examining cash disbursements made after the balance sheet date for expenditures for goods and services received prior to year-end and comparing them with the accounts payable trial balance, sending confirmations to vendors with zero balances, and reconciling payable balances with vendors' documentation.

Answer (A) is incorrect because confirmation is unlikely to detect unrecorded amounts owed to creditors not listed on the schedule. Answer (B) is incorrect because confirmation of zero balances might be more useful to detect unrecorded amounts than confirming amounts owed currently. Answer (C) is incorrect because this procedure is intended to detect overstatement, not understatement, of Year 2 payables.

14. Which is the best engagement procedure to obtain information to support the legal ownership of real property?

A. Examination of board resolutions with regard to approvals to acquire real property.

B. Examination of closing documents, deeds, and ownership documents registered and on file in local government records.

C. Discussion with the organization's legal counsel concerning the acquisition of a specific piece of property.

D. Confirmation with the title company that handled the escrow account and disbursement of proceeds on the closing of the property.

Answer (B) is correct. *(CIA, adapted)*

REQUIRED: The best audit procedure for obtaining evidence to support the legal ownership of real property.

DISCUSSION: Examination of title documents, the deed, and any other supporting documents, such as closing documents, will be helpful in verifying ownership. But these records are not conclusive. An inspection of public records will determine whether any interests in the property (e.g., mortgages, judgment liens, or claims to the title) exist that do not appear in the engagement client's records.

Answer (A) is incorrect because an examination of board resolutions will not provide information about actual ownership, only approval to acquire the property. Answer (C) is incorrect because the testimony of legal counsel provides only corroborating information. Answer (D) is incorrect because confirmation with an escrow agent provides information only about the closing. It does not provide information regarding subsequent transactions, such as a mortgage liability not recorded in the accounting records.

Question 15 is based on the following information. The internal auditor of a construction enterprise that builds foundations for bridges and large buildings performed a review of the expense accounts for equipment (augers) used to drill holes in rocks to set the foundation for the buildings. During the review, the internal auditor noted that the expenses related to some of the auger accounts had increased dramatically during the year. The internal auditor inquired of the construction manager who offered the explanation that the augers last 2 to 3 years and are expensed when purchased. Thus, the internal auditor should see a decrease in the expense accounts for these augers in the next year but would expect an increase in the expenses of other augers. The internal auditor also found out that the construction manager is responsible for the inventorying and receiving of the augers and is a part owner of a business that supplies augers to the organization. The supplier was approved by the president to improve the quality of equipment.

15. Which of the following procedures would be the least appropriate engagement procedure to address these analytical observations?

A. Note the explanation in the working papers for investigation during the next engagement and perform no further work at this time.

B. Develop a comparative analysis of auger expense over the past few years to determine if the relationship held in previous years.

C. Take a sample of debits to the auger expense account and trace to independent shipping documents and to invoices for the augers.

D. Arrange to take an inventory of augers to determine if the augers purchased this year were on hand and would be available for use in the next 2 years.

Answer (A) is correct. *(CIA, adapted)*

REQUIRED: The least appropriate audit procedure to address the findings.

DISCUSSION: Performing no further work is the least appropriate engagement procedure because it defers the investigation to the following year. The construction manager's conflict of interest provides the motive for fraud, and the ineffective controls allow its commission and concealment.

Answer (B) is incorrect because a comparative analysis is an effective procedure to establish the reasonableness of the manager's explanation. If the relationship is valid, it should also have held in previous years. Answer (C) is incorrect because the internal auditor should obtain independent information as to whether the goods invoiced were received. The internal auditor should search for receiving reports signed by parties other than the construction manager and should verify that those individuals exist. The construction manager is in a position to bill the organization for more augers than are actually received and to conceal the shortage. Answer (D) is incorrect because taking an inventory of the augers enables the internal auditor to verify their existence and condition.

16. The internal auditors are evaluating the adequacy of the new policies and procedures in maintaining an appropriate risk profile. Which of the following engagement procedures is least relevant to the accomplishment of the engagement objective?

A. Meet with operational management to determine its interpretation of those procedures that are not clear.

B. Meet with senior management or a board member, if necessary, to clarify policy issues.

C. Test a sample of investments for compliance with the new procedures.

D. Review recent regulatory pronouncements to determine whether the new procedures are consistent with regulatory requirements.

Answer (C) is correct. *(CIA, adapted)*

REQUIRED: The audit procedure least relevant to the evaluation of new controls over investing and lending activities.

DISCUSSION: Based on the results of the risk assessment, the internal audit activity should evaluate the adequacy and effectiveness of controls (for example, the new policies and procedures for monitoring investments and loans) encompassing the organization's governance, operations, and information systems. This should include, among other things, the reliability and integrity of financial information (Standard 2120.A1). Adequacy of risk management, control, and governance processes is present when management plans and designs them so that they provide reasonable assurance that organizational objectives and goals will be achieved efficiently and economically. Testing for compliance with controls is a procedure to determine their effectiveness, that is, whether management has directed processes so that they provide reasonable assurance that organizational objectives and goals will be achieved (PA 2100-1).

Answer (A) is incorrect because the internal auditors must seek authoritative interpretations of vague operating standards. Answer (B) is incorrect because policy issues that are not clear should be clarified by upper management or the board. Answer (D) is incorrect because the auditors should determine whether the criteria used by the organization comply with laws, regulations, and contracts.

Questions 17 and 18 are based on the following information. A company maintains production data on personal computers, connected by a local area network (LAN), and uses the data to generate automatic purchases via electronic data interchange. Purchases are made from authorized vendors based on production plans for the next month and on an authorized materials requirements plan (MRP) which identifies the parts needed for each unit of production.

17. The production line has experienced shut-downs because needed production parts were not on hand. Which of the following audit procedures would best identify the cause of the parts shortages?

A. Determine if access controls are sufficient to restrict the input of incorrect data into the production database.

B. Use generalized audit software to develop a complete list of the parts shortages that caused each of the production shutdowns, and analyze this data.

C. Select a random sample of parts on hand per the personal computer databases and compare with actual parts on hand.

D. Select a random sample of production information for selected days and trace input into the production database maintained on the LAN.

Answer (B) is correct. *(CIA, adapted)*

REQUIRED: The audit procedure that best identifies the cause of the parts shortages.

DISCUSSION: Internal auditors apply engagement (audit) procedures to obtain sufficient, competent, relevant, and useful information (evidence) to achieve the internal audit engagement's objectives. Analysis results in an understanding of a situation, set of circumstances, or process. It means understanding a whole by studying its parts. Analysis of a complete list of parts shortages establishes the cause.

Answer (A) is incorrect because access controls are not necessarily directly relevant. Authorized but incorrect data also could be the problem. Answer (C) is incorrect because testing a sample provides useful information, but it is not as comprehensive as analyzing the complete list of parts shortages. Answer (D) is incorrect because this procedure tests only one source of the data inaccuracy (that is, the input of production data). Other sources of potential error are ignored.

18. Which of the following audit procedures would be most effective in determining if purchasing requirements have been updated for changes in production techniques?

A. Recalculate parts needed based on current production estimates and the MRP for the revised production techniques. Compare these needs with purchase orders generated from the system for the same period.

B. Develop test data to input into the LAN and compare purchase orders generated from test data with purchase orders generated from production data.

C. Use generalized audit software to develop a report of excess inventory. Compare the inventory with current production volume.

D. Select a sample of production estimates and MRPs for several periods and trace them into the system to determine that input is accurate.

Answer (A) is correct. *(CIA, adapted)*

REQUIRED: The most effective auditing procedure for determining whether purchasing requirements have been updated.

DISCUSSION: Recalculating parts needed based on current information and comparing current purchase orders is the most appropriate procedure to determine the cause of the already known problem. This direct comparison of current parts requirements with purchase orders being generated allows for differences to be identified and corrective action taken.

Answer (B) is incorrect because the test data approach provides evidence that all items entered are processed. Comparison of these results with currently generated purchase orders does not provide evidence about whether the correct parts are being ordered. Answer (C) is incorrect because generalized audit software is a good method to identify an inventory problem. However, the excess inventory may not be the result of a revised production technique. Answer (D) is incorrect because this procedure provides evidence about the input of data into the system, but it does not provide evidence about whether changes in the production process have been implemented.

19. To ascertain that all credit sales are recorded in accounts receivable, an internal auditor should

A. Confirm selected accounts receivable balances by direct correspondence with customers.

B. Vouch a sample of subsidiary ledger entries to related sales invoices and to related shipping documents.

C. Compare a sample of customer purchase orders with related shipping documents.

D. Trace a sample of shipping documents to related sales invoices and the subsidiary ledger.

Answer (D) is correct. *(CIA, adapted)*

REQUIRED: The audit procedure to ascertain that all credit sales are recorded in accounts receivable.

DISCUSSION: Customer orders should be approved and sales invoices prepared before shipping documents are created. To determine that all credit sales are recorded, the proper direction of testing is from the shipping records, such as bills of lading, to the sales invoices and the accounts receivable subsidiary ledger.

Answer (A) is incorrect because confirming accounts receivable will not detect an unrecorded and unbilled receivable. Answer (B) is incorrect because vouching entries will not detect an unrecorded and unbilled receivable. Answer (C) is incorrect because comparing customer orders with shipping documents does not determine whether goods shipped were billed.

20. Divisional management stated that a recent gross margin increase was due to increased efficiency in manufacturing operations. Which of the following audit procedures would be most relevant to that assertion?

A. Obtain a physical count of inventory.

B. Select a sample of products, then compare costs-per-unit this year to those of last year, test cost buildups, and analyze standard cost variances.

C. Take a physical inventory of equipment to determine if there were significant changes.

D. Select a sample of finished goods inventory and trace raw materials cost back to purchase prices in order to determine the accuracy of the recorded raw materials price.

Answer (B) is correct. *(CIA, adapted)*

REQUIRED: The most relevant audit procedure when management states that a recent gross margin increase is due to increased efficiency in manufacturing operations.

DISCUSSION: An analysis of operations is relevant to determining the efficiency of operations. An increase in gross margin (sales – cost of sales) may result from an increase in unit sales or cost of sales, a decrease in unit cost of sales, an increase in inventory, or a combination of these factors. An increase in efficiency implies a greater output for a given level of cost. Accordingly, tests of unit costs and cost balance and analysis of variances are relevant procedures.

Answer (A) is incorrect because a physical inventory count is useful only to determine whether the gross margin increase was due to overstated inventory. Answer (C) is incorrect because simply counting equipment has little relevance to determining whether manufacturing costs per unit have decreased. The count does not determine whether the new equipment (if any) is more efficient. Answer (D) is incorrect because this procedure is relevant in determining the correctness of materials purchases, but it does not provide any evidence regarding the efficiency of operations.

10.2 Perspective on Ethics

21. A code of conduct was developed several years ago and distributed by a large financial institution to all its officers and employees. What is the internal auditor's best approach to providing the board with the highest level of comfort about the code of conduct?

A. Fully evaluate the comprehensiveness of the code and compliance with it and report the results to the board.

B. Fully evaluate organizational practices for compliance with the code, and report to the board.

C. Review employee activities for compliance with provisions of the code, and report to the board.

D. Perform tests on various employee transactions to detect potential violations of the code of conduct.

Answer (A) is correct. *(CIA, adapted)*

REQUIRED: The approach that provides the highest level of comfort about the code of conduct.

DISCUSSION: When evaluating a code of conduct, it is important to consider two items: comprehensiveness and compliance. The code should address the ethical issues that the employees are expected to encounter and provide suitable guidance. The internal auditor also must consider the extent to which employees are complying with the standards established.

Answer (B) is incorrect because evaluating practices and reporting to the board is not the best approach. Answer (C) is incorrect because reviewing employee activities does not provide as much comfort about the code of conduct as evaluation of comprehensiveness. Answer (D) is incorrect because performing tests on employee transactions is not the best approach.

22. A primary purpose of establishing a code of conduct within a professional organization is to

A. Reduce the likelihood that members of the profession will be sued for substandard work.

B. Ensure that all members of the profession perform at approximately the same level of competence.

C. Promote an ethical culture among professionals who serve others.

D. Require members of the profession to exhibit loyalty in all matters pertaining to the affairs of their organization.

Answer (C) is correct. *(CIA, adapted)*

REQUIRED: The primary purpose of establishing a code of conduct within a professional organization.

DISCUSSION: The IIA Code of Ethics is typical. Its purpose is "to promote an ethical culture in the profession of internal auditing." The definition of internal auditing states that it is "an independent, objective assurance and consulting activity." Moreover, internal auditing is founded on "the trust placed in its objective assurance about risk management, control, and governance." The IIA Code of Ethics further emphasizes that it provides guidance to internal auditors "serving others."

Answer (A) is incorrect because, although this result may follow from establishing a code of conduct, it is not the primary purpose. To consider it so would be self-serving. Answer (B) is incorrect because a code of conduct may help to establish minimum standards of competence, but it would be impossible to legislate equality of competence by all members of a profession. Answer (D) is incorrect because, in some situations, responsibility to the public at large may conflict with, and be more important than, loyalty to one's organization.

23. An accounting association established a code of ethics for all members. What is one of the association's primary purposes of establishing the code of ethics?

A. To outline criteria for professional behavior to maintain standards of integrity and objectivity.

B. To establish standards to follow for effective accounting practice.

C. To provide a framework within which accounting policies could be effectively developed and executed.

D. To outline criteria that can be used in conducting interviews of potential new accountants.

Answer (A) is correct. *(CIA, adapted)*

REQUIRED: The primary purpose of establishing a code of ethics.

DISCUSSION: The IIA Code of Ethics includes Principles and Rules of Conduct. Internal auditors are expected to apply and uphold four principles: integrity, objectivity, confidentiality, and competence.

Answer (B) is incorrect because national standard-setting bodies, not a code of ethics, provide guidance for effective accounting practice. Answer (C) is incorrect because a code of ethics does not provide the framework within which accounting policies are developed. Answer (D) is incorrect because the primary purpose is not for interviewing new accountants.

24. A review of an organization's code of conduct revealed that it contained comprehensive guidelines designed to inspire high levels of ethical behavior. The review also revealed that employees were knowledgeable of its provisions. However, some employees still did not comply with the code. What element should a code of conduct contain to enhance its effectiveness?

A. Periodic review and acknowledgment by all employees.

B. Employee involvement in its development.

C. Public knowledge of its contents and purpose.

D. Provisions for disciplinary action in the event of violations.

Answer (D) is correct. *(CIA, adapted)*

REQUIRED: The element that enhances the effectiveness of a code of conduct.

DISCUSSION: Penalties for violations of a code of conduct should enhance its effectiveness. Some individuals will be deterred from misconduct if they expect it to be detected and punished.

Answer (A) is incorrect because periodic review and acknowledgment would ensure employee knowledge and acceptance of the code, which are not at issue. Answer (B) is incorrect because employee involvement in development would encourage employee acceptance, which is not at issue. Answer (C) is incorrect because public knowledge might affect the behavior of some individuals but not to the same extent as the perceived likelihood of sanctions for wrongdoing.

25. In analyzing the differences between two recently merged businesses, the chief audit executive of Organization A notes that it has a formal code of ethics and Organization B does not. The code of ethics covers such things as purchase agreements, relationships with vendors, and other issues. Its purpose is to guide individual behavior within the firm. Which of the following statements regarding the existence of the code of ethics in A can be logically inferred?

I. A exhibits a higher standard of ethical behavior than does B.

II. A has established objective criteria by which an individual's actions can be evaluated.

III. The absence of a formal code of ethics in B would prevent a successful review of ethical behavior in that organization.

A. I and II.

B. II only.

C. III only.

D. II and III.

Answer (B) is correct. *(CIA, adapted)*

REQUIRED: The inference(s) regarding the existence or absence of a formal code of ethics.

DISCUSSION: A formal code of ethics effectively communicates acceptable values to all members, provides a method of policing and disciplining members for violations, establishes objective standards against which individuals can measure their own performance, and communicates the organization's value system to outsiders.

26. The best reason for establishing a code of conduct within an organization is that such codes

A. Are typically required by governments.

B. Express standards of individual behavior for members of the organization.

C. Provide a quantifiable basis for personnel evaluations.

D. Have tremendous public relations potential.

Answer (B) is correct. *(CIA, adapted)*

REQUIRED: The best reason for an organizational code of conduct.

DISCUSSION: An organization's code of ethical conduct is the established general value system the organization wishes to apply to its members' activities by communicating organizational purposes and beliefs and establishing uniform ethical guidelines for members, which include guidance on behavior for members in making decisions. Because laws and specific rules cannot cover all situations, organizations can benefit from having an established ethical code. It effectively communicates acceptable values to all members, including recruits and subcontractors. It also provides a method of policing and disciplining members for violations through formal review panels and group pressure (informal). A code establishes high standards against which individuals can measure their own performance and communicates to those outside the organization the value system from which its members must not be asked to deviate.

Answer (A) is incorrect because governments typically have no such requirement. Answer (C) is incorrect because codes of conduct provide qualitative, not quantitative, standards. Answer (D) is incorrect because other purposes of a code of conduct are much more significant.

27. Which of the following statements is not appropriate to include in a manufacturer's conflict of interest policy? An employee shall not

A. Accept money, gifts, or services from a customer.

B. Participate (directly or indirectly) in the management of a public agency.

C. Borrow from or lend money to vendors.

D. Use organizational information for private purposes.

Answer (B) is correct. *(CIA, adapted)*

REQUIRED: The item not included in a manufacturer's conflict of interest policy.

DISCUSSION: A prohibition on public service is ordinarily inappropriate. Public service is a right, if not a duty, of all citizens.

Answer (A) is incorrect because a conflict of interest policy should prohibit the transfer of benefits between an employee and those with whom the organization deals. Answer (C) is incorrect because a conflict of interest policy should prohibit financial dealings between an employee and those with whom the organization deals. Answer (D) is incorrect because The IIA Code of Ethics prohibits use of information for personal gain (Rule of Conduct 3.2).

10.3 The IIA Code of Ethics

28. In applying the Rules of Conduct set forth in The IIA Code of Ethics, internal auditors are expected to

A. Not be unduly influenced by their own interests in forming judgments.

B. Compare them with standards of other professions.

C. Be guided by the desires of the engagement client.

D. Use discretion in deciding whether to use them.

Answer (A) is correct. *(CIA, adapted)*

REQUIRED: The responsibility of internal auditors under The IIA Code of Ethics.

DISCUSSION: According to the objectivity principle stated in The IIA Code of Ethics, internal auditors exhibit the highest level of professional objectivity in gathering, evaluating, and communicating information about the activity or process being examined. Internal auditors make a balanced assessment of all the relevant circumstances and are not unduly influenced by their own interests or by others in forming judgments.

Answer (B) is incorrect because standards of other professions are not intended to provide guidance to internal auditors serving others. Answer (C) is incorrect because auditors should be independent of the engagement client. Answer (D) is incorrect because internal auditors must follow The IIA Code of Ethics.

29. The IIA Rules of Conduct set forth in The IIA Code of Ethics

A. Describe behavior norms expected of internal auditors.

B. Are guidelines to assist internal auditors in dealing with engagement clients.

C. Are interpreted by the Principles.

D. Apply only to particular conduct specifically mentioned.

Answer (A) is correct. *(CIA, adapted)*

REQUIRED: The true statement about The IIA Code of Ethics.

DISCUSSION: A code of ethics is necessary and appropriate for the profession of internal auditing, founded as it is on the trust placed in its objective assurance about risk management, control, and governance. The Institute's Code of Ethics extends beyond the definition of internal auditing to include two essential components: (1) Principles that are relevant to the profession and practice of internal auditing and (2) Rules of Conduct that describe behavior norms expected of internal auditors. These rules are an aid to interpreting the Principles into practical applications and are intended to guide the ethical conduct of internal auditors.

Answer (B) is incorrect because the Rules of Conduct provide guidance to internal auditors in the discharge of their responsibility to all those whom they serve. Engagement clients are not the only parties served by internal auditing. Answer (C) is incorrect because the Rules of Conduct are an aid in interpreting the Principles. Answer (D) is incorrect because the conduct may be unacceptable or discreditable although not mentioned in the Rules of Conduct.

30. The IIA Code of Ethics requires internal auditors to perform their work with

A. Honesty, diligence, and responsibility.

B. Timeliness, sobriety, and clarity.

C. Knowledge, skills, and competencies.

D. Punctuality, objectivity, and responsibility.

Answer (A) is correct. *(CIA, adapted)*

REQUIRED: The qualities internal auditors should exhibit in the performance of their work.

DISCUSSION: Four rules are stated under the integrity principle. According to Rule of Conduct 1.1 of The IIA Code of Ethics, "Internal auditors shall perform their work with honesty, diligence, and responsibility."

Answer (B) is incorrect because timeliness, sobriety, and clarity are not mentioned in the Code. Answer (C) is incorrect because knowledge, skills, and competencies are mentioned in the *Standards for the Professional Practice of Internal Auditing*. Answer (D) is incorrect because punctuality is not mentioned in the Code.

31. Which of the following is permissible under The IIA Code of Ethics?

A. Disclosing confidential, engagement-related, information that is potentially damaging to the organization in response to a court order.

B. Using engagement-related information in a decision to buy an ownership interest in the employer organization.

C. Accepting an unexpected gift from an employee whom the internal auditor has praised in a recent engagement communication.

D. Not reporting significant observations and recommendations about illegal activity to the board because management has indicated it will address the issue.

Answer (A) is correct. *(CIA, adapted)*

REQUIRED: The action permissible under The IIA Code of Ethics.

DISCUSSION: Under Rule of Conduct 1.2, "Internal auditors shall observe the law and make disclosures expected by the law and the profession." Thus, the requirement not to use information in any manner detrimental to the legitimate and ethical objectives of the organization (Rule of Conduct 3.2) does not override the legal obligation to respond to a court order.

Answer (B) is incorrect because Rule of Conduct 3.2 prohibits internal auditors from using information for personal gain. Answer (C) is incorrect because Rule of Conduct 2.2 prohibits internal auditors from accepting anything that may impair or be presumed to impair their professional judgment. Answer (D) is incorrect because Rule of Conduct 1.3 prohibits knowingly being a party to any illegal activity. Internal auditors must also disclose all material facts known to them that, if not disclosed, might distort the reporting of activities under review (Rule of Conduct 2.3).

32. An internal auditor, working for a chemical manufacturer, believed that toxic waste was being dumped in violation of the law. Out of loyalty to the organization, no information regarding the dumping was collected. The internal auditor

A. Violated the Code of Ethics by knowingly becoming a party to an illegal act.

B. Violated the Code of Ethics by failing to protect the well-being of the general public.

C. Did not violate the Code of Ethics. Loyalty to the employer in all matters is required.

D. Did not violate the Code of Ethics. Conclusive information about wrongdoing was not gathered.

Answer (A) is correct. *(CIA, adapted)*

REQUIRED: The ethical implication of failing to gather information about the organization's illegal act.

DISCUSSION: Rule of Conduct 1.3 prohibits knowingly being a party to any illegal activity. Internal auditors must also disclose all material facts known to them that, if not disclosed, might distort the reporting of activities under review (Rule of Conduct 2.3). The internal auditor apparently also failed to perform his/her work with diligence (Rule of Conduct 1.1).

Answer (B) is incorrect because The IIA Code of Ethics does not impose a duty to the general public. Answer (C) is incorrect because an internal auditor may not use information in any manner detrimental to the legitimate and ethical objectives of the organization (Rule of Conduct 3.2) and must respect and contribute to such objectives (Rule of Conduct 1.4). However, illegal dumping of toxic waste is neither legitimate nor ethical. Answer (D) is incorrect because the internal auditor should have collected and reported such information in accordance with the SPPIA.

33. An internal auditor discovered some material inefficiencies in a purchasing function. The purchasing manager is the internal auditor's next-door neighbor and best friend. In accordance with The IIA Code of Ethics, the internal auditor should

A. Objectively include the facts of the case in the engagement communications.

B. Not report the incident because of loyalty to the friend.

C. Include the facts of the case in a special communication submitted only to the friend.

D. Not report the friend unless the activity is illegal.

Answer (A) is correct. *(CIA, adapted)*

REQUIRED: The proper internal auditor action given a conflict between professional duty and friendship.

DISCUSSION: Under Rule of Conduct 2.3, "Internal auditors shall disclose all material facts known to them that, if not disclosed, may distort the reporting of activities under review." Furthermore, under Rule of Conduct 1.4, "Internal auditors shall respect and contribute to the legitimate and ethical objectives of the organization."

34. The chief audit executive (CAE) has been appointed to a committee to evaluate the appointment of the external auditors. The engagement partner for the external accounting firm wants the CAE to join her for a week of hunting at her private lodge. The CAE should

A. Accept, assuming both their schedules allow it.

B. Refuse on the grounds of conflict of interest.

C. Accept as long as it is not charged to employer time.

D. Ask the comptroller whether accepting the invitation is a violation of the organization's code of ethics.

Answer (B) is correct. *(CIA, adapted)*

REQUIRED: The CAE's response to a social invitation by an external auditor who is subject to evaluation by a committee on which the CAE serves.

DISCUSSION: Under Rule of Conduct 2.1, "Internal auditors shall not participate in any activity or relationship that may impair or be presumed to impair their unbiased assessment. This participation includes those activities or relationships that may be in conflict with the interests of the organization." Furthermore, under Rule of Conduct 2.2, "Internal auditors shall not accept anything that may impair or be presumed to impair their professional judgment."

Answer (A) is incorrect because the auditor should not accept. Answer (C) is incorrect because not changing the time to the company is not sufficient to eliminate conflict-of-interest concerns. Answer (D) is incorrect because the auditor should know that accepting the invitation raises conflict of interest issues.

35. An internal auditor for a large regional bank was asked to serve on the board of directors of a local bank. The bank competes in many of the same markets as the regional bank but focuses more on consumer financing than on business financing. In accepting this position, the internal auditor

I. Violates The IIA Code of Ethics because serving on the board may be in conflict with the best interests of the internal auditor's employer

II. Violates The IIA Code of Ethics because the information gained while serving on the board of directors of the local bank may influence recommendations regarding potential acquisitions

A. I only.

B. II only.

C. I and II.

D. Neither I nor II.

Answer (C) is correct. *(CIA, adapted)*

REQUIRED: The possible violation(s), if any, of The IIA Code of Ethics.

DISCUSSION: Under Rule of Conduct 2.1, "Internal auditors shall not participate in any activity or relationship that may impair or be presumed to impair their unbiased assessment. This participation includes those activities or relationships that may be in conflict with the interests of the organization." Accordingly, service on the board of the local bank constitutes a conflict of interest and may prejudice the internal auditor's ability to carry out objectively his or her duties regarding potential acquisitions.

36. Which of the following concurrent occupations could appear to subvert the ethical behavior of an internal auditor?

A. Internal auditor and a well-known charitable organization's local in-house chairperson.

B. Internal auditor and part-time business insurance broker.

C. Internal auditor and adjunct faculty member of a local business college that educates potential employees.

D. Internal auditor and landlord of multiple housing that publicly advertises for tenants in a local community newspaper listing monthly rental fees.

Answer (B) is correct. *(CIA, adapted)*

REQUIRED: The concurrent occupations that could create an ethical issue.

DISCUSSION: Under Rule of Conduct 2.1, "Internal auditors shall not participate in any activity or relationship that may impair or be presumed to impair their unbiased assessment. This participation includes those activities or relationships that may be in conflict with the interests of the organization." As a business insurance broker, the internal auditor may lose his or her objectivity because (s)he might benefit from a change in the employer's insurance coverage.

Answer (A) is incorrect because the activities of a charity are unlikely to be contrary to the interests of the organization. Answer (C) is incorrect because teaching is compatible with internal auditing. Answer (D) is incorrect because, whereas dealing in commercial properties might involve a conflict, renting residential units most likely does not.

37. Internal auditors should be prudent in their relationships with persons and organizations external to their employers. Which of the following activities will most likely not adversely affect internal auditors' ethical behavior?

A. Accepting compensation from professional organizations for consulting work.

B. Serving as consultants to competitor organizations.

C. Serving as consultants to suppliers.

D. Discussing engagement plans or results with external parties.

Answer (A) is correct. *(CIA, adapted)*

REQUIRED: The external relationship most likely not to involve an ethics violation.

DISCUSSION: Professional organizations are unlikely to be employees, clients, customers, suppliers, or business associates of the organization. Hence, the consulting fees are not likely to impair or be presumed to impair the internal auditors' professional judgment (Rule of Conduct 2.2). Moreover, relationships with professional organizations are not likely to create a conflict of interest or impair or be presumed to impair internal auditors' unbiased judgment (Rule of Conduct 2.1). Also, the consulting engagement should not result in the improper use of information (Rule of Conduct 3.2).

Answer (B) is incorrect because serving as a consultant to competitors might create a conflict of interest. Answer (C) is incorrect because serving as a consultant to suppliers might create a conflict of interest. Answer (D) is incorrect because internal auditors should "be prudent in the use and protection of information acquired in the course of their duties" (Rule of Conduct 3.1). Furthermore, such discussion might be "detrimental to the legitimate and ethical objectives of the organization" (Rule of Conduct 3.2).

38. An internal auditor has been assigned to an engagement at a foreign subsidiary. The internal auditor is aware that the social climate of the country is such that "facilitating payments" (bribes) are an accepted part of doing business. The internal auditor has completed the engagement and has found significant weaknesses relating to important controls. The subsidiary's manager offers the internal auditor a substantial "facilitating payment" to omit the observations from the final engagement communication with a provision that the internal auditor could revisit the subsidiary in 6 months to verify that the problem areas have been properly addressed. The internal auditor should

A. Not accept the payment because such acceptance is in conflict with the Code of Ethics.

B. Not accept the payment, but omit the observations as long as a verification visit is made in 6 months.

C. Accept the offer because it is consistent with the ethical concepts of the country in which the subsidiary is doing business.

D. Accept the payment because it has the effect of doing the greatest good for the greatest number; the internal auditor is better off, the subsidiary is better off, and the organization is better off because there is strong motivation to correct the deficiencies.

Answer (A) is correct. *(CIA, adapted)*

REQUIRED: The proper action an internal auditor should take when offered a bribe.

DISCUSSION: Rule of Conduct 2.2 states, "Internal auditors shall not accept anything that may impair or be presumed to impair their professional judgment."

Answer (B) is incorrect because Rule of Conduct 2.3 requires internal auditors to "disclose all material facts known to them that, if not disclosed, may distort the reporting of activities under review." Answer (C) is incorrect because the profession's standards, not the customs of individual countries or regions, should guide the internal auditor's conduct. Answer (D) is incorrect because the action is explicitly prohibited by the Code of Ethics.

39. An internal auditor engages in the preparation of income tax forms during the tax season. For which of the following activities will the internal auditor most likely be in violation of The IIA Code of Ethics?

A. Writing a tax guide intended for publication and sale to the general public.

B. Preparing the personal tax return, for a fee, for one of the organization's division managers.

C. Teaching an evening tax seminar, for a fee, at a local university.

D. Preparing tax returns for elderly citizens, regardless of their associations, as a public service.

Answer (B) is correct. *(CIA, adapted)*

REQUIRED: The activity most likely a violation of The IIA Code of Ethics.

DISCUSSION: Rule of Conduct 2.2 states, "Internal auditors shall not accept anything that may impair or be presumed to impair their professional judgment." Preparing a personal tax return for a division manager for a fee falls under this prohibition.

40. An internal auditing team has made observations and recommendations that should significantly improve a division's operating efficiency. Out of appreciation of this work, and because it is the holiday season, the division manager presents the in-charge internal auditor with a gift of moderate value. Which of the following best describes the action prescribed by The IIA Code of Ethics?

A. Not accept it prior to submission of the final engagement communication.

B. Not accept it if the gift is presumed to impair the internal auditor's judgment.

C. Not accept it, regardless of other circumstances, because its value is significant.

D. Accept it, regardless of other circumstances, because its value is insignificant.

Answer (B) is correct. *(CIA, adapted)*

REQUIRED: The action prescribed by The IIA Code of Ethics when an engagement client makes a gift to an internal auditor.

DISCUSSION: Rule of Conduct 2.2 states, "Internal auditors shall not accept anything that may impair or be presumed to impair their professional judgment."

Answer (A) is incorrect because the timing of the gift is irrelevant. Answer (C) is incorrect because, according to Rule of Conduct 2.2, the decision whether to accept a gift should be based on the potential impairment of the auditor's judgment. Answer (D) is incorrect because the gift's acceptance should be based on whether the internal auditor's professional judgment will be impaired or be presumed to be impaired.

41. A CIA is working in a noninternal-auditing position as the director of purchasing. The CIA signed a contract to procure a large order from the supplier with the best price, quality, and performance. Shortly after signing the contract, the supplier presented the CIA with a gift of significant monetary value. Which of the following statements regarding the acceptance of the gift is true?

A. Acceptance of the gift is prohibited only if it is not customary.

B. Acceptance of the gift violates The IIA Code of Ethics and is prohibited for a CIA.

C. Because the CIA is no longer acting as an internal auditor, acceptance of the gift is governed only by the organization's code of conduct.

D. Because the contract was signed before the gift was offered, acceptance of the gift does not violate either The IIA Code of Ethics or the organization's code of conduct.

Answer (B) is correct. *(CIA, adapted)*

REQUIRED: The true statement about acceptance of a gift from a supplier.

DISCUSSION: Members of The Institute of Internal Auditors and recipients of, or candidates for, IIA professional certifications are subject to disciplinary action for breaches of The IIA Code of Ethics. Rule of Conduct 2.2 states, "Internal auditors shall not accept anything that may impair or be presumed to impair their professional judgment."

Answer (A) is incorrect because acceptance of the gift could easily be presumed to have impaired the CIA's professional judgment. Answer (C) is incorrect because the CIA is still governed by The IIA's code of conduct. Answer (D) is incorrect because the timing of signing the contract is irrelevant.

42. In some countries, governmental units have established audit standards. For example, in the United States, the Government Accountability Office has developed standards for the conduct of governmental audits, particularly those that relate to compliance with government grants. In performing governmental grant compliance audits, the auditor should

A. Be guided only by the governmental standards.

B. Be guided only by The IIA Standards because they are more encompassing.

C. Be guided by the more general standards that have been issued by the public accounting profession.

D. Follow both The IIA Standards and any additional governmental standards.

Answer (D) is correct. *(CIA, adapted)*

REQUIRED: The standards an auditor follows when performing governmental grant compliance audits.

DISCUSSION: Rule of Conduct 4.2 of The IIA Code of Ethics states, "Internal auditors shall perform internal auditing services in accordance with the *International Standards for the Professional Practice of Internal Auditing.*" Furthermore, an internal auditor is legally obligated to adhere to governmental standards when performing governmental grant compliance audits.

43. An organization has recently placed a former operating manager in the position of chief audit executive (CAE). The new CAE is not a member of The IIA and is not a CIA. Henceforth, the internal audit activity will be run strictly by the CAE's standards, not The IIA's. All four staff internal auditors are members of The IIA, but they are not CIAs. According to The IIA Code of Ethics, what is the best course of action for the staff internal auditors?

A. The Code does not apply because they are not CIAs.

B. They should comply with the Standards for the Professional Practice of Internal Auditing.

C. They must respect the legitimate and ethical objectives of the organization and ignore the Standards.

D. They must resign their jobs to avoid improper activities.

Answer (B) is correct. *(CIA, adapted)*

REQUIRED: The best course of action when the CAE is not a member of The IIA and not a CIA but the staff are members of The IIA.

DISCUSSION: Rule of Conduct 4.2 of The IIA Code of Ethics states, "Internal auditors shall perform internal auditing services in accordance with the *International Standards for the Professional Practice of Internal Auditing.*" Because the internal auditors are members of The Institute, The IIA Code of Ethics is enforceable against them even though they are not CIAs.

Answer (A) is incorrect because The IIA Code of Ethics may be enforced against IIA members and recipients of, or candidates for, IIA professional certifications. Answer (C) is incorrect because internal auditors should respect and contribute to the legitimate and ethical objectives of the organization, but an IIA member, a holder of an IIA professional certification, or a candidate for certification may be liable for disciplinary action for failure to adhere to the Standards. Answer (D) is incorrect because The IIA Code of Ethics says nothing about resignation to avoid improper activities.

44. A new staff internal auditor was told to perform an engagement in an area with which the internal auditor was not familiar. Because of time constraints, no supervision was provided. The assignment represented a good learning experience, but the area was clearly beyond the internal auditor's competence. Nonetheless, the internal auditor prepared comprehensive working papers and communicated the results to management. In this situation,

A. The internal audit activity violated the Standards by hiring an internal auditor without proficiency in the area.

B. The internal audit activity violated the Standards by not providing adequate supervision.

C. The chief audit executive has not violated The IIA Code of Ethics because it does not address supervision.

D. The Standards and The IIA Code of Ethics were followed by the internal audit activity.

Answer (B) is correct. *(CIA, adapted)*

REQUIRED: The effect of failing to supervise an internal auditor who lacks proficiency in the area of the engagement.

DISCUSSION: Although The IIA Code of Ethics does not address supervision directly, it does require that the Standards be followed (Rule of Conduct 4.2). The Standards require engagements to be performed with proficiency and due professional care (Standard 1200). They also should be properly supervised to ensure that objectives are achieved, quality is assured, and staff is developed (Standard 2340).

Answer (A) is incorrect because all internal auditors need not be proficient in all areas. The internal audit activity should have an appropriate mix of skills. Answer (C) is incorrect because the Code requires compliance with the Standards, and the Standards require proper supervision. Answer (D) is incorrect because the Standards and the Code were not followed.

45. Which situation most likely violates The IIA Code of Ethics and the Standards?

A. The chief audit executive (CAE) disagrees with the engagement client about the observations and recommendations in a sensitive area. The CAE discusses the detail of the observations and the proposed recommendations with a fellow CAE from another organization.

B. An organization's charter for the internal audit activity requires the chief audit executive (CAE) to present the yearly engagement work schedule to the board for its approval and suggestions.

C. The engagement manager has removed the most significant observations and recommendations from the final engagement communication. The in-charge internal auditor opposed the removal, explaining that (s)he knows the reported conditions exist. The in-charge internal auditor agrees that, technically, information is not sufficient to support the observations, but management cannot explain the conditions, and the observations are the only reasonable conclusions.

D. Because the internal audit activity lacks skill and knowledge in a specialty area, the chief audit executive (CAE) has hired an expert. The engagement manager has been asked to review the expert's approach to the assignment. Although knowledgeable about the area under review, the manager is hesitant to accept the assignment because of lack of expertise.

Answer (A) is correct. *(CIA, adapted)*

REQUIRED: The situation most likely to be considered a violation of The IIA Code of Ethics.

DISCUSSION: According to Rule of Conduct 3.1 of The IIA Code of Ethics, "Internal auditors shall be prudent in the use and protection of information acquired in the course of their duties." According to Rule of Conduct 3.2, "Internal auditors shall not use information for any personal gain or in any manner that would be contrary to the law or detrimental to the legitimate and ethical objectives of the organization." Consequently, discussion of sensitive matters with an unauthorized party is the situation most likely to be considered a Code violation. The information conveyed might be used to the detriment of the organization.

Answer (B) is incorrect because approval of the engagement work schedule by the board and senior management is required (Standard 2020). Answer (C) is incorrect because information must be sufficient to achieve engagement objectives (Standard 2300). Answer (D) is incorrect because the Standards allow use of experts when needed.

46. Which of the following situations is a violation of The IIA Code of Ethics?

A. An internal auditor was ordered to testify in a court case in which a merger partner claimed to have been defrauded by the internal auditor's organization. The internal auditor divulged confidential information to the court.

B. An internal auditor for a manufacturer of office products recently completed an engagement to evaluate the marketing function. Based on this experience, the internal auditor spent several hours one Saturday working as a paid consultant to a hospital in the local area that intended to conduct an engagement to evaluate its marketing function.

C. An internal auditor gave a speech at a local IIA chapter meeting outlining the contents of a program the internal auditor had developed for engagements relating to electronic data interchange (EDI) connections. Several internal auditors from major competitors were in the audience.

D. During an engagement, an internal auditor learned that the organization was about to introduce a new product that would revolutionize the industry. Because of the probable success of the new product, the product manager suggested that the internal auditor buy an additional interest in the organization, which the internal auditor did.

Answer (D) is correct. *(CIA, adapted)*

REQUIRED: The violation of The IIA Code of Ethics.

DISCUSSION: According to Rule of Conduct 3.2, "Internal auditors shall not use information for any personal gain or in any manner that would be contrary to the law or detrimental to the legitimate and ethical objectives of the organization."

Answer (A) is incorrect because, according to Rule of Conduct 1.2, "Internal auditors shall observe the law and make disclosures expected by the law and the profession." Failure to comply with a court order is illegal. Answer (B) is incorrect because the hospital is not a competitor or supplier of the internal auditor's employer. Hence, no conflict of interest is involved. Answer (C) is incorrect because giving a speech is not a violation of The IIA Code of Ethics. In fact, The IIA's motto is "progress through sharing."

47. During the course of an engagement, an internal auditor discovers that a clerk is embezzling funds from the organization. Although this is the first embezzlement ever encountered and the organization has a security department, the internal auditor decides to interrogate the suspect. If the internal auditor is violating The IIA Code of Ethics, the rule violated is most likely

A. Failing to exercise due diligence.

B. Lack of loyalty to the organization.

C. Lack of competence in this area.

D. Failing to comply with the law.

Answer (C) is correct. *(CIA, adapted)*

REQUIRED: The ethics rule most likely violated.

DISCUSSION: Rule of Conduct 4.1 under the competency principle states, "Internal auditors shall engage only in those services for which they have the necessary knowledge, skills, and experience." Internal auditors may not have and are not expected to have knowledge equivalent to that of a person whose primary responsibility is to detect and investigate fraud.

Answer (A) is incorrect because the requirement to perform work with diligence does not override the competency Rules of Conduct or the need to use good judgment. Answer (B) is incorrect because loyalty is better exhibited by consulting professionals and knowing the limits of competence. Answer (D) is incorrect because the internal auditor may violate the suspect's civil rights as a result of inexperience.

48. Which of the following actions taken by a chief audit executive (CAE) could be considered professionally ethical under The IIA Code of Ethics?

A. The CAE decides to delay an engagement at a branch so that his nephew, the branch manager, will have time to "clean things up."

B. To save organizational resources, the CAE cancels all staff training for the next 2 years on the basis that all staff are too new to benefit from training.

C. To save organizational resources, the CAE limits procedures at foreign branches to confirmations from branch managers that no major personnel changes have occurred.

D. The CAE refuses to provide information about organizational operations to his father, who is a part owner.

Answer (D) is correct. *(CIA, adapted)*

REQUIRED: Ethical actions under The IIA Code of Ethics.

DISCUSSION: According to Rule of Conduct 3.1 of The IIA Code of Ethics, "Internal auditors shall be prudent in the use and protection of information acquired in the course of their duties." According to Rule of Conduct 3.2, "Internal auditors shall not use information for any personal gain or in any manner that would be contrary to the law or detrimental to the legitimate and ethical objectives of the organization." Thus, such use of information by the CAE might be illegal under insider trading rules.

Answer (A) is incorrect because, according to Rule of Conduct 1.1, "Internal auditors shall perform their work with honesty, diligence, and responsibility." Answer (B) is incorrect because, according to Rule of Conduct 4.3, "Internal auditors shall continually improve their proficiency and the effectiveness and quality of their services." Answer (C) is incorrect because, according to Rule of Conduct 4.2, "Internal auditors shall perform internal auditing services in accordance with the Standards for the Professional Practice of Internal Auditing." The Standards require supporting information to be sufficient, reliable, relevant, and useful.

49. During an examination of grants awarded by a nonprofit organization, an internal auditor discovered a number of grants made without the approval of the grant authorization committee (which includes outside representatives), as required by the organization's charter. All the grants, however, were approved and documented by the president. The chair of the grant authorization committee, who is also a member of the board of directors, proposes that the committee meet and retroactively approve all the grants before the engagement communication is issued. If the committee meets and approves the grants before such issuance, the internal auditor should

A. Not report the grants in question because they were approved before the issuance of the engagement communication.

B. Discuss the matter with the chair of the grant committee to determine the rationale for not approving the grants earlier. If the grants are routine, discussion of the grant committee's inaction should be omitted from the engagement communication.

C. Include the items in the communication as an override of the organization's controls. Details about each grant should be reported, and the internal auditor should investigate further for fraud.

D. Report the override of control to the board.

Answer (D) is correct. *(CIA, adapted)*

REQUIRED: The action by an internal auditor if the committee retroactively authorizes certain grants.

DISCUSSION: Rule of Conduct 2.3 states, "Internal auditors shall disclose all material facts known to them that, if not disclosed, may distort the reporting of activities under review." The management override of an important control over approval of grants created a material risk exposure. Thus, the internal auditor is ethically obligated to report the matter to senior officials charged with performing the governance function.

Answer (A) is incorrect because the control override should be reported. Answer (B) is incorrect because the routine nature of the grants is irrelevant to the issue of the violation of the charter. Answer (C) is incorrect because details about each grant need not be included unless the internal auditor believes that fraud may have occurred. Moreover, the appropriate organizational authorities should be informed if wrongdoing is suspected.

50. A chief audit executive (CAE) learned that a staff internal auditor provided confidential information to a relative. Both the CAE and staff internal auditor are CIAs. Although the internal auditor did not benefit from the transaction, the relative used the information to make a significant profit. The most appropriate way for the CAE to deal with this problem is to

A. Verbally reprimand the internal auditor.

B. Summarily discharge the internal auditor and notify The IIA.

C. Take no action because the internal auditor did not benefit from the transaction.

D. Inform the Institute's Board of Directors and take the personnel action required by organizational policy.

Answer (D) is correct. *(CIA, adapted)*

REQUIRED: The CAE's appropriate action after learning that a staff internal auditor has provided confidential information to a relative.

DISCUSSION: The staff internal auditor has violated Rule of Conduct 3.2 regarding use of information. A violation of The IIA Code of Ethics is the basis for a complaint to the International Ethics Committee, which is responsible for receiving, interpreting, and investigating all complaints against members or CIAs on behalf of the Board of Directors of The IIA, and making recommendations to the Board on actions to be taken (Administrative Directive 5). In addition, organizational policy must be followed.

Answer (A) is incorrect because the internal auditor has violated Rule of Conduct 3.2 regarding use of information. The IIA should be notified. Answer (B) is incorrect because summary discharge may not be in accordance with company personnel policies. Answer (C) is incorrect because the auditor improperly used information and violated The IIA Code of Ethics. Some action is warranted.

51. In a review of travel and entertainment expenses, a certified internal auditor questioned the business purposes of an officer's reimbursed travel expenses. The officer promised to compensate for the questioned amounts by not claiming legitimate expenses in the future. If the officer makes good on the promise, the internal auditor

A. Can ignore the original charging of the non-business expenses.

B. Should inform the tax authorities in any event.

C. Should still include the finding in the final engagement communication.

D. Should recommend that the officer forfeit any frequent flyer miles received as part of the questionable travel.

Answer (C) is correct. *(CIA, adapted)*

REQUIRED: The internal auditor's action when an officer agrees to compensate for questionable expenses by not claiming legitimate expenses in the future.

DISCUSSION: Rule of Conduct 2.3 states, "Internal auditors shall disclose all material facts known to them that, if not disclosed, may distort the reporting of activities under review."

Answer (A) is incorrect because the possibly fraudulent behavior of the officer is a material fact that should be reported regardless of whether the questioned expenses are reimbursed. Answer (B) is incorrect because the Standards require the CAE to disseminate results to the appropriate individuals (Standard 2440). However, communication of results outside the organization is not required in the absence of a legal mandate. Answer (D) is incorrect because management should determine what constitutes just compensation.

52. An internal auditor, nearly finished with an engagement, discovers that the director of marketing has a gambling habit. The gambling issue is not directly related to the existing engagement, and the internal auditor is under pressure to complete it quickly. The internal auditor notes the problem and passes the information on to the chief audit executive but does no further follow-up. The internal auditor's actions

A. Are in violation of The IIA Code of Ethics for withholding meaningful information.

B. Are in violation of the Standards because the internal auditor did not properly follow up on a red flag that might indicate the existence of fraud.

C. Are not in violation of either The IIA Code of Ethics or the Standards.

D. Are in violation of The IIA Code of Ethics for withholding meaningful information and are in violation of the Standards because the internal auditor did not properly follow up on a red flag that might indicate the existence of fraud.

Answer (C) is correct. *(CIA, adapted)*

REQUIRED: The true statement(s) about an internal auditor's communication of personal information about an engagement client.

DISCUSSION: There is no violation of either The IIA Code of Ethics or the Standards. The internal auditor did not withhold information but properly followed up upon learning of the information.

53. An engagement at a foreign subsidiary disclosed payments to local government officials in return for orders. What action does The IIA Code of Ethics suggest for an internal auditor in such a case?

A. Refrain from any action that might be detrimental to the organization.

B. Report the incident to appropriate regulatory authorities.

C. Inform appropriate organizational officials.

D. Report the practice to the board of The Institute of Internal Auditors.

Answer (C) is correct. *(CIA, adapted)*

REQUIRED: The internal auditor's action after learning of payments to foreign officials in return for orders.

DISCUSSION: Such payments may be illegal. Rule of Conduct 2.3 states, "Internal auditors shall disclose all material facts known to them that, if not disclosed, may distort the reporting of activities under review."

Answer (A) is incorrect because informing organizational officials is not detrimental to the organization. Answer (B) is incorrect because the Code does not require that the incident be reported to regulatory authorities. Answer (D) is incorrect because the Code does not require reporting to The IIA.

54. During an engagement, an employee with whom you have developed a good working relationship informs you that she has some information about senior management that is damaging to the organization and may concern illegal activities. The employee does not want her name associated with the release of the information. Which of the following actions is considered to be inconsistent with The IIA Code of Ethics and the Standards?

A. Assure the employee that you can maintain her anonymity and listen to the information.

B. Suggest that the employee consider talking to legal counsel.

C. Inform the employee that you will attempt to keep the source of the information confidential and will look into the matter further.

D. Inform the employee of other methods of communicating this type of information.

Answer (A) is correct. *(CIA, adapted)*

REQUIRED: The action inconsistent with The IIA Code of Ethics and the Standards.

DISCUSSION: An internal auditor cannot guarantee anonymity. Information communicated to an internal auditor is not subject to a testimonial privilege. Moreover, Rule of Conduct 2.3 states, "Internal auditors shall disclose all material facts known to them that, if not disclosed, may distort the reporting of activities under review." The identity of the informant may be such a material fact.

Answer (B) is incorrect because suggesting that the person seek expert legal advice from a qualified individual is appropriate. Answer (C) is incorrect because promising merely to attempt to keep the source of the information confidential is allowable. This promise is not a guarantee of confidentiality. Answer (D) is incorrect because the employee could be directed to other methods of communicating the information in order to maintain her anonymity.

55. The chief audit executive is aware of a material inventory shortage caused by internal control deficiencies at one manufacturing plant. The shortage and related causes are of sufficient magnitude to affect the external auditor's report. Based on The IIA Code of Ethics, what is the CAE's most appropriate course of action?

A. Say nothing; guard against interfering with the independence of the external auditors.

B. Discuss the issue with management and take appropriate action to ensure that the external auditors are informed.

C. Inform the external auditors of the possibility of a shortage but allow them to make an independent assessment of the amount.

D. Communicate the shortages to the board and allow them to communicate it to the external auditor.

Answer (B) is correct. *(CIA, adapted)*

REQUIRED: The most appropriate action, given awareness by the CAE of a matter affecting the external auditor's report.

DISCUSSION: The IIA's Code of Ethics calls for compliance with the Standards (Rule of Conduct 4.2). The CAE should share information and coordinate activities with other internal and external providers of relevant assurance and consulting services (Standard 2050). In addition, all material facts known by the internal auditors should be disclosed (Rule of Conduct 2.3). Because the shortage affects the external auditor's work, in which the internal auditors are participating, the situation must be divulged.

Answer (A) is incorrect because the shortage is a material fact that could distort a report of activities under review if not revealed. Answer (C) is incorrect because the condition is known and the external auditors should be told more than that a possibility of a shortage exists. Answer (D) is incorrect because information should be shared and activities coordinated with the external auditor.

56. During an engagement performed at a manufacturing division of a defense contractor, the internal auditor discovered that the organization apparently was inappropriately adding costs to a cost-plus governmental contract. The internal auditor discussed the matter with senior management, which suggested that the internal auditor seek an opinion from legal counsel. Upon review, legal counsel indicated that the practice was questionable but was not technically in violation of the government contract. Based on legal counsel's decision, the internal auditor decided to omit any discussion of the practice in the final engagement communication sent to senior management and the board. However, the internal auditor did informally communicate legal counsel's decision to senior management. Did the internal auditor violate The IIA's Code of Ethics?

A. No. The internal auditor followed up the matter with appropriate personnel within the organization and reached a conclusion that no fraud was involved.

B. No. If a fraud is suspected, it should be resolved at the divisional level where it is taking place.

C. Yes. It is a violation because all important information, even if resolved, should be reported to the board.

D. Yes. Internal legal counsel's opinion is not sufficient. The internal auditor should have sought advice from outside legal counsel.

Answer (A) is correct. *(CIA, adapted)*

REQUIRED: The reason, if any, for a violation of The IIA's Code of Ethics.

DISCUSSION: Although an argument can be made that the internal auditor should report the matter to the board and senior management, there is no indication that the internal auditor is deliberately withholding material facts that, if not disclosed, may distort reports of activities under review (Rule of Conduct 2.3). Hence, no violation of the Code occurred.

Answer (B) is incorrect because material fraud, if suspected, should be brought to the attention of management. However, in this case, the internal auditor gathered sufficient information to dispel the suspicion of fraud. Answer (C) is incorrect because the internal auditor did not deliberately withhold important information. Answer (D) is incorrect because the internal auditor has gathered sufficient information. Internal legal counsel's opinion appears to be sufficient.

57. Which of the following most likely constitutes a violation of The IIA Code of Ethics?

A. Auditor A has accepted an assignment to perform an engagement at the electronics manufacturing division. Auditor A has recently joined the internal audit activity. But Auditor A was senior auditor for the external audit of that division and has audited many electronics organizations during the past 2 years.

B. Auditor B has been assigned to perform an engagement at the warehousing function 6 months from now. Auditor B has no expertise in that area but accepted the assignment anyway. Auditor B has signed up for continuing professional education courses in warehousing that will be completed before the assignment begins.

C. Auditor C is content as an internal auditor and has come to look at it as a regular 9-to-5 job. Auditor C has not engaged in continuing professional education or other activities to improve effectiveness during the last 3 years. However, Auditor C feels performance of quality work is the same as before.

D. Auditor D discovered an internal financial fraud during the year. The books were adjusted to properly reflect the loss associated with the fraud. Auditor D discussed the fraud with the external auditor when the external auditor reviewed working papers detailing the incident.

Answer (C) is correct. *(CIA, adapted)*

REQUIRED: The violation of The IIA Code of Ethics.

DISCUSSION: Rule of Conduct 4.3 states, "Internal auditors shall continually improve their proficiency and the effectiveness and quality of their services."

Answer (A) is incorrect because no professional conflict of interest exists per se, especially given that the internal auditor was previously in public accounting. However, the internal auditor should be aware of potential conflicts. Answer (B) is incorrect because, according to Rule of Conduct 4.1, "Internal auditors shall engage only in those services for which they have the necessary knowledge, skills, and experience." Thus, Auditor B may perform this service if the necessary knowledge, etc., is obtained. Answer (D) is incorrect because the information was disclosed as part of the normal process of cooperation between the internal and external auditor. Because the books were adjusted, the external auditor was expected to inquire as to the nature of the adjustment.

58. Through an engagement performed at the credit department, the chief audit executive (CAE) became aware of a material misstatement of the year-end accounts receivable balance. The external auditors have completed their engagement without detecting the misstatement. What should the CAE do in this situation?

A. Inform the external auditors of the misstatement.

B. Report the misstatement to management when the external auditors present a report.

C. Exclude the misstatement from the final engagement communication because the external auditors are responsible for expressing an opinion on the financial statements.

D. Perform additional engagement procedures on accounts receivable balances to benefit the external auditors.

Answer (A) is correct. *(CIA, adapted)*

REQUIRED: The proper action by the CAE after discovery of a material misstatement not found by the external auditor.

DISCUSSION: Rule of Conduct 2.3 states, "Internal auditors shall disclose all material facts known to them that, if not disclosed, may distort the reporting of activities under review."

Answer (B) is incorrect because the CAE should share information and coordinate activities with the external auditors (Standard 2050). Answer (C) is incorrect because, although the internal audit activity's main focus may be on risk management, control, and governance processes, a material misstatement must be communicated. Answer (D) is incorrect because, when performing an audit, the external auditors should determine what work should be performed by the internal auditor.

59. An internal auditor has uncovered facts that could be interpreted as indicating unlawful activity on the part of an engagement client. The internal auditor decides not to inform senior management and the board of these facts because of lack of proof. The internal auditor, however, decides that, if questions are raised regarding the omitted facts, they will be answered fully and truthfully. In taking this action, the internal auditor

A. Has not violated The IIA Code of Ethics or the Standards because confidentiality takes precedence over all other standards.

B. Has not violated The IIA Code of Ethics or the Standards because the internal auditor is committed to answering all questions fully and truthfully.

C. Has violated The IIA Code of Ethics because unlawful acts should have been reported to the appropriate regulatory agency to avoid potential "aiding and abetting" by the internal auditor.

D. Has violated the Standards because the internal auditor should inform the appropriate authorities in the organization if fraud may be indicated.

Answer (D) is correct. *(CIA, adapted)*

REQUIRED: The effect of not reporting a suspected irregularity.

DISCUSSION: The internal auditor should inform the appropriate authorities in the organization if the indicators of the commission of a fraud are sufficient to recommend an investigation. Hence, the internal auditor has a duty to act even though the available facts do not prove that an irregularity has occurred. Moreover, Rule of Conduct 2.3 states, "Internal auditors shall disclose all material facts known to them that, if not disclosed, may distort the reporting of activities under review."

Answer (A) is incorrect because reporting a possible irregularity to the appropriate organizational authorities is not a breach of the duty of confidentiality owed to the organization. Answer (B) is incorrect because the internal auditor has an affirmative duty to report the results of his or her work. Answer (C) is incorrect because the possibility of unlawful activities should be reported to the appropriate personnel within the organization.

60. Internal auditors who fail to maintain their proficiency through continuing education could be found to be in violation of

A. *The International Standards for the Professional Practice of Internal Auditing.*

B. The IIA's Code of Ethics.

C. Both the Standards for the Professional Practice of Internal Auditing and The IIA's Code of Ethics.

D. None of the answers are correct.

Answer (C) is correct. *(CIA, adapted)*

REQUIRED: The effect of failing to meet continuing education requirements.

DISCUSSION: The IIA's Code of Ethics (Rule of Conduct 4.3) states, "Internal auditors shall continually improve their proficiency and the effectiveness and quality of their services." The Code also requires compliance with the Standards (Rule of Conduct 4.2). Furthermore, Standard 1230 states, "Internal auditors should enhance their knowledge, skills, and competencies through continuing professional development." Hence, both The IIA's Code of Ethics and the Standards are violated by failing to earn continuing education credits.

61. Today's internal auditor will often encounter a wide range of potential ethical dilemmas, not all of which are explicitly addressed by The IIA's Code of Ethics. If the internal auditor encounters such a dilemma, the internal auditor should always

A. Seek counsel from an independent attorney to determine the personal consequences of potential actions.

B. Apply and uphold the principles embodied in The IIA Code of Ethics.

C. Seek the counsel of the board before deciding on an action.

D. Act consistently with the code of ethics adopted by the organization even if such action is not consistent with The IIA's Code of Ethics.

Answer (B) is correct. *(CIA, adapted)*

REQUIRED: The action taken when an internal auditor encounters an ethical dilemma.

DISCUSSION: The Code includes Principles (integrity, objectivity, confidentiality, and competency) relevant to the profession and practice of internal auditing and Rules of Conduct that describe behavioral norms for internal auditors and that interpret the Principles. Internal auditors are expected to apply and uphold the Principles. Furthermore, that a particular conduct is not mentioned in the Rules does not prevent it from being unacceptable or discreditable.

Answer (A) is incorrect because seeking the advice of legal counsel on all ethical decisions is impracticable. Answer (C) is incorrect because seeking the advice of the board on all ethical decisions is impracticable. Furthermore, the advice might not be consistent with the profession's standards. Answer (D) is incorrect because, if the organization's standards are not consistent with, or as high as, the profession's standards, the internal auditor is held to the standards of the profession.

62. Which of the following fraudulent entries is most likely to be made to conceal the theft of an asset?

A. Debit expenses, and credit the asset.

B. Debit the asset, and credit another asset account.

C. Debit revenue, and credit the asset.

D. Debit another asset account, and credit the asset.

Answer (A) is correct. *(CIA, adapted)*

REQUIRED: The fraudulent entry most likely to be made to conceal theft of an asset.

DISCUSSION: Most fraud perpetrators attempt to conceal their theft by charging it against an expense account. The result is that the recorded asset balance equals the actual amount on hand, and applying procedures to it will not detect the theft.

Answer (B) is incorrect because debiting the stolen asset account simply increases the discrepancy between the recorded amount and the amount on hand. Answer (C) is incorrect because an entry decreasing revenue is unusual and would attract attention. Answer (D) is incorrect because this entry would not permanently conceal the fraud. It would simply shift the irreconcilable balance to another asset account.

10.4 Fraud Responsibilities of Internal Auditors

63. After noting some red flags, an internal auditor has an increased awareness that fraud may be present. Which of the following best describes the internal auditor's responsibility?

A. Expand activities to determine whether an investigation is warranted.

B. Report the possibility of fraud to senior management and the board and ask them how they would like to proceed.

C. Consult with external legal counsel to determine the course of action to be taken, including the approval of the proposed engagement work program to make sure it is acceptable on legal grounds.

D. Report the matter to the audit committee and request funding for outside service providers to help investigate the possible fraud.

Answer (A) is correct. *(CIA, adapted)*

REQUIRED: The internal auditor's responsibility after noting some fraud indicators.

DISCUSSION: An internal auditor's responsibilities for detecting fraud include evaluating fraud indicators and deciding whether any additional action is necessary or whether an investigation should be recommended (PA 1210.A2-1).

Answer (B) is incorrect because the internal auditor should notify the appropriate authorities within the organization if (s)he has determined that the indicators of fraud are sufficient to recommend an investigation. Answer (C) is incorrect because the internal auditor does not have the authority to consult with external legal counsel. Answer (D) is incorrect because the internal auditor should report the matter and request funding for outside service providers only if (s)he has determined that the indicators of fraud are sufficient to recommend an investigation.

64. In the course of their work, internal auditors must be alert for fraud and other forms of white-collar crime. The important characteristic that distinguishes fraud from other varieties of white-collar crime is that

A. Fraud encompasses an array of irregularities and illegal acts that involve intentional deception.

B. Unlike other white-collar crimes, fraud is always perpetrated against an outside party.

C. White-collar crime is usually perpetrated for the benefit of an organization, but fraud benefits an individual.

D. White-collar crime is usually perpetrated by outsiders to the detriment of an organization, but fraud is perpetrated by insiders to benefit the organization.

Answer (A) is correct. *(CIA, adapted)*

REQUIRED: The trait distinguishing fraud from other white-collar crimes.

DISCUSSION: Fraud encompasses an array of irregularities and illegal acts characterized by intentional deception or misrepresentation. It can be perpetrated for the benefit of or to the detriment of the organization and by persons outside or inside the organization (PA 1210.A2-1).

Answer (B) is incorrect because fraud may be perpetrated internally. Answer (C) is incorrect because fraud may be perpetrated for the organization's benefit or for otherwise unselfish reasons. Answer (D) is incorrect because fraud may be perpetrated by insiders and outsiders, and it may be either beneficial or detrimental to an organization.

65. Which of the following statements is(are) true regarding the prevention of fraud?

I. The primary means of preventing fraud is through internal control established and maintained by management.

II. Internal auditors are responsible for assisting in the prevention of fraud by examining and evaluating the adequacy of the internal control system.

III. Internal auditors should assess the operating effectiveness of fraud-related communication systems.

A. I only.

B. I and II only.

C. II only.

D. I, II, and III.

Answer (D) is correct. *(CIA, adapted)*

REQUIRED: The true statement(s) about the prevention of fraud.

DISCUSSION: The principal mechanism for preventing fraud is internal control. Responsibility for establishing and maintaining control rests with management. Furthermore, internal auditors are responsible for assisting in the prevention of fraud by examining and evaluating the adequacy and the effectiveness of the system of internal control, commensurate with the extent of the potential exposure within the organization. Internal auditors also should assess the operating effectiveness of fraud-related communication systems and practices and support fraud-related training initiatives (PA 1210.A2-1).

Answer (A) is incorrect because internal auditors are responsible for assisting in the prevention of fraud by examining and evaluating the adequacy of the internal control system, and internal auditors should assess the operating effectiveness of fraud-related communication systems. Answer (B) is incorrect because internal auditors should assess the operating effectiveness of fraud-related communication systems. Answer (C) is incorrect because the primary means of preventing fraud is through internal control established and maintained by management, and internal auditors should assess the operating effectiveness of fraud-related communication systems.

66. The internal audit activity's responsibility for preventing fraud is to

A. Establish internal control.

B. Maintain internal control.

C. Evaluate the system of internal control.

D. Exercise operating authority over fraud prevention activities.

Answer (C) is correct. *(Publisher, adapted)*

REQUIRED: The internal audit activity's responsibility for preventing fraud.

DISCUSSION: The principal mechanism for preventing fraud is control, and management has the primary responsibility for establishing and maintaining control. Internal auditors are responsible for assisting in the prevention of fraud by examining and evaluating the adequacy and the effectiveness of the system of internal control (PA 1210.A2-1).

Answer (A) is incorrect because management's responsibility is to establish internal control. Answer (B) is incorrect because management's responsibility is to maintain internal control. Answer (D) is incorrect because the IAA will not be independent if it exercises operating authority.

67. An internal auditor who suspects fraud should

A. Determine that a loss has been incurred.

B. Interview those who have been involved in the control of assets.

C. Identify the employees who could be implicated in the case.

D. Recommend an investigation after determining that fraud has occurred.

Answer (D) is correct. *(CIA, adapted)*

REQUIRED: The action to be taken by an internal auditor who suspects fraud.

DISCUSSION: An internal auditor's responsibilities for detecting fraud include evaluating fraud indicators and deciding whether any additional action is necessary or whether an investigation should be recommended. The internal auditor should notify the appropriate authorities within the organization if (s)he has determined that the indicators of fraud are sufficient to recommend an investigation (PA 1210.A2-1).

Answer (A) is incorrect because determining the loss could alert the perpetrator of the fraud. The perpetrator could then destroy or compromise evidence. Answer (B) is incorrect because interviewing those who have been involved in the control of assets is part of the fraud investigation. Answer (C) is incorrect because identifying the employees who could be implicated in the case is part of the fraud investigation.

68. The internal auditors' responsibility regarding fraud includes all of the following except

A. Determining whether the control environment sets the appropriate tone at top.

B. Ensuring that fraud will not occur.

C. Being aware of activities in which fraud is likely to occur.

D. Evaluating the effectiveness of control activities.

Answer (B) is correct. *(CIA, adapted)*

REQUIRED: The item not part of the internal auditors' responsibility regarding fraud.

DISCUSSION: Control is the principal mechanism for preventing fraud. Internal auditors are responsible for assisting in the prevention of fraud by examining and evaluating the adequacy and the effectiveness of the system of internal control, commensurate with the extent of the potential exposure in the organization. However, management is responsible for establishing and maintaining internal control (PA 1210.A2-1). Moreover, due professional care requires the conduct of examinations and verifications to a reasonable extent but does not require detailed reviews of all transactions. Thus, the internal auditors cannot give absolute assurance that noncompliance or irregularities do not exist (PA 1220-1).

Answer (A) is incorrect because internal auditing is responsible for evaluating the organization's control environment. Answer (C) is incorrect because the internal auditor should have sufficient knowledge of fraud indicators and be alert to opportunities that could allow fraud. Answer (D) is incorrect because assessing the design and operating effectiveness of fraud-related controls is the responsibility of internal auditing.

69. A significant employee fraud took place shortly after an internal auditing engagement. The internal auditor may not have properly fulfilled the responsibility for the prevention of fraud by failing to note and report that

A. Policies, practices, and procedures to monitor activities and safeguard assets were less extensive in low-risk areas than in high-risk areas.

B. A system of control that depended upon separation of duties could be circumvented by collusion among three employees.

C. There were no written policies describing prohibited activities and the action required whenever violations are discovered.

D. Divisional employees had not been properly trained to distinguish between bona fide signatures and cleverly forged ones on authorization forms.

Answer (C) is correct. *(CIA, adapted)*

REQUIRED: The way in which the internal auditor may not have properly fulfilled the responsibility for the prevention of fraud.

DISCUSSION: Management is responsible for establishing and maintaining internal control. Thus, management also is responsible for the fraud prevention program. The control environment element of this program includes a code of conduct, ethics policy, or fraud policy to set the appropriate tone at the top. Moreover, organizations should establish effective fraud-related information and communication practices, for example, documentation and dissemination of policies, guidelines, and results (PA 1210.A2-1).

Answer (A) is incorrect because, for cost-benefit reasons, controls should be more extensive in high-risk areas. Answer (B) is incorrect because even the best system of control can often be circumvented by collusion. Answer (D) is incorrect because forgery, like collusion, can circumvent even an effective control.

70. In an organization with a separate division that is primarily responsible for the prevention of fraud, the internal audit activity is responsible for

A. Examining and evaluating the adequacy and effectiveness of that division's actions taken to prevent fraud.

B. Establishing and maintaining that division's system of internal control.

C. Planning that division's fraud prevention activities.

D. Controlling that division's fraud prevention activities.

Answer (A) is correct. *(CIA, adapted)*

REQUIRED: The responsibility of the IAA in an organization with a separate fraud prevention division.

DISCUSSION: Control is the principal mechanism for the prevention of fraud. Management, in turn, is primarily responsible for the establishment and maintenance of control. Internal auditors are primarily responsible for preventing fraud by examining and evaluating the adequacy and effectiveness of control (PA 1210.A2-1).

Answer (B) is incorrect because establishing and maintaining control is a responsibility of management. Answer (C) is incorrect because planning fraud prevention activities is a responsibility of management. Answer (D) is incorrect because controlling fraud prevention activities is a responsibility of management.

71. When conducting fraud investigations, internal auditors should

A. Clearly indicate the extent of the internal auditors' knowledge of the fraud when questioning suspects.

B. Assign personnel to the investigation in accordance with the engagement schedule established at the beginning of the fiscal year.

C. Perform its investigation independently of lawyers, security personnel, and specialists from outside the organization who are involved in the investigation.

D. Assess the probable level of, and the extent of complicity in, the fraud within the organization.

Answer (D) is correct. *(CIA, adapted)*

REQUIRED: The role of the internal auditors in fraud investigations.

DISCUSSION: When conducting fraud investigations, internal auditors or others should assess the probable level of, and the extent of complicity in, the fraud within the organization. This assessment can be critical to ensuring that (1) crucial evidence is not tainted or destroyed and (2) misleading information is not obtained from persons who may be involved (PA 1210.A2-2).

Answer (A) is incorrect because, by always giving the impression that additional evidence is in reserve, the internal auditors are more apt to obtain complete and truthful answers. Answer (B) is incorrect because fraud investigations usually occur unexpectedly and cannot be scheduled in advance. Also, the fraud investigation must be conducted by individuals having the appropriate expertise, even if another engagement must be delayed. Answer (C) is incorrect because the internal auditors should coordinate their activities with management, legal counsel, and other specialists.

72. The manager of a production line has the authority to order and receive replacement parts for all machinery that requires periodic maintenance. The internal auditor received an anonymous tip that the manager ordered substantially more parts than were necessary from a family member in the parts supply business. The unneeded parts were never delivered. Instead, the manager processed receiving documents and charged the parts to machinery maintenance accounts. The payments for the undelivered parts were sent to the supplier, and the money was divided between the manager and the family member. Which of the following tests would best assist the auditor in deciding whether to investigate this anonymous tip further?

A. Comparison of the current quarter's maintenance expense with prior-period activity.

B. Physical inventory testing of replacement parts for existence and valuation.

C. Analysis of repair parts charged to maintenance to review the reasonableness of the number of items replaced.

D. Review of a test sample of parts invoices for proper authorization and receipt.

Answer (C) is correct. *(CIA, adapted)*

REQUIRED: The test that would best assist the auditor in determining whether to further investigate the anonymous tip.

DISCUSSION: Analytical procedures are evaluations of financial information made by a study of plausible relationships among both financial and nonfinancial data. They involve comparisons of recorded amounts, or ratios developed from recorded amounts, with expectations developed by the internal auditor. A basic premise underlying the application of analytical procedures is that plausible relationships among data may reasonably be expected to exist and continue in the absence of known conditions to the contrary. Thus, an analysis of repair parts charged to maintenance would quantify the excessive number of items and raise a red flag that abuse may be occurring.

Answer (A) is incorrect because the current quarter's expense may not vary significantly from the prior period's unless the manager just started this fraud. The auditor has no information on how long this might have been occurring. Answer (B) is incorrect because physical testing would not locate nonexistent parts that already have been charged to maintenance. Answer (D) is incorrect because lack of segregation of duties allowed the fraud to occur. The manager was authorized to process both the purchase and receipt, so the test would only verify the fraudulent paperwork.

10.5 Fraud Indicators

73. Red flags are conditions that indicate a higher likelihood of fraud. Which of the following is not considered a red flag?

A. Management has delegated the authority to make purchases under a certain value to subordinates.

B. An individual has held the same cash-handling job for an extended period without any rotation of duties.

C. An individual handling marketable securities is responsible for making the purchases, recording the purchases, and reporting any discrepancies and gains/losses to senior management.

D. The assignment of responsibility and accountability in the accounts receivable department is not clear.

Answer (A) is correct. *(CIA, adapted)*

REQUIRED: The item that is not a red flag.

DISCUSSION: Delegating the authority to make purchases under a certain value to subordinates is an acceptable and common practice intended to limit risk while promoting efficiency. It is not, by itself, considered a red flag.

Answer (B) is incorrect because lack of rotation of duties or cross-training for sensitive jobs is a red flag. Such a person may have a greater opportunity to commit and conceal fraud. Answer (C) is incorrect because an inappropriate combination of duties is a red flag. Answer (D) is incorrect because establishing clear lines of authority and accountability not only helps to assign culpability but also has preventive effects.

74. Internal auditors have been advised to consider red flags to determine whether management is involved in a fraud. Which of the following does not represent a difficulty in using the red flags as fraud indicators?

A. Many common red flags are also associated with situations in which no fraud exists.

B. Some red flags are difficult to quantify or to evaluate.

C. Red flag information is not gathered as a normal part of an engagement.

D. The red flags literature is not well enough established to have a positive impact on internal auditing.

Answer (D) is correct. *(CIA, adapted)*

REQUIRED: The item not a difficulty in using red flags as fraud indicators.

DISCUSSION: The state of red flags literature is not a difficulty. It is well established and will be refined in the future as research is done. Thus, it does not preclude consideration of red flags.

Answer (A) is incorrect because red flags are developed by correlation analysis, not necessarily by causation analysis. Answer (B) is incorrect because many red flags, such as management's attitude, are difficult to quantify. Answer (C) is incorrect because internal auditors should be able to identify fraud indicators and should be alert to opportunities that could allow fraud. However, internal auditors do not normally perform procedures specifically to gather red flag information.

75. An internal auditor should be concerned about the possibility of fraud if

A. Cash receipts, net of the amounts used to pay petty cash-type expenditures, are deposited in the bank daily.

B. The monthly bank statement reconciliation is performed by the same employee who maintains the perpetual inventory records.

C. The accounts receivable subsidiary ledger and accounts payable subsidiary ledger are maintained by the same person.

D. One person, acting alone, has sole access to the petty cash fund (except for a provision for occasional surprise counts by a supervisor or auditor).

Answer (A) is correct. *(CIA, adapted)*

REQUIRED: The reason an internal auditor should be concerned about the possibility of fraud.

DISCUSSION: Paying petty cash expenditures from cash receipts facilitates the unauthorized removal of cash before deposit. All cash receipts should be deposited intact daily. Petty cash expenditures should be handled through an imprest fund.

Answer (B) is incorrect because the monthly bank reconciliation should not be performed by a person who makes deposits or writes checks, but the inventory clerk has no such responsibilities. Answer (C) is incorrect because there is no direct relationship between the transactions posted to the accounts receivable and accounts payable subsidiary ledgers; having the same person maintain both does not create a control weakness. Answer (D) is incorrect because, to establish accountability for petty cash, only one person should have access to the fund.

Questions 76 through 82 are based on the following information.

Randy and John had known each other for many years. They had become best friends in college, where they both majored in accounting. After graduation, Randy took over the family business from his father. His family had been in the grocery business for several generations. When John had difficulty finding a job, Randy offered him a job in the family store. John proved to be a very capable employee. As John demonstrated his abilities, Randy began delegating more and more responsibility to him. After a period of time, John was doing all of the general accounting and authorization functions for checks, cash, inventories, documents, records, and bank reconciliations. (1) *John was trusted completely and handled all financial functions.* No one checked his work.

Randy decided to expand the business and opened several new stores. (2) *Randy was always handling the most urgent problem ... crisis management is what his college professors had termed it.* John assisted with the problems when his other duties allowed him time.

Although successful at work, John had (3) *difficulties with personal financial problems.*

At first, the amounts stolen by John were small. John didn't even worry about making the accounts balance. But John became greedy. "How easy it is to take the money," he said. He felt that he was a critical member of the business team (4) *and that he contributed much more to the success of the company than was represented by his salary.* It would take two or three people to replace me, he often thought to himself. As the amounts became larger and larger, (5) *he made the books balance.* Because of these activities, John was able to purchase an expensive car and take his family on several trips each year. (6) *He also joined an expensive country club.* Things were changing at home, however. (7) *John's family observed that he was often argumentative and at other times very depressed.*

The fraud continued for 6 years. Each year the business performed more and more poorly. In the last year, the stores had a substantial net loss. Randy's bank required an audit. John confessed when he thought the auditors had discovered his embezzlements.

When discussing frauds, the pressures, opportunities, and rationalizations that cause/allow a perpetrator to commit the fraud are often identified. Symptoms of fraud are also studied.

76. Number 1, "John was trusted completely . . .," is an example of a(n)

A. Document symptom.

B. Situational pressure.

C. Opportunity to commit.

D. Physical symptom.

Answer (C) is correct. *(CIA, adapted)*

REQUIRED: The characteristic of which complete trust in an employee is an example.

DISCUSSION: Complete trust in an individual represents an opportunity to commit fraud. John's actions went unscrutinized because of the absence of an appropriate segregation of functions and his ability to override whatever control procedures were in place.

77. Number 2, "Randy was always handling the most urgent . . .," is an example of a(n)

A. Opportunity to commit.

B. Analytical symptom.

C. Situational pressure.

D. Rationalization.

Answer (A) is correct. *(CIA, adapted)*

REQUIRED: The characteristics of which crisis management is an example.

DISCUSSION: When a manager continually handles the most pressing issues of a company, an opportunity for the manager to commit fraud is created. The lack of long-range planning creates a potential for fraud because organizational objectives may have been replaced with individual initiatives.

78. Number 3, "Difficulties with personal financial problems," is an example of a(n)

A. Behavioral symptom.

B. Situational pressure.

C. Rationalization.

D. Opportunity to commit.

Answer (B) is correct. *(CIA, adapted)*

REQUIRED: The characteristic of which personal financial problems are an example.

DISCUSSION: Financial difficulties create situational pressures or temptations that may contribute to fraud. These situational pressures result from high personal indebtedness, extravagant lifestyles, gambling problems, etc.

79. Number 4, "and that he contributed much more . . .," is an example of a

A. Rationalization.

B. Behavioral symptom.

C. Situational pressure.

D. Physical symptom.

Answer (A) is correct. *(CIA, adapted)*

REQUIRED: The characteristic of which an inflated self-worth is an example.

DISCUSSION: Rationalization occurs when one attributes actions to rational and creditable motives without analysis of one's true and especially unconscious motives. Thus, a feeling that one is contributing more than one is paid would be a rationalization for committing fraud.

80. Number 5, "he made the books balance," is an example of a(n)

A. Physical symptom.

B. Analytical symptom.

C. Lifestyle symptom.

D. Document symptom.

Answer (D) is correct. *(CIA, adapted)*
REQUIRED: The characteristic of which covering fraud by tampering with company records is an example.
DISCUSSION: Tampering with the company's books is a document symptom. In other words, the indicator of fraud consists of the changes in actual company records.

81. Number 6, "He also joined an expensive country club," is an example of a

A. Rationalization.

B. Lifestyle symptom.

C. Behavioral symptom.

D. Physical symptom.

Answer (B) is correct. *(CIA, adapted)*
REQUIRED: The characteristic of which an extravagant lifestyle is an example.
DISCUSSION: John was living beyond his means. The change in lifestyle was a symptom that indicated the presence of fraud.

82. Number 7, "John's family observed that he was often argumentative . . .," is an example of a

A. Rationalization.

B. Lifestyle symptom.

C. Behavioral symptom.

D. Physical symptom.

Answer (C) is correct. *(CIA, adapted)*
REQUIRED: The characteristic of which an argumentative attitude is an example.
DISCUSSION: A drastic change in an employee's behavior may indicate the presence of fraud. The guilt and the other forms of stress associated with perpetrating and concealing the fraud may induce noticeable changes in behavior.

83. Which of the following policies is most likely to result in an environment conducive to the occurrence of fraud?

A. Budget preparation input by the employees who are responsible for meeting the budget.

B. Unreasonable sales and production goals.

C. The division's hiring process frequently results in the rejection of adequately trained applicants.

D. The application of some accounting controls on a sample basis.

Answer (B) is correct. *(CIA, adapted)*
REQUIRED: The policy most likely to result in an environment conducive to the occurrence of fraud.
DISCUSSION: Unrealistically high sales or production quotas can be an incentive to falsify the records or otherwise take inappropriate action to improve performance measures so that the quotas appear to have been met.

Answer (A) is incorrect because participatory budgeting can reduce antagonism to budgets and reduce the likelihood of inappropriate means of meeting the budget. Answer (C) is incorrect because hiring policies should be based on factors other than adequate training, such as the applicants' personal integrity. Furthermore, hiring of all adequately trained applicants is unlikely to be necessary. Answer (D) is incorrect because, under the reasonable assurance concept, the cost of controls should not exceed their benefits. The cost of applying controls to all relevant transactions rather than a sample may be greater than the resultant savings.

84. Internal auditors should have knowledge about factors (red flags) that have proven to be associated with management fraud. Which of the following factors have generally not been associated with management fraud?

A. Generous performance-based reward systems.

B. A domineering management.

C. Regular comparison of actual results with budgets.

D. A management preoccupation with increased financial performance.

Answer (C) is correct. *(CIA, adapted)*
REQUIRED: The factor not associated with management fraud.
DISCUSSION: Regular comparison of actual results to budgets provides feedback and is a normal and necessary part of the control loop. Ineffective control is an indicator of possible fraud.

Answer (A) is incorrect because generous reward systems provide incentives for management to distort performance. Answer (B) is incorrect because pressure from superiors provides an incentive for management to distort performance. Answer (D) is incorrect because a management preoccupation with increased financial performance provides an incentive for managers to distort performance.

85. Which of the following is an indicator of possible financial reporting fraud being perpetrated by management of a manufacturer?

A. A trend analysis discloses (1) sales increases of 50% and (2) cost of goods sold increases of 25%.

B. A ratio analysis discloses cost of goods sold is 50% of sales.

C. A cross-sectional analysis of common size statements discloses (1) the firm's percentage of cost of goods sold to sales is 40% and (2) the industry average percentage of cost of goods sold to sales is 50%.

D. A cross-sectional analysis of common size statements discloses (1) the firm's percentage of cost of goods sold to sales is 50% and (2) the industry average percentage of cost of goods sold to sales is 40%.

Answer (A) is correct. *(CIA, adapted)*

REQUIRED: The indicator of possible financial reporting fraud being perpetrated by management of a manufacturer.

DISCUSSION: A 50% increase in sales supported by a 25% increase in cost of goods sold is either fortuitous or fraudulent. Increases in sales are usually accompanied by close to proportional increases in cost of goods sold. Examples of situations in which increases in sales can be disproportionately larger than increases in cost of goods sold include (1) operations within the realm of economies of scale (increasing returns to scale) and (2) the introduction of a highly accepted fashion item. Cases in which disproportionately large sales increases indicate fraudulent conduct include (1) collusion by the host firm's sales personnel and the buying firm's purchasing personnel and (2) collusion by members of two departments within the host firm, such as sales and transportation. Because the internal auditor would not know whether the disproportionately large increase in sales is legitimate, the auditor should view this condition as an indicator of possible fraud.

Answer (B) is incorrect because a gross profit margin (GPM) of 50% is not an indicator of fraud. Manufacturers can expect a range of 40-60% for this ratio. Answer (C) is incorrect because these data indicate an industry GPM of 50% and host firm GPM of 40%. The greater GPM realized by the host firm may result from any number of reasonable causes. These include (1) greater efficiencies exercised by the host firm, (2) greater sales effort (or a more highly accepted product), and (3) measurement errors. Answer (D) is incorrect because these data indicate an industry GPM of 40% and a host firm GPM of 50%. The lower GPM realized by the host firm may result from such causes as (1) host firm inefficiencies; (2) less acceptance of host firm product, or less sales effort; and (3) measurement errors.

86. A company, which has many branch stores, has decided to benchmark one of its stores for the purpose of analyzing the accuracy and reliability of branch store financial reporting. Which one of the following is the most likely measure to be included in a financial benchmark?

A. High turnover of employees.

B. High level of employee participation in setting budgets.

C. High amount of bad debt write-offs.

D. High number of suppliers.

Answer (C) is correct. *(CIA, adapted)*

REQUIRED: The most likely measure included in a financial benchmark.

DISCUSSION: The level of bad debts written off as uncollectible is a benchmark stated in financial terms. A level exceeding the benchmark could indicate fraud, which compromises the accuracy and reliability of financial reports. Bad debt write-offs may result from recording fictitious sales.

Answer (A) is incorrect because turnover of employees is not a financial benchmark. Answer (B) is incorrect because employee participation in setting budgets is not a financial benchmark. Answer (D) is incorrect because the number of suppliers is not a financial benchmark.

87. When comparing perpetrators who have embezzled an organization's funds with perpetrators of financial statement fraud (falsified financial statements), those who have falsified financial statements are less likely to

A. Have experienced an autocratic management style.

B. Be living beyond their obvious means of support.

C. Rationalize the fraudulent behavior.

D. Use organizational expectations as justification for the act.

Answer (B) is correct. *(CIA, adapted)*

REQUIRED: The least likely characteristic of those who have falsified financial statements.

DISCUSSION: Living beyond one's means has been linked to employee fraud (embezzlement), not to financial statement fraud. Fraud perpetrated for the benefit of the organization ordinarily benefits the wrongdoer indirectly, whereas fraud that is detrimental to the organization provides immediate, direct benefits to the employee.

Answer (A) is incorrect because autocratic management styles have been linked to management (financial statement) fraud. Answer (C) is incorrect because rationalization is common to all fraud. Answer (D) is incorrect because high expectations are often given as a motivating factor by those who have committed financial statement fraud.

88. The following are facts about a subsidiary:

1. The subsidiary has been in business for several years and enjoyed good profit margins although the general economy was in a recession, which affected competitors.
2. The working capital ratio has declined from a healthy 3:1 to 0.9:1.
3. Turnover for the last several years has included three controllers, two supervisors of accounts receivable, four payables supervisors, and numerous staff in other financial positions.
4. Purchasing policy requires three bids. However, the supervisor of purchasing at the subsidiary has instituted a policy of sole-source procurement to reduce the number of suppliers.

When conducting a financial audit of the subsidiary, the internal auditor should

A. Most likely not detect 1., 2., or 3.

B. Ignore 2. since the economy had a downturn during this period.

C. Consider 3. to be normal turnover, but be concerned about 2. and 4. as warning signals of fraud.

D. Consider 1., 2., 3., and 4. as warning signals of fraud.

Answer (D) is correct. *(CIA, adapted)*

REQUIRED: The items an internal auditor should consider in a financial audit of a subsidiary.

DISCUSSION: That the organization has reported high profits when competitors have not may indicate a misstatement of the financial statements. Insufficient working capital may indicate such problems as overexpansion, decreases in revenues, transfers of funds to other organizations, insufficient credit, and excessive expenditures. The internal auditor should be alert for the diversion of funds for personal use through such methods as unrecorded sales and falsified expenditures. Rapid turnover in financial positions may signify existing problems with which the individuals feel uncomfortable but that they do not want to disclose. Accountability for funds and other resources should be determined upon termination of employment. Use of sole-source procurement does not encourage competition to assure that the organization is obtaining the required materials or equipment at the best price. Sole-source procurement, if not adequately justified, indicates potential favoritism or kickbacks.

Answer (A) is incorrect because the items described can be detected through usual procedures in a financial audit. Answer (B) is incorrect because, although the economy suffered a downturn, the change in working capital is unusual in light of the continuing strong profit margins and should be investigated. Answer (C) is incorrect because the working capital ratio, the high employee turnover rate, and the sole-source procurement policy are all warning signals of fraud.

89. The manager of a production line has the authority to order and receive replacement parts for all machinery that requires periodic maintenance. The internal auditor received an anonymous tip that the manager ordered substantially more parts than were necessary from a family member in the parts supply business. The unneeded parts were never delivered. Instead, the manager processed receiving documents and charged the parts to machinery maintenance accounts. The payments for the undelivered parts were sent to the supplier, and the money was divided between the manager and the family member. Which of the following internal controls would have most likely prevented this fraud from occurring?

A. Establishing predefined spending levels for all vendors during the bidding process.

B. Segregating the receiving function from the authorization of parts purchases.

C. Comparing the bill of lading for replacement parts to the approved purchase order.

D. Using the company's inventory system to match quantities requested with quantities received.

Answer (B) is correct. *(CIA, adapted)*

REQUIRED: The internal control most likely to have prevented the fraud from occurring.

DISCUSSION: Separating the parts authorization and receiving functions would have improved internal control. If the parts in question had been sent to the company and a receiving report had been prepared by an employee other than the one ordering the goods, the fraud could not have occurred. Moreover, the receiving department should not accept goods unless it has a blind copy of a properly approved purchase order for the items.

Answer (A) is incorrect because predefined spending levels would probably already include the fraudulent amounts and would only limit the size of the fraud. Answer (C) is incorrect because the bill of lading would agree with the purchase order. The quantity received (verified by a third party) should be compared to both the bill of lading and the purchase order. Answer (D) is incorrect because the computer matching would only verify the fraudulent paperwork.

10.6 Engagement Procedures Related to Fraud

90. Contributions to a nonprofit organization have been constant for the past 3 years. The audit committee has become concerned that the president may have embarked on a scheme in which some of the contributions from many sustaining members have been redirected to other organizations. The audit committee suspects that the scheme may involve taking major contributions and depositing them in alternative accounts or soliciting contributions to be made in the name of another organization. Which of the following procedures should be most effective in detecting the existence of such a fraud?

A. Use generalized audit software to take a sample of pledged receipts not yet collected and confirm the amounts due with the donors.

B. Take a sample that includes all large donors for the past 3 years and a statistical sample of others and request a confirmation of total contributions made to the organization or to affiliated organizations.

C. Take a discovery sample of cash receipts and confirm the amounts of the receipts with the donors. Investigate any differences.

D. Use analytical review procedures to compare contributions generated with those of other comparable institutions over the same period of time. If the amount is significantly less, take a detailed sample of cash receipts and trace to the bank statements.

Answer (B) is correct. *(CIA, adapted)*

REQUIRED: The procedure most effective for detecting misdirected contributions.

DISCUSSION: The engagement objective is to determine whether contributions have been wrongly directed to alternate accounts or solicited for other organizations. Consequently, an appropriate procedure is to send confirmation requests to donors. However, testing transactions recorded by the accounting system will not result in sufficient information about solicitation of contributions for other organizations. The internal auditor must therefore make inquiries of the sustaining members about such solicitations.

Answer (A) is incorrect because sampling amounts listed as unpaid does not provide evidence about contributions previously paid or shifted to another organization. Answer (C) is incorrect because sampling cash receipts that have been recorded by the organization provides no evidence about unrecorded receipts or contributions diverted elsewhere. Answer (D) is incorrect because analytical procedures are of limited use. Also, the follow-up procedure only provides evidence that recorded receipts were also deposited.

91. A production manager for a moderate-sized manufacturer began ordering excessive raw materials and had them delivered to a wholesale business that the manager was running on the side. The manager falsified receiving documents and approved the invoices for payment. Which of the following procedures is most likely to detect this fraud?

A. Take a sample of cash disbursements; compare purchase orders, receiving reports, invoices, and check copies.

B. Take a sample of cash disbursements and confirm the amount purchased, purchase price, and date of shipment with the vendors.

C. Observe the receiving dock and count materials received; compare the counts with receiving reports completed by receiving personnel.

D. Perform analytical tests, comparing production, materials purchased, and raw materials inventory levels; investigate differences.

Answer (D) is correct. *(CIA, adapted)*

REQUIRED: The procedure most likely to detect a purchasing fraud.

DISCUSSION: The application of analytical procedures is based on the premise that, in the absence of known conditions to the contrary, relationships among information may reasonably be expected to exist and continue. Examples of contrary conditions include unusual or nonrecurring transactions or events; accounting, organizational, operational, environmental, and technological changes; inefficiencies; ineffectiveness; errors; irregularities; or illegal acts. Hence, the analytical procedures should identify an unexplained increase in materials used.

Answer (A) is incorrect because, given that documents have been falsified, supporting documents exist for each cash disbursement. Answer (B) is incorrect because the vendors will confirm all transactions. Answer (C) is incorrect because, given that the improper orders are shipped to another location, observing receiving dock counts will not detect the fraud.

Questions 92 and 93 are based on the following information.

Jane Jackson had been the regional sales manager for an organization for over 10 years. During this time, she had become very close friends with Frank Hansen, an internal audit manager. In addition to being neighbors, Jane and Frank had many of the same interests and belonged to the same tennis club. They trusted each other. Frank had helped Jane solve some sales problems, and Jane had given Frank some information that led to significant engagement observations during the past three engagements.

Below are selected analytical data from the organization that have led staff internal auditors to believe that there has been a financial statement fraud. The perpetrator appears to have falsified sales information for the past 2 years. Frank is concerned because he recently completed an engagement in the area and accepted Jane's explanation for differences in the analytical data. Frank is now certain that Jane is involved in the fraud.

	Current Year	Last Year	–2 Year	–3 Year	–4 Year
Percent increase in sales	10%	8%	6%	4%	5%
Inventory turnover	5	4	5	3.5	4
Gross margin percentage	54	49	42	39	40
Percent change in sales returns	8%	6%	3%	2.5%	3%

92. Which combination of the following analytical data provides the strongest indication of the possibility of the fraud?

A. Percentage increase in sales and inventory turnover.

B. Gross margin percentage and change in sales returns.

C. Inventory turnover and change in sales returns.

D. Percentage increase in sales and gross margin percentage.

Answer (B) is correct. *(CIA, adapted)*

REQUIRED: The analytical data that provide the strongest indication of the possibility of fraud.

DISCUSSION: Rapid increases in gross margin percentage are expected if sales are fictitious, that is, if sales are recorded without shipments and a consequent increase in cost of sales. The large increase in returns is also symptomatic of falsified sales.

Answer (A) is incorrect because the increase in percentage change in sales is not unreasonable, and, given the constant increase, one might expect increases in inventory that could keep turnover constant. Answer (C) is incorrect because the turnover and return figures, when taken together, are not indications of sales overstatements. Answer (D) is incorrect because, if the increase in sales was due to a market sales price increase, one might expect these results.

93. The current dilemma in which Frank finds himself was least likely caused by

A. Not rotating engagements every year.

B. Accepting an engagement in an area where he was a close personal friend of management.

C. Failing to select the appropriate analytical procedures.

D. Accepting the response of management without additional testing.

Answer (C) is correct. *(CIA, adapted)*

REQUIRED: The least likely cause of the dilemma.

DISCUSSION: The information given suggests that Frank applied the proper analytical procedures but accepted management's explanation of the findings.

Answer (A) is incorrect because failure to rotate engagements seems to have contributed to Frank's decision to accept management's explanation for the analytical findings. Answer (B) is incorrect because Frank's friendship with Jane impaired his objectivity. Answer (D) is incorrect because Frank's acceptance of management's explanations apparently resulted in his failure to obtain sufficient information.

94. The chief of an organization's security received an anonymous call accusing a marketing manager of taking kickbacks from a media outlet. Thus, the marketing department is on the list of possible engagement clients for the coming year. The internal audit activity is assigned responsibility for investigating fraud by its charter. If obtaining access to outside media outlet records and personnel is not possible, the best action an internal auditor could take to investigate the allegation of marketing kickbacks is to

A. Search for unrecorded liabilities from media outlets.

B. Obtain a list of approved media outlets.

C. Develop a financial and behavioral profile of the suspect.

D. Vouch any material past charge-offs of receivables.

Answer (C) is correct. *(CIA, adapted)*

REQUIRED: The best action an internal auditor can take to investigate an allegation of kickbacks.

DISCUSSION: The best action is to develop a financial and behavioral profile of the marketing manager. A common indicator of fraud by an employee is an unexplained change in his/her financial status. A standard of living not commensurate with the employee's income may signify wrongdoing. The employee's behavior may also be suspicious (for example, constant association with, and entertainment by, a member of the media outlet's staff). The profile may help to corroborate illegal income and thereby provide a basis for tracing illegal payments to the employee.

Answer (A) is incorrect because, if the employee is taking kickbacks, unrecorded liabilities are not being created. Answer (B) is incorrect because a list of approved media outlets would not provide any information about kickbacks. Answer (D) is incorrect because the receipt of kickbacks would have no effect on accounts receivable.

Questions 95 through 97 are based on the following information. During an engagement performed at a smaller division, the internal auditor notes the following regarding the purchasing function:

- There are three purchasing agents. Agent 1 is responsible for ordering all large component parts, agent 2 for electric motors, and agent 3 for smaller parts such as fasteners.
- There are separate accounts payable and receiving departments.
- In order to hold vendors more responsible, all invoices are sent to the purchasing agent placing the order. The purchasing agent matches the vendor invoice, receiving slip, and purchase order. If all match, the purchasing agent sends the documents forward to the accounts payable department. Differences are investigated by the purchasing agent.
- Only the accounts payable department has the ability to authorize an item for payment.
- All recorded receipts are immediately recorded into a perpetual inventory record by the department to which the goods are transferred after receipt.

The internal auditor interviewed both management and the purchasing agents. Both groups were very satisfied with the current system because it helps maintain vendor accountability and provides sufficient segregation of duties given that only the accounts payable department can authorize an item for payment.

95. Which of the following engagement procedures is most effective in determining whether material fraud was taking place?

A. Take a random sample of cash disbursements and trace to approved purchase orders and receiving slips.

B. Reconcile the perpetual inventory to the general ledger and investigate any differences.

C. Take a random sample of purchase orders. Trace each purchase order to a receiving slip, vendor invoice, and approval by the accounts payable department.

D. Perform an analytical review of inventory by product line to determine whether a particular product line has increased. Inquire of the purchasing agent as to the reason for the inventory increase.

Answer (B) is correct. *(CIA, adapted)*

REQUIRED: The most effective procedure to determine whether material fraud occurred.

DISCUSSION: A fraud could result in an overstatement of inventory in the ledger. However, the perpetual inventory reflects the actual goods received.

Answer (A) is incorrect because cash disbursements are authorized by accounts payable and are not made in the absence of approved documents. Purchasing agents have control of these documents. Hence, if they are falsified by the purchasing agents, merely verifying that documents exist to support payments is ineffective. Answer (C) is incorrect because tracing purchase orders to receiving slips, invoices, and accounts payable approvals verifies only that purchase orders were processed. It would not detect fictitious purchase orders. Answer (D) is incorrect because analytical review of inventory by product line provides limited evidence on the possibility of fraud but would not be as effective as reconciling inventory.

96. The internal auditor is responsible for evaluating internal control to determine whether it allows undetected fraud. Based on the information presented, the most likely undetected fraud, if any, is that the

A. Purchasing agent is purchasing the majority of products from a favorite vendor because rotation among purchasing agents is not mandatory.

B. Purchasing agent is sending fake purchase orders to a dummy vendor, inserting a receiving slip, and having payments made to the dummy vendor.

C. Receiving department is diverting receipts to different locations and failing to create receiving reports.

D. Production department is deflating the price of products purchased and thereby increasing the reported gross margin of sales.

Answer (B) is correct. *(CIA, adapted)*

REQUIRED: The most likely undetected fraud.

DISCUSSION: Internal control is unlikely to detect the purchasing agent's fraud because this individual is in a position to perpetrate and conceal irregularities. Receiving documents and vendors' invoices should be sent to accounts payable, not to the purchasing agent.

Answer (A) is incorrect because purchasing most goods from a particular vendor may be justified. Answer (C) is incorrect because this possible fraud should be detected by the absence of receiving reports to support vendors' invoices. Answer (D) is incorrect because this response is unrelated to the purchasing environment.

97. Which of the following controls, if properly implemented, is most likely to decrease the likelihood of fraud?

A. Require periodic rotation of purchases among different vendors.

B. Require rotation of duties among the three purchasing agents.

C. Require that receiving reports be sent directly to accounts payable.

D. Require that the updates to the perpetual inventory record be made by the receiving department.

Answer (C) is correct. *(CIA, adapted)*

REQUIRED: The control most likely to decrease the likelihood of fraud.

DISCUSSION: This change in procedures prevents the purchasing agent from falsifying receiving reports. An even better procedure is to have both the receiving reports and the vendors' invoices sent to accounts payable.

Answer (A) is incorrect because rotation of vendors might partially alleviate the problem, but the purchasing agent could develop new dummy vendors. Answer (B) is incorrect because rotation of duties will not affect the type of fraud that could occur in this environment. The purchasing agent could develop another dummy vendor for the new product line. Answer (D) is incorrect because this procedure will create an additional opportunity for fraud by the receiving department.

98. During an engagement relating to purchasing, the internal auditor finds that the largest blanket purchase order is for tires, which are expensed as vehicle maintenance items. The fleet manager requisitions tires against the blanket order for the company's 400-vehicle service fleet based on a visual inspection of the cars and trucks in the parking lot each week. Sometimes the fleet manager picks up the tires but always signs the receiving report for payment. Vehicle service data are entered into a maintenance database by the mechanic after the tires are installed. What is the best course of action for the internal auditor in these circumstances?

A. Determine whether the number of tires purchased can be reconciled to maintenance records.

B. Count the number of tires on hand and trace them to the related receiving reports.

C. Select a judgmental sample of requisitions and verify that each one is signed by the fleet manager.

D. Compare the number of tires purchased under the blanket purchase order with the number of tires purchased in the prior year for reasonableness.

Answer (A) is correct. *(CIA, adapted)*

REQUIRED: The action to be taken by the internal auditor during a purchasing engagement.

DISCUSSION: The best course of action for the internal auditor is to determine whether the number of tires purchased can be reconciled to maintenance records. That the fleet manager both requisitions and receives the tires provides an opportunity for fraud. The internal auditor should verify whether fraud has occurred. A separate receiving function would diminish the possibility of fraud by providing an independent count of items received.

Answer (B) is incorrect because tracing the tires on hand to the receiving reports would not reveal a fraud. The manager signs the receiving report. Answer (C) is incorrect because testing for signed requisitions would not necessarily reveal whether fraud is present. Answer (D) is incorrect because a fraud could have occurred during the prior year also.

99. During a post-completion engagement related to a warehouse expansion, the internal auditor noted several invoices for redecorating services from a local merchant that were account-coded and signed for payment only by the cost engineer. The internal auditor should

A. Compare the cost and description of the services with the account code used in the construction project and with related estimates in the construction-project budget.

B. Consult with the cost engineer for assurance that these purchases were authorized for this construction project.

C. Obtain a facsimile of the cost engineer's signature from the accounts payable group and compare it with the signature on the invoices.

D. Recommend reclassifying the expenditure to the appropriate account code for redecorating services.

Answer (A) is correct. *(CIA, adapted)*

REQUIRED: The action taken when invoices are account-coded and approved by the cost engineer only.

DISCUSSION: The internal auditor needs to determine the validity of the transaction because the engineer is performing incompatible tasks. Comparing the cost and description of the services with the account code and the budget will verify the transaction. However, normal controls over disbursements need to be established.

Answer (B) is incorrect because the cost engineer's assurance would not confirm the authorization of these expenditures. Answer (C) is incorrect because the primary focus is the validity of the transaction within this construction project. Answer (D) is incorrect because there is no basis for reclassifying the transaction within this context.

100. The internal auditor reviewed documentation showing that a customer had recently returned three expensive products to the regional service center for warranty replacement. The documentation also showed that the warranty clerk had rejected the claim and sent it to the customer's local distributor. The claim was rejected because the serial numbers listed in the warranty claim were not found in the computer's sales history file. Subsequently, the distributor supplied three different serial numbers, all of which were validated by the computer system, and the clerk completed the warranty claim for replacements. What is the best course of action for the internal auditor under the circumstances?

A. Determine if the original serial numbers provided by the customer can be traced to other records, such as production and inventory records.

B. Notify the appropriate authorities within the organization that there are sufficient indicators that a fraud has been committed.

C. Verify with the appropriate supervisor that the warranty clerk had followed relevant procedures in the processing and disposition of this claim.

D. Summarize this item along with other valid transactions in the internal auditor's test of warranty transactions.

Answer (A) is correct. *(CIA, adapted)*

REQUIRED: The action to be taken by the internal auditor in investigating suspicious warranty claims.

DISCUSSION: The best course of action for the internal auditor is to determine whether the original serial numbers provided by the customer can be traced to other records, such as production and inventory records. The internal auditor should determine whether the related equipment had actually been reported in a sales transaction.

Answer (B) is incorrect because the internal auditor should pursue additional information before alerting authorities. Answer (C) is incorrect because verifying that the warranty clerk followed procedures does not provide more information about the validity of the warranty claim. Answer (D) is incorrect because the internal auditor should obtain more information about the validity of the transaction.

101. The internal auditor suspects a disbursements fraud in which an unknown employee(s) is submitting and approving invoices for payment. Before discussing the potential fraud with management, the internal auditor decides to gather additional information. Which of the following procedures is most helpful in providing the additional information?

A. Use software to develop a list of vendors with post office box numbers or other unusual features. Select a sample of those items and trace to supporting documents such as receiving reports.

B. Select a sample of payments made during the year and investigate each one for approval.

C. Select a sample of receiving reports representative of the period under investigation and trace to approved payment. Note any items not properly processed.

D. Take a sample of invoices received during the past month, examine to determine whether properly authorized for payment, and trace to underlying documents.

Answer (A) is correct. *(CIA, adapted)*

REQUIRED: The most helpful procedure related to a disbursements fraud.

DISCUSSION: A disbursements fraud may be accomplished through the use of fictitious vendors. Investigating vendors with suspicious characteristics appropriately focuses on payees as sources of additional information.

Answer (B) is incorrect because the individual perpetrating the fraud may have been in a position to obtain approvals. Answer (C) is incorrect because the problem is more likely to be with payments for which no valid support exists. Answer (D) is incorrect because sampling invoices for the past month is not as effective as investigating suspicious vendors. It focuses only on a short period of time, and it does not emphasize the items most likely to be fraudulent.

102. During an engagement, the internal auditor found a scheme in which the warehouse director and the purchasing agent for a retail organization diverted a significant amount of goods to their own warehouse, then sold the goods to third parties. The fraud was not noted earlier because the warehouse director forwarded receiving reports (after updating the perpetual inventory records) to the accounts payable department for processing. Which of the following procedures most likely led to the discovery of the missing materials and the fraud?

A. Take a random sample of receiving reports and trace to the recording in the perpetual inventory record. Note differences and investigate by type of product.

B. Take a random sample of purchase orders and trace them to receiving documents and to the records in the accounts payable department.

C. Take an annual physical inventory, reconciling amounts with the perpetual inventory, noting the pattern of differences and investigating.

D. Take a random sample of sales invoices and trace to the perpetual records to see if inventory was on hand. Investigate any differences.

Answer (C) is correct. *(CIA, adapted)*
REQUIRED: The audit procedure to detect the diversion of the goods.
DISCUSSION: Taking an annual physical inventory should lead to the identification of systematic shrinkages in the inventory. The pattern of the shrinkages should implicate the warehouse director. At that time, a fraud investigation should be undertaken.
Answer (A) is incorrect because sampling receiving reports would not have detected the fraud. The warehouse director updates the perpetual inventory records before forwarding the false receiving reports to accounts payable. Answer (B) is incorrect because taking a sample of purchase orders would not have detected the irregularities. All the goods were ordered, and the perpetrators colluded to falsify receiving reports even when the goods were diverted to another location. Answer (D) is incorrect because the warehouse director falsified the inventory records.

103. The internal auditor finds a situation in which one person has the ability to collect receivables, make deposits, issue credit memos, and record receipt of payments. The internal auditor suspects the individual may be stealing from cash receipts. Which of the following engagement procedures is most effective in discovering fraud in this scenario?

A. Send positive confirmations to a random selection of customers.

B. Send negative confirmations to all outstanding accounts receivable customers.

C. Perform a detailed review of debits to customer discounts, sales returns, or other debit accounts, excluding cash posted to the cash receipts journal.

D. Take a sample of bank deposits and trace the detail in each bank deposit back to the entry in the cash receipts journal.

Answer (C) is correct. *(CIA, adapted)*
REQUIRED: The engagement procedure most effective in detecting theft from cash receipts.
DISCUSSION: The most effective procedure is to perform a detailed review of debits to customer discounts, sales returns, etc. These accounts could be used to conceal a theft of cash payments without alerting customers. Seeking confirmation from customers and tracing bank balances will not detect the fraud because neither customer statements nor bank records will contain evidence of fraud.
Answer (A) is incorrect because an employee who performs asset custody, authorization, and recording functions can conceal the theft by debiting customer discounts or sales returns. Answer (B) is incorrect because seeking information from customers and tracing bank balances will not detect the fraud because neither customer statements nor bank records will contain evidence of fraud. Answer (D) is incorrect because bank deposits will agree with journal entries. The stolen amounts are never recorded.

104. Management has requested that the internal auditor investigate the possibility that a purchasing agent is receiving kickbacks. Which of the following procedures is least effective in addressing management's concern?

A. Confirm all contract terms with vendors.

B. Analyze, by purchasing agent, all increases in cost of procured goods from specific vendors.

C. Take a statistical sample of goods purchased and compare purchase prices for goods with those of other sources of similar goods, such as other organizations or catalogs.

D. Observe any changes in the lifestyles or individual consumption habits of the purchasing agents involved.

Answer (A) is correct. *(CIA, adapted)*
REQUIRED: The least effective procedure to discover whether a purchasing agent is receiving kickbacks.
DISCUSSION: Confirming contract terms is the least useful procedure because the contract terms are already known. The confirmation would have to be expanded to inquire as to whether the purchasing agent has pressured vendors to make kickbacks. That approach is useful only if the kickbacks were initiated by the purchasing agent rather than the vendor.
Answer (B) is incorrect because analyzing increases in the cost of procured goods from specific vendors provides insight as to what products and which purchasing agent may be involved. Answer (C) is incorrect because sampling goods purchased and comparing prices against other sources of similar goods provides information on excess purchase prices. Answer (D) is incorrect because unexplained changes in personal habits of purchasing agents may reveal the purchasing agent involved in receiving the kickbacks.

105. While reviewing a division's accounts, an internal auditor becomes concerned that the division's management may have shipped poor quality merchandise to boost sales and profitability and thereby increase the manager's bonus. For this reason, the internal auditor suspects that returned goods are being shipped to other customers as new products without full correction of their defects. Which of the following engagement procedures is the least effective in determining whether such shipments took place?

A. Examine credit memos issued after year-end for goods shipped before year-end.

B. Physically observe the shipping and receiving area for information of returned goods.

C. Interview customer service representatives regarding unusual amounts of customer complaints.

D. Require the division to take a complete physical inventory at year-end, and observe the taking of the inventory.

Answer (D) is correct. *(CIA, adapted)*

REQUIRED: The least effective procedure to determine whether merchandise returned has been reshipped without the correction of defects.

DISCUSSION: Taking a complete year-end inventory is an ineffective engagement procedure. The goods returned and reshipped without the correction of defects would not be on hand to be counted.

Answer (A) is incorrect because examining credit memos issued after year-end for goods shipped before year-end would show that customers are returning inferior goods. Answer (B) is incorrect because physically observing the shipping and receiving area might reveal goods returned that are not yet accounted for. Answer (C) is incorrect because unusual amounts of customer complaints may suggest a condition not explained by normal spoilage rates.

106. An investment portfolio manager has the authority to use financial derivatives to hedge transactions but is not supposed to take speculative positions. However, the manager launches a scheme that includes (1) taking a position larger than required by the hedge, (2) putting the speculative gains in a suspense account, and (3) transferring the funds to a nonexistent broker and from there to a personal account. Which of the following engagement procedures is least effective in detecting this fraud?

A. Examine individual trades to determine whether the trades violate the authorization limit for the manager.

B. Sample individual trades and determine the exact matching of a hedge. Schedule and investigate all differences.

C. Sample all debits to the suspense account and examine their disposition.

D. Sample fund transfers to brokers and determine if the brokers are on the organization's authorized list for transactions.

Answer (A) is correct. *(CIA, adapted)*

REQUIRED: The least effective engagement procedure for detecting the fraudulent use of derivatives.

DISCUSSION: Examining individual trades to determine whether they violate the authorization limit would not detect the fraud. The speculative nature of the transaction, not its amount, is the violation of policy.

Answer (B) is incorrect because sampling individual trades may detect an unauthorized speculation. Answer (C) is incorrect because all debits to the suspense account should be sampled given the potential for using such an account for irregularities. Answer (D) is incorrect because sampling fund transfers to brokers and determining whether the brokers are on the authorized list for transactions may detect a fictitious party.

10.7 Controls Related to Fraud

107. Which of the following controls is the least effective in preventing a fraud conducted by sending purchase orders to bogus vendors?

A. Require that all purchases be made from an authorized vendor list maintained independently of the individual placing the purchase order.

B. Require that only approved vendors be paid for purchases, based on actual production.

C. Require contracts with all major vendors from whom production components are purchased.

D. Require that total purchases for a month not exceed the total budgeted purchases for that month.

Answer (D) is correct. *(CIA, adapted)*

REQUIRED: The control least effective in preventing a fraud involving bogus vendors.

DISCUSSION: Requiring that total purchases for a month not exceed the total budgeted purchases for that month is the least effective procedure. It controls the total amount of expenditures, not whether a purchase has been requested and authorized, with whom the purchase orders are placed, or whether goods purchased are received.

Answer (A) is incorrect because segregating the selection and approval of reputable vendors from placement of actual orders is an effective means of preventing fraud. Answer (B) is incorrect because restricting payment to approved vendors is an effective means of preventing fraud. Answer (C) is incorrect because requiring contracts with major vendors is an effective means of preventing fraud.

108. A potential problem for a manufacturer is that purchasing agents may take kickbacks or receive gifts from vendors in exchange for favorable contracts. Which of the following is the least effective in preventing this problem?

A. A specific organizational policy prohibiting the acceptance of anything of value from a vendor.

B. An organizational code of ethics that prohibits such activity.

C. A requirement for the purchasing agent to develop a profile of all vendors before the vendors are added to the authorized vendor list.

D. The establishment of long-term contracts with major vendors, with the contract terms approved by senior management.

Answer (C) is correct. *(CIA, adapted)*

REQUIRED: The least effective control to prevent purchasing agents from taking kickbacks or gifts from vendors.

DISCUSSION: A requirement for the purchasing agent to develop a profile of all vendors is the least effective approach because it concerns only the authorization of vendors, a function that should be performed independently of the purchasing agent. It does not address the purchasing agent's relationships with approved vendors.

Answer (A) is incorrect because a policy prohibiting kickbacks and gifts from vendors provides guidance and influences behavior. Answer (B) is incorrect because a code of ethics gives direction to the purchasing agents and is helpful in influencing behavior. Answer (D) is incorrect because approval of long-term vendor contracts by senior management is an effective procedure that is increasingly being used by many organizations.

109. A purchasing agent received expensive gifts from a vendor in return for directing a significant amount of business to that vendor. Which of the following organizational policies most effectively prevents such an occurrence?

A. All purchases exceeding specified monetary amounts should be approved by an official who determines compliance with budgetary requirements.

B. Important high-volume materials should regularly be purchased from at least two different sources in order to afford supply protection.

C. The purchasing function should be decentralized so each department manager or supervisor does his/her own purchasing.

D. Competitive bids should be solicited on purchases to the maximum extent that is practicable.

Answer (D) is correct. *(CIA, adapted)*

REQUIRED: The policy that most effectively prevents or detects bribery by a vendor.

DISCUSSION: In the absence of special circumstances, competitive bidding is a legitimate and effective means of obtaining the lowest price consistent with quality. It is a practice that exploits competition in the market place. Competitive bidding also serves as a control over fraud by restricting the ability of a purchasing agent to reward a favored vendor.

Answer (A) is incorrect because the problem is vendor selection, not authorization of purchases. Answer (B) is incorrect because a purchasing agent could still display favoritism to one of the vendors. Answer (C) is incorrect because decentralization creates more opportunities for buyer fraud.

Questions 110 and 111 are based on the following information. A purchasing agent acquired items for personal use with the organization's funds. The organization allowed designated employees to purchase a specified amount per day in merchandise under open-ended contracts. Supervisory approval of the purchases was required, but that information was not communicated to the vendor. Instead of reviewing and authorizing each purchase order, supervisors routinely signed the authorization sheet at the end of the month without reviewing any of the supporting documentation. Because purchases of this nature were not subject to normal receiving policies, the dishonest employee picked up the supplies at the vendor's warehouse. All purchases were for items routinely ordered by the organization. During the past year, the employee amassed enough merchandise to start a printing and photography business.

110. Which of the following controls would have been most effective in preventing this fraud?

A. Allowing purchases only from a list of pre-approved vendors.

B. Requiring the use of prenumbered purchase orders for all purchases of merchandise.

C. Canceling supporting documents such as purchase orders and receiving reports at the time invoices are paid.

D. Establishing separation of duties between the ordering and receiving of merchandise.

Answer (D) is correct. *(CIA, adapted)*

REQUIRED: The most effective control to prevent a purchasing agent from purchasing items for personal use with the organization's funds.

DISCUSSION: Separating the purchasing and receiving functions would have improved internal control. If the supplies in question had been sent to the organization, and a receiving report had been prepared by an employee other than the one ordering the goods, the fraud could not have occurred. Moreover, the receiving department should not accept goods unless it has a blind copy of a properly approved purchase order for the items.

Answer (A) is incorrect because the facts do not suggest that the vendor's actions were inappropriate. Answer (B) is incorrect because prenumbering would not have prevented the fraud. The weakness is in the authorization and receiving procedures. Answer (C) is incorrect because canceling supporting documents when invoices are paid prevents the same document from being used to support two identical payments, but that is not the abuse here.

111. Which of the following engagement procedures, performed by the internal auditor, is most likely to detect this fraud?

A. Tracing selected canceled checks to the cash payments journal and to the related vendors' invoices.

B. Performing a trend analysis of printing supplies expenses for a 2-year period.

C. Tracing prices and quantities on selected vendors' invoices to the related purchase orders.

D. Recomputing the clerical accuracy of selected vendors' invoices, including discounts and sales taxes.

Answer (B) is correct. *(CIA, adapted)*

REQUIRED: The engagement procedure most likely to detect the fraud.

DISCUSSION: Analytical procedures are evaluations of financial information made by a study of plausible relationships among both financial and nonfinancial data. They involve comparisons of recorded amounts, or ratios developed from recorded amounts with expectations developed by the internal auditor. A basic premise underlying the application of analytical procedures is that plausible relationships among data may reasonably be expected to exist and continue in the absence of known conditions to the contrary. Thus, performing a trend analysis of printing supplies expenses for a 2-year period should identify an excess use of supplies.

Answer (A) is incorrect because a legitimate vendor's invoice existed for each cash payment related to this fraud. Answers (C) and (D) are incorrect because the issue is not whether the invoices are accurate but whether the transactions are authorized.

Questions 112 and 113 are based on the following information. A fraud was perpetrated in a moderate-sized organization when the accounting clerk was delegated too much responsibility. During the year, the organization switched suppliers of a service to a new vendor. The accounting clerk continued to submit fraudulent invoices from the "old supplier." Because contracting for services and approval of supplier invoices had been delegated to the clerk, it was possible for the clerk to continue billings from the old supplier and deposit the subsequent checks, which the clerk was responsible to mail, into a new account the clerk opened in the name of the old supplier. The clerk was considered an excellent employee and eventually was improperly given the added responsibility of preparing the department budgets. This added responsibility allowed the clerk to budget for the amount of the fraudulent payments.

112. Which of the following controls would have been least likely to prevent or detect the fraud described?

A. Requiring authorization of payments by someone other than the clerk negotiating the contract.

B. Comparison by the person signing checks of invoices with an independent verification of services received.

C. Budget preparation by someone other than the person signing contracts and approving payment.

D. Mailing of checks by someone other than the person responsible for check signing or invoice approval.

Answer (D) is correct. *(CIA, adapted)*

REQUIRED: The control least likely to prevent or detect the fraud.

DISCUSSION: Once invoices have been approved, and checks prepared and signed, the mailing of the check by an independent person provides no means of preventing improper payments. The person responsible for the treasury function should sign the checks, transmit them, and cancel the supporting documents.

Answer (A) is incorrect because separating contracting for services and approval of invoices would have prevented the fraud. Answer (B) is incorrect because an independent verification of services received reviewed by the check signer would have prevented payment for services not received. Answer (C) is incorrect because independent budget preparation would have allowed an actual-with-budget comparison to detect the payments.

113. Which of the following engagement procedures is most likely to detect the fraud?

A. Take a sample of paid invoices and verify receipt of services by departments involved.

B. Trace a sample of checks disbursed to approved invoices for services.

C. Perform a bank reconciliation and account for all outstanding checks.

D. Trace a sample of receiving documents to invoices and to checks disbursed.

Answer (A) is correct. *(CIA, adapted)*

REQUIRED: The engagement procedure most likely to detect the fraud.

DISCUSSION: Confirming with the using department the receipt of services that have been paid for would uncover the fraud.

Answer (B) is incorrect because the fraudulent invoices were approved by the clerk, and each check is therefore supported by an approved invoice. Answer (C) is incorrect because bank reconciliations do not test the validity of the cash payments. Answer (D) is incorrect because beginning with valid receiving reports will not detect the fraud. The direction of testing is inappropriate.

114. A programmer's accumulation of roundoff errors into one account, which is later accessed by the programmer, is a type of computer fraud. The best way to prevent this type of fraud is to

A. Build in judgment with reasonableness tests.

B. Independently test programs during development and limit access to the programs.

C. Segregate duties of systems development and programming.

D. Use control totals and check the results of the computer.

Answer (B) is correct. *(CIA, adapted)*

REQUIRED: The best way to prevent computer fraud.

DISCUSSION: Programmers should not have access to programs used in processing. The accumulation of roundoff errors into one person's account is a procedure written into the program. Independent testing of a program will lead to discovery of this programmed fraud.

Answer (A) is incorrect because reasonableness tests will not detect this irregularity. In this particular type of fraud, all of the amounts will balance. Answer (C) is incorrect because segregation of duties between systems development and programming would not prevent this type of error. The skills required to construct the program are possessed by programmers. Answer (D) is incorrect because this particular fraud will result in balanced entries. Thus, control totals would not detect the fraud.

The GLEIM CIA System Works!

This is a quick note from a happy and satisfied CIA On-Line Course user. I followed your study program and recommendations, making only a few personal preference changes. As the Gleim team professed, I did pass each part I took, without any need to retake any part. One time through on each part of the CIA and I was done. You have a good product and the program works.

Gregory White

It is my great pleasure to inform you that I have qualified CIA examination with the help of Gleim materials. Gleim materials, especially Online and CDs were really helpful to prepare for the examinations , which helped me to pass all the papers in my first attempt. Once again I thank you for my victory.

Sheji Valiyakath

I would like to share the great news that I passed my CIA exams. I must say that without your wonderful material i.e. both the books and the CDs I would not have achieved this. Thank you all for creating the study material that really helps candidates conquer the challenging CIA exams.
Thanks again.

Mohsin Jagani

Dr. Gleim and users: I appreciate the valuable service that Gleim has provided me. I recently passed the CIA Exam, even though the IIA raised the bar for the passing threshold. My confidence in Gleim is absolute, thus passing the more difficult CIA was not problematic. As a matter of fact, I have passed the Gleim offerings of CFM, CMA, and now CIA. For those interested parties who want to pass these tests, buy Gleim and pass!

Stephen Wills

Thanks so much!!!! The complete online course certainly works! I didn't start studying until August and just received notification that I passed all four parts of the exam on my first attempt.

Rebecca Neal

GLEIM KNOWLEDGE TRANSFER SYSTEMS®

APPENDIX A
THE IIA CONTENT SPECIFICATION OUTLINES (CSOs) AND CROSS REFERENCE

For your convenience, we have reproduced verbatim The IIA's Content Specification Outline (CSO), also known as a Content Syllabus, for each CIA exam part from their website (www.theiia.org). We also have provided cross references to the study units and subunits in this book that correspond to The IIA's more detailed CSO coverage. If one entry appears above a list, it applies to all items. Please visit The IIA's website for updates and more information about the exam. Rely on the Gleim materials to pass each part of the exam. We have researched and studied The IIA's CSOs as well as questions from prior exams to provide you with an excellent review program.

PART I – THE INTERNAL AUDIT ACTIVITY'S ROLE IN GOVERNANCE, RISK, AND CONTROL

A. **COMPLY WITH THE IIA'S ATTRIBUTE STANDARDS (15 - 25%)** (proficiency level) (1.2)

1. Define purpose, authority, and responsibility of the internal audit activity. (2.1)
   a. Determine if purpose, authority, and responsibility of internal audit activity are clearly documented/approved.
   b. Determine if purpose, authority, and responsibility of internal audit activity are communicated to engagement clients.
   c. Demonstrate an understanding of the purpose, authority, and responsibility of the internal audit activity.
2. Maintain independence and objectivity.
   a. Foster independence. (2.2, 2.4)
      1) Understand organizational independence.
      2) Recognize the importance of organizational independence.
      3) Determine if the internal audit activity is properly aligned to achieve organizational independence.
   b. Foster objectivity. (2.3, 2.4)
      1) Establish policies to promote objectivity.
      2) Assess individual objectivity.
      3) Maintain individual objectivity.
      4) Recognize and mitigate impairments to independence and objectivity.
3. Determine if the required knowledge, skills, and competencies are available. (1.5, 1.6)
   a. Understand the knowledge, skills, and competencies that an internal auditor needs to possess.
   b. Identify the knowledge, skills, and competencies required to fulfill the responsibilities of the internal audit activity.
4. Develop and/or procure necessary knowledge, skills, and competencies collectively required by internal audit activity. (1.5, 1.6)
5. Exercise due professional care. (1.6)
6. Promote continuing professional development. (1.7)
   a. Develop and implement a plan for continuing professional development for internal audit staff.
   b. Enhance individual competency through continuing professional development.
7. Promote quality assurance and improvement of the internal audit activity. (9.3-9.7)
   a. Establish and maintain a quality assurance and improvement program.
   b. Monitor the effectiveness of the quality assurance and improvement program.
   c. Report the results of the quality assurance and improvement program to the board or other governing body.
   d. Conduct quality assurance procedures and recommend improvements to the performance of the internal audit activity.
8. Abide by and promote compliance with The IIA Code of Ethics. (1.1, 1.5)

B. **ESTABLISH A RISK-BASED PLAN TO DETERMINE THE PRIORITIES OF THE INTERNAL AUDIT ACTIVITY (15 - 25%)** (proficiency level) (1.3)

1. Establish a framework for assessing risk. (8.1, 4.1)
2. Use the framework to: (8.1, 4.1)
   a. Identify sources of potential engagements (e.g., audit universe, management request, regulatory mandate)
   b. Assess organization-wide risk
   c. Solicit potential engagement topics from various sources
   d. Collect and analyze data on proposed engagements
   e. Rank and validate risk priorities
3. Identify internal audit resource requirements. (8.5)
4. Coordinate the internal audit activity's efforts with: (Intro of 9, 9.1, 9.2)
   a. External auditor
   b. Regulatory oversight bodies
   c. Other internal assurance functions (e.g., health and safety department)
5. Select engagements. (8.1, 8.2)
   a. Participate in the engagement selection process.
   b. Select engagements.
   c. Communicate and obtain approval of the engagement plan from board.

C. **UNDERSTAND THE INTERNAL AUDIT ACTIVITY'S ROLE IN ORGANIZATIONAL GOVERNANCE (10 - 20%)** (proficiency level) (1.3)

1. Obtain board's approval of audit charter. (2.1, 8.4)
2. Communicate plan of engagements. (8.2)
3. Report significant audit issues. (8.3)
4. Communicate key performance indicators to board on a regular basis. (8.3, 8.4)
5. Discuss areas of significant risk. (8.1, 4.1)
6. Support board in enterprise-wide risk assessment. (4.1, 5.2, 6.2, 8.1)
7. Review positioning of the internal audit function within the risk management framework within the org. (4.1)
8. Monitor compliance with the corporate code of conduct/business practices. (3.2)
9. Report on the effectiveness of the control framework. (5.1)
10. Assist board in assessing the independence of the external auditor. (9.2, 8.4)
11. Assess ethical climate of the board. (3.2)
12. Assess ethical climate of the organization. (3.2)
13. Assess compliance with policies in specific areas (e.g., derivatives). (3.3, 4.1)
14. Assess organization's reporting mechanism to the board. (3.3, 8.4, 5.4)
15. Conduct follow-up and report on management response to regulatory body reviews. (3.3)
16. Conduct follow-up and report on management response to external audit. (3.2)
17. Assess the adequacy of the performance measurement system, achievement of corporate objective. (3.1, 5.5)
18. Support a culture of fraud awareness and encourage the reporting of improprieties. (5.4)

D. **PERFORM OTHER INTERNAL AUDIT ROLES AND RESPONSIBILITIES (0 - 10%)** (proficiency level) (1.3)

1. Ethics/compliance (3.2)
   a. Investigate and recommend resolution for ethics/compliance complaints.
   b. Determine disposition of ethics violations.
   c. Foster healthy ethical climate.
   d. Maintain and administer business conduct policy (e.g., conflict of interest).
   e. Report on compliance.

2. Risk management (4.1)

   a. Develop and implement an organization-wide risk and control framework.
   b. Coordinate enterprise-wide risk assessment.
   c. Report corporate risk assessment to board.
   d. Review business continuity planning process.

3. Privacy (4.2)

   a. Determine privacy vulnerabilities.
   b. Report on compliance.

4. Information or physical security (4.2)

   a. Determine security vulnerabilities.
   b. Determine disposition of security violations.
   c. Report on compliance.

E. **GOVERNANCE, RISK, AND CONTROL KNOWLEDGE ELEMENTS (15 - 25%)**

1. Corporate governance principles (awareness level) (3.2)
2. Alternative control frameworks (awareness level) (6.2)
3. Risk vocabulary and concepts (proficiency level) (1.4, 6.1)
4. Risk management techniques (proficiency level) (4.1)
5. Risk/control implications of different organizational structures (proficiency level) (6.4)
6. Risk/control implications of different leadership styles (awareness level) (6.5)
7. Change management (awareness level) (6.6)
8. Conflict management (awareness level) (6.7)
9. Management control techniques (proficiency level) (6.3)
10. Types of control (preventive, detective, input, output) (proficiency level) (6.1)

F. **PLAN ENGAGEMENTS (15 - 25%)** (proficiency level) (1.3)

1. Initiate preliminary communication with engagement client. (7.1)
2. Conduct a preliminary survey of the area of engagement. (7.2)

   a. Obtain input from engagement client.
   b. Perform analytical reviews.
   c. Perform benchmarking.
   d. Conduct interviews.
   e. Review prior audit reports and other relevant documentation.
   f. Map processes.
   g. Develop checklists.

3. Complete a detailed risk assessment of the area (prioritize or evaluate risk/control factors). (7.2)
4. Coordinate audit engagement efforts with (9.1)

   a. External auditor
   b. Regulatory oversight bodies

5. Establish/refine engagement objectives and identify/finalize the scope of engagement. (7.2, 7.3)
6. Identify or develop criteria for assurance engagements (criteria against which to audit). (5.5)
7. Consider the potential for fraud when planning an engagement. (10.4-10.7)

   a. Be knowledgeable of the risk factors and red flags of fraud.
   b. Identify common types of fraud associated with the engagement area.
   c. Determine if risk of fraud requires special consideration when conducting an engagement.

8. Determine engagement procedures. (7.4, 10.1)
9. Determine the level of staff and resources needed for the engagement. (7.3)
10. Establish adequate planning and supervision of the engagement. (7.1, 7.5)
11. Prepare engagement work program. (7.4)

PART II – CONDUCTING THE INTERNAL AUDIT ENGAGEMENT

A. **CONDUCT ENGAGEMENTS (25 - 35%)** (proficiency level)

1. Research and apply appropriate standards: (10.1, 10.2)
   a. IIA Professional Practices Framework (Code of Ethics, Standards, and Practice Advisories)
   b. Other professional, legal, and regulatory standards
2. Maintain an awareness of potential for fraud when conducting an engagement. (10.3-10.8)
   a. Notice indicators or symptoms of fraud.
   b. Design appropriate engagement steps to address significant risk of fraud.
   c. Employ audit tests to detect fraud.
   d. Determine if any suspected fraud merits investigation.
3. Collect data. (1.1, 1.2)
4. Evaluate the relevance, sufficiency, and reliability of evidence. (1.1, 1.4, 1.7)
5. Analyze and interpret data. (1.2)
6. Develop workpapers. (1.8)
7. Review workpapers. (1.9)
8. Communicate interim progress. (2.2)
9. Draw conclusions. (2.2)
10. Develop recommendations when appropriate. (2.2)
11. Report engagement results. (2.4)
    a. Conduct exit conference.
    b. Prepare report or other communication.
    c. Approve engagement report.
    d. Determine distribution of report.
    e. Obtain management response to report.
12. Conduct client satisfaction survey. (1.3)
13. Complete performance appraisals of engagement staff. (1.3)

B. **CONDUCT SPECIFIC ENGAGEMENTS (25 - 35%)** (proficiency level)

1. Conduct assurance engagements.
   a. Fraud investigation (10.3-10.8)
      1) Determine appropriate parties to be involved with investigation.
      2) Establish facts and extent of fraud (e.g., interviews, interrogations, and data analysis).
      3) Report outcomes to appropriate parties.
      4) Complete a process review to improve controls to prevent fraud and recommend changes.
   b. Risk and control self-assessment (3.3)
      1) Facilitated approach
         a) Client-facilitated
         b) Audit-facilitated
      2) Questionnaire approach
      3) Self-certification approach
   c. Audits of third parties and contract auditing (4.6, 7.3, 7.4)
   d. Quality audit engagements (4.4)
   e. Due diligence audit engagements (4.3)
   f. Security audit engagements (4.5)
   g. Privacy audit engagements (4.5)
   h. Performance (key performance indicators) audit engagements (4.4)
   i. Operational (efficiency and effectiveness) audit engagements (Intro. SU 3, 4.6)
   j. Financial audit engagements (3.1)
   k. Information technology (IT) audit engagements
      1) Operating systems (5.2)
         a) Mainframe
         b) Workstations
         c) Server
      2) Application development (5.3)
         a) Application authentication
         b) Systems development methodology
         c) Change control
         d) End user computing

3) Data and network communications/connections (e.g., LAN, VAN, and WAN) (6.1)
4) Voice communications (6.1)
5) System security (e.g., firewalls, access control) (5.4)
6) Contingency planning (5.5)
7) Databases (6.2)
8) Functional areas of IT operations (e.g., data center operations) (5.1)
9) Web infrastructure (6.1)
10) Software licensing (5.3)
11) Electronic Funds Transfer (EFT)/Electronic Data Interchange (EDI) (6.3)
12) E-Commerce (6.3)
13) Information protection (viruses, privacy) (6.5)
14) Encryption (5.4)
15) Enterprise-wide resource planning (ERP) software (e.g., SAP R/3) (6.4)

l. Compliance audit engagements (4.1)

2. Conduct consulting engagements. (3.2)

a. Internal control training (4.6)
b. Business process review (4.4)
c. Benchmarking (4.4)
d. Information technology (IT) and systems development (7.1-7.3)
e. Design of performance measurement systems (4.4)

C. **MONITOR ENGAGEMENT OUTCOMES (5 - 15%)** (proficiency level)

1. Determine appropriate follow-up activity by the internal audit activity (2.5)
2. Identify appropriate method to monitor engagement outcomes (2.5)
3. Conduct follow-up activity (2.5)
4. Communicate monitoring plan and results (2.1, 2.3, 2.5)

D. **FRAUD KNOWLEDGE ELEMENTS (5 - 15%)**

1. Discovery sampling (awareness level) (8.5)
2. Interrogation techniques (awareness level) (9.3, 10.7)
3. Forensic auditing (awareness level) (10.5)
4. Use of computers in analyzing data (proficiency level) (5.3)
5. Red flag (proficiency level) (10.4)
6. Types of fraud (proficiency level) (10.4)

E. **ENGAGEMENT TOOLS (15 - 25%)**

1. Sampling (awareness level) (8.1-8.7)

a. Nonstatistical (judgmental)
b. Statistical

2. Statistical analyses (process control techniques) (awareness level) (8.8)
3. Data gathering tools (proficiency level) (9.3, 9.4)

a. Interviewing
b. Questionnaires
c. Checklists

4. Analytical review techniques (proficiency level)

a. Ratio estimation (1.2, 8.4)
b. Variance analysis (e.g., budget vs. actual) (1.2)
c. Other reasonableness tests (1.2)

5. Observation (proficiency level) (1.6, 9.4)
6. Problem solving (proficiency level) (9.5)
7. Risk and control self-assessment (CSA) (awareness level) (3.3)
8. Computerized audit tools and techniques (proficiency level)

a. Embedded audit modules (5.1)
b. Data extraction techniques (5.1)
c. Generalized audit software (e.g., ACL, IDEA) (5.1)
d. Spreadsheet analysis (1.8)
e. Automated workpapers (e.g., Lotus Notes, Auditor Assistant) (1.8)

9. Process mapping including flowcharting (proficiency level) (9.1, 9.2)

PART III – BUSINESS ANALYSIS AND INFORMATION TECHNOLOGY

A. **BUSINESS PROCESSES (15 - 25%)**

1. Quality management (e.g., TQM) (awareness level) (1.1)
2. The International Organization for Standardization (ISO) framework (awareness level) (1.3)
3. Forecasting (awareness level) (1.4)
4. Project management techniques (proficiency level) (1.5)
5. Business process analysis (e.g., workflow analysis and bottleneck management, theory of constraints) (proficiency level) (1.6)
6. Inventory management techniques and concepts (proficiency level) (2.1)
7. Marketing -- pricing objectives and policies (awareness level) (2.3)
8. Marketing -- supply chain management (awareness level) (2.2)
9. Human resources (individual performance management and measurement, supervision, environmental factors that affect performance, facilitation techniques, personnel sourcing/staffing, training and development, and safety) (proficiency level) (2.4)
10. Balanced scorecard (awareness level) (1.2)

B. **FINANCIAL ACCOUNTING AND FINANCE (15 - 25%)**

1. Basic concepts and underlying principles of financial accounting (statements, terminology, relationships) (proficiency level) (3.1-3.4)
2. Intermediate concepts of financial accounting (e.g., bonds, leases, pensions, intangible assets, R&D) (awareness level) (3.5-3.8, 4.1-4.9)
3. Advanced concepts of financial accounting (e.g., consolidation, partnerships, foreign currency transactions) (awareness level) (4.10-4.13)
4. Financial statement analysis (proficiency level) (5.9)
5. Cost of capital evaluation (awareness level) (5.3)
6. Types of debt and equity (awareness level) (5.1, 5.2, 4.8)
7. Financial instruments (e.g., derivatives) (awareness level) (5.5, 5.6, 5.8, 3.5)
8. Cash management (treasury functions) (awareness level) (5.4)
9. Valuation models (awareness level)
   a. Inventory valuation (3.6)
   b. Business valuation (5.7)
10. Business development life cycles (awareness level) (5.10)

C. **MANAGERIAL ACCOUNTING (10 - 20%)**

1. Cost concepts (e.g., absorption, variable, fixed) (proficiency level) (6.2)
2. Capital budgeting (awareness level) (6.10)
3. Operating budget (proficiency level) (6.9)
4. Transfer pricing (awareness level) (6.12)
5. Cost-volume-profit analysis (awareness level) (6.1)
6. Relevant cost (awareness level) (6.11)
7. Costing systems (e.g., activity-based, standard) (awareness level) (6.3-6.8)
8. Responsibility accounting (awareness level) (6.13)

D. **REGULATORY, LEGAL, AND ECONOMICS (5 - 15%)** (awareness level)

1. Impact of government legislation and regulation on business
2. Trade legislation and regulations (7.2)
3. Taxation schemes (7.3)
4. Contracts (7.6)
5. Nature and rules of legal evidence (7.5)
6. Key economic indicators (7.4)

E. **INFORMATION TECHNOLOGY (IT) (30 - 40%)** (awareness level)

1. Control frameworks (e.g., SAC, COBIT) (8.4, 8.5)
2. Data and network communications/connections (e.g., LAN, VAN, and WAN) (9.3)
3. Electronic funds transfer (EFT) (10.1)
4. E-Commerce (10.1)
5. Electronic data interchange (EDI) (10.1)
6. Functional areas of IT operations (e.g., data center operations) (8.1)
7. Encryption (9.1)
8. Information protection (e.g., viruses, privacy) (10.4)
9. Evaluate investment in IT (cost of ownership) (10.2)
10. Enterprise-wide resource planning (ERP) software (e.g., SAP R/3) (10.3)
11. Operating systems (8.2)
12. Application development (8.3)
13. Voice communications (9.3)
14. Contingency planning (9.2)
15. Systems security (e.g., firewalls, access control) (9.1)
16. Databases (9.4)
17. Software licensing (8.3)
18. Web infrastructure (9.3)

PART IV – BUSINESS MANAGEMENT SKILLS

A. **STRATEGIC MANAGEMENT (20 - 30%)** (awareness level)

1. Global analytical techniques
   a. Structural analysis of industries (1.2, 2.4)
   b. Competitive strategies (e.g., Porter's model) (1.1, 1.3, 1.4)
   c. Competitive analysis (2.1, 2.2)
   d. Market signals (2.3)
   e. Industry evolution (2.5)
2. Industry environments (2.4)
   a. Competitive strategies related to:
      1) Fragmented industries (3.1)
      2) Emerging industries (3.2)
      3) Declining industries (3.3)
   b. Competition in global industries (3.4)
      1) Sources/impediments
      2) Evolution of global markets
      3) Strategic alternatives
      4) Trends affecting competition
3. Strategic decisions
   a. Analysis of integration strategies (4.1)
   b. Capacity expansion (4.2)
   c. Entry into new businesses (4.3)
4. Portfolio techniques of competitive analysis (2.2)
5. Product life cycles (2.5)

B. **GLOBAL BUSINESS ENVIRONMENTS (15 - 25%)** (awareness level)

1. Cultural/legal/political environments
   a. Balancing global requirements and local imperatives (5.1)
   b. Global mindsets (personal characteristics/competencies) (5.3)
   c. Sources and methods for managing complexities and contradictions (5.1-5.3)
   d. Managing multicultural teams (5.4)
2. Economic/financial environments
   a. Global, multinational, international, and multilocal compared and contrasted (5.1)
   b. Requirements for entering the global market place (5.1)
   c. Creating organizational adaptability (5.3)
   d. Managing training and development (5.4)

C. **ORGANIZATIONAL BEHAVIOR (20 - 30%)** (awareness level)

1. Motivation (6.1, 6.2)
   a. Relevance and implication of various theories
   b. Impact of job design, rewards, work schedules, etc.
2. Communication
   a. The process (6.3, 6.4)
   b. Organizational dynamics (6.3)
   c. Impact of computerization (6.5)
3. Performance (7.1, 7.2)
   a. Productivity
   b. Effectiveness
4. Structure (7.4, 7.5)
   a. Centralized/decentralized (7.6)
   b. Departmentalization (7.3)
   c. New configurations (e.g., hourglass, cluster, network) (7.6)

D. **MANAGEMENT SKILLS (20 - 30%)** (awareness level)

1. Group dynamics
   a. Traits (cohesiveness, roles, norms, groupthink, etc.) (8.1)
   b. Stages of group development (8.2)
   c. Organizational politics (8.3)
   d. Criteria and determinants of effectiveness (8.4)
2. Team building (8.4)
   a. Methods used in team building
   b. Assessing team performance
3. Leadership skills
   a. Theories compared/contrasted (9.1, 9.2)
   b. Leadership grid (topology of leadership styles) (9.2)
   c. Mentoring (9.2)
4. Personal time management (10.1)

E. **NEGOTIATING (5 - 15%)** (awareness level)

1. Conflict resolution (10.2)
   a. Competitive/cooperative
   b. Compromise, forcing, smoothing, etc.
2. Added-value negotiating (10.3)
   a. Description
   b. Specific steps

APPENDIX B
THE IIA EXAMINATION BIBLIOGRAPHY

The Institute has prepared a listing of references for the CIA exam, reproduced beginning below. These publications have been chosen by the Board of Regents as reasonably representative of the common body of knowledge for internal auditors. However, all of the information in these texts will not be tested. When possible, questions will be written based on the information contained in the suggested reference list. This bibliography is reorganized in an alphabetical listing by part to give you an overview of the scope of each part. The IIA also indicates that the examination scope includes

1. Articles from *Internal Auditor* (The IIA periodical)
2. IIA research reports
3. IIA pronouncements, e.g., The IIA Code of Ethics and SIASs
4. Past published CIA examinations

The IIA bibliography is reproduced for your information only. The texts you will need to acquire (use) to prepare for the CIA exam will depend on many factors, including

1. Innate ability
2. Length of time out of school
3. Thoroughness of your undergraduate education
4. Familiarity with internal auditing due to relevant experience

SUGGESTED REFERENCES FOR THE CIA EXAM

PART I: THE INTERNAL AUDIT ACTIVITY'S ROLE IN GOVERNANCE, RISK, AND CONTROL

Sawyer, et al, *Sawyer's Internal Auditing*, 5th Ed., The Institute of Internal Auditors.

OR Sears, *Internal Auditing Manual*, WG&L Financial Reporting & Management.

The American Institute of Certified Public Accountants, *Internal Control - Integrated Framework*, 1994.

The Institute of Internal Auditors, Inc., *Professional Practices Framework*, 2002.

OR *Other Control and Governance Frameworks.*

Supplemental:

Albrecht, Wernz, and Williams, *Fraud: Bringing Light to the Dark Side of Business*, Irwin Professional Publishing.

Murphy and Parker, *Handbook of IT Auditing*, Warren, Gorham & Lamont.

Reider, *Complete Guide to Operational Auditing*, John Wiley & Sons, Inc.

PART II: CONDUCTING THE INTERNAL AUDIT ENGAGEMENT

Sawyer, et al, *Sawyer's Internal Auditing*, 5th Ed., The Institute of Internal Auditors.

OR Sears, *Internal Auditing Manual*, WG&L Financial Reporting & Management.

The Institute of Internal Auditors, Inc., *Professional Practices Framework*, 2002.

Supplemental:

Kreitner, *Management*, 9th Ed., Houghton Mifflin Co., 2004.

PART III: BUSINESS ANALYSIS AND INFORMATION TECHNOLOGY

Information Systems and Control Foundation, *Cobit: Governance, Control, and Audit for Information and Related Technology*, 3rd Ed., 2000.

International Accounting Standards Committee, *International Accounting Standards*, 2002.

Kieso, Warfield, and Weygandt, *Intermediate Accounting*, 11th Ed., John Wiley & Sons, Inc., 2004.

Kreitner, *Management*, 9th Ed., Houghton Mifflin Co., 2004.

Sawyer, et al, *Sawyer's Internal Auditing*, 5th Ed., the Institute of Internal Auditors.

OR Sears, *Internal Auditing Manual*, WG&L Financial Reporting & Management.

The Institute of Internal Auditors Research Foundation, *Systems Assurance and Control*, 2003.

Weber, *Information Systems Control and Audit*, Prentice Hall, 1998.

PART IV: BUSINESS MANAGEMENT SKILLS

Bruner, Eaker, Freeman, Spelkman, Teisberg, and Venkataraman, *The Portable MBA*, 4th Ed., John Wiley & Sons, 2002.

Fisher, Ury, and Patton, *Getting to Yes, Negotiating Agreement Without Giving In*, Penguin USA.

Hill, *International Business with Global Resource CD, Powerweb and World Map*, 4th Ed., McGraw-Hill/Irwin, 2002.

Kreitner, *Management*, 9th Ed., Houghton Mifflin Co., 2004.

Kotler, *Marketing Management*, 11th Ed., Prentice Hall, 2002.

PUBLICATIONS AVAILABLE FROM THE IIA

The listing on the previous pages presents only some of the current technical literature available. Quantity discounts are provided. Inquiries should be sent to

Customer Service
Institute of Internal Auditors
249 Maitland Avenue
Altamonte Springs, FL 32701-4201

Request a current catalog by mail or call
(407) 830-7600, ext. 1

Book orders can be placed directly by calling (877) 867-4957 (toll-free) or (770) 442-8633, extension 275.

ORDERING TEXTUAL MATERIAL

The IIA does not carry all of the reference books. Write directly to the publisher if you cannot obtain the desired texts from your local bookstore. Begin your study program with *CIA Review*, Parts I through IV, which most candidates find sufficient. If you need additional reference material, borrow books from colleagues, professors, or a library.

Addison-Wesley Publishing Company
Reading, MA 01867

Basic Books, Inc.
Harper & Row Publishers
10 East 53rd Street
New York, NY 10022

Business Publications, Inc.
1700 Alma, Suite 390
Plano, TX 75075

The Dryden Press
One Salt Creek Lane
Hinsdale, IL 60521-2902

Harcourt Brace Jovanovich
1250 Sixth Avenue
San Diego, CA 92101

Harper & Row
10 East 53rd Street
New York, NY 10022

Holt, Rinehart, Winston
383 Madison Avenue
New York, NY 10017

Houghton Mifflin Company
One Beacon Street
Boston, MA 02108

Richard D. Irwin, Inc.
1818 Ridge Road
Homewood, IL 60430

Kent Publishing Company
20 Park Plaza
Boston, MA 02116

McGraw-Hill Book Company
1221 Avenue of the Americas
New York, NY 10020

Mitchell Publishing, Inc.
915 River Street
Santa Cruz, CA 95060

Prentice-Hall, Inc.
Englewood Cliffs, NJ 07632

Reston Publishing Company
11480 Sunset Hills Road
Reston, VA 22090

South-Western Publishing Company
5101 Madison Road
Cincinnati, OH 45227

West Publishing Company
P.O. Box 55165
St. Paul, MN 55101

John Wiley & Sons, Inc.
605 Third Avenue
New York, NY 10016

PRACTICE ADVISORY INDEX

Practice Advisory

INDEX

NOTE: Practice Advisories are listed in the Practice Advisory Index.

CPA

COMPLETE GLEIM CPA SYSTEM

All 4 sections, including Gleim Online, books*, *Test Prep CD-Rom*, *Test Prep for Pocket PC*, Audio CDs, plus bonus book bag. ☐ $989.95

Also available by exam section @ $274.95 (does not include book bag).

*Fifth book: *CPA Review: A System for Success*

$________

CMA

COMPLETE GLEIM CMA SYSTEM

Includes: Gleim Online, books*, *Test Prep CD-Rom*, *Test Prep for Pocket PC*, Audio CDs, plus bonus book bag. ☐ $739.95

Also available by exam part @ $213.95 (does not include book bag).

*Fifth book: *CMA Review: A System for Success*

$________

CIA

COMPLETE GLEIM CIA SYSTEM

Includes: Gleim Online, books*, *Test Prep CD-Rom*, *Test Prep for Pocket PC*, Audio CDs, plus bonus book bag. ☐ $824.95

Also available by exam part @ $224.95 (does not include book bag).

*Fifth book: *CIA Review: A System for Success*

$________

EA

GLEIM EA REVIEW SYSTEM

Includes: Gleim Online, books, *Test Prep CD-Rom*, *Test Prep for Pocket PC*, Audio CDs, plus bonus book bag. ☐ $629.95

Also available by exam part @ $224.95 (does not include book bag).

$________

EQE

"THE GLEIM SERIES" EXAM QUESTIONS AND EXPLANATIONS

Includes: 5 books and *Test Prep CD-Rom*. ☐ $112.25

Also available by part @ $29.95.

$________

CPE

GLEIM ONLINE CPE

Try a FREE 4 hour course at gleim.com/cpe

- Easy-to-Complete
- Informative
- Effective

Contact **GLEIM PUBLICATIONS** for further assistance:

gleim.com
800.874.5346
sales@gleim.com

SUBTOTAL $________

Complete your order on the next page

GLEIM PUBLICATIONS, INC.

P. O. Box 12848 Gainesville, FL 32604

TOLL FREE: 800.874.5346
LOCAL: 352.375.0772
FAX: 352.375.6940
INTERNET: gleim.com
E-MAIL: sales@gleim.com

Customer service is available (Eastern Time):
8:00 a.m. - 7:00 p.m., Mon. - Fri.
9:00 a.m. - 2:00 p.m., Saturday
Please have your credit card ready, or save time by ordering online!

SUBTOTAL (from previous page) $______
Add applicable sales tax for shipments within Florida. ______
Shipping (nonrefundable) 25.00

TOTAL $______

Fax or write for prices/instructions on shipments outside the 48 contiguous states, or simply order online.

NAME (please print) ______________________

ADDRESS ______________________ Apt. ______
(street address required for UPS)

CITY ______________ STATE ______ ZIP ______

____ MC/VISA/DISC ____ Check/M.O. Daytime Telephone (___) ______

Credit Card No. ______ - ______ - ______ - ______

Exp. ____ / ____ Signature ______________________
Month / Year

E-mail address ______________________

1. We process and ship orders daily, within one business day over 98.8% of the time. Call by 3:00 pm for same day service.
2. Please PHOTOCOPY this order form for others.
3. No CODs. Orders from individuals must be prepaid.
4. Gleim Publications, Inc. guarantees the immediate refund of all resalable texts and unopened software and audios if returned within 30 days. Applies only to items purchased direct from Gleim Publications, Inc. Our shipping charge is nonrefundable.
5. Components of specially priced package deals are nonrefundable.

Prices subject to change without notice.
02/08

For updates and other important information, visit our website.

GLEIM KNOWLEDGE TRANSFER SYSTEMS®

gleim.com

Please forward your suggestions, corrections, and comments concerning typographical errors, etc., to **Irvin N. Gleim • c/o Gleim Publications, Inc. • P.O. Box 12848 • University Station • Gainesville, Florida • 32604.** Please include your name and address so we can properly thank you for your interest.

1. ______________________________

2. ______________________________

3. ______________________________

4. ______________________________

5. ______________________________

6. ______________________________

7. ______________________________

8. ______________________________

9. ______________________________

10. ______________________________

11. ______________________________

12. ______________________________

13. ______________________________

14. ______________________________

15. ______________________________

16. ______________________________

17. ______________________________

18. ______________________________

Remember, for superior service: Mail, email, or fax questions about our materials.
Telephone questions about orders, prices, shipments, or payments.

Name: ______________________________

Address: ______________________________

City/State/Zip: ______________________________

Telephone: Home: __________ Work: __________ Fax: __________

Email: ______________________________

GLEIM Bookmark

Dr. Gleim's Advice: Cover the answers and explanations in our book with this bookmark. Answers will not be alongside questions when you take an exam. Use our Online course, Test Prep CD-Rom, and audios to complete your study program. Gleim's Test Prep CD-Rom will emulate actual exam conditions and track your progress.

Professor-Led

Review

- **LIVE weekly study sessions**
- **Leadership of a Professor**
- **Interactive Online Community**
- **Gleim's proven self-study materials**
- **CPA, CMA, CIA, and EA Reviews**

Contact GLEIM for the location nearest you.

800.874.5346
gleim.com